Dictionary of Statuses within EU Law

Antonio Bartolini • Roberto Cippitani •
Valentina Colcelli
Editors

Dictionary of Statuses within EU Law

The Individual Statuses as Pillar of European Union Integration

Springer

Editors
Antonio Bartolini
Department of Law
University of Perugia
Perugia, Italy

Roberto Cippitani
Department of Medicine
University of Perugia
Perugia, Italy

Valentina Colcelli
National Research Council
IFAC Institute, Sesto Fiorentino
Firenze, Italy

The present work has been carried out within the activities of the Eurostatus Project of the Department of Law of the Università degli Studi di Perugia, with the support of the Programme Erasmus+-Jean Monnet of the European Union (Grant Decision no. n.2016-3354_001-001).

ISBN 978-3-030-00553-5 ISBN 978-3-030-00554-2 (eBook)
https://doi.org/10.1007/978-3-030-00554-2

Library of Congress Control Number: 2018966515

This Springer imprint is published by the registered company Springer Nature Switzerland AG
The registered company address is: Gewerbestrasse 11, 6330 Cham, Switzerland

Foreword[1]

Inquiry into individual statuses within the European integration process is, without doubt, a multi-layered and interdisciplinary topic. It can be approached from a variety of disciplines and perspectives, including, but certainly not limited to, law. Still, individual statuses play an essential—even primordial—role in the European integration process and, in particular, in European Union ('EU') law, to which this volume makes a valuable contribution in mapping out the contours of specific individual statuses in numerous fields.

Indeed, statuses pervade EU law and are continuously shaped by it. This is illustrated by the ways in which the Court of Justice of the European Union ('the Court')[2] uses the concept of individual statuses in its case law. Thus, I would like to provide some reflections on individual statuses in the European context, considering the impact of the EU and the Court's jurisprudence in this regard.

As one useful approach, the concept of 'status' may generally be viewed as a tree with different branches. The root of the tree may be called the 'constitutional status', which is composed of four key elements: (1) the concept of citizenship, (2) the fundamental principles that provide common grounding for this status, (3) the rights and duties to realise this status and (4) the guarantees that afford judicial protection to enforce those rights and duties. Then, there are the many branches of the tree that denote the various types of statuses found in the different spheres, such as those in the workplace and private life. It should be noted, however, that this is not a hierarchical construction.

With regard to the impact of the EU on statuses, there is another tree conception. Importantly, however, it is not an absolute replica of the first tree, since the EU is not a State. Thus, the EU is not characterised as having a constitution in the national sense, though the EU has a 'constitutional charter', as recognised initially by the

[1] All opinions expressed herein are strictly personal.

[2] Under the first paragraph of Article 19(1) of the Treaty on European Union ('TEU'), the institution of the Court of Justice of the European Union encompasses the Court of Justice, the General Court and specialised courts. This contribution refers to the Court of Justice as the Court in the sense of the highest court of this institution.

Court in its landmark judgment in *Les Verts v. European Parliament* (1986).[3] The EU, therefore, is not a replica of the existing national structures. Nevertheless, the two trees coincide—they are connected (or entangled) to some degree. This is because, for instance, when it comes to Union citizenship, it is 'additional to and [does] not replace national citizenship', as established in the Treaties.[4] As for the branches of this tree, they represent the various statuses recognised in EU law. Here, too, there is no hierarchy: the rights and duties afforded to statuses are functionally linked, one not being more important than another. In effect, the rights and duties associated with a particular status may be considered two sides of the same coin.[5]

The Court's jurisprudence has an important role in this setting, in terms of the ways in which individual statuses are recognised, shaped and developed by the Court in the case law. By and large, the Court's case law involving individual statuses cuts across many spheres of EU law, and it can be classified (and sub-classified) in many ways. In part, the Court's case law may 'follow in the footsteps' of the Union legislator, for example, in the context of Union measures that implicate matters of 'civil status', such as those involving succession.[6] Moreover, certain statuses may intersect with significant events affecting the EU, such as the global economic crisis or the Syrian 'refugee' crisis, which, in turn, prompt litigation before the EU courts and bring those statuses to centre stage. Thus, without claiming to be exhaustive, I would like to draw your attention to a few salient examples which help to illustrate some interesting features of the Court's case law on statuses.

One of the first references to 'status' in the case law concerned the Court's engagement with the status of 'worker' in its 1964 judgment in *Unger*.[7] This was in connection with the interpretation of a measure on social security for migrant workers, whereby the Court proclaimed it to be an autonomous EU concept not dependent on national law. Recently, in its judgment in *Matzak*,[8] the Court held that both professional and volunteer firefighters qualify as a 'worker' within the autonomous meaning given to that term under the so-called Working Time Directive,[9] irrespective of classifications under national law.

---

[3] Judgment of 23 April 1986, *Les Verts* v *European Parliament* (294/83, EU:C:1986:166, paragraph 23).

[4] Article 20(1) of the TFEU.

[5] In regard to the status of Union citizenship, see also note 25.

[6] Regulation (EU) No 650/2012 of the European Parliament and of the Council of 4 July 2012 on jurisdiction, applicable law, recognition and enforcement of decisions and acceptance and enforcement of authentic instruments in matters of succession and on the creation of a European Certificate of Succession (OJ 2012 L 201, p. 107). See, in that regard, judgments of 12 October 2017, *Kubicka* (C-218/16, EU:C:2017:755), and of 1 March 2018, *Mahnkopf* (C-558/16, EU:C:2018:138). For other measures, see, e.g., the Commission's website, https://ec.europa.eu/info/policies/justice-and-fundamental-rights/civil-justice_en.

[7] Judgment of 19 March 1964, *Unger* (75/63, EU:C:1964:19, paragraph 2).

[8] Judgment of 18 February 2018, *Matzak* (C-518/15, EU:C:2018:XX, points 28–31).

[9] Directive 2003/88/EC of the European Parliament and of the Council of 4 November 2003 concerning certain aspects of the organisation of working time (OJ 2003 L 299, p. 9).

Likewise, the status of 'consumer' commands a growing body of case law that traverses various spheres of EU law. A salient example is the Court's judgment in *Schrems*.[10] The Court held, inter alia, that a private Facebook account user did not lose his or her 'consumer' status within the context of EU rules on private international law (the 'Brussels I Regulation'[11]) on account of his or her activities of publishing books, lecturing, operating websites, fundraising and being assigned the claims of other consumers for the purposes of their enforcement.[12]

In his Opinion, Advocate General Bobek stressed the following in light of the provision at issue:

> [T]he determination of consumer status must be made by reference to the position of that person in a particular contract, having regard to the nature and aim of that contract. Thus, … as confirmed by the Court, the concept of 'consumer' is 'objective in nature and is distinct from the concrete knowledge the person in question may have, or from the information that person actually has'. This means that the same person can, even on the same day, be acting as a professional and a consumer, depending on the nature and aim of the contract that has been concluded. For example, a professional lawyer specialising in consumer law may still be a consumer, despite his professional activity and knowledge, whenever he enters into a contractual relationship for private purposes.[13]

In fact, as cited in that Opinion, the Court held as much in its judgment in *Costea,*[14] within the context of the interpretation of the so-called Unfair Contract Terms Directive,[15] which lays down a set of common rules to protect consumers against unfair clauses in standard form contracts drawn up by traders. The Court ruled that a natural person who practises as a lawyer and concludes a credit agreement with a bank has the status of 'consumer' under that directive where that agreement is not linked to the lawyer's profession. The fact that the debt arising out of that credit agreement is secured by a mortgage taken out by that person in his or her capacity as representative of his or her law firm and involving goods intended for the exercise of that person's profession, such as a building belonging to that firm, was not relevant.[16]

---

[10] Judgment of 25 January 2018, *Schrems* (C-498/16, EU:C:2018:37).

[11] Council Regulation (EC) No 44/2001 of 22 December 2000 on jurisdiction and the recognition and enforcement of judgments in civil and commercial matters (OJ 2001 L 12, p. 1). It has been repealed by Regulation (EU) No 1215/2012 of the European Parliament and of the Council of 12 December 2012 on jurisdiction and the recognition and enforcement of judgments in civil and commercial matters (OJ 2012 L 351, p. 1).

[12] Judgment of 25 January 2018, *Schrems* (C-498/16, EU:C:2018:37, paragraphs 25–41).

[13] Opinion of Advocate General Bobek in *Schrems* (C-498/16, EU:C:2017/863, points 32–33) (citations omitted).

[14] Judgment of 3 September 2015, *Costea* (C-110/14, EU:C:2015:538).

[15] Council Directive 93/13/EEC of 5 April 1993 on unfair terms in consumer contracts (OJ 1993 L 95, p. 29).

[16] Judgment of 3 September 2015, *Costea* (C-110/14, EU:C:2015:538, paragraph 30).

Of note, the Unfair Contract Terms Directive has been the focal point of a growing body of the Court's case law that involves the *ex officio* application of EU law, obliging the national courts to assess the unfairness of contract terms of their own motion, so as to guarantee the system of consumer protection intended by that directive.[17] As such, the status of 'consumer' under this directive is crucial since it allows the person concerned to be afforded such protections under EU law.

Surely, one of the preeminent spheres involving individual statuses concerns the Court's case law on Union citizenship—the 'vast jurisprudential endeavour by means of which the Court has made citizenship of the Union an effective reality'.[18] The Court has consistently held, starting in *Grzelczyk*,[19] that:

> Union citizenship is destined to *the fundamental status* of nationals of the Member States, enabling those who find themselves in the same situation to enjoy the same treatment in law irrespective of their nationality, subject to such exceptions as are expressly provided for.[20]

The Court's famous declaration in that case built on the previous Opinion of Advocate General La Pergola in *Martínez Sala*,[21] which heralded EU citizenship as 'the *fundamental* legal status' guaranteed to the citizens of the Member States by the Union legal order.[22] It has been further stated in many Opinions of the Advocates General thereafter, such as Advocate General Szpunar's Opinion in *Chavez-Vilchez and Others*,[23] which emphasised:

> As the fundamental status of Union citizens, Union citizenship embodies, particularly for new generations, the opportunity to build a Europe in which all citizens may, as human beings, move, reside, work, study, provide a service or settle in another Member State, prosper, marry or choose to live in an equivalent form of partnership, found a family, if they so wish, and live in peace and security.[24]

This finds expression in the Court's recent rulings on Union citizenship, in the light of the relevant provisions of primary and secondary EU law.[25] For example, in

---

[17] See recently, e.g., judgment of 17 May 2018, *Karel de Grote* (C-147/16, EU:C:2018:320, paragraphs 26–37 and citations therein). See also *ibid.*, paragraphs 45–60: the Court held that an educational establishment had the status of 'seller or supplier' within the meaning of the Unfair Contract Terms Directive and in the circumstances of those proceedings.

[18] Opinion of Advocate General Szpunar in *Rendón Marín* (C-165/14, EU:C:2016:75, point 110).

[19] Judgment of 20 September 2001, *Grzelczyk* (C-184/99, EU:C:2001:458, paragraph 31).

[20] Emphasis added.

[21] Opinion of Advocate General La Pergola in *Martínez Sala* (C-85/96, EU:C:1997:335, points 18, 20–21).

[22] *Ibid.*, point 18.

[23] Opinion of Advocate General Szpunar in *Chavez-Vilchez and Others* (C-133/15, EU:C:2016:659, points 80–84 and citations therein). See also, e.g., Opinion of Advocate General Poiares Maduro in *Huber* (C-524/06, EU:C:2008:194, points 18–19).

[24] Opinion of Advocate General Szpunar in *Chavez-Vilchez and Others* (C-133/15, EU:C:2016:659, point 80).

[25] For a listing of the rights attached to the status of Union citizen under primary Union law, see, in particular, Articles 20–25 of the TFEU and Title V of the Charter of Fundamental Rights of the European Union ('the Charter'), titled 'Citizens' Rights' (Articles 39–45). For a recent application

K.A. and Others,[26] the Court reiterated that although the Treaty provisions on Union citizenship do not confer any autonomous rights on third-country nationals, there are 'very specific situations' developed in the case law, whereby a right of residence is granted to a third-country national who is a family member of a Union citizen who has not made use of his or her free movement rights under certain circumstances, so as to ensure that the effectiveness of Union citizenship is not undermined if, as a consequence of refusal of such a right, that citizen would be obliged in practice to leave the territory of the EU as a whole, thus depriving him of the 'genuine enjoyment of the substance of the rights conferred by that status'.[27]

On that basis, the Court held, inter alia, that Article 20 of the Treaty on the Functioning of the European Union ('TFEU') precluded a Member State's practice of not examining applications for a residence permit by third-country nationals for the purposes of family reunification with a Union citizen who has never exercised his or her free movement rights, solely on the grounds that the third-country national is the subject of a ban on entering the territory of that Member State without any examination of whether there exists a relationship of dependency of such a nature that the Union citizen would in practice be compelled to leave the EU territory as a whole and, hence, be deprived of the genuine enjoyment of the substance of the rights conferred by that status.[28]

Moreover, in *Coman and Others*,[29] the Court recalled the 'fundamental status' of Union citizenship and confirmed the rights that nationals of Member States enjoy under Article 21(1) of the TFEU include the right to lead a normal family life, together with their family members, both in the host Member State and in the Member State of which they are nationals upon return.[30] The Court also pointed out that even though 'a person's status, which is relevant to the rules on marriage', is a matter falling within the competence of the Member States, it is well established that the Member States must comply with EU law, including the Treaty provisions on the freedom conferred on all citizens to move and reside in the territory of the Member States.[31] Consequently, the Court held that the refusal by the authorities of a Member State to recognise, for the sole purpose of granting a derived right of residence to a third-country national, the marriage of that national to a Union citizen of the same sex and lawfully concluded during their genuine residence in the host

involving the political dimension of the status of Union citizen, see judgment of 6 October 2015, *Delvigne* (C-650/13, EU:C:2015:648). Further, it should not be overlooked that the Treaties refer to both rights and duties in respect of Union citizenship. The first sentence of Article 20(2) of the TFEU states: 'Citizens of the Union shall enjoy the rights and be subject to the duties provided for in the Treaties.'

[26] Judgment of 8 May 2018, *K.A. and Others* (C-82/16, EU:C:2018:308).

[27] *Ibid.*, paragraph 51.

[28] *Ibid.*, paragraphs 52–62.

[29] Judgment of 5 June 2018, *Coman and Others* (C-673/16, EU:C:2018:385).

[30] *Ibid.*, paragraphs 30–32.

[31] *Ibid.*, paragraphs 37–38.

Member State[32] would interfere with the rights conferred on that citizen to move and reside freely because it would have the effect of denying that citizen of the possibility of returning to the Member State of which he or she is a national together with his or her spouse.[33] Thus, Article 21(1) of the TFEU precluded the competent authorities of the Member State of which the Union citizen is a national from refusing to grant a third-country national of the same sex—to whom that citizen is lawfully married—a right of residence on the grounds that the law of that Member State does not recognise same-sex marriage.[34]

Along similar lines, in *Freitag*,[35] the Court underlined—in the light of settled case law—that although the rules governing the way in which a person's surname is entered on certificates of civil status are matters falling within the competence of the Member States, those competences must be exercised in compliance with EU law, including the Treaty provisions on the freedom of every citizen to move and reside in the territory of the Member States.[36] Therefore, it follows from the case law that the refusal by the authorities of a Member State to recognise the name of a national of that Member State who exercised their right to free movement in the territory of another Member State, as determined in that second Member State, is likely to hinder the exercise of the right to move and reside freely under Article 21(1) of the TFEU on account of the confusion and inconvenience arising from the divergence between the two names used for the same person.[37] In the circumstances of that case, the Court made clear that the discretion enjoyed by the competent national authorities—in respect of an existing procedure allowing for changes of name—must be exercised so as to give full effect to Article 21 of the TFEU.[38]

These foregoing cases help to illustrate some interesting features of the Court's case law on statuses. First, statuses are context dependent. Statuses under EU law may differ from their counterparts under national law. Moreover, depending on the

---

[32] In accordance with the conditions laid down in Article 7(1) of Directive 2004/38/EC of the European Parliament and of the Council of 29 April 2004 on the right of citizens in the Union and their family members to move and reside freely within the territory of the Member States amending Regulation (EEC) No 1612/68 and repealing Directives 64/221/EEC, 68/360/EEC, 72/194/EEC, 73/148/EEC, 75/34/EEC, 75/35/EEC, 90/364/EEC, 90/365/EEC and 93/96/EEC (OJ 2004 L 158, p. 77; corrigenda OJ 2004 L 229, p. 35, and OJ 2005 L 197, p. 34). In regard to the Court's interpretation of the term 'spouse' within the meaning of that directive, see *ibid.*, paragraphs 33–36, and Opinion of Advocate General Wathelet in *Coman and Others* (C-673/16, EU:C:2018:2, points 33–80).

[33] Judgment of 5 June 2018, *Coman and Others* (C-673/16, EU:C:2018:385, paragraphs 39–40).

[34] *Ibid.*, paragraph 51. The Court hastened to add that an obligation to recognise same-sex marriage, for the sole purpose of granting a derived right of residence to a third-country national in the circumstances of the present proceedings, did not undermine the national identity or pose a threat to the public policy of the Member State concerned, and that the right to respect for private and family life guaranteed by the Charter is a fundamental right. See *ibid.*, paragraphs 42–50.

[35] Judgment of 8 June 2017, *Freitag* (C-541/15, EU:C:2017:432).

[36] *Ibid.*, paragraph 33 and citations therein.

[37] *Ibid.*, paragraphs 35–39.

[38] See *ibid.*, paragraphs 40–46.

case, there is not just one status, as demonstrated by the statuses of 'citizen' and 'spouse' in *Coman and Others*. Second, these cases highlight the influence of EU law on the 'upgrading' of individual statuses within the sense of affording key rights and protections as a matter of EU law to persons holding such statuses that are part of the overall 'package'. Recently, certain commentators observed:

> What we see emerging is that EU law is engaged in the production of statuses. Status does not refer here to the pre-modern concept of an individual inextricably attached to a particular community … It also goes beyond the mere attribution of functional roles. Status is something which makes the exercise of individual rights possible, an '*underlying idea*' of what it means to be a citizen, a student or a child in relation to others within society.[39]

In this way, the Court's jurisprudence will no doubt prove to be a lens through which to examine the dynamic interplay of individual statuses and EU law as the process of European integration continues to unfold.

Court of Justice of the European Union
Kirchberg, Luxembourg
University of Sofia 'St. Kliment Ohridski'
Sofia, Bulgaria

Evgeni Tanchev

[39] L. Azoulai, S. Barbou des Places and E. Pataut, 'Being a Person in the European Union', in *Constructing the Person in EU Law* (Hart, 2016), p. 10 (citing J. Waldron, 'Is Dignity the Foundation of Human Rights?' (2013) NYU School of Law, Public Law Research Paper No 12-73) (emphasis added).

Contents

Introduction

Antonio Bartolini, Roberto Cippitani, and Valentina Colcelli

This Dictionary aims to analyse the way in which the individual status of European citizens is being profoundly affected by contemporary EU law.

The concept of individual legal status finds its origins in Roman law, and remains an important feature of modern legal systems. It persists in juridical language and legislative texts, but only as a rather vague and opaque idea. EU law is providing new criteria that may be employed to define the significance and contours of individual legal status. The process of EU integration has been accompanied by structural and economic changes, which have influenced the individual's legal status in distinct and varying ways. In order to enhance the functioning of its internal market, certain legal statuses (such as those of worker, producer etc.) have been brought to the fore by the EU, while, at the same time, EU law has made great modifications to these statuses.

The status of EU citizen is a general status that encompasses, as if it were a holdall, all the statuses that European law grants to each individual. Citizenship rights are granted not only to European citizens, but also to non-European citizens.

The features of the status of an EU citizen may not be efficient for reaching the goal of deep integration in the EU area: EU citizenship is a dual citizenship (as it is derived from national citizenship) but it does not have the typical characteristics of national citizenship; it is a citizenship without duties; and it is able to create a

A. Bartolini (✉)
Department of Law, University of Perugia, Perugia, Italy
e-mail: antonio.bartolini@unipg.it

R. Cippitani
Department of Medicine, University of Perugia, Perugia, Italy
e-mail: roberto.cippitani@unipg.it

V. Colcelli
National Research Council, IFAC Institute, Sesto Fiorentino, Firenze, Italy
e-mail: valentina.colcelli@cnr.it

A. Bartolini et al. (eds.), *Dictionary of Statuses within EU Law*,
https://doi.org/10.1007/978-3-030-00554-2_1

proliferation of special statuses (as is shown in this Dictionary) that assist with market integration, but not with a strong social and political integration.

The European Court of Justice has used the expression 'fundamental status' to refer to citizenship status (in Cases C-184/99 (*Grzelczyk*), C-413/99) and has also invoked 'individual legal status' in various other judgments (Cases C-256/11, C162/09, C34/09, etc.).

EU recognition of particular individual rights is contributing to the definition and re-definition of the legal status of the person in the light of the process of European integration. The attention paid to individual status and to the relationships between private actors within the EU legal order is crucial for understanding the development of EU law.

In order to explain the general focus, it is important to define the meaning of individual legal status as a starting point:

(i) An individual legal status could be defined as a public and personal condition from which stems certain rights and duties. It is able to encompass various activities and dimensions of the individual life of an EU citizen.
(ii) An individual status and its corollaries should be recognised wherever a person holding that particular legal status may travel. When that person moves, so does her/his status and his/her attributes within society'.
(iii) Promoting freedom of movement requires that the identification of individual status be regarded as of direct interest to European Union law as a preliminary requisite for applying EU law.

Why is it possible to say that EU law has influenced the concept of individual legal status in various ways?

This is the case because the European Court of Justice has held that the EU legal system is based on the direct recognition of individual rights by the EU Treaties. While originally this approach was primarily concerned with economic actors and the free market, it now extends into many aspects of the lives of EU citizens, as EU law increasingly regulates matters that have an impact on work, travel, market, family, the status of children: on the status of persons in sum. Thus, recognition of the rights of individuals and their legal positions (their statuses) is fundamental to the process of integrating the EU.

Under EU law, individuals are defined by virtue of their activity or status and they are regarded as being of direct interest to EU law as follows:

(a) They are of interest in themselves and without reference to any connection they may have with any other specific individual (as concerns the requirements for defining a person as engaged in a certain activity).
(b) An individual may also benefit to some extent from EU law because of the relationship he/she enjoys with another person (e.g. as a family member).
(c) The EU legislator also introduces or amends laws by classifying them on the basis of the status ascribed to the subjects to whom the law is addressed in order to achieve its goals (Arts. 2, 3 and 6 Treaty on the European Union (TEU)).

In this scenario, the Dictionary provides the research data for an analysis of the relations between individuals and EU institutions and bureaucracies, in view of the process of legal harmonisation within the EU.

In particular, the Dictionary will provide answers to the following questions: Has the process of European integration modified the traditional juridical definition of individual status? Has the concept of legal status now acquired a new function? What role has EU law played in developing a new modern function for the concept of individual status? Is the selection of a specific individual status by EU law and the proliferation of such statuses, which is synonymous with the creation of new privileges, undermining the goal of achieving substantive equality between EU citizens? Is this a return to the past? Under EU law, is it possible to build a unitary definition of the legal status of the person, over and above the definition that is constructed by a particular Member State's legal system?

The transformation of the meaning of public interest within the EU legal system has also altered the preconditions for the identification of new individual statuses, currently creating difficulties of definition. The EU legal system aims, above all, to protect the public interest. In Articles 2, 3 and 6 of the TEU, the elimination of obstacles to equality is presented as the function of the construction of the EU legal system itself, with the number of individual statuses being restricted to those statuses which constitute a necessary individual precondition for the operation of EU law and which do not detract from the necessary promotion of the centrality of the person in the legal systems of Member States and of the European Union as a whole.

Thus this academic study of particular individual statuses (as worker, consumer, family member etc.) could help pave the way for a reconsideration of individual status at the EU level.

It is certainly true that if, under EU law, individuals are defined by virtue of their activities, and they are regarded as being of direct interest to EU law, then (1) their activities might become of interest as a requirement for a certain activity or status; and (2) they may benefit in some measure from EU law because of a relationship that they enjoy with another person, such as a family member (Barrett 2003). It has been proved that EU laws and jurisprudence have had an impact on the European social model (Collins 2008), and this impact has always been caused by the imposition of a new social paradigm, which is likened to a European economic constitution.

The 'European social model' is an intricate concept that lacks normative references and has indistinct political formulations. It is situated between two poles: (a) its connection with the tradition of social constitutionalism, and (b) the claims for modernisation and transformation imposed by the Union itself (Buelga 2006).

The exercise by citizens of their right to free circulation in the EU and the associated right to access health services and social services in the host EU Member State could correspond to distributive justice by the acceptance of essential services, thereby granting compensation for the insufficient resources of the original Member State.

In the EU Charter of Fundamental Rights, public services become, more properly, public services of general interest, and thus, they are specifically ranked as 'social services', social security and welfare services (Article 14 of the Treaty on the Functioning of the EU). Article 34 (social security and social assistance) of the EU Charter of Fundamental Rights recognises the 'right of access to social security benefits and social services providing protection in cases such as maternity, illness, industrial accidents, dependency or old age, and in cases of job loss, according to rules laid down by Community law and national laws and practices'.

The rules on services of general interest aim to protect users, persons, consumers or businesses who access the services. Ultimately, in particular, in order to combat social exclusion and poverty, the EU recognises the 'right to social and housing assistance so as to ensure a decent existence for all those who lack sufficient resources' (Article 34, par. 3). It also prescribes a 'right of access to preventive health care and to obtain medical treatment' (Article 35). Access to social services is not just for the citizens of a particular Member State under the principle of EU solidarity: 'Everyone residing and moving legally within the European Union is entitled to social security benefits and social advantages in accordance with Community law and national laws and practices' (Article 34, par. 2) (Cippitani 2011).

Social rights are deeply engraved on the social position of persons, which has had an impact on citizens of the Member States (Colcelli 2015).

Within the domain of EU law, all EU citizens possess the same features of a joint and fundamental EU status. This is also true in the social dimension (C-413/99 Baumbast v R, Racc., I-7091, p. 82).

Indeed, EU citizenship does not rest on the set of laws applicable to the citizenship of Member States. The EU Court of Justice has consistently held that EU citizenship is of no relevance in situations that are solely internal, but it has stated that non-discrimination is the main aim of the EU and is an instrumental right for building the 'European Union welfare state' (see Arts. 2 and 3 TFEU).

If national citizenship is mistakenly used as grounds for discrimination, this would in all cases be divergent from the aims of the Union and the Treaties. There is an intricate 'European social model', in which EU citizenship is an 'individual fundamental status', grounded on non-discrimination. The citizen's social dimension, which is formed in the national state and relates directly to the host state's social system, circulates with EU citizenship and the freedom of movement that accompanies it. The freedom of movement and individual status cannot be separated from the social nature that accompanies an individual's pre-border crossing status and his/her settlement in another Member State.

After a period of three months and after five years of residence in a host Member State, a conflict can arise between a number of claims: (a) the Member States' rights to maintain the integrity of their welfare systems; (b) the Member States' rights to shelter their welfare systems from the claims of 'outsider insiders'; (c) claims to equal treatment based on EU citizenship law; and (d) claims arising because the policy has generated problems that have exceeded the liberalising trend of a free market ideology.

Internal rights are guaranteed in the EU host country through EU citizenship; however, this is not adequate to ensure the complete recognition of the social dimension of EU citizenship.

Inevitably, a key question has emerged from the Euro zone crisis: what will the impact of this be on the future of the EU social model? In any case, with the growing implementation of EU citizenship as a fundamental status and of the freedom of movement of citizens, the same harmful effect may occur regarding the level of sustainability of the internal welfare states.

Citizenship status, free movement, and individual well-being in regional migration flows have an effect on income distribution and the sustainability of the national welfare states.

In a scenario involving the full implementation of EU citizenship status, what are the consequences of the freedom of movement on the well-being of individuals and on the sustainability of the national welfare states? To what extent would regional migration flows be driven by fiscal competition, with more generous welfare state contexts attracting low-income immigrants in search of stronger protection? How will this reverberate in relation to inequality and the growth of origin and destination regions?

Looking at the historical function of the Court of Justice in the building of the EU, what is very relevant is the increase in the number of people who can rely on the primacy of Community/EU law: more rights mean a greater number of people who can rely on Community law. The recognition of fundamental economic rights and, above all, of freedom of movement, even for people who are not European citizens, is therefore to be welcomed. The Court of Justice has extended the range of 'community subjectivity', setting people as the guardians of EU law (Margiotta 2014).

This has led to the proliferation of special statuses that are sometimes recognised regardless of European citizenship.

The proliferation of statuses opens up a world of plural citizenship and the shattering of the concept of citizenship.

The index to the present volume offers a cross-section of this plurality of statuses and particular nationalities.

In this framework, EU citizenship status seems to be a sum of individual positions rather than a political synthesis of different positions.

The next step is the fulfilment of the normative content of EU social citizenship, to contribute to the implementation of the European Pillar of Social Rights and to put forward recommendations on the exercise of EU social rights as an integral part of EU citizenship and upward convergence.

It seems to be the case that—not only at the European level but also at the global level—the constitutionalisation of fundamental rights (which also takes place through the international charters on this topic) allows a transition from national citizenship towards a 'citizenship of rights' (Bartolini and Pioggia 2016, p. 14). Citizenship changes its nature and presents itself as a set of rights that make up the heritage of every person, wherever that person is (Rodotà 2012, p. 4).

This global and constitutional idea of citizenship rights as fundamental rights, attributed to the person as such, is accompanied, in the EU context, by the idea of integration through rights. Citizenship thus opens up plural and differentiated models, and 'the idea of a multi-city citizenship or rather of a citizenship with multiple dimensions' is growing (Grosso 2014, p. 141).

References

Barrett, G. (2003). Family matters: European community law and third-country family members. *Common Market Law Review, 40*, 369–421.

Bartolini, A., & Pioggia, A. (2016). Cittadinanze amministrative. In L. Ferrara & D. Storace (Eds.), *A 150 anni dall'Unificazione Amministrativa Italiana* (Vol. VIII). Firenze: Firenze University Press.

Buelga, G. (2006). El Impacto De La Ampliación De La U.E. *Revista de Derecho Comunitario Europeo, 23*, 7–45.

Cippitani, R. (2011). *La solidarietà giuridica tra pubblico e privato*. Roma: ISEG srl.

Colcelli, V. (2015). The solidarity principle in new EU Member States. In C. Perugini & F. Pompei (Eds.), *Inequalities during and after transition in Central and Eastern Europe* (pp. 247–265). Basingstoke: Palgrave Macmillan.

Collins, H. (2008). *The European Civil Code*. Cambridge: Cambridge University Press.

Grosso, E. (2014). La cittadinanza: appartenenza, identità e partecipazione dallo Stato liberale alla democrazia contemporanea. In L. Violante (Ed.), *Storia d'Italia, Legge Diritto Giustizia, Torino* (14) (pp. 141 ff). Torino: Enaudi.

Margiotta, C. (2014). *Cittadinanza europea*. Bari: Laterza.

Rodotà, S. (2012). *Il diritto di avere diritti*. Bari: Laterza.

Part I
Historical and Juridical Contexts for the Status Within European Union Law

Historical Overview of the Status Topic

Andrea Trisciuoglio

1 *Status* in Ancient Rome

1.1 *Status* in the Language of the Romans

The etymology of the word *status* (from *stare*) particularly refers to a stable condition in which a person is taken into consideration, not as an individual, but as a member belonging to a group. It is believed that the term has preserved, in the Latin language, the characteristics of a substantivised verbal voice, properly indicating an effective and permanent situation of a man related to a group and not an abstract concept (Ricciardi 2008, p. 57 f.). In modern language, it is usual to establish a correspondence with the terms 'condition', 'position' and 'situation' (personal). In Roman legal language, the term '*condicio*' is also used, but unlike *status*, it indicates a non-stable, transitory personal situation, as that of the slave that can be manumitted (*condicio servilis*) (Melillo 2006, p. 16 ff.). In Seneca (*De Benef.* 3.18.2), however, '*status*' refers to the slave, and this one, when manumitted in a testament under the suspensive condition, is qualified with the expression '*statuliber*', which has an uncertain etymology (Donatuti 1940, p. 6 ff.; Bretone 1971, p. 380).

It should also be highlighted that the condition recalled by *status* is not only the person's juridical condition, which can be identified, for example, in section 1.5 of the Digest (*De statu hominum*) or in a well-known Hermogenian's text, which is still accepted in the Digest *sub eodem titulo* (D.1.5.2: *Cum igitur hominum causa omne ius constitutum sit, primo de personarum statu ... dicemus*); *status* also refers to a social condition (*status dignitatis* = *dignitas*) (Peppe 2012, p. 228 ff.) defined by laws and customary rules, as is the condition of a man of good reputation

A. Trisciuoglio (✉)
Department of Law, University of Torino, Torino, Italy
e-mail: andrea.trisciuoglio@unito.it

A. Bartolini et al. (eds.), *Dictionary of Statuses within EU Law*,
https://doi.org/10.1007/978-3-030-00554-2_2

(D.50.13.5.1: *Existimatio est dignitatis inlaesae status, legibus ac moribus comprobatus*).

However, '*status*' in the Latin language is not only related to the person. In rhetorical terms, the word is also connected to '*causa*' (*status causae*) and in this case it indicates, based on the theory of *status* dating back to the Greek rhetorician Ermagora of Temno (see *Rhetorica ad Herennium*), the nucleus of an issue in which two statements of accusation and defence are set against each other; it will be up to the judge to choose the most well-founded among them and to decide. Thus, in the aforesaid theory, a conjectural *status* is distinguished (the fact is accomplished—the fact is not accomplished, *an sit*), a defining *status* (the accused has committed the crime A—the accused has committed the crime B; *quid sit*), a qualitative *status* (there is a cause of justification—there is no cause of justification, *qualis sit*). Moreover, in rhetoric works, the rational *status* described above stands opposite the legal *status*, regarding which there are discussions on a written text rather than on a fact, aimed at providing an interpretation (see Quint., *Inst. Or.* 3.6.86 ff.) (Crifò 2000, p. 210 f.; Martini 2004, p. 30 ff.; Procchi 2009, p. 237 ff.).

On the opposite, in the famous definition of *ius publicum* from Ulpian (D.1.1.1.2: *Publicum ius est quod ad statum rei Romanae spectat*), the term refers to the organisational structure of the Roman community, and it is appropriate to remember that the Italian derivative 'stato', in the meaning of an abstract public entity, will be used only since the fifteenth century, and especially by Machiavelli (Orestano 1968, p. 187 nt. 5; Sicari 2006, p. 1680 ff.).

1.2 The Community Concept of Personal Status Within the Romans

The community vision of the Romans—community vision implies that the person is considered in the legal world not as a single individual but as belonging to a group—clearly emerges in classical jurisprudential thought, but not in relation to the moment in which a *status* is acquired—normally at birth (e.g. *status* of a free individual, of a citizen), exceptionally by negotiation (e.g. *status* of freedom by manumission), by public concession (e.g. *status* of a citizen), by constitutive sentence (e.g. *status* of freedom based on the presumption of a non-executed fideicommissary manumission) or, for certain purposes, by legal fiction—but with reference to the moment in which a *status* is lost and another one is acquired. In fact, the reading of this phenomenon provided by Gaius in his Institutes does not stress an individual story, but the vicissitudes of a group that loses its 'head'. The *permutatio prioris status* of a person is primarily a *capitis deminutio* of a group (Gai., *Inst.* 1.159). Therefore, the loss of freedom suffered by a person is seen as a numeric decrease in the group of free individuals (and citizens), the loss of citizenship is considered as a reduction of the corps of Roman citizens, the emancipation of a child (with the entry into the *status* of *sui iuris*) or his/her adoption is intended as a reduction of the agnatic family of origin (Arangio-Ruiz 1998, p. 45; Cannata 2001, p. 55; Palma 2014, p. 18). It is significant in this regard that '*civitas*' indicates, at the same time, both the legal situation (*status*) of the citizen and the citizens as a whole (the group).

Belonging to a group in the Romans' vision implies not only the recognition of rights or privileges but also of duties. The *status* of citizen, for example, in private law relationships, allows the successful conclusion of certain conveyancing of property stores which is forbidden to foreigners (*mancipatio*, *in iure cessio*) or to acquire property by usucapion. In the field of public law, only the *civis* can invoke the constitutional guarantees to protect his personal safety threatened by the magistrate (see especially Cic., *In Verr.* 2.5.162) (Mancini 2014, p. 351; Mandas 2017, p. 22 ff., with reference to the trial against Paul of Tarsus); the citizen is also entitled to take part in public tenders (Trisciuoglio 1998, p. 186 ff.). However, specific duties are connected to citizenship, such as the obligation of military service in the republican age or obligations of a fiscal nature (before the second century BC, and especially after the extension of citizenship to almost all the subjects of the empire with the edict of Caracalla of AD 212). Thus, in the Roman concept of status, we cannot find the widespread vision of our times in which we tend to emphasise the rights connected to a certain juridical position (mostly of a subject considered to be weak) and to obscure the relevant duties.

Furthermore, it is believed in recent philosophical studies (Esposito) (see Garofalo 2014, p. 102) that the Roman law first, through the attribution of the *status* to certain individuals, created inequalities which were unknown in the state of nature. Due to this legal system, a fracture between nature and institution would have occurred; in accordance with the Greek philosophical language (Plato, Aristotle), a fracture between *zoé* and *bíos*, that is between the individual made of flesh and bones and the holder of legal subjective situations. The human rights theory that places man as such at the centre, with his dignity, is intended to recompose this fracture.

1.3 The Stability of Personal Status

The personal *status*, which in later Romanistic thoughts composes the legal capacity (see below, Sect. 3), are the *status libertatis*, the *status civitatis*, the *status familiae*, that is, evaluating the tripartition in positive terms, the condition of a free individual, of a Roman citizen, of *sui iuris* (that is of a subject who has no legitimate male sex ascendants within his/her family). However, only the expression *status libertatis*, among those mentioned above, finds confirmation in the Roman sources (Orestano 1971, p. 383; Cannata 2001, p. 52). These personal legal conditions, once acquired, only exceptionally can be lost and changed with others: this happens for example in case of war imprisonment, which involves the loss of freedom and citizenship, or in case of *adrogatio*, which implies for a *pater familias* the loss of the *status* of *sui iuris*. Therefore, Romans show quite clearly a conservative tendency towards the *status*, as we can infer for example from the rule which forbids to affix a resolutory condition to the negotiations granting a new *status* (e.g. manumission of the slave, *adrogatio*, *emancipatio*) (Marrone 2000, p. 175). With reference then to the uncertainty that can derive from trials (*praeiudicia*) regarding the personal *status*—including those of women (Donadio 2011, p. 128 f.)—Romans punish rash initiatives: in such cases, the actor can be summoned to appear in court through the *actio iniuriarum* by the person who, as affected by an unfounded complaint concerning his/her *status* (of free individual), is considered defamed (Atzeri 2014, p. 18 ff.); in addition, the beneficiary *ex testamento* who questioned the *status* of a deceased person is hit by indignity and loses the legacy in favour of the *Fiscus* (D.34.9.9.2).

In the late Roman Empire, the *status* tendential stability extended to socio-economic categories with legal relevance. This choice is explained by the fact that certain trades (for example the boatmen gathered in a guild) or certain dignities (for example that of *decuriones*, the senators of the cities of the empire) were necessary to ensure essential public services (public transport, collection of taxes). The imperial provisions, starting from the fourth century AD, are intended to prevent flights from their own category and to affirm their hereditariness, so that *decuriones*' children can belong only to that order, which is made responsible for the collection of taxes. Belonging to such types of socio-economic groups implies, in the late Roman Empire, the subjection to obligations rather than the enjoyment of rights or privileges (Grosso 1965, p. 430 f.; Veyne 1981, p. 341 f.; Mancini 2014, p. 384).

2 *Status* in the Medieval Age

In the medieval dictionary of the Middle Ages '*status*' indicates the class, the social rank (Grossi 2009, p. 16), revealing a socio-juridical meaning, based on belonging to a group, quite similar in concept to that of the most ancient Roman experience. Therefore, the person is not considered as a single actor in the view of the legal system, but as a member of a group of individuals (mainly linked together on the basis of a socio-economic or even religious criterion), which is regulated by its own statute and to which he/she belongs in a mostly involuntary and stable way (Lenti 1999, p. 30 f.; Cianferotti 2013, p. 6 ff.; Alpa 2013, p. 650). In fact, the legal concept of personal status considered by St. Thomas in the Summa Theologiae (II.II, q.183 a.1) is still the Roman one, since he emphasises a permanent condition, free or slave, which implies obligations rather than rights; and in the aforesaid text, St. Thomas underlines the diversity between the legal *status* and the economic condition (of rich or poor) or the social one (of *dignus* or of *plebeius*), that may change and therefore cannot be called '*status*' (Ricciardi 2008, p. 58 ff.).

It is possible, however, in the feudal legal system, to also change durably one's own overall personal legal situation by contract, as in the case of *homagium*, an agreement able to establish the condition of vassal for oneself and his children, with the related obligations of *fidelitas* towards the lord, recognising to the latter a sort of proprietary right over the person of the vassal, almost a possession of his status (Conte 1996, pp. spec. 196 ff., 210 ff.; Conte 2009, p. 152).

The meaning of (public) organisation, which emerged already with reference to the definition of *ius publicum* provided by Ulpian (see above, Sect. 1.1), can be widely found in medieval sources (Post 1964, p. spec. 335 ff.).

3 *Status* and Legal Capacity: The Theory of the Three *Status* (XVI–XVIII Centuries)

The representation of the legal capacity in Rome as the presence in the individual of the three *status* of freedom, Roman citizen and *sui iuris* has no basis in the Roman sources, but it is the result of a subsequent elaboration (in the XVI–XVIII centuries) provided by interpreters (Burdese 1975, p. 136) and perfected by Savigny. Therefore, in the Roman legal view, *status* does not refer to something similar to our legal capacity, recognised to the subject of law considered *uti singulus*, but it recalls only a subjective position (with its rights and duties) with respect to a group, in particular that of Roman citizens, or the family one, given that the group of free individuals, if detached from that of citizens, does not reflect a specific legal relevance (Betti 1935, p. 80; Orestano 1971, p. 383 f.; Talamanca 1990, p. 76 f.; Prosperi 2013, p. 3). The concept of legal capacity, on the other hand, was elaborated—it is not peacefully stated—by Thibaut only at the beginning of the nineteenth century (Alpa 1993, p. 63 f.; Stanzione 2017, p. 23 nt. 44).

4 French Revolution

The French revolutionaries, with the Déclaration des Droits de l'Homme et du Citoyen (1789), following natural-law thinking in which a *status naturalis* is countered with the artificial state (*status civilis*) created by a human arbitrary act (Corasaniti 1990, p. 955), place at the centre of the legal system the individual (citizen), free and equal to other individuals, in place of the person-member of an intermediate social class named at that time 'state' (nobility, clergy, third state or people). Since this moment, the individual considers himself/herself, in the legal world, *uti singulus* and not artificially *uti socius* (Lenti 1999, p. 31; Ago and Vidotto 2006, pp. 71, 220; Lanza 2012, p. 63 ff.; Cianferotti 2013, p. 12 ff.; Stanzione 2017, p. 28 ff.). However, we should remember that a widespread implementation of an egalitarian system, in opposition to a system based on the criteria of family and social *status*, can be found only in the contemporary age (Pani 2010, p. 110 f.).

5 Henry Sumner Maine's Theory (*Ancient Law*: 1861)

This historic passage is perspicaciously highlighted by Henry Sumner Maine (1822–1888), versatile Scottish author, comparatist–internationalist–anthropologist but above all Romanist (Stein 1980, p. 86 ff.). He considers the successful formula: 'from the status to the contract', useful to illustrate the passage from the Roman and medieval age to the modern one, but not exempt of criticism (see, for example, Perozzi 1948, p. 721). In particular, Maine observes that contractual relations at this time have replaced potestative relationships, once permanently established within the family according to the *status* which individuals belonged to: there is no longer the *servus* without freedom and subject to a *dominus*, but in its place we find the servant who is able to sign, as a free individual, contracts with the master; likewise, children undertake obligations contractually towards their father, women are no longer subject to the protection of other individuals different from their husband and have also acquired the capacity to be a part in a juridical act; in short, relations derive now from the free agreement of individuals even when there are parental bonds between them (Maine 1970, pp. spec. 163–165, 302 f., 356 f.; Palma 2014, p. 19 f.; Stanzione 2017, p. 48 f.).

6 *Status* and State

The re-elaborated concept of *status* also has a certain success in the public law doctrines of the nineteenth century. In Jellinek's theory of subjective public rights, later resumed by Santi Romano, four '*status*' are identified that characterise the relationship between the individual and the state: the '*status subiectionis*, *libertatis, civitatis*, *activae civitatis*'; a plurality of positions that prefigured duties but also rights (of citizenship and political), conferred by the state to the citizen (Corasaniti 1990, p. 963; Cianferotti 2013, pp. 32 ff.; 79 ff.).

7 Persistence of Community Theories in the Face of Individualistic–Egalitarian Theories in the Most Recent Civil Doctrine

We can say that the individualistic and egalitarian vision of *status* (*personae*) has not definitively prevailed with respect to the older community vision of the *status* of Roman origin and, on the contrary, we can notice a crisis of the single universal subject (Vincenti 2007, p. 193 ff.) and, however, the scholars discuss a return to the status (Alpa 1993, p. 205 ff.), giving new meanings to the term. On the one hand, old *status* is brought to a shape, from a legislative point of view, on different bases: for example, we do not tend so much to identify the *status familiae* on the basis of the traditional marital and blood ties, but rather on the basis of an affective relationship, even established *extra ordinem*, as is the case of homosexual unions (Busnelli 2005, p. 42 ff.). On the other hand, the communities of reference are no longer only familiar and political, or socio-economic as in the Roman and medieval age, but they also include groups of subjects who are in the same disadvantaged condition and should therefore be protected—eventually with specific group statutes, with special laws (Irti 1999, p. 40 ff.)—creating an effective, not only formal, equality (Mazzù 2009, p. 1140 ff.); the example of consumers, in this regard, is very frequent (for the BGB see Rescigno 2005, p. 16 f.; Mazzù 2009, p. 1148 ff.). In this new meaning of *status*, however, the traditional elements of the stability and of the necessary (non-voluntary) belonging to the group cannot be found and the term also risks being vague and legally irrelevant (Carboni 1998, pp. 9 ff.; 47 ff.; 117 ff.; Stanzione 2017, p. 52 ff.).

References

Ago, R., & Vidotto, V. (2006). *Storia moderna*. Bari: Laterza.

Alpa, G. (1993). *Status e capacità. La costruzione giuridica delle differenze individuali*. Bari: Laterza.

Alpa, G. (2013). Status. In M. I. Álvarez Ledesma & R. Cippitani (Eds.), *Diccionario Analítico de Derechos Humanos e Integración Jurídica*. Roma-Perugia-México: ISEG.

Arangio-Ruiz, V. (1998). *Istituzioni di diritto romano (XIV)*. Napoli: Jovene.

Atzeri, L. (2014). L'infamia nei rescritti di Diocleziano. In W. Brandes, L. M. Hoffmann, & K. Maksimovič (Eds.), *Fontes Minores (XII)*. Frankfurt am Main: Löwenklau.

Betti, E. (1935). *Diritto romano (I). Parte generale*. Padova: Cedam.

Bretone, M. (1971). Statuliber. In *Novissimo Digesto Italiano (XVIII)*. Torino: Utet.

Burdese, A. (1975). *Manuale di diritto privato romano (III)*. Torino: Utet.

Busnelli, F. D. (2005). Nascere per contratto? In M. Paradiso (Ed.), *I mobili confini dell'autonomia privata*. Milano: Giuffrè.

Cannata, C. A. (2001). *Corso di Istituzioni di diritto romano (I)*. Torino: Giappichelli.

Carboni, B. (1998). *Status e soggettività giuridica*. Milano: Giuffrè.

Cianferotti, G. (2013). *Il concetto di status nella scienza giuridica del Novecento*. Milano: Giuffrè.

Conte, E. (1996). *Servi medievali. Dinamiche del diritto comune*. Roma: Viella.

Conte, E. (2009). *Diritto comune*. Bologna: Il Mulino.

Corasaniti, A. (1990). Stato delle persone. In *Enciclopedia del diritto (XLIII)*. Milano: Giuffrè.

Crifò, G. (2000). *Lezioni di storia del diritto romano (III)*. Bologna: Monduzzi.

Donadio, N. (2011). Donne e quaestiones di status nel mondo romano: ancora sul 'processo di Giusta'. In A. Maffi & L. Gagliardi (Eds.), *I diritti degli altri in Grecia e a Roma*. Sankt Augustin: Academia Verlag.

Donatuti, G. (1940). *Lo statulibero*. Milano: Giuffrè.

Garofalo, L. (2014). Principi e ordinamento romano: una riflessione sulle orme di Fritz Schulz. In F. Reinoso Barbero (Ed.), *Principios generales del derecho. Antecedentes históricos y horizonte actual*. Madrid: Aranzadi.

Grossi, P. (2009). *L'Europa del diritto (IV)*. Bari: Laterza.

Grosso, G. (1965). *Lezioni di storia del diritto romano (V)*. Torino: Giappichelli.

Irti, N. (1999). *L'età della decodificazione (IV)*. Milano: Giuffrè.

Lanza, C. (2012). *Concezioni giuridiche in forma storica*. Napoli: Satura.

Lenti, L. (1999). Status. In *Digesto Discipline privatistiche. Sezione civile (XIX)*. Torino: Utet.

Maine, H. S. (1970). *Ancient law. Its connection with the early history of society and its relations to modern ideas*. Gloucester, MA: P. Smith.

Mancini, G. (2014). Integrazione ed esclusione nell'esperienza giuridica romana. Dalle politiche di integrazione dello straniero alla generalizzazione della condizione di "straniero in patria": le norme su capacità matrimoniale e filiazione come strumenti della frammentazione degli status in età tardoantica. In F. Rimoli (Ed.), *Immigrazione e integrazione. Dalla prospettiva globale alle realtà locali (I)*. Napoli: Editoriale Scientifica.

Mandas, A. M. (2017). *Il processo contro Paolo di Tarso. Una lettura giuridica degli Atti degli Apostoli (21.27 - 28.31)*. Napoli: Jovene.

Marrone, M. (2000). *Istituzioni di diritto romano (II)*. Palermo: Palumbo.

Martini, R. (2004). Antica retorica giudiziaria (Gli 'status causae'). In *Studi Senesi (CXVI)*. Siena: Università degli Studi di Siena.

Mazzù, C. (2009). Riflessioni sullo status tra passato e futuro. *Rivista del notariato, 5*(LXIII), 1135 ff.

Melillo, G. (2006). *Personae e status in Roma antica*. Napoli: Jovene.

Orestano, R. (1968). *Il «problema delle persone giuridiche» in diritto romano (I)*. Torino: Giappichelli.

Orestano, R. (1971). Status libertatis, civitatis, familiae. In *Novissimo Digesto Italiano (XVIII)*. Torino: Utet.

Palma, A. (2014). Note in tema di cittadinanza romana e sovranità. In S. Masuelli & S. Zandrino (Eds.), *Linguaggio e sistematica nella prospettiva di un romanista*. Napoli: ESI.

Pani, M. (2010). *Il costituzionalismo di Roma antica*. Bari: Laterza.

Peppe, L. (2012). Note sulla dignitas. In *Bullettino dell'Istituto di Diritto Romano (CVI)*. Milano: Giuffrè.

Perozzi, S. (1948). Gli studi di H. Sumner Maine e la filosofia del diritto. In U. Brasiello (Ed.), *Scritti giuridici (III)*. Milano: Giuffrè.

Post, G. (1964). *Studies in medieval legal thought. Public law and the state (1100–1322)*. Princeton, NJ: Princeton University Press.

Procchi, F. (2009). 'Medium quiddam tenere'. Tra retorica e diritto: considerazioni a margine di Plin. Ep. 4.9. In *Studi in onore di Remo Martini (III)*. Milano: Giuffrè.

Prosperi, F. (2013). Rilevanza della persona e nozione di status. *Civilistica.com 4(II) = Rassegna di diritto civile (IV)*, 1997, 810 ff.

Rescigno, P. (2005). Status e capacità. In M. Paradiso (Ed.), *I mobili confini dell'autonomia privata*. Milano: Giuffrè.

Ricciardi, M. (2008). *Status. Genealogia di un concetto giuridico*. Milano: Giuffrè.

Sicari, A. (2006). Realtà antiche e categorie moderne. Osservazioni metodologiche. In L. Labruna, M. P. Baccari, & C. Cascione (Eds.), *Tradizione romanistica e Costituzione (II)*. Napoli: ESI.

Stanzione, P. (2017). Il soggetto. II. Capacità, legittimazione, status. In A. Cicu, F. Messineo, L. Mengoni, & P. Schlesinger (Eds.), *Trattato di diritto civile e commerciale*. Milano: Giuffrè.

Stein, P. (1980). *Legal evolution: The story of an idea*. Cambridge: Cambridge University Press.

Talamanca, M. (1990). *Istituzioni di diritto romano*. Milano: Giuffrè.

Trisciuoglio, A. (1998). *'Sarta tecta, ultrotributa, opus publicum faciendum locare'. Sugli appalti relativi alle opere pubbliche nell'età repubblicana e augustea*. Napoli: Jovene.

Veyne, P. (1981). Clientèle et corruption au service de l'État: la vénalité des offices dans le Bas-Empire romain. *Annales. Économies, Sociétés, Civilisations, 3*(XXXVI), 339–361.

Vincenti, U. (2007). Persona e diritto: trasformazioni della categoria giuridica fondamentale. In G. Boniolo, G. De Anna, & U. Vincenti (Eds.), *Individuo e persona. Tre saggi su chi siamo*. Milano: Bompiani.

From Cosmopolitan Individual Status (French Civil Code of 1804) and "*l'exercice des droits civils*" to EU Citizenship

Valentina Colcelli

1 Introduction

The EU Court of Justice has introduced the expression 'fundamental status' when referring to ideas of European citizenship. The notion of status, which was first seen in Roman law, is retained in present-day juridical idioms and legal language. However, its meaning remains vague (Cicu 1965, p. 181).

An individual's legal status is an on-going private and public condition (Rescigno 1973, p. 209). Common to all these ideas, however, is that status is the description of the person/group in relation to the state and/or to other private and public entities (Palazzo 2003, p. 23). Rather, individual legal status was described in terms of category, class or caste (Alpa 2013, p. 100).

As a matter of fact, the EU Court of Justice does not, in its notion of 'status' use the view of category, class or caste mentioned above. The meaning of EU citizenship being a 'fundamental status' is deeply linked to the fundamental right of free circulation in Europe, and therefore is far away from the historical idea of status that we have just described.

Starting from the characteristics of EU citizenship we demonstrate that the idea of a super-regional status for individual citizens can be found in the French civil code of Napoleon.

Of course, the above-mentioned private law tradition, as a starting point for understanding EU citizenship status as a super-regional condition, also has to be read in the light of provisions relating to fundamental rights and the international and European declarations on these. In this framework, the status is based on universal concepts and not on the fixed or formal value of a person.

V. Colcelli (✉)
National Research Council, IFAC Institute, 50019, Via Madonna del Piano 10, Sesto Fiorentino, Firenze, Italy
e-mail: valentina.colcelli@cnr.it

A. Bartolini et al. (eds.), *Dictionary of Statuses within EU Law*,
https://doi.org/10.1007/978-3-030-00554-2_3

This chapter will therefore try to explain the historical reasons behind the evolution of ideas regarding super-regional citizenship, which are grounded in the European private law tradition (the Napoleonic Code) as a precursor to modern EU citizenship and as an instrument for making the principle of non-discrimination effective.

To achieve this aim, this chapter will proceed as follows. First of all, we will examine Article 7 of the Napoleonic Civil Code. In Sect. 3, we will analyse the ways in which the exercise of civil rights contributes to a person's legal status in the light of the European process of integration. Individual rights were once primarily concerned with economic actors and the free market. Now, these rights extend to many aspects of citizens' lives. They have an impact on employment, free movement, the market, family law and the status of the individual. Next (Sect. 4), we will examine how the enlargement of legal capacity across boundaries, despite the principle of reciprocity, gives a concrete realization to the principle of non-discrimination among EU citizens. In Sect. 5, we conclude.

In this part of the book we do not consider the whole definition and description of EU citizenship, but instead look at the exercise of civil rights by EU citizens as a concrete manifestation of the rights of free circulation of people.

We make this choice for two main reasons: on the one hand, there is a specific chapter containing a complete analysis of EU citizenship (e.g. chapter "EU Citizen"); on the other hand, for the purpose of these pages the relevant aspect of EU citizenship is "the right to move and reside freely within the territory of the Member States" that is established by Article 20(2)(a) TFEU.

This is because there is a direct relationship between the exercise of civil rights, the right of free movement and EU citizenship status. The principle of non-discrimination in the exercise of civil rights for those who have moved from their native Member State to another EU country is the direct link to the European tradition of private law derived from the Napoleonic Civil Code.

To regard EU citizenship as a fundamental status is hence similar to saying that it enriches national citizenship and reduces discrimination.

To say that an EU citizen is really free in the exercise of civil rights in a host country is something more than subscribing to a contract. It is the concrete awareness that non-discrimination is a central focus of EU rights and a distinctive feature of citizens' fundamental individual legal status. This change was foreseen in Article 7 of the Napoleonic Code, where, for the first time in European history, an individual's legal status was not related to his or her legal capacity in private law within nationally defined boundaries.

2 Code Napoléon and How the Concept of Legal Capacity Has Evolved into Individual Supra-Regional Status

In the private law tradition, the idea developed that individual legal status was closely related to the concept of the legal capacity of the person across national boundaries. In private law, an individual's legal status and the attributes of this are set by (a) the law of the person's nationality (if the person was born in a civil law state); or and (b) the law of the person's domicile (if the person was born in a common-law state).

The idea that status was linked to social class ended after the French Revolution, with the principle of equality and the affirmation of equal rights for all. Equal rights do not override the limits of formal equality (Palazzo 2012, p. 218). However, the idea of the French Revolution, where universal, equal rights for free individuals were protected equally by the law, is sufficient for all citizens to be understood to possess the same formal legal position in private law, according to the *Code civil des Français*.

The legal capacity of all persons—not only French citizens—to exercise their property rights and their legal capacity to negotiate, to make a will, to bear witness, etc., was affirmed in the *Code Napoléon* (enacted on 8 March 1803 and promulgated on 18 March 1803), in Article 7 of Book I, Title I 'Of the Enjoyment and Privation of Civil Rights', Chapter I, 'Of the Enjoyment of Civil Rights', which states: "*L'exercice des droits civil est indépendant de la qualité de Citoyen, la quelle ne s'acquiert et ne se conserve que conformément à la loi constitutionnelle.*"

By the French Civil Code, the enjoyment of civil rights was expanded to those who were not French citizens, as well as to French people born outside France, those who were born in France to foreigners once they had reached their majority, women who were married to Frenchmen, and children born outside France to fathers who had lost their French citizenship.

All citizens had the legal capacity to negotiate, to make a will, to bear witness, and to exercise property rights because formally there was no longer a difference between rich and poor, nobleman and commoner, free man and servant (Palazzo 2012, p. 218). Although, State Councillor Treilhard distinguished between foreigners who chose to live in France, and therefore deserved greater attention because of the principle of reciprocity, and foreigners who only stayed temporarily in France (Palazzo 2012, p. 218), Anyway, we can affirm that Article 7 of the *Code Napoléon* is the starting point for an enlarged view of citizenship status that goes beyond national boundaries.

The preliminary address on the first draft of the *Code Napoléon*, members of the government-appointed commission, made a statement on the public function that was assigned to private law.

> Every revolution is a conquest. (…) The concern is no longer for the private relationships among men; there is only a political and general purpose. One seeks confederates rather than fellow citizens. All becomes public law. Good private laws are the greatest good that men can give and receive (Singh 2016, p. 4).

The spirit of the *Code civil des Français* has long been presented as a '*hymne à l'individu*', and as the '*triomphe de l'individualisme libéral*'. In other words, the spirit of the individual '*défendu par les philosophes du XVIIIe siècle*' was extolled by the elevation ('*not amment spiritualiste*') of the human being (Cornu 1990, pp. 106–107).

This point requires further clarification. Portalis means that the individual is the primary social atom in the social structure (Fenet 1827, p. 112). However, despite the fact that it has no formal legal status within the *Code Napoléon*, the family nevertheless remains an essential socio-political cell (Portalis 1801, pp. 102–103 and 105). Can individual freedom be guaranteed in private law? Portalis has a concise answer to this question: "*S'agit-il du droit, l'individu n'est rien; la loi est tout*" (Fenet 1827, p. 120). Francis X. Martin has shown that the principal drafters of the *Code Napoléon* did not legislate to consecrate and 'philosophically' exalt the freedom of the individual. Rather, they sought to integrate a social dimension that might restore order and stability to a French society shattered by revolutionary disorder.

In this way, in the *Code Napoléon* all people have rights and powers guaranteed by private law. All discrimination between free people and slaves falls away in the sphere of private law. Immunities and privileges cease to distinguish between individuals in a discriminatory manner. The law, however, is a fictitious means by which to facilitate the organization and representation of socio-economic relations in a society. As such, its function is purely utilitarian. It is sufficient, then, to organize and regulate the legal relationships between the individuals making up French society, and basic rights are not denied to wives, children, vagrants or beggars of no fixed abode.

Article 8 of the *Code Napoléon* states that '*Tout Français jouira des droits civils*', and that enjoyment lies within larger or smaller limits, ranging from simple inability to enjoy rights to the loss of that enjoyment. In other words, there are no universal civil rights for individuals in the *Code Napoléon*. The individual is at the core of the *Code Napoléon*, but not in the guise of a human being. Rather, she or he is the individual legal owner of property. This status dictates the way in which her or his social and economic relations are conducted. In this sense, it is not the individual but the individual property owner who is at the core of the *Code Napoléon* (Arnaud 1973).

Worse, it may even be said that this core is represented by the regulation of the property itself (Weil and Terré 1979, p. 98).

Portalis said that "*il n'y a que des individus dans la société, comme dans la nature*" (Portalis 1820, p. 256). Certainly, Portalis said that people are the overarching concern of the law. The value of the legislature is derived from the individuals who make use of it (Portalis 1801/2004, p. 100).

Anyway, the contents of the *Code civil des Français* are a reflection of French Enlightenment ideas, in which order is dictated by nature and man must adjust himself to the natural order (Palazzo 2012, p. 218). Therefore, a person is seen as a fragment of nature, but also as a member of society, where the essence of the law is to regulate the ability of that person (Portalis 1804, p. 14). For this reason, the enjoyment of civil rights is extended by the Civil Code to non-French persons.

The *Code civil des Français* used the enjoyment of civil rights, and thus private law instruments, to realize the philosophical and political idea of equal rights for free individuals who were protected equally by the law: 'Men are born and remain free and equal in rights. Social distinctions may be founded only upon the general good' (Art. 1, *Déclaration des droits de l'homme et du citoyen*, August 1789). From this choice, grounded on French Enlightenment ideas and '*l'exercice des droits civils*', begins a truly enlarged view of citizenship status.

3 EU Citizenship As Fundamental to EU Individuals' Status and "l'exercice des droits civils" in the Member State of Destination

The European Union, through a 'functional use' of private law instruments and the expansion of legal capacity across national boundaries, despite the principle of reciprocity (Cippitani 2015, p. 4), also gives material validity to the principle that there should be no discrimination.

There is a strong relationship between the issues surrounding private law and workers' rights to free movement, and this relationship has existed since the foundation of the European Community in 1957.

Free movement therefore means the possibility of seeking a job in another country, working in another country without special permission, living in another country not just for the purpose of working there, remaining in another country after one's employment ends, and enjoying treatment equal to that of local workers in access to employment, in working conditions, and in all other social and fiscal aspects of the host country (see Article 45 TFEU).

At this time, according to Article 21 TFEU and Article 3 TEU, free movement is guaranteed for all EU citizens. The articles mentioned above therefore extend the right of residence, the right to receive social benefits, and the right to agree contracts (not only work contracts) to all EU citizens. Certain rights are also extended to workers' family members.

For these reasons, free movement has both a direct and an indirect effect on the individual legal status of a person with respect to national family law and the law governing all types of contract (sales, rental, employment etc.), acting in addition to the principle of reciprocity that formally still survives in, for example, the Italian Civil Code 1942 (see Article 16 of *Pre leggi*).

Right to freedom of movement can grant individuals a different status to that enjoyed in their original Member State (Case 69/79 Jordens-Vosters [1980] ECR 75, par. 6). According to EU law regarding freedom of movement, the status of the person travels with the individual.

Taking into account the secondary legislation, the Preamble to Council Regulation 1612/68 calls for "the fundamental right of workers to improve their standard of living which must be exercised in freedom and dignity" (Kostakopoulou 2014, p. 428).

Instruments of European private law may change the regulatory approach to both the market for goods and products and the labour market (Colcelli 2013, p. 575). Thus, the regulation of the rights usually connected with the status of the person is—typically—a way of having a deep impact on a person's social position (Kostakopoulou 2014, p. 432; The Free Movement of Workers in the Countries of the European Economic Community, Bull. EC 6/61, pp. 5–10, p. 6; Regulation 1612/68).

4 The 'Enjoyment of Civil Rights' As an Instrument for Fulfilment of the Non-discrimination Principle

EU citizenship is, without doubt, connected with the conditions for citizenship under national law. Citizenship of the EU, established by the former Article 17 TEC, is not, however, intended to extend beyond the scope of the *ratione materiae* (also known as the subject-matter jurisdiction) of the Treaty and thus to include domestic situations that have no link to EU law (see 2 October 2003 Case C-148/02, Carlos Garcia Avello v État Belge). 'Fundamental status' cannot, therefore, usurp the citizenship of Member States. National citizenship could, however, be a limitation to the freedoms established by the Treaties that are incorporated in the notion of EU citizenship.

In the Grzelczyk case, EU citizenship was pronounced to be a fundamental status of Member State nationals, "(31) enabling those who find themselves in the same situation to enjoy the same treatment in law irrespective of their nationality" (ECJ, 20 September 2011, C-184/99, Grzelczy, I-6193, p. 31).

EU Court of Justice has consistently held that EU citizenship is of no relevance to domestic situations (ECJ, 17 September 2002, C-413/99, Baumbast and R., I-7091, p. 82).

Discrimination founded on Member State citizenship is something that EU law intends to overcome. If national citizenship becomes a ground for discrimination, it finds itself in conflict with the aims of the EU and its Treaties (see Articles 2 and 3 TFEU). As such, national citizenship must cede to fully egalitarian EU citizenship. The EU is fundamental in the sense that it is a safety net should national citizenship fail to meet the rights of the people.

Expression 'fundamental status' refers to the elimination of discrimination through the enjoyment of civil rights because of the exercise of free movement (ECJ C-184/99; ECJ C-413/99 etc.).

EU Court of Justice's reasoning in cases such as Martinez Sala v Freistaat Bayern (Case C-85/96 [1998] ECR I-2691) shows the way EU citizenship has been used to increase the protection offered by Community law against discrimination based on nationality.

5 Conclusions

The modern ideas of EU citizenship, founded in concepts of regional integration and also the European Convention of Human Rights, take private law as their starting point (Colcelli 2015, p. 247). Starting from the characteristic marks of EU citizenship, we can affirm that the idea of a super-regional status for individual citizens can be found in the French civil code of Napoleon. The *Code civil des Français* used the enjoyment of civil rights, and thus private law instruments, to realize the philosophical and political idea of equal rights for free individuals to be protected equally by the law.

The European Union, through a 'functional' use of private law instruments and the enlargement across boundaries of the legal capacity of citizens despite the principle of reciprocity, realized, in a concrete way, the principle of non-discrimination among EU citizens (Colcelli and Arnold 2015, p. 35).

If an EU citizen is really to be free to exercise civil rights in a host country, this requires something more than subscribing to a contract (Acemoglu 2010, pp. 17–32).

The historical moment in which we live offers us a vantage point from which to deepen the connection between history and the social dimension of private law (Amable 2003). Scholars (Alpa 1982, p. 194; Pocar 1989, p. 36; Baliba 2010, p. 21) who are concerned about the connections between status and legal capacity have shown for a long time that these connections are defeated by arranged international rules.

References

Acemoglu, D. (2010). Theory, general equilibrium, and political economy in development economics. *Journal of Economic Perspectives, 24*(3), 17–32.

Alpa, G. (1982). *Status e capacità*. Bari: Laterza.

Alpa, G. (2013). Status. In M. I. Álvarez Ledesma & R. Cippitani (Eds.), *Diccionario analíticode derechos humanose integración jurídica* (p. 649 ff). Rome, Perugia, Mexico City: ISEG srl.

Amable, B. (2003). *The diversity of modern capitalism*. Oxford: Oxford University Press.

Arnaud, A. J. (1973). *La règle du jeu dans la paix bourgeoise*. Paris: LGDJ.

Baliba, E. (2010). *La proposition de l'egaliberté*. Paris: PUF.

Cicu, A. (1965). Il concetto di status. In A. Cicu (Ed.), *Scritti minori* (Vol. 1). Milan: Giuffrè.

Cippitani, R. (2015). The 'contractual enforcement' of human rights in Europe. In A. Diver & J. Miller (Eds.), *Justiciability of human rights law in domestic jurisdictions* (pp. 307–332). Switzerland: Springer International Publishing.

Colcelli, V. (2013). Private law instruments as way of EU regional integration. In M. I. Álvarez Ledesma & R. Cippitani (Eds.), *Derechos Individuales e Integración regonal (antología)* (pp. 575–597). Rome, Perugia, Mexico City: ISEG srl.

Colcelli, V. (2015). The solidarity principle in new EU Member States. In C. Perugini & F. Pompei (Eds.), *Inequalities during and after transition in Central and Eastern Europe* (pp. 247–265). Basingstoke Hampshire: Palgrave Macmillan.

Colcelli, V., & Arnold, R. (2015). Individual rights as construction of the EU legal system. In V. Colcelli & R. Arnold (Eds.), *Europeanization through private law instruments. Arnold, R. (dir.) Entwicklungen im Europischen Recht-Developments in European Law - Developpements en droit europen* (pp. 35–38). Regensburg: Universitätsverlag.

Cornu, G. (1990). *Droit civil, introduction/les personnes/les biens* (pp. 106–107 and 122). Paris: Dalloz.

Fenet, P. A. (1827). *Recueil complet des travaux préparatoires au Code civil* (Vol. 11). Paris: Au depot, rue Saint-Andre des Arcs.

Kostakopoulou, D. (2014). European Union citizenship rights and duties: Civil, political and social. In E. Isin & P. Nyers (Eds.), *Handbook of global citizenship studies* (pp. 427–436). London: Routledge.

Palazzo, A. (2003). Interesse legittimi e tutela dei diritti del private. In *Nuove forme di tutela delle situazioni giuridiche soggettive, Atti della Tavola rotonda in memoria di Lorenzo Migliorini (Perugia, 7 dicembre 2001)*. Turin: Giappichelli.
Palazzo, A. (2012). Cittadinanza, ambiente e costituzione dei beni comuni. *Diritto e Processo, unique*, 217–237.
Pocar, F. (1989). *I diritti umani a 40 anni dalla Dichiarazione universale*. Padua: Cedam.
Portalis, J. E. M. (1801/2004). *Discours préliminaire du premier projet de Code civil. Titre original: Motifs et discours prononcés lors de la publication du Code civil. Discours prononcé le 21 janvier 1801 et le Code civil promulgué le 21 mars 1804. Preface by Michel Massenet*. Bordeaux: Éditions Confluences.
Portalis, J. E. M. (1804). *Code civil des français suivi de l'exposé des motifs*. Paris: Dalloz.
Portalis, J. É. M. (1820). *De l'usage et de l'abus de l'esprit philosophique durant le XVIII siècle* (Vol. II). Paris: Dalloz.
Rescigno, P. (1973). Situazione e status nell'esperienza del diritto. *Riv. Di dir. Civ.*, (I), 21 ff.
Singh, R. (2016). Preliminary address on the first draft of the civil code (1801) (Jean-Étienne-Marie Portalis (1746-1807), Trans). *Montesquieu Law Review*, 4.
Weil, A., & Terré, F. (1979). *General introduction to law*. Paris: Précis Dalloz.

Part II
Dictionary of European Union Statuses

Administrative Judges in Europe

Fabrizio Figorilli

1 The Reasons Why There Are Administrative Judges in European Legal Systems

It is well known that most of the issues concerning the judicial protection of legal subjects against public administrations can only be understood within the area of administrative law.

The matter of the judge who, in European legal systems, is called upon to resolve disputes between citizens and public authorities is no exception.

In the 19th Century in France was established a body—originally within the administration—to entrust quarrels between the administration and citizens who needed to protect their subjective legal position is a good example.

The first problem that arose when the executive power was submitted to control, as a result of the progressive implementation of the rule of law, was whether or not to identify a special judge to whom the resolution of conflicts should be entrusted. (Harlow and Rawlings 2009).

This led to the (almost automatic) choice in the so-called *droit administratif* countries to opt for a specific judicial body, taking into account the specificity of the rules governing the actions of public administrations.

This is the perspective of the position in Germany, Spain and Italy where, albeit following different paths and at different times, the idea was formed that only through the use of a dualist model could the aspiration of ensuring adequate methods (increasingly shaped over time according to the principle of effectiveness) for the protection of citizens against the unlawful measures of public authorities really be realized (Garcia de Enterria 2003).

F. Figorilli (✉)
Department of Law, Università degli Studi di Perugia, Perugia, Italy
e-mail: fabrizio.figorilli@unipg.it

A. Bartolini et al. (eds.), *Dictionary of Statuses within EU Law*,
https://doi.org/10.1007/978-3-030-00554-2_4

The genesis of the evolution of the administrative procedural system in the so-called common law systems is very different. As matter of fact, in that model substantive reasons led to the identification of a single judge to whom to entrust all kinds of controversy, regardless of the public or private nature of the author of the decision that was being made subject to judicial review.

Thus, since the same rules had to be applied to all types of legal relationships, there was no need to create a special judge to resolve conflicts in which one of the parties was a public authority.

However, over time, in these systems too, disciplines derogating from the rules of the common law were progressively adopted. This had several consequences for the procedural instruments and, especially in the latter part of the last century, led to the introduction, even in the United Kingdom, of forms of special protection in relation to public administrations that, by synthesis, have numerous points of contact with the dualist models described above (Chirulli 2017).

At the same time, the simultaneous presence of an administrative judge alongside an ordinary judge, although on the one hand representing the attainment of a goal (albeit with the inescapable differences that continue to run through the various national legal systems that adhere to the European Union), on the other hand is a source of uncertainty and complication with regard to the criterion by which disputes are submitted to each legal system.

More specifically, the criterion is the one that was already used two centuries ago in the French model, that is to say the nature of the activity carried out by the administration (*service public*), on the basis of the principle that any determination regarding the care of the public interest falls within the competence of the *Juge administratif*.

This approach has, in fact, not been able to prevent the fact that, over time, even in an apparently well-defined general context—a sort of watershed between the rules of public law and those of private law—it would be necessary to assign disputes in certain fields that are apparently of public importance (think of industrial and commercial public services) to the knowledge of the ordinary judge (Truchet 2005).

There is also the eternal debate in this area about the granting of jurisdiction to certain sections of the Italian Council of State, focusing on the choice of submitting the dispute to a particular judge on the basis of the nature of the subjective legal situation that led to the dispute.

This choice has therefore favoured the development, within the academic context, of a reflection on the consistency and relevance of the legitimate interest, since this is a prerequisite for the competence of the administrative judge, which, however, has been and still is the cause of difficulties with regard to the identification of the competent judge. This is particularly true when the Court of Cassation, in the exercise of its function as the judge of conflicts of jurisdiction, is called upon to settle the dispute.

For this reason, the most effective system seems to be the one adopted by Germany, in which all disputes involving a public administration (with the exception of matters relating to public contracts) fall within the competence of the administrative courts, since these matters arise from legal relations that are governed by public law.

2 The Characteristics of the Review Carried Out by the Administrative Judge in Some European Legal Systems

Once the reasons for the need to submit disputes between a public administration and the addressees of its action to an administrative judge have been clarified, it is worth dwelling briefly on the characteristics of this submission in the various European experiences.

In this perspective, it is useful recalling the French experience, which, in turn, has had a strong impact on the genesis and nature of the Italian administrative process and which has always represented an obligatory benchmark for scholars of European administrative justice systems (Scoca 2013).

More specifically, it should be pointed out that the judicial control of public decisions by the *Conseil d'État* represents the main instrument for ensuring the mere legitimacy of the choices and conduct of the administration, giving rise to a predominantly objective decision (Rivero 1974).

In fact, both the private and the special enforcement cases make it possible to establish if there are any deviations from the legal framework typical of the measures in question, in order to establish whether there is compliance with the parameters of the legitimacy of the administrative action.

For this reason, a wide-ranging right of action is granted to those who assert the defect just mentioned, almost as if it were a popular action, with the consequent *erga omnes* effectiveness of the judge's rulings.

The new powers of *astreintes* and *injaunctions*, with specific reference to the procedures for enforcing judgments (this is the result of the amendments made in the 1980, 1995 and 2000 reforms), and of *refères* as regards protective measures, changed the basic approach of the French administrative justice system.

The interests of the citizen have received renewed attention through the *recours objectif de pleine jurisdiction*. This allows a more incisive protection of the subjective position of the applicant that goes beyond the mere ascertainment of the unlawfulness of the censured decision and also allows the judge to condemn the administration or to reform the effect of the choice that was judged to be harmful.

Similar considerations can be seen in the development of the Italian system. It is interesting to note that even in this model we have progressively freed ourselves from a structure created and developed for over a century, to ensure an essentially objective protection (focused on a type of judgment whose purpose is to ascertain the defects in the legitimacy of the administrative measure without any connection to the claims of the applicant). This has been a long process that has required the case law and legal doctrine to change their points of view significantly, deepening and maximizing the subjective situation (called the legitimate interest) to legitimize the position of the applicant, as opposed to that of the holder of public authority. The administrative judge has therefore become the judge of legitimate interests, and has in fact been assimilated by the Italian Constitution to the classic situation that is typical of relations between civilians, understanding however by this notion a subjective situation, no longer quantitatively but only qualitatively different from subjective rights.

There is therefore an increased importance in the evaluation of the decisions of the administrative court in relation to the satisfaction of the claims of the applicant in substantive terms and the exercise of power once the dispute is concluded with a decision to accept or reject the application. This has all taken place while the institutions and a model of judgment based on the typical action of cancellation have been maintained for almost 150 years.

It was only in 2010 that the administrative trial took on its final shape, thanks to the provision of a code governing all stages of the proceedings. The code provides for a number of actions (constituting, convicting, ascertaining, enforcing) that can be taken to promote effective protection, in line with the principles of the Italian Constitution.

No less interesting are the changes that have taken place in the legal system of the United Kingdom, particularly in view of the fact that, in this context, disputes with public authorities were usually settled on the basis of the rules laid down by the ordinary law. In this model, therefore, the primary objective of the system of guarantees provided by the institutions of the civil trial was to achieve uniformity in the application of the provisions in force and not the protection of the subjective situation of the citizen.

Nor, in this regard, did prerogative orders play an incisive role, in the context of the 1977 reform concerning the procedure of application for judicial review. In this model, the principal requirement of the legal system is to verify the legitimacy or otherwise of a determination by the public authorities, rather than to recognize the right of the applicant.

However, exactly 40 years later, with the Tribunals, Courts and Enforcement Act of 2007, the United Kingdom decided once again to intervene, reshaping the functions of a figure who was beginning to assume the characteristics of an administrative judge (Craig 1998) and to whom the review of administrative decisions and also the satisfaction of the legitimate expectations of those who brought the dispute were entrusted (Marchetti 2014). This is the case despite the wide discretionary powers granted to the judge regarding the admissibility of the claim, with a view to a wise balance between the need to protect the citizen and the efficiency of administrative action (including the costs of procedures).

According to the German model—which is focused on offering full protection of the subjective (public) right—the judge's position is absolutely independent, and the judge has wide decision-making powers with reference to disputes where the parties involved are considered as equals (Schmidt-Aßmann et al. 2016).

Consequently, the norms regulating administrative trials are closely modelled on those for civil trials, with the aim of attributing to the applicant, in the event of the successful outcome of the dispute, the benefit that is the subject of his application, without limiting him to the mere quashing of the measure considered unlawful. Hence there is a need to assign a role of primary importance to the judge, so that the judge has the power to ascertain the facts on which the contested measure is based and to evaluate them, even going beyond the formal arguments put forward by the parties (Folkert Geert 2014).

3 The Role of the Case Law of the Court of Justice and the European Court of Human Rights as the Main Instrument for the Progressive Establishment of a European Process Model

Last but not least, we shall make a few brief comments on the influence, on the models of administrative justice in the Member States, of European integration over recent decades, together with the increasing influence of the case law of the Court of Justice and the European Court of Human Rights.

The mechanism of the so-called Europeanization of national procedural rights proves to be of particular interest, giving rise to a real process of cross-fertilization, capable of ensuring the circulation of principles and rules within the domestic legal systems of the countries that are members of the European Union (De Pretis 2005).

This is, in essence, a sort of triangulation that allows rules, of both a substantive and a procedural nature, to create a virtuous path between European law and the national laws, thus creating a multi-level system as the result of a progressive interconnection between the regulatory sources for national and European judgments, within which a leading role must be attributed to jurisprudential sources.

This is all a result of the attention given by the European Courts to one of the new generation of fundamental rights, namely the right to an 'effective remedy'. In recent years, this has on several occasions committed the European judges to giving concrete answers, in accordance with what is solemnly provided for by Article 47 of the European Charter of Human Rights.

This trend has also had direct consequences on the way national judges behave when they are called upon to confront these new realities, making judicious use of the instrument of so-called 'counter-limits' (by virtue of which the decisions of the European Courts must be implemented on condition that they do not conflict with the constitutional principles of the internal system, in the light of the verification made by the Constitutional Courts).

This is the case with the evolution that has accompanied precautionary protection in Italy and the driving role played by positive Euro-unitary regulations, as well as the contributions made by the case law of the Court of Justice regarding the introduction of new instruments to protect the applicant, compared to the original scheme that had been set up and remained in force for a long time in the Italian administrative justice system and also in France (Caranta 2007).

All this is a consequence of the numerous judgments issued by the Court of Justice on the matter, from the 1990s onwards when the Luxembourg judges, on the one hand, imposed on the Member States respect for the principles and levels of protection imposed by the discipline of the Treaty (in the *Factortame* judgments of 1990, the *Zuckerfabrik* decision of 1991, and the *Atlanta* decision of 1995) and, on the other hand, dictated an alternative discipline to the one in force in the national procedural models (De Pretis 2002).

In Italy, there was a significant introduction in 2000 of the possibility for the applicant, in extremely serious cases, to obtain from the administrative judge a unilateral measure that allows him to take all appropriate measures to safeguard his subjective situation even before the collective hearing in which the precautionary application is addressed.

No less worthy of attention is the issue of the strength of the judicial review of the administrative judge in those cases in which the injury to the interested party derives from the passing of an administrative measure of a technical discretionary nature. At EU level, the idea seems to be to give the judicial body wide powers of investigation, not least to prevent possible infringements of Article 6(1) of the European Convention of Human Rights, which requires the principle of fair proceedings to be upheld, in opposition to the much more cautious positions traditionally adopted by the Italian administrative judges (European Court of Human Rights, 21 January 2014, Ref. No. 48754/11, *Placì* v *Italy*).

Finally, there is the very delicate problem of the intangibility of *res judicata* that is causing so many questions for the Italian procedural model, as it affects one of the rules that have always governed the way in which an incontrovertible judgment is reached, and the ability to establish definitively the legal relationship following the making of an unchangeable judgment by the competent court.

On these aspects, the Court of Justice has also failed to act consistently and firmly on the openings expressed by the EDU Court, sometimes proclaiming the need to respect legal certainty (in the *Kapferer* judgment, Court of Justice Case-234/04), and at other times declaring its support for substantive restrictions on this rule.

These brief reminders are sufficient to give an understanding that there is still a long way to go. At the same time, the experience gained during the controversies referred to above gives a perfect idea of the type of development taking place and the difficulties, but at the same time the opportunities, that the dialogue between the courts, which has been going on for some decades, can offer in terms of European legal integration (De Pretis 2007). Not surprisingly, development has also taken place through the contribution made by the protection of human rights, on the one hand, and of the fundamental rights closely connected to them, on the other hand, as a result of the wise work of stitching that has been carried out by interpreters both on the theoretical level and in the application of case law, operating a complex systematization of principles and rules regulated at a conventional level and at a positive level, as well as being read and interpreted by European and national judges.

References

Caranta, R. (2007). La tutela giurisdizionale (italiana, sotto l'influenza comunitaria). In M. P. Chiti & G. Greco (Eds.), *Trattato di diritto amministrativo europeo*. Milano: Giuffrè.

Chirulli, P. (2017). Standing e funzione della giustizia amministrativa. Una riflessione comparata. *Quaderni Dir. Proc. Amm.*, pp. 77 ff.

Craig, P. (1998). Ultra vires and the foundations of judicial review. *Cambridge Law Journal, 57,* 63 ff.

De Pretis, D. (2002). La tutela giurisdizionale amministrativa europea e i principi del processo. *Riv. trim. dir. pubbl.*, pp. 687 ff.

De Pretis, D. (2005). La tutela giurisdizionale amministrativa in Europa tra integrazione e diversità. *Riv. it. dir. Pubbl. e comunitario*, pp. 13 ff.

De Pretis, D. (2007). La giustizia amministrativa. In G. Napolitano (Ed.), *Diritto amministrativo comparato* (pp. 283–323). Milano: Giuffrè.

Folkert Geert, W. (2014). *The vigilance of individuals: How, when and why the EU legislates to facilitate the private enforcement of EU law before national courts* (pp. 71 ff). Leiden: Leiden University.

Garcia de Enterria, E. (2003). *La justicia administrativa en el cambio de siglo* (pp. 83 ff). Ciudad de Mexico: Fundap.

Harlow, C., & Rawlings, R. (2009). *Law and administration*. Cambridge: Cambridge Press.

Marchetti, B. (2014). Il giudice amministrativo tra tutela soggettiva e oggettiva: riflessioni di diritto comparato. *Dir. Proc. Amm.*, pp. 74 ff.

Rivero, J. (1974). Le juge administratif gardien de la lègalitè administrative ou gardien administratif de la lègalitè? In M. M. Waline (Ed.), *Le juge et le droit public* (pp. 701–717). Paris: L. G. D. J.

Schmidt-Aßmann, E., De Lucia, L., & Romano, M. C. (2016). Prospettive della tutela giurisdizionale amministrativa in Germania e in Italia. *Dir. Proc. Amm.*, pp. 711 ff.

Scoca, F. G. (2013). Recours pour excès de pouvoir e ricorso al giudice amministrativo. Stesse radici, simili problemi, soluzioni diverse. *Dir. Proc. Amm.*, pp. 1 ff.

Truchet, D. (2005). Playdoyer pour une cause perdue; la fin du dualisme juridictionnnel. In *Actualitè juridique* (pp. 1767 ff). Droti administratif.

Artist

Carlos Francisco Molina del Pozo and Covadonga Reyes Assiego

1 Introduction

To accurately address the status of artists in the present legal framework, one must look backward. Explaining the material content of artistic activities is not an easy task due to the dynamism and subjectivity of perception.

The etymological root of the lexeme ("ars, artis") refers to those works in which talent, technique, and creativity have been reflected. Nevertheless, such meaning has evolved over time, being susceptible to changes (e.g. new technologies have led to new ways to express the arts) and circumstantial interpretations. We have previously discussed the difficulty in defining artistic activity due to the linguistic disambiguation that has taken place over time, and also due to the innovation resulting from the best technical teams or methods exploiting its exercise.

Before carrying on with this matter we must first classify the activities presently considered to be an art. Painting, sculpture, poetry, drama, and music are all classical art media. In the last few decades, and especially in the last century, new platforms and disciplines have been introduced where art has been expressed in a new way, such as cinema, architecture, photos, and even some artisan works. In conclusion, now even the most skeptical recognise that art can include those whose works contain an aesthetic value.

Going into the objective status, as a result of the critical view of society, artists, their activities, and their defining have suffered some ups and downs according to the time period in which they have practised and created their art. However, we can appreciate the fact that they always have satisfied some requests, which we will explain below.

C. F. Molina del Pozo (✉) · C. Reyes Assiego
Department of Law, Universidad de Alcalá de Henares, Alcalá de Henares, Spain
e-mail: carlosf.molina@uah.es

A. Bartolini et al. (eds.), *Dictionary of Statuses within EU Law*,
https://doi.org/10.1007/978-3-030-00554-2_5

2 The Legal Scheme

We must expound upon the current legal framework, including the legal situation for artists for several reasons.

Art concerns a job related to the freedom recognised both within the European Union and globally: the Universal Human Rights Treaty (Arts. 19, 29), the International Agreement of Civil and Political Rights (Arts. 19, 29), the Convention of the Children's Rights (Art. 13). Concerning European law, we must consider the European Convention for the Protection of the Fundamental Rights and Public Freedom, Art. 10.

The law is bound to recognise artists' roles, but not to regulate their work.

The law establishes a few limits, for cases in which situations arise where artistic freedom could harm another right of the same range or legal importance.

The European Union and some cooperative States have bestowed through Treaties greater opportunities for artistic movement within Europe.

Grants and subsidies are endowed to different arts. One of the most important grants is the STEP Beyond Travel grant. Some grants are oriented toward artists and cultural workers, supplied by the European Culture Foundation, and focused mainly on persons under 35.

3 European Union and International Legal Framework

At the European level, it is important to mention the treaties signed by the majority of European Union member countries. The agreements provide for a harmonisation and homogeneity that has been the root of later Treaties of the European Union. They have been inspired by some principles already found in the treaties, which will be discussed later. Because of them, the European artists, protected by such a norm, behold not just copyright protection, but also the related derivative rights. The artists collective in general will be able to see their artworks protected in other countries, which have ratified the texts giving some guarantees; they will even be able to know the limits of protection in some specific cases.

The following agreements are limited to a work's protection. There are also regulations that ease its dispersal and commercialisation.

Probably the first international agreement that protects and safeguards the artist and professionals of culture is Copyright Acts: Berne Convention for the Protection of Literary and Artistic Works about the copyright, that regulates the first conception of a work that will later be complemented with other, more modern, international treaties. The 1886 text of the Berne Convention for the Protection of Literary and Artistic Works has been revised on several occasions, adapting to different events and the evolution of law at the national level in different countries that have adopted the agreement. It has been modified to protect what is referred to as the artistic work's creation, its use, and its dissemination, along with many others that had been affected by technological evolution. The first review of the text was in 1908 in Berlin, later in Rome in 1928, and then again in Stockholm in 1967. The last review was in Paris in 1971. The text was not adopted due to greater copyright protection at the international level, but dealt with possible harmonisation at a legal level among countries, which gave shape to the agreement.

Two principles are reflected in the Act of Paris and the Berna Treaty in 1971. The first declares the legal protection at a national level, affirming that a realised work inside one member country of the treaty would be protected by the other countries. The second principle affects minimum rights, meaning that the member States' laws must provide minimum levels of the protection already declared in the text. The treaty fails to add that many states have joined the Treaty of Berna due to the commercialisation and globalisation supplied by telematics and emerging technologies. Article 2 of the agreement declares that the context and works protected include all the productions in the literary, scientific and artistic field, whatever it could be the way of expression. Article 2.6 declares that the coverage of protection is given to the author with certain exceptions or modalities referred to cinematographic works, Art. 14 bis. Article 3 declares that the protected subject is the nation's author, or residents in any member country. Articles 8, 9, 11, 11bis, 11ter, 12, and 14 contain and create a list of the typologies of protected works. The rest of the agreement exposes their patrimonial limitations or free use (see quotations, special cases), or non-voluntary licenses, such as broadcasting and public communications.

The right, arising since the technological boom, is an offshoot of copyright. Rights of the artists, interpreters, executors and phonograms producers of the musical protected by the copyright. The broadcasting which are title of the exclusive right to realize, forbid or authorize, can also profit of the related rights (Treaty of Brussels about the distribution of signal carrier of programs transmitted by satellites, 1974).

Consequently, at the end of the 1980 it was evident that new international rules were necessary.

Therefore, the work of WIPO Internet treaties (WIPO Copyright Treaty (WCT) and the WIPO Performances and Phonograms Treaty (WPPT)) about interpretation or phonogram execution was started to prepare new instruments in both copyright and related right.

The European Union embraced the most important aspects of the Berna Treaty, respecting the rules of the member States that had developed competent legislation and that again faced a new framework established by Europeans agreements.

In the European Union Treaty, or Maastricht, was produced the official recognition of the cultural dimension inside the idea of European Integration. A range of competence remains inside the cultural action of the European Community.

These are some treaties disposing of normative content about culture, but the key words are limited to recognize as they do not indicate either an imperative of action.

The culture as its contents is recognized as a common feature in Europe, where a legislative labor will raise after the treaty that recognizes such presence in common. With the wish to improve the solidarity between its countries whit the respect due to their history, culture and traditions. The cultural peculiarities of each region in the EU must be recognized.

It is necessary to enhance the rules of how the different institutions cooperate in matters with other organisations of the European Union, with other member states, and even with international organisations, such as the European Council (30.3.2010 Official Diary of European Union C 83/121).

Directive 92/100/CEE of the Council of 19th November 1992 about the rent, loan rights, and other copyrights in the field of the intellectual property has been modified substantially on several occasions. In the interest of greater rationality and clarity, it is best to look to the coding of this directive. It has been modified on several occasions. One of the biggest challenges the artist must cope with is the protection of his or her work of art, which is more vulnerable to new technologies used for plagiarism, intellectual appropriation, or illegal spreading. Interest in this issue has had a big increase in trade; therefore, artists can express their work with a larger audience due to easy access and distribution.

The European Union has not ignored these events, nor does it have a desire to regulate this situation.

The most recent legislative overview included a directive, with the goal of reaching the level of the EU. The Directive provides a spark in the debate about the content of an artistic activity. The rent and the loan of some protected work by the copyright as the objects protected by similar rights have each time more importance particularly for the authors, artists, interpreters, some executors and phonograms and filmmakers. As we have previously exposed the task has incorporated new modalities of creation and expressions.

Inside the scheme of the Directive some points of interest and legal relevance are noted.

It is fair to say that the exercise and the realised works by the art and cultural professionals become more important and "they can be considered of capital importance for the economic and cultural development of the community" as is recognised in the preamble in the third paragraph.

Enhance the importance of the benefits trade, declaring the necessity of increasing such need with the time and support of the Treaties and Directives. This has remained the same since 2006. Establish a legal framework for increased labor harmonisation of the collective. Benefits must be equally provided through an harmonised establishment of a legal frame in the Community.

It alludes to the obligatory nature of remuneration through an equitable benefit for the services in a direct or indirect way. Art. 5. The following articles establish some measures, such as the distribution. Art. 9.

Regulation (EU) No 1295/2013 of the European Parliament and of the Council of 11 December 2013 establishing the Creative Europe Programme (2014 to 2020) and repealing Decisions No 1718/2006/EC, No 1855/2006/EC and No 1041/2009/EC Text with EEA relevance, concerns one of the most ambitious ideas and Project of the Union, in the short term, establishes a series of objectives: Support the promotion of cultural and artistic expression, so as to establish some requirements for a sustainable and necessary competitiveness that mobilises the expectation of the

Union face as European cultural face time. Its foundation is in the TFUE and in the United Nations Educational, Scientific and Cultural Organization (UNESCO), celebrated in 2005.

The Union's support of cultural and creative sectors: the mix of programmes the Union continues to support. The directives and European rules that created on this issue are as follows: (a) Decision number 1718/2006/CE of the European Parliament and the Council. Programme Media; (b) La Decision number 1855/2006/CE. The European Parliament and The Council Programme Culture; (c) Decision number 1041/2009/CE; (d) programme MEDIA Mundus; (e) The Decision number 1622/2006/CE; (f) The Decision number 1194/201.

In the European Parliament and the Council, relative action to the hallmark of the European patrimony. They define what is understood as a cultural and creative sector, declaring that the artistic expressions, as defined, remain inflated, affecting the reach of the project. It is important to note that it provides that those who are outside the agreement are able to sell their products.

The mobility programmes find its foundation in the art 4 Rule (UE) Number 1295/2013. The European Union safeguards the employment, study, research, coproduction and participation in stay and exchange programmes designated to promote the professional trajectory of artists and culture professionals. For several artists, the mobility provides not an option found in the willing, but in an imperative in the face of competitiveness. The EU recognises the importance of mobility and integration inside its competitive field and territory, providing therefore:

- Improvement of professional opportunity;
- Access to a new markets;
- Promotion of a cultural diversity and intercultural dialogue;
  Increase and spreading of the audience;
- Establishment of associations and contracts; and
- Creation of networks

The role of the European Commission is to support, encourage, and facilitate complementary measures of the member States in order to reduce the obstacles to mobility faced by workers in this trade. So, a correct framework must be offered next for a complete guide about questions related to mobility. It is worth mentioning that since 2008 the member States of the EU have collaborated regarding mobility and have offered greater flexibility to travel in different European regions or within other states; to this end, they have signed agreements of reciprocity and collaboration. Currently, through an open method of coordination, increased mobility in the field of culture is promoted, facilitating the exchange of ideas, techniques, knowledge, good habits, and the peer-learning. In April 2013 and June 2014 the Commission convened a series of seminars about artist mobility. Three issues were highlighted: visa Schengen; insurance; and cross-border taxation.

4 Conclusion

The artist observes the revaluation of their rights in Europe, which have been adjusted to accommodate modernism (i.e. the technological revolution). Both national and international laws are limited in recognizing some of artists' rights without further limits on author protection, plagiarism, or any dissemination without consent.

Maybe we are facing a legal status with both greater discretion without any legislative oversight, as even the national legal systems are able to regulate these issues, thereby establishing a link with freedom, as art remains in international and communitarian treaties.

Asylum Seeker

Jeanise Dalli

1 Introduction

Originally, international law on asylum, the existence of which preceded by decades European Union (EU) asylum law, provided no specific definition of 'asylum seeker' and lacked a formal distinction between this figure and that of the 'refugee', in that they were construed to have a similar meaning. By contrast, EU asylum law, at its inception, included an explicit definition of 'asylum seeker'. This definition has, however, been removed following recent amendments to the legal instruments that laid it down and the focus now is on the 'applicant' (for international protection), rather than the 'asylum seeker'.

This chapter starts by analysing the orthodox understanding of 'asylum seeker' in international law, and then proceeds to compare this with the applicable definition under EU law before 2013, when only the term, 'applicant', was kept in the text of the law. Then, the final section analyses the key factors that are contributing to defining and re-defining asylum seekers and shows how European integration has led to a new understanding of this figure, namely as a legal classification and an unofficial civil status. With reference to the Maltese asylum regime, the chapter also highlights some of the negative consequences, resulting from this newly developed status at EU level.

J. Dalli (✉)
Department of Civil Law, Faculty of Laws, University of Malta, Msida, Malta
e-mail: jbonn09@um.edu.mt

A. Bartolini et al. (eds.), *Dictionary of Statuses within EU Law*,
https://doi.org/10.1007/978-3-030-00554-2_6

2 The Traditional Understanding of 'Asylum Seeker' in International Law

Historically, the 1951 Geneva Convention Relating to the Status of Refugees (1951 Convention)–deemed to be the foundation of international refugee protection today–has lacked not only a specific definition of 'asylum seeker', but also a specific reference to the term *per se.* Rather, the focus was more on defining the 'refugee' and on laying down basic minimum standards of protection for those who fitted within this legal definition. In fact, the title of the Convention itself immediately sets the 'refugee', rather than the 'asylum seeker', as the focal point and the main object of protection. Additionally, some Articles in the Convention, particularly those dealing with expulsion and return, are rather ambiguous about the term 'refugee'. For instance, Article 31 is headed, 'Refugees unlawfully in the country of refuge', and provides that these should 'present themselves without delay to the authorities and show good cause for their illegal entry or presence'. Taken literally, the Article seems to be referring to asylum seekers who have already been granted refugee status; however, on a close reading, one understands that the term, 'refugees', is referring, instead, to asylum seekers who not only lack a legal status but who also have not yet presented themselves to the authorities.

The main reason, for the above omissions and apparent ambiguities, is because traditionally, refugee status has been declaratory in nature, i.e., not a status that is granted by states but simply, *ipso facto*, recognised by them, as the same status is defined by virtue of facts–namely, the search for asylum–rather than formalities (Hathaway and Foster 2017, p. 1). In fact, UNHCR emphasises that asylum seekers do not become refugees because of recognition of their refugee status, but they are recognised as such *because* they are refugees (UNHCR 2011, para. 28). Thus, the drafters of the 1951 Convention felt there was no need for a conceptual understanding of 'asylum seeker' or for any explicit definition in the Convention. Furthermore, there was no necessity to distinguish between asylum seekers and refugees or to classify them within separate legal categories; thus, the real distinction is between those who fit the refugee definition and those who are excluded (1951 Convention, respectively at Arts. 1A[2], 1D-F).

Nonetheless, international organisations working within the field of asylum, such as UNHCR (UNHCR 2018) and Amnesty International (Amnesty 2018) *do* provide a specific definition of asylum seekers and attempt to distinguish them from refugees. Whilst these organisations define the refugee in accordance with the 1951 Convention, they refer to asylum seekers as persons who are seeking sanctuary but whose request has not yet been processed and hence, not yet formally recognised as refugees by the state of asylum.

3 The Definition of 'Asylum Seeker' in EU Law

Although EU asylum law was 'based on the full and inclusive application of the 1951 Convention' (see, e.g., dir. 2011/95/EU, preamble, para. 2), unlike this Convention, two of its legal instruments, namely regulation 343/2003 (Dublin II Regulation) and directive 2003/9/EC (Reception Directive), provided a specific definition of 'asylum seeker'; this definition was the same as that of an 'applicant' (for international protection) (respectively, Art. 2[c] & Art. 2[b]). However, initially, this definition was not the same for these two legal instruments because, whilst the Dublin II Regulation defined the 'applicant' and the 'asylum seeker' as 'a third country national [TCN] who has made an application for asylum in respect of which a final decision has not yet been taken' (Art. 2[d]), the Reception Directive also included stateless persons in its definition (Art. 2[c]). However, this was remedied in 2013, when amendments to the Regulation extended protection to stateless persons.

From the given definitions of 'asylum seeker' and (asylum) 'applicant', one may understand that the EU legislators, at the time, intended to limit the scope of the definition to TCNs–i.e. nationals of states outside the EU, who do not enjoy the right to free movement within the EU (see, e.g., dir. 2008/115/EC, Art. 3[1])–and to stateless persons, thereby excluding EU nationals from their protective scope. Interestingly, before the 1967 Protocol Relating to the Status of Refugees (1967 Protocol), which removed the temporal and geographical limitations of the 1951 Convention, the Convention was applicable solely to persons fleeing events occurring in Europe or elsewhere before 1st January 1951 (Art. 1B); the *raison d'être* being that the Convention was originally drafted as a post-Second World War instrument of humanitarian protection. However, the Protocol did not affect those states that had made reservations about granting asylum only to people fleeing events occurring within Europe before 1951 (Art. 1[3]), notably to people from European countries. Hence, EU accession required those European states that had made such reservations to revoke them; meaning that the geographical limitations they had assented to, would now be reversed to exclude EU citizens. Consequently, the conceptual understanding of TCNs has changed from meaning a European national to a non-EU citizen (or stateless person).

Indeed, the concepts of TCNs and statelessness are also implicit in one of the underlying criteria constituting the definition of 'refugee' in the 1951 Convention, namely, that in order to qualify as refugees, asylum seekers must seek refuge outside their country of nationality, or if they have no nationality, outside the country of their former habitual residence (Art. 1A[2]); thereby excluding internally displaced persons (IDPs) from the definition. In the EU context, since EU citizens are perceived to belong to the same Union and to enjoy free movement there within, IDPs can be construed as referring to EU nationals who seek asylum in another EU state and thus, excluded from protection.

It is noteworthy that, in international human rights law instruments, the right to be granted asylum, is not expressly recognised. Thus, the principle of state sovereignty allows EU states to remain in control of their territorial borders, and the right to decide who does and who does not qualify for international protection, according to the criteria established by law. At the same time, given the universal recognition of the Human Right (HR) to seek and to enjoy asylum, laid down under the 1948 Universal Declaration of HRs (Art. 14) and the EU Charter of Fundamental Rights (Art. 18)–a right which should be enjoyed equally by all human beings–EU states remain duty-bound to respect this HR, irrespective of one's country of origin (COO). Despite this fact, Protocol 24 on asylum for EU nationals (12008E/PRO/24), lays down this indirect prohibition by stating, in its sole article, that EU states are to declare applications by EU nationals as admissible, only in the exceptions stipulated therein, including if the member-state so decides unilaterally. This prohibition is based, *inter alia,* on the argument that EU countries are regarded as "safe" countries[1] since they all respect HRs, including the principle of *non-refoulment [prohibition of forced return]* (see, e.g., reg. 604/2013, preamble, para. 3). Nonetheless, although the position taken by EU legislators could be seen as impinging upon EU nationals' HR to seek asylum, states remain free to process such applications, in view of directive 2011/95/EU (Qualifications Directive, Art. 3) which gives EU states the discretion to lay down more favourable standards for determining who qualifies for international protection and Article 3 of the 1951 Convention, not to discriminate on the grounds of COO (Gil-Bazo 2006, p. 10).

The 2013 amendments to the Dublin II Regulation and the Reception Directive, which produced regulation 604/2013 (Dublin III Regulation) and directive 2013/33/EU (Recast Reception Directive), left the EU asylum legal framework without a specific definition of 'asylum seeker', much like international law. In both instruments, the term, 'asylum seeker', was removed from the list of definitions and only the term, 'applicant', was maintained. The term, 'asylum seekers', was also removed from the title of the Recast Reception Directive and replaced with 'applicants for international protection'. Interestingly, Gil-Bazo (2015, p. 2) observes that, under EU law, the concept of 'asylum' is gradually being replaced by the concept of 'international protection', based on a system of statuses, namely the refugee and subsidiary statuses–this could be one of the reasons why the figure of the asylum seeker was removed. Arguably, these amendments could also be seen as superfluous because essentially, the terms, 'applicant' (for international protection) and 'asylum seeker', have the same connotations. Furthermore, without prejudice to the exceptions abovementioned, the same criterion that qualifies 'applicants for international protection', that was applicable before the term, 'asylum seeker', was taken out, applies today–namely that applicants have to be TCNs or stateless persons.

[1] Nonetheless, the ongoing case of Russian whistleblower, Maria Efimova, currently wanted by the Maltese courts to face fraud allegations, has challenged both the long held perception of EU countries as "safe" COO and the narrow definition of asylum seeker under EU asylum law—see Caruana (2018).

4 The Asylum Seeker as a Legal Category & Implications Thereof Within the EU

As indicated above, the introduction of an *exclusive* definition, defining people in search of sanctuary within the EU, was purely an EU legal construction. Certainly, the objective of EU states in constructing this definition was not to attempt to establish a universal interpretation of an 'asylum seeker' or (asylum) 'applicant'. In fact, the legal instruments abovementioned, clearly state that the definitions listed therein, are specific to these instruments and, hence, are meant to be exclusively applicable within the EU asylum system, binding upon EU states only.

It must be emphasised, however, that the figure of the (asylum) 'applicant', both under the original and the recast legislation, reflects an understanding of the 'asylum seeker' as a distinct legal category. Once asylum seekers make a formal application for asylum, they are automatically transferred from the social to the legal category. In practice, this has developed as a result of the duty of EU states to grant asylum, or rather, to award a legal status to those who qualify. This is implicit in and imposed by the Qualifications Directive (Gil-Bazo 2006, p. 7), as well as denoted by the wording, 'Member states *shall [emphasis added]* grant' refugee or subsidiary status (Arts. 13, 18). This duty has created a corresponding subjective right *to receive* asylum and a space for asylum seekers to navigate in a "legal limbo" pending the outcome of their asylum application. This space necessarily required the development of an *ad hoc* legal status, for the duration of the asylum process.

Although, as opposed to refugee and subsidiary status, the 'asylum seeker', is not formally recognised as a distinct legal status in EU law, the rights relating to reception under the Recast Reception Directive (including the rights to information, documentation certifying one's legal status as an asylum seeker, accommodation and employment) and the procedural guarantees under directive 2013/32/EU–the Recast Procedures Directive–(including the right to *non-refoulement* and the right to appeal or to make a subsequent application in the case of a rejected claim), can be perceived, both as an acknowledgment of the asylum claim and the award of an *ad hoc* informal legal status to asylum seekers awaiting a decision on their claim for protection. These rights become applicable once an asylum application is lodged.

This informal status carries with it rights but also duties. In fact, the contemporary emphasis on the 'applicant' (for international protection), rather than on the 'asylum seeker', sheds light on the duty of asylum seekers–especially those who enter in an irregular manner–to present themselves to the asylum authorities for the purpose of making a formal claim for asylum and to co-operate with these authorities as much as possible (see, e.g., Recast Reception Dir. Art. 7[5]).

The initial introduction of the figures of the 'asylum seeker' and the 'applicant' can be perceived as a positive development, particularly since, unlike the 1951 Convention, EU law aims to provide a comprehensive legal framework for their protection. However, this mode of conceptualising asylum seekers as merely 'applicants', instead of refugees *a priori*, who still need to be recognised as such, has created several problems. In fact, in addition to the argument made above, this could be another reason why the figure of the asylum seeker was removed from EU law. Originally, the Reception Directive made the automatic detention of asylum seekers permissible. This mode of "reception" was deemed contrary to the 1951 Convention, which provides that refugees should not be penalised 'on account of their illegal entry or stay' (Art. 31[1]). Malta, for instance, was one of the EU countries with a reception policy imposing the automatic detention of asylum seekers entering the country illegally. Up till 2015, upon arrival, all asylum seekers were issued a return decision and a removal order, in terms of Maltese Immigration Law, and immediately placed in detention, with certain exceptions (aida 2018, p. 57). A lot of criticism was levelled at the Maltese state and the European Court of Human Rights also found the state in breach of HRs due to poor conditions and long waiting periods in detention.[2] This problem has now been remedied with the prohibition of holding persons in detention for the sole reason that they are seeking asylum; rather, the Recast Reception Directive now provides that resort to detention should only occur when necessary, for the reasons and under the guarantees and conditions specified in the Directive (Arts. 8–11).

5 Conclusion

European integration has largely modified the traditional understanding of asylum seekers in international law. Although the term, 'asylum seeker', was removed from EU law and only the term, 'applicant' was kept, the definition of 'applicant' still focuses on TCNs and stateless persons. Indeed, EU law has reproduced the principles of TCN and statelessness found in the 1951 Convention. However, the understanding of TCNs has been narrowed down to exclude EU citizens, mainly due to the perception of EU states as "safe" countries. Thus, apart from their main activity–the search for asylum–asylum seekers are also defined by virtue of their COO, which has become an additional criterion for the determination of their asylum claim, in addition to those set in the Qualifications Directive. Nonetheless, it has been argued that EU nationals' HR to seek asylum in other EU states is still protected under other EU legal provisions and under the 1951 Convention.

It has also been observed that under EU law, the asylum seeker, has acquired a new characteristic, namely as a legal identity sanctioned by EU asylum law (Collier et al. 1995, p. 18), albeit not formally recognised. The removal of the figure of the asylum seeker under the recast legal instruments and the emphasis on the (asylum) 'applicant', reflects the conceptual understanding of asylum seekers under EU law, where from refugees *a priori*, as understood in international law, these persons are now merely considered as (asylum) 'applicants' and only considered as refugees once a legal status has been granted to them. This understanding has created a legal gap and the need for an *ad hoc* protection status for this category of persons.

[2] See, for example, European Court of Human Rights, *Suso Musa v Malta*, App. No. 42337/12, 9 December 2013.

Consequently, persons seeking refuge in the EU must now be recognised as 'asylum seekers' by means of a formal application before their claim can be determined.

Furthermore, despite that the figure of the asylum seeker has been removed from the text of the law, the concept prevails, *ipso facto*. It has also been shown that under the previous EU reception regime, the construction of this new status has led to adverse consequences in certain EU states, as those who fled persecution and who eventually qualified for protection, had to suffer further persecution by the same state which ultimately, granted them protection.

References

Asylum Information Database (aida). (2018). Country Report: Malta. Retrieved June 27, 2018, from http://www.asylumineurope.org/reports/country/malta

Asylum Seekers (UNHCR: The UN Refugee Agency, 2018). Retrieved June 27, 2018, from http://www.unhcr.org/asylum-seekers.html

Caruana, C. (2018). Pilatus whistleblower Efimova will not be extradited: Greek courts refuse prosecutor appeal. *Times of Malta*. Retrieved June 27, 2018, from https://www.timesofmalta.com/articles/view/20180614/local/pilatus-whistleblower-efimova-will-not-be-extradited.681745

Collier, J. F., Maurer, B., & Suarez-Navaz, L. (1995). Sanctioned identities: Legal constructions of modern personhood. *Identities, 2*(1–2), 1–27. https://doi.org/10.1080/1070289X.1997.9962524

Gil-Bazo, M. (2006, November). *Refugee Status, subsidiary protection, and the right to be granted asylum under EC law* (Research paper No. 136). UNHCR.

Gil-Bazo, M. (2015). Asylum as a general principle of international law. *International Journal of Refugee Law, 27*(1), 3–28. https://doi.org/10.1093/ijrl/eeu062

Hathaway, J. C., & Foster, M. (2017). *The law of refugee status*., 2nd edn. Cambridge: Cambridge University Press.

Refugees, Asylum-Seekers and Migrants (Amnesty International, 2018). Retrieved June 27, 2018, from https://www.amnesty.org/en/what-we-do/refugees-asylum-seekers-and-migrants/

UN High Commissioner for Refugees (UNHCR). (2011). Handbook and guidelines on procedures and criteria for determining refugee status under the 1951 Convention and the 1967 protocol relating to the status of refugees, HCR/1P/4/ENG/REV. 3.

Author

Maurizio Borghi

1 Introduction

The notion of the author, as a status bearing specific rights and obligations, emerged back in eighteenth Century Europe and received stable legal recognition in the course of the nineteenth Century (Borghi 2018). The legal traditions of civil law and common law countries partially converged in the Berne Convention for the Protection of Literary and Artistic Works, signed in 1886.[1] The Convention established a principle of equal treatment for foreign authors subject to certain minimum requirements, which triggered a process of narrowing gaps between national legal regimes internationally (Ricketson and Ginsburg 2006). Based on this common ground, in the 1990s the European Union (EU) started a process of harmonisation of the laws of Member States, which progressively developed a rich and coherent body of laws and decisions of the EU Court of Justice (Pila and Torremans 2016, p. 247). Yet, despite the *acquis communautaire*, the protection of author's rights remains subject to national law, and the legal traditions of the Member States still have a bearing on the way in which this status is recognised and governed by law.

[1] The Convention was signed by Belgium, France, Germany, Haiti, Italy, Liberia, Spain, Switzerland, Tunisia, and the United Kingdom in 1886, and it was lastly amended in 1979. In 1994, the Convention was incorporated in the Agreement on Trade Related Aspects of Intellectual Property (TRIPS) and then made applicable to the member nations of the World Trade Organisation (WTO).

M. Borghi (✉)
Centre for Intellectual Property Policy & Management (CIPPM), Bournemouth University, Fern Barrow, Poole, UK
e-mail: mborghi@bournemouth.ac.uk

A. Bartolini et al. (eds.), *Dictionary of Statuses within EU Law*,
https://doi.org/10.1007/978-3-030-00554-2_7

2 The Status of Author in the European Legal Traditions

In the common law world, the status of the author has been classically interpreted through the lenses of natural-right theories of original acquisition, coupled with utilitarian-instrumentalist approaches.[2] The theory of original acquisition postulates that property rights arise by effect of 'mixing' one's own labour with the resources available in nature. Likewise, authorship is a particular case of labour-intensive processes where common resources (e.g., language, notes and colours) are transformed into ideal instances (e.g. poems, music and paintings) in which the person who invested their own labour has legitimate interests. The scope of these interests is determined by state-created property rights, which in turn provide incentives to the creation of new works (i.e., similar to how patents operates in the realm of inventions) and further public interest goals, such as the advancement of knowledge and dissemination of culture.[3] In the British judicial tradition, the author is the person who has invested 'skills, labour and judgement' in the creation of a work.[4] The author is mainly seen as a person bearing economic interests, to whom statutory law confers transferable property rights aimed at the commercial exploitation of the fruits of their labour (Saunders 1992).

As opposed to the common-law tradition, the civil-law tradition of Continental Europe is characterised by a stronger emphasis on the personality elements of authorship. The author is primarily seen as a person who expresses their own individuality in the creation of a work, or alternatively a person who communicates their thought to others through visible signs of language.[5] The status of an author encompasses a range of interests that go beyond the commercial ones and include freedom of expression, protection of reputation and economic livelihood. Accordingly, the author is vested a complex bundle of exclusive and non-exclusive rights (i.e., so-called 'remuneration rights'), as well as a robust system of inalienable personality rights (i.e., so-called 'moral rights'). The exercise and enforcement of those rights are often handed over to collective management organisations that administer economic interests on behalf of authors.

The EU Harmonisation of Author's Rights Rights pertaining to authors are governed by the laws of Member States, but they are subject to extensive EU regulation. As a general principle, EU law requires that works of authorship are protected by copyright as a form of intellectual property, and it recognises such protection as a fundamental right under Art. 17(2) of the Charter of Fundamental Rights. This prin-

---

[2]The acquisition theory originates from John Locke's *Treaties of Government* (1690), while classical legal utilitarianism has developed under the influence of authors like Jeremy Bentham (1748–1832) and John Stuart Mill (1806–1873).

[3]The 'Statute of Anne', the first British copyright act, was termed *An Act for the Encouragement of Learning* (8 Anne c. 19, 1710).

[4]*Ladbroke v William Hill*; House of Lords (1964), 1 All ER 465.

[5]The 'personality theory' is traditionally traced back to the legal theory of Hegel, while the 'communication theory' is based on Kant's philosophy of right.

ciple finds application in about ten directives, which in fact—also by virtue of the interpretation given by an expansive jurisprudence of the Court of Justice of the European Union (CJEU)—expand the scope of authors' protection beyond the requirements of international law.

The process of harmonisation of author's rights is rooted in the Green Paper on Copyright and the Challenge of Technology, adopted by the European Commission (EC) in 1988, and its follow-up (EC 1988, 1995). The main driver of this process was the need to secure adequate protection to European's intellectual labour, in times where the economic activity of industrialised countries shifted away from the production of 'staple commodities' towards 'the production of goods to which considerable value has been added through the application of technology, skill and creativity' (EC 1988, § 1.2.2). In line with this market-oriented approach, EU harmonisation has focused primarily on removing the inconsistencies in national legislations that hindered the functioning of the internal market (Montagnani and Borghi 2008). Therefore, harmonisation has addressed mainly the author's economic rights and has left personality rights outside the scope of the legislation.

Of central importance in this process is the Information Society Directive of 2001 (Directive 2001/29/EC of the European Parliament and of the Council of 22 May 2001 on the harmonisation of certain aspects of copyright and related rights in the information society. Official Journal L 167, 22/06/2001) which has 'horizontally' harmonised the key economic rights of authors. These include the rights of reproduction, distribution and communication to the public of their works via electronic means (including making available on demand). In addition, the Directive provides for remuneration rights in the form of 'fair compensation' for reproductions made by means of reprographic techniques (e.g., photocopying machines)[6] and for the 'harm' caused by unauthorised copies made for personal private use.[7] The reasons for not extending the author's exclusive rights to those cases are both practical and principled, as enforcing exclusive rights in private spheres would be both unfeasible and in conflict with fundamental rights of users (Karapapa 2012). Collectively, the economic rights provided for under the Information Society Directive cover a broad range of ways in which authorial works are exploited commercially in today's digital economy. Indeed, one of the key and most-cited objectives of the Directive is to secure 'a high level of protection'[8] to authors, and it is in this connection that EU law has had a significant influence on the juridical definition of the status of an author.

[6] So-called 'reprography exception': Directive 2001/29/EC, art. 5(2)(a).

[7] So-called 'private copying exception': *ibid.*, art. 5(2)(b).

[8] Directive 2001/29/EC, Rec. 4 and 9 (as frequently referred to in the CJEU jurisprudence, see Favale et al. 2016).

3 Author as First Owner of Rights

The *aquis communautaire* identifies the author as the first owner of rights in 'works'. The notion covers any form of expression in the literary, scientific and artistic domain, including cinematographic works,[9] photographs,[10] computer programmes[11] and original databases[12]; however it is distinct from other protected subject-matter, such as performances, phonograms and broadcasts. Accordingly, the author is distinct from the performer, the phonogram producer and the broadcasting organisation, and all these categories of owners are collectively referred to in the legislation and in policy documents as 'rightholders' (Walter & Von Lewinski 2010).

The term 'rightholder' lends itself to some ambiguity. Since exclusive rights can be, and normally are, transferred by the author to other parties (e.g., a publisher, a record company or a broadcaster, in view of the commercial exploitation of the work), the category of 'rightholders' may end up incorporating indefinite categories of natural or legal persons who 'own' the relevant rights. The question arises as to whether those persons are entitled to benefit from the same level of rights and 'high level of protection' that the legislation affords to authors, or whether EU law provides for standards that are specific and unique to the status of an author.

Some guidance has been given in a 2013 CJEU decision about author's fair compensation for photocopies and private copying (Case C-572/13 *Hewlett-Packard Belgium v Reprobel* [2013]). While the Information Society Directive (Directive 2001/ 29/EC) in these cases, provides for remuneration rights for 'rightholders',[13] some Member States have extended remuneration schemes to publishers and other subjects. However, the CJEU declared that these schemes are incompatible with EU law. To the Court, the term 'rightholder' must be interpreted narrowly, as covering only the subjects specifically referred to in the text of the Directive. Accordingly, fair compensation cannot be extended to "publishers of works created by authors', especially where those publishers are 'under no obligation to ensure that the authors benefit, even indirectly, from some of the compensation of which they have been deprived" (Case C.572/13, § 43) To the Court, the rights in question are a prerogative of the status of an author, and Member States are not allowed to transfer, albeit partially, this prerogative to other subjects as well.

---

[9] Directive 2006/116/EC of the European Parliament and of the Council of 12 December 2006 on the term of protection of copyright and certain related rights (codified version). Official Journal L 372, 27/12/2006, art. 2(1).

[10] Ibid., art. 6.

[11] Directive 2009/24/EC of the European Parliament and of the Council of 23 April 2009 on the legal protection of computer programs (codified version). Official Journal L 111, 5/5/2009, art. 1(1): 'Member States shall protect computer programs, by copyright, as literary works [...]'.

[12] Directive 96/9/EC of the European Parliament and of the Council of 11 March 1996 on the legal protection of databases. Official Journal L 77, 27/3/1996.

[13] Directive 2001/29/EC, art. 5(2)(a) ('reprography exception') and 5(2)(b) ('private copying exception').

EU law also mandates for the recognition of the status of the author in specific circumstances. One of these is the creation of cinematographic works. While some Member States vest the film producer with the initial ownership of rights in a film, EU law requires that the 'principal director' be recognised as the 'author or one of the authors' of the film as well.[14] In *Luksan v. van der Let* (2012) the CJEU declared incompatible with EU law national legislation, excluding the principal director from the exercise of certain exclusive rights and remuneration rights provided for by the Information Society Directive. Stressing the aim of securing a 'high level of protection' to authors, the Court affirmed that 'since the status of author has been accorded to the principal director of a cinematographic work, it would prove incompatible with the aim pursued by [the Directive] to accept that that creator be denied the exploitation rights at issue"(Case C-277/10, *Luksan v van der Let* [2012], § 67.)

4 The Author as Creator of the Work

Although there is no unequivocal definition in the acquis, the notion of author can be understood by reference to the basic principle: copyright originally vests in the person who has created the work. The principle is expressly stated in relation to computer programmes and original databases.[15] Unless otherwise provided by national legislation, the author is assumed to be a natural person and not a legal person.

'Creation' is not defined in the legislation, and its meaning may vary depending on the nature of the work. In case of works of informational nature, such as computer programmes and databases, 'creation' refers to the form in which the informational content has been expressed and arranged, and not to the way in which the underlying content has been devised. So, protection of computer programmes extends to the "expression in any form of a computer program" but not to the underlying "ideas and principles" (Directive 2009/24/EC, art. 1(2)). The CJEU reaffirmed this principle in *SAS Institute v. World Programming* (2012), where it held that the functionality of a computer programme cannot be protected by copyright, as this "would amount to making it possible to monopolise ideas, to the detriment of technological progress and industrial development".[16] Similarly, copyright protection of databases applies to the 'selection and arrangement' of the database's content, but it has no bearing on the content as such.[17]

---

[14] Directive 2006/116/EC, art. 2(1).

[15] *See* Directive 2009/24/EC on the legal protection of computer programs (codified version), art. 2(1), and Directive 96/9/EC on the legal protection of databases, art. 4(1): 'The author of a [computer programme or database] shall be the natural person or group of natural persons who has created [it] or, where legislation of the Member States so permits, the legal person designated as the right holder by the legislation'.

[16] Case C-406/10 *SAS Institute v World Programming* (2012), § 39–40.

[17] Directive 96/9/EC, art. 3.

Hence, as a general principle, author's rights subsist only in the elements of the work that are expressions of the author. However, what determines the subsistence of these elements? While the Information Society Directive is silent on this crucial aspect, the CJEU, in a line of cases starting from *Infopaq v. DDF* (2009),[18] has clarified what must be the criterion to determine the subsistence of author's rights in a work. In *Infopaq* (2009), a case on unauthorised reproduction of extracts from newspaper articles by a news monitoring service, the Court was called to determine whether an extract of eleven words could attract protection as 'part' of a work.[19] Based on a broadened reading of the acquis on computer programmes, photographs and databases,[20] the Court affirmed that the sole criterion to determine subsistence of rights is whether the part contains "elements which are such as to express the intellectual creation of the author of that work".[21] While it is for national courts to make this determination on a case-by-case basis, no other criterion should be considered compatible with EU law.

The consequences of *Infopaq* on the acquis are twofold. On the one side, protection can in principle be extended to any intellectual creation that meets the authorial criterion, without limits as to the subject matter. This was confirmed in a subsequent case on computer programmes, in which the CJEU held that although a graphic user interface cannot be regarded as a computer programme, it can still receive protection under 'the ordinary law of copyright' if it is original in the sense of its 'author's own intellectual creation'.[22] On the other side, only works that originate from the natural person of the author—or, as stated by the CJEU in another post-*Infopaq* case that 'reflect the author's personality' and their 'personal touch'[23]—receive protection under EU law. Works or parts thereof that lack this personality imprint are outside the scope of author's rights.

5 Conclusion

The EU recognition of the status of the author has evolved from purely economic considerations (i.e., the author as a right holder in the 'knowledge economy') to a more comprehensive appreciation of its specific legal nature. As we have seen, CJEU jurisprudence has backed the uniqueness of the author in EU copyright law as a determinant in the subsistence of rights and as an exclusive beneficiary of

---

[18] Case C-312/10 *Infopaq v DDF* [2009] ("Infopaq I").

[19] Under art. 2 of the Information Society Directive, authors have the right to authorise or prohibit reproduction of their works "in whole or in part" (Directive 2001/29/EC, art. 2).

[20] Directive 96/9/EC (databases), Directive 2006/116/EC (term of protection) and Directive 2009/24/EC (computer programs).

[21] Case C-312/10, § 50.

[22] Case C-393/09 *Bezpečnostní softwarová asociace – Svaz softwarové ochrany v Ministerstvo kultury* (2010), § 44–46.

[23] Case C-145/10 *Painer v Standard Verlags GmbH* [2011], § 92.

certain rights. This has affected the way national laws operate, both in civil law and common law countries (Rahmatian 2013). In the UK, courts may no longer be able to find copyright subsistence in editorial interventions[24] or deny protection to authorial creations like the scene of a photographic setting,[25] an edited video performance[26] or the Stormtrooper's helmets of Star Trek.[27] Likewise, continental European countries are no longer allowed to restrict the exercise of rights that are specific to authors or transfer their benefits to publishers in the framework of levy collection systems. It is to be hoped that such trend in the recognition of the specificity of the status of authors can pave the way for more ambitious harmonisation objectives, eventually providing a substantial rebalancing of rights among all the parties involved in the European creative economy.

References

Borghi, M. (2018). Copyright and the commodification of authorship in 18th and 19th century Europe. *Oxford Research Encyclopaedia of Literature*. http://literature.oxfordre.com/page/recently-published

Favale, M., Kretschmer, M., & Torremans, P. C. (2016). Is there a EU copyright jurisprudence? An empirical analysis of the workings of the European court of justice. *Modern Law Review, 79*(1), 31–75. https://doi.org/10.1111/1468-2230.12166

Karapapa, S. (2012). *Private copying*. London, UK: Routledge.

Montagnani, M. L., & Borghi, M. (2008). Promises and pitfalls of the European copyright law harmonisation process. In D. Ward (Ed.), *The European Union and the culture industries: Regulation and the public interest* (pp. 213–240). London, UK: Ashgate.

Pila, J., & Torremans, P. (2016). *European intellectual property law*. Oxford, UK: Oxford University Press.

Rahmatian, A. (2013). Originality in UK copyright law: The old 'skill and labour' doctrine under pressure. *International Review of Intellectual Property and Competition Law, 44*(1), 4–34. https://doi.org/10.1007/s40319-012-0003-4

Ricketson, S., & Ginsburg, J. C. (2006). *International copyright and neighbouring rights: The Berne Convention and beyond*. New York: Oxford University Press.

Saunders, D. (1992). *Authorship and copyright*. London, UK: Routledge.

Walter, M. M., & Von Lewinski, S. (2010). *European copyright law. A commentary*. Oxford, UK: Oxford University Press.

[24] *Sawkins v. Hyperion Records Ltd* [2005] RPC 32 (CA).

[25] *Creation Records v. News Group* [1997] EMLR 444.

[26] *Norowzian v. Arks Ltd* [1999] All ER (D) 1214.

[27] *Lucasfilm v. Ainsworth* [2011] 3 WLR 487.

Banker

Andrea Pierini

1 Introduction

In common language, the term banker refers to "a person engaged in banking as owner, manager, administrator, or large shareholder of a credit institution" (Treccani Encyclopedia at http://www.treccani.it/vocabulario/banchiere).

This definition identifies the *status* assumed by people associated in various ways with the control and management of a banking enterprise, which traditionally has included fundraising and lending activities.

Banks provide necessary financial resources for the working of the real economy, in that the utilisation in lending operations of the financial provisions obtained through the gathering of deposits and the concurrent management of payment services ensure the transfer of financial resources from actors and sectors who have a surplus of savings to those, on the other hand, who are in need of financial resources (because they spend more than their income for consumption, investments, and goods).

Because of the banking system's central role in the market economy's proper functioning, banking enterprises and, consequently, the individuals who work in them, have always been subject to a special legal framework and a distinct system of public controls and restrictions compared both with the generality of other enterprises (individual and collective) and with other types of intermediaries operating in the financial markets (such as insurers and intermediaries in real property transactions).

This special treatment is a function of the primary need to safeguard savings invested in bank deposits. Credit market regulation has at its center the stability of such deposits and the prevention of systemic risks, such as those deriving from

A. Pierini (✉)
Department of Law, University of Perugia, Perugia, Italy
e-mail: andrea.pierini@unipg.it

A. Bartolini et al. (eds.), *Dictionary of Statuses within EU Law*,
https://doi.org/10.1007/978-3-030-00554-2_8

repeated episodes of depositor panic and bank runs underlying the banking system's periodic crises.

2 From Dirigisme to the Great Moderation

The traditional categorisation—established by legislation enacted after the so-called Great Depression of the 1930s—of persons variously involved in banking activity, either as owners of capital holdings (*shareholders*) or as persons interested in the products, services, and healthy condition of banks (so-called *stakeholders*), such as customers, investors, suppliers, and employees of the enterprise—within the sphere of a credit market characterised by strong governmental intervention, applying to the market, in the terminology of Italian public law, the definition of "*ordinamento sezionale*" or "sectional legal order" (Giannini 1970).

In this sectional order, in fact, administrative law prevails over private law. Endowing the exercise of banking with the function of fundraising and safeguarding of savings (understood, that is, as a function in the public interest) entails the utilisation of structural supervision incident to the competition and autonomy of those operating in the sector. This gives special reference toward balancing the traditional principle of maximising shareholder value (*shareholder view*) and the principle of protecting savings and banking institutions' stability.

This regulatory framework, characterised by public intervention and the primacy of national governments in the introduction of penetrating restrictions (both territorial and functional) apt to limit so-called banking freedom was subjected to the considerable impact of successive structural transformations starting in the 1980s, influenced by the effects of so-called neo-liberal globalisation and the consequent internationalisation of the financial markets. This process was favoured by multiple market forces. These included: the so-called information technology revolution, with the consequent change in the way banking and financial services are made accessible to consumers; financial innovation, brought about by the emergence of new products (such as so-called derivatives); and new services and financial intermediaries, operating in special multifunctional sales networks for those same products.

With respect to the regulatory framework, the effect of these transformations was the liberalisation and deregulation of the financial markets. Consequently, this led to reduction of the former structural restrictions, with territorial and functional barriers to the exercise of banking activities and of the traditional segmentation of the financial markets (insofar as they were divided into the traditional compartments of banking, insurance, and real estate). It is evident, therefore, that the trend toward internationalisation and integration of the financial markets (and of the ownership structures of the enterprises operating in those markets) as well as the trend toward consolidation of credit institutions into large banking groups with trans-border operations, posed multiple challenges to the European legal framework governing financial markets. This led to more frequent intervention by community legislators and the consequent Europeanisation of banking law.

3 The Europeanisation of Banking Regulation

It is equally indubitable that the process of transferring away from European Union member states the authority over banking sector regulation and control was favoured, following approval of the Treaty of Maastrict (1992) not only by the necessity to reinforce the free circulation of capital (as recognised by Art. 56 ECT, today Art. 63 TFEU) but also by the creation of an economic and monetary union (Title VII TEU) with attribution to the European System of Central Banks and International Organisations (ESCB) composed of the European Central Bank (ECB) and the national central banks, of powers over monetary policy (whereby banks, through the granting of credit and management of payment systems, constitute a fundamental node for the implementation of monetary policy choices).

This process of banking law federalisation has been translated into a series of community legislative acts, driven initially to achieve a minimal harmonisation of the regulatory framework, in which banking enterprises (and thus the persons managing and controlling them) are called upon to operate in such a way as to limit the risks of forum shopping and protectionist behavior on the part of national governments, liable to limit the free circulation of capital and competition among operators.

Initially, this legislation gave rise to a series of directives aimed at introducing a framework of common rules regarding access to the credit market, prudential standards necessary to guarantee the healthy and prudent management of credit institutions, systems guaranteeing deposits, and the recovery and resolution of credit institutions.

This effort included directives aimed, first of all, at introducing uniform requirements for access to credit markets with final introduction of the principle of "single authorisation." That is, the "European passport," by which every enterprise that had obtained authorisation to conduct credit activity in a member state would be equally authorised to conduct its activity in any member state of the Community, in actualisation of the principle of freedom of establishment and free provision of services (See First Council Directive 77/780/EEC of 12 December 1977 and Second Council Directive 89/646/EEC of 15 December 1989 on the coordination of laws, regulations and administrative provisions relating to the taking up and pursuit of the business of credit institutions).

The mutual recognition of authorisations obtained by banks in their home states and the services provided in the exercise of freedom of establishment were further modified, however, by the organisational principle. This provided that the entitlement and exercise of settlement and supervisory functions in the same credit markets remained with the purview of national banking authorities (*home country control*).

To limit forum-shopping, deriving from different regulations and controls in the various member countries, directives were enacted to harmonise the rules relative to prudential standards applied to banking activity (so as to reinforce the adequacy of banks' levels of capitalisation with respect to assumed risks) and to create protective mechanisms for the various categories of stakeholders, the first among them being depositors.

Some of these directives (since revoked) including the following: 89/299/EEC (Own funds directive); 89/647/EEC (Solvency ratio directive); 92/121/EEC (Large exposures directive); and 94/19/EC19 (Deposit guarantee directive). Subsequently, Dir. 2000/12/EEC of March 2000 was approved, which coordinated and integrated the contents of the previous banking directives.

This process of constructing a uniform European scheme of prudential standards applicable to the operations of banks and investment enterprises was later reinforced through the adoption of a series of directives entitled *Capital Requirement Directives* (CRD). This began with the so-called CRD 1 packet, constituted by directives 2006/48/ED and 2006/49/EC, which adopted the 2004 Agreement known as Basel II. With the CRD, the Union implemented packets of rules and proposals, having the nature and effect of *soft law*, elaborated by the Basel Committee on Bank Supervision (BCBS).

The framework was completed by Directive (CE) n. 19/1994, on deposit guarantee systems, and the subsequent Directive 2001/24/CE on the recovery and resolution of credit institutions.

4 The Effects of the Last Great Financial Crisis: The Federalising Process of Banking Regulation and the Banking Union

The process of normative homogenisation received a final push from the need to respond to the grave financial crisis starting in 2007–2008. This crisis further evolved in Europe, starting in 2010, from a mortgage crisis to a sovereign debt crisis due to deteriorating public finances throughout the Eurozone. This led to a "vicious circle" of growing private debt of banks involved in the mortgage crisis and growing public debt from the bank bailout measures adopted by the affected countries. Consequently, the European Union promulgated broader banking system reforms aimed at reinforcing the above-mentioned process of federalisation of banking and credit market regulation.

This context forms the backdrop for the process, in progress within the European Union, of creating a banking union based on various factors. On the one hand, it reinforced the *corpus* of uniform rules regulating the capital requirement of banks, deposit guarantees, and the prevention and management of bank failures. On the other, it contemporaneously transferred supervisory responsibilities over credit institutions and the resolution of banking system crises from the competent authorities of national governments to European authorities (thus bringing about a federalisation of such competencies).

Particularly important in the process of legislative and regulatory harmonisation were: a further packet of three directives on bank capital requirements, CRD II, (2009/27/EC, 2009/83/EC and 2009/111/EC) covering supervisory capital, large exposures, securitisation, liquidity, colleges of supervisors, cooperation among authorities in times of crisis, public information; the subsequent packet CRD III (including directive 2010/76/EC) regarding the capital requirements applicable to securitisation operations and the revision remuneration policies; and finally, the CRD IV packet, including the capital requirement regulation (CRR) n. 575/2013, containing a series of provisions directed at implementing requirements regarding capital, liquidity, and limitations on recourse to financial leverage set forth in the Basel 3 rules and the Directive on capital requirements (CRD) 2013/36/UE, also regarding additional requirements for capital conservation buffers and specific countercyclical capital conservation buffers, as well as prudential supervision.

With regard to structural reforms of credit market governance, the process of federalising credit market supervision was initiated by the creation of a European System of Financial Supervision (ESFS). The ESFS is composed of the European sector authorities (including the European Banking Authority [EBA]), charged with participating in the development of secondary norms (technical, regulatory, and implementation norms) for market supervision, coordinating the application of supervisory regulations, and ensuring cooperation among national control authorities (Lamandini and Ramos Munõz 2016).

Subsequently, countries in the Eurosystem took a more decisive step toward the integration of credit service markets. This was done by instituting and implementing a proper European Banking Union, a model of credit market regulation based on centralisation within the European Central Bank of prudential supervision over the large banking groups operating in the Eurozone, the introduction of a single resolution mechanism for bank failures, and a European deposit insurance fund (Busch and Ferrarini 2015).

This process led to approval of Reg. 1024/2013, instituting the Single Supervisory Mechanism (SSM) of credit institutions and Reg. 806/2014, which introduced the Single Resolution Mechanism (SRM) for failing credit institutions.

A set of institutional instruments for the management of bank crises completed by Directive 2014/59/UE of the European Parliament and the Council (BRRD), institute a harmonised framework of recovery and resolution tools for banks and investment companies.

Finally, it must be noted that the extensive process of Europeanisation of the system of regulation and control of the banking business has also involved the regulation of banks' internal organisational models, based on the now-consolidated opinion that there exists a cause and effect relationship between deficiencies in corporate governance and the economic-financial crises of recent years.

Problems incident to the governance of banking institutions have, in fact, profoundly influenced the incisiveness and persistence of crisis effects. Deep flaws, often connected to defects in the functioning of governing bodies in terms of insufficient professionalism, misunderstanding of risks, defective coordination, confusion of roles, and distorted incentivisation, have harmed customers and the entire system's sustainability.

Major banking law reforms have included the issuance of international and community rules of conduct and the adoption of primary and secondary domestic legislation: Principles for Enhancing Corporate Governance by the Basel Committee 2010; Corporate Governance and the Financial Crisis: Key Findings and Main Messages by the OECD 2009; Thematic Review on Risk Governance—Peer Review Report del Financial Stability Board 2013, Directive 2013/36/UE known as CRD IV; Guidelines on Internal Governance 2011; and Guidelines on the Assessment of the Suitability of Members of the Management Body and Key Function Holders 2013 by the E.B.A. These have had a significant impact on models of corporate governance, particularly with reference to the number of governing bodies, the configuration of such bodies, the establishment *ex lege* of the number of their independent components, the reorganisation of the so-called cooperative banks, and, furthermore, have become requisites for access to leadership positions within the internal hierarchy of individual banks.

5 General Effects on Freedom of Establishment of Banks and to Provide Banking Services in the European Union

In conclusion, what has emerged is a radical reform of the system of public oversight and of the stabilisation mechanisms of the banking system (Chiti and Santoro 2016). This has led to a new configuration of the principles governing the exercise of banking activity and so-called banking freedom in the dual dimension of autonomy of choice relative to the initiation of entrepreneurial activity and to the identification of objectives of such activity, as well as the tools to be used in the conduct of the activity.

From all points of view, in fact, the Union's new banking law introduces a series of innovations with regard to the division of competences within the legal order of credit markets, characterised by the objective of constructing, by way of federalising its regulatory and control systems, a single market of credit services within which banks can operate on a level playing field. This objective is capable of enhancing within the banking sector the founding freedoms of the Treaty of Rome, with particular reference to the freedom of establishment, the freedom to provide services, and the free movement of capital.

The legislative framework provides useful elements for resolving interpretive problems, recently amplified by the increased public intervention in the credit market, resulting from the renewed special nature of banking enterprises with respect to the general freedom of private economic initiative.

A context determined both by the increase of public restrictions and controls over the exercise of the banking business (with the consequent revitalisation of the so-called "regulatory state") and by the escalation of bank recapitalisation and rescue interventions by the government, with the consequent acquisition of public holdings of bank capital (giving rise to talk of the "savior state" or "insurer state.")

Such a significant increase in the public law regulation of credit markets (following the preceding phase of liberalisation and privatisation of those markets) could be termed a new dirigisme and/or a new functionalisation of the banking enterprise, such as to limit the freedom of economic initiative in the credit sector in the name of safeguarding concurrent interests such as the protection of savings (Art. 47 of the Italian Constitution).

In attempting to evaluate the soundness of this approach, what emerges from this survey of community law is a European notion of banking, which, while keeping in place the enterprising nature of credit institutions, identifies the general purpose of banking in the traditional activities of fundraising and lending (Art. 4 Reg. 575/2013). Provided, however, that the same institutions can offer a wide range of additional financial services (subject to of mutual recognition), particularly those of intermediation of securities and the acquisition of industrial holdings (activities listed in Attachment I of Dir. 2013/36/EU).

Hence, the continued prevalence of a banking business model that, notwithstanding its special nature deriving from the peculiar institutional functions of fundraising and lending (with the consequent subjugation to the publically-imposed restrictions outlined above), continues to fall within the traditional European polyfunctional model of the universal bank (Dragomir 2010), specialised in providing services both as a commercial bank and as an investment bank.

References

Busch, D., & Ferrarini, G. (Eds.). (2015). *European banking union*. Oxford: Oxford University Press.

Chiti, M. P., & Santoro, V. (Eds.). (2016). *L'unione bancaria Europea*. Florence: Pacini Editore.

Corporate Governance and the Financial Crisis: Key Findings and Main Messages by the OECD. (2009). Retrieved http://www.oecd.org/daf/ca/corporategovernanceprinciples/43056196.pdf

Dragomir, L. (2010). *European banking regulation and prudential supervision*. Abingdon/Oxon, UK: Routledge.

Giannini, M. S. (1970). *Diritto amministrativo*. Milan: Giuffrè.

Guidelines on Internal Governance. (2011). Retrieved https://www.eba.europa.eu/documents/10180/103861/EBA-BS-2011-116-final-EBA-Guidelines-on-Internal-Governance-(2)_1.pdf

Guidelines on the Assessment of the Suitability of Members of the Management Body and Key Function Holders. (2013). Retrieved https://www.eba.europa.eu/documents/10180/1972984/Joint+ESMA+and+EBA+Guidelines+on+the+assessment+of+suitability+of+members+of+the+management+body+and+key+function+holders+%28EBA-GL-2017-12%29.pdf

Lamandini, M., & Ramos Munõz, D. (2016). *EU financial law*. Milan: Wolters Kluwer Italia.

Principles for Enhancing Corporate Governance by the Basel Committee. (2010). Retrieved https://www.bis.org/publ/bcbs168.pdf

Thematic Review on Risk Governance – Peer Review Report del Financial Stability Board. (2013). Retrieved http://www.fsb.org/wp-content/uploads/r_130212.pdf

Treccani Encyclopedia. Retrieved http://www.treccani.it/vocabulario/banchiere

Biological Mother

Stefania Stefanelli

1 Introduction

The discussion concerning the possible ways of identifying a child's mother is complex since, according to Italian law, the woman who gives birth is the child's mother (Art. 269 paragraph 3 of the Civil Code, Bianca 2015), but so is the woman who has a genetic link with the child (Art. 269, paragraph 2 of the Civil Code). Specific precedents are missing, due to the prohibition of surrogacy, but the answers offered by judges when the identification of the mother is questioned, in cases of ART, are contradictory.

Italian case law shows two fundamental cases. First, due to a mistake of the health staff, the embryos of two different couples who had needed a homologous Artificial Reproductive technique (ART) were exchanged. One of the two pregnancies never occurred, while the other one led to the birth of a pair of twins. The Court of Rome (Court of first Instance of Roma 8.8.2014; Court of first Instance of Roma 22.4.2015; Court of first Instance of Roma 10.5.2016) decided that the mother was the woman who had given birth, despite the fact that she was not the genetic mother, since the ovum used to produce embryos did not belong to her. The decision was based on the principle of *mater semper certa est*, set forth by Art. 269, paragraph 3, C.C.

In the second case, a woman who gave birth in Spain had procreated using her partner's ovum. The Supreme Court ordered the recognition of the birth certificate drawn up in Spain identifying two mothers, ruling that the woman who did not give birth was the genetic mother of the child, who has the right to have her biological maternity legally recognized (Supreme Court of Cassation 30.9.2016, n. 19599, Sassi et al. 2018) That decision was based on Art. 269, comma 2, C.C.

The Italian law on medically assisted reproduction, no. 40/2004, was very restrictive and placed Italy at the most conservative place on the European spectrum. The

S. Stefanelli (✉)
Department of Law, University of Perugia, Perugia, Italy
e-mail: stefania.stefanelli@unipg.it

A. Bartolini et al. (eds.), *Dictionary of Statuses within EU Law*,
https://doi.org/10.1007/978-3-030-00554-2_9

law was widely criticized, and many couples seeking medically assisted reproduction brought their cases before the Italian Civil Courts with regard to pre-implantation genetic diagnosis (PGD), donor insemination and the issue of consent.

Thirteen years later, having suffered the blows of the Italian Constitutional Court, a small part of law 40/2004 remains: in 2009, the Italian Constitutional Court declared that the maximum limit of the number of embryos to be produced and transferred for each cycle (i.e. three), as stated in the original version of the law, was constitutionally illegitimate. In 2014, the same Court declared unconstitutional the ban on donor insemination, thus opening the way to heterologous assisted reproduction. In 2015 the Constitutional Court granted the right to access medically assisted reproduction to couples who are fertile but carriers of genetic diseases: a ban on selecting embryos for fertility treatments to avoid the transmission of some serious disease was illegitimate. Also the European Court of Human Rights in Strasbourg in 2012 had rejected the law. In 2016 the Italian Constitutional Court reaffirmed the legitimacy of a ban on human embryo research, in the case of a couple wishing to donate their non-viable embryos to scientific research.

2 Surrogacy

However, there is still much room for criticism.

Italian law states that access to medically assisted reproduction should be limited to adults of different genders, of fertile age, with medically certified sterility or infertility. They should be married or living together, and both living. Same-sex couples, single women, post-mortem insemination, surrogacy and gestational carriers are still banned.

Italian Law no. 40 of 2004 expressly prohibits surrogacy (Art 12 paragraph 6). Various justifications are offered for this prohibition: first, the state has an interest in preventing children from being turned into commodities; moreover, surrogacy makes maternity uncertain, due to the separation of the various mother figures, which has negative consequences on the psychological and social development of the child.

The ban under Italian law is also rooted in the claim that surrogacy involves the exploitation of women because it treats the surrogate mother as a means to an end, relegating her from a person worthy of respect to a mere object. According to this view, a woman acting as a surrogate is often persuaded by the substantial amount of compensation offered and is thus not able to decide freely to grant the child to whom she has just given birth.

Among Italian scholars, there is greater acceptance of the practice by which the surrogate mother is inseminated with the commissioning couple's gametes, as the woman then only carries a child who has genetic links with both intended parents. According to this view, the existence of this biological relationship, which is particularly significant for the identity of the child, can justify the child's being 'handed over' to the couple immediately after birth.

Under Italian law, when a child has been born of an unmarried surrogate mother and there is a genetic link with the commissioning father, the fact that the two have acted illegally cannot constitute a valid reason for a refusal to perform a DNA test to confirm the paternity of the latter: the intended father can formally recognise the child and will be registered as the father on the birth certificate.

However, if the child was born of a married surrogate mother, the presumption of paternity within the marriage would result in the surrogate mother's husband being considered the legal father of the child. This presumption could again be rebutted by a DNA test, but only the surrogate mother, her husband and the child, at the age of 18, can bring this action, not the intended parents.

The discussion concerning the possible ways of identifying a child's mother is more complex since, according to Italian law, the woman who gives birth is the child's mother (Art. 269 paragraph 3 of the Civil Code), but so is the woman who has a genetic link with the child (Art. 269, paragraph 2 of the Civil Code). However, the reasons influencing the decision of the surrogate mother to provide an infertile couple with a child may not always be financial; in some cases, it may result from an altruistic desire. Recent changes to social attitudes are provoking new, positive reactions among legal scholars in Italy. Some of them argue that the sole biological fact of giving birth should be put into this perspective and that the focus should be placed on evaluating the reasons for free procreative choices; emphasizing notions such as the protection of human health and solidarity among women, they attempt to legitimise surrogacy agreements by framing them as a 'gift relationship' (Stefanelli 2016).

In support of this view, we can underline the relevance acquired by a concept of parenthood that is founded both on the notion of 'procreative choice' and on the notion of 'procreative responsibility' (Palazzo 2012).

A survey of practical outcomes reveals that courts have adopted different positions. Some couples, when they return to Italy, provide the civil registry office with foreign documents in which the commissioning couple are stated to be the legal parents. Some documents are judicial decisions while others are simply birth certificates. In some cases, the documents presented are not valid in Italy because they are not accepted by the national authorities as attesting to the status of the child, who consequently will not be able to be legally recognised as an Italian citizen.

On the one hand, the lower courts tend to endorse the acceptance of the commissioning couple as the legal parents when at least the man has contributed genetically to the surrogacy process. On the other hand, the Court of Cassation in 2014 (Supreme Court of Cassation 11.11.2014, n. 24001) rejected surrogate motherhood outright when neither the commissioning man nor the commissioning woman has a genetic link with the child.

In a decision of 24 January 2017, the European Court of Human Rights[1] stated that Italy did not violate the intended parents' rights in taking a child born from a surrogate mother in Russia: since the DNA test revealed that the baby was not bio-

[1] E.C.H.R., Application no. 25358/12, *Paradiso and Campanelli vs. Italy*, [2017].

logically related to either intended parent, Italian authorities refused to honour the birth certificate that the Russian government had issued and, 6 months after the return of the family to Italy, deemed the child abandoned. The child was placed for adoption by another couple. The ECHR initially stated that the Italian government's action was a violation of the intended parents' rights and imposed legal fees on the government, but the child remained with the adoptive parents, by that time having established strong emotional ties, protected by Art. 8 of the Convention. The Grand Chamber overturned the decision, concluding that 'no family life existed between the intended parents and the child' in light of the absence of any biological tie between the child and the intended parents, the short duration of the intended parents' relationship with the child and the uncertainty of the ties from a legal perspective. It is important to note that the Court did not examine the case from the perspective of child protection, but only for the recognition of the impact of an irreversible separation from the child on the applicants' family life. 'While the Convention does not recognise a right to become a parent (…) the Court accepts that the Italian courts, having assessed that the child would not suffer grave or irreparable harm from the separation, struck a fair balance between the different interests at stake, while remaining within the wide margin of appreciation available to them in this case.'

In July 2016, the Court of Appeal of Milan, in a case of surrogacy acted in India by an unmarried heterosexual couple, filed a question of constitutional legitimacy on Art. 263 of the Italian Civil Code, which consented to rebut the child's maternity even in contrast with the child's interest in preserving his/her legal ties with the intended mother in the absence of biological ties between the child and the intended mother. The decision of the Italian Constitutional Court can be influenced by the fundamental principle of the best interest of the child, but also by the appreciation of the right to have a child, also without biological ties, affirmed by the same Court in 2014, declaring the ban on donor insemination unconstitutional.

However, the protection of the best interest of the child does not appear to be compatible with contrasting decisions which jeopardise the right of all children to the same legal status. Under Italian law, children have acquired a unique legal status since the enactment of the legislation reforming the law on filiation (by Law 10 December 2012 no. 219 and Legislative Decree 28 December 2013 no. 154). Hence, it is necessary to respect the principle of non-discrimination on the basis of the circumstances of conception or birth.

The most recent decision states in favour of the legal recognition of parentage between the newborn child and the intended parents in certain cases, specifically when the process has been completed in accordance with the laws of another state and the child needs to continue in Italy the family relationship previously established with the intended parents.

In February 2017, the Court of Appeal of Trento of 23.02.2017 decided that two gay partners should be legally recognised as the fathers of two surrogate children, rather than only the parent who is biologically related, because parental relationships should not be determined only by the biological link. 'On the contrary, one must consider the importance of parental responsibility, which is manifested in the conscious decision to raise and care for the child.' The consequences of the violation of the rules set forth by Law no. 40 of 2014 (which prohibits couples from using a surrogate mother) 'committed by adults should not fall back on the newborn'. The Court relied on the recent judgment of the Italian Supreme Court, no. 19599/2016, to assert that a child's right to the continuity of the status lawfully acquired abroad is grounded in Art. 8 of the European Convention of Human Rights and in Art. 3 and Art. 8 of the United Nations Convention on the Rights of the Child, all aimed at granting that all actions concerning the child must be based on his or her best interest.

Finally, as a result of the prohibition of surrogacy, the child who was born eventually in Italy from a surrogate mother must necessarily be recognised by her, since Art. 9 of the Law 40/2004 does not allow childbirth in anonymity in case of pregnancy obtained through medical techniques.

Nobody can ask the performance of a surrogacy agreement, since it is a void contract prohibited by law. At the same time, if the birth from a surrogate mother is not ascertained—for example, because the practice has been carried out secretly, in order to avoid being punished by the law—or if the birth occurred abroad, the child has no specific rights towards the surrogate mother, not even to know her identity or that of other children eventually procreated by her.

3 Personal Identity and Heterologous Medically Assisted Reproduction

Other issues have arisen as a result of the recent lifting of the ban on heterologous medically assisted reproduction. Following the decision of the Constitutional Court, Law no. 190/2014, Art. 1 section 298 introduces the unpaid and voluntary nature of gamete donation and the anonymity of gamete donors.

The donation of gamete is required to be free with not even a refund of the costs of donation provided, since Art. 1, paragraph 298, Law no. 190 of 23 December 2014 applies to the case in point the general discipline set forth with respect to the donation of human organs and tissues for transplant purposes. The same reason imposes absolute anonymity on the donor, and the donors have no rights, not even to know the number of children born thanks to the collection of their gametes, and they have neither rights nor obligations towards them (Art. 9, Law no. 40/2004). As a consequence, the son or daughter has no right to know either the identity of the donors or the existence of other brothers/sisters: the child and his/her parents can only know the contents of the donor's health file, created at the moment of collection of the gametes, when necessary to treat his/her health, but this is very different from any guarantee of a right to know his/her own origins, as stated by the Italian Constitutional Court.

This is the critical point of the law in force, given that the decision of the unconstitutionality of the prohibition of heterologous procreation, which has been cited several times, brought the legislature's attention to the necessity, imposed by the constitutional protection of the right to personal identity arising from Art. 2 Cost., to ensure to the child born through heterologous ART the ability to find out the possibility of knowing is/her biological origins, as guaranteed to the child born from anonymous childbirth,[2] on the principle that the child's right to know his or her biological lineage is fundamental for his or her offspring's wellbeing and for the understanding of his or her own identity, as well as for choices to be made later in life.

Nonetheless, the debate on open or anonymous gamete donation continues unabated. While anonymous gamete donation has long been the preferred practice, a new focus on the rights and interests of donor-conceived children has led a number of countries to shift towards an open-identity system.

The recent lifting of the ban on heterologous medically assisted reproduction has led to a number of proposals, whichever they are: the introduction of a maximum number of births from the same donor; the introduction of a minimum and maximum age for donors; the introduction of adequate technical provisions for the selection of donors and the safety of the donation in compliance with the EU Tissue and Cells Directive (EUTCD) (Directive 2004/23/EC) and the supplementary technical directives 2006/17/EC and 2008/86/EC; and the establishment of a national registry for tracing donor and child.

An evolving debate is now underway regarding the other parties involved: some authors affirm that parents have a right to privacy which would be violated if the details of conception are disclosed; others scholars affirm that it is not in the best interests of the child to know, because if facts about a child's conception are spread throughout the family and school environment, this could lead to isolation and stigmatization. But a debate on the possible right of donors to be informed about the offspring conceived by their donation is also emerging.

References

Bianca, C. M. (2015). *La riforma della filiazione*. Padova: Cedam.

Palazzo, A. (2012). La filiazione. In A. Cicu, F. Messineo, L. Mengoni, & P. Schlesinger (Eds.), *Trattato di diritto civile e commerciale*. Milano: Giuffré.

Sassi, A., Scaglione, F., & Stefanelli, S. (2018). La filiazione e i minori. In Sacco, R. (Ed.), *Trattato di diritto civile Le persone e la famiglia* (pp. 4 ff). Torino: Wolters Kluwer.

Stefanelli, S. (2016). Accertamento della maternità nella gestazione per altri. *BioLaw Journal, 1*, 17 ff.

[2] See no. 2; Corte cost. n. 162/2014, cit.

Child and Adolescent

Tunjica Petrašević

1 Introduction

The aim of this chapter is to outline the status of the child and the adolescent in EU law. No single and formal definition of *child* or of *adolescent* exists, either in EU law sources or in the case law of the Court of Justice of the EU (hereinafter: CJEU). Legal EU documents usually refer to the UN Convention on the Rights of the Child (hereinafter: CRC), which defines a *child* as '*every human being below the age of 18 years unless under the law applicable to the child, majority is attained earlier*' (Art. 1 CRC). The Convention does not define the term *adolescent*.

The definition of *child* in EU law varies according to the regulatory context. Thus, for example, Directive 2004/38/EC defines children as direct descendants under the age of 21 (Art. 2(2)). In general, EU law does not regulate the rights of adolescents separately and differently from the rights of children. However, Directive 94/33/EC does recognize and define the terms *child*, *adolescent* and *young person*. The term *young people* covers both *adolescents* (aged 15–18 years) and *children* (under the age of 15).

Irrespective of this confusion of terms under Directive 94/33/EC, this chapter will use the single term *child*, and this normally also includes adolescents.

After defining the basic terms, the chapter will provide an overview of the status and the rights of children in the periods before and after the adoption of the Lisbon Treaty, from 2009 until today. Lastly, the chapter will offer conclusions and suggestions on how the status of the child (including the adolescent) in EU can be improved.[1]

[1] This book chapter is partially based on the author's previous research: Petrašević (2009, pp. 273–295; 2016, pp. 44–57).

T. Petrašević (✉)
Law Faculty Osijek, Josip Juraj Strossmayer University of Osijek, Osijek, Croatia
e-mail: tpetrase@pravos.hr

A. Bartolini et al. (eds.), *Dictionary of Statuses within EU Law*,
https://doi.org/10.1007/978-3-030-00554-2_10

2 Definition of a Child and Adolescent Within EU

EU law does not provide a uniform and formal definition of *child* or *adolescent*. In this regard, EU law documents usually refer to the CRC, which defines a *child* as '*every human being below the age of 18 years unless under the law applicable to the child, majority is attained earlier*' (FRA/CoE 2015, p. 15). The age of majority in the EU is 18, except that in Scotland full legal capacity is attained at 16. The CRC does not recognize terms such as *adolescent, minor* etc.

The definition of *child* in EU law varies according to the regulatory context. A *child* is viewed from the biological, age-based or dependency-based standpoint (the latter concerns an individual's economic or social dependence on parents or legal representatives) (Stalford 2012, p. 21 cited in Hrabar 2013, p. 56). As previously mentioned, Directive 2004/38 defines children as '*direct descendants who are under the age of 21 or are dependent*'. Further, Directive 94/33/EC on the protection of young people at work applies the term *young person* to denote a person aged under 18 and *child* to denote a person aged under 15 (FRA/CoE 2015, p. 18). Directive 94/33/EC differentiates between *adolescents* (aged 15–18 years) and *children* (under the age of 15). Occasionally EU law refers to national legislation that regulates the subject matter, as is the case with Regulation 1408/71 (Ackers and Stalford 2004, p. 72).

Since the concept of *child* is usually attached to the concept of *family*, the definition of *child* may also be dependent on the traditional understanding of family. Thus, for instance, the definition of *child* under Art. 10 of Regulation 1612/68 includes only a child of both spouses. In the case of *Netherlands v Reed*, the Court took the position that '*the term spouse refers to a marital relationship only*' (59/85, par. 15). In the case of *Baumbast*, the Court broadened the definition to include stepchildren (C-413/99). The new Directive 2004/38/EC formally confirmed this view of the CJEU. The term *family* under Directive 2004/38 includes spouses and registered partners, but only where national legislation treats registered partnerships as equivalent to marriage (Art. 2 Directive 2004/38/EC) (McGlynn 2006, p. 47; Petrašević 2009, p. 276). The CJEU broadened the scope and the concept of the rights of the child to the greatest extent possible, but the Court itself is limited in its own competence (Petrašević 2016, p. 47).

Regardless of the different definitions and understandings of the concept of *child*, in discussing the rights of children below, this chapter will use the single term *child* but by this will refer also to (the rights of) adolescents.

3 Children's Rights in the Pre-Lisbon Period

Historically, children's rights developed in a piecemeal and unsystematic manner, usually when the aim was to address other economic and/or political goals. It was not until recently that children's rights have become subject to a more coordinated

EU agenda (FRA/CoE 2015, p. 20). As the Lisbon Treaty is indisputably a milestone in the development of children's rights, these rights can thus be observed in two development phases: the pre-Lisbon period and the post-Lisbon period.[2] The pre-Lisbon period will be discussed first.

The EU (or its predecessors, the European Communities) was established primarily for economic integration. The founding Treaties (primarily the EEC Treaty (1957)) contained no specific provisions on the rights of children or on human rights in general (Petrašević 2016, p. 44). One possible explanation is that the protection of human rights was administered by a different international organization—the Council of Europe (CoE), as a result of which human rights in general as well as children's rights were neglected in the EU for quite some time (Duić and Petrašević 2015, pp. 253–255). Another explanation might be that the ability of the EC (later EU) to regulate children's rights was very limited because of the lack of a legal basis for this in the founding Treaties.

Aside from the context of human rights protection, children's rights may be viewed through the prism of the family, which has also been largely outside the EU's competence (Majstorović 2013, pp. 1–21; 2015, pp. 323–340). The premise is therefore the lack of EU competence in regulating both human rights protection and family matters.

Despite an explicit legal basis being lacking in the Treaties, children's rights in the EU were recognized for the first time in the domain of the free movement of workers. To encourage free movement, the EU adopted two legal documents that indirectly addressed children's rights: Regulation 1612/68 on freedom of movement of workers, and Regulation 1408/71 on the coordination of the social security system. A new Family Reunification Directive 2003/86/EC was later also adopted. In the area of free movement, children were only referred to in the context of certain social rights and the right to family reunification (Goldner Lang 2005, pp. 163–164). The rights of children were still only incidental in the evolution of the rights of their parents as workers (Ackers and Stalford 2004, p. 5; Petrašević 2016, p. 46). Children, in this context, were merely an instrument for achieving freedom of movement, that is, a means for ensuring the success of the common market project (McGlynn 2006, p. 46; Petrašević 2016, p. 46).

The next stage in the development of children's rights in the EU was the adoption of the Treaty of Amsterdam (1997) and the creation of an area of freedom, security and justice (hereinafter: FSJ). The creation of the FSJ area marked a new milestone in the development of the Union by leading to a transition from a predominantly economic and monetary union to a common legal and political order. As the result of this transition, the Union moved from being a purely economic entity, and took on a more humane form (Đurđević 2006; Petrašević 2009, p. 282; 2016, p. 50). The Amsterdam Treaty expressly mentions children in two Articles: Art. 13 TEC (combating discrimination) and Art. 29 TEU (intergovernmental measures for combating

[2]European Parliament. (2012). *EU Framework of Law for Children's Rights*, 2012. Retrieved from http://www.europarl.europa.eu/RegData/etudes/note/join/2012/462445/IPOLLIBE_NT(2012)462445_EN.pdf.

crime against children). These two articles laid the groundwork for the adoption of measures for the protection of children from trafficking, sexual exploitation and violence. This protection was founded upon the notion of children as vulnerable and passive persons in need of protection (Petrašević 2009, p. 282). In other words, children were viewed as objects of protection. Other provisions indirectly related to children include Articles 61 and 65 TEC, which allowed the EU to expand its competence to family matters (Majstorović 2015, p 326). This formed the basis for adopting the next two key legal documents: the Brussels II and Brussels II *bis* Regulations (Rešetar 2008, pp. 224–258; Župan 2016, pp. 125–167). In this domain, the EU adopted an entire series of measures for the protection of children (Petrašević 2009, p. 283).

The status of *child* can also be studied in the context of EU citizenship as established by the Treaty of Maastricht (TEU 1992): '*Any person who is a national of a Member State of the EU is considered a citizen of the EU*' (Art. 20 TFEU, previously Art. 17 TEC). This provision indisputably includes children, but only those who are nationals of a Member State. Protection of children under EU citizenship regulations did not cover children who were nationals of third countries, who were therefore in a less favourable position (Ruxton 2005, p. 16). Furthermore, the list of rights enjoyed by EU citizens demonstrates that they are in fact rights of adults, not rights of children (Petrašević 2009, p. 283; Stalford 2000, pp. 101–132). The rights of children are set in the framework of their parents' or families' rights, meaning that children are regarded only as citizens *in statu nascendi* (Ackers and Stalford 2004, p. 5; Petrašević 2016, p. 51).

A significant development in children's rights in the domain of EU citizenship is seen in the decision of the CJEU in the case of *Zhu and Chen* (C-200/02) (Craig and De Burca 2011, pp. 827–829). By granting the right of residence to the parents of a minor child, the CJEU judgment recognized children as fully-fledged EU citizens with independent rights (Petrašević 2009, p. 284).

The development and the protection of children's rights can be seen in the context of the protection of human rights within the EU. In this context, children's rights follow the 'fate' of human rights protection in the EU in general (Craig and De Burca 2011, pp. 362–406; Duić and Petrašević 2015, pp. 251–266). Despite having protected human rights even before the formal adoption of the Charter of Fundamental Rights (hereinafter: the Charter), under general principles of law, the EU (specifically the CJEU) did not acknowledge human rights *per se*, but rather viewed them as a means of achieving certain economic goals (McGlynn 2006, p. 9). The Charter represents a new direction in the development of EU law, and a shift in the preoccupation of the Union with economic goals and the regulation of the common market, in that it recognizes for the first time the impact of the Union's policies on families and children (McGlynn 2006, p. 18).

To a certain extent, the Charter does carry over the rights from the European Convention on Human Rights (ECHR), but it also introduces certain 'new' rights, such as the rights of children. Given that EU law (Art. 6(3) TEU) explicitly refers to the ECHR, Art. 52(3) of Charter is relevant to the relationship between these two documents.

Even though the Charter was adopted in 2000, it only entered into force in 2009 as an integral part of the Lisbon Treaty. From its adoption to 2009, the Charter was merely a soft law instrument (yet this did not preclude the CJEU from invoking it in its judgment in C-540/03 *Parliament v Council*). The section below gives the details of the status of the child in the context of the Charter.

4 Children's Rights in the Post-Lisbon Period

The Charter of Fundamental Rights refers either directly or indirectly to the rights of children in several Articles. The main provision is that of Art. 24, entitled '*The rights of the child*', which embodies the three principal rights of children: the right to express their own views (Art. 24(1)), the right to have their best interests as the primary consideration (Art. 24(2)), and the right to live with both parents (Art. 24(3)).

These rights are merely a selection from the rich directory of the CRC. Emphasizing the rights of children in a separate Article does not imply that children do not enjoy the other rights guaranteed by the Charter, but rather that its authors felt the need to highlight the rights they viewed as being of particular importance to children as separate rights in the EU (Korač Graovac 2013, p. 45). The right to express one's own view and the respect of the best interests of the child are two essential procedural rights of children (Lenaerts 2013; Župan 2017).

Other provisions refer to children either explicitly (right to education (Art. 14(3)), prohibition of discrimination based on age (Art. 21(1)) and prohibition of child labour (Art. 32)) or indirectly (equality before the law (Art. 20), respect for private and family life (Art. 7) and the legal, economic and social protection of the family (Art. 33)).

The rights of children might be the most notable accomplishment of the Charter, although there has been criticism that they are the result of a compromise between different concepts of children's rights (McGlynn 2006, p. 21; Petrašević 2009, p. 287). Children's rights as guaranteed under the Charter recognize the child as an independent subject of EU law with individual interests and needs. The introduction of children's rights into the Charter reflects the development of children's rights on the international level (McGlynn 2006, pp. 67–70; Petrašević 2016, p. 52; EU Agenda 2011, p. 3). Nevertheless, the mere listing of children's rights in the Charter is only the first step in their protection and promotion. The challenge is to put them into practice, and the responsibility for this lies with both the national courts and the CJEU (Petrašević 2009, p. 286).

As previously mentioned, the ability of the Union to regulate the rights of children was limited by the lack of a legal basis in the founding Treaties. The Lisbon Treaty recognized the protection of children's rights as one of the objectives of both the internal and the external policy of the EU (Petrašević 2016, p. 52). The Lisbon Treaty ultimately created the legal basis for this, in Articles 5(3) and 5(5) TEU. Children are referred to more specifically in the TFEU, thus enabling the EU to enact legislative measures aimed at combating sexual exploitation and human trafficking (Art. 79(2) and Art. 83(1) TFEU) (FRA/CoE 2015, p. 21). It seems that the Lisbon Treaty finally recognized the impact of certain policies of the Union on the rights of children. In doing this, the Lisbon Treaty did not produce new powers for the EU, but rather allowed certain measures to be taken in the areas of EU competence for protecting the rights of children (Petrašević 2009, p. 290). The Lisbon Treaty thus indisputably represents a significant advance in the protection of children's rights.

What are the rights of children in the EU today? The rights of children in the EU derive from multiple sources: the national law of the Member States (28 legal systems), European law (from the EU and the CoE) and international law (the UN CRC). There is a link between these sources. All EU Member States are parties to the CRC and the ECHR. These two documents are not formal sources of EU law. Rather, the standards and principles of the CRC must continue to guide EU policies and actions that affect the rights of children (EU Agenda 2011, p. 3). In spite of adopting its own Charter, the EU is still in the process of acceding to the ECHR (Duić and Petrašević 2015).

However, this chapter has focused solely on a selection of formal EU law sources applicable to children. As children's rights arise in various fields of law, there exists a lengthy catalogue of EU documents applicable to children (FRA/CoE 2015, pp. 22, 33–212; EC JUST.C2/MT-TC, 2017). This chapter highlighted three key documents:

1. Treaty on the European Union (TEU 2009) – Arts. 5(3) and (5);
2. EU Charter of Fundamental Rights (2009) – 7, 14(2), 20, 21(1), 24, 32 and 33.
3. Agenda for the Rights of the Child (2011) – 11 concrete actions.

Although the Agenda is not legally binding (but is, instead, soft law), it does reinforce the full commitment of the EU and all Member States to the promotion, protection and fulfilment of the rights of the child in all relevant EU policies, as well as to ensuring this has tangible results (EU Agenda 2011, p. 3).

5 Concluding Remarks

The first part of the chapter points to these conclusions. First, there is no uniform and single definition of *child* in EU law. Second, the EU considers all persons below the age of 18 to be children. This is a standard taken from the CRC, with exceptions that depend on the regulatory context (e.g. Directive 2004/38). Third, in certain cases EU law also refers to national legislation (Regulation 1408/71). Fourth, the status of children covers the status of adolescents.

The second part may be outlined as follows. First, children's rights were neglected for a long time. This was due to the lack of interest of the EU in human rights protection, but also due to the lack of a legal basis in the founding Treaties. Second, in spite of the lack of an explicit legal basis, children's rights were recognized in regulations on free movement, but only with the aim of encouraging mobility. Third, in the area of the FSJ, children were perceived as passive subjects of protection from violence and trafficking. However, this resulted in the adoption of key documents for their protection. Fourth, in terms of EU citizenship, children were perceived only as citizens *in statu nascendi,* but the CJEU in its case law recognized children as fully-fledged EU citizens with their own independent rights.

The third part may be summarised in the following points. First, the Charter recognizes the child as a subject of EU law with his or her own independent rights (EU Agenda 2011, p. 3). Second, the Lisbon Treaty could serve as a basis for the adoption of a 'children policy'. Third, the CJEU was and is the driving force in the protection and advancement of children's rights within the EU (FRA/CoE 2015, pp. 233–240, Petrašević 2016, p. 54).

In brief, the status of the *child* (and the *adolescent*) in the EU has changed and has significantly moved forward since the 1950s. The child has finally been recognized as a subject of EU law. Nevertheless, in spite of these significant advances, the approach to the protection of children's rights is still largely *ad hoc* and unsystematic. There is therefore still a need to strengthen the protection and promotion of children's rights. However, the limited possibilities and powers of the EU must be taken into account. In a visionary manner, certain authors advocate the adoption of a separate EU charter on the rights of children, modelled on the UN CRC. They expand this idea by proposing the establishment of a specialized EU court for the rights of children (Hrabar 2013, pp. 69–70, 2014, pp. 181–198). Even if one supports such an idea, it cannot reasonably be seen as a possibility, at least in terms of a specialized court. The abolition of the specialized Civil Service Tribunal only confirms that the EU has abandoned the concept of specialized courts as a whole.[3]

References

Ackers, L., & Stalford, H. (2004). *A community for children – children, citizenship and internal migration in the EU*. Hampshire: Ashgate Publishing Limited.

Craig, P., & De Burca, G. (2011). *EU law, text, cases and materials* (4th ed.). Oxford: Oxford University Press.

Duić, D., & Petrašević, T. (2015). Opinion 2/13 on the EU accession to the ECHR. In M. Vinković (Ed.), *New developments in the eu labour, equality and human rights law* (pp. 251–267). Osijek: J.J. Strossmayer University of Osijek, Faculty of Law.

Đurđević, Z. (2006). Pravda, sloboda i sigurnost. *Pravo azila, 1*, 3–11.

EU Agenda for the Rights of the Child – COM(2011) 60 final.

FRA/CoE. (2015). *Handbook on European Law relating to the rights of the children*. Retrieved January 7, 2018, from http://fra.europa.eu/en/publication/2015/handbook-european-law-child-rights

Goldner Lang, I. (2005). Family reunification of European Community nationals. *Croatian Yearbook of European Law and Policy, 1*, 163–200.

[3]More on the CJEU's reform can be found at http://www.consilium.europa.eu/en/press/press-releases/2015/12/03/cu-court-of-justice-general-court-reform/.

Hrabar, D. (2013). Prava djece u Europskoj uniji – pravni okvir. In A. Korač Graovac & I. Majstorović (Eds.), *Europsko obiteljsko pravo* (pp. 53–72). Zagreb: Narodne novine.

Hrabar, D. (2014). The establishment of a European Court for the rights of the child as a new contribution to the area of freedom, security and justice. *Zbornik Pravnog fakulteta u Zagrebu, 64*(2), 181–198.

Korač Graovac, A. (2013). *Povelja o temeljnim pravima EU i obiteljsko pravo / Europsko obiteljsko pravo, Narodne novine* (pp. 25–52). Zagreb.

Lenaerts, K. (2013). The best interests of the child always come first: The Brussels II bis regulation and the European Court of Justice. *Jurisprudence, 20*(4), 1302–1328.

Majstorović, I. (2013). Obiteljsko pravo kao različitost u jedinstvu: Europska unija i Hrvatska. In A. Korač Graovac & I. Majstorović (Eds.), *Europsko obiteljsko pravo* (pp. 53–72). Zagreb: Narodne novine.

Majstorović, I. (2015). Family law and the EU – At the crossroads? In M. Vinković (Ed.), *New developments in the EU labour, equality and human rights law* (pp. 251–267). Osijek: J.J. Strossmayer University of Osijek, Faculty of Law.

McGlynn, C. (2006). *Families and the European Union*. New York: Cambridge University Press.

Petrašević, T. (2009). Dijete u pravu Europske Unije. In B. Rešetar (Ed.), *Dijete i pravo* (pp. 273–295). Osijek: Pravni fakultet Osijek.

Petrašević, T. (2016). The rights of children in the EU. *European Scientific Journal, special edition*, 44–57. Retrieved from https://eujournal.org/index.php/esj/article/view/7665

Rešetar, B. (2008). *Pravna zaštita prava na susrete i druženje u obiteljskom pravu*. Doctoral thesis, Faculty of Law, University of Zagreb.

Ruxton, S. (2005). What about us? Children's rights in the European Union – Next steps. *EURONET*, Retrieved from http://www.crin.org/docs/ Ruxton%20 Report_WhatAboutUs.pdf

Stalford, H. (2000). The citizenship status of children in the European Union. *The International Journal of Children's Rights, 8*, 101–132.

Stalford, H. (2012). *Children and the European Union – rights, welfare and accountability*. Oxford: Hart Publishing.

Župan, M. (2016). Europski obiteljski postupci. In T. Petrašević & I. Vuletić (Eds.), *Europsko procesno pravo* (pp. 125–167). Osijek: Pravni fakultet.

Župan, M. (2017). The best interest of the child – A guiding principle in administering cross-border child related matters? In T. Liefaard & J. Sloth-Nielsen (Eds.), *The United Nations Convention on the rights of the child. Taking stock after 25 years and looking ahead* (pp. 213–229). Leiden: Brill|Nijhoff.

Climate Change Activist

Carlos Francisco Molina del Pozo and Francisco Barquín Domínguez

1 Introduction

The *Real Academia Española de la Lengua* defines activism as the tendency to behave in an extremely dynamic way or as the exercise of proselytism and social action of a public character.

Thus, activists in the fight against climate change may considered to be people or organisations working to promote solutions to mitigate the phenomenon of climate change, as well as supporting policies, agreements and international treaties that aim at reducing greenhouse gas emissions.

Environmental activists have been characterised, from their origins until now, as seeing and defining nature as a subject as important as any other living being and not as an object that can be used at anyone's whim.

In addition, they disseminate awareness of the negative consequences that the harmful acts we carry out have on the environment in which today's society lives and performs its daily activities.

We can say that the ultimate goal of environmental activism is none other than the conservation of nature in its purest state, so that a better development of humanity can be achieved in important matters such as health. The mission of this activism is to build a society together in which the guiding principle is the continuity of life in a sustainable way, with the aim of leaving an equal or better planet to future generations.

However, it must be concluded that its task is not an easy one, because climate change is a complex issue. This is first because it is a problem of a global nature; in other words, it affects all of us and therefore cannot be solved by a single group of countries. And secondly, the effects of this phenomenon, although already perceived, have not yet caused irreversible effects, as they are long term, which implies

C. F. Molina del Pozo (✉) · F. Barquín Domínguez
Department of Law, Universidad de Alcalá de Henares, Alcalá de Henares, Spain
e-mail: carlosf.molina@uah.es; Bernardo.Carnicero.Dominguez@esa.int

A. Bartolini et al. (eds.), *Dictionary of Statuses within EU Law*,
https://doi.org/10.1007/978-3-030-00554-2_11

that today, governments, businesses and society are aware of and refrain from carrying out certain actions to achieve a benefit that future generations will be able to see (which makes it very difficult to reach a meeting point due to political, cultural and socio-economic factors).

But what is climate change? According to the United Nations Framework Convention on Climate Change (UNFCCC), this phenomenon is defined as: "a change of climate which is attributed directly or indirectly to human activity that alters the composition of the global atmosphere and which is in addition to natural climate variability observed over comparable time periods" (see Article 1).

The reasons for this climate change can be multiple, that is to say, it can be due to natural variations in the climate (temperature, rainfall, cloud cover, etc.), or it can be the result of human action.

On the other hand, the same text of the Convention defines greenhouse gases as "those gaseous constituents of the atmosphere, both natural and anthropogenic, that absorb and re-emit infrared radiation" (Article 1). In other words, they are the retention of the sun's heat in the earth's atmosphere by a layer of gases in the atmosphere. Without them, life as we know it would not be possible, as the planet would be too cold. These gases include carbon dioxide, nitrous oxide and methane, which are released by industry, agriculture and the burning of fossil fuels.

A very broad interpretation of this phenomenon is that the energy radiated by the sun enters the earth's atmosphere (which is made up of 78% nitrogen, 21% oxygen, and 0.33% carbon dioxide, with the rest made up of various gases such as methane) in the form of ultraviolet rays and heats the earth's crust. This, in turn, radiates energy into space in the form of infrared rays, but some of these rays are trapped in the atmosphere and are reflected back into the earth's crust by a kind of curtain composed of the so-called greenhouse gases; this causes a warming of the climate in general. The greater the amount of these gases, the greater the amount of energy that is trapped, which, in turn, increases the temperature.

Although anyone can contribute to the fight against climate change by participating in activities aimed at defending and protecting the environment, activists in this field must be familiar with the legal and scientific aspects of climate action so that their management can lead to greater effectiveness and significance.

Therefore, these activists must have a specific knowledge about, among other things: the greenhouse effect; what climate change is and what its consequences are; what acid rain is; what the hole in the ozone layer is and its causes; alternative energies and their types, etc. Moreover, they should be aware of the most important environmental policies that are carried out to combat this phenomenon, such as: the Kyoto Protocol, the Emissions Trading Scheme (EU ETS), the Paris Agreement, etc.

We are convinced that activists must show initiative, leadership and clear persuasive skills that make them capable of recruiting followers or of obtaining donations. Although society is becoming more and more familiar with this phenomenon, in fact, it knows very little about how it originates, about the impact it causes and about how it—not only governments and NGOs—can help to mitigate its effects.

According to Greenpeace, one of the best known NGOs due to its protection of nature worldwide, the solution to climate change lies in the energy revolution. The organisation emphasises that renewable energies will mitigate the effects of climate change and achieve energy efficiency that will create jobs and reduce electricity costs.

With the Paris Accord, which was reached in December 2015 after years of failed attempts, it can be said that the first universal climate agreement was achieved during the Conference of the Parties held in Paris (COP21), which was unanimously adopted and entered into force on 4 November 2016.

The Agreement aims at establishing a comprehensive and legally binding global framework that requires implementation by all major economies. However, this Agreement suffered a major setback when a country of such importance as the United States of America withdrew from it, on the grounds that its president, Donald Trump, does not consider it transcendental in terms of climate action, and that his country's economy would be seriously undermined by its inclusion in the Agreement.

In spite of this, environmental NGOs have not surrendered. In this sense, it can be said that an increasing number of researchers, activists and citizens are concerned about mitigating climate change. In recent years, with the emergence of new grassroots movements and knowledge on sustainable development, the perception of the population is different. Social networks have played an enormously important role in improving the understanding of the consequences of climate change and its solutions on a global scale.

Climate activists are now well known for their efforts to make the world a better place, especially during and after the Paris COP. One of the most well-founded reasons for this success was the enormous political and media momentum of the Conference of the Parties, as well as the fact that weather events can be seen today that are more extreme than ever before and occur with great intensity, such as heat waves, extreme snowfall, loss of entire harvests due to droughts, force and repetition of seismic movements, etc.

Therefore, we can confirm, now, in the current post-Paris Accord period, that environmentalists need to collaborate at the national level with other actors such as governments, businesses, NGOs and local authorities. This is something that will only be possible if environmental activism matures and cooperates with other grassroots movements and activists. However, let us note that this must also be done on an individual basis, that is to say, all citizens who believe in climate change have a moral and civic obligation to change their behaviour and decisions in daily life and to follow concrete and agreed guidelines to reduce their carbon footprint. On the other hand, we must also note the fact that, at present, many conferences, meetings at the highest level, study days, as well as quite a few events and activities of all kinds are being held, but, in our opinion, there must be a greater degree of cooperation between the various parties involved in these events. The report presented during the Climate Summit in Bonn (Germany) in 2017 concluded with the clear idea that, despite the Paris Climate Agreement, countries are not making great efforts, and therefore, we cannot affirm that they are doing enough work to put a stop to the existing situation of global warming.

In addition, the report coincided with a request signed by 15,364 scientists from 184 countries around the world alerting humanity about the growing dangers of climate change. The text of the document indicated that the situation is now much worse than in 1992, when some 1700 scientists signed a similar letter warning about the problems of global warming.

Such objectives seem difficult to achieve in a world mainly influenced by the capitalist system. However, in spite of the utopia that for some people means being able to combine actions against the climate with the economies of the countries, environmental activism aims to motivate modern society to transform it into a community that is aware of the ravages that this phenomenon involves and, in this way, does not cause more of the damage to the planet that it is currently suffering.

Thus, in summary, it can be said that the fight against climate change has become a priority agenda for most governments, which has led to the establishment and consolidation of non-governmental organisations (NGOs) dedicated to protecting the environment, as well as to the implementation of initiatives aimed at improving the planet, which are among the most important at the international level in terms of their fight against climate change, as detailed in the paragraphs below.

2 WWF (World Wildlife Fund)

This well-known NGO's panda bear logo has set a global trend since its foundation in 1961. The WWF is currently one of the world's leading environmental conservation NGOs, along with Greenpeace.

The organisation we mention is one of the most prestigious NGOs in the field of wildlife and ecosystem conservation. It has about five million people in constant service in its various activities around the world.

Its headquarters are located in Switzerland, but it has offices all over the world, with some 27 national organisations as partners. Also, it is important to highlight that one of its greatest allies is the United Nations Organisation (UNO), which has been one of the flags of the world conservation movement since its foundation, as well as the European Union and the World Bank.

We can point out that one of the most important missions or objectives that the NGO must fulfil is being able to stop the current degeneration of the environment, promoting environmental activism to raise awareness and create a state of harmony between human beings, natural life and the efficient management of natural resources. In addition, another equally important task carried out by this NGO is to try to reduce the footprint of human beings, which seems increasingly indelible, in ecosystems marked by deforestation, logging, burning, as well as pollution of all kinds.

3 Greenpeace

Greenpeace is the flagship NGO of the global ecological conservation movement. Founded in 1971, when the environmental movement was at its height, and based in Vancouver, Canada, Greenpeace has an extensive network of activists around the world (approximately three million), making it the largest in existence today after the WWF.

Greenpeace proposes the conservation of the ecosystem and the defence of the environment, and intervention is necessary when acts are perpetrated against the protection of nature: hence, its constant protest activities and campaigns against these polluting acts. It also has the following objectives: nuclear disarmament; non-proliferation of biological weapons; protection of all types of biodiversity; elimination of transgenics; prevention of water pollutants in oceans, rivers and seas; prevention of abuse in the use of non-renewable natural resources.

We can agree that Greenpeace's essential basis in terms of climate change is focused and directed towards the electricity sector, aiming at achieving a model based on clean energy, free of greenhouse gases derived from the use of fossil fuels.

Over the years, this organisation has gained considerable prestige thanks to its achievements, mainly through the creation and consolidation of a vast plurality of conservation networks around the world, in stopping toxic waste pollution, in promoting corporate responsibility for environmental issues, and in raising awareness of the damage caused by oil spills along the coast.

4 The Nature Conservancy

This global organisation has the prestige of having protected some 48 million hectares of forests on land and having conserved water in major rivers around the globe. The Nature Conservancy has 400 offices with a total number of 4000 members in a network covering 35 countries around the world.

Founded in 1951 and extended to Latin America in 1975 in 16 countries in the region, its work has been focused on the creation of national parks and nature reserves in the territories of the different countries where the organisation operates. Therefore, it has been a great ally in terms of the conservation and enforcement of green policies in the main natural lungs of the earth, having and offering a wide variety of plans to be carried out in the aforementioned regions of the world, which are within its objectives, as special areas where major change can be generated.

It could be said that the Conservancy has applied the standardised use of applied science to everything involved in the development of conservation actions, especially in relation to water and land use. It has both public and private partners in order to achieve the objectives set out in its action plans. In this sense, it should be noted that, during its more than 60 years of activity, the organisation has managed to improve its experience in everything related to and affecting the implementation of a wide and varied range of conservation plans, having the professionalism to work at the local level, making the implementation of projects for the defence of nature more effective.

5 Friends of the Earth Network

The Friends of the Earth Network was born as an anti-nuclear organisation that, of course, is against the proliferation of nuclear weapons, nuclear energy and all kinds of nuclear material. Currently, its objectives go beyond environmental conservationism, as it has expanded in terms of its activities and plans related to economic policies aimed at sustainability.

The Friends of the Earth Network comprises 74 countries around the world, working through partnerships with a wide range of small and medium-sized non-governmental organisations, all of which are active in the field of environmental conservation, and whose policies cover the following areas: Arctic and Antarctic conservation; food sovereignty; nuclear disarmament and non-proliferation of biological weapons; halting the development of the use of GMOs in food; promoting sustainable development; the protection of environmental rights; responsible use of natural resources.

Many of the policies promoted in this organisation are oriented and aimed at the strict achievement of the conservation of a society in harmony with nature, which is why, although it is not very renowned or known in comparison to the organisations previously mentioned, it is true that it currently presents a rather important boom in terms of its campaigns and promotion of ecological alliances to preserve biodiversity on earth.

6 Climate Action Network

Climate Action Network (CAN) is a global network of more than 1100 non-governmental organisations, located in more than 120 countries around the world, working to promote governmental and individual action to mitigate human-induced climate change and to reduce it to ecologically sustainable levels.

The members of this organisation work to achieve the above objective by seeking to establish an effective use of information exchange and to pursue the coordinated development of NGO strategy on international, regional and national climate issues. This organisation maintains regional network centres that coordinate these efforts around the world.

Likewise, its members give high priority in their actions both to achieve a healthy environment and to promote development that meets the needs of the present, without compromising future generations in the satisfaction of their own needs.

The primary mission of this NGO is basically to protect the atmosphere while enabling harmonious, sustainable and equitable development around the world.

Finally, it should be pointed out that it is not only NGOs that are fighting against climate change on our planet. At the same time, there are also those who are researching alternative ways to manipulate the climate and the ecosystem with advanced technologies to mitigate its causes and consequences. Thus, in this order of things, we could highlight the following:

The Laval University (Quebec, Canada) project to detect the effects of climate change on the Arctic Ocean: the Argo drone. This device can be submerged up to 2000 m, measuring the temperature and salinity variables associated with pressure. This improves the monitoring and prediction of phenomena such as the loss of ice cover in summer and the invasion of marine species from the south. Similarly, both the World Meteorological Organisation (WMO) and UNESCO launched the Argo Programme with the clear aim of forming a global network of floating platforms and submarine drones for ocean observation.

In order to solve the problems caused by climate change, such as the rise of the ocean level, or the droughts and floods that we can see today on our planet, a team of researchers from the Desert Research Institute (DRI) is carrying out tests in the Nevada Desert (USA) in which they use unmanned aircraft that try to deposit certain elements in the clouds to cause or avoid rain. For the time being, the work is focused on solving the first of the above-mentioned assumptions, and a drone named Savant has been used for this purpose.

On the other hand, it is also worth mentioning, albeit very briefly, the work and effort of Japanese researchers at the Advanced Institute of Industrial Science and Technology (AIST) who have developed small drones capable of pollinating flowers. These drones are covered with the hair of an insect, the bee, and bathed with a sticky gel, which allows the pollen to be trapped when it lands on one flower and then released on another. This has emerged as a very interesting experiment in the context we are studying.

7 Conclusion

Finally, it is necessary to make a minimal reference to the remarkable impetus that is today being given to the field of clean energies, which is becoming a maxim for mitigating the effects of climate change, even more so with the entry into force of the Paris Agreement. In this way, we can see how wind energy is paradigmatic and stands as one of the main sources of clean energy production, so that many companies in all countries are constantly launching new products on the market with the aim of making their contribution, even if modest, to the achievement of respect for a cleaner environment, as well as reinforcing the fight against climate change on all possible fronts. The French company New Find, for example, offers a solution to the landscape impact of wind turbines that generate wind energy, the Wind Tree, which is a wind turbine that is camouflaged, thanks to its shape, between urban trees. Each blade, called Aerolaf, works like a small wind turbine that, together with the rest, can produce enough electricity to provide up to 80% of the average electrical power of a European home.

Cohabiting (Status of)

Nataša Lucić

1 Introduction

The term cohabitation is derived from the Latin verb 'cohabitare', meaning joint dwelling or co-tenancy in general (Klaić 1990, p. 702). Although cohabitation may imply various forms of joint living; in the legal sense, cohabitation usually denotes a couple living together without being legally married. Accordingly, the law regards persons living in a life union without being married as cohabitants.

Considering the fact that there is no legal definition of cohabitation in European law and that national legislations in Europe have rather different requirements for obtaining the legal status of 'cohabitant' and its subsequent legal benefits, it is not easy to formulate the exact features of a life union, which could be deemed as the requirement for obtaining the status of a cohabitant. Some national legislations do afford cohabitants living in *de facto* unions legal protection; some offer them the possibility to register their union and some differentiate between heterosexual and homosexual cohabitants, while some have the same regulations for all types of relationships (see, for example, Boele-Woelki 2015).

The grounds for acquiring certain rights depends on the potential cohabitants' family status. In this regard, it should be emphasised that EU law contains neither a definition of cohabitation nor a clear definition of the family. In the wider context of European—not just EU—law, one can say that European law first started to take cohabitants into consideration through the case law of the European Court of Human Rights (ECHR) and its protection of the right to family life. Therefore, the following chapter first examines the respective cases of the ECHR and then the individual status of cohabitants in EU law. It also tries to answer whether cohabitants are affected by European law, whether the process of European integration has affected

N. Lucić (✉)
Faculty of Law Osijek, Josip Juraj Strossmayer University of Osijek, Osijek, Croatia
e-mail: nlucic@pravos.hr

A. Bartolini et al. (eds.), *Dictionary of Statuses within EU Law*,
https://doi.org/10.1007/978-3-030-00554-2_12

the individual status of cohabitants and, if so, to realise the scope of such an influence.

2 Protection of the Right to Family Life Under the European Convention on Human Rights

Under European law, the status of a cohabitant was first recognised using the protection of the right to family life under Article 8 of the European Convention on Human Rights (hereinafter: the Convention). Even though at the time of the Convention's preparation, family life entailed the life union of married heterosexual partners (Kiernan 2003, p. 2; Probert and Barlow 2000, p. 153), the contemporary changes in family forms have prompted the extension of the legal protection of the right to family life stipulated by Article 8 of the Convention to other family forms. In a number of its judgments, the ECHR has revealed that the existence of family life depends on the existence of close ties, mutual affiliation, emotional bonds and dependence between family members and not exclusively on the existence of a formal legal act or consanguinity. For instance, in the case of *X, Y, Z v. United Kingdom,* the ECHR explicitly indicated that the notion of family life under Article 8 of the Convention is not solely confined to marriage-based families and may comprise *de facto* relationships too, which can be disclosed by considering several factors such as whether a couple live together, the length of their relationship and whether they have demonstrated their commitment to each other by having children together or by any other means. The family status of heterosexual cohabitants living in long-standing and stable unions and their right to protection of family life in the sense of Article 8 of the Convention has remained unchallenged for decades. The first time the ECHR decided on the existence of family life between homosexual cohabitants was in the case of *Schalk and Kopf v. Austria.* In this judgment, the ECHR held that in light of the changes in national legislations and the rapid evolution of social attitudes towards same-sex couples, it would be insincere to have a different view and so consequently concluded that the relationship of the applicants, a cohabiting same-sex couple living in a stable partnership, fell within the notion of "family life" under Article 8 of the Convention, just as the relationship of a heterosexual couple in the same situation would.

Heterosexual cohabitants have not frequently submitted applications for legal protection before the ECHR. What supports this thesis is the case of *Quintana Zapata v. Spain,* in which the applicant believed that the State violated Article 14 (prohibition of discrimination), in conjunction with Article 8 of the Convention. The violation allegedly resulted from a refusal to pay a widow's pension to the applicant who had lived with the deceased for 65 years and could not exercise the pension rights granted to a surviving spouse. The ECHR assumed that, in the context of widows' pensions, differences in the treatment between spouses and persons who lived together outside marriage pursue a legitimate aim and are based on an objective and reasonable justification; in this case, the objective and reasonable justification was the protection of the traditional family and so there was no violation of Article 14 of the Convention. A similar argument was utilised by the ECHR in the cases of *Shackell v. United Kingdom* and *Saucedo Gomez v. Spain.* In the case of *Van der Heijden v. the Netherlands,* the ECHR excluded a possible violation of Articles 8 and 14 of the Convention; a national court had not given the applicant the right to a denial of testimony in criminal proceedings against her longstanding cohabitant with whom she was in a stable family relationship. The applicant claimed that the relationship with her partner did not differ from those of spouses and registered partners who are, in compliance with the rules of the Dutch criminal procedure, permitted to refuse to testify against each other.

It is homosexual cohabitants who have much more frequently requested protection from discriminatory action before the ECHR if in accordance whit national legislation they cannot conclude marriage and exercise the associated rights or to exercise rights granted to heterosexual cohabitants. For example, in the case of *P.B. and J.S. v. Austria* the ECHR was invited to decide on a refusal to extend sickness insurance cover to the homosexual partner of an insured person, which resulted in a judgment partially confirming the violation of Article 14 taken in conjunction with Article 8 of the ECHR (for the period after the respective legislative amendment allowing relevant insurance rights to heterosexual cohabitants). The *Aldeguer Tomás v. Spain* case concerned a denial of a survivor's pension rights on the ground of the applicant's sexual orientation, but no violation of Article 14 was found. The case of *Mata Estevez v. Spain* also concerned the applicant's eligibility for a survivor's pension after experiencing treatment by the law that contrasted with the experiences of both spouses and even heterosexual cohabitants. The application was rejected because the ECHR ruled that the difference in treatment could fall within the State's margin of appreciation. In the case of *Gas and Dubois v. France*, the applicants were two cohabiting women. The case related to a refusal for adoption in respect of the second applicant's child. The ECHR saw no violation of Articles 8 or 14 of the Convention since the applicants' legal situation in this view did not resemble that of married couples and no discrimination based on sexual orientation was detected. The case of *X and Others v. Austria* largely resembled *Gas and Dubois*, though the outcome was different; it concerned two homosexual women, one of whom wanted to adopt the son of the other. The ECHR recognised the alleged violation since, unlike French law, Austrian law permits heterosexual cohabitants to undergo second parent adoption; the ECHR therefore recognised discrimination based on sexual orientation.

It can be concluded that today both heterosexual and homosexual cohabitants in longstanding and stable life unions enjoy the protection of their family life under Article 8 of the Convention and that putting homosexual cohabitants in an underprivileged position represents discrimination in the sense of Article 14 of the Convention. However, regulation of the legal relationships between cohabitants is a matter of national legislation and despite the fact that marriage is not a requirement for obtaining the protection of family life under Article 8 of the Convention, the Convention does not at all bind national legislators to equalise the legal status of cohabitants with that of spouses.

3 Cohabitants and EU Law

3.1 *Family Status of Cohabitants*

EU law neither governs the individual status of cohabitants nor considerably refers thereto. For the time being, there are only three areas of EU law where cohabitants really matter and these are free movement of persons and their family members, asylum and immigration issues and benefits in the context of employment law (Miles 2016, p. 90). However, EU rights and entitlements are advanced to families rather than to individuals (McGlynn 2006, p. 113), so the family status of cohabitants represents, if existing, the foundation for acquiring certain rights in those legal areas.

The Charter of Fundamental Rights of the European Union (hereinafter: the Charter) guarantees, like the Convention, the right to respect for private and family life (see Article 7). Since it appeared a half-century after the Convention, the Charter has adapted to the contemporary changes in family forms in society and law due to, among other things, a growing number of cohabitants. In this view, Article 9 of the Charter, in contrast to the Convention, refers to the right to marry and the right to found a family as a twos separate rights. However, the Charter also puts the burden of responsibility for the manner of exercising the right to marry and the right to found a family on national legislations, prescribing in the same Article that these rights "shall be guaranteed in accordance with the national laws governing the exercise of these rights". To summarise, the question of whether cohabitants have family status and under which conditions it can be obtained is, according to the Charter, a matter for the national legislation of the Member State.

As highlighted by De Baere and Gutman, one should bear in mind that as matters stand now, there are no legal bases governing the EU, which allows its institutions to adopt measures concerning substantive family law (De Baere and Gutman 2016, p. 13). When EU law touches upon the rights of couples based on their family ties, it still explicitly refers to spouses and, in some newer documents, to cohabitants who have registered their union (see, for example, Regulation No 31 (EEC), 11 (EAEC), laying down the Staff Regulations of Officials and the Conditions of Employment of Other Servants of the European Economic Community and the European Atomic Energy Community). Moreover, when it comes to *de facto* cohabitants, EU law is still reluctant to make a significant move towards legally equalising cohabitants with spouses.

3.2 *Freedom of Movement of Persons*

The majority of cohabitants who do not want to enter into marriage in Europe are largely considered by EU law only when prescribing measures to ensure freedom of movement of persons. As neatly noted by Miles, the fullest recognition of cohabiting couples in EU law relates to free movement, but cohabitants' recognition is substantially inferior to that afforded to workers' spouses (Miles 2016, p. 91).

Directive 2004/38/EC of the European Parliament and of the Council of 29 April 2004 on the right of citizens of the Union and their family members to move and reside freely within the territories of the Member States (hereinafter: Directive 2004/38/EZ) refers to cohabitants with EU citizenship who have resided in a Member State other than his/her country of origin. Regarding the formulations of its Articles, Directive 2004/38/EZ is not concerned about the sexual orientation of cohabitants, so one can draw the conclusion that its implementation refers to both heterosexual and homosexual cohabitants, but the ultimate answer to the question of which cohabitants are provided with the regard to freely move and reside in a concrete Member State should be found in the national legislation of that Member State. This is derived from Article 2, Paragraph 2b of Directive 2004/38/EZ, which regards a registered partner as a family member addressed therein, thus opening up the possibility of the host Member State to facilitate the entry and residence of the unregistered partner with whom the EU citizen is in a longstanding and stable (durable) relationship (see Article 3, Paragraph 2b of the Directive). Whether there is a possibility of registering the applicants' cohabitation before the competent body of a particular Member State, whether both heterosexual and homosexual partners qualify for the registration and the attitude of the Member States towards *de facto* unions, considering the possibility of exercising the rights regulated by Directive 2004/38/EZ, are all questions tackled by the national legislation of the Member State concerned (Lucić 2015. pp. 106–107).

3.3 *Case Law of the Court of Justice of the European Union*

The first case that left a considerable mark on the case law of the Court of Justice of the European Union with regard to *de facto* heterosexual cohabitations is the case of *Reed*; the Court expressed the opinion that the notion of "partners" in Article 10 of Regulation (EEC) No 1612/68 of the Council of 15 October 1968 in the context of freedom of movement for workers within the European Economic Community refers only to spouses and not to cohabitants and that legal equalisation of marital and extramarital unions does not belong to the domain of European law but to the domain of national legislations. In the case of *Grant,* due to a lack of a general consensus among the Member States on homosexual life unions, the Court excluded discrimination resulting from an unequal treatment of heterosexual and homosexual cohabitants (see also the *Eyüp* case). However, as stated by Swennen, in this case the Court at least recognised the existence of protected heterosexual cohabitations (Swennen 2007, p. 414). Still, a considerable amount of time has lapsed since these cases; it needs to be considered that between now and then a whole different awareness of cohabitations in Europe has developed. E. Goossens rightly notes that the latest EU documents deviate from the traditional unreserved "sympathy for marriage" and that a tendency to recognise registered partnerships in substantive EU law has developed in recent years (Goossens 2012, pp. 633–634). The first case which determined the attitude of the Court towards cohabitants in registered partnerships dates back to 2001, in the form of *D and Sweden*. In this case, the Court first conveyed the viewpoint that a difference in the status between registered partners and spouses is not unlawful due to the difference between the "nature" of registered partnerships and the "nature" of marriage which was, at that time, reserved only for heterosexual partners. In later cases, e.g. in the cases of *Maruko* and *Römer*, the Court held that the difference in the legal status of registered partners and spouses is only unlawful in national legislations in which same-sex registered partnerships serve as a substitute for marriage, i.e. where same-sex marriage has not yet been legalised. Hence, it can be concluded that there is no unlawfulness in cases where national legislations rule that there is a difference between marriage and heterosexual registered partnerships since heterosexual partners have an alternative—they can enter into marriage. By analogy, there is no discrimination against homosexual registered partners who do not enjoy the same rights as spouses if homosexual partners can, in line with the respective national legislation, conclude marriage (see Goossens 2012, pp. 642–643).

4 Conclusion

Although the continuous rise in the number of cohabiting couples in Europe imposes numerous questions on European legislation, legislators still hesitate to appropriately respond and continue to put the burden of responsibility on national legislation. Consequently, one may deduce that for the time being, European integration has no significant influence on the individual status of cohabitants. Speaking in the context of EU law only, we can say that it still confines its concern for cohabitants to the area of free movement of persons; even in this field, when an issue concerns cohabitants in *de facto* life unions, it mostly forwards the cases to national legislation.

Therefore, it would make more sense to draw a conclusion on the impact of cohabitants on European law than on the impact of European law on cohabitants. In fact, European law cannot ignore the fact that marriage is no longer the only way to found a family and that the number of cohabitants who opt for extramarital unions is growing. European law should not be reluctant to respond to such changes in family forms and it should take them into account in order to be able to satisfy the needs of European society as a whole. We can be certain, therefore, that the adaptation of European law to these changes will be neither swift nor easy, since European law is facing a number of obstacles arising from traditional, cultural, religious and other diversities which exist among the Member States. Those diversities account for the huge difference in the status of cohabitants between the Member States; we can, therefore, only hope that European law will devise adequate mechanisms to contribute to the harmonisation of national legislations in this legal area.

References

Boele-Woelki, K. (2015). *European family law in action, Volume V: Informal relationships*. Cambridge/Antwerp/Portland: Intersentia.

De Baere, G., & Gutman, K. (2016). The impact of the European Union and the European Court of Justice on the European family law. In J. M. Scherpe (Ed.), *European family law, Volume I: The impact of institutions and organisations on European family law* (pp. 5–48). Cheltenham/Northampton: Edward Elgar Publishing Limited.

Goossens, E. (2012). Different regulatory regimes for registered partnership and marriage: Outdated or indispensable? A European perspective on the Belgian model. In A. L. Verbeke et al. (Eds.), *Confronting the frontiers of family and succession law* (pp. 633–650). Antwerp: Intersentia.

Kiernan, K. (2003). *Cohabitation and divorce across nations and generations* (CASE paper 65). London: Centre for Analysis of Social Exclusion.

Klaić, B. (1990). *Rječnik stranih riječi* (Dictionary of Foreign Words). Zagreb: Nakladni zavod MH.

Lucić, N. (2015). *Izvanbračna zajednica i pravna sigurnost* (Cohabitation and Legal Security). Dissertation, University of Zagreb

McGlynn, C. (2006). *Families and the European Union: Law, politics and pluralism*. Cambridge/New York: Cambridge University Press.

Mileš, J. (2016). Unmarried cohabitation in a European perspective. In J. M. Scherpe (Ed.), *European family law, Volume III: Family law in a European perspective* (pp. 82–115). Cheltenham/Northampton: Edward Elgar Publishing Limited.

Probert, R., & Barlow, A. (2000). Displacing marriage – diversification and harmonisation within Europe. *Child and Family Law Quarterly, 12*(2), 153–166.

Swennen, F. (2007). Atypical families in EU (private international) family law. In J. Meeusen et al. (Eds.), *International family law for the European Union* (pp. 389–423). Antwerp/Oxford: Intersentia.

Consumer

Joaquín Sarrión Esteve

1 Introduction

Consumer protection was used primarily under European Communities legislation as an instrument to drive economic integration (Chalmers et al. 2014, p. 669), but with the creation of an internal market, it has developed as a 'driving force' in the EU integration process (Benöhr 2013, p. 9).[1] Consumer protection is not only a key legal instrument to achieve the internal market but also to reinforce EU citizens' and residents' economic, legal, and constitutional status as equality players in the market. After all, there is a duality in the images of the consumer: as a person who is in the mind of EU institutions and as a (projected and finally real) person who will emerge as a result of the EU regulation (Leczykiewicz and Weatherill 2016).[2]

Moreover, the European Court of Justice (ECJ) case law is relevant in the development of EU consumer concept and status which must be applied by national courts.

Nevertheless, it is impossible to understand well the concept of an EU consumer, and therefore the consumer EuroStatus within, without using a multilevel methodology because of the complex European legal order comprised of systems with different levels increasingly interconnected (Gómez Sánchez 2011, p. 20). We need this theoretical basis to approach and try to study any EU legal institution which always includes legal elements derived from these related and interconnected legal systems,

[1] In fact, the EU market success depends on cross-border consumer activity (see de Vries 2012).

[2] Nevertheless, consumer law configuration depends on the 'underlying consumer image', and EU consumer law is forcing national legislators and courts to overcome a rigid and uniform national concept of consumer (Rott 2014).

J. Sarrión Esteve (✉)
Ramón y Cajal Programme, Departamento de Derecho Constitucional, Universidad Nacional de Educación a Distancia (UNED), Madrid, Spain
e-mail: jsarrion@der.uned.es

A. Bartolini et al. (eds.), *Dictionary of Statuses within EU Law*,
https://doi.org/10.1007/978-3-030-00554-2_13

particularly with the constitutional horizon opened in the EU after the Lisbon Treaty (Sarrión 2011, 2014a).

2 Consumer Protection Configuration, the Notion of 'Consumer', and the Development of a Consumer Legal Framework in the EU

2.1 EU Consumer Protection Configuration

EU consumer protection is essential for EU integration and development (European Commission 2017a). But one of the questions that challenges consumer protection is if we are facing a 'fundamental right'. Certainly, consumer protection is recognised in the EU Charter of Fundamental Rights[3] in title IV, Solidarity, under article 38: Union policies shall ensure a high level of consumer protection.

We can understand, however, that 'not all rights are granted equal status', and we can see several differences (Sarrión 2010, pp. 88–89) due to the configuration of consumer protection as a policy clause,[4] i.e. the recognition of consumer protection under the EU Charter is limited to a mandate to the EU institutions—and, of course, for EU member state authorities in the implementation—to ensure in their policies 'a high level of consumer protection'. Therefore, consumer protection is more like a principle and depends on its regulation in the treaties and the legal development of the policies in the EU.

Moreover, consumer protection is also part of the social dimension of the EU, and as ECJ pointed out before in Viking[5] regarding social rights, the European community doesn't have a unique economic aim, and there is a need of balance between the economic and social dimensions (Sarrión 2010).

This legal configuration is confirmed in the articles 52(5) (principles which may be implemented by legislative and executive acts of the EU institutions, and by Member states when implementing EU law in the exercise of their competences) and 51(1) of the EU Charter.[6] The ECJ interprets the implementation of EU law as being linked to the concept of the scope of EU law (Sarrión 2015); the Explanations of the EU Charter indicates for article 38 that the principles set out were based on article 169 TFEU.

---

[3] The Charter of Fundamental Rights of the European Union, better known as the EU Charter, was elaborated in 2000, adopted in 2007, and entered into force with the Lisbon Treaty on 1 December, 2009.

[4] In fact, as Menendez (2003, pp. 183–187) pointed out, we can distinguish a typology of legal positions: fundamental rights, ordinary rights, and policy clauses; consumer protection is a policy clause.

[5] C-438/05 Viking Line.

[6] EU Charter provisions are addressed not only to EU institutions but also to the EU Member States when they are implementing EU law.

2.2 The Notion of 'Consumer'

The notion of *consumer* is a negative concept in contrast to a professional person, i.e., it is a natural person—in EU Law—who acts outside the scope of an economic, professional, trade, or business activity.[7] In this way, the consumer establishes a contractual relationship with a professional or a trader, a natural or legal/juristic person. There is a concrete contractual relation between a business and a consumer (a Business to Consumer [B2C] contract), in contrast to a Business to Business (B2B) contract (Hedegaard and Wrbka 2016, p. 71). The consumer is the weaker party due to his non-professionalism and therefore his lower degree of knowledge about the contract and its conditions in contrast to the professional who is supposed to be an expert in the field (Lazíková and Rumanovská 2016, p. 2).

Although the EU legislation approach to the consumer notion can be seen as partial (there is not a common definition), the differences are minor and consider consumer as a natural person who, in contracts covered by the respective directive, is acting for purposes which are not related to or which are outside his trade, business, craft, or profession.[8] Moreover, the ECJ helps with a restrictive and standard interpretation of the consumer as a natural person position (personal criterion)[9] linked not to the connection with his/her professional activity (functional criterion), meaning that the judgement of the adjudication of the consumer position needs to consider the nature and aim of the specific contract.[10]

Of course with this concept we can always see complex cases including mixed-purpose contract situations such as Gruber (a person living in a building in which one part was used as a family home and the rest for the farm) where the ECJ clarified that the existence of private elements was irrelevant and it denied the notion of consumer, stating that person who concludes a contract concerning goods intended partly for purposes which are in part within and in part outside his profession may not rely on the notion of consumer unless the professional or trade aim is so limited as to be ineligible in the context.[11] There also was the case of Costa in which the ECJ stated that a lawyer who concluded a credit agreement with a bank, in which the purpose of the credit was not specified, may be regarded as a consumer if the agreement was not linked to that lawyer's profession.[12]

[7] The ECJ is clear about the interpretation of EU consumer which exclude legal persons although they have a non-business character.

[8] In fact, it is the secondary EU law, each statute, which makes individual definitions for any of the statute purposes. The different approaches already have been subject of several interesting contributions outlining differences and similitudes (see Lazíková and Rumanovská 2016; Hedegaard and Wrbka 2016).

[9] C-541/99 and 542/99 Cape Snc and Idealserive joined cases.

[10] C-361/89 Di Pinto and C–269/95 Francesco Benincasa v Dentalkit Sr.

[11] C–464/01 Johann Gruber.

[12] C–110/14 Costea.

This strong restrictive approach to defining consumers has been criticized. There is a lack of protection for a person who can be acting as the weaker party—which is supposed to be the aim of consumer protection—and there also is overprotection for a well-informed person (for example, a lawyer) in a private purpose contractual relationship.[13] Therefore, perhaps criteria based on the person and not functional criteria could be better as Lazíková and Rumanovská (2016, p. 10) suggested *de lege ferenda*.

Being a consumer implies having the status of consumer (the Consumer EuroStatus) in a legal sense, and therefore the application of the EU Consumer regulation.[14] It is well known that national laws include legal entities in the concept of consumer when they act in a private way, as in Austria or Czech Republic, or when they act as final users as in Greece or Spain (Mańko 2013). This re-interpretation of consumer in national legislation and problems of national courts regarding the existence of a consumer relation may be required for an EU legal presumption (European Commission 2017b, p. 29).[15] Nevertheless, it is interesting to consider the advantages of leaving sufficient discretion for courts to value the existence of a weaker party and to protect its position as a consumer (Lazíková and Rumanovská 2016, p. 2).

One might suggest that the consumer concept may be included in the national civil codes, but the truth is that it did not appear at all in the codes until recently in someone's. The concept is included usually in a special status for consumer protection—a type of compilation of consumer rules or a 'special body of norms for the protection of consumers'. This is the case of Spain, where consumer protection rules are included in the Consumer Protection Act except for the Unfair Contract Terms Directive the transposition of which is out of this act, and of Austria, France, and the United Kingdom.[16] Nevertheless, some countries recently decided to introduce the concept in the civil codes, as is the case of Netherlands and Germany. The Dutch Civil Code introduced the consumer concept in the reform of 1992, and Germany in the reform of 2002 included EU consumer protection regulation. It is important to outline the case of Germany modifying the civil code with the so-called 'great solution'; it may be the most important since the code entered into

[13] See Stuyck (2010, p. 29), Schueller (2012, p. 123), Lazíková and Rumanovská (2016, p. 2), Hedegaard and Wrbka (2016, p. 87).

[14] In the notion of consumer, it is important to know the status of the parties, i.e. the rights and obligations, because the legal consequences are different. Some authors speak about two sides of the consumer notion; the external side is whether or not a person can be called or not a consumer in a legal sense, while the internal side determines the differences between consumers (groups or classes of consumers) who need a special protection and those who do not, and it is linked to the consumer protection model (see Hedegaard and Wrbka 2016, pp. 76–77).

[15] The European Commission's recent report suggests as a solution to provide for a legal presumption of being a consumer 'whenever a natural person concludes a contract for sale and/or services with a salesman or a business' (European Commission 2017b, p. 29).

[16] In the case of UK is the recent Consumer Rights Act of 2015 which seeks to consolidate, simplify, and modernise the consumer protection legislation in UK absorbing and consolidating the EU directives. See Giliker (2018).

force in 1900 and realized a Europeanization of the Bürgerliches Gesetzbuch (BGB). Others, such as Italy and Austria, have used an intermediate solution which introduced new provisions in their respective civil codes (Martínez Velencoso 2017, pp. 254–263).

3 EU Consumer Protection Legal Framework Development

Consumer protection was not included in the original European Community Treaty but it was mentioned in the competition and the common agricultural policy. The EC assumed its competence under the flexibility clause (former article 235 EECT and then article 308 ECT), a general clause which allowed EC institutions to adopt any measure needed to achieve one of the aims of the community required for the functioning of the common market in cases where the treaty had not provided it. Also, as Rossi (2012, p. 86) outlines, the practice expanded the flexibility clause application, creating new competences including consumer protection.

After that, consumer protection was included with the Single European Act (1986, article 100a) and reinforced under the Treaty of Maastricht with the attribution to the European Community of the competence to consumer protection (1992, article 129a ECT).

The ECJ considered that although the scope of article 129a is limited, it provides the European Community the duty to contribute to the achievement of a high consumer-protection level and a competence to do it, and although it is one of the objectives, it is not the sole one,[17] meaning that the consumer protection policy 'is a cross-sectional' one, creating the objectives with the internal market (Lazíková 2016, p. 21).

While consumer protection was a key instrument to achieve the internal market, we also can see its interesting development in the treaties. In fact, the Treaty of Amsterdam introduced the competence for promoting consumer rights in 1997 (article 153 ECT), and it confirmed the cross-sectional nature of the competence (Lazíková 2016, p. 22). Also, the Treaty of Lisbon included consumer protection in the 'shared competences' list (a non-exhaustive catalogue) between the EU and member states (article 4(2) of the Treaty of the Functioning of the European Union, TFEU 2009).

Article 2 TFEU recognised three types of competences: exclusive, shared, and supporting. While the treaties conferred to the EU a shared competence, both the EU and member states may legislate and adopt legally binding acts in the referred area, according to article 2(2) TFEU.

This inclusion of consumer protection in shared competences means that member states may adopt rules in this area, and that the EU harmonisation legislation is subject to the subsidiarity principle. A shared competence, however, does not mean

[17] See C-192/04 Lagardère and C-233/94 Germany v. European Parliament and EU Council.

a concurrent one, that is, the EU and member states may act, and therefore state action is not excluded, but the national competence can be exercised to the extent that the EU has not exercised or ceased to exercise the shared competence. The latter may occur when the EU decides to repeal an EU act.[18]

Nevertheless, the existence of the competence depends on the specific regulation because one can interpret that EU regulation is free to go from a minimum harmonisation to a less flexible total harmonisation (with a uniform standard). The EU traditionally followed a minimum harmonisation approach until the recent directive in which EU adopted a maximum harmonisation approach.[19]

The EU consumer protection is regulated in article 169 TFEU. And although it is true that today that consumer protection is still an internal market key instrument (Chalmers et al. 2014, p. 671), there is a relevant change because we are developing, as article 3(3) of the Treaty of the European Union (TEU) identifies, a ‘social market economy’ (Barnard 2010, pp. 27–30). Furthermore, consumer protection, from my point of view, is a key for the development of legal and constitutional status of EU citizens and residents as equality players in the market as part of the social dimension.[20]

According to article 169(1) TFEU, EU institutions must guarantee a high level of protection for consumers through (a) measures adopted within article 114 TFEU in the completion of the internal market, article 169(2a), and (b) measures adopted to support, supplement, and monitor the policy pursued by member states, according to article 169(2b), without preventing national measures which maintain or introduce a higher protection following article 169(4) TFEU.[21]

Certainly, one can ask if the dormant competence or the so-called pre-emption doctrine can be applied to this area of consumer protection shared competences, preventing member states from regulating in a way that jeopardises an existing EU regulation.[22] But in reading both legal bases, article 169(2b) in connection with

[18] In fact, Declaration N. 28 in relation to the delimitation of competences states that the EU may decide to repeal an act to ensure a constant respect of the proportional and subsidiarity principles (Tridimas 2012, p. 63, note 55).

[19] The traditional minimum approach allowed member states to maintain their national pre-existing approaches (Kunnecke 2014, pp. 427–428).

[20] Some authors argue, however, that EU consumer law has focused until today principally in the development of the internal market (see Howes et al. 2017).

[21] Therefore, we can see two bases to legislate. The first one is not a general competence or legislative power for EU harmonisation (Weatherill 2013, p. 352; Lazíková 2016, p. 23; Micossi 2016, p. 11), but the limits can be unclear and it is an important legal base to legislate. One can interpret that the EU has the flexibility to develop a traditional minimum harmonisation approach or a maximum one. The second legal base is clearly complementary to the member states in the sense that EU measures are adopted to support, supplement, and monitor national policies (article 169(2b) TFEU), without preventing national measures which maintain or introduce a higher protection following article 169(4) TFEU.

[22] Certainly, authors argue about the application of the USA Constitutional Dormant Doctrine or the pre-emption doctrine to the EU shared competences. In this sense, EU law can be interpreted to incorporate a restraining effect on national powers, that is, member states shall, when imple-

article 169(2a), one can argue that the pre-emption doctrine is explicitly limited in consumer protection and member states are free to maintain or introduce measures in consumer protection if they guarantee a higher protection, that is, member states are only precluded from regulating a lower protection for consumers (also according to article 169(4) TFEU).

Of course, to ensure a better harmonisation of consumer protection, the former EC and later the EU developed several initiatives to ensure a better harmonisation. We can outline, particularly, the Directive on Consumer Rights (2011/83/EU),[23] the Directive 1999/44/EC on certain aspects of the sale of consumer goods and associated guarantees,[24] and the Council Directive 93/13/EEC on unfair terms in consumer contracts.[25]

Moreover, the European Commission outlined in several communications that consumer protection is an essential part of its strategic plan, as under the Europe 2020 Strategy for smart, sustainable and inclusive growth, and the action plan implementing the Stockholm Programme, the Citizenship Report, and the Digital Agenda (European Commission 2017a).

The European Commission also adopted directives on resolution mechanisms on alternative dispute resolution[26] and online dispute resolution for consumer disputes,[27] but as a relevant report pointed recently, there is no EU instrument on EU consumer protection in civil proceedings (European Commission 2017b, p. 28).

Nevertheless, the role of the ECJ in the development of EU consumer protection is relevant, and in fact, the court developed through the effective judicial protection principle (Sarrión 2014a, b) a constitutional procedural EuroStatus for consumers which must be applied by national courts in civil proceedings (Sarrión 2018).

menting their own legislation in shared competences, guarantee EU law, including EU principles, and must avoid jeopardising the EU regulation (Luif 2014; Rossi 2012; Schütze 2006; Tridimas 2012; Weatherill 2002).

[23] Directive 2011/83/EU of the European Parliament and of the Council of 25 October 2011 on consumer rights, amending Council Directive 93/13/EEC and Directive 1999/44/EC of the European Parliament and of the Council and repealing Council Directive 85/577/EEC and Directive 97/7/EC of the European Parliament and of the Council. OJEU L304/64 22.11.2011.

[24] Directive 1999/44/EC of the European Parliament and of the Council of 25 May 1999 on certain aspects of the sale of consumer goods and associated guarantees. OJ L 171 7.7.1999.

[25] Council Directive 93/13/EEC of 5 April 1993 on unfair terms in consumer contracts. OJ L 95 21.4.1993.

[26] Directive 2013/11/EU of 21 May 2013 on alternative dispute resolution for consumer disputes and amending Regulation (EC) No 2006/2004 and Directive 2009/22/EC OJL 165 18.06.2013.

[27] Regulation (EC) No 524/2013 of 21 May 2013 on online dispute resolution for consumer disputes OJ L165/1 18.06.2013.

4 Development of a Consumer Constitutional Procedural Status: The Ex-officio Doctrine and Equal Arms Principle

In the absence of EU legislation, EU member states are free to regulate the procedure for implementation of EU law, according to each domestic legal system, therefore, including the EU consumer protection legal framework.

Nevertheless, according to the principle of cooperation laid down in article 4 EUT, member states shall take the necessary measures to ensure fulfilment of the obligations under the treaty, and in particular national courts shall provide appropriate judicial protection of rights which EU law confers on individuals.

In this sense, we can say that the principle of procedural autonomy implies that the EU member states are free to configure the appropriate procedural rules to guarantee EU law, and particularly rights recognized in EU legislation, because national judges are the EU ordinary judges and courts.

As the ECJ considered in the Unibet case in 2007,[28] in the treaty there is no national procedural remedy for the preservation of EU law other than those laid down in national law. EU law requires, however, the national configuration of procedural rules to ensure the respect for rights deriving from EU law. That national regulation must not be less favourable than those governing similar domestic actions (principle of equivalence), and nor should it render impossible in practice or excessively difficult the exercise of rights conferred by EU law (principle of effectiveness). The national courts are to interpret ‘as far as possible’ the procedural rules so that the application of these rules contributes to the goal of ensuring effective judicial protection of EU law rights attributed to litigants (Unibet, paragraphs 38–44 and 54). Thus, the procedural autonomy would be strongly held by the principles of equivalence and effectiveness, changing the old procedural autonomy freedom to a limited one (Sarrión 2014b, p. 446).

The so-called ex officio (control) doctrine (Mickilitz 2013) started in 1998 with the Oceano Grupo[29] case as a tool which could be used by national courts to enforce and apply EU consumer law (European Commission 2017b, pp. 188–189). There has been a coherent development of this doctrine, however, reinforcing the effectiveness of the consumer protection (Sarrión 2014a).[30] In fact, in the Pannon case in 2009,[31] the court stated that the specific characteristics of judicial proceedings between professionals and consumers, in national law, cannot be an element that may affect the legal protection they enjoy under EU law. Also, the national court is required to examine ex officio the unfairness of a contractual term as soon as he/she has the facts and law that need to do it. Moreover, in the Pénzügyi case a year later, the ECJ ruled that a national court can examine ex officio and declare a contractual

[28] C-432/05 Unibet.

[29] C-240/98 to 244/98 Oceano Grupo joined cases.

[30] Some authors argue that there is a unpredictability application of ex officio doctrine by the ECJ (see Trstenjak and Beysen 2011; report of the European Commission 2017b, p. 189).

[31] C-243/08 Pannon GSM.

term unfair, although in the case that the parties have not requested it, and under national procedural law the tests can be performed only at the request of a party in the civil process.[32]

The *ex officio doctrine* is an application of the principle of effectiveness that involves not a simple interpretation of national procedural law, but it allows the courts an ex officio action not provided under national procedural law and therefore against national legislation (Sarrión 2014b, p. 442).

Although in the Dominguez case in 2012,[33] the ECJ's ruling may seem a backward step, it is not. The ECJ said the national court must determine the applicable procedural rules and, considering all elements of the national legislation and applying the interpretative methods recognized in this, do everything within its power to ensure the full effectiveness of EU law (Sarrión 2014b, p. 443). After that case, the court confirmed that when there is no possibility to guarantee an effective protection for consumers, national courts should exercise ex officio control, overcoming national law (although national law doesn't allow the national court to do it), i.e. they must apply the Pénzügyi doctrine. We can see this action confirmed in several cases focused on Spain as Banco Español de Crédito in 2012,[34] Aziz in 2013,[35] Sánchez Morcillo (in which the ECJ tried to reinforce the consumer position to

[32] C-137/08 Pénzügyi.

[33] C-282/10 Dominguez, paragraph 27.

[34] C-618/10 Banco Español de Crédito. The ECJ stated that the Spanish procedural rules about the payment procedure were contrary to the principle of effectiveness in preventing consumer protection. The reason is that the Spanish legislation did not allow the national court when it had the facts and law elements to examine ex officio the unfairness of a contractual default interest clause contained in a contact held between a professional and a consumer when the consumer did not raise opposition to it.

[35] C-415/11Mohamed Aziz. The ECJ stated that Spanish legislation was incompatible with EU law because in regulating mortgage enforcement proceedings, it did not provide the possibility of formulating grounds of opposition based on the unfairness of a contractual term (which is the basis of an ejection title). At the same time, the law did not allow the judge of the declarative process (which is the power to assess the unfairness of the clause) to take precautionary measures, including the suspension of the mortgage enforcement proceeding when it is necessary to ensure the full effectiveness of the court's final decision. The problem with the Spanish legislation was that it did not cover and guarantee the rights of a consumer in relation to banks because they could discuss the unfairness of a clause only in the declarative process, not in the mortgage enforcement proceedings. At the same time, in the mortgage enforcement proceedings, the consumer could not argue the unfairness of a clause. In this sense, according to that legislation, the consumer usually lost the mortgage enforcement proceedings, and after that if he/she won the declarative process, it would be impossible to gain recuperation of the house, impacting the protection of rights of the Spanish consumer.

guarantee the equal arms principle in the judicial process) in 2014,[36] and in Gutiérrez Naranjo in 2016.[37]

Therefore, we can say that the so called procedural autonomy principle is greatly reduced, and that EU member states, when implementing and regulating their legal system, must always guarantee the exercise of rights covered in EU law including consumer protection framework. Of course, the national court may use national law to provide EU consumer protection, but the court should overcome national rules when they can affect the EU consumer status; within this we can see included a strictly equal arms principle in the judiciary process.

The effectiveness and primacy of EU law thus limits the freedom of the procedural autonomy of the national power, and today there is only a functionalized or oriented procedural autonomy to ensure the EU legal framework (Arzoz Santiesteban 2013; Galetta 2011; Sarrión 2014b). It is a good solution from the perspective of a multilevel system: EU member states have the competence to regulate national procedures, but this regulation must guarantee rights covered not only at national level but also at the EU level (Sarrión 2018).

5 Conclusions

Being an EU consumer implies having the status of a 'consumer', and therefore the Consumer EuroStatus, in a legal sense, with the guarantees of the EU consumer regulation. The consumer notion as part of EU consumer regulation is not only a key for the consolidation of the internal market but also for the development of the legal and constitutional status for EU citizens and residents within the market.

The EU is clearly contributing to the Europeanization of national legislation regarding consumers thanks to the development of legal EU instruments and to important ECJ case law. In fact, we can outline that the ECJ has been playing an important role regarding the EU consumer concept and position, including the establishment of a consumer constitutional procedural EuroStatus which must be applied by national courts in civil proceedings.

[36] C-169/14 Sánchez Morcillo. The ECJ mentioned the Banesto and Aziz cases, and observed that Spanish legislation in relation to mortgage enforcement 'gives the seller or supplier, as a creditor seeking enforcement, the rights to bring an appeal against a decision ordering a stay of enforcement or declaring an unfair clause inapplicable, but does not permit, by contrast, the consumer to exercise a right of appeal against a decision dismissing and objection to enforcement'.

[37] C-154/15 Gutiérrez Naranjo. The ECJ rules incompatible to the EU consumer protection framework a national case law such as the Spanish Supreme Court doctrine which restricts the restitutory effects connected with the invalidity of an unfair term to the amounts overpaid after the delivery of the decision; from the ECJ perspective, the restoring effect has a retroactive effect.

References

Arzoz Santiesteban, X. (2013). La autonomía institucional y procedimental de los Estados miembros en la Unión Europea: Mito y realidad. *Revista de Administración Pública, 191*, 159–197.

Barnard, C. (2010). *The substantive law of the EU* (3rd ed.). Oxford, England: Oxford University Press.

Benöhr, I. (2013). *EU consumer law and human rights*. Oxford, England: Oxford University Press.

Chalmers, D., Davies, G., & Monti, G. (2014). *European Union law* (3rd ed.). Cambridge, England: Cambridge University Press.

de Vries, S. (2012). Consumer protection and the EU single market rules – The search for the 'paradigm consumer. *Journal of European Consumer and Market Law, 5*(4), 228–242.

European Commission. (2017a). *Consumer rights and law*. Retrieved from http://ec.europa.eu/consumers/consumer_rights/index_en.htm

European Commission. (2017b). *An evaluation study of national procedural laws and practices in terms of their impact on the free circulation of judgements and on the equivalence and effectiveness of the procedural protection of consumers under EU consumer law*. JUST/2014/RCON/PR/CIVI/0082. Retrieved from http://ec.europa.eu/newsroom/just/item-detail.cfm?item_id=612847

Galetta, D.-U. (2011). *Procedural autonomy of EU member states: Paradise lost?* Heidelberg, Germany: Springer.

Giliker, P. (2018). The Consumer Rights Act 2015 – a bastion of European consumer rights? *Legal Studies, 37*(1), 78–102. https://doi.org/10.1111/lest.12139.

Gómez Sánchez, Y. (2011). *Constitucionalismo multinivel: Derechos Fundamentales*. Madrid, Spain: Sanz y Torres.

Hedegaard, J. S., & Wrbka, S. (2016). The notion of consumer under EU legislation and EU case law: Between the poles of legal certainty and flexibility. In M. Fenwick & S. Wrbka (Eds.), *Legal certainty in a contemporary context: Private and criminal law perspectives* (pp. 69–88). Cham, Switzerland: Springer International Publishing AG.

Howes, G., Twigg-Flesner, C., & Wilhelmsson, T. (2017). *Rethinking EU consumer law*. New York: Routledge.

Kunnecke, A. (2014). New standards in EU consumer rights protection? The new directive 2011/83/EU. *European Scientific Journal, 1*, 426–437.

Lazíková, J. (2016). The consumer policy in the EU law. *EU Agrarian Law, 5*(1), 21–26. https://doi.org/10.1515/eual-2016-0003.

Lazíková, J., & Rumanovská, L. (2016). The notion of consumer in the EU law. *EU Agrarian Law, 5*(2), 1–12. https://doi.org/10.1515/eual-2016-0006.

Leczykiewicz, D., & Weatherill, S. (2016). The images of the consumer in EU law. In D. Leczykiewicz & S. Weatherill (Eds.), *The images of the consumer in EU law: Legislation, free movement and competition law.* Oxford, England: Hart Publishing. Oxford Legal Studies Research Paper 9/2016. Retrieved from https://ssrn.com/abstract=2743283

Luif, P. (2014). The division of powers/competences between the EU and the member states: What can we learn from pre-emption in the United States. In L. S. Rossi & F. Casorali (Eds.), *The EU after Lisbon. Amending or coping with the existing treaties* (pp. 37–56). Cham, Switzerland: Springer International Publishing AG.

Mańko, R. (2013, May 6). The notion of 'consumer' in EU law. Library Briefing. *Library of the European Parliament*. Retrieved from http://www.europarl.europa.eu/RegData/bibliotheque/briefing/2013/130477/LDM_BRI130477_REV1_EN.pdf

Martínez Velencoso, L. M. (2017). The impact of harmonized European private law and the *Aquis Communautaire* on national law around Europe. In A. Solanes Corella & E. M. Górriz Royo (dir). *Legal challenges of the XXI century* (pp. 247–298). Valencia, Spain: Tirant lo Blanch.

Menendez, J. A. (2003). Rights to solidarity': Balancing solidarity and economic freedoms. In E. Eriksen, J. Fossum, & J. Menéndez (Eds.), *Chartering of Europe, the European charter of fundamental rights and its constitutional implications* (pp. 179–198). Baden-Baden, Germany: Nomos Verlagsgesellschaft Mbh & Co.

Mickilitz, H. W. (2013). Mohamed Aziz-sympathetic and activist, but did the court get it wrong? In *ECLN Conference Florence When the ECJ gets it wrong*. Retrieved from http://www.ecln.net/tl_files/ECLN/Florence%202013/Micklitz%20-%20The%20ECJ%20gets%20it%20wrong%20Aziz-30-11-14.pdf

Micossi, S. (2016). *Thirty years of the single European market* (CEPS Special Report, No. 148). Retrieved from https://www.ceps.eu/publications/thirty-years-single-european-market

Rossi, L. S. (2012). Does the Lisbon treaty provide a clear separation of competences between EU and member states? In A. Biondi, P. Eeckhout, & S. Ripley (Eds.), *EU after Lisbon* (pp. 85–106). Oxford, England: Oxford University Press.

Rott, P. (2014). The low-income consumer in European private law. In K. Purnhagen & P. Rott (Eds.), *Varieties of European economic law and regulation. Studies in European economic law and regulation* (Vol. 3, pp. 675–691). Cham, Switzerland: Springer International Publishing AG.

Sarrión, J. (2010). Social rights protection problems in conflicting situations with market freedoms in European Union Law. *Revista Universitaria Europea, 13*, 85–102.

Sarrión, J. (2011). El nuevo horizonte constitucional para la Unión Europea: A propósito de la entrada en vigor del Tratado de Lisboa y la Carta de Derechos Fundamentales. *CEFLegal: Revista Práctica del Derecho, 162*, 53–111.

Sarrión, J. (2014a). *Effective judicial protection in consumer protection in the ECJ's Case Law*. Retrieved from https://ssrn.com/abstract=2526709

Sarrión, J. (2014b). Sobre la necesaria reforma de la legislación española a la luz de la STJUE de 14 de marzo de 2013, Aziz c. CatalunyaCaixa, C-415/11. In *Il diritto patrimoniale di fronte alla crisi economica in Italia e in Spagna* (pp. 437–448). Milano, Italy: CEDAM.

Sarrión, J. (2015). *Actual trends and challenges of the constitutional fundamental rights and principles in the ECJ case law from the perspective of multilevel constitutionalism*. Retrieved from https://ssrn.com/abstract=2656394

Sarrión, J. (2018). The configuration of an EU constitutional procedural status for consumer protection. In A. Bartolini & D. Zammit (Eds.), *European dimensions of individual status*. Perugia: ISEG. (in press).

Schueller, B. (2012). The definition of consumers in EU consumer law. In J. Devenney & M. Kenny (Eds.), *European consumer protection: Theory and practice* (pp. 123–142). Cambridge, England: Cambridge University Press.

Schütze, R. (2006). Supremacy without pre-emption? The very slowly emergent doctrine of community pre-emption. *Common Market Law Review, 43*(4), 1023–1048.

Stuyck, J. (2010). Setting the scene. In H.-W. Micklitz, J. Stuck, & E. Terryn (Eds.), *Cases, materials and text on consumer law* (pp. 1–69). Oxford, England: Hart Publishing.

Tridimas, T. (2012). Competence after Lisbon. The elusive search for bright lines. In D. Ashiagbor, N. Countouris, & I. Lianos (Eds.), *The European Union after the Lisbon treaty* (pp. 47–77). Cambridge, England: Cambridge University Press.

Trstenjak, V., & Beysen, E. (2011). European consumer protection law: Curia semper dabit remedium? *Common Market Law Review, 48*(1), 95–124.

Weatherill, S. (2002). Pre-emption, harmonisation and distribution of competences to regulate the internal market. In C. Barnard & J. Scott (Eds.), *The law of the single market: Unpacking the premises* (pp. 41–74). Oxford, England: Hart Publishing.

Weatherill, S. (2013). *EU consumer law and policy*. Cheltenham, England: Elgar Publishing.

Creditor and Debtor

Angela Guerrieri

1 Introduction

Creditor and debtor are two faces of the same coin: these statuses appear when a contractual or non-contractual obligation begins, in addition to those already existing, in reference to natural or legal persons. Speaking about these statuses, therefore, we will often refer at the same time to both figures, with the European normative dictated, in a transversal way, to favour the creditor, but also involving, for obvious reasons, the debtor.

The meaning of the terms 'creditor' and 'debtor', as used within European legislation, is essentially content-based according to economics; since the first historical phase of the European project, it has been well known that the safeguarding of trades, exchanges, and all kind of commercial transactions—and consequently the credit-debt relationship among the parts—is central to the project.

Obviously, we are well aware that in the European landscape—especially since the economic crisis that hit Europe in late 2009—one may refer also to creditor/debtor status in relation to member states. Indeed, and in particular since the Greek public deficit and sovereign debt problem emerged in full light, a new division has started to gain ground with regard to states; that between creditor and debtor countries. But for the purposes of this chapter, we will set aside this separate issue.

So, with reference to the 'subjective' meaning of the creditor/debtor terms, first of all we have to say that the European Union has focused its action in this area primarily on the protection of economic operators—in their capacity as creditors—and on facilitating business. In this sense we will see a number of legislative actions designed to improve the safety of credit.

In particular, the focus will be both on the creditor-debtor relation between private parties and between a private party and a public administration. In those two

A. Guerrieri (✉)
Department of Law, University of Perugia, Perugia, Italy
e-mail: angela_guerrieri@libero.it

A. Bartolini et al. (eds.), *Dictionary of Statuses within EU Law*,
https://doi.org/10.1007/978-3-030-00554-2_14

domains, what changes is the role of the debtor, and we will see some differences in terms of discipline.

In the background, with particular connection to the concept of status, one may also wonder, in the EU context, about individuals having credit rights—if, in terms of theory and protections, this is close to property rights. At the end of this brief overview, thus, we will examine the most recent position of EU jurisprudence on this issue.

2 Credit Relationship Between Private Parties

The discipline of the credit domain is not among the exclusive competences of the European Union, so we find no detailed regulation that deals exactly with the creditor/debtor status. However, over the years, new tools for safeguarding the position of creditors have been promoted within the EU.

The first important European legislation about creditor/debtor relations was Directive (2011/7/EU) on combating late payments in commercial transactions, which was adopted on 16 February 2011 and was due to be integrated into national law by EU countries by 16 March 2013 at the latest. This directive actually followed another one on the same subject: Directive 2000/35/EC, issued in 2000. But despite the implementation of the 2000 directive in 2002, the European Commission concluded in 2008 that late payments were still widespread in the EU. It also turned out that public authorities in certain member states were stipulating unjustifiably long contractual payment periods for transactions. For these reasons, the Commission prepared in 2009 a proposal for a new European regulation on combating late payments in commercial transactions and, from this, the Directive 2011/7/EU.

In particular, this legislation has been aimed at protecting European businesses, especially small and medium-sized enterprises, against late payment, improving their competitiveness. The directive has put in place strict measures to contribute significantly to growth and to improve the liquidity of businesses. These include stipulations that enterprises have to pay their invoices within 60 days, unless they expressly agree otherwise and provided it is not grossly unfair; and that there is an automatic entitlement to interest for late payment—statutory interest that is at least 8% above the European Central Bank's reference rate. At the same time, EU countries may continue maintaining or bringing into force laws and regulations that are more favourable to the creditor than the provisions of the directive. Thus we may say that the concept of creditor, from the European Union point of view, is essentially linked to aspects of payment.

On the other side, and in close connection, the status of debtors is something that can be 'quantified' in relation to the number of days of non-payment from an economic operator or a public administration.

The discipline on combating late payments is not confined to the credits-safeguard panorama. In the same direction, we can read the introduction, in 2004, of legislation about a European enforcement order (Regulation 805/2004); this was followed in 2006 by an order for payment procedures (Regulation n. 1896/2006).

Briefly, Regulation 805/2004 created a European enforcement order for claims that are uncontested by debtors. By means of the enforcement order, judgments, court settlements, and authentic instruments on uncontested claims can be recognised and enforced automatically in another EU country, without any intermediate proceedings.

The second regulation created a European order for payment procedure, for claims not contested by the defendant. This aimed to simplify, speed up, and reduce the costs of litigation in cases involving more than one EU country. It also permitted the free circulation of European orders for payment that are recognised and enforced in all EU countries. According to the regulation, "The swift and efficient recovery of outstanding debts over which no legal controversy exists is of paramount importance for economic operators in the European Union, as late payments constitute a major reason for insolvency threatening the survival of businesses, particularly small and medium-sized enterprises, and resulting in numerous job losses". So, in this case also the EU legislature acted with the primary aim of safeguarding enterprises within the European economic area.

In regard to debtors, the late or non-payment of debts is damaging to businesses and customers alike, especially when no information is available on the debtor's assets. Indeed, the search for the address of a debtor and information on his financial situation is often the starting point for enforcement proceedings.

To accelerate the process, in a green paper titled 'Effective Enforcement of Judgments in the European Union: The Transparency of Debtors' Assets' (COM 2008/128), the Commission recommended four kinds of measures to help the creditor obtain reliable information on the debtor's assets within a reasonable period of time. Those measures included: drawing up a manual of national enforcement laws and practices containing all the sources of information, accessible in all EU countries, about a person's assets as well as contact information for people who can obtain that information if access is limited, including the costs of access and other relevant details; increasing the information available and improving access to registers, including commercial registers, population registers, and social security and tax registers; the specific rules of each EU country in the field of data protection as well as social and fiscal privacy, which should still be considered; enhancing exchange of information between enforcement authorities so that national enforcement bodies are able to directly access the (non-public) registers of other EU countries; implementing international instruments dealing with the exchange of information between national enforcement bodies, which may be an additional solution; and harmonising measures relating to the debtor's declaration, for example, through the introduction of a European assets declaration, which obliges debtors to disclose all assets in the European area of justice. In this way, the transparency of the debtor's assets would not be limited by the territoriality of the enforcement proceedings.

3 Creditor Status Before a Public Administration

For this domain too, we must refer to the directive on combating late payments in commercial transactions (2011/7/UE), which reads, "This Directive should regulate all commercial transactions irrespective of whether they are carried out between private or public undertakings or between undertakings and public authorities, given that public authorities handle a considerable volume of payments to undertakings. It should therefore also regulate all commercial transactions between main contractors and their suppliers and subcontractors."

Therefore, questions related to the obligations between public administrations and private parties are of primary interest for the European legislature, which is well aware of many problems that affect member states in relation to times and ways of credit satisfaction by public authorities.

The directive goes on to read (recital n. 22), "As a general rule, public authorities benefit from more secure, predictable and continuous revenue streams than undertakings. In addition, many public authorities can obtain financing at more attractive conditions than undertakings. At the same time, public authorities depend less than undertakings on building stable commercial relationships for the achievement of their aims. Long payment periods and late payment by public authorities for goods and services lead to unjustified costs for undertakings. It is therefore appropriate to introduce specific rules as regards commercial transactions for the supply of goods or services by undertakings to public authorities, which should provide in particular for payment periods normally not exceeding 30 calendar days, unless otherwise expressly agreed in the contract and provided it is objectively justified in the light of the particular nature or features of the contract, and in any event not exceeding 60 calendar days".

This directive acknowledges full awareness, therefore, that the negative consequences arising from late payments affect the entire financial system and not just a single contractual relationship.

In general, from the directive text emerges the idea of a careful European legislature that wants to safeguard the weakest contractual part (small and medium-sized enterprises, in this case), to rebalance the juridical positions. It wants, in other words, to avoid strengthening the economically stronger contractor (a public administration, in this case) against the weaker, exposed to the economic-juridical abuse of the counterpart.

Therefore, after a series of European disciplines was created to favour the rebalancing of all situations related to consumers and enterprises, the attention of the European legislature seems to have moved towards other typologies of economic and commercial relationships, in which a contractual 'disharmony' is potentially present. One of these is between private parties and public authorities in their contractual relationship. In this potential contractual imbalance, as for cases of safeguarding consumers, one may see the economically stronger part exercising an abuse of its position. So we can see that those with the status of creditor (private companies) and those with the status of debtor (public administrations) are functional to the European legislature for its primary purpose of ensuring fair competition and balancing relations in the EU market.

4 Conclusions: Some Suggestions About Property Rights

Turning to the EU Court of Justice, also in this case there is no specific jurisprudence that has dealt with this theme. Judgements of the Luxembourg Court that have decided, directly, with respect to safeguarding the rights of creditors and their juridical qualifications are nearly non-existent. However, the tenor of some cases of law, linked to the more general question of property rights, gives us some guidelines related to the European Community approach on this matter.

For our purpose, it is useful to remember that the EU Court of Justice has repeatedly said that the right to property is among the fundamental rights protected by EU law. In particular, since the historic judgement *Hauer* (ECJ 14 May 1974 C- 4/73), the concept of property has started to be regarded from the point of view of the 'productive use' of the asset, more than the classical point of view of the individual and exclusive sphere.

Due to this strict connection between property and private economic initiatives, the Court of Justice, in some cases, seems to have implicitly embraced the notion of property of common law tradition, where the concept doesn't mean only the relation of exclusive belonging between the owner and the asset, but includes all the rights that involve the use or the enjoyment of a good, and also in relation to intangible goods. So, this notion of property embraces all the rights that arise from the exercise of economic activities and all the financial utilities obtainable from the use of properties.

The Court, therefore, seems to move the idea of property towards the freedom to pursue an economic activity, by adopting a wide notion of property and by including, among owners' guarantees, all the rights, including those of a personal nature and those linked to the utilities obtainable from the use of the asset. This kind of configuration aids in linking a credit right (and its holder) to this meaning of property that we have seen, in a sort of *genus ad speciem* relation. And this assertion is also supported by article 52 of the Nice Charter, which states that when considering a certain right provided for in both the Charter of Fundamental Rights of the European Union and the ECHR, we must follow the Strasbourg Court interpretation when it is more favourable and protective of the interests of individual citizens.

In fact, the latter, in relation to the notion of good (*bien*) protected under Protocol 1, Article 1, ECHR, provides an interpretation of property rights that seems to also include credit rights. In this regard, we recall the two Strasbourg judgments *Pennino v. Italy* and *De Luca v. Italy* (ECHR 270-271/2013), in which the Court reiterated that a 'claim' could constitute a 'possession' within the meaning of Article 1 of Protocol No. 1 if it was sufficiently established to be enforceable. In that light, the creditor position is getting closer to that of the owner, in the European landscape.

In conclusion, in light of the above, looking both to European legislation and jurisprudence, the status of private creditors appears strengthened, from a substantive point of view and in terms of protections. On the one hand, it is because the concept of property—in its process of 'dematerialization'—is widening its own boundaries, including those positions of credit/debit (as opposed to other legal systems, anchored to traditional meaning of property). On the other hand, it is undeniable that the European legislature has also paid attention to full and effective safeguards for creditors, in particular in relation to the circulation of the rights in the European context and to the restriction of public prerogatives, when not expressly justified.

Further Readings

Akkermans, B. (2011). The European Union development of European property law. *Maastricht European Private Law Institute, Working Paper 30.*

Bastion, S. (2003). Direttive comunitarie e tutela del creditore in caso di ritardato pagamento nelle transazioni commerciali: prime osservazioni a proposito del d.lgs. n. 231/2002. *Il diritto dell'Unione Europea*, 395.

Candian, A., Gambaro, A., & Pozzo, B. (1992). *Property, Proprietà, Eigentum* (p. 13). Padova: Cedam.

Caranta, R. (1994). Intorno al problema delle individuazioni delle posizioni giuridiche sogg. del cittadino comunitario. *Riv Ital Dir Pubbl comunit*, 983.

Carss-Frisk, M. (2000). The right to property: A guide to the implementation of Article 1 of Protocol No. 1 to the European Convention on Human Rights. In *Council of Europe, The right to property: A guide to the implementation of Article 1 Protocol No. 1 of the European Convention on Human Rights*, August 2003, Human rights handbooks, No. 4. Retrieved July 1, 2018, from http://www.refworld.org/docid/49f1810d2.html

Crifò, C. (2004). *Cross-border enforcement of debts in the European Union, default judgments, summary judgments and orders for payment.* Hague: Kluwer Law International.

Gnes, M. (2011). La disciplina europea sui ritardi dei pagamenti. *Giornale Diritto Amministrativo*, 821.

Guerrieri, A. (2014). La Corte di Strasburgo e la normativa italiana sul dissesto degli enti locali. In *Rivista italiana di diritto pubblico comunitario*, 320.

Gutman, K. (2014). *The constitutional foundations of European contract law: A comparative analysis*. Oxford: Oxford University Press.

Jaeger, M. (2011). Il diritto di proprietà quale diritto fondamentale nella giurisprudenza della Corte di giustizia. *Europa e dir priv.*, 362.

Mata Munoz, A. (2011). *Typical personal security rights in the EU: Comparative law and economics in Italy, Spain and other EU countries in the light of EU law, Basel II and the financial crisis*. Tubingen: Mohr Siebeck.

Tarrant, J. (2011). Obligations as property. *University of New South Wales Law Journal, 34*, 677.

Van Erp, S. (2011). EU charter of fundamental human rights and property rights. In D. Wallis & S. Allanson (Eds.), *European property rights and wrongs* (pp. 44–49). Brussels: Wallis.

Data Manager

Anna Maria Emili

1 Introduction and Legal Framework

The 2012/417 Commission Recommendation of 17 July 2012, firstly establishes and recommends the professional figure of the data manager. The paragraph recites that member states:

Further develop e-infrastructures underpinning the system for disseminating scientific information by supporting scientific data infrastructures for dissemination of knowledge, research institutions and funding entities to address all stages of the data life cycle. These stages should include acquisition, curation, metadata, provenance, persistent identifiers, authorization, authentication and data integrity. Approaches need to be developed to provide a common look and feel to data discovery across disciplines, thus reducing the learning curve required to achieve productivity, supporting the development and training of new cohorts of data-intensive computational science experts, including data specialists, technicians and data managers. (See Paragraph 5, 'E-infrastructures', Commission Recommendation 2012/417).

The establishment of this professional figure falls within a wider set of guidelines where the European Commission (the Commission) takes into consideration the targets set by the Europe 2020 strategy, more specifically detailed in the following flagship initiatives: 'Digital Agenda for Europe' and 'Innovation Union'. Among the actions to be taken under the 'Digital Agenda', publicly funded research should be widely disseminated through open access publications of scientific data and papers. The 'Innovation Union' initiative calls for a European Research Area (ERA) framework to be set up in order to help remove obstacles to mobility and cross-border cooperation. It states that open access to publications and data from publicly funded research should be promoted, and that access to publications should

A. M. Emili (✉)
Rights and Science Jean Monnet Centre of Excellence, Department of Medicine,
University of Perugia, Perugia, Italy

A. Bartolini et al. (eds.), *Dictionary of Statuses within EU Law*,
https://doi.org/10.1007/978-3-030-00554-2_15

be the general principle for projects funded by the E.U. research framework programmes.

It is to be noted that the abovementioned recommendation is in line with the 'Revised Strategy on UNESCO's Contribution to the Promotion of Open Access to Scientific Information and Research' and the 'OECD Declaration on Access to Research Data from Public Funding' (See Recital 14 of 2012/417 Commission Recommendation above mentioned[1]).

Furthermore, it is evident that solid e-infrastructures underpinning the scientific information system will improve access to scientific information and its long-term preservation. The data manager would, hence, represent a guarantor of sensitive data management.

Notwithstanding the vast recognition of the data manager, regulation varies significantly among European countries. For instance, in 2007, it implemented the 'Nederlandse Vereninging Van Oncologie Datamanagers',[2] an official register, following a qualitative evaluation of data manager activities. Other countries, such as Italy, do not regulate or precisely define—not even as far as specific competencies are concerned—the professional figure of the data manager[3] (Rota and Perfetti 2001).

2 Data Manager Definition and Operation Sector

The data manager is a professional figure of uneasy classification since there is not yet a univocal regulatory and definitory framework within the EU. The data manager carries out his activity in the field of clinical research, acting as a supporting figure in the coordination and management of the same. When talking about clinical research or experimentation, the latter is intended as experiments on human subjects, aimed at identifying and verifying the clinical effects of one or more drugs and non-pharmacological medicinal products or procedures (e.g., surgery, radiotherapy protocol, experimental medical devices or identifying any adverse reactions).

In the case of experimental drugs, clinical research may be designed to study their pharmacodynamic effects, action mechanisms, absorption, distribution, metabolism and elimination with the aim of assessing their safety and effectiveness. Clinical trials can be either 'profit' trials (i.e., promoted by the pharmaceutical industry and medical industry, and the outcomes are the property of industries and can be used for industrial and commercial purposes) or 'non-profit' trials (i.e., promoted by public

[1] European Commission (2012) Recommendations Commission Recommendation of 17 July 2012 on access to and preservation of scientific information (2012/417/EU) 21.7.2012, Official Journal of the European Union L. 194/39, Brussels.

[2] See, https://www.nvvod.nl/.

[3] As highlighted by numerous National Association, including the Italian Medical Oncology Association: www.aiom.it/C_Common/Download.asp?file=/$Site$/files/doc/documenti.

or not-for-profit research institutes with the ultimate aim of enlarging therapeutic perspectives and promoting general public health).

Over the past decades, clinical research has undergone a profound evolution in terms of both quality and quantity. Research has, indeed, increasingly been shifting from a widespread practice of observational studies conducted on limited cases to randomised, controlled clinical trials (CCTs), which tend to be based on larger sample cases, often resulting from a cooperation between national or international bodies in order to determine the effectiveness of a therapeutic intervention.

Since a large number of patients is required to determine whether the effects of a treatment are statistically and clinically meaningful, most of the clinical studies are now multi-pooling and carried out in different research units (e.g., local health agencies and hospitals, universities, research institutes, cancer recovery and care units of scientific institutions, private clinics, etc.). Hence, both at the European and international level—in order to be deemed scientifically valid, reliable and the result of innovation and knowledge—clinical research is to strictly comply with the methodology and principles that guide clinical studies. Those principles also include the fundamental good clinical practices (GCPs)[4] ethical considerations that draw their original inspiration from the Helsinki Declaration[5] (Bennett and Murray 2009). Furthermore, clinical research has to comply with the legislation of the country of origin and the European Community (EC) legislation as referred to in Regulation (EU) No 536/2014 of the European Parliament and of the Council of 16 April 2014 on clinical trials on medicinal products for human use; repealing Directive 2001/20/EC.

Precisely because of the increasing complexity of recent research and clinical trials, the figure of the data manager has become an essential one. The data manager is not only required to perform a thorough analysis on the loyalty and reliability of the data collected as part of the research, but the data manager is also required to manage contacts with the investigator and other professionals and establish the research parameters together with the promoter and the ethics committee (Perfetti 2004/2005). The data manager is to ensure that the study is designed, carried out and concluded in compliance with GCPs and the specific internal company regulations (Schnapper et al. 2018).

The data manager may work with and under the direction of the principal investigator by supporting, facilitating and coordinating daily activities. The data man-

[4] See, http://ichgcp.net/it/.

[5] Declaration of Helsinki—Ethical Principles for Medical Research Involving Human Subjects was adopted by the 18th World Medical Association (WMA) General Assembly, Helsinki, Finland, June 1964 and amended by the 29th WMA General Assembly, Tokyo, Japan, October 1975; 35th WMA General Assembly, Venice, Italy, October 1983; 41st WMA General Assembly, Hong Kong, September 1989; 48th WMA General Assembly, Somerset West, Republic of South Africa, October 1996; 52nd WMA General Assembly, Edinburgh, Scotland, October 2000; 53rd WMA General Assembly, Washington DC, USA, October 2002 (Note of Clarification added); 55th WMA General Assembly, Tokyo, Japan, October 2004 (Note of Clarification added); 59th WMA General Assembly, Seoul, Republic of Korea, October 2008; 64th WMA General Assembly, Fortaleza, Brazil, October 2013.

ager may also represent a reference point for both the clinical team who is conducting the research (including doctors, nurses, pharmacists, radiologists, laboratory technicians, administrative staff, etc.) and the local and external regulatory structures, such as health directions, pharmaceutical companies, Haematological Oncological Research Centre (CREO), Oncological Research Centre (CRO), trial start-up and auditors.

Depending on the type of activity, there should be a distinction between the central and the local data manager. The central data manager carries out his activities at the Central Coordinating Centre and cooperates with the investigator and creator of the research protocol, the statistician, and the practical and organisational management of the trial. On the contrary, the local data manager is the person who works in a hospital ward or a research institute, coordinating the technical and management aspects of the trial, and deals with the gathering and quality of data (Perfetti 2004/2005).

3 Roles and Responsibilities of the Data Manager

The data manager plays a key role in all phases of the study: beforehand, during the trial and finally in the verification of the data collected (Rico-Villademoros et al. 2004). In particular, prior to the activation of the trial, the data manager discusses the management and organisational aspects relating to the feasibility of the study with the experimenter and checks the possible competition with other studies already being carried out at the research institute, the adequacy of the institute in conducting the trial, the completeness and the clarity of the research protocol.

Furthermore, the data manager is to arrange the start-up procedures of the study, such as the preparing and submitting the requests for authorisation to the ethics committee and contacting the coordinating centre for documentation and information relating to the experimental drug. The data manager is also responsible for preparing and updating the internal standard operating procedures of the O.U. (Operational Unit) for the conduct of the trial. The data manager also collaborates in the preparation of the research protocol and other relevant study documents, meets with the research team to evaluate the organisational feasibility, outlines the required procedures to obtain the informed consent, and prepares the documents to be submitted to the authorities.

Moreover, the data manager is to define and analyse the budget of the study, organise the reception and the storage of the drugs to be studied, develop a monitoring plan and ensure that all personnel involved are aware of the protocols, the investigator's brochures, the Case Report Form (CRF) and the procedures implemented to report adverse events.

During the study, the data manager should implement the required quality control procedures: monitoring patient recruitment, verifying compliance with eligibility criteria, handling registration procedures and randomisation, data collecting from medical records and their interpretation or transcript in CRF according to the

Food and Drug Administration (FDA) and ALCOA standard (Grimm and Tainter 2017). Equally important is the safety supervision of the study, through the management of serious adverse events, adverse reactions, and central and peripheral monitoring management, through the coordination of the monitors during the visits, and cooperation in any audits. Lastly, the data manager is to inform the ethics committee of the trial closing, store the documentation of the study, deal with the residual material and medication and balance any economic contract signed.

In the exercise of his or her functions, as described above, the data manager is to comply with Standard Operating Procedure (SOP)[6] auditing requirements and supply all the relevant documentation. The auditor is to be independent and ascertain that the research was conducted in accordance with GCPs and, therefore, in accordance with research protocols.

4 The Role of the Data Manager as a Sensitive Health Data Guarantor

As well as coordinating the various aspects of a clinical research trial, the data manager is responsible for the relevant data processing. Moreover, as widely stated, the data manager deals with the collection of data from medical records and their interpretation and transcription in the CRF, according to the FDA and ALCOA standards, which constitute one of the pillars of the GCPs.

Medical records, whether paper or electronic, are extremely important for the management of the data collected. They represent an essential tool in patient care since the entire medical history of a patient is recorded here (Vantongelen et al. 1989). Medical records contain the physician diagnosis, the various treatments administered, eventual laboratory or instrumental examinations and permit to share information among the various operators for a responsible sharing of the clinical trial management (Kim 2016).

One of the many duties and responsibilities of the data manager is, indeed, to verify whether the data collected comply with the ALCOA standards. In order to be deemed valid, data need to be attributed (i.e., data sources are to be known and traceable by signature and date, the identity of any health operator participating to the study is to be disclosed and time of all interventions is to be specified); data need to be recorded and readable; data meaning is to be notified at the time of their observation and not retrospectively; data are to be original (i.e., observed data and transcripts); and, finally, data are to be accurate because they are to reflect the situation observed in its entirety. No approximation may be accepted.

The highly sensitive nature of biometric and genetic health data and the position held by the data manager within the experiment suggest that the latter may qualify as the person effectively responsible for the treatment and management of such data

[6] See, among other, http://www.uhhospitals.org/clinical-research/research-credentialing/research-standard-operating-procedures.

on behalf of the data controller. Hence, the data manager is called to ensure a correct handling, treatment and storage of the data related to the clinical studies carried out by healthcare facilities. Simultaneously, the data manger is to verify the reliability of the data by checking against the clinical database and in compliance with the diagnosis and treatment quality indicators and by monitoring the quality of the interventions during diagnosis and therapy administration. This would enable the core-team to act promptly on any critical issues and ensure a high-quality standard of therapies.

It is evident that the data manager—in the framework of clinical researches—may be considered as the person responsible for sensitive data treatment. In consideration of a health care system that has become increasingly 'dependent' on personal data processing, the total respect of data protection principles (including lawfulness, fairness, transparency, accuracy, integrity and security) is a prerequisite for the proper conduct of the professional role of data manager, which shall be better defined and implemented in the near future.

5 Conclusion

Although the EU recognises the professional figure of the data manager, no job description has been provided, as well as in the Regulation (EU) No 2016/679 on the protection of natural persons with regard to the processing of personal data and on the free movement of such data. Thus, it should be highlighted that the data manager has a primary role in the implementation of clinical trials, particularly in case of oncology clinical trials. Furthermore, the data manager operates as a mediator among the various members of health care staff and between the health structure and the general public. The data manager is the person who ensures continuity of information disclosure and updating among researchers, data elaboration centres, the pharmacy industry, clinical research organisations, and ethical committees. It should be mentioned, also, that the data manager is pivotal in ensuring that correct procedures are implemented and followed, resulting in highly reliable research outcomes, even in terms of drugs and treatments. Finally, it should be highlighted that further research is needed to systematically evaluate the role of a data manager in every area of the European health system.

References

Bennett, M., & Murray, J. (2009). *Conducting clinical trials in the US and abroad: Navigating the rising tide of regulation and risk*. [online]. Available at: https://www.squirepattonboggs.com/~/media/files/insights/publications/2009/10/conducting-clinical-trials-in-the-us-and-abroad-__/files/ssdcentral68696v2draftwhitepaperconductingclinic__/fileattachment/ssdcentral68696v-2draftwhitepaperconductingclinic__.pdf

Good Clinical Practice. (n.d.). Retrieved from: http://ichgcp.net/it/

Grimm, N. L., & Tainter, D. M. (2017). Role of the clinical research coordinator in orthopaedic research: Making research less onerous. *The Duke Orthopaedic Journal, 7*(1), 1–2. https://doi.org/10.5005/jp-journals-10017-1073

Home Associazione Italiana di Oncologia Medica. (n.d.). Retrieved from: www.aiom.it/C_Common/Download.asp?file=/$Site$/files/doc/documenti.

Home NVvOD. (n.d.). Retrieved from: https://www.nvvod.nl/v

Kim, S. S. (2016). Mutual authentication scheme between biosensor device and data manager in healthcare environment. *The Journal of Supercomputing, 72*(1), 177–184.

Perfetti, E. (2004/2005). *La sperimentazione clinica in oncologia: ruolo e contributo del data manager al miglioramento dei trials clinici in ambito oncologico*. Master's thesis, University of Pavia. Retrieved from: http://www.thinktag.it/system/files/6815/data_manage.pdf?1292164652

Research Standard Operating Procedures. (n.d.). Retrieved from: http://www.uhhospitals.org/clinical-research/research-credentialing/research-standard-operating-procedures

Rico-Villademoros, F., Hernando, T., Sanz, J., López-Alonso, A., Salamanca, O., Camps, C., et al. (2004). The role of the clinical research coordinator – data manager – in oncology clinical trials. *BMC Medical Research Methodology, 4*(1).

Rota, S., & Perfetti, E. (2001). *Il data manager in Italia: figura professionale o utopia della ricerca?*, A.I.O.M. anno I n°1. [online]. Available at: http://www.medinews.it/bin/Aiom1.pdf

Schnapper, G., Marotti, L., Casella, D., Mano, M. P., Mansel, R. E., & Ponti, A. (2018). Data managers: A survey of the European Society of Breast Cancer Specialists in certified multidisciplinary breast centers. *The Breast Journal*. https://doi.org/10.1111/tbj.13043

Vantongelen, K., Rotmensz, N., & Schueren, E. V. (1989). Quality control of validity of data collected in clinical trials. *European Journal of Cancer and Clinical Oncology, 25*(8), 1241–1247.

WMA - The World Medical Association-WMA Declaration of Helsinki. (n.d.). *Ethical principles for medical research involving human subjects*. Retrieved from: https://www.wma.net/policies-post/wma-declaration-of-helsinki-ethical-principles-for-medical-research-involving-human-subjects/

Data Protection Officer

Anna Maria Emili

1 Personal Data Protection Is Intended to Be a Fundamental Right

The European Union (EU) law recognizes personal data protection as one of the fundamental human rights. Article 8 of the EU Charter of Fundamental Rights expressly states that:

1. Everyone has the right to the protection of personal data concerning him or her. 2. Such data must be processed fairly for specified purposes and on the basis of the consent of the person concerned or some other legitimate basis laid down by law. Everyone has the right of access to data which has been collected concerning him or her, and the right to have it rectified. 3. Compliance with these rules shall be subject to control by an independent authority.[1]

Following the entry into force of the Treaty of Lisbon in December, 2009, and of the Charter of Fundamental Rights of the EU, the right to the protection of personal data was elevated to the status of a fundamental right. However, it is not intended to be an absolute right, since it must be considered in relation to its function in society[2] (Pizzetti 2016).

Personal data protection law and regulation may be the response to the digital era and ongoing technological development. Simultaneously, it strengthens citizens' fundamental rights and facilitates business relationships by simplifying rules. Furthermore, a single law eliminates the current fragmentation and costly adminis-

[1] European Parliament, the Council and the Commission (2012), Charter of Fundamental Rights of the European Union, (2012/C 326/02), 26.10.2012, O.J. (C 326) 391, Brussels.

[2] *See*, for example, joined cases C-92/09 and C-93/09, Volker and Markus Schecke GbR and Hartmut Eifert v. Land Hessen, 2010, E.C.R. I-11063.

A. M. Emili (✉)
Rights and Science Jean Monnet Centre of Excellence, Department of Medicine,
University of Perugia, Perugia, Italy

A. Bartolini et al. (eds.), *Dictionary of Statuses within EU Law*,
https://doi.org/10.1007/978-3-030-00554-2_16

trative burdens of multiple laws. In May 2016, the EU adopted a new data protection package, consisting of two different deeds. Firstly, Directive 95/46/EC was repealed by Regulation EU/2016/679 of the European Parliament and of the Council on the Protection of Natural Persons with regard to the processing of personal data and on the free movement of such data.[3] Secondly, Council Framework Decision 2008/977/JHA was repealed by the Directive (EU) 2016/680 of 27 April 2016 of the European Parliament and of the Council on the Protection of Natural Persons with regard to the processing of personal data by the competent authorities for the purpose of the prevention, investigation, detection or prosecution of criminal offences or the execution of criminal penalties, and on the free movement of such data.[4]

The data protection package aims to make the EU fit for the digital age, ensuring that the same data protection rights apply across the EU, regardless of where they are processed. The regulation came into force on 24 May 2016 and was implemented on 25 May 2018. Regulation EU/2016/679 (also, General Data Protection Regulation or GDPR) should be recognized for the merit of interpreting the most pressing and urgent issues of the modern digital society. Indeed, it consolidates all those positions and resolutions that have been elaborated by Article 29 of the Data Protection Working Party[5] and the jurisprudence of the European Court of Justice (ECJ) and confirms, widens and updates the set of principles deriving from the Directive 95/46/EC.

It is a timely and clear piece of legislation with a vocation for the completion of its goals, in compliance with the regulatory framework of a self-executing deed, such as the GDPR at hand, as well as introducing the innovative professional figure of the DPO.

2 Data Protection Officer

The DPO may be seen as a 'supervisor' as far as personal data protection within a company or a public law body is concerned. In fact, the DPO monitors the correct application of European regulation for each treatment, by assessing the risks according to the nature of the data processed, the area of application, and the scope of processing.

The DPO is a professional figure distinguished and independent from the data controller and data processor. Article 4 (7) GDPR defines the controller as 'the per-

---

[3] Regulation (EU) 2016/679 of the European Parliament and of the Council of 27 April 2016, also called General Data Protection Regulation (GDPR), 2016, O.J. (L 119) 1.

[4] European Parliament and the Council of the European Union, Directive (EU) 2016/680 of the European Parliament and of the Council of 27 April 2016, 2016, O.J. (L 119) 89.

[5] The Article 29 Data Protection Working Party (WP29) is an advisory body made up of a representative from the data protection authority of each EU Member State, the European Data Protection Supervisor and the European Commission. The composition and purpose of WP29 was set out in Article 29 of the Data Protection Directive 95/46/EC, and it was launched in 1996.

son or body that determines the purposes and means of the processing,' whereas Article 4 (8) GDPR defines the processor as 'the person or body that processes data on behalf of the controller.' The appointment of a DPO may be mandatory or discretionary.

According to EU law, the controller and the processor must designate a mandatory DPO in three cases. First, when the processing is carried out by a public authority or body,[6] except for courts acting in their judicial capacity; secondly, when the core activities[7] of the controller or the processor consist of processing operations which, by virtue of their nature, their scope or their purposes, require regular and systematic monitoring of data subjects[8] on a large scale; and lastly, when the core activities of the controller or the processor consist of processing, on a large scale, special categories of data and personal data relating to criminal convictions and offences. In such cases, the designation of a DPO is mandatory.

Regulation EU/2016/679 permits the designation of a single DPO to be responsible for several entities, according to their organisational structure and size, as long as the DPO is accessible to each establishment. The controller must ensure that a single DPO can perform his or her tasks efficiently (Art. 29 WP, 2016 revised 2017).

Easy accessibility for each establishment is a fundamental requisite, taking into account that a DPO represents a reference and contact point for each of the processor, controller, and staff dealing with data and public authorities. The same applies in the case of a group of public authorities.

In order to fulfil EU law requirements, the DPO's contact details must be published and communicated to the supervisory authority.[9] In keeping with the principle of accessibility of the DPO, the European guarantor recommends the appointment of a professional who is located in the EU, regardless of whether the controller and

[6] The GDPR does not define what constitutes a 'public authority or body.' The WP29 considers that such a notion is to be determined under national law. Accordingly, public authorities and bodies include national, regional and local authorities, but the concept, under the applicable national laws, typically also includes a range of other bodies governed by public law. In such cases, the designation of a DPO is mandatory. WP29 Guidelines on Data Protection Officers adopted on 13 December 2016.

[7] Core activities are intended to be 'the key operations necessary to achieve the controller's or processor's goals'; however, they should not be interpreted as excluding activities where the processing of data forms an inextricable part of the controller's or processor's activity. *See* GDPR, *supra* n. 3.

[8] The notion of regular and systematic monitoring of data subjects is not defined in the GDPR, but the concept of 'monitoring the behaviour of data subjects' is mentioned in recital 2415 and clearly includes all forms of tracking and profiling on the internet. However, the notion of monitoring is not restricted to the online environment, and online tracking should only be considered by way of example. WP29 interprets 'regular' as meaning one or more of the following: ongoing or occurring at particular intervals for a particular period; recurring or repeated at fixed times and constantly or periodically taking place. Whereas, WP29 interprets 'systematic' as meaning one or more of the following: occurring according to a system; pre-arranged, organised or methodical; taking place as part of a general plan for data collection and carried out as part of a strategy.

[9] According to the WP29 Guidelines, the contact details of the DPO should include information allowing data subjects and the supervisory authorities to reach the DPO easily: a postal address, a dedicated telephone number, and a dedicated e-mail address, etc.

the processor are established inside or outside the EU's territory. However, it is possible that the national legislation of a Member State will provide for the mandatory appointment of a DPO. In any case, if not mandatory, a company or other body may voluntarily appoint a DPO who shall be equally answerable by law.

3 Knowledge, Expertise and Skills of the DPO

The DPO 'shall be designated on the basis of professional qualities and, in particular, expert knowledge of data protection law and practices and the ability to fulfil the tasks referred to in article 39.'[10] According to Article 29 WP 243 (2016, revised 2017) the necessary level of expert knowledge should be determined according to the data processing operations carried out and the protection required for the personal data being processed.[11]

The required level of expertise is not strictly defined, but it is to be commensurate with the sensitivity, complexity and amount of data organisation processes. Generally, where a data processing activity is particularly complex, or where a large amount of sensitive data is involved, the DPO may need a higher level of expertise and support. There is also a difference depending on whether the organisation systematically transfers personal data outside the EU or whether such transfers are occasional. The DPO should thus be chosen carefully, with due regard to the data protection issues that arise within the organisation.

In consideration of the fluidity of proceedings, supervisory authorities should be encouraged to promote adequate and regular training for DPOs. An in-depth knowledge of the business sector and of the organisation of the controller (information systems, data security, administrative rules and procedures) is also fundamental.

The ability to fulfil the tasks incumbent on the DPO should be interpreted as both referring to their personal qualities and knowledge, and to their position within the organisation. Personal qualities should include, for instance, integrity and a high level of professional ethics.

The DPO plays a key role in fostering a data protection culture within the organisation and helps to implement essential elements of the GDPR, such as the principles of data processing, data subjects' rights, data protection by design and by default, records of processing activities, security of processing and notification and communication of data breaches. The function of the DPO can also be exercised on the basis of a service contract concluded with an individual or an organisation outside of the controller's-processor's organisation. In fact, Article 38 (6) GDPR allows DPOs to 'fulfil other tasks and duties.' However, it requires the organisation to ensure that 'any such tasks and duties do not result in a conflict of interests.' In consideration of the fact that a DPO must act independently, he or she may not hold a position within the organisation, which would lead him or her to determine the

[10] See art. 37 (5) GDPR, *supra* n. 3.

[11] See Recital 97 GDPR, *supra* n. 3.

purposes and the means of the processing of personal data. On the other hand, the GDPR guarantees a DPO's independence by ensuring that he or she shall not receive instructions regarding the exercise of his or her tasks and by protecting him or her from unfair termination of contract or dismissal or any other form of penalty.

For the sake of legal clarity and good organisation, it is recommended that tasks be clearly allocated within the DPO team and that there be an appointment of a single individual as a lead contact and person 'in charge' for each client.[12]

4 Tasks of the DPO

Article 39 GDPR identifies six main tasks and duties that the DPO shall fulfil. Recital 97 GDPR further specifies that DPO 'should assist the controller or the processor to monitor internal compliance with this Regulation.' Thus, it should inform and advise the controller and processors, as well as any employees involved in data processing, of their obligation under European and National law, and secondly DPO monitoring compliance with the GDPR. In particular, DPOs may collect information to identify processing activities, analyse and check the compliance of processing activities, and issue recommendations to the controller or the processor. However, the legal responsibility for implementing appropriate technical and organisational measures to ensure and demonstrate that processing is performed in accordance with the GDPR lies with the processor.

The DPO has the duty to assist the controller during the Data Protection Impact Assessment (DPIA). However, one has to be aware that data protection compliance is a corporate responsibility of the data controller, not of the DPO (Comellini 2018).

Article 35, clause 1 of the GDPR directs that it is the task of the controller to carry out, where necessary, a DPIA, though DPO assistance may be highly useful. Following the principle of data protection by design, specifically, the controller 'shall seek advice' from the DPO when carrying out a DPIA. Article 39 (1c), in turn, tasks the DPO with the duty to 'provide advice where requested as regards the DPIA and monitor its performance.' Moreover, Article 39 (2) of the GDPR requires that the DPO have 'due regard to the risk associated with the processing operations, taking into account the nature, scope, context and purposes of processing.' This article recalls a general and common sense principle, which may be relevant to many aspects of a DPO's day-to-day work. In a nutshell, it requires DPOs to prioritize their activities and focus their efforts on issues that present higher data protection risks. This does not mean that they should neglect monitoring compliance of data processing operations that have comparatively lower level of risks, but it does indicate that they should focus, primarily, on the higher-risk areas.

[12] Article 38(2) of the GDPR requires the organization to support its DPO by 'providing resources necessary to carry out [their] tasks and access to personal data and processing operations, and to maintain his or her expert knowledge.' The data protection function must be effective and sufficiently well-resourced in relation to the data processing being carried out.

Furthermore, according to Article 30 (1, 2), it is the controller or the processor, not the DPO, who is required to 'maintain a record of processing operations under its responsibility' or 'maintain a record of all categories of processing activities carried out on behalf of a controller.' These records should also be considered a tool allowing the controller and the supervisory authority, upon request, to have an overview of all the personal data processing activities an organisation is carrying out. It is thus a prerequisite for compliance, and as such, an effective accountability measure.

5 Conclusion

A close examination of DPO tasks and competences reveals the DPO's crucial role in all issues relating to personal data protection.

A DPO should, in fact, be seen as facilitating the implementation and respect of the GDPR provisions by the processor and the controller and should be consulted at the outset of processing to help guarantee compliance (Garante per la Protezione dei Dati Personali 2018[13]). Moreover, the organisation should ensure, for example, that the DPO is invited to participate regularly in management meetings and decision-making where data protection implications are involved. All relevant information must be passed on to the DPO in a timely manner in order to allow the DPO to provide adequate advice; the opinion of the DPO must always be given due weight.[14] DPOs need to have autonomy in order to fulfill their mandate; however, this should not be interpreted as an extension of their decision-making powers beyond their tasks. The controller or processor remain the persons in charge for compliance with data protection law and must be able to demonstrate as much.

References

Article 29 Data Protection Working Party. (2016). Guidelines on Data Protection Officers ('DPOs') (16/EN WP 243, revised and adopted on 05 April 2017). Available at: http://ec.europa.eu/justice/data-protection/index_en.htm

Comellini, S. (2018). *Il responsabile della protezione dei dati (Data Protection Officer – DPO), Soluzioni di Diritto*. Bologna: Maggioli Editore.

Home Garante per la protezione dei dati personali. (2018). Retrieved from http://www.garanteprivacy.it/web/guest/home/docweb/-/docweb-display/docweb/8036793

Pizzetti, F. (2016). *Privacy e il diritto europeo alla protezione dei dati personali, II: Il Regolamento europeo 2016/679* (pp. 6–9). Torino: G. Giappichelli.

[13] See the website: https://www.gpdp.it/.

[14] In case of a disagreement, the WP29 recommends, as good practice, to document the reasons for not following the DPO's advice. The DPO must be promptly consulted once a data breach or another incident has occurred.

Data Subject

Anna Maria Emili

1 Data Subject: Definition and Legal Framework

The data subject (DS) is a natural person whose personal data is processed by a controller or processor.[1] In fact, article 4 of Regulation 2016/679 designates the DS as an identified or identifiable natural person who can be identified, directly or indirectly, is identifiable through a name, an identification number, location data, an online identifier or one or more factors specific to the physical, physiological, genetic, mental, economic, cultural, or social identity of that natural person. However, before going any further, 'personal data' needs to be defined. This concerns any information that is related to an identified or identifiable natural person regarding genetic data, biometric data, and health data.[2]

Uddin (2017) observes that the GDPR lacks information about the DS's nature, since it defines it as a 'natural individual'. This is due to the fact that no information is given about this natural person, and does not limit the DS to those with EU citizenship or residency. In fact, Recital 14 states that the GDPR should be applied with no prejudice to any natural person, as long as it concerns the EU's territory in relation to the processing of their personal data. Moreover, Recital 22 of the GDPR focuses on the 'establishment'. Recital 22 concerns the controller or processor as well as effective and real exercise. In the first case, the controller or processor are settled in the Union, regardless of whether the processing itself takes place within the EU. On the other hand, establishment implies the effective and real exercise of activity through stable arrangements. Moreover, the GDPR covers both goods and services offered by a third country within the Union that utilizes personal data of EU

[1] https://www.eugdpr.org/glossary-of-terms.html.

[2] See Article 4 (1, 13-15) GDPR.

A. M. Emili (✉)
Rights and Science Jean Monnet Centre of Excellence, Department of Medicine, University of Perugia, Perugia, Italy

A. Bartolini et al. (eds.), *Dictionary of Statuses within EU Law*,
https://doi.org/10.1007/978-3-030-00554-2_17

citizens as well as the Territorial Scope.[3] To ensure that the natural person is not deprived of his/her rights, two main factors need to be applied. Firstly, language or currency shall be used in one or more Member States, enabling the DS to order goods and services in the other language. Secondly, mentioning customers or users who are in the Union, which may make it apparent that the controller envisages offering goods or services to data subjects in the Union.[4]

However, DS rights concern not only different citizenships, but also differing implementation and interpretation of the legislation by EU Member States, Courts, and Data Protection Authorities (DPAs). According to Custers et al. (2017), EU decision-making process brings out the heterogeneity on the decision-making process at the national level. Therefore, in order to smooth over implementation issues, the authors suggest further simplification into workable, sector-specific, and context-specific rules and practices (p. 235).

2 DS' Categories

The concept of 'natural person' includes not only individuals able to understand the matter, but also those who might have difficulty in understanding due to physical and psychological disabilities and age. Unlike the other categories, the GDPR claims that children merit specific consideration due to the fact they may be less aware of the risks and consequences of using their personal data.[5] For instance, Recital 58 of the GDPR explicitly highlights the importance of clear and plain language that a child can easily understand. Transparency is a fundamental requirement, especially in the electronic data field, when information is targeted toward individuals, in this case children, through websites.

The development of the internet shaped the notion of protecting informational privacy and personal data, and there is a high level of internet usage throughout the EU. For instance, the Eurobarometer Survey 431 (2015) states that 57% of EU citizens use social networks at least once per week, with Irish and Swedish residents using it the most; German and French residents have the lowest usage (p. 109).[6] Moreover, the Eurobarometer Survey 341 (2015) found that 17% of EU citizens shop online at least once per week, with those in the UK and Ireland shopping online more frequently than the average EU resident. Thus, one can conclude that the internet plays a crucial role in EU citizens' lives. However, it is important to understand how EU citizens use technology and spread their personal data, espe-

[3] See Directive 95/46/EC; Article 3(2) GDPR; European Court Justice (ECJ), 13 May 2014 C-131/12 *Google Spain SL, Google Inc. Agencia Española de Protección de Datos (AEPD) c/ Mario Costeja González.*

[4] Recital 23–24 GDPR.

[5] See Recital 38 GDPR.

[6] Eurobarometer Survey 431 (2015). *Attitudes on data protection and electronic identity in the European Union*. Bruxelles, June, p. 109.

cially minors. The youngest population under 18 uses the internet for the largest variety of different objectives, such as playing, creating, learning, self-expressing, and experimenting with relationships and identities (Macenaite and Kosta 2017, p. 146). In fact, investigations have found that privacy risks are ordinary on the internet, especially among the youngest generation, since they do not rationally evaluate a situation and do not think about the long-term consequences of their virtual actions (p. 147).

To prevent the youngest generations from being misled, the EU intervened by repealing Directive 95/46/EC with the GDPR to specifically protect minors. Unlike the previous Directive, article 8 of the new Regulation 2016/679/EC provides stricter rules, such as child-appropriate information, a stricter right to erasure, and stronger protection against marketing and profiling (p. 148). For instance, the GDPR establishes that an individual must be at least 16 years old to consent to the use and processing of his or her personal data. However, a Member State may lower the minimum age to 13 years, but no younger, only through parental consent. These mechanisms were made possible through the rights introduced and safeguarded by the UN Convention on the Rights of the Child (UN CRC), which sought to balance children's rights with the 'digital age'. However, Macenaite and Kosta (2017) claim that article 8 of the GDPR lacks justification for the final decision establishing the age for self-consent. Thus, article 8 GDPR is weakened by the perceived lack of justification.

3 The Rights of the Data Subject

The core of the GDPR is driven by DS' rights, which are empowered by certain rights assuring the protection and privacy of personal data. Chapter III of the GDPR explicitly mentions DS' rights in five separate sections. The first concerns transparency and modalities; the second focuses on information and access to personal data; the third section outlines rectification and erasure; the fourth sets forth the rights to object and automated individual decision-making; and the final one aims at presenting restrictions.

This paper, however, analyses only the right to data portability (article 20 GDPR) since it is an innovation brought by the GDPR, thus fulfilling literature gaps. Before going any further, a definition of this right is needed. Van der Auwermeulen (2017) attributed to article 20 GDPR the right to control DS' data by the ability to transfer and share the data (p. 59). Hert et al. (2018) stated that article 20 GDPR is composed by three rights: the right to receive data concerning the data subject that he/she has provided; the right to transmit those data to another controller; and the right to have personal data transmitted directly from one controller to another (p. 197).

Natural individuals are able to move with no difficulty across different network spaces and to reuse their own data while controlling their own privacy and respecting others' privacy as well (p. 59). On the other hand, Hert et al. (2018) stated that this new right might also mislead natural individuals, since it can also be used as a competition tool for digital services and platform interoperability (p. 193). An example might be found in digital services, i.e. telephone numbers, which constituted a crucial development in user-centric privacy (p. 194). According to Malgieri and Custers (2018) personal data have their own monetary value in the data economy, although the majority of natural individuals treat it as a 'free' digital service or a discount for online products. In other words, customers' data and profiling algorithms are considered business instruments (p. 290).

However, this problem might be solved by informing individuals about the monetary value of their personal data, meaning their economic power in the economic flow. Thus, by informing individuals and consequently putting an end to what to Malgieri and Custers (2018) defined as a 'core element' (p. 290), individuals' attention and awareness might increase, while the data-driven economy decreases (p. 290). Van der Auwermeulen (2017) stated that the right of data portability brings advantages to both users and service providers. With regard to users, article 20 GDPR allows them to directly transfer their personal data from one service to another where technically feasible (p. 60). Thus, the format that data assumes is a crucial feature, since it is structured, commonly-used, and 'machine-readable' (Hert et al. 2018, p. 196). On the other hand, it is convenient for services providers, since, while providing transparency to their clients, they earn economic interest as well as their costumers' trust (p. 60).

4 Conclusion

This paper focuses on the impact of the new GDPR that came into force on 25 May 2018 about DS' rights. The analysis has been operationalised in the definition and legal framework of the DS. It proceeded by outlining DS' categories and by focusing only on children; it concluded by mentioning DS' rights, but analysed only the right to data portability. The DS is an identified or identifiable natural person who can be identified, directly or indirectly, is identifiable through a name, an identification number, location data, an online identifier or one or more factors specific to the physical, physiological, genetic, mental, economic, cultural, or social identity of that natural person. The DS does not have absolute rights, but rather can be used only in appropriate occasions. Moreover, the Regulation at issue concerns different categories, such as natural persons able to understand data privacy, as well as those who might have difficulties in understanding due to physical and psychological disabilities and age. The GDPR focuses on children because they are considered more fragile than others. Moreover, the issue of personal data is considered to be a sensitive issue in the technological field, including the internet. The youngest generation, under 18, are the most frequent users of the internet. This is further justification for the analysis in this paper. The GDPR provides that an individual must be at least 16 years old to consent to the using and processing of his or her personal data. However, a Member State may lower that age to a minimum of 13 years, but not below, only by obtaining parental consent. Furthermore, the GDPR includes several rights in

Charter III, such as rights to data portability (article 20 GDPR). This provision controls DS data through its ability to transfer and share data, bringing advantages to both users and service providers. One has to be aware that this paper presents several limitations. For this reason, in order to have a broader view of the matter, one could continue this research by analysing the implementation of the Regulation 2016/679/EC across different Member States. In this way, the validity of this research might be strengthened, as well. Moreover, further research might be conducted about the concept of 'natural persons' due to its lack of justification in the GDPR and the varied interpretations given by the different Member States.

References

Auwermeulen, B. V. (2017). How to attribute the right to data portability in Europe: A comparative analysis of legislations. *Computer Law & Security Review, 33*(1), 57–72. https://doi.org/10.1016/j.clsr.2016.11.012.

Custers, B., Dechesne, F., Sears, A. M., Tani, T., & Hof, S. V. (2017). A comparison of data protection legislation and policies across the EU. *SSRN Electronic Journal.*

Hert, P. D., Papakonstantinou, V., Malgieri, G., Beslay, L., & Sanchez, I. (2018). The right to data portability in the GDPR: Towards user-centric interoperability of digital services. *Computer Law & Security Review, 34*(2), 193–203. https://doi.org/10.1016/j.clsr.2017.10.003

Macenaite, M., & Kosta, E. (2017). Consent for processing children's personal data in the EU: Following in US footsteps? *Information & Communications Technology Law, 26*(2), 146–197. https://doi.org/10.1080/13600834.2017.1321096.

Malgieri, G., & Custers, B. (2018). Pricing privacy – the right to know the value of your personal data. *Computer Law & Security Review, 34*(2), 289–303. https://doi.org/10.1016/j.clsr.2017.08.006.

Uddin, M. (2017, May 17). *GDPR – The data subject, citizen or resident?* Retrieved from https://cybercounsel.co.uk/data-subjects/

Diplomatic Agent

Cristina Blanco Sío-López

1 Introduction: Conceptual Historical Overview

The emerging states of Europe in the modern age slowly began to institutionalise formal diplomatic customs and conventions in the fourteenth, fifteenth, and sixteenth centuries, forced as they were to engage with one another for political, geographic, economic, symbolic, and strategic reasons. Traditionally—and very especially since the Renaissance—diplomacy has been conducted by ambassadors and consuls, that is, by professional diplomats who functioned as resident agents of their respective governments in foreign states (Atkinson 2011).

From an etymological viewpoint, this legal status refers to the practice of diplomatic agents, more specifically to negotiations, but also to the skill in the conduct of international relations. Leira also notes that such a status is also used as a synonym for foreign policy (Leira 2016).

The term 'diplomacy' comes originally from ancient Greek, in which it was used both as a verb (*diploo*), to designate double folding (*diploun*), and as a noun (*diploma*), making a direct reference to official documents that were folded, and which gave the bearer a specific set of rights. How the concept expanded to cover not only the total body of treaties but also those engaged in negotiating such treaties remains unclear (Leira 2016). In this regard, Koselleck indicates that during the age of absolutism, diplomacy rested on a conceptual dichotomy where the state monopolised 'politics', leaving ethical considerations to the subjects (Koselleck 1988).

During the Enlightenment, the notion of 'diplomatic agency' gradually evolved, but it included intertwined connotations. For instance, the link "with written

C. Blanco Sío-López (✉)
European Studies Centre, St. Antony's College, University of Oxford, Oxford, UK

Global Young Academy (GYA), Halle, Germany

Institute of Contemporary History (IHC), New University of Lisbon, Lisbon, Portugal
e-mail: cristina.blanco.sio-lopez@eui.eu

A. Bartolini et al. (eds.), *Dictionary of Statuses within EU Law*,
https://doi.org/10.1007/978-3-030-00554-2_18

diplomas suggests a connection between a form of specialised handicraft and statecraft, and the roots in the accrediting authority of diplomas" (Constantinou 1996, pp. 83–88). From this source, the status of diplomatic agents gradually mutated from the background of treaties to the realm of privilege, duplicity, and secrecy.

Against this backdrop, calls for a 'New Diplomacy' focused on trade priorities started to proliferate, implying a fairer and simpler role for 'diplomatic agents' (Ducher 1793, p. 75). Indeed, this approach entailed an instance of legal status survival, because during the 18th century many key players advocated for the abolishment of the whole existing diplomatic apparatus as a solution to its critical flaws. As a result, from the end of the eighteenth century onwards, there was a shift in focus towards issues concerned with trade and science (Martin 2012, pp. 5–10).

Despite this conflict and attempt at a dissociation in the secretive status, the direct connection between diplomacy and military conflict persisted, and the expected and promoted distinction between an old political diplomacy and a new diplomacy, focused on trade, was maintained as a liberal critique throughout the nineteenth century (Rogers and James 1866, p. 496; Leira 2016).

It is also important to note that the concept of diplomatic agent permeated not only the domain of politics but also the academic one, especially from the perspective of the newly created discipline of international relations in the early nineteenth century. In this context, Reinsch indicates how "the old kinds of treaties—which upheld the purpose of conciliation and compromise of conflicting political interests—were balanced with the new economic treaties seeking to find a basis for a wider cooperation" (Reinsch 1909, p. 14).

In short, this new phase is marked by the consideration that 'traditional diplomacy' was in essence defined by its flaws, by its secrecy, and by its failure to prevent war. The new diplomacy, however, promised pathways of peace and cooperation (Leira 2016). Nonetheless, the downfall of the League of Nations and the coming of the Second World War would unavoidably shift such high 'Kantian-perpetual-peace'-inspired considerations of diplomacy into a complex and multilevel political signifier.

2 Challenges to the Polysemy of 'Diplomatic Agent': The Case of the Configuration of a European Diplomatic Agency

After the Second World War, such a shift influenced the emergence of a so-called 'composite diplomacy', in which new players, scenarios, issues, and modalities of interaction attempted to monopolise their own diplomatic legitimacy and accountability. Nowadays, state agents—and more specifically, national foreign services—have acquired a dominant position in what can be conceptualised as the European diplomatic field (AdlerNissen 2014). It is also significant to indicate that, in such a context, there is a preeminent presence of non-state actors—from private companies to non-governmental organisations— increasingly engaged in their own parallel diplomatic realms (Cooper and Hocking 2000). Actually, we can observe new symbolic articulations of collective representation differing from the traditional promotion of national interests, such as the 'No Logo' movement, the Seattle demonstrations, and various attempts to create a challenging transnational public sphere in a new global governance mindset (AdlerNissen 2014). Also, global media, technological developments, and increased parliamentary control of foreign policy represent a further test to traditional diplomacy (AdlerNissen 2014), which has seen a relative decline of the foreign services in relation to other parts of the state apparatus (Spence 2005). However, it is precisely the process of gatekeeping and rebuffing national diplomats that also transformed their own practice: One chief example is the process of Europeanisation (Adler-Nissen 2009). Indeed, since the 1970s, European Community (EC) member states have sought to collaborate under the aegis of the European Political Cooperation (EPC), the forerunner of the Common Foreign and Security Policy (CFSP). The EPC, which was kept separate from the EC (and hence the Commission), led to a rapid increase of high-level meetings, working groups, and coordination among diplomats from different EC member states, discussing a variety of topics from non-proliferation to development issues in Africa (Mérand 2010). One key turning point in this Europeanisation of the diplomatic process was the Maastricht Treaty (1992), which proposed major initiatives to coordinate under broad and mutually acceptable terms (Smith 2008).

Nonetheless, it was only with the Lisbon Treaty (2009) that the EU achieved its own diplomatic service, separate from national foreign policy systems. In this sense, the European External Action Service (EEAS) represented a novelty: a quasi-supranational diplomatic corps (Van Vooren 2011).

3 Triggers and Potentialities of the European External Action Service

It is important to acknowledge that—from the perspective of the Europeanisation of diplomacy—the consolidation of the role of the EU High Representative for Foreign and Security Policy and of the EEAS constitutes one of the Treaty of Lisbon's most controversial innovations. Indeed, since the 1st of December 2010, the EEAS has been given the task "to serve the EU's common foreign policy, represent the European Union (EU) around the world, and develop common strategies on everything from EU peacekeeping missions to humanitarian aid and possibly consular affairs for EU citizens abroad" (TEU art. 10A).

The EEAS as a new diplomatic body would then bring together—for the first time—national diplomats, civil servants from the Commission, and officials from the Council Secretariat under the same roof. Adler-Nissen interprets such a new setting as a Bourdieu-inspired framework conceptualising a European diplomatic domain as a structured social space, where different state and non-state actors struggle for dominant positions (AdlerNissen 2014). This approach becomes especially relevant in light of a much neglected symbolic power analysis as a central dynamic in diplomacy (Neumann 2011). Some of the main issues at stake in this quasi-supranational diplomatic setting include the recruitment and position-taking of three subgroups: seconded national diplomats, civil servants from the European Commission, and officials from the Council Secretariat, who together may effectively construct a newly dynamic diplomatic *ésprit de corps* (AdlerNissen 2014).

Such aspirations reconnect with classical definitions of diplomacy, which emphasise "the process of dialogue and negotiation by which states in a system conduct their relations and pursue their purposes by means short of war". In this sense, these emerging diplomatic agents are also viewed and valued as "a form of knowledge production" (Neumann 2011).

The production of foreign policy innovation based on negotiation and dialogue at a quasi-supranational level stands high in the diplomatic agency agenda-setting of the EEAS. These self-defining principles also correspond with their status as newcomers in the European diplomatic arena. Indeed, the EEAS is different from a foreign ministry, especially because it fuses pre-existing Council and Commission institutions and tools. In this respect, it is meaningful to signal that the EEAS "was built on existing Commission and Council structures, but shaped by the language of national diplomacy" (Petrov et al. 2012, p. 2). That is why Bátora features the EEAS as an "interstitial organisation", due to this hybrid status emerging in liminal spaces between various organisations. In fact, the EEAS is more than a EU agency, it is not just a Commission DirectorateGeneral, and it equally does not fit the definition of an independent institution such as the European Central Bank. Hence, the scholarly analyses on this case have not reached an agreement on the nature and role of the EEAS, but they converge in these conventional definitions: The EEAS is the EU's first common diplomatic body, as formally established in 2010; it supports the EU foreign affairs chief (High Representative for Foreign Affairs and Security Policy) in conducting the EU's Common Foreign and Security Policy; and it has delegations around the world working on behalf of the people of Europe and representing the EU as a whole (AdlerNissen 2014). This compound nature of the EEAS also includes the designation of the leading roles within this organisation. For instance, in the final version of the Constitutional Treaty, the High Representative was denominated 'Union Minister for Foreign Affairs', thus multiplying its layers of simultaneous identity and legal outreach (Working Group—WG VII, Working Document—WD 55, by I. Méndez. de Vigo, 2002). Nevertheless, beyond issues of nomenclature and mutable status, what makes the EEAS controversial is its potential to challenge the dominant position of national diplomats by pushing the boundaries of the state's reach and overtaking its functions. In sum, "it is future growth, which makes some national diplomats anxious about cut-downs and replacement. EU diplomats should not only be concerned with high politics, but also everyday consular service, that is, with 'diplomacy for people'" (AdlerNissen 2014, p. 679). At the same time, the EU's diplomatic service makes originally national diplomats aware of their uniqueness as both national and supranational diplomatic agents.

Therefore, a key question arises: Are we witnessing an implosive duplicity or a creative entanglement?

In this sense, the European Commission "has attempted to convince member states to hand over consular affairs to the Commission's overseas delegations for years" (Fernández 2008, p. 27). And, indeed, some EU member states and observers actively support this idea; they see it as a welcome support to national consular services in light of globalization, seemingly resulting in a convergence of national interests (Emerson et al. 2011).

In institutional terms, the shift towards a hybrid EU diplomatic culture, in terms of recruitment and career development, started on the 1st of January 2010, "when all former 'European Commission delegations' were renamed 'European Union delegations' and were gradually upgraded into embassy-type missions invested with more power than the regular delegations" (AdlerNissen 2014, p. 673).

From a procedural viewpoint, and following the formal construction of the EEAS, a recruitment system was set up with assessment centres that pre-select candidates. While the EU member states may propose their own candidates, the EEAS makes the decision on whom to appoint. The drafters of the Council Decision found it necessary to write a characteristic EU compromise in Art 6(6) in this regard: "All appointments in the EEAS shall be based on merit and on the broadest possible geographical basis. The staff of the EEAS shall comprise a meaningful presence of nationals from all the Member States" (AdlerNissen 2014, p. 675). Hence, it is feared that instead of representing the whole Union, the EEAS will be controlled by some of the larger member states. The question of national balance is definitely sensitive, but it is not the most important issue when it comes to the EU's diplomatic service. What is really at stake is the capacity of the EEAS to be seen as a competent and legitimate diplomatic body. While EU member states compete among themselves, they increasingly also position themselves, collectively, against the EEAS. In short, diplomats in the EU member states see themselves as sharing a particular professional culture: "They are arguably trained to be 'strategic', to 'share knowledge', to follow a 'political line'. This culture does not include the civil servants from the Commission: they have different dispositions, loyalties, and experiences and have entered the EU institutions through the EU *concours* system" (AdlerNissen 2014, p. 676).

Therefore, we could argue that the status of diplomatic agent in the EEAS was initially imbued with a wider perspective of allegiances and responsibilities. Indeed, its members are expected to both expand the scope and impact of their interventions and to be subject to a sense of deepening accountability in correlation with the European integration *acquis*.

4 Conclusions

In conclusion, the crucial change in the European diplomatic field lies not so much in the fact that the EU seeks to construct a common foreign policy, but in the creation of a new institution, the EEAS, entrusted with diplomatic tasks and, more importantly, with symbolic functions that were hitherto reserved for states only (AdlerNissen 2014).

Furthermore, a new frontier for a pan-European conception of diplomatic agency is constituted by the emerging dynamism of regional integration vectors and organisations within new modes of global governance. From this perspective, it will subsequently be fundamental to closely study the development of cases, practices, and conventionally agreed policy innovations in terms of interregional relations across the globe.

Such a game changer is, in any case, dependent on the never-fixed, necessary approach to peace as a primary objective in diplomatic relations throughout history. Even if the European integration process and various comparative processes of regional integration in global governance nominally allude to peace as a primary goal of international relations, this priority is secondary to an overstated notion of security. As a matter of fact, peace means more than the presence of security and the absence of conflict. It entails a community building and a constant search for consensus, which lies at the basis of democracy itself. Thus, the status of diplomatic agent is also imbued with the expected role of fulfilling this historic aspiration of transforming walls into bridges of cooperation and stumbling blocks into stepping stones. The key question is then: How should the diplomatic role and nature be crafted in order to move away from war, privilege, and lack of transparency and to foster an actual implementation of qualitative democratic principles and fundamental rights?

References

AdlerNissen, R. (2014). Symbolic power in European diplomacy: The struggle between national foreign services and the EU's External Action Service. *Review of International Studies, 40*(4), 657–681.

Adler-Nissen, R. (2009). Late sovereign diplomacy. *The Hague Journal of Diplomacy, 4*(2), 121–141.

Atkinson, D. (2011). *History of diplomacy, international relations*, ISBN: 9780199743292. doi:https://doi.org/10.1093/OBO/9780199743292-0013. [online], Retrieved March 14, 2018, from http://oxfordindex.oup.com/view/10.1093/obo/9780199743292-0013

Constantinou, C. M. (1996). *On the way to diplomacy*. Minneapolis, MN: University of Minnesota Press.

Cooper, A. F., & Hocking, B. (2000). Governments, non-governmental organizations and the recalibration of diplomacy. *Global Society, 14*(3), 361–367.

Ducher, G. J. A. (1793). *Acte de navigation, avec ses rapports au commerce, aux finances, à la nouvelle diplomatie des Français. Partie 1*. Paris: Impr. Nationale.

Emerson, M., Balfour, R., Corthaut, T., Wouters, J., Kaczyński, P., & Thomas, R. (2011). *Upgrading the EU's role as a global actor*. [online], Retrieved March 14, 2018, from http://www.epc.eu/documents/uploads/pub_1218_upgrading_the_eu_as_global_actor_e-version%5B1%5D.pdf

Fernández, A. M. (2008). Consular affairs in the EU: Visa policy as a catalyst for integration? *The Hague Journal of Diplomacy, 1*(3), 27.

Koselleck, R. (1988). *Critique and crisis: Enlightenment and the pathogenesis of modern society*. Cambridge, MA: MIT Press.

Leira, H. (2016). *A conceptual history of diplomacy. The SAGE handbook of diplomacy*. Thousand Oaks, CA: Sage Publications.

Martin, V. (2012). 'Les enjeux diplomatiques dans le Magasin encyclopédique (1795–1799): du rejet des systèmes politiques à la redéfinition des rapports entre les nations'. *La Révolution française*, (2), [online], Retrieved March 14, 2018, from http://lrf.revues.org/610

Méndez de Vigo, I. (2002). *Working Group - WG VII - External Action, Working Document - WD 55 - Towards the establishment of a common European diplomacy, The Convention, The Secretariat*, Source/COMM/PPE/Méndez de Vigo [online], Retrieved March 14, 2018, from http://ec.europa.eu/dorie/fileDownload.do;jsessionid=HbHNTbjVJgLYTQXlPJrZD2jwcRD23NQnW2NqTpH0cxjl616YfpTG!689158481?docId=281699&cardId=281699

Mérand, F. (2010). Pierre Bourdieu and the birth of European defense. *Security Studies, 19*, 342–374.

Neumann, I. B. (2011). *At home with the diplomats: Inside a European foreign ministry*. Ithaca, NY: Cornell University Press.

Petrov, P., Pomorska, K., & Vanhoonacker, S. (2012). Introduction: The emerging EU diplomatic system: Opportunities and challenges after Lisbon. *The Hague Journal of Diplomacy, 7*, 1–9.

Reinsch, P. (1909). International administrative law and national sovereignty. *The American Journal of International Law, 3*(1), 1–45.

Rogers, T., & James, E. (1866). Opening address of the President of Section F (Economic Science and Statistics) of the British Association for the Advancement of Science, Thirty-Sixth Meeting, Nottingham, August, 1866. *Journal of the Statistical Society of London, 29*(4), 493–503.

Smith, K. E. (2008). *European Union foreign policy in a changing world* (pp. 3–9). Cambridge: Polity Press.

Spence, D. (2005). The evolving role of foreign ministries in the conduct of European Union affairs. In B. Hocking & D. Spence (Eds.), *Foreign ministries in the European Union: Integrating diplomats* (pp. 18–36). New York: Palgrave.

Van Vooren, B. (2011). A legal institutional perspective on the European External Action Service. *Common Market Law Review, 48*, 457–502.

Disabled

Susana Sanz Caballero

1 Concept (Definition of the Status of "Persons with Disability")

While there are several landmark United Nations human rights treaties that protect the rights of specific vulnerable groups, it was not until the Convention on the Rights of Persons with Disabilities entered into force in 2008 that we finally had a global treaty addressing the needs of the world's largest minority, namely, disabled persons (Sanz Caballero 2003). It is worth mentioning that about 10% of the total world population experience various forms of disabilities, according to the World Health Organization (WHO) (15% of the population according to United Nations data) (UN: *The Convention on the Rights of Persons with Disabilities* 2014, p. 1).

At that time, many people contended that since existing treaties covered persons with disabilities along with everybody else, a specific treaty containing the rights of persons with disabilities was useless. However, social movements and associations of persons with disabilities worldwide maintained that without a legally binding treaty that spelled out their rights, persons with disabilities would continue being legally "invisible" both at national and international levels.

The UN Convention on the Rights of Persons with Disabilities of 2006 was drafted by an ad hoc committee which was agreed by the General Assembly resolution 56/168 of 19 December 2001. This committee was mandated to consider proposals for an integral international convention to promote and protect the rights and dignity of persons with disabilities which should be based on the holistic approach

This paper is one of the results of the Jean Monnet Project 587457-EPP-1-2017-1-ES-EPPJMO-CHAIR.

S. Sanz Caballero (✉)
Faculty of Law, Business and Political Science, CEU Cardenal Herrera University, Moncada, Valencian Community, Spain
e-mail: ssanz@uchceu.es

A. Bartolini et al. (eds.), *Dictionary of Statuses within EU Law*,
https://doi.org/10.1007/978-3-030-00554-2_19

of previous UN work carried out in the fields of human rights, social development and non-discrimination.

One controversial issue that was the object of discussion during the drafting was whether the future convention should include a definition of the expression "persons with disabilities", the risk being the unintentional exclusion from the scope of the convention of certain groups in case the definition provided was too restrictive (Lawson 2007, p. 594). The *United Nations Standard Rules on the Equalization of Opportunities for Persons with Disabilities* had already provided a quite accurate explanation in 1993: *"The term 'disability' summarizes a great number of different functional limitations occurring in any population in any country of the world. People may be disabled by physical, intellectual or sensory impairment, medical conditions or mental illness. Such impairments, conditions or illnesses may be permanent or transitory in nature*".[1] Finally, a workable solution was achieved where article 1 of the Convention does not give a strict or exclusive definition of the term but instead provides some useful guidelines to identify a person with a disability. In so doing, the Convention includes all disabilities.

Article 1 establishes the following: *"Persons with disabilities include those who have long-term physical, mental, intellectual or sensory impairments which in interaction with various barriers may hinder their full and effective participation in society on an equal basis with others"*. It is important to note that article 1 says that "persons with disabilities include", not "persons with disabilities are". The legal provision uses the verb *to include* instead of the verb *to be*. Like this, it shows that the text is not intended to give a *numerus clausus* of reasons or origins of disability but only an illustrative list of them. Article 2 of the Convention complements the former by saying: "*Discrimination on the basis of disability" means any distinction, exclusion or restriction on the basis of disability which has the purpose or effect of impairing or nullifying the recognition, enjoyment or exercise, on an equal basis with others, of all human rights and fundamental freedoms in the political, economic, social, cultural, civil or any other field. It includes all forms of discrimination, including denial of reasonable accommodation . . .*"

Article 1 of the Convention presents an evolving concept of disability that results from the interaction between impairments and the external environment (both physical and attitudinal barriers). It is not a fixed concept because it adapts to different societies and depends on how welcoming or hostile a given environment is. It does not deny the existence of physical, sensory, intellectual or mental impairments but fights against the deprivation of rights because of those impairments.

The most relevant message of this already universal convention (having received 177 ratifications) is that persons with disabilities are entitled to all human rights. It could not be otherwise since persons with disabilities are human beings and human rights are the rights all humans are entitled to. The second message of this convention is that reasonable accommodation has to be ensured so that persons with disabilities enjoy their rights with dignity, on an equal footing with others, and without discrimination.

[1] UNGA: Res. 48/96 of 20 December 1993, para. 17.

As for the origins of these impairments, the Convention names long-term physical, mental, intellectual and sensory limitations. However, it insists on the importance external barriers play as constituting factors of disability. Thus, the Convention makes clear that it is barriers which must be categorized and dismantled, not the persons with long-term physical, mental, intellectual and sensory limitations since categorisation is a dangerous step towards exclusion.

2 Evolution (from the Traditional Status of Persons with Disabilities to the Current International Approach)

To say that the status of disability and of the persons with disability has evolved over time, is not to sufficiently honour the tremendous change of focus that this issue has undergone in recent decades. Few areas of study have suffered a more radical change of historic paradigm than this one. Disability has been a real challenging arena, and one of the actors and promoters of this change of perception, attitude and even paradigm has been the European Union.

The change of focus in this area does not only affect the existing social perceptions of the persons with disabilities. It also impacts the role that society at large and States have to play in order to make an all-inclusive environment with universal accessibility (Cardona and Sanjosé 2005, p. 149). Additionally, there has been a significant terminological shift which reveals a change of mentality and philosophy in the way we treat persons pertaining to this category. As it is easy to understand, these aspects interconnect and forge a new ground in disability research and studies, which should also lead to an improvement in the well-being and status of the disabled.

Traditionally, disability was understood as a medical and biological condition that impaired the person and prevented a normal functioning in society. The focus was put on the person's individualized condition and, as a result, persons with disability were stigmatised. They had to be assisted and cared for and became the object of charity. They were often hidden and removed from society. Persons with disabilities were considered as suffering from a pathology or an abnormality that had to be clinically cured: they had to be rehabilitated so as to become "normal" according to the then-ongoing societal standards—or at least they had to be as "normalized" as possible. In this paternalistic model, the disadvantage was perceived as intrinsic to the nature of the person with disability. The underlying idea was that of a broken body.[2]

Over time, this narrow-minded perception—where the person is felt as a burden and where the emphasis is put on his or her impairment—has slowly but steadily changed. The new approach to disability drives our attention to the concept of functional diversity since each person has different abilities in private, family and social

[2] *Training guide*, p. 17.

life. This new approach focuses also on the society's responsibility, on the characteristics of the external environment and on how and to what extent cultural barriers influence their opportunities depending on each one's abilities and capacities (Traustadóttir 2009, p. 9). As the preamble of the UN Convention goes, disability results from the interaction between a person with impairments and the social barriers that prevent this person from participating in public life and society. In this way, the surrounding environment has an important part of responsibility in settling the status of disability. In this new model, the notion of disability becomes more flexible and less centred on the person's condition since the prevailing social attitudes and the persistence or removal of the existing environmental barriers will make the difference between isolation and integration and full participation of the person in society. When accommodation measures are foreseen and adequately introduced, persons with disabilities compete in conditions of equality with others, and they are no longer "special". However, for integration to be true, not only are external adjustments required, attitudes have to be also in line. Interaction with persons with disabilities has to be founded on respect and on the inherent dignity of the human being. In other words, this interaction needs to have a human rights approach. In this model, the disadvantage for the person with a disability very much depends on the obstacles of the surrounding environment, which are often avoidable. From this, it follows that denial of reasonable accommodation which does not impose an undue or disproportionate burden, as article 2 of the Convention states, is a form of discrimination in itself and a violation of the Convention.

Before the UN Convention was adopted, other international human rights tools considered the rights of persons with disabilities—both *hard law* and *soft law* instruments and both generic and specific instruments. As for the *hard law*—be it in the form of international treaties in force or international customary law—the general provisions against discrimination of article 2 of the *Universal Declaration of Human Rights*, of the *International Covenant on Economic, Social and Cultural Rights* and of the *International Covenant on Civil and Political Rights* clearly apply to persons with disabilities despite the lack of explicit mention of this condition in the texts. Under the formula "*without distinction of any kind such as . . . or other status*" the discrimination of persons with disabilities is understood to be included. The first human rights treaty to explicitly reference protection against discrimination on grounds of disability was the *UN Convention on the Rights of the Child* of 1989. Mention should also be made of the work done by the bodies of the human rights treaties of the UN.

As far as *soft law* instruments are concerned, despite a sometimes inadequate use of language, the General Assembly adopted in 1971 the *Declaration on the Rights of Mentally Retarded Persons*[3] and in 1975 the *Declaration on the Rights of Disabled Persons*.[4] The former document contains inaccuracies that evidence that, at this early stage, there was little scientific knowledge of mental disabilities. Indeed, WHO in its 1980 *International Classification of Impairments, Disabilities and*

[3] UNGA: Res. 2856 (XXVI) of 20 December 1971.

[4] UNGA: Res. 3447 (XXX) of 9 December 1975.

Handicaps stated that "*[i]n the context of health experience, a disability is any restriction or lack (resulting from an impairment) of ability to perform an activity in the manner or within the range considered normal for a human being*" (WHO: *International Classification of Impairments, Disabilities and Handicaps. A Manual of Classification Relating to the Consequences of Disease,* May 1976, Geneva, p. 143) therefore restricting disability to a strict medical problem. The document went on in its elaboration of this notion by establishing disability as a strict individual problem of the person with disability and ignoring the role of attitudinal, societal and environmental obstacles: "*Disability represents a departure from the norm in terms of performance of the individual, as opposed to that of the organ or mechanism. The concept is characterized by excesses or deficiencies of customarily expected behavior or activity, and these may be temporary or permanent, reversible or irreversible, and progressive or regressive. The key feature relates to objectification. This is the process through which a functional limitation expresses itself as a reality in everyday life, the problem being made objective because the activities of the body are interfered with. In other words, disability takes form as the individual becomes aware of a change in his identity*".[5] Again, this classification took disability for a disease or disorder as shown in the subtitle of this document as well: "*A manual of classification relating to the consequences of disease*".

In the 1990s, a new vindication period started when very interesting *soft law* norms were adopted. On the one hand, the *Final Declaration of the UN Summit on Human Rights* that took place in Vienna made clear that the person with a disability is not an object of protection but a subject of the law.[6] Despite its lack of compulsory character, the Final Declaration symbolised the political and ethical commitment achieved by the international community so far regarding human rights. Ever since, persons with disabilities started being recognized as rights holders and not as dependent persons lacking autonomy. Among their rights, they were entitled to the right of removal or minimisation of the social, economic and cultural barriers that produce their discrimination. In that same decade, the *Principles on the protection of persons with mental illness and the improvement of mental health care*[7] were adopted. Their goal was to provide guidelines on how States should address and treat persons with mental disabilities.

On the other hand, in 1993 the General Assembly adopted the *Standard Rules on the Equalization of Opportunities for Persons with Disabilities*,[8] the most emblematic and relevant resolution for the recognition of the rights of persons with disabilities until the 2006 UN Convention. The Standard Rules depart from the old medical and charity approach that had led to an assistance- and protection-based mindset. Instead, the Standard Rules took a human rights–based approach. They proclaim the right to equality and to improvements in life conditions in accordance with eco-

[5] ibid p. 29.

[6] E/CN.4/2002/18/Add. 1, p. 3.

[7] UNGA: Res. 46/119 of 7 December 1991.

[8] UNGA: Res. 48/96 of 20 December 1993.

nomic and social development. The content of the UN Convention largely follows this resolution.

The following year, a long-term strategy was issued to promote the application of the Standard Rules. This was done through a new General Assembly resolution under the heading: *Towards full integration of persons with disabilities in society: implementation of the Standard Rules on the Equalization of Opportunities for Persons with Disabilities, and of the Long-Term Strategy to Implement the World Programme of Action concerning Disabled Persons to the Year 2000 and Beyond.*[9]

The role that all this *soft law* played in the subsequent drafting of the UN Convention cannot be denied. These resolutions paved the way towards a change of paradigm in the way how persons with disabilities were perceived. NGOs and social movements, including many associations representing the disabled, played a major role in this historical shift. Persons with disabilities were very active in international forums and activities, such as the first long-term strategy to implement the world programme of action concerning disabled persons. Persons with disabilities and the organisations representing them put in place strong advocacy action to make society understand that they enjoy the same rights as everyone else, but that sometimes further steps need to be taken, by both States and society, so as to ensure they can fully enjoy these rights.

Persons with disabilities stood up for their rights. They were no longer considered as passive recipients of services but as rights holders on an equal footing as the rest of the population. Persons with disabilities demanded the use of a part of the benefits of economic and social development to dismantle the external barriers that produce disability and exclusion. They questioned States by affirming that the latter had positive obligations towards them. These positive obligations were being ignored and neglected, and this prevented both their full participation in society and the adequate satisfaction of their rights. The level of implementation of some of these rights would depend on the country's level of development, especially those rights needing reasonable adjustments.

3 Role of the EU (Influence of the European Union in the Adoption of the Contemporary Status of Persons with Disabilities)

Once acknowledged that there has been a change of paradigm and perspective in the international status of disability, it is the moment to delve into the question of the role played by EU law in this shift, if any.

It has to be said that the EU has been active in the emergence and adoption of this new trend that promotes social justice and social equality. The EU was an influential

[9] UNGA: Res. 49/153 of 23 December 1994.

international actor that soon recognized disability as a social construct and advocated inclusion and accessible development. Before the UN Convention on disability, the EU was already bound by *Council Directive 2000/78/EC of 27 November 2000 establishing a general framework for equal treatment in employment and occupation* ((Biel Portero and Rey Aneiros 2008, pp. 205–230; Biel Portero 2008, pp. 135–162). However, this Directive is focused on the field of employment and disregards any other field. This is why a new directive has been proposed by the European Commission to apply the principle of equal treatment outside the employment field, but this proposal has met with reservations by some Member States. Once agreed and in force, this proposal will supplement the existing EU legal framework under which the prohibition of discrimination on grounds of religion or belief, disability, age, or sexual orientation applies only to employment, occupational and vocational training.[10] As for the 2000/78 Directive, this norm shied away from providing a specific definition of the term disability. Instead, article 5 defined the expression "reasonable accommodation for disabled persons" as follows: "*In order to guarantee compliance with the principle of equal treatment in relation to persons with disabilities, reasonable accommodation shall be provided. This means that employers shall take appropriate measures, where needed in a particular case, to enable a person with a disability to have access to, participate in, or advance in employment, or to undergo training, unless such measures would impose a disproportionate burden on the employer* (. . .)."

The lack of a definition of disability or of who deserves protection against discrimination on grounds of disability in the Directive derives from the fact that the legislation of EU Member States approached this subject differently, and at least four models exist on the issue of how and whether to define disability. A first group of States have not included a definition of disability in their non-discrimination legislation at all (e.g. Belgium, Slovakia and Italy). A second group has defined disability in the context of their non-discrimination legislation (e.g. Malta and the UK). A third group have taken a risky path by borrowing restrictive definitions of disability from other fields of law, often from social security law (e.g. Czech Republic and Slovenia) which do not match well with the non-discrimination legislation. A fourth group of States have adopted a dual approach to defining disability for the purposes of non-discrimination legislation (e.g. France and Germany). In the latter, on the one hand, a general non-discrimination law provides for a broad definition of disability whilst, on the other hand, a second law addressing reasonable accommodation makes use of a more limited definition of disability, typically drawn from the social security field. The third and fourth models could result in a violation of the 2000/78 Directive.[11]

---

[10] Proposal for a Council Directive on implementing the principle of equal treatment between persons irrespective of religion or belief, disability, age or sexual orientation {SEC(2008) 2180} {SEC(2008) 2181}.

[11] European Network of Legal Experts in the Non-discrimination Field: *Disability and non-discrimination law in the EU. An analysis of disability discrimination law within and beyond the employment field*, POEU (2009), p. 7.

As is often the case in the EU realm, the lack of a clear uniform definition set in primary or secondary EU law forced the European Court of Justice (ECJ) to act and fill the void. In a first case, the ECJ gave a restrictive definition of disability that incited criticism. In *Chacón Navas*, the Court stated: "*[T]he concept of 'disability' must be understood as referring to a limitation which results in particular from physical, mental or psychological impairments and which hinders the participation of the person concerned in professional life. However, by using the concept of 'disability' in Article 1 of that directive, the legislature deliberately chose a term which differs from 'sickness'. The two concepts cannot therefore simply be treated as being the same*".[12] This definition was controversial in that it demanded an almost permanent status of impairment as well as the inability to work of the person concerned. Moreover, it did not take into account the role played by an unwelcoming external environment for disability to manifest itself.

Some years later, the Court nuanced its interpretation of the concept by stating in *HK Danmark* that "*The concept of 'disability' must be interpreted as including a condition caused by an illness medically diagnosed as curable or incurable where that illness entails a limitation which results in particular from physical, mental or psychological impairments which in interaction with various barriers may hinder the full and effective participation of the person concerned in professional life on an equal basis with other workers, and the limitation is a long-term one*".[13] However, the ECJ's definition is still limited in comparison with the level of protection of the UN Convention in that it demands that disability represents an obstacle for work. Not without reason, some authors have argued that European legislation should remove the reference to professional life in the interpretation given to disability. It should be enough that individual impairments, in interaction with various barriers, hinder the person's full and effective participation in society on an equal basis with others, regardless of whether it specifically affects the person's work life (Carrasquero Cepeda 2018, p. 42). Moreover, the ECJ's ruling still demands that the limitation be a long-term one.

As for the role played by the EU in the drafting of the UN Convention, it is worth mentioning that the *Convention on the Rights of the Persons with Disabilities* is the first human rights treaty where the European Union as such stands as one of its 177 parties, together with the 28 EU Member States. Both the European Commission and the then-27 Member States sent delegations to the negotiations. It was also the first time in history that an international organisation as such participated in a human rights treaty. The EU struggled to be considered as a party and to see its international legal personality recognised in the future treaty. Not without reason, disabil-

---

[12] ECJ, C-13/05, Judgment of 11 July 2006, *Sonia Chacón Navas v. Eurest Colectividades SA*, paras. 43 and 44.

[13] ECJ, Joined Cases C-335/11 and C-337/11, Judgment of 11 April 2013, HK Danmark, acting on behalf of Jette Ring, Dansk almennyttigt Boligselskab & HK Danmark, acting on behalf of Lone Skouboe Werge, v Dansk Arbejdsgiverforening, acting on behalf of Pro Display A/S, para. 93. ECJ, C-270/16, Judgment of 18 of January of 2018, *Carlos Enrique Ruiz Conejero v. Ferroser Servicios Auxiliares S.A. y Ministerio Fiscal* repeats the same idea in para. 28.

ity is an area where the competences of the EU and its Member States converge. On the one hand, article 13 TFEU authorizes the EU to take appropriate action to combat discrimination based, among other grounds, on disability. On the other hand, article 2 TFEU establishes that "*the Member States shall coordinate their economic and employment policies within arrangements as determined by this Treaty, which the Union shall have competence to provide*" whereas article 4 establishes that "*shared competence between the Union and the Member States applies in the following principal areas: . . . social policy, for the aspects defined in this Treaty*".

Despite the fact that at the onset, the EU was sceptical about the need for an internationally binding treaty on disability, once a general consensus emerged on this issue, the EU changed its position and tried at least to influence the future treaty's content so that it matched the EU legislation. Two main reasons can be found for why the EU was unconvinced about drafting a disability covenant. First, it was more inclined to strengthen *the UN Standard Rules for the Equalization of Opportunities of Persons with Disabilities* despite it being a soft law instrument. Second, it was of the opinion that the drafting of a new human rights treaty meant for the benefit of a particular vulnerable group could have the undesired effect of signalizing and segregating this group rather than integrating it (De Búrca 2009, p. 179). But once the process of adoption of the treaty started, the EU was, unlike the USA, an active negotiator that pressed for a social approach for the status of disability, as practiced by the European institutions themselves within the EU's internal policies. It also tried to avoid any potential conflict with EU legislation. However, the position of the EU during the negotiations was sometimes weak. This was due, on the one hand, to differences of opinion between Member States, whose views on disability were not always uniform. On the other hand, the European Commission—as the EU negotiator—was interested in agreeing with its Member States on a consensual position so that they could all speak with a single voice. The price to be paid was often a weakening of the arguments when Member States had different viewpoints.

The social model advocated by the EU, which diverged from the traditional medical approach, was embraced by the rest of negotiators. The EU framework on disability, based on a non-discriminatory, rights-based approach, was also partially followed, with the Disability Convention containing a holistic, hybrid model of rights. The EU's view, in the sense that a closed definition of disability or of the expression "persons with disabilities" would be counterproductive for the future UN treaty, was also accepted. This way, article 2, on "Definitions", does not provide a precise and detailed definition, whereas article 1, on "Purpose", provides some nonexclusive guidelines to identify what disability means. Another evidence of the influence of the EU in the final text is that, in line with the long history of fight of the EU against discrimination, the agreed draft UN Convention includes a strong and broad definition of discrimination on grounds of disability in article 2. The EU also succeeded in obtaining the inclusion of the denial of reasonable accommodation as a motive of discrimination, something new in human rights treaties (De Búrca 2009, p. 192). In this respect, the inclusion of the concept of reasonable accommodation was largely due to EU negotiators.

In some other issues, the European Commission simply supported other States' views. This was the case with the discussion on the need for national monitoring mechanisms to be established. In this respect, the EU did not have strong feelings. It followed the Caribbean and Latin American States as well as NGOs who had adamantly defended the need to adopt a clear stance in favour of the settlement of national mechanisms for the convention to be useful (De Búrca 2009, p. 190).

4 Conclusion

The role played by the EU in the historical change of paradigm of disability (from a medical condition to a social one and in the status of the persons with disability (from a personal problem to one involving societal responsibility) should not be denied. In the framework of its non-discrimination law, the EU legislated on disability years before the UN Convention was adopted. Also, despite the fact that during the drafting of the UN Convention, NGOs and Latin American countries, especially Mexico, were the most visible negotiators, the EU was also a prominent actor that struggled to transpose the EU model into the new document. The EU was also active in trying to avoid the inclusion in the UN treaty of concepts and ideas that were alien to the EU. In this way, the contribution of the EU in the redefinition of the term disability and in the recognition of the current international status of persons with disabilities should be valued.

References

Biel Portero, I. (2008). Discapacidad, Derecho Internacional y ¿Cooperación al desarrollo? In J. Ferrer & S. Sanz Caballero (Eds.), *Protección de Personas y Grupos Vulnerables. Especial Referencia al Derecho Internacional y Europeo* (pp. 135–162). Valencia: Tirant Lo Blanch.

Biel Portero, I. & Rey Aneiros, A. (2008). Las Personas con Discapacidad ante la UE: del Paternalismo Inicial al Reconocimiento de Derechos. In F. Aldecoa, & Others (Eds.), *Los Tratados de Roma en su Cincuenta Aniversario* (pp. 205–230). Madrid: Marcial Pons.

Cardona, J. & Sanjosé, A. (2005). La promoción y la protección de los derechos humanos de las personas con discapacidad en el camino de su reconocimiento universal. In C. Courtis (Ed.), *Protección Internacional de Derechos Humanos. Nuevos Desafíos* (pp. 149 ff). México: Porrúa S.A.

Carrasquero Cepeda, M. (2018). Los Ajustes Razonables para Personas con Discapacidad en la UE. *REE, 71*, 42 ff.

De Búrca, G. (2009). The EU in the negotiation of the UN Disability Convention. *European Law Review, 35*(2), 179 ff.

European Network of Legal Experts in the Non-discrimination Field: Disability and Non-Discrimination Law in the EU. (2009). *An analysis of disability discrimination law within and beyond the employment field, POEU*. Retrieved from https://publications.europa.eu/en/publication-detail/-/publication/cf7bc8c8-2c84-46ff-83b5-202a6fb805a1/language-en

Lawson, A. (2007). The United Nations Convention on the rights of persons with disabilities new era or false dawn? *Syracuse Journal of International Law and Commerce, 34*(2), 594.

Sanz Caballero, S. (2003). Personas con Discapacidad. In M. Álvarez & R. Cippitani (Eds.), *Diccionario Analítico de Derechos Humanos e Integración Jurídica*. Roma, Perugia: ISEG.

Traustadóttir, R. (2009) Disability studies, the social model and legal developments. In O. M. Arnardóttit & G. Quinn (Eds.), *The UN Convention on the rights of persons with disabilities: European and Scandinavian perspectives* (pp. 9 ff). Leiden: Martinus Nijhoff, Brill

UN. (2014). The Convention on the rights of persons with disabilities. *Training Guide*, 19.

WHO. (1976, May). *International classification of impairments, disabilities and handicaps. A manual of classification relating to the consequences of disease*. Geneva, p. 143.

Disabled Person

Carlos Vidal Prado

1 The Attitude of EU Law Towards People with Disabilities at the End of the 20th Century

The EU initiated significant activity through social policies in the mid '70s. Social policy, and consequently policies concerning persons with disabilities, was part of the sphere of responsibility of the Member States who, in turn, sought international guidelines for their policies on disabilities and disabled persons. The first Social Action Programme, an initiative of the European Commission, was adopted in 1974 and, with the exception of measures of greater draught on equal opportunities, safety and the health of workers, included programmes of action in favour of disabled people, those living in poverty and elderly people.

At the end of the 1980s, the European Union adopted major initiatives in the field of social policy aimed at persons with disabilities; a resolution was adopted by the Council on 21 December 1981, which focused on the social integration of disabled people and which invited Member States to promote and intensify actions specified in this objective.[1]

The UN's Standard Rules were the framework relied upon by Member States when creating policies focusing on disabilities, the initiatives of the EU itself and other agencies as the Council of Europe (EUAFR, ECHR, CE 2011) and the World Health Organization. Its adoption inaugurated a new phase in the history of disability policies; its standards served as an instrument for policy-makers and as a basis

[1] Resolution of the representatives of the Governments of the Member States of the European Communities meeting within the Council of 21 December 1981 on the social integration of handicapped people. Official Journal C 347, 31/12/1981, 1.

C. Vidal Prado (✉)
Faculty of Law, Universidad Nacional de Educación a Distancia (UNED), Madrid, Spain
e-mail: cvidal@der.uned.es

A. Bartolini et al. (eds.), *Dictionary of Statuses within EU Law*,
https://doi.org/10.1007/978-3-030-00554-2_20

for the development of technical and economic cooperation activities (Blanco Egido and Sánchez Salcedo 2006; Cabra de Luna et al. 2007; Quinn and Degener 2002).

Upon Recommendation 86/379/EEC of 24 July 1986 on the employment of disabled people in the Community,[2] the Council established a guideline framework setting out examples of positive actions promoting the employment and training of disabled people, and in its Resolution of 17 June 1999 on equal employment opportunities for people with disabilities,[3] affirmed the importance of giving specific attention, among other things, to the recruitment, retention, training and lifelong learning of disabled persons.

The 1988 adoption of the Community Action Programme "Helios" on behalf of people with disabilities (1988–1992) was the result of the Resolution of the European Parliament of 11 March 1981 on the economic, social and vocational integration of disabled people in the European Community,[4] and facilitated the meeting, common actions and policies that were under way in different countries through the study and exchange of experiences through networking. A new Programme "Helios II" was approved for the period of 1993–1996[5] and highlighted the active role of non-governmental organisations and the inclusion of new issues, such as accessibility, transport and technological solutions for communication and autonomy; these issues would get a leading role in the following years.

The most significant changes in the management of the EU's approach to disability started from 1996. The Commission, through its Communication of 30 July 1996 on the equality of opportunities for people with disabilities: A New European Community Disability Strategy,[6] proposed a new model "which implie[d] effective equality in the exercise of rights by persons with disabilities" (Biel Portero 2011, pp. 245–266). This step represented a change in approach because the actions of the European Union thereon aimed to protect persons with disabilities and to give them equal opportunities; this step was based on the EU's respect for the human rights of these people.

A few months later, the EU approved the Resolution of the Council of 20 December 1996 on equal opportunities for people with disabilities.[7] The Council reaffirmed its commitment to equal opportunities for disabled people and to avoid or abolish all forms of negative discrimination based on disability. The Resolution called upon Member States to ascertain whether their policies considered the need to eliminate all obstacles to disabled peoples' full participation in social life and to educate the public about the abilities of disabled people. Member States were equally encouraged to promote the participation of disabled people in the implementation and investigation of these policies. The Council called upon the

---

[2] OJ L 225, 12.8.1986, 43.

[3] OJ C 186, 2.7.1999, 3.

[4] OJ C 77, 6.4.1981, 27.

[5] 88/231/EEC: Council Decision of 18 April 1988 establishing a second Community action programme for disabled people (Helios), OJ L 104, 23/04/1988, 0038–0044.

[6] COM 96, 406 final.

[7] OJ C 12, 13.01.1997.

Commission to integrate the dimension of "equality of opportunity for people with disabilities" (part III of the Resolution) into all its relevant proposals and to encourage the exchange of useful information and experience, particularly with regard to innovative policies and good practice.

A High Level Group centring on disability, with representatives from each Member State, was created in order to follow the political progress and to gather information and experience. It also welcomed in 1996 the creation of the new European Disability Forum. Both instruments have developed a work of great value in the recognition of equal opportunities for disabled people and towards the guarantee of their human rights.

In 1997, the Amsterdam Treaty amended Article 13 of the Treaty establishing the European Community and introduced, for the first time in a conventional text, an express reference to discrimination based on disability in Paragraph 1: "Without prejudice to the other provisions of this Treaty and within the limits of the powers conferred by it upon the Community, the Council, acting unanimously on a proposal from the Commission and after consulting the European Parliament, may take appropriate action to combat discrimination based on sex, racial or ethnic origin, religion or belief, disability, age or sexual orientation" (art. 13.1).

The Intergovernmental Conference, which prepared the Amsterdam Treaty, strengthened the warranty set forth in Article 13 through Declaration No. 22: "the institutions of the Community shall take account of the needs of persons with a disability".

Throughout 1998 and 1999, the Council drew up Council Recommendation 98/376/EC of 4 June 1998 thereby providing a parking card for people with disabilities,[8] known as a Blue Badge, and the Resolution of the Council and of the Representatives of the Governments of the Member States meeting within the Council of 17 June 1999 on equal employment opportunities for people with disabilities.[9]

2 A New Stage: The Council Directive 2000/78/EC of 27 November 2000

In 2000, European legislation on equal opportunities and the prohibition of discrimination acquired an important role in the EU. During the same year, the Commission also presented the Communication "towards a barrier free Europe for people with disabilities",[10] whilst the Council adopted two important instruments: the Council Directive 2000/78/EC of 27 November 2000, establishing a general

---

[8] OJ L 167, 12.6.1998, 25–28.

[9] OJ C 186, 02.07.1999.

[10] COM/2000/0284 final. Communication from the Commission - Towards a barrier free Europe for people with disabilities.

framework for equal treatment in employment,[11] and the Community Action Programme to combat discrimination (2001 to 2006).[12]

Directive 2000/78/EC was the legal norm that regulated, for the first time, discrimination in employment by reason of disability and has had a significant impact on the level of protection offered to victims of disability discrimination in Member States.

The objective of the Directive is to put in place a general framework that would ensure equal treatment of individuals in the European Union, regardless of their religion or belief, disability, age or sexual orientation, as regards access to employment or occupation and membership of certain organisations.

Although today the Directive remains the most important legal instrument in the EU within the field of disability, its transposition and implementation has not been completely comprehensive in every Member State. The definitions and criteria applicable to disabilities are currently established in national legislation and differ from one Member State to another (European Commission 2002).

The EU Charter of Fundamental Rights makes direct reference to disability in two Articles: 21 (Non-discrimination) and 26 (Integration of persons with disabilities: "The Union recognises and respects the right of persons with disabilities to benefit from measures designed to ensure their independence, social and occupational integration and participation in the life of the community".).

3 Equal Opportunities for People with Disabilities: A European Action Plan (2004–2010)

Building on the momentum created and the results achieved in 2003 by the "European Year of People with Disabilities",[13] the Commission planned to introduce a multiannual action plan through to 2010, aiming at mainstreaming disability issues in relevant Community policies and implementing specific measures in key areas with a view to enhancing the economic and social integration of people with disabilities.[14]

In recent years, the EU has been moving forward on legislative matters in specific areas. In 2006, the European Parliament and the Council adopted Regulation (EC) No 1107/2006 of 5 July 2006 concerning the rights of disabled persons and

[11] OJ L 303, 2.12.2000, 16–22.

[12] Council Decision 2000/750/EC of 27 November 2000 establishing a Community action programme to combat discrimination (2001 to 2006). OJ L 303, 2.12.2000, 23–28.

[13] Council Decision 2001/903/EC of 3 December 2001 on the European Year of People with Disabilities 2003. OJ L 335, 19.12.2001, 15–20.

[14] Communication of 30 October 2003, Equal opportunities for people with disabilities: a European action plan. COM (2003) 650 final; and Communication—Situation of disabled people in the European Union: the European Action Plan 2008-2009 (COM (2007) 738 final).

persons with reduced mobility when travelling by air[15]; the first Regulation focusing exclusively on protecting the rights of persons with disabilities (Biel Portero 2007).

However, one of the most striking developments on legislative matters on disability was the conclusion of the United Nations Convention on the Rights of Persons with Disabilities,[16] the first international legally binding instrument setting minimum standards for rights for people with disabilities, and the first human rights convention to which the EU has become a party (Biel Portero 2010). The core elements of the UN Convention are reflected in the European Disability Strategy 2010–2020.[17]

Article 27 of the Convention prohibits "discrimination on the basis of disability with regard to all matters concerning all forms of employment, including conditions of recruitment, hiring and employment, continuance of employment, career advancement and safe and healthy working conditions". However, Directive 2000/78 allows Member States to exempt the principle of equal treatment in the field of the Armed Forces. Thus, Article 3.4 of the Directive established that "Member States may provide that this Directive, in so far as it relates to discrimination on the grounds of disability and age, shall not apply to the Armed Forces". In accordance with this, the EU has made a reservation concerning this part during the signing of the Convention.

The Renewed Social Agenda,[18] designed to ensure that EU policies respond effectively to today's economic and social challenges, was adopted by the European Commission on 2 July 2008. The agenda aimed to create more opportunities for EU citizens, improve access to quality services and demonstrate solidarity with those who are affected negatively by change. One of the priorities of the Agenda was the reinforcement of the principle of non-discrimination, promoting, among other measures, the Proposal for a Council Directive of 2 July 2008 on the implementation of the principle of equal treatment between persons irrespective of religion or belief, disability, age or sexual orientation.[19]

[15] OJ L 204, 26.7.2006, 1–9.

[16] https://www.un.org/development/desa/disabilities/convention-on-the-rights-of-persons-with-disabilities.html Accessed 16 March 2018; Council Decision of 26 November 2009 concerning the conclusion, by the European Community, of the United Nations Convention on the Rights of Persons with Disabilities (2010/48/EC). Official Journal L 23, 27.01.2010.

[17] COM(2010) 636 final, European Disability Strategy 2010-2020: A Renewed Commitment to a Barrier-Free Europe.

[18] COM(2008) 412 final, Renewed social agenda: Opportunities, access and solidarity in twenty-first century Europe.

[19] https://eur-lex.europa.eu/legal-content/EN/TXT/HTML/?uri=LEGISSUM:em0008&from=ES Accessed 16 March 2018.

4 The Concept of Disability and the Role of the Court of Justice of the European Union

EU Law does not offer a definition of disability or guidance to identify if a person meets this criterion. In relevant literature (Threlfall 2003; Waddington and Lawson 2010), the case of Chacón Navas, the first related to equal treatment in the employment Directive,[20] is usually used to give a definition.

The Court of Justice of the European Union (CJEU) affirm that the "concept of 'disability' must be understood as referring to a limitation which results in particular from physical, mental or psychological impairments and which hinders the participation of the person concerned in professional life". The most applicable criticism to argue against this definition is that it is founded on the medical concept of disability, which today is rejected by major European and international institutions, and not on a social model.

The CJEU dealt with the concept of disability in a judgment in 2008.[21] The Court said that "Directive 2000/78, and, in particular, Articles 1 and 2(1) and (2)(a) thereof, must be interpreted as meaning that the prohibition of direct discrimination laid down by those provisions is not limited only to people who are themselves disabled. Where an employer treats an employee who is not himself disabled less favourably than another employee is, has been or would be treated in a comparable situation, and it is established that the less favourable treatment of that employee is based on the disability of his child, whose care is provided primarily by that employee, such treatment is contrary to the prohibition of direct discrimination laid down by Article 2(2)(a)" (n. 56) (Muñoz Ruiz 2009).

Later the Court affirmed: "Consequently, it does not follow from those provisions of Directive 2000/78 that the principle of equal treatment which it is designed to safeguard is limited to people who themselves have a disability within the meaning of the directive. On the contrary, the purpose of the directive, as regards employment and occupation, is to combat all forms of discrimination on grounds of disability. The principle of equal treatment enshrined in the directive in that area applies not to a particular category of person but by reference to the grounds mentioned in Article 1. That interpretation is supported by the wording of Article 13 EC, which constitutes the legal basis of Directive 2000/78, and which confers on the Community the competence to take appropriate action to combat discrimination based, inter alia, on disability" (n. 38).

In both judgments, the CJEU supplements the lack of a definition of disability under EU Law. If we make a global interpretation of the two rulings, we can conclude that although the scope of the directive does not extend beyond discrimination on grounds of religion or belief, disability, age or sexual orientation, in a case in which there is discrimination for one of these reasons it will extend the scope of the application beyond the person who professes a certain religion, suffers from a dis-

[20] Judgment of the Court (Grand Chamber) of 11 July 2006. Sonia Chacón Navas v Eurest Colectividades SA. Case C-13/05. ECLI:EU:C:2006:456.

[21] Judgment of the Court (Grand Chamber) of 17 July 2008. S. Coleman v Attridge Law and Steve Law. ECLI:EU:C:2008:415.

ability or is of a certain age or gender, protecting even the people who care for the disabled person and who they directly depend on.

5 Recent Initiatives

In 2009 upon the signing of the Treaty of Lisbon, the contents of Article 13 of the Treaty establishing the European Community were replaced by Article 19 of the Treaty on the Functioning of the European Union (TFEU). In addition, Article 10 of the TFEU was included with the signing of the Treaty of Lisbon: "In defining and implementing its policies and activities, the Union shall aim to combat discrimination based on sex, racial or ethnic origin, religion or belief, disability, age or sexual orientation". This means that, among the objectives of the European Union, a person will be able to challenge discrimination on grounds of disability.

The EU promotes the active inclusion and full participation of disabled people in society, in line with the EU's human rights approach to disability issues. Disability is a rights issue and not a matter of discretion. This approach is also at the core of the UN Convention on the Rights of Persons with Disabilities (UNCRPD), to which the EU is a party.

The European Commission's European Disability Strategy 2010–2020,[22] adopted in 2010, builds on the UNCRPD. A Progress Report[23] presenting the achievements of the implementation of the Strategy was published in February 2017. It lists some tangible successes and describes the implementation of the UNCRPD by the EU, including within EU institutions. It also confirms the need for a European Strategy that will continue to deliver its objectives, taking into account the UN's Concluding Observations.[24]

The Commission also supports the Academic Network of European Disability Experts (ANED[25]), which provides the Commission with an analysis of national situations, policies and data. ANED also manages the DOTCOM Online Tool,[26] which provides an overview of key instruments in Member States and in the EU needed for the implementation of the UNCRPD. The creation of the Tool was one of the actions foreseen in the List of Actions (2010–2015)[27] accompanying the

[22] COM(2010) 636 final: European Disability Strategy 2010–2020: A Renewed Commitment to a Barrier-Free Europe, http://eur-lex.europa.eu/LexUriServ/LexUriServ.do?uri=COM:2010:0636:FIN:en:PDF Accessed 16 March 2018.

[23] Commission staff working document, Progress Report on the implementation of the European Disability Strategy (2010–2020) http://ec.europa.eu/social/BlobServlet?docId=16995&langId=en Accessed 16 March 2018.

[24] United Nations, Committee on the Rights of Persons with Disabilities, Concluding observations on the initial report of the European Union, Adopted by the Committee at its fourteenth session (17 August-4 September 2015). http://ec.europa.eu/social/BlobServlet?docId=14429&langId=en Accessed 16 March 2018.

[25] http://www.disability-europe.net/ Accessed 16 March 2018.

[26] http://www.disability-europe.net/dotcom Accessed 16 March 2018.

[27] Commission staff working document. Initial plan to implement the European Disability Strategy 2010–2020. List of Actions 2010–2015. http://eur-lex.europa.eu/LexUriServ/LexUriServ.do?uri=SEC:2010:1324:FIN:en:PDF Accessed 16 March 2018.

European Disability Strategy. Published in May 2012, the DOTCOM Tool is updated every year.

References

Biel Portero, I. (2007). Los derechos de las personas con discapacidad y las personas con movilidad reducida en el transporte aéreo. Comentario al Reglamento (CE) n° 1107/2006 del Parlamento Europeo y del Consejo, de 5 de julio de 2006. *Revista General de Derecho Europeo, 13*, 1–16.

Biel Portero, I. (2010). El primer Tratado de Derechos Humanos celebrado por la Unión Europea: La Convención de Naciones Unidas sobre los derechos de las Personas con Discapacidad. *Revista General de Derecho Europeo*, 21.

Biel Portero, I. (2011). *Los derechos humanos de las personas con discapacidad*. Valencia: Tirant lo Blanch.

Blanco Egido, E., & Sánchez Salcedo, A. M. (2006). El enfoque de la discapacidad en los organismos internacionales. *Revista del Ministerio de Trabajo y Asuntos Sociales, 65.*

Cabra de Luna, M. Á., Bariffi, F., & Palacios, A. (2007). *Derechos humanos de las personas con discapacidad: la Convención Internacional de las Naciones Unidas*. Madrid: Editorial Universitaria Ramón Areces.

European Commission. (2002, September). Definition of disability in Europe: A comparative analysis. Retrieved March 17, 2018, from http://ec.europa.eu/social/BlobServlet?docId=2088&langId=en

European Union Agency for Fundamental Rights, European Court of Human Rights. Council of Europe. (2011). Handbook on European non-discrimination law. Luxemburg: Publications Office of the European Union, 2011. Retrieved March 17, 2018, from https://www.echr.coe.int/Pages/home.aspx?p=caselaw/otherpublications/handbooks

Muñoz Ruiz, A. B. (2009). El caso Coleman: un paso más en la construcción del modelo social de discapacidad de la unión Europea y su extensión a los cuidadores. *Temas laborales: Revista andaluza de trabajo y bienestar social, 101*, 321–339.

Quinn, G., & Degener, T. (2002). *Derechos humanos y discapacidad. Uso actual y posibilidades futuras de los instrumentos de derechos humanos de las Naciones Unidas en el contexto de la discapacidad*. New York: United Nations.

Threlfall, M. (2003). European integration: Harmonization, convergence and single areas. *Journal of European Social Policy, 13*(2), 121–139.

Waddington, L., & Lawson, A. (2010). *European Network of Legal Experts in the non-discrimination field. Handicap et droit européen contre la discrimination*. Luxemburg: Office des Publications de l'Union Européenne.

Economic Operator

Viviana Di Capua

1 The Economic Operator in the European Union (EU): A Status Under Construction

The status of the economic operator is created by the European lawmaker and jurisprudence during the harmonisation process of procedure for the award of public contracts in ordinary and specialised sectors. The first legal reference can be found in the 2004/18/CE directive (Art. 1, par. 2, let. *a*), in which 'public contract' includes the economic operator amongst the contracting parties, and Article 1, paragraph 8, specifies that this term 'shall cover equally the concepts of contractor, supplier and service provider': it is 'any natural or legal person or public entity or group of such persons [or] bodies, which offers on the market, respectively, the execution of works [or] a work, products or services', and that '[i]t [is] used merely in the interest of simplification'.

The creation of a unitary legal category, which includes the different figures disciplined by the previous directive on the public contracts in specific sectors (i.e., services, products and works), is perfectly coordinate with the process of integration which is the objective of the European order in this field—enabling the identification of subjects that are able to participate in award procedures issued by member States.

Subsequently, the European jurisprudence specified further requisites for the status of economic operator—which has extended the qualification to subjects excluded from single national organisations—in order to guarantee, through the principles of *favor partecipationis* e *par condicio*,[1] the opening to the competition in public tenders in the widest possible way.[2]

[1] CJEU, Case C-538/7 *Assitur s.r.l. v Camera di Commercio, Industria, Artigianato e Agricoltura di Milano*[2009].

[2] CJEU, Case C-526/13 *IVD GmbH & Co. KG v Ärztekammer Westfalen-Lippe*[2013].

V. Di Capua (✉)
Faculty of Law, University of Naples "Federico II", Naples, Italy

A. Bartolini et al. (eds.), *Dictionary of Statuses within EU Law*,
https://doi.org/10.1007/978-3-030-00554-2_21

In fact, notwithstanding the legal definition, the indifference of the European order for the *status* of the natural or legal person of the candidates or tender, the national lawmaker and jurisprudence have frequently adopted a restrictive orientation as opposed to the *ratio* of the directive.

The Courts of Justice of the European Union (hereinafter: CJEU) has intervened in a significantly and exemplifying manner on the question with two judgments; respectively, in the fields of public contract and public services. In the Frigerio sentence, on 18 December 2007, regarding litigation before the Italian administrative judge and brought about on the basis of a petition presented by *Frigerio Luigi & C. S.N.C.* against the Municipality of Triuggio for excluding the tender issued for the award of a contract for the management of environmental hygiene services, pursuant to provisions of Article 113, par. 5, d.lgs. n. 267/2000, which permits the participation of limited liability companies alone. The European judges declared the principle of neutrality of legal forms, specifying that European law precludes national provisions, which exclude candidates or tenderers entitled under the law of the Member State or concerned to provide the service in question, including those composed of groups of service providers, from submitting a tender, in a procedure for the award of a public service contract with a value greater than the European threshold solely on the ground that those candidates or tenderers do not have a legal form corresponding to a specific category of legal persons, namely that of a company with share capital.[3]

In the *CoNISMa* sentence, on 23 December 2009, the European judges push even further, confirming the total indifference of the European order for the legal nature (i.e., private or public) and the aim sought after by the subjects, in order to participate in public tenders. The *Consiglio di Stato* raised a preliminary ruling in the occasion of an extraordinary appeal to the President of the Republic. The dispute referred to the exclusion of CoNISMa from a tender issued by the Marche Region for the acquisition of marine stratigraphic seismic surveys (i.e., core borings and collection of samples of marine water) and, therefore, more generally the possibility for subjects which are not principally profit making entities, do not have a business organisation and do not ensure a regular presence on the market, such as Universities and Research Institutions, as well as groups constituted by Universities and public administrations, to participate in award procedures of public contracts. The European judges concluded affirmatively, specifying that a restrictive interpretation of the concept of economic operator would be that contracts concluded between contracting authorities and bodies which are primarily non-profit-making would not be regarded as 'public contracts', could be awarded by mutual agreement and would thus not be covered by Community rules on equal treatment and transparency, which would be inconsistent with the aim of those rules.[4]

In synthesis, the European judges—considering the risk of impairment of the principle *favor partecipationis*, which derives from the tight requirements to participate in public award procedures—have sustained 'a broad definition of economic

[3] See CJUE, Case C-357/06 *Frigerio Luigi & C. s.n.c. c. Comune di Triuggio*[2007].

[4] CJUE, Case C-305/08 *Consorzio Nazionale Interuniversitario Scienze del Mare (CoNISMa) v Regione Marche*[2009].

operator, based on an objective-substantial presupposition: the offer of good and services on the market'. The favoured competition is not precluded to compare the offers presented by economic operators organised in a different way, allowing them to participate in the procedure for awarding public contracts to any person or authority that offers works, supplies and services on the market, regardless of the organisational structure, the regular presence on the market, the non-profit-making and the public financing (Foà 2014, p. 26).[5]

The affirmation of the freedom of forms for the participation in tenders has, in this way, extended the status of trader, even to public non-economic bodies (e.g., universities), only if the activity is instrumental to the final institutional objective of the participating public body, it has been authorised by the State member in which it is based to operate on the market and there has not been a precise national ruling that precludes such activity[6] (Bartolini 2013; Di Capua 2014; Mazzamuto 2013).

2 The Ruling of the CJEU Becomes Law: The Status of Economic Operator in the New Directives 2014/24/UE, 2014/25/UE and 2014/23/UE

The new directives 2014/24/UE, 2014/25/UE and 2014/23/UE of 26 February 2014, regarding public procurement and the award of concession contracts, outlines (respectively, at Art. 2, par. 1, n. 10; Art. 2, par. 1, n. 6; and Art. 5, par. 1, n. 2) a wider idea of economic operator, which includes any natural or legal person, or public entity, or a group of such persons or entities, including temporary associations of undertakings, which offers the execution of works or a work, the supply of products or the provision of services on the market. The total acceptance of the praetorian orientation is clear when reading *Considerando 14* of the directive 2014/24/UE, which clarifies that the notion of economic operators should be interpreted in a broad manner so as to include any persons or entities that offer the execution of works, the supply of products or the provision of services on the market, irrespective of the legal form under which they have chosen to operate. Thus, firms, branches, subsidiaries, partnerships, cooperative societies, limited companies, universities, public or private, and other forms of entities than natural persons should all fall within the notion of economic operator, whether or not they are 'legal persons' in all circumstances. This is merely an illustrative list, put together in order to extend the status of economic operator to the various subjects that are different in form, nature and legal discipline regarding the new European legislation for public tenders and concession contracts (Caranta and Dragos 2014; De Quesada 2014; Kotsonis 2014). The new directive extends, widens and completes the field of

[5] See also CJUE, Case C-568/13 *Azienda Ospedaliero-Universitaria di Careggi-Firenze v Data Medical Service s.r.l.*[2014].

[6] CJUE, Case C-159/11 *Azienda Sanitaria Locale di Lecce e Università del Salento v Ordine degli Ingegneri della Provincia di Lecce e altri*[2012].

application of the discipline, as well as and above all a subjective profile; thus, reaffirming and strengthening 'the neutral nature of the economic operator's notions, regardless of a specific legal form and exempt from typing obligations'. In this way, 'the preference of European lawmaker for freedom of forms of private law, here considered as freedom of choice under the profile of legal form and organization structure of the subjects that want to participate to the adjudication' (Torchia 2016, p. 131).

The new definition of economic operator represents the result of European integration, which has found its most complete manifestation in the public tender sector. The creation of an internal market passes, in fact, necessarily through the elimination of national barriers that prevent or limit the free circulation of people, services and assets. Necessary in the realisation of this aim is the definition of common rules that allow a smoothing out of the dissimilarities that exist between the national legal systems, as well as the construction of status that has the aim of overcoming the standardisation of national administrative rights. The standardisation of subjects who are able to participate in public tenders satisfies the need, particularly of the national orders, to find within the definition *ex ante* of the type of operator the necessary guarantees (Torchia 2016, p. 137). To the contrary, the European order requires that the existence of these guarantees must be verified *ex post*, whilst ignoring the form that the trader has chosen to assume. These considerations are reflected in the European regulations regarding participation in award procedures of traders. Article 19 of the directive 2014/24/UE, from one viewpoint, prohibits the contracting authority to prevent the participation or presentation of an offer to groups that are not a specific legal form (par. 2). Nevertheless, from the other viewpoint, Article 19 allows the contracting authority, once they have been awarded the tender, to impose a change of the original legal form when it is deemed necessary for the positive outcome of the tender (par. 3) or in cases where a jointly liable responsibility is to be assumed (par. 15, first line).

3 The Effects of the European Integration: The Trader as the Centre of Legal Relations in Active and Passive Subjective Situations

The status of the trader can be defined as a product of the European integration procedures that have its most complete implementation. European law takes into consideration the potential competitors under a material respect, in accordance with their suitability to operate on the market (i.e., through contracting, supplies or services), regardless of evaluations of any other type. The subject holder of the relevant status becomes the recipient of subjective legal situations (i.e., rights and obligations) that are expressly recognised and protected by the European order. One example is the discipline of the reasons for exclusion, mentioned in Article 57 of the directive 2014/24/UE, which outlines the general and moral requirements that must be legitimately possessed in order to participate in a public tender.

The presence of convictions—ascertained by a final judgment for one of the offences specifically mentioned in the regulations (e.g., participation in criminal organizations, corruption, terrorism, etc.) or for tax and social irregularities—determine the mandatory exclusion; whereas, bankruptcy, a relevant dispute or the realisation of serious professional offences are potential causes of an optional exclusion. In order to avoid exclusion from the procedures, the regulations permit the trader the right to demonstrate his integrity; thus, the regulations allow the trader to produce evidence of efficient remedial and precautionary measures aimed at repaying any damages incurred and preventing the perpetration of further criminal offences or misconduct. The exercise of this right is carried out in the contradictory procedures with the contracting authority, which, if he or she still considers the exclusion to be necessary, must justify the motivations. Moreover, these are active subjective situations that come about directly from the right to good administration and laid out in Article 41 of the EU Bill of Rights, which—following the Lisbon Treaty—assumes the same legal value as the European treaties (Della Cananea and Franchini 2017).

The substantial prospective, adopted by the European lawmakers, can also be seen in the rules on derogations (subjective) to the application of procedures with public evidence. Article 12 of the directive 2014/24/UE concerns public tenders between public-sector bodies, foreseeing the hypothesis of in house providing and of the agreements concluded between contracting authorities, who, in some conditions, make up a free zone of the relevant regulations. The ratio of the derogations does not lie in the public nature of the in house company or of the contracting authority in the case of cooperation agreements, provided that even the public bodies can be traders. To the contrary, it can be observed in the absence of impartiality of the in-house subject regarding the public body and, therefore, in the absence of a subjective alternative by reason of an analogical control to which it is subjected and which place it in the same position of an office or a service, and as the reason for differences between an organisational agreement and a contract for services (i.e., cooperation and exchange) (Janssen 2014; Volpe 2016). The circumstance that both parties of an agreement are public authorities, in fact, does not automatically exclude the application of regulations for the protection of competition.

References

Bartolini, A. (2013). Accordi organizzativi e diritto europeo: La cooperazione pubblico-pubblico (CPP) e la disciplina degli appalti. *Urb e app, 12*, 1260–1265.

Caranta, R., & Dragos, D. C. (2014). La mini-rivoluzione del diritto europeo dei contratti pubblici. *Urb e app, 5*, 493–504.

De Quesada, C. E. (2014). Competition and transparency in public procurement markets. *Public Procurement Law Review, 3*, 229–244.

Della Cananea, G., & Franchini, C. (2017). *I principi dell'amministrazione europea*. Torino: Giappichelli.
Di Capua, V. (2014). Accordi tra Amministrazioni e inderogabilità del diritto dell'Unione Europea in materia di appalti pubblici. La tutela della concorrenza diventa un "superprincipio". Retrieved from http://www.giustamm.it
Foà, S. (2014). I soggetti partecipanti alle gare. In C. E. Gallo (Ed.), *Autorità e consenso nei contratti pubblici alla luce delle direttive* (p. 25 ff.). Torino: Giappichelli.
Janssen, W. A. (2014). The institutionalised and non-institutionalised exemptions from EU public procurement law: Towards a more coherent approach? *Utrecht Law Review, 10*(5), 168–186.
Kotsonis, T. (2014). The 2014 utilities directive of EU: Codification, flexibilisation and other misdemeanours. *Public Procurement Law Review, 4*, 169–187.
Mazzamuto, M. (2013). *L'apparente neutralità comunitaria sull'autoproduzione pubblica: Dall'in house al Partenariato "Pubblico-Pubblico"* (Vol. 6, pp. 1416–1420). Italian Jurisprudence.
Torchia, L. (2016). La nuova direttiva europea in materia di appalti servizi e forniture nei settori ordinari. In G. Della Torre (Ed.), *La nuova disciplina dei contratti pubblici tra esigenze di semplificazione, rilancio dell'economia e contrasto alla corruzione: Proceedings of the Atti del LXI Convegno di Studi di Scienza dell'Amministrazione, Varenna-Villa Monastero - 17-18-19 Settembre 2015* (pp. 131–186). Milano: Giuffrè.
Volpe, C. (2016). Le nuove direttive sui contratti pubblici e l'in house providing: problemi vecchi e nuovi. In G. Della Torre (Ed.), *La nuova disciplina dei contratti pubblici tra esigenze di semplificazione, rilancio dell'economia e contrasto alla corruzione: Proceedings of the Atti del LXI Convegno di Studi di Scienza dell'Amministrazione, Varenna-Villa Monastero - 17-18-19 Settembre 2015* (pp. 225–261). Milano: Giuffrè.

Economic Operator of Third Countries

Valentina Colcelli

1 Introduction

Directive 2014/24/UE defines 'economic operator' as any natural or legal person or public entity or group of such persons and/or entities, including any temporary association of undertakings, which offers the execution of works and/or a work, the supply of products or the provision of services on the market (art. 2, par. 1, point 10). The Directive explains how

> . . . the notion of "economic operators" should be interpreted in a broad manner so as to include any persons and/or entities which offer the execution of works, the supply of products or the provision of services on the market, irrespective of the legal form under which they have chosen to operate. Thus, firms, branches, subsidiaries, partnerships, cooperative societies, limited companies, universities, public or private, and other forms of entities than natural persons should all fall within the notion of economic operator, whether or not they are "legal persons" in all circumstances. (Directive 2014/24/UE, Whereas n. 14).

In short, these definitions confirm the 'substantial prospective, adopted by the European lawmakers' (e.g. chapter "Economic Operators of Third Countries") on the status of the economic operator as a derogation of a subjective prospective for the application of procedures with public evidence.

In this legal framework, this paper focalises its analysis on the definition of the status of 'economic operators of third countries' in the application of Directive 2014/24/UE on public procurement.

This analysis takes into consideration how the status of the economic operators of third countries must conscientiously respect the principle of reciprocity, meaning that contracting authorities must apply the principle of non-discrimination in the treatment of all economic operators, whether or not they come from European

V. Colcelli (✉)
National Research Council, IFAC Institute, Sesto Fiorentino, Firenze, Italy
e-mail: valentina.colcelli@cnr.it

A. Bartolini et al. (eds.), *Dictionary of Statuses within EU Law*,
https://doi.org/10.1007/978-3-030-00554-2_22

Union (EU) Member States, if they fall under the conditions established by Article 25 of Directive 2014/24/UE.

To reach this goal, the starting point of the paper will be the analysis of the principle of non-discrimination among the economic operators of EU Member States for the purposes of analysing how the principle is applied to economic operators of third countries and when it is not. This paper will study the case of the economic operators of third countries within the multilateral framework of balanced rights and obligations relating to public contracts under the World Trade Organisation Agreement on Government Procurement (the GPA) and other international agreements. We will use the Italian application of Article 49 of the Code of Public Procurement as the parameters for the previously mentioned distinction. In section 4, we provide our conclusion, taking into consideration the situation of the United Kingdom (UK) economic operators after the European Union exit.

2 The Principle of Equality Among the Economic Operators

Since February 2014, when the EU legislature adopted the three most recent significant measures in the (…) field (…) of EU public procurement regime (…) [Directive 2014/23/EU, Directive 2014/24/EU and Directive 2014/25/EU], [the EU] supplements the general principles of EU law applied under the Treaty on the Functioning of the EU ("TFEU"), particularly the fundamental freedoms [for enterprises and economic operators]: the free movement of goods, the freedom to provide services and the right of establishment in any Member State (Brexit paper 9 2017, p. 3).

"Contracting authorities shall treat economic operators equally and without discrimination and shall act in a transparent and proportionate manner" (Article 18 of Directive 2014/24/EU). "The principle of equality ensures that all candidates in public procurement processes are subject to exactly the same conditions for submission and evaluation of tenders and are treated in exactly the same way" (Georgieva 2017, p. 6).

Article 18 imposes, for public procurement, the more general principle underpinning the internal market established in the Article 34 TFUE (Graells 2015, p. 275). The principle of non-discrimination is the fundamental principles of the internal market (i.e., different treatment under the same circumstances) on grounds of nationality (*Dassonville*, case C-8/74). It is well known that, as regards the movement of goods, with the judgment in *Dassonville*, and "cassis de dijon" (C-120/78) too, the European Court of Justice extended the review of compatibilities to directly discriminatory national measures and, later, to indirectly discriminatory national measures—in force in the Member State of destination—with regard to the discipline of freedoms of the Economic Community. These historic rulings provide for the system's recourse to mutual recognition by introducing the assessment of the compatibilities of State measures—even indirectly applicable—which constitute an obstacle to the free movement of goods. Under the former Article 12 EC Treaty, treating imported goods differently from domestic goods was prohibited.

The jurisprudence of the European Court of Justice extended the same principle to freedom of movement for workers (*Bosman*, C-415/93), in respect of professional qualifications, banking, insurance and financial services. Furthermore, there is a broader meaning with regard to the principle of mutual recognition, freedom of movement of persons and the right of establishment.

The principle was stressed by the European Court of Justice and adapted to services, where the discrimination was considered from the point of view of both nationality and residence (*Säger*, case C-76/90). Additionally, this principle also firmly applies in the field of company law, especially in the area of 'freedom of establishment of the companies' in the European Single Market (*Gebhard*, case C-55/94), grounding the Freedom of Establishment of Companies 49, from TFEU.

The principle of non-discrimination is one of the rules intended to safeguard, structure and preserve the EU internal market under the light of EU discipline of competition and the area of European public and private law (Arts. 101, 102 et seq., TFUE). The 'economic' regulation has to guarantee allocative efficiency, but also must covenant with externalities and informational asymmetries. In the field of public procurement, the principle of non-discrimination is close to the principle of transparency, where it is 'mainly to do with the amount of information to be provided on orders and procedures, and the publicity of the actions/inactions of the contracting authorities on selection of a contractor' (Georgieva 2017, p. 3). As matter a of fact, in the field of completion law, 'the obligation not to discriminate applies to the institutions of central governments as well as to the institution of regional or local public authorities (see *Stopover Tax*, case C-169/08)' (Torino 2017, p. 12), so the principle must also work for the public procurements.

3 Economic Operators of Third Countries Above and Below Thresholds

The principle of non-discrimination works only among economic operators from EU Member States and economic operators of third countries that fall under the condition established in 'Whereas n. 17' and Article 25 of Directive 2004/18/EC.

According to Council Decision 94/800/EC, by which the European Community approved the World Trade Organisation Agreement on Government Procurement, there was established a 'multilateral framework of balanced rights and obligations relating to public contracts with a view to achieving the liberalisation and expansion of world trade.' This means that 'for contracts covered by Annexes 1, 2, 4 and 5 and the General Notes to the European Union's Appendix I to the GPA, as well as by other relevant international agreements by which the Union is bound, contracting authorities should fulfil the obligations under those agreements by applying' the Directive 2014/24/EU 'to economic operators of third countries that are signatories to the agreements.'

The Agreement on Government Procurement (GPA) is a multilateral arrangement within the framework of the World Trade Organisation that ensures open, fair and transparent conditions of competition in the government procurement markets. The GPA applies to those WTO members that have negotiated the Agreement and applies to contracts above certain thresholds. These thresholds are different from the thresholds laid down by the Directive 2014/24/ECU, but in any case are very high.

Directive 2014/24/EU takes into consideration the 1994 version of the GPA, the coverage of which was structured in 5 annexes plus general notes. 'In the revised 2011 version (effective 2014), the coverage was reorganised in 7 annexes, the last being the general notes themselves. Both annex structures however have in common that Annex 3 deals with the coverage of "other entities." Directive 2014/24/EU refers to the 1994 version of the GPA (still in force when it was approved)' (Telles and Sanchez-Graells 2016), as amended—with reference to Council Decision 2014/115/EU on the conclusion of the Protocol Amending the Agreement on Government Procurement, which means 'everything but Annex 3 on other entities' (Telles and Sanchez-Graells 2016).

So, economic operators of third countries will benefit from equal treatment with EU economic operators if the third country—where they came from—signed the GPA and apply for public procurement of supplies, works and services by EU governments, regional and local authorities and non-governmental entities that cover specific minimum threshold values bounded by the latter GPA or other international agreements. Under these conditions, the economic operators of third countries do not have the same rights as the EU economic operator applying public procurement that is realized in one of the EU Member States by contracting authorities.

We have also referred to 'other relevant international agreements by which the Union is bound.' We mean, for instance, the Comprehensive Economic and Trade Agreement between Canada and the European Union (CETA) or the Transatlantic Trade and Investment Partnership between the United States and the European Union (TTIP). Both CETA and TTIP have a chapter on public procurement market access open in the negotiations. As regards these international agreements, the treatment of the economic operator of third country in EU public procurement is conditioned by thresholds of the public contracts established in these international agreements.

In the Italian legal system, Article 25 of Directive 2014/24/EU is encompassed in Article 49 of the Public Procurement Code (Legislative Decree No. 50 of 18 April 2016), nearly verbatim:

In so far as they are covered by Annexes 1, 2, 4 and 5 and the General Notes to the European Union's Appendix I to the GPA and by the other international agreements by which the Union is bound, contracting authorities shall accord to the works, supplies, services and economic operators of the signatories to those agreements treatment no less favourable than the treatment accorded to the works, supplies, services and economic operators of the Union.

Article 49 clarifies—compared to the wording of Article 47 of the former Italian Public Procurement Code—how the principle of non-discrimination governs access in the Italian public market by economic operators coming from the signatory countries of international agreements or established in the EU legal system.

To recognise whether or not a non-EU economic operator is established in the internal market, the Italian Regional Administrative Courts ruled the following criteria: the secondary offices of an enterprise (even if organised in a corporate form) do not count as autonomous centres of legal imputation if the activity carried out by the person in charge of the secondary office—both in substance and in procedure—is under the responsibility of the undertaking as a whole (Regional Administrative Courts of Veneto, section I, 14 August 2006, n. 2453). Although, with regard to the World Trade Organisation system (Article 5, para. 5, sec. b) and the section entitled 'permanent establishment', it could be possible qualified as a 'branch' the company that, while an articulation of the parent company, only operates as a subsidiary. In the case analysed by the Italian Regional Administrative Court, the applicant was the head office of the parent company, which was located in the United States, and as such could not serve as an independent centre of legal imputation; despite this branch's permanent establishment in Italy, it could not be imbued with the autonomic decisions of the parent company in the United States. Therefore, in this situation, involving the tender, a company under U.S. law could be precisely applicable in Appendix 1 to the GPA, as referred to in Article 3 of the GPA. (Regional Administrative Courts of Lazio, 15 September 2017, no. 9734).

It is not part of the obligations already imposed on states and administrations by the EU legal system for purchases from economic operators in third countries below the threshold. For instance, the Legislative Decree No. 50 of 18 April 2016 excludes U.S. companies from supplies under 200,000 SDRs.

Purchases by economic operators in third countries that are monetarily below the threshold are outside the scope of Article 49. In the previous situation, at the time of making a choice, there can be no total equivalence among Italian or EU or non-EU suppliers of economic operators from third countries that are established in the EU when the economic operators from third countries are not set in the EU. Otherwise, the value of Article 49 would be nullified. There is a duty applied to contracting authorities to not buy, at purchase values below the threshold, 'widespread/general' supplies or services from economic operators in third countries. A purchase from an economic operator of a third country—outside the scope of Article 49—must be justified by the fact that the economic operator of the third country is the only specific supplier capable of supplying the goods or services in question, and that there are no reasonable alternatives or substitute products or services for reasons such as a lack of competition in a particular area of technology, etc. The economic advantage alone cannot be a sufficient reason.

4 Extra-Territorial Application of EU Directives on Procurement. Some Conclusions

Starting from the article of chapter "Economic Operators of Third Countries", which explores the status of the economic operator as qualified by the European lawmaker and jurisprudence, this paper focalises its analysis on the definition of the economic operator of third countries in the application of the Directive 2014/24/UE on public procurement. This analysis will take into consideration how the status of the economic operator of third countries must conscientiously respect the principle of reciprocity. This means that contracting authorities have to apply the principle of non-discrimination in the treatment of all economic operators, whether or not they come from EU Member States, if the latter fall under the multilateral framework of balanced rights and obligations relating to public contracts under the GPA or other international agreements.

Two requirements are established by 'Whereas n. 17' and Article 25 of Directive 2004/18/EC for the extra-territorial application of directives on public procurement: (a) to be Members that have negotiated the GPA or other international agreements; and, (b) public procurement of supplies, works and services by EU governments, regional and local authorities and non-governmental entities specify the minimum threshold values bounded by the GPA and other international agreements.

The first requirement explains how the 'EU competence in the area of public procurement brings benefits beyond the EU internal market' (*Brexit Paper 9: Public procurement post-Brexit*, Brexit Working Group/European Law Committee, April 2017, p. 10).

So, to determine who could be qualified as economic operators of third countries according to Directive 2004/18/EC, we have to take into consideration the economic operators that come from countries that are parties to the GPA and other agreements. On the other side, if a country is part of one of international agreements, its economic operators could not be qualified to take part in public procurement of supplies, works and services by EU governments, regional and local authorities and non-governmental entities if the public contract is under the minimum threshold values.

In this framework, we take into consideration the UK situation after Brexit, and whether British economic operators can continue to access significant procurement in the EU market, given that Brexit could have economically different consequences in terms of procurement (Sandulli 2017).

First, the United Kingdom, as a single country, is not part of the GPA; its participation in the GPA was tied to its membership in the EU. After Brexit, UK enterprises can only continue to be qualified as economic operators of a third country if the UK applies to join WTO rules. In so doing, the United Kingdom will continue to benefit from WTO rights and may, in due course, negotiate trade agreements with third countries close to the position reached by the EU in its trade agreements. Outside of taking this action, the United Kingdom's economic operators can no longer apply for public procurement in the EU. Of course, it is possible that there could be the adoption of specific rules going beyond or deviating from EU rules designed for UK economic operators, but such accommodations clearly would have to be extended to SMEs or other specific categories of suppliers. Even if the UK joins the GPA, such does not guarantee liberalised access to public procurement and other services markets in public contracts with values under the minimum threshold values. Usually, the SMEs are able to apply for public procurements under the minimum threshold values, not above the threshold.

References

Brexit Working Group/European Law Committee. (2017). *Brexit Paper: Public Procurement Post-Brexit*, 9. Retrieved from http://www.europarl.europa.eu/RegData/etudes/STUD/2017/602028/IPOL_STU(2017)602028_EN.pdf

Georgieva, I. (2017). The EU principles in public procurement. Transparency – Origin and main characteristics. Using transparency against corruption in public procurement. *Studies in European Economic Law and Regulation, 11*, 5–46.

Graells, A. S. (2015). *Public procurement and the EU competition rules* (pp. 3–314). Oxford: Hart Publishing.

Sandulli, M. A. (2017). I possibili effetti della Brexit sull'affidamento dei contratti pubblici di appalto e di concessione disciplinati dalle direttive UE 23, 24 e 25 del 2014. *Federalismi.it, 16*, 3–14.

Telles, P., & Sanchez-Graells, A. (2016). Regulation 25 – Conditions relating to the GPA and other international agreements. *Public Contracts Regulations 2015 Commentary*. http://pcr2015.uk/regulations/regulation-25-conditions-relating-to-the-gpa-and-other-international-agreements/ (last visited 11.06.2018)

Torino, R. (2017). The internal market short history and basic concepts. In R. Torino (Ed.), *Introduction to European Union internal market law* (pp. 1–33). Rome: Roma TrePress.

Elderly People

Francesca Polacchini

1 Introduction

The higher life expectancy is probably one of the most notable change in the European Union (EU) context, and it is determining a transition towards a much older population structure. Ageing is undoubtedly a challenge for society and for all generations in Europe, and it is also a matter for intergenerational solidarity and for the family, as underlined by Decision No. 940/2011/EU of the European Parliament and of the Council of 14 September 2011 on the European Year for Active Ageing and Solidarity between Generations. This demographic development is likely to have a considerable impact on a wide range of policy areas: with respect to the different health and care requirements of the elderly, to the labour market, social security and pension systems, economic resources, as well as government finances. This article will explore the EU legal and political system in the matter of elderly people and analyse the status of elderly rights recognised by the EU legal order and by the case law of the Court of Justice of the EU (the Court).

2 A Brief Overview on the Rights of Elderly People in International Treaties

Before analysing the status of the elderly people in the context of the EU, it is useful to mention some of the international instruments of protection of rights of elderly people. These international documents demonstrate that regional organisations

---

F. Polacchini (✉)
Department of Legal Science, University of Bologna, Bologna, Italy
e-mail: francesca.polacchini@unibo.it

A. Bartolini et al. (eds.), *Dictionary of Statuses within EU Law*,
https://doi.org/10.1007/978-3-030-00554-2_23

promoting human rights have recently opted for a legally binding instrument specifically devoted to the rights of elderly people.

Three regional human rights instruments expressly mention elderly people as a group that needs special protection. The African Charter on Human and Peoples' Rights stipulates that the 'Older Persons and people with disabilities shall also have the right to special measures of protection in keeping with their physical or moral needs' (Article 18, para. 4). In January 2006, the African Union adopted the Protocol to the African Charter on the Rights of Older Persons in Africa, which aims to promote and protect the rights of elderly people and guarantee that they fully contribute and participate in social and political life.

The Inter-American Convention on Protecting the Human Rights of Older Persons (the Convention) recognises several elderly rights, such as the right to life and dignity in old age, the right to independence and autonomy, the right to participation and community integration, the right to safety and to a life free of violence of any kind, the right to receive long-term care, the right to social security, the right to work, etc. The purpose of the Convention—the first regional instrument of its kind in the world—is to promote and ensure the recognition and the full enjoyment and exercise, on an equal basis, of all human rights and fundamental freedoms by elderly people, in order to contribute to their full inclusion, integration and participation in society (Rodriguez-Pinzón and Martin 2003).

Within the framework of the Council of Europe (the Council), the Revised European Social Charter sets the right to social protection for the elderly in Article 23, which states that the parties undertake to adopt appropriate measures: (a) to enable the elderly to remain full members of society for as long as possible by providing adequate resources and information about available services; (b) to enable the elderly to choose their life-style freely and live independently for as long as possible by providing adequate housing and services; and (c) to guarantee support for older persons living in institutions.

3 The EU Legal and Political Framework on Elderly People in a Diachronic Perspective

The process of EU integration is marked by an increasing attention on the figure of the elderly people and their role in society, although a definition of 'elderly' is still lacking. The most common ages used for statistical and practical purposes are 60 and 65 years, which may also be the ages at which retirement from work officially takes place and a state pension becomes available (Cole and Cole 1997). Originally, in fact, the EU definition of 'elderly' referred to the work status of the citizen. Certainly, the question of the worker or the former worker status of an elderly person must be understood within the context of the economical aims of the EU (Article 3 of the Treaty on European Union [TEU]). However, flowing from the fundamental changes within the EU, from a purely economic EU to a supranational organisation with general aims, elderly people are no longer defined by their labour status. They have become citizens at the Member State and Union levels. The concept of citizenship now encompasses civil, political and cultural rights, and it extends beyond solely social and economic rights (Evrard and Lacour 2012).

In 1997, the Treaty of Amsterdam assigned to the EU the competence to combat discrimination based on sex, ethnic origin, religion or belief, age or sexual orientation (see Article 13 of the Treaty Establishing the European Community (TEC). Indeed, the 'age' question had been on the policy agenda since 1982, when the European Parliament issued a resolution on the situation and problems of the elderly in the European Community. It was followed in 1986 by a European Parliament resolution on services for the elderly and a European Parliament resolution on Community measures to improve the situation of elderly people. The year 1986 was also proposed by the European Parliament as the European Year of the Elderly.

Article 13 of the TEU provided a specific legal basis for the development of legislation on age-based discrimination, which was absent until this juncture. The power contained in Article 13 TEU was subsequently used as a basis for the enactment of the Council Directive 2000/78/EC of 27 November 2000 (the 'Framework Employment Equality Directive'), which established a general framework for equal treatment in employment and occupation (Bell 2002). According to Article 1 of the Directive 2000/78/EC:

> The purpose of this Directive is to lay down a general framework for combating discrimination on the grounds of religion or belief, disability, age or sexual orientation as regards employment and occupation, with a view to putting into effect in the Member States the principle of equal treatment. (Article 1).

By virtue of Article 6 of the Directive 2000/78/EC, Member States may provide differences of treatment on grounds of age solely if, 'within the context of national law, they are objectively and reasonably justified by a legitimate aim, including legitimate employment policy, labour market and vocational training objectives, and if the means of achieving that aim are appropriate and necessary'.

In 2000, the Charter of Fundamental Rights of the EU (the Charter of Rights) was adopted. Article 21 prohibits discrimination on the grounds of age, and Article 25—titled 'The Rights of Elderly'—states that the 'Union recognises and respects the rights of the elderly to lead a life of dignity and independence and to participate in social and cultural life'. Dignity, independence and participation are the core rights recognised to elderly people. This provision included for the first time a specific reference to rights of elderly people and would potentially change the Court landscape in this specific field. The explanatory report to the Charter of Rights indicates that the rights referred to in Article 25 must be interpreted in light of Article 23 of the Revised Social Charter and the Community Charter of the Fundamental Social Rights of Workers, and that participation in social life includes the right to participate in political life. In 2009, the Treaty of Lisbon conferred binding force to the Charter of Rights, which provide an abundant range of civil, political, economic and social rights relevant for elderly people, such as the rights to non-discrimination, social security, health care and education. Until the entry into force of the Treaty of

Lisbon and the recognition of the legal binding value to the Charter of Rights, the 'elderly' were not recognised as individuals who have their own subjective legal status (Doron 2013).

Article 3, paragraph 3 of the TEU states that the EU should 'combat social exclusion and discrimination, and shall promote social justice and protection, equality between women and men, solidarity between generations and protection of the rights of the child'.

Within the framework of the Treaty on the Functioning of the European Union (TFEU), Article 10 sets that, 'in defining and implementing its policies and activities, the Union shall aim to combat discrimination based on sex, racial or ethnic origin, religion or belief, disability, age or sexual orientation'. Article 19 of the TFEU (formerly known as Article 13 of the TEC) contemplates:

> Without prejudice to the other provisions of the Treaties and within the limits of the powers conferred by them upon the Union, the Council, acting unanimously in accordance with a special legislative procedure and after obtaining the consent of the European Parliament, may take appropriate action to combat discrimination based on sex, racial or ethnic origin, religion or belief, disability, age or sexual orientation. (Article 19).

Finally, it is important to recall that the United Nation Convention on the Rights of Persons with Disabilities was the first international convention on human rights ratified in 2011 by the EU, which considered the needs of the ageing population in its application (Fredvang and Biggs 2012).

4 Some Instruments for the Implementation of Article 25 of the Charter of Fundamental Rights of the EU

It is possible to identify several legal measures that can be regarded as a form of implementation of Article 25 of the Charter of Rights. Following a chronologically descending approach, the Decision (EU) 2017/864 of the European Parliament and of the Council of 17 May 2017 on a European Year of Cultural Heritage (2018) underlines the importance to make the cultural heritage of cities accessible for persons with disabilities, elderly people and those with reduced mobility or other types of temporary impairments. Moreover, among the objectives of the European Year, there is the raising of the awareness of the importance of Europe's cultural heritage through education and lifelong learning; in particular, by focusing on children, young and elderly people, local communities and hard-to-reach groups.

Another significative action is the Directive (EU) 2016/2102 of the European Parliament and of the Council of 26 October 2016 on the accessibility of the websites and mobile applications of public sector bodies (the Web Accessibility Directive), which should make it easier for disabled and elderly people to access data and services on the internet (e.g., to file a tax declaration, apply for an allowance, pay fees or enrol at a university). This directive lays down the first EU-wide rules to ensure that the websites and apps of public sector bodies are made more accessible to users, in particular, elderly people and persons with disabilities. The right of the elderly to participate and be integrated in the social and cultural life of the EU is, in fact, inextricably linked to the provision of accessible audio-visual media services.

The importance of the use of technologies by elderly people had already been highlighted by the Decision No. 742/2008/EC of the European Parliament and of the Council of 9 July 2008 on the Community's participation in a research and development programme undertaken by several Member States aimed at enhancing the quality of life of older people through the use of new information and communication technologies. In the European Communication of 12 October 2006, entitled 'The demographic future of Europe - from challenge to opportunity', the European Commission (the Commission) underlined that demographic ageing is one of the main challenges facing all countries in the EU and that the increasing use of new technologies could help to control costs, improve well-being and promote the active participation in society of elderly people, as well as foster the competitiveness of the European economy, in support of the revised Lisbon Strategy for growth and jobs. In the field of information and communication technologies (ICT), the ageing of the population can be seen as an opportunity for an emerging market for new goods and services that respond to the needs of the elderly.

Finally, it is important to mention the Decision No. 940/2011/EU, which designated 2012 as the European Year for Active Ageing and Solidarity between Generations (EY2012). Promoting active and healthy ageing is also one of the investment priorities of the new European Social Fund for 2014–2020 (Davies 2014).

5 Active Ageing: The Key Principle of the EU Political and Legal Framework on Elderly People

Decision No. 940/2011/EU has the overall objective of changing attitudes towards elderly people, in order to offer them better opportunities to remain active and to participate as full members of society. Numerous soft law acts preceded Decision No. 940/2011/EU, as it can be inferred from its recitals. The importance of the concept of active ageing is, therefore, chorally recognised by EU institutions.

Decision No. 940/2011/EU recalls the definition of active ageing, as determined in 2002 by the World Health Organization's (WHO) policy framework. According to the WHO, active ageing is:

> the process of optimizing opportunities for health, participation and security in order to enhance quality of life as people age. It allows people to realise their potential for wellbeing throughout their lives and to participate in society according to their needs, desires and capabilities, while providing them with adequate protection, security and care when they need assistance. (2002 World Health Organization's policy framework).

Decision No. 940/2011/EU established the objectives, content of measures and the budget for this initiative. It contained specific provisions on the coordination with Member States at the EU and international level. It also obliged the Commission to assess its implementation and results, especially with regard to any lasting effects that were to be produced for the promotion of active ageing across the EU.

The contents and the objectives of the active ageing culture are expressed by Article 2 of the Decision No. 940/2011/EU, which states:

> Promoting active ageing means creating better opportunities so that older women and men can play their part in the labour market, combating poverty, particularly that of women, and social exclusion, fostering volunteering and active participation in family life and society and encouraging healthy ageing in dignity. (Article 2).

It is significant to note the succession with which Decision No. 940/2011/EU lists the contents of active aging, which initially valorises the participation in the labour market and only ultimately supports healthy ageing in dignified conditions. This is in line with what is expressed in the recital 11 of Decision No. 940/2011/EU: 'healthy ageing can help to raise the labour market participation of older people, enable them to be active in society for longer, improve their individual quality of life and limit pressure on health, social care and pension systems'. Therefore, active ageing encompasses two distinct profiles: one that shows a narrow economic focus on elderly workers, and the other shows a social focus on elderly people, which includes the whole life course.

The Council issued, on 6 December 2012, Guiding Principles on Active Ageing and Solidarity between Generations (the Principles), which operate as the basis for preserving and further developing the legacy of EY2012 at a European, national, regional and local level. The Principles comprise a preamble—starting with a reference to the projected 50% increase of the ration of people above 65 to those of working age (ages 15–64) by 2050—and are divided into three parts: (1) employment (including continuing vocational education and training, healthy work conditions, age management strategies, employment services for elder workers, preventing age discrimination, employment-friendly tax and benefit systems, transfer of experience and reconciliation of work and care), (2) participation in society (including income security, social inclusion, senior volunteering, life-long learning, participation in decision making and support for informal carers) and (3) independent living (including health promotion and disease prevention, adapted housing and services, accessible and affordable transport, age-friendly environments and goods and services and maximising autonomy in long-term care).

In summation, active aging policy aims to facilitate the capacity of elderly people to remain healthy (i.e., reducing the costs of health and social care), remain in employment longer (i.e., reducing pension costs) and also participate in social and political life. Rather than equating the oldest phase of life purely with a period of rest and inactivity, active aging discourse seeks to enable the participation of elderly people in society (Barrett and McGoldrick 2013).

6 The Prohibition of Discrimination on Grounds of Age as a General Principle of EU Law

Another form of protection enjoyed by the elderly is the indirect one that derives from the Court case law on the matter of non-discrimination. The principle of non-discrimination on grounds of age must be regarded as a general principle of Community law, as the Court affirmed in several judgments.

Starting with *Werner Mangold v. Rüdiger Helm* (2005),[1] the Court interpreted the specific prohibitions of discrimination in the new anti-discrimination law as an expression of a general principle of equality, to be regarded as a general principle of Community law, which already finds its source in various international instruments and in the constitutional traditions common to the Member States. From this principle the Court has drawn an unprecedented consequence, namely, the direct application of the principle of non-discrimination on grounds of age. Precisely, as affirmed in paragraph 76 and 77 of the *Mangold* decision:

> observance of the general principle of equal treatment, in particular in respect of age, cannot as such be conditional upon the expiry of the period allowed the Member States for the transposition of a directive intended to lay down a general framework for combating discrimination on the grounds of age, in particular so far as the organisation of appropriate legal remedies, the burden of proof, protection against victimisation, social dialogue, affirmative action and other specific measures to implement such a directive are concerned. In those circumstances it is the responsibility of the national court, hearing a dispute involving the principle of non-discrimination in respect of age, to provide, in a case within its jurisdiction, the legal protection which individuals derive from the rules of Community law and to ensure that those rules are fully effective, setting aside any provision of national law which may conflict with that law (para. 76, 77).

In *Kücükdeveci v. Swedex GmbH & Co. KG.* (2010),[2] the Court confirmed that 'the principle of non-discrimination on grounds of age is a general principle of European Union law in that it constitutes a specific application of the general principle of equal treatment' (para. 50).

More recently, in *Dansk Industry (DI) v. Estate of Karsten Eigil Rasmussen* (2016),[3] the Court reaffirmed that:

> the source of the general principle prohibiting discrimination on grounds of age, as given concrete expression by Directive 2000/78, is to be found, as is clear from recitals 1 and 4 of the directive, in various international instruments and in the constitutional traditions common to the Member States (see judgments in Mangold, C-144/04, EU:C:2005:709, paragraph 74, and Kücükdeveci, C-555/07, EU:C:2010:21, paragraphs 20 and 21). It is also apparent from the Court's case-law that that principle, now enshrined in Article 21 of the Charter of Fundamental Rights of the European Union, must be regarded as a general principle of EU law. (para. 22)

---

[1] Case C-144/04 *Werner Mangold v Rüdiger Helm* [2005].

[2] Case C-555/07 *Kücükdeveci v Swedex GmbH & Co. KG.* [2010].

[3] Case C-441/14 *Dansk Industry (DI) v Estate of Karsten Eigil Rasmussen* [2016].

The importance of the aforementioned case law of the Court in elderly people issues is clearly evident: through the direct application of the principle of non-discrimination on the grounds of age, the elderly can receive protection if they are affected by measures that, without a legitimate aim, determine discrimination against them because of their old age.

Apart from the disputes involving discriminations on the grounds of age, the Court—in its 'typical' elder rights case law—had to deal with legal issues of pensions relating to state funded pensions or employer-based occupational pensions. The rest of the cases were mostly age discrimination, mandatory retirement or attendance and home care (Doron 2013).

7 Conclusion

In light of the aforementioned EU legal and political framework, it is possible to try to outline the status of elderly people, which emerges from the EU legal system and the protection granted to elderly. EU policy responses to population ageing globally comprise both negative and positive strands. On the one hand, old age is commonly portrayed as a period of inactivity and dependency; while, on the other hand, elderly people are viewed as a social and economic resource (Foster and Walker 2015). Therefore, the legal protection of the elderly develops on two main fronts: the negative one, relating the prohibition of discrimination based on age in an overall perspective of anti-discriminatory law and the protection of elderly as a vulnerable person; and the positive one, concerning the active ageing and social promotion of the elderly.

The first dimension underlines that all elderly people should be able to live their lives in dignity and security, free from discrimination, isolation, violence, neglect and abuse. The second perspective stresses that elderly persons should be able to fully and effectively participate in social and political life and should be included in society. In line with the economistic aim that originally drawn inspiration to the European integration process and from which the EU has only partly emancipated, the figure of the elderly is valued in an active ageing dimension, such as to allow the elderly to remain an active subject of social and economic processes and to continue to be a consumer. Active ageing has emerged as the paramount policy response to the challenges of population aging.

Unlike the provisions of the international instruments mentioned above (paragraph 2), the needs of older people are dealt with within a purely generic framework in the EU legal system. This occurs because a construction of the elderly, as a social category that deserves an autonomous legal consideration, is still lacking. Specific legal safeguards tailored to the situation of older persons, protecting their specific needs, are still lacking (Martin et al. 2015). However, the European social model will have to face the effects of ageing population. In the Preamble of the Charter of Rights, a provision states: 'it is necessary to strengthen the protection of fundamental rights in the light of changes in society, social progress and scientific and technological developments by making those rights more visible in a Charter'. Certainly, one of the most significant changes in society is the ageing of the population, in which it will be necessary to rethink the protection of rights of the elderly. In this perspective, solidarity, intergenerational responsibility and respect between generations should likely be the key principles to be recognised and promoted as an essential feature of an active ageing policy that involves fairness between generations.

References

Barrett, G., & McGoldrick, C. (2013). Narratives of (in)active ageing in poor deprived areas of Liverpool. *International Journal of Sociology and Social Policy, 33*, 347–366.

Bell, M. (2002) *Anti-discrimination law and the European Union*. Oxford, England: Oxford University Press.

Cole, J., & Cole, F. (1997). *A geography of the European Union* (2nd ed.). London, England: Routledge.

Davies, R. (2014). *Older people in Europe: EU policies and programmes* [Briefing]. Retrieved from https://www.europarl.europa.eu/RegData/bibliotheque/briefing/2014/140811/LDM_BRI(2014)140811_REV1_EN.pdf

Doron, I. (2013). Older Europeans and the European Court of Justice. *Age and Ageing, 42*(5), 604–608.

Evrard, A., & Lacour, C. (2012). A European approach to developing the field of law and ageing. In I. Doron & A. Soden (Eds.), *Beyond elder law* (pp. 149–173). Berlin, Heidelberg: Springer.

Foster, L., & Walker, A. (2015). Active and successful aging: A European policy perspective. *The Gerontologist, 55*(1), 83–90.

Fredvang, M., & Biggs, S. (2012). *The rights of older persons: Protection and gaps under human rights law* (Social Policy Working Paper No. 16). Retrieved from https://social.un.org/ageing-working-group/documents/fourth/Rightsofolderpersons.pdf

Martin, C., Rodriguez-Pinzón, D., & Brown, B. (2015). *Human rights of older people: Universal and regional legal perspectives*. New York: Springer.

Rodriguez-Pinzón, D., & Martin, C. (2003). The international human rights status of elderly persons. *American University International Law Review, 18*(4), 915–1008.

Entrepreneur

Rainer Arnold and Lukas Cerny

1 Introduction

The entrepreneur is the central actor in the free market system of the European Union. EU primary and secondary law establishes rules on enabling, facilitating and restricting entrepreneurial activity. Article 16 of the EU Fundamental Rights Charter expresses the constitutional guarantee for doing business freely. However, the concept and substance of this right have not comprehensively been defined by legal texts or by jurisprudence. The restrictions of this right have to comply with the requirements of Article 52. The aim of this paper is to analyse the status of the "entrepreneur" and its adaptation to the transnational dimension of the common market.

2 On the Concept of Entrepreneur

Neither primary nor secondary EU law defines what an *entrepreneur* is. It seems possible to explain this concept only in a rather indirect way. One aspect is that Article 3.3 TEU qualifies as the general economic structure of the EU a highly competitive social market economy. The economic activity within this framework can only be that of an entrepreneur, defined by inherent characteristics: The entrepreneur's activity is creative, innovative and dynamic by introducing an economic profit-oriented action into the market process, based on the deployment of one's own capital, anticipation of the chances for economic success and the acceptance of economic risk.[1]

[1] See https://de.wikipedia.org/wiki/Unternehmer.

R. Arnold (✉) · L. Cerny
Faculty of Law - University of Regensburg, Regensburg, Germany

A. Bartolini et al. (eds.), *Dictionary of Statuses within EU Law*,
https://doi.org/10.1007/978-3-030-00554-2_24

EU law is characterised by a considerable terminological diversity indicating the typical fields of entrepreneurial activity: trader (Directive 85/577/EC; 2011/83/EU), supplier (Directive 97/7/EC), and "doing business" in Article 16 of the EU Fundamental Rights Charter[2] (a term which comes close to "entrepreneurial" but is rather neutral) while other (German, French or Spanish) language versions of this Article are terminologically much more precise,[3] though without providing a definition.

While the Charter has introduced—at least in some of the linguistic versions of Article 16—the term "enterprise, entrepreneurial", though without explaining its content, the period before has also been characterised by terminological uncertainty. The term, initially used often, has been broad and relatively weak: the unwritten principle of free "economic activity", as already expressed in the early *Nold*[4] case. The existence of an explicit fundamental right guaranteeing free entrepreneurial activity by article 16 of the Charter has inspired the successive jurisprudence to reflect on the reach and nature of this right. Thus, the decision in the *Sky Österreich* case (EuGH, 22.01.2013 - C-283/11) gives insight into a spectrum of substantive aspects which belong to this freedom. Quite generally it is said that the freedom to conduct a business (a formulation used by Article 16 of the Charter which can conceptually be equated to the above-mentioned formulation in the German, French and Spanish versions of Article 16) covers the freedom to exercise an economic or commercial activity, the freedom of contract, and free competition, an interpretation which is methodologically drawn from the explanations of the Convention *Praesidium* relating to the Charter, which are a "valuable tool of interpretation" for it.[5] Besides this, the Court specifies that the freedom of contract includes the freedom "to choose with whom to do business"[6] and the freedom "to determine the price of a service".[7] This decision indicates some of the important aspects of the entrepreneurial activity, introduces free competition into the argumentation and qualifies this element, consequently, as a right as well as the objective condition for the deployment of this activity. The term "free exercise of an economic activity" (which

---

[2] In the following text called "Charter".

[3] German: "unternehmerische Freiheit"; French: "liberté d'entreprise"; Spanish: "libertad de empresa".

[4] ECLI:EU:C:1974:51; Case 4/73, Judgment May 14, 1974, paras. 14, 15. However, this judgement uses also the word "undertaking" and speaks of the right "freely to choose and practice (their) trained profession" (para. 14) as well as of "economic activity", which needs the appropriate evaluation of the economic situation and the necessary steps for adaptation, referring to the "uncertainties" inherent in economic activity, that means to the inherent element of "risk". By this, the judgement characterises essential aspects of entrepreneurial activity without putting forward a clear-cut definition of it.

[5] Off. Journal EU, December 14, 2007, C 303/17. See for the applicability of the explanations article 52 (7) of the Charter. See also Case C-279/09 *DEB* [2010] ECR I-13849, para. 32 as referred to by the Court in Sky Österreich (EuGH, 22.01.2013 - C-283/11), para. 42.

[6] Referring to Joined Cases C-90/90 and C-91/90 *Neu* [1991] ECR I-3617, paragraph 13.

[7] Referring to Case C-437/04 *Commission* v *Belgium* [2007] ECR I-2513, paragraph 51, and Case C-213/10 *F-TEX* [2012] ECR, paragraph 45.

includes a commercial activity) indicates the very basic right in this context, but does not characterize clearly the entrepreneurial specificities. This corresponds to a broad and rather indeterminate concept of Article 16 of the charter in literature, such as "the offer of goods and services on a certain market" (what gets close to the field of competition). (Wollenschläger 2015, S. 287). The EU CJ jurisprudence after the *Sky Österreich* case does not essentially contribute to a further clarification, while Article 16 of the Charter is used as an argument relatively often. The decision of June 30, 2016, *Lidl GmbH & Co v. Freistaat Sachsen* (ECLI:EU:C:2016:498), summarises[8] that this activity covers essentially the "right of every undertaking to freely dispose of its own economic, technical and financial resources within the limits of its responsibility for its own actions". This means that the undertaking has the right to use its resources for economic finalities, a right which underlies restrictions for legitimate social needs. The successive jurisprudence does not contribute to a more precise notion of entrepreneur. The formulas developed by the precedent jurisprudence are continuously repeated.

What could be mentioned is the distinction between the exercise of economic and of commercial activity, both terms used as aspects of the freedom to do business covered by Article 16 of the Charter. (ECLI:EU:C:2017:989). This could be understood in the way that commercial activity is profit-oriented while economic activity is broader and could also be carried out by charitable, non-profit enterprises. However, the English term for the Article 16 protection is *doing business*, which gives a slight preference, in contrast to the other linguistic versions of Article 16 of the Charter,[9] for an overall understanding of Article 16 as a protection of *commercial*, profit-oriented activity.

In a first conclusion, the fundamental rights protection of the entrepreneur as embodied by Article 16 has to be conceived in a broad way, quite generally as the freedom of *economic activity on the market*, essentially determined by the free market system, with a detailed spectrum of subcategories. Much more attention is paid to the question of how far these fundamental rights can be restricted.

Article 15 of the Charter covers the freedom of professional activity, meaning the freedom to take up and exercise a certain profession which is able to satisfy a person's living. Independent entrepreneurial activity can be a special aspect of Article 15 (Wollenschläger 2015, p. 287) which refers to both dependent and independent professional activities. Article 17 of the Charter protects property as a substance and not the processes to gain property by professional or entrepreneurial activity. The fundamental rights of Articles 15 to 17 of the Charter are the cornerstones of the economic constitutional order of the European Union (Bernsdorff, in: Meyer 2014, para. 1), accompanied by the principle of the free market system based on free competition which, of course, has to comply with the societal interests and therefore is a social market system.

---

[8] Referring to the decision of March 27, 2014, UPC Telekabel Wien, C-314/12, EU:C:2014:192, para. 49: http://curia.europa.eu/juris/celex.jsf?celex=62012CJ0314&lang1=de&type=TXT&ancre=.

[9] See *supra* note 3.

Apart from the charter rights, EU primary and secondary law specify the rights and duties of the entrepreneur in certain fields (competition, public procurement, etc.). The interpretation of "undertakings" or of similar terms is essentially related to the functions of the EU provisions in the correspondent fields; a functional approach is therefore needed. Of course, authorisations of and restrictions on economic activity (as entrepreneurial activity) have to comply with Article 16 of the Charter: in the field of secondary law being compatible with this fundamental right, and in the field of primary law (which has the same rank as the charter) an adequate concordance between Article 16 of the Charter and the other primary law provisions has to be found.

3 Entrepreneurial Activity as a Freedom Protected by the Fundamental Rights Charter

3.1 The Field of Application of Article 16 of the Charter

A fundamental right exercises its protective function within the field of protection which is expressly laid down in the charter or in other parts of the primary law or implicitly existent in unwritten form to be made manifest by interpretation. A dynamic interpretation which is based on the idea of *effet utile* is practice of the EU courts as well as (with methodological influence on the EU jurisprudence) of the European Court of Human Rights. Unwritten aspects of a written guarantee can be deployed by interpretation. As Article 6(3) TEU shows, interpretation can also result in pointing out general principles of EU law which are complementary to the written (or unwritten) Charter rights.

The field of application of Article 16 of the Charter is broad; it embraces the starting, continuing and termination of an entrepreneurial activity (Bernsdorff in Meyer 2014, para. 10a).

Not only physical but also legal persons are entitled to invoke this right. (Sasse 2012, p. 628ff.)

It should be mentioned in this context that the main substantive freedoms which the entrepreneur enjoys are protected by the fundamental freedoms, in particular by the freedom of establishment (Art. 49 TFEU). They complement the fundamental right and give substance to it. While the fundamental freedoms are primarily directed against discrimination and not justified restrictions established by the Member States, they are also orientations and even limits for EU secondary law. Therefore, the fundamental freedoms reinforce the fundamental right of doing business. As to the freedom of establishment, it protects the whole process of independent business action, the core activity of the entrepreneur. The free movement of goods and services has also essential relevance in this field. It is evident that the free movement of workers is of great importance for an efficient transnational organization of business. As entrepreneurship is the fundamental type of economic activity within an open market system, basically all the essential provisions of EU primary and secondary law are entrepreneur-related, either liberalising transnational business or restricting what has to be legitimised under Article 16 of the Charter and the fundamental freedoms.

3.2 The Restrictions of the Entrepreneurial Freedom

The restriction of the fundamental right covered by Article 16 of the Charter is a frequent issue in jurisprudence. The interventions into this right are numerous; the social (societal) function of this right is often expressed by the Court.[10]

The freedom to do business (freedom of entrepreneurial activity) is "recognised" by Article 16 of the Charter; however, it is a fully efficient fundamental right in the classic sense as the right of defence against public power (EU and, according to Article 51(1) of the Charter, Member States') intervention (Wollenschläger 2015, p. 286).

The text of Article 16 of the Charter guarantees the right only "in accordance with Union law and national laws and practices". Is this the door for a large, indefinite number of restrictions which can be easily formulated by the national legislators profiting from a broad political discretionary power? Jurisprudence as well as literature keep the possibility for restrictions in compliance with Article 52 (1) of the Charter. This means in particular that the restrictions have to be proportional and are not allowed to affect the very essence of the fundamental right (von der Groeben et al. 2015, Art. 52 paras. 5–9). Proportionality is conceived, in accordance with the preceding jurisprudence of the ECJ[11] and the understanding developed by the German Constitutional Court, in three elements.[12] The intervention must be *apt* to fulfil or to contribute to the fulfilment of a legitimate public interest, must be *necessary* (that means that no less intervening measure is possible to obtain the same result) and must be *proportional* in a narrow sense. This last element presupposes the comparison of the individual and the public interest. The intensity and seriousness of the intervention must be adequate to the finality to be pursued.[13]

4 Normative Concretions of Entrepreneurial Activity

EU primary and secondary law contains many provisions which enable, facilitate or restrict entrepreneurial activity. Only some of the most important can be indicated here. An important field is competition law which gives room to free economic and

[10] See, for example, C-157/14, Neptune Distribution SNC, judgement of 17 December 2015, para. 66 or C-277/16, Polkomtel, judgement of 20 December 2017, para. 50.

[11] See ECJ Hauer case, ECLI:EU:C:1979:290, para. 5 and many subsequent decisions.

[12] See the early decision of the German Federal Constitutional Court vol. 16, pp. 194, 204.

[13] See EUCJ C-157/14, Neptune Distribution SNC, para. 68.

entrepreneurial transactions. Articles 101 and 102 TFEU are central for the efficient and free deployment of business; the entrepreneur could not freely act if the market is not open but distorted by unlawful agreements or practices or dominant market power is abused. Public undertakings (Art. 106 TFEU) as important market actors are also submitted to the competition rules. A preventive control to ensure the free market is effectuated with regard to fusion of economic actors with significant market power. The free market as a precondition for the efficiency of transnational entrepreneurial activity is also ensured by the prohibition of financial aids from side of the Member States protecting own enterprises (Arts. 107–109 TEU). An important complex of entrepreneur-related (secondary law) provisions are those on public procurement ensuring transparency and fair competition for enterprises throughout the European Union.

Many other fields of action are relevant for the entrepreneurs: in particular environmental protection law with manifold detailed obligations which affects directly the market activities.[14] The energy policy also impacts importantly the economic sector and has therefore relevance for transnational business.[15] The same can be said for research and technology, for the fields of labour and social policy.[16] The European Data Protection Regulation will be applicable as of 25 May 2018 in all Member States to harmonise data privacy laws across Europe.[17]

5 The Transnationalisation of Business Activities: The New Status of the Entrepreneur

The European Union has transformed the role of the entrepreneur from one with a predominantly national field of activity into one who exists in the transnational context comprising the economic area of all the Member States. This integration process has embedded the entrepreneur into a new supranational legal order.

EU law and jurisprudence have significant impact on the entrepreneur's daily activity. This has not only transformed the entrepreneur into a transnational actor but also has a decisive influence on business management. This implies the necessity for all forms of entrepreneurship to be aware of this interconnection with supranational legal and economic developments.

---

[14] For example, Regulation (EU) No. 517/2014 on fluorinated greenhouse gases; see also Directive 2009/29/EC concerning the greenhouse gas emission allowance trading scheme of the Community.

[15] See the Directive 2009/28/EC on the promotion of the use of energy from renewable sources or Directive 2009/72/EC concerning common rules for the internal market in electricity.

[16] See the Directive 2003/88/EC of the European Parliament and of the Council of 4 November 2003 concerning certain aspects of the organization of working time.

[17] Regulation (EU) 2016/679 on the protection of natural persons with regard to the processing of personal data and on the free movement of such data.

References

Meyer, J. (2014). *Charta der Grundrechte der Europäischen Union*. Baden-Baden: Nomos Verlag.

Sasse, T. (2012). Die Grundrechtsberechtigung juristischer Personen durch die unternehmerische Freiheit gemäß Art. 16 der Europäischen Grundrechtecharta. *Europarecht (EuR)*, 628–654.

von der Groeben, H., Schwarze, J., & Hatje, A. (2015). *Europäisches Unionsrecht, (I)* (7th ed.). Baden-Baden: Nomos Verlag.

Wollenschläger, F. (2015). Die unternehmerische Freiheit (Art. 16 GRCh) als grundrechtlicher Pfeiler der EU-Wirtschaftsverfassung. In *Konturen in der Charta-Rechtsprechung des EuGH* (pp. 285–288). EuZW.

Ethics Advisor on Research Projects

Roberto Cippitani

1 Ethical Dimensions of Europe as a Knowledge-Based Society

Legal sources and other institutional documents of the European Union (hereinafter 'the EU') refer to Europe as a 'knowledge-based' society and economy (Cippitani 2012).

Officially, the first among such documents was the 1995 White Paper on 'Growth, Competitiveness and Employment' that was drawn up by the Commission led by Jacques Delors. Other texts have developed the idea, until the moment when knowledge became the hub of the European institutions' policy in the so-called 'Lisbon Strategy' launched by the European Council in March 2000.

According to these documents, in order to solve the problems of the European economy and society (i.e. low growth and low employment levels), the Union had to become 'the most competitive and dynamic knowledge-based economy in the world, capable of sustainable economic growth with more and better jobs and greater social cohesion' (Presidency Conclusions of European Council of Lisbon).

The political process that began in Lisbon was confirmed over the next decade by the 'Europe 2020' strategy[1] proposed by the Commission and approved by the European Council in June 2010.

[1] European Commission, 'Europe 2020 A strategy for smart, sustainable and inclusive growth', COM(2010) 2020 final, 3 March 2010.

R. Cippitani (✉)
Department of Medicine, Università degli Studi di Perugia, Perugia, Italia
e-mail: roberto.cippitani@unipg.it

A. Bartolini et al. (eds.), *Dictionary of Statuses within EU Law*,
https://doi.org/10.1007/978-3-030-00554-2_25

'Knowledge', in EU sources, consists of the interrelation of three elements: research, innovation, and education and training.[2]

In particular, an important role in the integration process is played by research (in relation to EU politics on research, see Molina del Pozo (2009)).[3]

As matter of fact, one of the objectives of the EU is to establishing the European Research Area ('ERA'), which is defined by Article 179, para. 1, of the Treaty of Functioning of the European Union (hereinafter referred to as the 'TFEU') as an area where 'researchers, scientific knowledge and technology circulate freely, and encouraging it to become more competitive, including in its industry'.

In order to build a true European Research Area,[4] the Union has to encourage the free circulation of researchers and cooperation between undertakings, research centres and universities, removing obstacles (particularly legal and fiscal ones) to this circulation and cooperation.

The EU texts underline the need to increase investment in research and innovation at a European level, as the main instrument for both economic and social development.[5]

Furthermore, according to EU law, freedom of research is considered as a fundamental right (Article 13 Charter of Fundamental Rights of the European Union, hereinafter referred to as the 'EU Charter') (Cippitani 2015).

However, to achieve the objective of building the European Research Area it is necessary to face the risks arising from scientific research and innovation.

As matter of fact, the EU Charter affirms that 'it is necessary to strengthen the protection of fundamental rights in the light of changes in society, social progress and scientific and technological developments' (see the Preamble of the EU Charter).

Therefore, in order to reinforce the protection of fundamental rights in a 'knowledge-based' society, Europe has to develop a system of shared values, through debate at various levels.[6]

In particular, the European Union has committed itself in recent years to identifying and elaborating 'ethical fundamental principles', that is to say, legal provisions as well as other kinds of rules (e.g. those established by case law, codes of practice, and opinions of ethics committees), whose scope is the protection of fundamental interests that may be affected by techno-science.

---

[2] See para. 3.3 of the Communication of the Commission to the Spring European Council, 'Working together for growth and jobs – A new start for the Lisbon Strategy', COM(2005) 24 final, 2 February 2005.

[3] Where 'Research and experimental development (R&D) comprise creative work undertaken on a systematic basis in order to increase the stock of knowledge, including knowledge of man, culture and society, and the use of this stock of knowledge to devise new applications'. (see OECD, 'Frascati Manual', 2002, para. 63).

[4] Communication of the Commission, 'Towards a European Research Area', COM (2000) 6 final, 18 January 2000.

[5] See Communication of the Commission to the Spring European Council, 'Working together for growth and jobs – A new start for the Lisbon Strategy', n. 2.

[6] Communication of the Commission, 'Towards a European Research Area', n. 4, para. 7.2.

This concern is expressed in the EU Charter, in particular; this is the first constitutional text to provide bioethical rules that establish the rights and limits to research and innovation activities (Mathieu 2009, p. 8).

2 Ethical Assessment of Projects Funded by EU Programmes

The EU takes into consideration the need to respect ethical rules, especially within the funding of the Framework Programmes. These are the main instruments that implement the European policy on research and technological development (see Article 180 TFEU).

The legal basis of the present Framework Programme, 'Horizon 2020', and of the other EU programmes, provides rules in order to ensure that projects funded by the European Union will comply with its ethics rules (see the entry for 'Recipient of EU Programmes' in this Dictionary).

According to Article 19, para. 1, Regulation (EU) No. 1291/2013, all research and innovation activities carried out under Horizon 2020 must comply with ethical principles and relevant national, Union and international norms, including the EU Charter and the European Convention on Human Rights and its Supplementary Protocol.

The legal basis of Horizon 2020 refers to the ethical principles established under European Union law (see Article 19, para. 1, 2nd line, Regulation (EU) No. 1291/2013; see also Recital 29 Regulation No. 1291/2013).

An ethics appraisal within Horizon 2020 must be in place during the entire lifetime of a project.

As matter of fact, each proposal considered for funding is subject to an ethics review by ethics experts of the European Commission (Article 14 Regulation (EU) No. 1290/2013). If the proposal does not meet the ethical standards, the project will not be financed (Article 13, para. 3, Regulation (EU) No. 1290/2013).

Afterwards, if the grant is awarded, the project will be subject to a continuous ethics assessment. The European Commission (or the EU agencies) is entitled to carry out checks and audits in order to verify compliance with ethical principles. If there is a breach, the project may be terminated (Article 34 Grant Agreement of Horizon 2020).

The Commission or the agency may object to the transfer of the results in the case of a breach of ethical principles or the security of the Union (Article 44, para. 3, Regulation (EU) No. 1290/2013, Article 30.4 Grant Agreement of Horizon 2020).

Because of the relevance of ethical issues for research programmes, the European Commission has developed several documents on practice in order to ensure that research activities comply with fundamental ethical principles; these documents include: 'Guidance – How to complete your ethics self-assessment' (see version 5.2 of 12 July 2016); 'Roles and functions of ethics advisors/ethics advisory boards in EC-funded projects'; 'European textbook on ethics in research'; and 'Syllabus on ethics in research. Addendum to the European textbook on ethics in research'.

These documents refer to the EU legislation and to the case law of the Court of Justice, as well as to opinions and advice prepared by committees of experts such as the European Group on Ethics in Science and New Technologies (EGE) and the Article 29 Working Party (on the protection of personal data).

3 Ethics Advisors Within EU Programmes

According to the documents of the European Commission, the consortium of beneficiaries of a research programme should be supported by experts to ensure that it complies appropriately with ethical requirements.

In particular, the consortium is requested to appoint one or more 'ethics advisors'.[7] A group of advisors with varied expertise (forming an 'advisory board') is suggested where there are several ethical issues or the issues are particularly sensitive. This allows the many perspectives arising from the ethical issues to be taken into consideration (Hunter 2007).

The advisor is expected to be external to the project and to the host institution, totally independent and free from any conflict of interest.[8]

In order to make the independence of the ethics advisor effective, the EU sources recommend that the appointment is not gratuitous.

The ethics advisor should have expertise in law, data protection/privacy and research ethics, and experience in the assessment of ethics issues in the specific area of the topic of the project.[9]

It may be necessary to involve many experts with specific competences, depending on the particular nature of the project or the ethical issues concerned.

The documents of the Commission underline that is easier to find experts in some fields, such as medical research and animal welfare, than in other areas (e.g. dual use, biosecurity, privacy, or the societal implications of research).[10]

The activities and the role of the ethics advisor must be outlined in regulations adopted by the consortium and within agreements (e.g. in a Memorandum of Understanding) drawn up with the expert.[11]

The role of an ethics advisor is to provide the consortium as a whole, its bodies (steering committees, general assembly, etc.) and each beneficiary, with advice on specific issues or general opinions about the ethical aspects of the research activities, including the regulations adopted by the body of the consortium. Therefore, the

[7] European Commission, 'Guidance – How to complete your ethics self-assessment', Introductory page 'Important notice'.

[8] Ibid. p. 38.

[9] European Commission, 'Roles and functions of ethics advisors/ethics advisory boards in EC-funded projects', December, 2012, p. 3.

[10] Ibid.

[11] Ibid., p. 5.

ethics advisor usually plays a consultancy role, and does not have a decision-making function.

The ethics advisor carries out a continuous ethical assessment of the project in cooperation with the governance body for the project, taking into account the dynamicity of the research activities, and gives support with drawing up a report for the funding authorities.

Nevertheless, it is possible to attribute to the ethics advisor power to authorise the beneficiaries to carry out particular activities (e.g. to transfer data or material), to draw up a template (e.g. an informed consent form or information sheet), and to adopt specific regulations that are relevant from an ethical viewpoint.

Furthermore, other functions or powers can be attributed to the ethics advisor, depending on the 'rules of engagement' agreed by the partnership carrying out the research project.

As matter of fact, an ethics advisor can act as a 'research regulator'. This implies 'monitoring research, which can be carried out in a variety of ways such as requiring reports at regular intervals or at the end of a project, or even in some cases by carrying out *ad hoc* inspections or audits of research'.[12] Also, an ethics advisor might be responsible for applying sanctions, such as the suspension or termination of research or the exclusion of researchers in cases of misconduct.

In any case, as stated in the Commission documents, 'An Ethics Advisor must not simply become a symbolic cipher without any effective power to influence the direction of the research activities or the methodology that will be used. The advisory role is a proactive one. The cultivation of mutual understanding between advisors and partners can see differences resolved through diplomacy and clear communications. Problems can be forestalled through cooperative endeavour and a culture of collaborative working.'[13]

4 Differences Between the Role of an Ethics Advisor and That of an Ethics Committee

The establishment of committees of ethics advisors for research projects arises from experience with ethics committees, particularly for clinical studies (for an overview of this matter, see Monnier (2009)).

For example, UNESCO's 2005 Guide No. 1, 'Establishing bioethics committees' is built on the idea that an ethics committee 'systematically and continually addresses the ethical dimensions of (a) the health sciences, (b) the life sciences and (c) innovative health policies'.

[12] European Commission, *European Textbook on Ethics in Research*, 2005, pp. 30 ff., especially p. 32.

[13] Ibid., p. 5.

Within EU law, according to Article 2, para. 2, No. 11 of Regulation (EU) No. 536/2014, concerning clinical trials on medicinal products for human use, an 'ethics committee' is 'an independent body established in a Member State in accordance with the law of that Member State and empowered to give opinions for the purposes of this Regulation, taking into account the views of laypersons, in particular patients or patients' organisations'.

Therefore, ethics committees are usually established in clinical studies, as provided by the relevant legislation.

On the other hand, the committees of ethics advisors envisaged in the legal rules underlying EU research programmes have similar functions to ethics committees in clinical studies, but may be distinguished from several viewpoints: they deal with ethical issues other than medical ones; they are established at the level of the consortium and not at the level of each legal entity; and they are linked to a specific project and not to the general activity of a beneficiary.

Ethics advisors should collaborate, and coordinate their activities, with the ethics committees established in each beneficiary or with other bodies, such as the bodies involved in the protection of personal data (such as the 'Data Protection Officer', see the entry in this Dictionary by A.M. Emili). This is in order to improve the ethics assessment of research activities at every level.

However, the distinction between the above-mentioned committees cannot be too strict. As matter of fact, the ethics committee of a legal entity may deal with issues other than the clinical studies, and a local ethics committee may be appointed for the ethical assessment of a research project. On the other hand, the ethics committee established for a specific project may be institutionalised.

In reality, ethics advisors in research projects and ethics committees established at the level of particular legal entities are all useful instruments to ensure the elaboration and implementation of ethical principles.

5 Applicable Norms

As mentioned above, the beneficiaries of EU research programmes have to comply with all applicable international, EU and national legislation with respect to the ethical issues arising from their projects.

However, ethics advisors, who collaborate with the consortium as a whole, are particularly required to apply EU ethical standards, which are normally more rigorous than local ones.[14]

If it is possible to identify several bioethical principles recognised by international law (Andorno 2013), EU law contains many provisions dealing with ethical issues.

[14] European Commission, 'Roles and functions of ethics advisors/ethics advisory boards in EC-funded projects', n. 9, p. 11.

Ethics advisors have to take into consideration the fact that EU law protects several fundamental interests that might be affected by research activities, such as: (a) human rights (Art. 6 Treaty of Functioning of the European Union, hereinafter referred to as 'TEU'; Art. 1 EU Charter; including the protection of personal data, see Art. 8 EU Charter and Art. 16 FEU), not only within Europe but also in research activities carried out in and in collaboration with third countries; (b) respect for the beginning of human life (Article 18, para. 1, Convention of Oviedo)[15]; (c) the rights of vulnerable persons (Articles 24, 25, 26 EU Charter); (d) the integrity of genetic patrimony (Article 3 EU Charter); (e) Security[16]; (f) the environment (Article 37 EU Charter); and (g) the wellbeing of animals (Article 13 TEU).

In order to protect these fundamental interests and to achieve an equilibrium with freedom of research, some ethical principles arising from the European legal system should be implemented: (i) dignity (Article 2 TEU; Preamble of EU Charter), which represents a pivotal principle of the European ethical system[17]; (ii) self-determination (Article 3, para. 2, EU Charter; Article 5 Convention of Oviedo); (iii) precaution (Article 191 TFEU); (iv) proportionality (Article 12 Convention of Oviedo); and (v) solidarity (Article 2 TEU).[18]

Furthermore, ethics advisors are required to apply EU law in specific fields that are relevant in the protection of fundamental interests, such as laws relating to the protection of personal data (Regulation (EU) No. 2016/679), clinical experimentation (Regulation (EU) No. 536/2014) and human tissues (Directive 2004/23/EC), animals in experimental activities (Directive 2010/63/EU), 'double-use' technologies (Council Regulation (EC) no, 428/2009), the use of the genetic resources of third countries (Regulation (EU) No. 511/2014), etc.

It is important to remember that the above-mentioned ethical and legal framework arising from European law may be different from the ethical principles applied in other countries. For example, in recent years, the Court of Justice has issued several judgments underlining the differences between European rules concerning the protection of personal data and the legislation of other countries, in particular the United States (for a more general discussion with respect to the differences between the ethical systems of the EU and the USA, see Busnelli (2010)).[19]

---

[15] Convention for the Protection of Human Rights and Dignity of the Human Being with regard to the Application of Biology and Medicine: Convention on Human Rights and Biomedicine (ETS No 164), opened for signature on 4 April 1997 in Oviedo.

[16] European Council, 2010, 'Internal security strategy for the EU. Towards a European security model'.

[17] See ECJ, judgment 14 October 2004, C-36/02, *Omega Spielhallen- und Automatenaufstellungs-GmbH* v *Oberbürgermeisterin der Bundesstadt Bonn*, ECLI:EU:C:2004:614.

[18] According to the 'traditional' north American literature on bioethics, ethical principles are respect for autonomy, beneficence, non maleficence, and justice (Beauchamp and Childress 2009).

[19] See, for example, the judgment of 6 October 2015, C–362/14, *Schrems* v *Data Protection Commissioner*, ECLI:EU:C:2015:650.

However, the ethics advisor and the consortium must implement the fundamental European ethical principles even in research activities carried out within third countries and in collaboration with legal entities from such countries.

References

Andorno, R. (2013). *Principles of international bio law: Seeking common ground at the intersection of bioethics and human rights*. Brussels: Bruylant.

Beauchamp, T. L., & Childress, J. F. (2009). *Principles of biomedical ethics*. Oxford: Oxford University Press.

Busnelli, F. D. (2010). Towards a 'European Bioethics'? *Ethically Speaking, 14*, 11.

Cippitani, R. (2012). *El Derecho de la Sociedad del Conocimiento*. Rome-Perugia: ISEG.

Cippitani, R. (2015). *Academic freedom as a fundamental right*. Paper presented at the 1st International Conference on Higher Education Advances, HEAd'15, Universitat Politècnica de València.

Hunter, D. (2007). Proportional ethical review and the identification of ethical issues. *Journal of Medical Ethics, 33*, 241–245.

Mathieu, B. (2009). *La bioéthique*. Paris: Dalloz.

Molina del Pozo, C. F. (2009). *El Derecho comunitario y la I+D+T. Hacia el diseño de un perfil para el futuro*. Madrid: UAH.

Monnier, S. (2009). *Les comités d'éthique et le droit: Eléments d'analyse sur le système normatif de la bioéthique*. Paris: PUF.

EU Citizen

Antonio Bartolini

1 The Idea of Citizenship Through History

It is certainly true that the common foundation of European law is the status of citizenship.

Citizenship since the classical era (that of ancient Greece and ancient Rome) has indicated a condition that belongs to the subject (called the *cives*). At the same time, citizenship is moulded in opposition to the legal condition of being a foreigner. Thus, citizens enjoy the rights, and are subject to the duties, of the community to which they belong, because they are under the *pòlis* or the *civitas*.

Roman law recognised citizenship for those who enjoyed the *civitatis* status: only those who had the *civitatis* legal status had the right to vote, could set up the solemn contract provided by the civil code, had dominion over things and slaves and could exercise rights linked to owning land. In ancient Rome the *civitatis* status was granted only to Roman *cives*; in the Republican era, it was granted to all freemen from certain countries. Only with the Emperor Caracalla (212 AD) was this status recognised for all freemen of the Roman Empire. After the fall of the Roman Empire, the idea of citizenship was eclipsed by the idea of a subject (the *subiectionis* status) (Costa 2005).

Renewed interest in the idea of citizenship surfaced in the Middle Ages (Ascheri 2011, pp. 299 ff.). It reappeared in a more concrete manner only during the Enlightenment, first, and after that during the French Revolution. As matter of fact, it was during the latter that the political dimension of the idea of citizenship was seriously developed. The status of citizenship allows the citizen to have universal rights as a man because all men were born free and equal in relation to rights, especially before the law and the state; in particular, citizens had the right to vote, as

A. Bartolini (✉)
Law Department University of Perugia, 06100, via Pascoli, Perugia, Italy
e-mail: antonio.bartolini@unipg.it

A. Bartolini et al. (eds.), *Dictionary of Statuses within EU Law*,
https://doi.org/10.1007/978-3-030-00554-2_26

asserted by the principle of the sovereignty of the people (Art. 6[1] *Déclaration des droits de l'homme et du citoyen de 1789*).

Citizenship, as a status, is a set of rights and duties: the rights start from the freedom of expression that is one of the most precious rights of man (Art. 11, *Déclaration des droits de l'homme et du citoyen de 1789*), but a citizen also has duties, such as the common contribution for the maintenance of public order, the expenses of public administration and the payment of public taxation (Art. 13[2] and Art. 14,[3] *Déclaration des droits de l'homme et du citoyen de 1789*) (Furia 2002, pp. 39 ff.).

The conception of citizenship as universal (always and everywhere having more of a political than a legal meaning) disappeared again with the Restoration, and re-emerged in western Europe (and, then, in eastern Europe, but after the fall of the Berlin Wall) only after the Second World War. The so-called second generation constitutions recognised, for all citizens, men and women, rights and duties borne out of their citizenship, first of all active and passive voting rights, and then the fundamental rights—the right to equality and the right to freedom.

In Europe, by means of the constitutions that were written after the Second World War, citizenship as a universal status was fully created, recognising, for citizens of every age and without any distinction based on sex, all the rights and duties recognised by the particular legal system.

'European citizenship' was born in 1992, when it was recognised by the Treaty of Maastricht.

At the same time, however, in international declarations like the United Nations Universal Declaration of Human Rights (1948) and the Convention for the Protection of Human Rights and Fundamental Freedoms (Council of Europe, Rome, 1950), 'citizenship rights' and fundamental and inalienable human rights stand out; these are recognised as belonging to each individual, regardless of whether or not he/she belongs to a particular state. From these declarations on human rights taken as a whole, a new type of citizenship emerged: this citizenship is independent of belonging to a community or a state, it is universally attributed to everybody, regardless of their nationality or their territorial identity, and it is therefore a 'global citizenship'.

[1] Art. 6: *la Loi est l'expression de la volonté générale. Tous les Citoyens ont droit de concourir personnellement, ou par leurs Représentants, à sa formation. Elle doit être la même pour tous, soit qu'elle protège, soit qu'elle punisse. Tous les Citoyens étant égaux à ses yeux sont également admissibles à toutes dignités, places et emplois publics, selon leur capacité, et sans autre distinction que celle de leurs vertus et de leurs talents.*

[2] Art. 13: *pour l'entretien de la force publique, et pour les dépenses d'administration, une contribution commune est indispensable: elle doit être également répartie entre tous les citoyens, en raison de leurs facultés.*

[3] Art. 14: *tous les Citoyens ont le droit de constater, par eux-mêmes ou par leurs représentants, la nécessité de la contribution publique, de la consentir librement, d'en suivre l'emploi, et d'en déterminer la quotité, l'assiette, le recouvrement et la durée.*

2 Citizenship of the EU Member States: *ius sanguinis* and *ius soli*

The ways in which citizenship is acquired can be traced back to two paradigms: *ius sanguinis* and *ius soli*.

Citizenship by *ius sanguinis* is transmitted by inheritance by the members of a nation: in other words, by *ius sanguinis*, a child acquires the citizenship of one of his/her parents (and, in some jurisdictions, that of one of his/her ancestors).

Citizenship by *ius soli* is acquired regardless of family relationships, and purely by reason of being born in the territory: in other words, through *ius soli*, citizenship is acquired in the nation of a person's birth.

Also, citizenship can be acquired after birth through naturalisation: here we are talking about *ius domicilii*, whereby citizenship can be acquired after birth, for example after a person has resided for some years in the state of which he/she wishes to become a citizen.

In France, the *ius sanguinis* was affirmed after the French Revolution, and was supported by the Enlightenment culture and, years after this, through the romantic idea of belonging to a nation. This is why this way of acquiring citizenship is still the most widespread in Europe.

By contrast, the *ius soli* arose from the experience of the common law, where the aim was to affirm the sovereignty of the monarch over citizens who had been born and lived in the kingdom. This idea was reinforced by the needs of the British colonial empire, which required that sovereignty be extended to subjects who were not born to British citizens. At this time, the *ius soli* is mainly applicable in the Commonwealth and in former British colonies such as the United States of America (USA).

The *ius sanguinis* aims to protect the idea of the nation, while the *ius soli* favours the integration of the different races who coexist in a territory.

Comparing the position across the world, at this time only the USA conservers an unmitigated *ius soli* rule: in 1868, after the Civil War, the 14th Amendment to the Constitution introduced the so-called citizenship clause: 'all persons born [...] in the United States, and subject to the jurisdiction thereof, are citizens of the United States'.

In the rest of the world the *ius soli*, if compared with USA model, is attenuated. As matter of fact, the USA model (which is difficult to modify since the citizenship clause is contained in the Constitution) provides a strong incentive for immigration: for example, children of irregular immigrants become American citizens if they are born in the United States.

The *ius soli* model is also present in the European Union, although with some variations. Usually, it qualifies as temperate/moderate form of *ius soli*, as citizenship is not acquired just by virtue of the fact that a person is born in a state, but usually is conditional on certain requirements being met by the parents. It could, for instance, be necessary for a parent to have been regularly resident in the state for a large number of years (Belgium, Germany, Greece, Ireland, or Portugal), or it could be mandatory that a parent was born in the same state for which the person is asking for citizenship (the so-called double *ius soli*), which is the case in France, Luxembourg, the Netherlands and Spain.

In *ius sanguinis* countries, citizenship can be acquired through naturalisation. Usually this is possible (although this is not a complete list) at the moment a person reaches his/her majority, provided that she/he has resided for a certain period of time in the country in which she/he is applying for citizenship; at the same time, the person has to demonstrate that she/he has studied in that country for a certain number of years (*ius culturae*) (this is the case in Austria, Bulgaria, Croatia, Denmark, Estonia, Finland, Hungary, Italy, Lithuania, Latvia, Poland, the Czech Republic, Romania, Slovenia and Sweden).

The *ius sanguinis*, in its purest form, is applied by Malta (even though the rule of citizenship by investment in Malta also applies).

There is, therefore, a mosaic of rules, which vary from country to country, but one can see a clear predominance of the *ius sanguinis* rule, even if significant countries, with high immigration, have adopted the *ius soli* rule (primarily Germany, France and Spain).

3 European Citizenship

European citizenship is a 'dual' citizenship, which means that it is acquired not directly but in a derived way. Every person who is a citizen of a Member State is a citizen of the Union, so citizenship of the Union is additional to and not a replacement of national citizenship (Article 20(1) TFEU).

European citizenship is the fundamental status of European citizens: as the EU Court of Justice has clarified, 'Union citizenship is destined to be the fundamental status of nationals of the Member States, enabling those who find themselves in the same situation to enjoy the same treatment in law irrespective of their nationality' (Court of Justice, EU, C-184/99, 20 September 2001, *Grzelczyk*).

First of all, the status of European citizen attributes to the individual a set of legal positions recognised by the European institutions and EU law, such as the right to vote in elections of the European Parliament, the right to petition the European Parliament or to complain to the Ombudsman, and more broadly the right to claim European justice (Article 20 TFEU). The Charter of Fundamental Rights of the European Union (CFREU) also recognises the right to good administration (Article 40 of the Charter) and the right of access to administrative documents (Article 41 of the Charter).

Above all, the Treaties give EU citizens 'the right to move and reside freely within the territory of the Member States' (Article 20 TFEU and Article 45 CFREU).

The right of freedom of movement and residence is a sort of key that enables citizens of a Member State to take the rights that have been formed in their own country to a Member State of destination; at same time, citizens of a Member State can acquire rights in another Member State if their own country does not recognise those rights (status shopping).

As regards mutual recognition, the paradigm of the problem was the argument that was unleashed in France about Polish workers in relation to the so-called Bolkestein Directive (Directive 2006/123/CE). This Directive, on services in the internal market, establishes general provisions facilitating the exercise of the freedom of establishment for service providers and the free movement of services, and so allows European citizens to take with them to another Member State the professional or provider status acquired in their country of origin of which they are (national) citizens.

In contrast, it is possible to acquire a status in a country that is different from one's status in one's own country: this is the case, for example, for the qualification as a lawyer that has resulted in a veritable form of 'tourism', with Spain as the destination of Italian law graduates. In this case, European citizenship is the gateway to acquiring a status recognised by European law in the country in which forms of access and acquisition are easiest or most advantageous.

The market of rules, and therefore these forms of 'status tourism', also concern the way in which citizenship is acquired.

In other words, we are witnessing a phenomenon whereby tourist or market situations are created that, in this case, involve not European citizens but non-EU citizens who want to become European citizens.

They seek the EU country that recognizes national citizenship in the easiest or most advantageous way.

Two cases in particular should be mentioned.

The first is Case C-200/02, *Zhu and Chen*: Mrs Chen, a Chinese national, decided to give birth to her second child in the Irish Republic in order to obtain a long-term residence permit in the United Kingdom (which she would not have been able to obtain with Chinese nationality), because at the time in Ireland the *ius soli* applied. In this way, Mrs Chen's daughter acquired both Irish and European citizenship. Immediately after giving birth, Mrs Chen returned to the United Kingdom and applied for a long-stay permit on the basis that her second child was a European citizen. The United Kingdom denied Mrs Chen's request, essentially on the grounds that she was sheltering under an abuse of rights. The matter came before the European Court. The Commission replied that if the mother were to be prevented from exercising her right to move, the child would be prevented from exercising that same right: that is why, according to the Luxembourg court, every European citizen, even a minor, has the right to reside freely throughout the European area. That right would be compromised if a child's parent, even if she/he were not a European citizen, were denied her/his right of long-term residence.

The *Chen* case shows that, even in the field of citizenship rights, there is a search for the most favourable national law (rule-shopping): Mrs Chen, in order to obtain a long-stay permit in the United Kingdom, chose for her second birth the country where it is easiest to obtain European citizenship (Ireland, where at the time the pure principle of *ius soli* applied), so that once she had obtained European citizenship for her daughter, her daughter obtained the status of a European citizen. This status, as we have seen, also allowed the child to be recognised as having various rights to freedom of movement. The acquisition by the child of this status, and in order to prevent the child from being unable to exercise these rights, forced the recognition of some European prerogatives to the parent (non-EU), as the child necessarily, in order to exercise her rights, had to bring with her, and be assisted by, those upon whom she was dependent. The *Chen* case, among others, forced Ireland, in a referendum, to change the constitutional provision of the pure *ius soli*, introducing a tempered/moderate *ius soli*, in order to prevent a repetition of such situations.

It turns out that there is a very interesting (and, at the same time, worrying) case in relation to Maltese citizenship by investment. The Maltese legal system allows non-EU citizens to acquire Maltese citizenship, if they intend to invest locally: in particular, they must make financial commitments (a contribution of 650,000 € is payable on application) and invest at least 150,000 in Maltese government bonds, as well as buying a property worth at least 350,000, or renting a property at a rental of at least 16,000 per year. The property, whether purchased or rented, must be kept for at least 5 years, and the same applies to the Maltese financial securities (Maltese Citizenship Act). To sum up, this formula makes it possible to buy European citizenship and acquire the status of a European citizen, with all the benefits related to this status.

Because 'a number of Member States have introduced schemes which directly or indirectly result in the sale of EU citizenship to third-country nationals' (European Parliament resolution of 16 January 2014 on EU citizenship for sale, 2013/2995(RSp)), the acquisition of EU citizenship is open to abuse. The European Union is therefore beginning to prepare regulatory measures, and the European Parliament has condemned this type of scheme with the resolution mentioned above. This would be an important innovation, since European law would begin to regulate an issue, that of the acquisition of citizenship, that until now has jealously remained a matter of national sovereignty.

It would probably be appropriate to start preparing (weak) harmonisation by prohibiting distorting practices. Therefore, we need to think about a common policy on this issue too.

In this respect, however, the Council of Europe Convention on Citizenship should not be forgotten. This calls on the contracting countries to facilitate the acquisition of nationality for those who are born and reside legally and ordinarily on their territory (Article 6(4)(e) of the European Convention on Nationality, STCE No 166, Council of Europe, Strasbourg, 6.XI.1997).

4 European Citizenship as a General Status of Community Law

The status of EU citizenship is a general status that encompasses, as if it were a kind of holdall, all the special statuses that European law grants to individuals.

The rights of citizenship are granted not only to European citizens, but also to non-European citizens: the *Chen* case is a paradigm.

European citizenship is, therefore, weak because, in addition to being dual (and therefore derived from national citizenship), it does not manifest some typical characteristics of national citizenship. First of all, it is a citizenship without duties (Kochenov 2014), in contrast to the concept of citizenship as a status that confers not only rights but also duties and, first and foremost, solidarity.

This is an element of weakness that shows how European citizenship is instrumental to market integration, but not to social and political integration.

To this end, the recognition of the right to vote in local government elections does not appear to be sufficient either, since a real point of action to meet the criticism would be to recognise genuine political citizenship expressed in the right to vote for a truly sovereign European Parliament.

From this point of view, the Commission's proposals to strengthen European citizenship through a programme of actions aimed at, among other things, strengthening European voluntary service, monitoring the granting of national citizenship by investment, etc., are inadequate (see European Commission, EU Citizenship Report, 2017).

The objective should be much more ambitious, and should be to reduce the democratic deficit by giving European citizens, as such, sovereignty over the Union, in the light of the idea of a multi-city citizenship (Grosso 1998, p. 141) derived from the constitutionalisation of fundamental rights (Bartolini and Pioggia 2016, p. 14).

References

Ascheri, M. (2011). Nella città medievale italiana: la cittadinanza o le cittadinanze. *Initium: Revista catalana d'història del dret, 16*, 299–312.

Bartolini, A., & Pioggia, A. (2016). Cittadinanze amministrative. In L. Ferrara & D. Storace (Eds.), *A 150 anni dall'Unificazione Amministrativa Italiana* (Vol. VIII). Florence: Firenze University Press.

Costa, P. (2005). *Cittadinanza*. Bari: Laterza.

Furia, A. (2002). La cittadinanza durante la rivoluzione francese (1789–1799). *Scienza e Politica, 27*, 39 ff.

Grosso, E. (1998). La cittadinanza: appartenenza, identità e partecipazione dal Stato liberale alla democrazia contemporanea. In L. Violante (Ed.), *Storia d'Italia, Annali 14, Legge Diritto Giustizia* (p. 141). Torino: Enaudi.

Kochenov, D. (2014). EU citizenship without duties. *European Law Journal, 20*, 482 ff.

EU Investor

Michele Siri and Shanshan Zhu

1 Introduction and Legal Framework

Following the financial turmoil in 2007, and considered the increasing complexity of financial markets, the EU strengthened its regulatory efforts to set a proper level of protection and transparency in investment services.[1] In particular, by introducing the Directive on Markets in Financial Instruments (MiFID),[2] the related Markets in Financial Instruments Regulation (MiFIR),[3] the Insurance Distribution Directive[4] and the Regulation on key information documents for packaged retail and insurance-based investment products (PRIIPs),[5] the EU recently provided the main—sometimes overlapping—criteria to be followed by financial intermediaries in the performance of their activities.

2 Investor Protection: The EU Path Towards Harmonisation

We can define 'investor protection' as the set of rules and principles expected to preserve the interests and the rights of a person in its role as the investor, or the 'defensive protection of the vulnerable investor against unscrupulous market participants' (Clark 1976). The aim of the regulation concerning investor protection is

[1] *See* Recital 3 and 4 of Directive 2014/65/EU.

[2] Directive 2004/39/EC (MiFID I), recently revised with the Directive 2014/65/EU (MiFID II).

[3] Regulation 648/2012/EU.

[4] Directive 2016/97/EU.

[5] Regulation 1286/2014/EU.

M. Siri (✉) · S. Zhu
University of Genoa, Genoa, Italy
e-mail: michele.siri@unige.it; shanshan.zhu@guri.unige.it

A. Bartolini et al. (eds.), *Dictionary of Statuses within EU Law*,
https://doi.org/10.1007/978-3-030-00554-2_27

to allow the investors to make informed financial decisions that are better aligned with their interests and profile.

In particular, based on previous contributions on the subject (Colaert 2017; Moloney 2010; Moloney 2015), we distinguish among four main dimensions of EU investor protection regulation: (1) disclosure of product information, (2) conduct of business (COB) rules, (3) product governance and intervention and (4) financial education.[6]

2.1 Disclosure of Product Information

The first focus area that EU financial authorities addressed is represented by the obligation to disclose information on the provided financial product. The disclosure of information—aiming not only at protecting unsophisticated investors' trading in the securities market but also at ensuring the efficiency of the financial markets and reducing agency costs (Enriques and Gilotta 2015)—has become an essential requirement since the introduction of the obligation to produce a prospectus.[7] This obligation, which was first harmonised at the EU level in 1985 and initially targeted only undertakings for collective investment in transferable securities UCITS funds,[8] evolved in order to introduce the so-called 'Key Investor Information Document' (KIID), a two-page document containing the essential features of the fund,[9] and finally extend to a larger range of financial products with the 'Key Investor Document' (KID).

The KID, modelled after the UCITS KIID and introduced with the PRIIPs Regulation,[10] targets 'PRIIP manufacturers' (i.e., fund managers, insurance undertakings, credit institutions and investment firms).[11] Moreover, it applies to 'all products, regardless of their form or construction, that are manufactured by the financial services industry to provide investment opportunities to retail investors'; therefore, it covers financial instruments pertaining to the banking, investment and insurance sector.[12] The KID should be a three-page, stand-alone document that is clearly sepa-

[6]In this paper, we decided not to treat enforcement mechanisms in order to focus on *ex-ante* mechanisms.

[7]Articles 27 and 28 of Directive 1985/611/EEC on the coordination of laws, regulations and administrative provisions relating to undertakings for collective investment in transferable securities (UCITS Directive).

[8]Article 1 of the UCITS Directive.

[9]Art 78 of Directive 2009/65/EC (UCITS IV).

[10]Regulation (EU) No. 1286/2014 on key information documents for packaged retail and insurance-based investment products (PRIIPs).

[11]Recital 12 of PRIIPs Regulation.

[12]Recital 6 of PRIIPs Regulation.

rated from other marketing material, easily readable and contain 'accurate, fair, clear and not misleading' information.[13]

The European Commission recently proposed to introduce a similar requirement in the context of a Regulation on a pan-European Personal Pension Product (PEPP).[14] This regulatory effort can be explained with the EU's intention to deal with the problems of information overload (Paredes 2003), investors limited rationality, deviant behaviour[15] and non-uniformity among different types of financial products.

2.2 *Conduct of Business (COB) Rules*

COB regulation, originally deriving from the fiduciary doctrine (Tuch 2015), aims at protecting investors from harm caused by the conduct of financial intermediaries during the operations performed for the investors or on their behalf. The first attempt to provide a minimum harmonised set of standards among the Member States was realised in 1993, with the issuance of the Investment Services Directive,[16] which is modelled after the International Conduct of Business Principles, published by the International Organisation of Securities Commissions (IOSCO) in 1990.[17] However, this original and rather simple regulatory scheme did not provide sufficient investor protection, nor did it establish a completely harmonised system (Davies et al. 2006).

A more extensive set of rules was introduced in 2004 with the 'Markets in Financial Instruments Directive' (MiFID I)[18] and its Implementing Directive (2006/39/EC), which replaced the ISD standards and revised many times in the years that followed.[19] Under the Directive 2014/65/EU (MiFID II) and its implementing Standards, the current COB rules provides a stricter and more detailed set of rules governing a large range of financial services. MiFID II, in particular, applies to all investment firms, credit institutions and UCITS management firms when providing investment services or ancillary services; thus, it generally requires financial intermediaries to 'act honestly, fairly and professionally in accordance with the best interests of (their) clients'.[20]

---

[13] Article 6(1), (2) and (4) of PRIIPs Regulation.

[14] Art 23 of the Proposal for a Regulation of the European Parliament and of the Council on a pan-European Personal Pension Product (PEPP) (COM (2017) 343 final).

[15] For a review of the literature on behavioural finance, see Barberis and Thaler (2003).

[16] Directive 93/33/EEC. This followed the European Recommendation to introduce some basic COB rules (Recommendation 77/534/EEC, OJ L 212/37).

[17] International Organisation of Securities Commissions (IOSCO), 'International Conduct of Business Principles' (1990).

[18] Directive 2004/39/EC on Markets in financial instruments (MiFID I).

[19] Directive 2006/31/EC, Directive 2007/44/EC, Directive 2008/10/EC, and Directive 2010/78/EC.

[20] Article 24(1) MiFID II.

Within this complex reforming process, we can identify some fundamental tendency lines that were followed by the European authorities. These concern: (1) widening the scope of the COB rules, (2) distinguishing between independent and non-independent financial advice, (3) specifying the duty to act in the client's best interest and (4) strengthening the information obligation.

The first relevant change concerns widening the scope and target of the COB rules. Even though the Investment Services Directive covered investment services in general, some common practices (such as financial advice and commodity derivatives) were not included since they were not identified as financial services. MiFID I upgraded investment advice from an ancillary service to a core investment service, and certain commodity derivatives were included among the financial instruments.[21] Moreover, MiFID II now draws a distinction between independent and non-independent financial advice. In detail, investment firms are required to disclose whether they provide investment advice on an independent basis,[22] and in such a case, they should assess a sufficiently diverse range of financial products—in terms of issuers and product providers—before making their recommendation.[23]

In order to avoid conflicts of interest, MiFID II establishes specific restrictions to the possibility for investment firms to accept or retain fees, commissions or any monetary and non-monetary benefits from third parties ('inducements'). With reference to independent advice, these should be immediately returned to the clients, except for certain minor non-monetary benefits that are capable of enhancing the quality of service provided—investment research included (Silverentand et al. 2017)—which should, however, be clearly disclosed.[24] As for non-independent advice, inducements are allowed if they are (a) designed to enhance the quality of client services, (b) consistent with the firm's duty to act in a client's best interest and (c) clearly disclosed to the affected client. Thus, the European legislator chose not to follow the United Kingdom (UK) experience of the Retail Distribution Review, which put an inducement ban on both 'independent' and 'restricted' advice (Giudici 2017). In the Commission proposal for a PEPP regulation, the EU authorities introduce a similar CBR for PEPP distributors.[25]

The third area of EU intervention is regarded as the general principle to which investment firms should act in the clients' best interests when dealing.[26] MiFID II strengthened this general standard that represents a key interpretation of what is further specified in other provisions (Enriques and Gargantini 2017), such as those

[21] Section 1, Annex I (5), Recital 4 and Par. I, Annex II of MiFID I.

[22] Recital 72 and Article 24(4) of MiFID II.

[23] Recital 73 and Article 24(7)(a) of MiFID II.

[24] Recital 74 and Article 24(7)(b) of MiFID II.

[25] Article 23 of the Proposal for a Regulation of the European Parliament and of the Council on a PEPP (COM (2017) 343 final).

[26] Article 24(1) of MiFID II.

concerning conflict of interest,[27] inducements,[28] staff remuneration practices,[29] best execution[30] and the suitability of appropriateness assessment.[31]

The fourth fundamental subject of reform is represented by the strengthened information obligations. While the ISD provided only the obligation for the investment firm to adequately disclose the 'relevant material information on its dealings with its client',[32] MiFID I—as well as MiFID II—poses a new set of information duties on financial intermediaries. All information addressed from the investment firm to clients or potential clients should be 'fair, clear and not misleading'.[33] Appropriate information should include the investment firm and its services, the financial instruments and proposed investment strategies, execution venues, appropriate guidance on and warnings of the risks associated and the costs and associated charges. In reference to financial advice, investment firms should also inform the client on whether their advice is based on a broad or on a more restricted analysis of different types of financial instruments, especially if the firm will periodically assess the suitability of the recommended financial instruments.[34] Specific information duties have been introduced in relation to investment services offered together with other services or as a part of a package.[35] Moreover, MiFID II now requires the producers to provide information about the product; therefore, an amplified cooperation with product manufacturers is necessary (Colaert 2017).

[27] Article 23 and Recital 56 of MiFID II. MiFID II does not define or prohibit conflicts of interest. Instead, conflicts of interest shall be avoided, taken into account and managed (Brenncke 2017; Herbst 2015, p. 94). For further discussion, see also Grundmann and Hacker (2017).

[28] Article 24(8) and (9) of MiFID II.

[29] Article 24(10) of MiFID II. Staff should not be remunerated in such a way that they recommend a particular financial instrument without taking into account the retail client's best interest.

[30] Article 27 of MiFID II. Investment firms shall take all reasonable steps to obtain the best possible result in the execution of clients' orders, with a different regime depending on the nature of the investor (i.e., either professional or retail).

[31] Article 25(2) and (3). In particular, the suitability assessment (Art. 25(2)) requires that portfolio managers and financial advisors shall gather information about their client's knowledge, experience, investment objective and risk tolerance—in relation to investment products and services—in order to recommend to the client the investment services and financial instruments that are best aligned with the client's profile. The appropriateness requirement provides that the investment firm gather information on the client in order to assess if the product or services offered or demanded were appropriate.

[32] Article 11 of ISD.

[33] Article 24(3) of MiFID II.

[34] Article 24(4)(a) of MiFID II.

[35] Article 24(11) of MiFID II.

2.3 Product Governance and Intervention

In opposition to the approach previously adopted by the EU policymaker,[36] the last financial crisis and the recent scandals showed the need to protect clients from harmful financial products by preventing them to even access to the market. The first attempts to govern the quality of financial instruments were realised by the UCITS Directive,[37] which regulated the conditions under which an investment fund could be allowed to use the label 'UCITS'. Other attempts were made by the Alternative Investment Fund Managers Directive (AIFMD),[38] which intervened on (non-UCITS) funds' managers by requiring them to fulfil certain quality requirements. In the meantime, some Member States, such as the UK, started issuing some principles regulating product governance.[39] Finally, encouraged by the ESMA opinion,[40] MiFID II and IDD established specific product governance and intervention rules.

Investment and insurance intermediaries shall now undergo a product approval process before marketing and distributing a financial instrument. In particular, they shall 'specify an identified target market for each product, ensure that all relevant risks to such identified target market are assessed and that the intended distribution strategy is consistent with the identified target market, and take reasonable steps to ensure that the insurance product is distributed to the identified target market'.[41]

Moreover, a review process shall be regularly performed in order to assess whether the financial instrument remains consistent with the needs of the identified target market and whether the intended distribution strategy remains appropriate. In such a way, the quality assessment of financial product covers its entire life cycle, starting at the design phase and ending with the review phase. MiFID II clearly assign to the management body the duty to define, oversee and implement the policy in relation to the products offered or provided.[42]

In addition, MiFID II and PRIIPs Regulation, in order to address an investor protection concern or preserve the integrity of the financial system, attributed some product intervention powers to European Supervisory Authorities,[43] according to which these authorities may temporarily prohibit the marketing, distribution and

[36] In the past, in order to support market innovation, the EU legislator avoided to impose any quality requirement for financial products (Colaert 2017).

[37] Original directive 1985/611/ECC.

[38] Directive 2011/61/EU on Alternative Investment Fund Managers Directive (AIFMD).

[39] See Colaert (2017).

[40] European Securities and Markets Authority (ESMA), 'Opinion. Structured Retail Products – Good practices for product governance arrangements' (ESMA/2014/332, March 2016).

[41] Article 16(3) of MiFID II and Article 25 of the IDD. See also ESMA, 'Final Report: Guidelines on MiFID II product governance requirements' (2017), ESMA35-43-620.

[42] See Article 9(3)(b) of MiFID II.

[43] To ESMA for financial instruments, to EBA with reference to structured deposits, to the European Insurance and Occupational Pensions Authority (EIOPA) in relation to insurance-based investment products.

sale of certain products to retail investors or a type of financial activity or practice.[44] These stricter *ex-ante* and *ex-post* product governance mechanisms will probably entail some extra costs for firms, but they are deemed acceptable, especially considered the damages that can derive from an inadequate investor protection framework (Busch 2017).

2.4 Financial Education

A final segment of intervention for the reinforcement of investor protection concerns the improvement of financial literacy in the context of Member States. In the view of EU authorities, the financial crisis confirmed that 'financial education is not a substitute for consumer protection, but a key element of the consumer protection framework'; however, since it fails to represent 'the underlying cause for the crisis ... it may have contributed to worsening the impact of the financial crisis in Europe in the autumn of 2008'.[45] As one of the 'post-crisis top priorities', financial education has been at the centre of many institutional documents and initiatives. At the international level, it has been mainly promoted by the Organisation for Economic Co-operation and Development (OECD) and its International Network on Financial Education (INFE), whereas it took form at the domestic level, especially in terms of cooperation between supervisors and various entities involved in consumer protection and of cooperation between supervisors and schools and the academic sector.[46]

In 2017, the European Banking Authority (EBA) established a repository in which is gathers financial education initiatives promoted by national authorities and those that fall within the scope of its competence.[47] To date, the repository consists of 84 initiatives, most of which are established in Ireland, Portugal and Sweden and consist of online resources. However, in line with the strive to reach harmonisation at a cross-sectoral level among financial services, the objective for the future is to publish reports via the Joint Committee of the European Supervisory Authorities (i.e., ESMA, EBA and EIOPA).[48]

[44] Article 40–41 of MiFIR and Article 16 of PRIIPs Regulation.

[45] Expert Group on Financial Education, The Financial Crisis and Financial Education (2009).

[46] EIOPA, 'Report on Financial Literacy and Education Initiatives by Competent Authorities' (2011).

[47] EBA, 'EBA Financial Education Report 2017/2018' (2018).

[48] EIOPA, 'Report on Financial Literacy and Education Initiatives by Competent Authorities' (2011).

3 Conclusion

Starting from the publication of the de Larosière Group report,[49] the European initiated an increasingly intense process of reforming investor protection instruments in the context of the European Capital Markets Law, marking a shift from a minimum to a maximum harmonisation approach (Möllers 2016). Nowadays, all financial intermediaries on a cross-sectoral basis—pertaining to the securities, banking and insurance sector—shall provide all the information necessary for both retail and professional investors to make the investment choices that are aligned with their best interests. The new rules concerning the obligation to provide a KID or KIID, the distinction between financial and non-financial advice, the related limitation to inducements and the new process of product governance and intervention have been the most discussed. However, their effectiveness has to be evaluated in the next years.

References

Barberis, N., & Thaler, R. (2003). A survey of behavioural finance. In G. Constantinides, M. Harris, & R. M. Stulz (Eds.), *Handbook of the economics of finance: Financial markets and asset pricing* (pp. 1051–1121). Amsterdam: North-Holland. https://doi.org/10.1016/S1574-0102(03)01027-6

Brenncke, M. (2017). Commentary on MiFID II conduct of business rules, Arts 21-30 MiFID II. In M. Lehmann & C. Kumpan (Eds.), *Financial Services Law* (1st ed.). Oxford, UK: Hart Publishing.

Busch, D. (2017). Product governance and product intervention under MiFID II/MiFIR. In D. Busch & G. Ferrarini (Eds.), *Regulation of the EU financial markets: MiFID II and MiFIR* (pp. 123–146). Oxford, UK: Oxford University Press.

Clark, R. C. (1976). The soundness of financial intermediaries. *Yale Law Journal, 86*(1), 1–102.

Colaert, V. (2017). Building blocks of investor protection: All-embracing regulation tightens its grip. *Journal of European Consumer and Market Law*, (6), 229–244.

Davies, R., Dufour, A., & Scott-Quinn, B. (2006). The MiFID: Competition in a new European equity market regulatory structure. In G. Ferrarini & E. Wymeersch (Eds.), *Investor protection in Europe: Corporate law making, the MiFID and beyond* (pp. 163–198). Oxford, UK: Oxford University Press.

Enriques, L., & Gargantini, M. (2017). The overarching duty to act in the best interest of the client in MiFID II. In D. Busch & G. Ferrarini (Eds.), *Regulation of the EU financial markets: MiFID II and MiFIR* (pp. 85–122). Oxford, UK: Oxford University Press.

Enriques, L., & Gilotta, S. (2015). Disclosure and financial market regulation. In N. Moloney, E. Ferran, & J. Payne (Eds.), *The Oxford handbook on financial regulation* (pp. 511–536). Oxford, UK: Oxford University Press.

Giudici, P. (2017). Independent financial advice. In D. Busch & G. Ferrarini (Eds.), *Regulation of the EU financial markets: MiFID II and MiFIR* (pp. 147–163). Oxford, UK: Oxford University Press.

Grundmann, S., & Hacker, P. (2017). Conflict of interest. In D. Busch & G. Ferrarini (Eds.), *Regulation of the EU financial markets* (pp. 165–204). Oxford, UK: Oxford University Press.

[49] de Larosière, The High-Level Group on Financial Supervision in the EU, Report (2009).

Herbst, J. (2015). *A practitioner's guide to MiFID II* (2nd ed.). London, England: Sweet & Maxwell/Thomas Reuters.
Möllers, T. M. J. (2016). European legislative practice 2.0: Dynamic harmonisation of capital markets law – MiFID II and PRIIP. *Banking & Finance Law Review, 31*(1), 141–176.
Moloney, N. (2010). *How to protect investors: Lessons from the EC and the UK*. Cambridge, UK: Cambridge University Press.
Moloney, N. (2015). Regulating the retail markets. In N. Moloney, E. Ferran, & J. Payne (Eds.), *The Oxford handbook of financial regulation* (pp. 736–765). Oxford, UK: Oxford University Press.
Paredes, T. A. (2003). Blinded by the light: Information overload and its consequences for securities regulation. *Washington University Law Quarterly, 81*, 417–485.
Silverentand, L., Sprecher, J., & Simons, L. (2017). Inducements. In D. Busch & G. Ferrarini (Eds.), *Regulation of the EU financial markets: MiFID II and MiFIR* (pp. 205–225). Oxford, UK: Oxford University Press.
Tuch, A. F. (2015). Conduct of business regulation. In N. Moloney, E. Ferran, & J. Payne (Eds.), *The Oxford handbook on financial regulation* (pp. 537–567). Oxford, UK: Oxford University Press.

EU Judge

Rainer Arnold and Lukas Cerny

1 Introduction

Jurisdiction is of high importance within the European Union (EU). Rule of law, which is recognised as a basic principle, requires far-reaching judicial competence. The independence of the EU judge is an essential element. The particular status and function of the EU judge, the Court of Justice (CJ), and of the General Court (GC) are analyzed in the following contribution.

2 Rule of Law and Jurisdiction

The European Union is essentially based on the rule of law. This means that all activities of the EU have to comply with law, primary law, which is functionally constitutional law, and secondary law, which has to conform to primary law. Judges, who are necessarily independent institutions, must interpret and apply the law in cases and controversies. It is manifest that the judicial courts efficiently fulfill these basic functions.

3 Judicial Organisation of the EU[1]

Article (Art.) 19 TEU is the constitutional foundation for judicial organisation in the EU, establishing the CJ, the GC, and specialised courts. These three types of EU courts form the European Court of Justice. The number of judges on the CJ is

[1] The structural parts of EU (primary) law provisions are cited as follows:

- a paragraph marked as such in the EU text will be marked in the same way, e.g. Art. 19 (1) TEU

R. Arnold (✉) · L. Cerny
Faculty of Law, University of Regensburg, Regensburg, Germany

A. Bartolini et al. (eds.), *Dictionary of Statuses within EU Law*,
https://doi.org/10.1007/978-3-030-00554-2_28

equivalent to the number of member states. EU jurisdiction requires the participation of judges from the various legal cultures of the member states, which is the basis behind why the CJ shall be composed of one judge from each member state (although not necessarily its citizen[2]).[3]

Acting within the given procedural rules, the judges exercise decision power by applying EU law and are assisted by Advocates-General (AG).[4]

The Statute of the Court (Court Statute) and Art. 254 TFEU enumerate rules on the organisation of the GC.

In accordance with Art. 257 TFEU, specialised courts can be established; the Civil Service Tribunal existed from 2005 until 2016 for the resolution of disputes of EC/EU civil servants.[5]

The distribution of judicial competences between the three types of courts is determined by Art. 256 TFEU and the Court Statute.

4 Qualification, Appointment, Specific Conditions, and Independence of EU Judges

Judges of the CJ must be persons whose "independence is beyond doubt" and "who possess the qualifications required for appointment to the highest judicial offices in their respective countries", or "who are *jurisconsults* of recognised competence".[6] There is no age limit. According to Art. 255 TFEU, an evaluation panel gives an opinion on the candidates' suitability to perform the respective duties of judge or

- a paragraph not marked as a paragraph in the EU text will be indicated as §.., e.g. Art. 267 § 1 TFEU
- a subparagraph will be indicated by §.., subsequently to the marked paragraph, e.g. Art. 19 (1) § 2 TEU (means subparagraph 2 of paragraph 1 of Art. 19 TEU)
- a sentence will be indicated by a number following paragraph…, e.g. Art. 19 (2) § 3.2 (the CJ is assisted by Advocates General).

[2] What is disputed, see Gaitanides, in: von der Groeben, Schwarze, Hatje, Europäisches Unionsrecht, vol. I, 7th ed., 2015, Art. 19 para. 61.

[3] This is a minimum requirement for the GC ("at least", Art. 19 (2) 2 TEU). Forty-six judges have been in office since October 1, 2017 (https://curia.europa.eu/jcms/jcms/Jo2_7033/de/). See Art. 48 of the Court Statute (47 from September 1, 2016 on; two judges from each member state from September one, 2019).

[4] According to Art. 252 TFEU: Eight Advocates-General; the number can be increased (currently there are 11 Advocates-General) in accordance with Art. 252 (1)2 TFEU.
(https://eur-lex.europa.eu/legal-content/EN/TXT/?uri=LEGISSUM%3Aai0049).

[5] For more details, see: https://curia.europa.eu/jcms/jcms/T5_5230/en/.

[6] The GC Judges' qualifications slightly diverge: "… who possess the ability required for appointment to high judicial office" (Art. 254 § 2 TFEU). Slightly diverging also for members of specialised courts: "…ability required for appointment to judicial office." (Art. 257 § 4 TFEU).

AG.[7] The appointment of judges and AGs takes place, after consultation of the evaluation panel, by common accord of the governments of the member states[8] (Art. 253 § 1; 254 § 2.2 TFEU). Their term is 6 years, but reappointment is possible. The president and the vice president of the CJ and GC are elected (with the possibility of re-election) by the judges for a period of 3 years.[9]

Impartiality and independence are elements inherent in judicial function and indispensable to EU judges and AGs. Before taking up their duties, they have to take an oath before the CJ on impartiality, conscientiousness, and preserving secrecy of deliberations (Arts. 2 and 8 Court Statute). To avoid conflicts of interest and to ensure independence and impartiality, they are prohibited from holding any political or administrative office or engaging in any occupation (gainful or voluntary).[10]

Judges and AGs are immune from legal proceedings. Immunity for acts performed in their official capacity extends to the time after their termination of the office.[11]

A judge or AG can be deprived of his/her function (or their pension or other benefits) only under strict conditions. The process includes a deliberation (without the participation of the concerned court member) resulting in the unanimous opinion of all judges and of the CJ (after consultation of the GC or specialised court if one of its members is concerned).[12]

5 Organisation of the CJ and the GC

The CJ is a permanent court (Art. 15 Court Statute) with variable configurations. The judges can act in Chambers of three or five judges, the Grand Chamber, consisting of 15 judges and presided over by the CJ president,[13] or they can sit as a full

[7] See https://eur-lex.europa.eu/legal-content/EN/TXT/?uri=CELEX%3A32010D0124. For the appointment of the panel members from March 1, 2018 onward, see: https://eur-lex.europa.eu/legal-content/EN/TXT/?uri=CELEX%3A32017D2262.

[8] The judges of specialised courts are appointed unanimously by the Council (Art. 257 § 4.2 TEU).

[9] With regard to the partial replacement of the Judges and GAs every three years, see Art. 9 of the Court Statute, Art. 253 § 2, and Art. 254 § 2.3 TFEU.

[10] See Arts. 4 § 1 and § 2 of the Court Statute, exemption to § 2 possible by Council's consent. Integrity and discretion as to the acceptance of appointments and benefits are required for the judges and AGs after the termination of their function; in case of doubt the CJ will decide (if a GC or specialised court member is concerned, the CJ will hear these courts before), Art.4 § 3,4 Court Statute).

[11] See Art. 3 § 1, 2 (for further details § 3, 4) Court Statute as well as Art. 11 a) of the Protocol on the Privileges and Immunities of the European Union.
(https://eurlex.europa.eu/legalcontent/EN/TXT/?uri=CELEX%3A12012E%2FPRO%2F07). Arts. 3 § 4 Court Statute makes reference furthermore to Arts. 11–14 and 17 of the mentioned Protocol; for details see these provisions.

[12] See Art. 6 of the Court Statute.

[13] If a member state or an EU institution that is a party to the proceedings so requests (Art. 16 § 3 Court Statute).

Court.[14] The GC sits in Chambers with three or five judges, as set forth by the procedural rules, as a full Court,[15] as the Grand Chamber,[16] or as a single judge (Art. 50 Court Statute).[17] Judges can be designated as AGs for GC proceedings.[18]

6 Judges Acting Within Their Competences

6.1 The Application of EU Law

The CJ, the GC, and the specialised courts are charged by Art. 19 (1) 2 TEU to interpret and to apply EU "law". This includes all types of EU law: primary law (in particular the TEU, the TFEU, and the fundamental rights charter); secondary law (regulations, directives, decisions as typical compulsory acts, recommendations, opinions as typical, noncompulsory acts, and the large spectrum of atypical acts of the EU institutions); the unwritten general principles of EU law; and the (less important) customary EU law. General principles have been important EU legal sources since the beginning and continue to be relevant today; they complement written structural principles or fill gaps in the law. The ECJ's jurisprudence has developed, starting in the 1960s, fundamental rights and rules of law through unwritten, general principles based on common constitutional traditions of the member states, and also on international treaties of a regional (e.g. the European Convention of Human Rights) or universal character (Sarrión Esteve 2015, pp. 33–49). The interpretative methodology was that of a "selective comparison",[19] creating an EU general principle that neither a minimum nor a maximum solution would be found in the national or international reference order, but that the courts would seek the *optimum* solution inspired by these orders that fits in the "structure and objectives of the community".[20] Today the function of unwritten general principles of EU law is more limited since the adoption of the fundamental rights charter in 2009; they complement, in accordance with Art. 6 (3) TEU, the Charter. International treaties entered into by the EU are incorporated as sources of international law into the EU internal legal order and enjoy a rank between secondary and

[14] In the proceedings on the dismissal of the ombudsman (Art. 228 (2) TFEU); dismissal of a Commissioner (Art. 245 (2)TFEU and Art. 247 TFEU) or on the dismissal of a member of the Court of Auditors (Art. 286 (6) TFEU).

[15] Plenum, Art. 47 Rules of Procedure (RP) GC (https://eur-lex.europa.eu/legal-content/EN/TXT/?uri=CELEX%3A32015Q0423%2801%29).

[16] Art. 28 and Art.15 RP GC (15 judges).

[17] Art 29 RP GC.

[18] Arts. 30, 31 RP GC.

[19] In German often called "wertende Rechtsvergleichung", Gaitanides, Artikel 19 para. 22.

[20] For information on the methodology, see ECJ Internationale Handelsgesellschaft, ECLI:EU:C:1970:114, para. 4, which is "ensured within the framECLI:EU:C:1974:41ework of the structure and objectives of the community" (para 4 of this decision).

primary EU law (Art. 216 (2) 2 TFEU). As they form an integral part of the supranational legal order,[21] EU judges must apply them (Arnold and Meindl 2017).

The EU courts do not decide whether to apply national law. The limits of national law drawn by EU law are submitted to the EU's jurisdiction. The exception clauses of the fundamental freedoms (e.g. Art. 36 TFEU for the free movement of goods) are to be regarded as EU law, as determined, and therefore under the review, by the EU courts. Furthermore, national law can be helpful for interpreting EU law. A significant example is Art. 52 (4) of the fundamental rights charter, which establishes rules for interpreting the charter rights in light of the common constitutional traditions of the member states, in so far as these charter rights are inspired by the member states' legal orders.

The task of interpreting EU law is given not only to EU courts, but also to the national courts applying EU law. EU law is predominantly exercised or implemented by national institutions and, quite generally, directly affects the national order. It is important in this context to refer to the mechanisms of cooperation between EU CJ and national courts through the proceedings of preliminary questions (Art. 267 TFEU). This mechanism enables national courts to involve the CJ and keep the CJ informed of interpretations of EU law, which are relevant in the national proceedings. This process ensures the uniform interpretation of EU law, which is a necessary complement to the primacy rule.

For the CJ to review the compatibility of secondary and primary EU law, all national courts, not only the last instance courts, are obliged to address the CJ.

While rule of law is a basic principle within the EU legal order, and forms the basis for the efficient and comprehensive review of EU legal and political actions (or omissions), the field of common foreign and security policy is exempt from EU courts' jurisdiction (Art. 24 (1) § 6 TEU; 275 TFEU).[22] Other topics exempt from EU court review are issues of freedom, security, and justice (Arts. 82 to 89 TFEU), according to Art. 276 TFEU.

6.2 *Types of Action in Which EU Judges Apply EU Law*

There are three main types of legal actions: (1) actions against a member state for non-fulfillment of obligations resulting from EU law (Arts. 258, and 259 TFEU); (2) preliminary ruling procedures[23] (Art. 267 TFEU); and (3) direct actions (Arts. 263, 265, 268 TFEU). The CJ can also deliver opinions on the compatibility of international treaties with EU primary law (proceedings prior to the conclusion of the treaty) (Art. 218 (11) TFEU), and others.

[21] See ECJ Haegeman, ECLI:EU:C:1974:41,para. 5 and subsequent jurisprudence.

[22] For exceptions see Art. 40 TEU and 275 § 2 TFEU.

[23] For the expedited procedure see Arts. 105, 106 of the Rules of Procedure for the CJ (RP CJ); for the urgent procedure see Arts. 103 to 114 RP CJ.

Art. 256 TFEU regulates the distribution of judicial competences among the different branches of the EU courts; actions types (1) and (2) in the above list are resolved by the CJ.[24]

First instance proceedings of direct actions triggering Arts. 263 (legality review), 265 (infringement for failure to act), 268 (compensation for damage), 270 (dispute EU and its servants),[25] and 272 TFEU (judgment pursuant to arbitration clause) fall within the competence of the GC, with the exception of proceedings reserved to specialised courts or to the CJ, per the Court Statute.

Article 51 modifies processes in multiple ways. It does so by modifying: actions initiated by a member state or by an EU institution against European Parliament or Council or against both in cooperation (see Art. 289 TFEU); initiated by or actions initiated by a member state against the Commission in the framework of enhanced cooperation (Art. 331 (1) TFEU); and actions of EU institutions against the European Central Bank do not fall in first instance into the competence of the GC but of the CJ.[26] The CJ reviews appeals of first instance decisions by the GC.

7 The Importance of the Judges' Activities for EU Integration

"Integration by jurisprudence" is a well-known saying that characterises the important rule the judges within the EU system. The supranational EU law is dynamic and has to be interpreted in an evolutionary, *effet utile*-oriented way (Potacs 2009). EC/EU judges have developed, in a rich jurisprudence, principles that are indispensable for a successful integration process: the direct effect and primacy of EC/EU law; the fundamental rights of the individual; the concept of rule of law; an integration-oriented interpretation methodology; the principles of proportionality and subsidiarity (later expressed by own provisions); and others. It can be said that judges have created the EC/EU constitutional order.

8 The Particular Status of the EU Judge

The status of the supranational judge of the European Union is quite different from that of the traditional national judge. The judge's task is to interpret and apply multinational law. A transnational methodology has to be applied. The dynamism

[24] The attribution of preliminary ruling proceedings to the GC in certain fields in accordance with Art. 256 (3) TFEU through specific provisions of the Court Statute has not yet been realised.

[25] See Art. 50, a Court Statute that clearly establishes the GC competence (re-attributed from a specialised court that no longer exists).

[26] See also the exceptions from the CJ competence made by Art. 51 a) Court Statute.

of the integration process has been duly considered as an inherent element in the understanding of the normative text. Different legal cultures, which form the educational bases of the judges coming from different countries, flow together. The various perspectives the judges introduced into the common deliberation process enrich the transnational vision, which is necessary for ruling on integration matters.

References

Arnold, R., & Meindl, E. (2017). Außenhandelsrecht. Grundlagen. In M. Dauses & M. Ludwigs (Eds.), 43th ed. K (I).

Gaitanides, Ch. (2015). Art. 19 TEU. In H. von der Groeben, J. Schwarze, & A. Hatje (Eds.), Europäisches Unionsrecht. (I), (pp. 307–330).

Potacs, M. (2009). Effet utile als Auslegungsgrundsatz. *Europarecht (EuR)*, (4), 465–487.

Sarrión Esteve, J. (2015) *El Tribunal de Justicia de Luxemburgo como Garante de los Derechos Fundamentales*. Madrid: Ed. Dykinson.

EU Officer

Carlos Francisco Molina del Pozo and Pablo Molina del Pozo Martín

1 Introduction

It could be concluded that, among the changes that have taken place in international law, the creation and subsequent consolidation of an international civil service has had the biggest impact. It would be interesting to analyse the direction of the historical development of international law that followed this. However, we shall limit ourselves to highlighting the way in which, in our opinion, this branch of law first stemmed from international administrative law and, secondly, was fed by international constitutional law. The result of this was that international officials began to be actors in a kind of permanent cooperation between different states.

All types of officials were recognized as international. Even regional organizations employed international officials. It was inevitable and absolutely necessary that these officials would make a contribution, in terms of their culture, education, and ways and methods, since such international organizations ought to be enriched by the contributions that could be offered by the diversity of countries, in order to improve the spirit of the organization. In this regard, the status of international officials is recognized as something that is necessary for the common interest, even though it might be strongly rejected by certain states that see part of their sovereignty being sacrificed for the sake of the sound functioning of the organization as a whole.

Over the years, the law governing all the aforementioned relationships continued to evolve. In the early days of international organizations, the relationships between these organizations and their staff were essentially based on contracts; the relationships that

C. F. Molina del Pozo (✉)
Department of Law, Universidad de Alcalá de Henares, Alcalá de Henares, Spain
e-mail: carlosf.molina@uah.es

P. Molina del Pozo Martín
DG DEVCO - Unit 4 International Cooperation and Development, Bruxelles, Belgium

A. Bartolini et al. (eds.), *Dictionary of Statuses within EU Law*,
https://doi.org/10.1007/978-3-030-00554-2_29

were established were thus contractual. At the same time, the organization used to define, for each official, the remuneration arrangements and the various advantages that were granted. Nevertheless, the general trend, in contrast to the above, was to replace the bulk of the conventional and specific provisions with an objective set of staff regulations, without fully abandoning the contractual nature, and this contractual nature is still maintained even today in some international organizations. Therefore, staff regulations appear as something specific to each organization. In any case, we can identify three families of organizations that have tried to coordinate their respective regulations for their officials. These families are the UN, Western organizations and the European Union.

2 Legal Definition, Past, Present and Future Developments of the Legal Status of EU Officials and the Impact of These Developments on EU Legislation

The total number of institutions that constitute the structure of the EU was not perfectly defined at the very beginning. On the contrary, the institutions were created as a result of various concerns that appeared over the years and required the use of quite diverse techniques and procedures. However, we can see that there was a desire for unification at an institutional level. What we now call the EU staff administration originates from the entry into force of the ECSC Treaty in 1952. Later, in 1956, staff regulations were laid down within the ECSC. In 1958 two other communities were established, the EEC and the EAEC, and a number of common services were put in place for the two communities. Subsequently, the merger of the executive bodies of the three communities took place in 1967 once the crisis had been overcome. The culmination of all the above events was the succession of enlargements that we witnessed in 1973, 1981 and 1986.

In particular, 1962 proved to be an important year as it was then that the common regulations were created, covering all officials and other types of staff linked to the European Union. As Plantey suggests (1977, pp. 54 and 55), each organization had its own personality, its own rules, its own regulations, its own finance and its own staff[1]; but even then the tendency was to establish a single EU civil service career path within the then European communities. Since 1958 both the Court of Justice and the Assembly have been common institutions. However, staff recruited before 1958 maintained their affiliation to the scheme laid down by the ECSC Treaty, whereas the rules and regime provided for in the former Treaty applied to those who joined thereafter.[2] Each institution began setting up a series of employment contracts for their staff.

In 1956, the ECSC's own staff regulations entered into force but, as we have already said, from 1962 onwards there were uniform standards for all staff. On 29

[1] See Joined Cases 27/59 and 39/59, Alberto Campolongo v High Authority of the ECSC, ECR [1960], 391.

[2] See Cases-25/60De Bruyn/Common Assembly, ECR [1962] 21.

February 1968, the Council decided to apply one single regulation, although in certain cases transitional measures were still applied. Therefore, with the conclusion of the Merger Treaty on 8 April 1965, all officials and other staff of the various institutions were integrated as part of a single administration. The same legal status has been applied since then to all the different categories of staff in the European Union. However, it should be noted that, even today, there is not complete administrative unification. Hierarchical authority is still shared on the basis of the existing division or classification of the institutions: the Council, the Commission and the Court of Justice. The case of the Economic and Social Committee deserves special mention,[3] as well as all the institutions that emerged afterwards, such as the Court of Auditors, and those that may emerge in the future.

Accordingly, it can be concluded that, since the merger of the executive bodies of the three communities, there has been a clear trend towards a single career path within the European Union. The Commission services, which have the largest number of employees among the institutions, constitute one single administration, according to Article 17 of the Rules of Procedure of the European Commission. Moreover, the existence of jurisdictional unity has contributed decisively to emphasizing the aforementioned trend, especially through the development of consultation and other forms of conflict resolution.[4]

As is suggested by the staff regulations that were published in 1968, the general implementing provisions thereof are to be adopted by each institution, after consulting the staff committee. In 2000 the Commission published a white paper on the reform of the Commission, reflecting the objective of the strategy for reform—introducing changes in order to ensure the application of principles such as efficiency, accountability, transparency, responsibility and universal labour agreements in this unique multinational public administration. The document stated that, with regard to human resources, the aim of the reform process was to foster an independent, permanent European civil service that is complete and effective, thereby enabling the Commission to function in its capacity as an organization that is a global player.

The Prodi Commission began to act on this basis. For example, it applied the principle of mobility for officials of higher grades, and on 18 September 1999 it decided to initiate the rotation of a large number of officials. Thus, on 8 December 1999 it adopted guidelines for promoting officials to level AD16 (Director-General) and AD15 (Director), and carried out a robust review of the mechanisms for the evaluation of merit, bearing in mind the imperatives of geographical balance and equal opportunities.

These initiatives, supported by a comprehensive reform of the human resources policy, allowed the approval and adoption of Council Regulation No 723/2004 of 22 March 2004 amending the staff regulations of officials of the European Communities and the conditions of employment of other servants of the European Communities. Thus, this reform ensured the following: a better balance between work and family

---

[3] Protocol (No 7) on the Privileges and Immunities of the European Union, Art. 2.

[4] See Joined Cases 27/59 and 39/59, Alberto Campolongo v High Authority of the ECSC, ECR [1960], 391.

life for officials by introducing a new statutory ability to take parental or family leave, and opening the possibility for part-time working[5]; a necessary and attractive update of the remuneration and pension scheme; the independence of officials, by not allowing them to deal with any matter in which, directly or indirectly, they had any personal interest that might impair their independence and, in particular, any family or financial interests; the requirement to know a third EU official language; freedom of expression; the legal recognition of the spouses of EU officials, etc. Consequently, this reform enabled a genuine modernization of the European public service, making it ethically adapted to social change (Gervasoni 2005).

3 General Provisions, Rights and Obligations of EU Officials

Who can be considered as an EU official? The answer can be found in Article 1b of the Staff Regulations, according to which an official is any person who has been appointed, as provided for in the Staff Regulations, to an established post on the staff of one of the European institutions; the appointment must take place on the basis of an instrument issued by the appointing authority of that institution.[6] The act of appointment of an official must specify the exact date from which the appointment takes effect, and this date may not be earlier than the official starting date of his activities (Article 3).

The content of Article 5 is of significant importance, as it lays down a classification into different function groups depending on the qualifications required. Thus, we see that function groups are classified according to the nature and importance of the duties to which they relate, leading to the existence of three function groups: the administrators' function group ('*AD*'), the assistants' function group ('*AST*') and a third group called '*AST/SC*' that brings together secretarial and office staff.[7,8]

[5] Article 56b of the Staff Regulations.

[6] See CJEU C-102-75 Petersen v Commission, ECLI:EU:C:1976:172: the appointment of an official should be based on a unilateral decision of the appointing authority. Thus, the established link between an official and his institution is statutory and not contractual in nature: CJEU, 27 October 2004, (T-508/93, RecFP P. II-761).

[7] Before the 2004 reform, there were four broad categories of officials (and not 'function groups'), which were identified in descending order in Article 5.1 by the letters A (superior career), B (intermediate career), C (average career) and D (normal career), as well as language grades designated by letters L/A for translation and interpretation tasks; all these categories were further divided into different grades (Art. 5-1). On this issue, readers should consult the work of Rogalla (1982, pp. 48–49). See also Molina Del Pozo (1988). However, these categories have not, in general, disappeared. They were actually recast in a more flexible and appropriate qualification system. The Commission decided, with the support of the Council, to create two function groups, a group of administrators consisting of officials of Category A, such as linguists for example, and a group of assistants consisting of officials in the former categories B, C and D, thus allowing an improvement, taking into account merit and the right to a more linear career development.

[8] Likewise, see Regulation (EU, EURATOM) No 1023/2013 of the European Parliament and of the Council of 22 October 2013 amending the Staff Regulations of Officials of the European Union

The function group AD comprises twelve grades, corresponding to administrative, advisory, linguistic and scientific duties.[9] Appointment to this function group requires a level of education that corresponds to completed university studies, or professional training of an equivalent level.[10] The twelve grades of the AD function group correspond to the following posts[11]:

- AD16 Director General.
- AD15 Director.
- AD13/AD14 Administrator working as e.g. Director/Head of Unit/Adviser/linguistic expert; economic expert; legal expert; medical expert; veterinary expert; scientific expert; research expert; financial expert, audit expert.
- AD11/AD12 Administrator working as Head of Unit/principal translator, principal interpreter, principal economist; principal lawyer; principal medical officer; principal veterinary inspector; principal scientist; principal researcher; principal financial officer, principal audit officer.
- AD9/AD10 Administrator working as Head of Unit/senior translator; senior interpreter; senior economist; senior lawyer etc.
- AD7/AD8 Administrator working as translator; interpreter; economist; lawyer; medical officer; veterinary inspector; scientist; researcher; financial officer, auditor.
- AD5/AD6 Administrator working as junior translator; junior interpreter; junior economist; junior lawyer; junior medical officer; junior veterinary inspector; junior scientist; junior researcher; junior financial officer, junior auditor.[12]

The function group AST comprises eleven grades, corresponding to executive, technical and clerical duties.[13] The eleven grades of the AST function group correspond to the following posts:

- AST11 Assistant working as personal assistant (p.a.);
- AST10/AST9 Assistant working as: personal assistant (p.a.); clerical officer; technical officer; IT officer
- AST8/AST7 Assistant working as: senior clerk; senior documentalist; senior technician; senior IT operative
- AST6/AST5 Assistant working as: clerk; documentalist; technician; IT operative

---

and the Conditions of Employment of Other Servants of the European Union (OJ L 287/19 of 29 October 2013).

[9] Article 5.2 §1 of amended Staff Regulations of 1 May 2004.

[10] Article 5.3 (b) and (c).

[11] Annex I Types of posts in each function group, as provided for in Article 5(3) of the Staff Regulations.

[12] The jobs described in grade AD5 also correspond to those in grade AST5, but the latter does not require the same education and training level.

[13] Article 5.2 § 2 of the Staff Regulations.

- AST4/AST3 Assistant working as: junior clerk; junior documentalist; junior technician, junior IT operative
- AST2/AST1 Assistant working as: filing clerk; technical attendant; IT attendant, parliamentary usher

Identical conditions for recruitment and service career apply to all officials belonging to the same function group or to the same grade.

Finally, we need to indicate that the various institutions also employ staff on a contractual basis. The employment contracts for these staff are in conformity with the rules on the conditions of employment of other servants of the European Union, laid down in Council Regulation No 259/68 of 29 February 1968.[14] This regulation identifies four groups/profiles: temporary staff, contract staff,[15] local staff and special advisers.[16]

Contract staff should perform their duties and conduct themselves in accordance with the strict aims and interests of the European Union, and they cannot accept or seek instructions from any government, authority, organization or person outside their institution. In addition, before appointing an official, the appointing authority must examine whether the candidate has any personal interest that might impair his independence, or any other conflict of interest. To that end, the candidate, using a specific form, must inform the appointing authority of any actual or potential conflicts of interest. In our opinion, the imposition of all these restrictions on the actions and conduct of the official is aimed at maintaining the highest degree of independence: the official is not allowed to compromise his independence in the performance of his duties and in relation to any authority that is external to the institution in which he works.[17]

Article 19 is perhaps one of the most important in terms of the obligations and responsibilities of EU officials. Indeed, this article refers to a key area: the rule of confidentiality. This rule is observed in court, whatever the cause or the capacity in which the officer appears in court, unless there is explicit permission from the competent authority.[18] The duty of EU officials to maintain secrecy is so important that, even after the expiry of their employment relationship, they remain obliged to comply fully. We should also highlight Article 23, which is dedicated to the issue of privileges and immunities. In the exclusive interest of the European Union, certain privileges and immunities are conferred on European civil servants.

---

[14] OJ L 56, 4.3.1968, 1.

[15] Contractual agents, who may not exceed 75% of the relevant staff.

[16] See Rogalla (1982, pp. 104–113). Previously, there were also auxiliary staff on fixed-term contracts with the possibility of extensions until 31 December 2007. From 31 December 2006 it was possible to employ new auxiliary agents under Article 52 of the Staff Regulations, which was inserted by Regulation No 723/2004 of the Council of 22 March 2004, OJ L 123, 27.4.2004, page 1. However, there is now a category of auxiliary contract agents, laid down by Articles 3b and 3c of the Regulation, applicable to other servants who perform manual or administrative support service tasks.

[17] CJEU, T-273/94 N v Commission, Rec Fp P. II-289 §126-132.

[18] See CJEU, C-54/90, Weddel v Commission, Rec. [1992] I-871 §20.

4 Conclusions

On the indisputable basis that the primary objective, not only in EU administration but also in the national administrations of the Member States, is the provision of a public service, it is clear that all administrations have had to adapt to the developments that have taken place in recent decades with regard to citizens' needs, since it is citizens who are, logically, the recipients of these services. The major societal changes to which we refer are mainly due to these three factors:

- Innovation in the field of new technology: both the creation and the further evolution of informatics, with the expansion of knowledge and data handling, ensure that information is available with efficiency and speed. Undoubtedly, the European Union has also benefited from innovation.
- Changes in social structures: in this regard, we can highlight the major change that society has experienced in education. An ever increasing number of people now have access to university education. To this we can add another development, which is the fact that all levels of society, to a large extent, no longer accept the mere imposition of authority without prior discussion.
- Tendency to budgetary restrictions: both the Member States and the European Union itself have decided to align themselves with the effort, at a global level, to limit budget excesses.

We are faced with an administration the problems and objectives of which differ very little from those of national administrations, apart, of course, from the particularly important territorial and human dimension that they are addressing. In the future, the trend will be to aim to structure perfect coordination between the central administration, with its headquarters in Brussels and Luxembourg, and the national administrations of many other Member States. Through their integration into the central administration, the latter will function as management and coordination centres of a huge institutional construction, which is the European civil service.

References

Gervasoni, S. (2005, February). Un nouveau statut pour les fonctionnaires des Communautés européennes: les principales dispositions de la réforme. *CFP*, 8–13.

Molina Del Pozo, C. F. (1988). *Europa y los funcionarios*. Madrid: Fundación Universidad Empresa.

Rogalla, D. (1982). *Fonction publique européenne*. Brussels: Fernand Nathan and Editions Labour, Collection Europe.

EU Representative to a Third Country

Carlos Francisco Molina del Pozo and Pablo Molina del Pozo Martín

1 Introduction

The European External Action Service (EEAS) started to become a reality when the Council established the organization and functioning of this service on 26 July 2010. Its legal framework makes it a functionally autonomous body of the EU, having its headquarters in Brussels, being separate from the General Secretariat of the Council and from the Commission and having the legal capacity necessary to perform its tasks and attain its objectives.[1] The most important conclusion to be drawn from this is that the EEAS is not an 'institution' as referred to in Article 13 TEU, and that it lacks the legal powers of the other institutions (Van Vooren 2011, p. 486). The idea of an EU diplomatic service is the fruit of an attractive and enriching debate that took place more than ten years ago during a Working Group meeting in 2002, when the participants drew very interesting conclusions about the future in this area.[2]

Diplomatic relations have always been regarded as a privilege and a monopoly of sovereign states (Plantey 2000, pp. 18 ff.).[3] It should be noted that, as has already been said, the EU is sui generis and was created as a consequence of a gradual negotiation process (Erkelens and Blockmans 2012). The Member States have

---

[1] See Article 1(2) of Council Decision 2010/427/EU of 26 July 2010 establishing the organisation and functioning of the European External Action Service, OJEU 2010, L 201/30 of 3 August 2010 ('Council Decision EEAS').

[2] CONV 459/02, Final Report of Working Group VII on External Action, Brussels, 16 December 2002, pp. 6, 7.

[3] According to Plantey, sovereignty is also a necessary condition for the development of diplomacy. The international diplomatic scheme has a strong national nature.

C. F. Molina del Pozo (✉)
Department of Law, Universidad de Alcalá de Henares, Alcalá de Henares, Spain
e-mail: carlosf.molina@uah.es

P. Molina del Pozo Martín
DG DEVCO - Unit 4 International Cooperation and Development, Bruxelles, Belgium

A. Bartolini et al. (eds.), *Dictionary of Statuses within EU Law*,
https://doi.org/10.1007/978-3-030-00554-2_30

gradually granted the EU various powers, including those enabling it to operate outside its borders.[4] On the other hand, given that the EU is not a nation state, some authors, from a purely national point of view, argue that international diplomatic law should not have jurisdiction.

The 1961 Vienna Convention on Diplomatic Relations[5] and customary international diplomatic law constitute the legal framework for inter-state diplomatic relations. States are parties to the Vienna Convention. However, this raises a crucial question: we refer to the application of international diplomatic law to an actor that is not a state as such, namely the EU. Over the years, the scope and the number of diplomatic missions have increased significantly (Ambast and Tyagi 2008, p. 16). The EU has an active and passive *ius legationis*, based on its bilateral and multilateral diplomatic relations around the world, in order to manage its international relations. Although Articles 48 and 50 of the above-mentioned Convention[6] prevent the EU from being a partner, they are widely applied in the bilateral diplomatic relations of the EU through several agreements.

2 Principles and Values Governing the EEAS and the Heads of Delegation

To be able to understand more clearly the legal status of the head of an EU delegation, we should start from the basics, which are the principles underlying the activities of the EEAS. First, the principle of autonomy is the basis of the service. This, as has already been said, was established by a Council Decision as an autonomous body separate from the General Secretariat of the Council and from the Commission and having the legal capacity necessary to perform its tasks and attain its objectives.[7] The EEAS, however, does not have the power to adopt individual and binding decisions vis-à-vis third parties. However, despite this lack of power, an exception might be found under Article 263 TFEU with regard to service level agreements that may be concluded by the EEAS.[8] This type of act could have legal effects in relation to third parties (Van Vooren 2010). Despite this autonomy, the EEAS is placed

[4] The European Union, pursuant to Art. 4(2) TEU, must respect the Member States' essential state functions in the exercise of the powers transferred by them.

[5] The Vienna Convention on Diplomatic Relations was signed in Vienna on 18 April 1961 and entered into force on 24 April 1964. See United Nations Treaty Series (UNTS), Volume 500.

[6] According to Article 48, 'The present Convention shall be open for signature by all States Members of the United Nations or of any of the specialized agencies or of the International Atomic Energy Agency or parties to the Statute of the International Court of Justice, and by any other State invited by the General Assembly of the United Nations to become a party to the Convention,…'. Article 50: 'This Convention shall remain open for accession by any State belonging to any of the categories mentioned in Article 48'.

[7] See Article 1(2) Council Decision EEAS.

[8] See Article 3(4) and 4(5) Council Decision EEAS.

under the authority of the High Representative of the Union for Foreign Affairs and Security Policy ('the High Representative').[9]

We must pay attention to the principles of cooperation and coordination that are clearly reflected in the strategic planning and programming of the EEAS, as these principles are essential for development and decision-making in the field of external action. Therefore, a sound interaction between the EEAS and the Member States, through the structures that are based in Brussels (COREPER, PSC and the working parties), through key figures within the EEAS and through political mandates, remains essential (Lefebvre and Hillion 2010).

The principle of loyal cooperation between the Member States and the EU institutional actors is at the heart of the European integration process. The European practice, and in particular the judgments of the Court of Justice of the EU, has demonstrated the proper functioning of the system of governance as it is defined (Halberstam 2004). This principle of loyalty or cooperation, which can also be seen in international law, and, in particular, the principle of good faith, is common in federal systems. The requirement of unity is always emphasized in the process of European integration (Mortelmans 1998).

Account has been taken of loyal cooperation in the various aspects of EU action, and the duty of loyalty was put in place to ensure the external and internal functioning of the Union. In addition, the principle of loyalty can be combined with other principles such as the principle of efficiency and the principle of supremacy. In this way, we stress the importance of the principle that, in our opinion, plays a key role in the creation of greater efficiency in the representation of the EU on the international stage (Casolari 2012).

3 Context and Framework of European Diplomacy: Beginning and Evolution to Date

The Maastricht Treaty was signed on 7 February 1992 by the ministers for foreign affairs of the then 12 member states, following the agreement reached by the heads of state and government participating in the summit held in the Dutch city of Maastricht from 9 to 11 December 1991. It entered into force on 1 November 1993, allowing the implementation of the political integration of the EU.

This Treaty came in the wake of the Single European Act, which carried out the most important reform of the 1957 Treaty of Rome and created the European political cooperation policy, the forerunner of the Common Foreign Policy. Launching the Treaty was rather complex, and the only possible compromise was to base it on three pillars, the pillars of integration and cooperation that formed the European Union. The Treaty stands on top of the entire structure and integrates it as part of a harmonized superstructure: the European Communities, the Common Foreign and Security Policy (CFSP) and cooperation in home and judicial affairs.

[9] See Article 1(3) Council Decision EEAS.

The second pillar, which concerns us most, is defined by the provisions of Title V and relates to the CFSP. It deepens the intergovernmental approach and reduces the supranationality that is represented by the Community. It replaces the provisions of the Single European Act and allows Member States to take joint action in foreign policy. The text of the Treaty is mitigated by the declaration that the decisions of the Council of Ministers on the CFSP must be taken unanimously. However, for specific measures in this area, the Council of Ministers may unanimously decide that decisions can be taken by a qualified majority. Thus, it can be shown that the first steps in the European foreign policy were very different from what we know today, and Member States are still very reluctant to relinquish part of their sovereignty to the EU in these areas. The role of the Commission and the Parliament was modest and the jurisdiction of the Court of Justice is not applicable in this field (Molina del Pozo 2002, 2015).

There was some small progress in the 1997 Treaty of Amsterdam and the 2001 Treaty of Nice, but nevertheless, the huge leap forward took place in 2004 with the so-called 'non nato' constitutional treaty that established a constitution for Europe. This was signed by all the Member States on 27 October 2004, but ultimately did not enter into force because France and the Netherlands refused to ratify it. One of the main innovations of this Treaty was the creation of a minister for CFSP, a position that was later renamed the minister of foreign affairs; the minister would also be responsible for the co-ordination of the defence policy. However, this designation did not reach the text of the Treaty that was signed in Lisbon, because some Member States did not approve of the use and insertion into the Treaty of terms evoking federalism or supranational integration. In the end, the title 'High Representative of the EU for Foreign Affairs and Security Policy' was agreed in Lisbon. With the so-called Constitutional Treaty, the CFSP remains in a blurred field of intergovernmental cooperation. The Treaty establishing a constitution for Europe was aimed at preventing the selection of shared competences between the European Union and its Member States, and it simply stated that countries should 'actively and unreservedly' support the Union's common foreign and security policy and they 'should therefore refrain from any action contrary to the Union's interests'.[10]

From the outset, among the priorities of the Treaty of Lisbon was the improvement, modernization and strengthening of the role of the EU in the global arena (Duke 2009). One of the other main objectives of the Treaty was to provide the EU with proper tools and instruments to allow it to assume its responsibilities in the world and establish a foreign policy with third countries (Wouters et al. 2008). As was explained previously, new actors have appeared who need to learn to coexist and maintain a good relationship with each other. On the one hand, there is the high representative[11]—currently Federica Mogherini, who has the general task of

[10] See the Treaty establishing a Constitution for Europe, Chapter II, Section 1, Article III-294.2.

[11] The change of title of the post reflects the fact that it has become clear that human resources represent the Union and not the Member States. The President of the European Council, and not the EU, exercises the powers of this post, without prejudice to the powers of the Department of Human Resources and Security Policy of the Union.

conducting the EU's CFSP with the support of the EEAS[12]—and, on the other, there is the president of the European Council, currently Donald Tusk, who at this level and in this capacity ensures the external representation of the Union on issues concerning the CFSP.[13]

4 A 'Traditional' Legal Definition of the Head of an EU Delegation

Each delegation or embassy has a head of delegation with the same power as an ambassador. An ambassador exercises his authority over all staff in the delegation and is responsible for all its activities.[14] He is accountable to the high representative—from whom he receives instructions—for the overall management of the work of the delegation. Whenever the Commission, within the scope of its powers, gives instructions to the delegations on certain policy areas, those instructions are executed under the responsibility of the head of the delegation. The head of the delegation has the authority to commit and implement operational funding that the EU grants in his area of competence, in accordance with the financial rules of the Commission. The head of delegation also has the power to represent the Union fully in the country where the delegation is accredited, particularly for the conclusion of contracts, and as a party to legal proceedings. EU ambassadors are appointed by the high representative with the approval of the Council and after a hearing before the Foreign Affairs Committee of the European Parliament.

The Vienna Convention establishes, in particular in its Article 3 which is of especial importance, the five functions of a diplomatic mission,[15] as well as what each function includes. However, EU diplomacy provides that the head of a delegation carries out his tasks as a person directly appointed by the European Union to carry out these tasks. EU diplomacy grants him the power to conclude contracts on behalf of the EU in the country where the delegation is accredited.[16] Similarly, embassies may sometimes be allowed to defend legal proceedings on behalf of the European Union. Therefore, the EEAS must be informed of every situation, particularly situations occurring in a third country.

[12] See Articles 18 and 27(2) TEU.

[13] See Article 15(6) TEU.

[14] See Article 5(1) of Council Decision EEAS.

[15] Article 3: The functions of a diplomatic mission consist, inter alia, in: (a) Representing the sending State in the receiving State; (b) Protecting in the receiving State the interests of the sending State and of its nationals, within the limits permitted by international law; (c) Negotiating with the Government of the receiving State; (d) Ascertaining by all lawful means conditions and developments in the receiving State, and reporting thereon to the Government of the sending State; (e) Promoting friendly relations between the sending State and the receiving State, and developing their economic, cultural and scientific relations.

[16] See Article 5(8) of Council Decision EEAS.

Below, we will refer to the internal ranking of diplomatic missions. Indeed, the Vienna Convention foresees, in addition to the ambassador, several categories of staff, such as the administrative and technical staff, the service staff and the private servants (or domestic service staff) of the mission.[17] Each delegation proposes the classification of staff in the diplomatic list, and this proposal may be accepted or refused by the host state.[18] The EEAS uses its own classification system for diplomatic staff, which reflects the different grades in the internal administration. This classification is translated into equivalent diplomatic titles and is sent to the host state.

5 Special Provisions

The Council Decision of 26 July 2010 made a number of changes to the staff regulations for EU officials in order to accommodate the needs of the new EEAS, ensuring that these officials enjoy a special status and the advantages that are mentioned in Title VIII(b) of the staff regulations.[19]

The Council Decision EEAS refers to the EEAS staff. In this regard, the powers conferred by the staff regulations on the appointing authority are exercised by the high representative, then the high representative determines who may determine who within the EEAS should exercise those powers. Article 2(2) of the Council Decision applies.

Furthermore, in respect of heads of delegation, the powers concerning appointments are to be exercised, using a thorough selection procedure based on merit and having regard to gender and geographical balance, on the basis of a final list of candidates on which the Commission has agreed within the framework of the powers conferred on it by the Treaties. This applies mutatis mutandis to transfers in the interest of the service made in exceptional circumstances and for a defined temporary period to a post of head of delegation. In addition, in cases where staff have to carry out tasks for the Commission as part of their duties, the appointing authority must initiate administrative inquiries and disciplinary proceedings, as referred to in Articles 22 and 86 and Annex IX, if the Commission so requests.[20]

Notwithstanding Article 11, a Commission official working in a Union delegation must take instructions from the head of the delegation in accordance with the latter's role, as provided for in Article 5 of the Council Decision.[21] An EEAS official who has to carry out tasks for the Commission as part of his duties takes instructions from the Commission with regard to those tasks, in accordance with Article 221(2)

[17] See Article 37 of the Vienna Convention on Diplomatic Relations.

[18] See Article 17 of the Vienna Convention on Diplomatic Relations.

[19] See Regulation (EU, EURATOM) No 1080/2010 of the European Parliament and of the Council of 24 November 2010, published in OJEU L 311 of 26 November 2010.

[20] See OJ L 311 of 26 November 2010, amended Article 95.

[21] See *Council Decision EEAS*.

of the Treaty on the Functioning of the European Union.[22] In addition, with regard to those officials who have been transferred to the EEAS, by way of derogation from Articles 4 and 29 of the staff regulations and under the conditions set out in Article 7(1) thereof, the appointing authorities of the institutions concerned may, in exceptional cases, acting by common agreement and solely in the interest of the service, after having heard the official concerned, transfer an EEAS official from the EEAS to a vacant post of the same grade in the General Secretariat of the Council or in the Commission, without notifying staff of the vacant post.[23]

For the purposes of Article 29(1)(a), when filling a vacant post in the EEAS, the appointing authority must consider applications from officials of the General Secretariat of the Council, the Commission and the EEAS, from temporary staff to whom Article 2(e) of the Conditions of Employment of Other Servants applies and from staff from national diplomatic services of the Member States, without giving priority to any of those categories. However, in exceptional cases and after having exhausted the possibilities of recruiting in accordance with these provisions, the appointing authority may decide to recruit technical support staff from outside the sources mentioned above at AD level if this is necessary for the good functioning of the EEAS; such staff may be specialists in the areas of crisis management, security or IT.[24]

6 Conclusions

As we have seen in the course of this chapter, the Common Foreign and Security Policy of the EU has had a clear evolution, after the various reforms of the Treaties. The position of head of delegation to a third country found its turning point in the European legal framework with the creation of the EEAS. Since the creation of the EEAS, the staff regulations have undergone numerous modifications and have been adapted to the times and circumstances, noting that the law, as a reference framework for different administrative situations and those related to the civil service, is quite dynamic and does not remain static in time but adapts to the needs that may arise in the international and the EU context.

Therefore, we can conclude that the rights and obligations that are associated with the ambassadors of the Member States have undergone an enormous metamorphosis. The functions of the ambassadors have expanded steadily, giving greater importance to the relationships between the EU and third countries. However, it is also true that, however positive the improvements may be, there is still a long way to go in order to achieve an optimal regulation of the legal status of the head of delegation.

[22] See OJ L 311 of 26 November 2010, amended Article 96.

[23] See OJ L 311 of 26 November 2010, amended Article 97.

[24] See OJ L 311 of 26 November 2010, amended Article 98.

References

Ambast, R., & Tyagi, V. (2008). Ambassadors of Europe: An insight into the evolution of the European Union and international diplomatic law. *Studia Diplomatica, LXI*(4), 173–189.

Casolari, F. (2012). The principle of loyal co-operation: A 'master key' for EU external representation? In S. Blockmans & R. A. Wessel (Eds.), *Principles and practices for external representation of the EU* (pp. 33–35). Centre for the Law of EU External Relations (CLEER) Working Paper 2012/5. Maastricht: The Haug.

Duke, S. (2009). Providing for European-level diplomacy after Lisbon: The case of the European External Action Service. *The Hague Journal of Diplomacy, 4*(2), 211–233.

Erkelens, L., & Blockmans, S. (2012). *Setting up the European External Action Service: An act of institutional balance*. CLEER Working Paper 2012/1. Maastricht: The Haug.

Halberstam, D. (2004). The political morality of federal systems. *Virginia Law Review, 90*, 731–834.

Lefebvre, M., & Hillion, C. (2010, June). The European External Action Service: Towards a common diplomacy? *European Policy Analysis*, SIEPS.

Molina del Pozo, C. F. (2002). *Manual de Derecho de la Comunidad Europea* (4th ed.). Madrid: Verlag Dijusa.

Molina del Pozo, C. F. (2015). *Tratado de Derecho de la Unión Europea* (Vol. III). Lisbon: Editorial Juruá Curitiba.

Mortelmans, K. (1998). The principle of loyalty to the Community (Article 5 EC) and the obligations of the Community institutions. *Maastricht Journal of European and Comparative Law, 5*(1), 67–88.

Plantey, A. (2000). *Principles of diplomacy*. Paris: Editions A. Pedone.

Van Vooren, B. (2010, July). *A legal-institutional perspective on the. European External Action Service* (Centre for the Law of EU External Relations working papers), pp. 21 and 23.

Van Vooren, B. (2011). A legal–institutional perspective on the European External Action Service. *Common Market Law Review, 48*(2), 475–502.

Wouters, J., Coppens, D., & Meester, B. (2008). The European Union's external relations after the Lisbon Treaty. In S. Griller & J. Ziller (Eds.), *The Lisbon Treaty: European constitutionalism without a constitutional treaty?* (pp. 143–203). Vienna: Springer.

Expert in Renewable Energies

Carlos Francisco Molina Del Pozo and Francisco Barquín Domínguez

1 Introduction

Energy can be defined as the potential capacity of bodies to produce work or heat, manifested by a change in their physical state. Energy sources can be renewable as opposed to conventional. Within conventional energies, we find coal, oil and its derivatives, nuclear energy and natural gas, all of which are exhaustible.

As is well known, the negative environmental effects of all these conventional energies are serious, including the greenhouse effect, acid rain, the loss of biodiversity and the depletion of the ozone layer.

The European Union, as a pillar and vanguard in the fight against pollution and climate change, plans to achieve 20% of its energy from renewable sources by 2020 and to improve its energy efficiency by 20%. And by the year 2030, at least 27% of its energy is to be obtained from renewable sources.

Thus, we can affirm that the use of renewable energies is occurring with increasing frequency and is considerably more transcendental within the terrestrial world. This is due to the effects produced by the phenomenon of the fight against climate change. Thus, more and more nations are promoting the implementation of these types of energy, also called alternatives, since their use not only avoids economic dependence on oil-producing countries, but also has clear environmental benefits. The sun, the wind, biomass, the tides and waves of the sea, hydrogen, the river currents or heat from the earth's interior produce renewable energy, which is continuous and inexhaustible.

However, it should be noted that the use of such renewable energies requires specialised knowledge of the area in order to know how and where to exploit them. On the basis of this consideration, at present, the role played in European society by

C. F. Molina Del Pozo (✉) · F. Barquín Domínguez
Department of Law, Universidad de Alcalá de Henares, Alcalá de Henares, Spain
e-mail: carlosf.molina@uah.es; Bernardo.Carnicero.Dominguez@esa.int

A. Bartolini et al. (eds.), *Dictionary of Statuses within EU Law*,
https://doi.org/10.1007/978-3-030-00554-2_31

the so-called experts in renewable energies, who have emerged and proliferated within each of the Member States of the European Union, is absolutely essential.

An expert in renewable energies is a person who has an in-depth knowledge—both theoretical and practical—of everything related to this subject. The current energy framework implies the need for the aforementioned experts in renewable energies to know the situation regarding energy sources, as well as the variety of types of renewable energies (wind, solar, photovoltaic, thermal, hydro, biomass, etc.), the existing or potential funding lines, the somewhat complicated issue of achieving what is known as energy efficiency, as well as everything related to the wide and complex world of renewable energies. This is imperative so that they can be progressively developed and implemented throughout the territory of the European Union and also, of course, at the level of all the countries that make up the international social reality.

We must stress that an expert in renewable energies will be able, among other things, to carry out the following actions:

- Develop projects in the field of renewable energies (photovoltaic, wind, solar, thermal, geothermal, energy generation and storage technologies, etc.).
- Evaluate renewable energy resources.
- Audit energy installations in buildings and infrastructures, both public and private.
- Study the fundamental principles of a system for using photovoltaic solar energy to generate electricity.
- Know the process for generating electricity from water and the typology and constituent elements of a mini-hydroelectric power plant, as well as how to design and study the feasibility of a mini-hydraulic installation.
- Acquire knowledge of the main characteristics that define wind energy and understand the basic principles governing the main components of a wind farm and the different types of installations.
- Know the systems for the energetic use of biomass, that is to say, the ways in which it is possible to obtain energy through biomass.
- Perform and interpret detailed climate analyses to obtain passive design strategies adapted to the climate.
- Efficiently design and regulate solar thermal installations, and the inclination and orientation of the collectors, and determine the radiation losses caused by possible shadows projected by nearby obstacles.

At present, given the increasing interference of States and companies in mitigating the adverse effects of climate change, the numbers of this kind of expert and specialist in the field are constantly and clearly increasing. In view of the diversity of existing renewable energies, they have become more and more specialised regarding the variety of typologies found in the field of specific energies, such as: wind, solar, hydraulic, geothermal, and biomass, among others.

2 Expert in Wind Energy

Wind energy uses the force of the wind to generate electricity. For this purpose, wind turbines are used, whereby wind moves a turbine and transforms the kinetic energy of the wind into mechanical energy. The amount of energy that can be obtained depends on the size of the mill. The longer the blades are, the more power and therefore the more energy is produced. However, we are currently learning about new revolutionary technologies and methods which, applied in all their breadth to the subject of wind energy, allow us to use much smaller mills and are capable of achieving a greater production of electrical energy by means of the installation of shorter blades which act in a vertical position and rotate on themselves. These new systems undoubtedly minimise the visual environmental impact.

In general, we can observe that wind energy is currently mainly used to generate electricity for sale to the grid. This is done by installing a set of mills which, once they are set up, are called wind farms. Wind turbines are often grouped together in these wind farms in order to make better use of the energy, and this reduces their environmental impact. The machines have a service life of 20 years.

Thus, wind energy experts will be specialised in the assembly, logistics, environmental requirements, operation and maintenance of wind farms. They will also be able to identify the energy possibilities of each area in terms of wind; analyse both the interconnection of the wind turbines and the high and low voltage components; identify the maintenance tasks necessary for the proper functioning of the installation; and, finally, know the environmental impacts of these installations and the necessary safety devices.

This energy, due to its high efficiency, has become the most important renewable energy source worldwide. Therefore, it can be argued that there is an increasing demand for people who are specialised in this area.

3 Expert in Solar Energy

Solar energy is the energy contained in solar radiation that is transformed by means of corresponding devices into a thermal or electrical form for later consumption wherever it is needed. The element for capturing solar radiation and transforming it into useful energy is the solar panel. Solar panels can be of different types depending on the mechanism chosen for the use of solar energy (by means of thermal solar collectors, photovoltaic modules or without any external element).

Today, there are basically three ways to harness solar energy: passive solar energy, photovoltaic solar energy and thermal solar energy.

Thus, experts in solar energy will be specialised in the operation of systems for the use of photovoltaic solar energy to generate electricity; quantify the electrical energy that can be generated depending on the energy received from the sun and the projected installation; determine the collector surface needed to guarantee a solar contribution to the supply of hot water; evaluate solar installations for the conditioning of pool water, both open and covered, as well as for providing heat to enclosures.

4 Expert in Biomass

Biomass is organic matter produced by plants and animals, such as wood and tree leaves, nutshells, animal droppings, pruning waste and other agricultural waste.

However, when we talk about biomass as a renewable energy source, we are referring to the process that uses this organic matter to produce energy. This process begins when plants, through photosynthesis, store the sun's radiant energy and convert it into chemical energy, commonly known as bioenergy. This same energy will finally be used to transform it into fuel.

There are two types of procedures for obtaining energy from biomass: direct and indirect. The simplest method is direct combustion (e.g. by burning wood). However, this is not the only use of biomass, as it is also employed to produce biogas and other biofuels such as biodiesel. Biodiesel is a substitute for diesel originating from vegetable oils and animal fats. It is a cleaner, non-toxic and much safer fuel that can be used as fuel in any current vehicle.

Among the advantages of using biomass as a renewable energy source, we can mention the following: first, this energy converts waste into resources; second, it is a non-polluting and environmentally friendly source of energy; third, it has the ability to contribute to forest clearing, avoiding possible fires, erosion and soil degradation; and, finally, this type of energy produces the same result as other types of energy, only at a much cheaper price.

Thus, it can be stated that more and more companies need experts in this area, who should have extensive knowledge of all types of biomass and waste with energy use or composting, and must be able to demonstrate their knowledge of everything related to the conversion processes, available technologies, the advantages and disadvantages of using biomass, and the management of a project for a biomass energy installation. In addition to the above, this class of experts should be familiar with the current energy environment, the possible lines of financing and aid, the characteristics and situation of biomass as a renewable energy source, as well as the bases for setting up a business project in this area.

5 Expert in Geothermal Energy

One of the most widespread renewable energy sources in Europe is geothermal energy. It is defined as the energy generated by geological heat sources.

This type of energy is based on the principles of the exploitation of the earth's natural heat. This heat is naturally released by the processes of the nuclear decomposition of the radioactive elements within the nucleus, mantle and crust of the earth. Some of these elements are the uranium, thorium and potassium that are contained in the innermost areas of the planet.

The use of geothermal energy is mainly manifested through one of the following methods: the direct use of heat for industrial purposes or in those known as hot spring waters, heating and water heating, absorption cooling, and electricity generation, among others. Everything seems to indicate, as is established by the vast majority of the doctrine, that geothermal energy offers the most resources. This type of energy is considered to be capable of providing more energy than all the energy produced based on oil, natural gas, coal and uranium worldwide. However, its insufficient development, the limitations on its implementation and the fact that it cannot be transported represent the main disadvantages for the normal use of the aforementioned geothermal energy.

In the same vein, we can conclude that experts in geothermal energy should be people with extensive knowledge of all the types of uses of geothermal energy, as well as the conversion processes, available technologies, and advantages and disadvantages of using this energy. They must also be proficient in the use of the basic principles, the applications according to the thermal level, the associated costs, the current regulations (RITE) and the methods for the sizing, installation and commissioning of systems based on the geothermal heat pump. Finally, they will also require extensive training in the handling and management of the corresponding projects that articulate the start-up of installations for this type of energy.

The exploitation of the so-called geothermal energy originated in Larderello (Italy) in 1904. Today, it is present in many volcanically active countries such as Iceland, New Zealand, Japan, the Philippines and the United States, with Iceland as the country with the greatest geothermal activity in the world. It should be noted that, at the international level, its use for heating is 33%.

6 Expert in Hydropower

Hydropower is the use of the kinetic energy of a body of water. Water moves a turbine whose rotating movement is transferred, by means of an axis, to an electricity generator.

There are two main types of hydroelectric power plants:

First, the so-called flowing water plants: These are those uses which work by means of an intake to capture part of the flow circulating through a river and take it to a plant to be turbined. This flow is then returned to the riverbed. These plants are characterised by a practically constant useful head and a highly variable turbine flow rate, depending on the hydrological time period or, in other words, on the time of year taken as a reference. Therefore, in this type of use, the installed power is directly related to the flow that passes through the river.

Second, the so-called dam-side plants: They are located downstream from reservoirs for hydroelectric or other purposes such as supplying water to towns or irrigating them. They are capable of producing electricity, and they do not consume any volume of water. They have the advantage of storing energy (water) and being able to use it when it is most needed. Normally, these are the plants that make it possible to regulate the capacity of the electricity system and, in a better way, to achieve a balance between consumption and production.

Thus, we can observe that the important and essential task of experts in hydropower will be none other than to know the components and characteristics of hydropower. Thus, they must also have the ability to design and develop a project for a hydraulic power plant, as well as to perform an economic viability analysis of the designed plant in order to evaluate and carry out its complete implementation.

7 Experts in Energy Coming from Hydrogen

Although different types of experts in renewable energy have been listed as the most prominent, it should be noted that, at present, more and more researchers and experts seem to be committed to reviewing and resolutely targeting hydrogen as a renewable energy source for the future.

This because hydrogen is the simplest and the most abundant element found in the universe (it is confirmed that today, approximately 90% of matter is made up of hydrogen). Thus, it can be almost unanimously maintained that energy that takes as its essential base or is derived from hydrogen seems to be an alternative energy with many possibilities for the future.

Quite often, hydrogen is combined with other elements in its composition, such as water and other organic elements. It is an element that is odourless, colourless and tasteless in its natural, non-gaseous form. In addition, it should be noted that it is non-toxic and safe to breathe. It can also be characterised as being extremely light, which is why it rises rapidly from the Earth's surface to the atmosphere. Therefore, scientists insist on the remarkable fact that hydrogen can be used as a renewable energy, even though it cannot be sustained as a tangible reality that it is, in itself, an energy-producing force.

This means that if we want to use hydrogen for any purpose, it must first be generated, which is a process that always consumes more energy than will later be produced. This is why it is necessary to assess in detail whether or not the use of alternative energy derived from hydrogen is appropriate.

On the basis of the above, it appears that hydrogen energy is an alternative energy source that can be used instead of coal or oil. Hydrogen can be transformed thanks to a technology similar to that used for the manufacture of batteries, so we can resolutely appreciate the fact that energy from hydrogen is a viable source of energy which does not pollute the planet as fossil fuels can do. In addition, among its advantageous characteristics, we find that it does not pollute, is not toxic, has a high efficiency, is silent and has a long life and power.

Perhaps the most impressive application of hydrogen is found in the new prototypes of motor vehicles recently launched on the world market by various European,

Japanese and American brands. The generalisation and progressive incorporation of this type of car into the market and its increasing use will require the creation of a hydrogen distribution network using hydrogenerators (service stations similar to petrol stations but which will supply hydrogen).

However, although it is a promising source of energy, this gas is not free on Earth, so it is necessary to find sources of it. However, it is desirable that based on technological advances, it can be created in quantities that will make it one of the most remarkable renewable energies of the future.

8 Companies and Renewable Energies

Finally, we will refer briefly to the relationship between companies and renewable energies. Thus, we will point out the following five companies, which are among the best at the international level in renewable energy production:

8.1 First Solar

This company is dedicated to the production of photovoltaic modules, with its headquarters in the United States and production plants in Germany, Malaysia and the USA. It should be noted that First Solar is dedicated to the manufacture of thin-film photovoltaic modules and offers integral solutions for photovoltaic systems.

8.2 Global Pvq SE Ill

This company is based in Germany and is active in the field of photovoltaics. The company divides its commercial activities into two segments: products and systems. The products segment comprises the production and sale of solar cells from monocrystalline and polycrystalline silicon, and the production and sale of the corresponding modules. In addition, the product segment covers the development, production and sale of modules based on CIGS thin-film technology. The systems segment includes the development and installation of photovoltaic systems, which include both large-scale systems and medium-sized industrial and commercial systems. The company operates through a number of subsidiaries in Germany, China, Canada, Australia, Mexico, the United States and other countries.

8.3 Siemens Gamesa Renewable Energy

Founded in 1976, this is a leading wind energy solutions company with customers all over the world. It presents and offers onshore and offshore wind energy, and has one of the most extensive and flexible portfolios in terms of solutions and the maintenance and optimisation of wind turbines. The company thus offers and ensures a holistic and lifelong service through innovation and digitisation.

8.4 SunPower

Since 1985, SunPower has been a leading US company in global solar innovation. Its solar panels consistently deliver more power and long-term peace of mind with the highest performing solar power systems available. It has a diversified global portfolio of clients, which reaches both the commercial and public service levels.

In addition, it should be noted that this company holds more than 750 patents for solar technology.

8.5 Vestas

This is a Danish company dedicated exclusively to wind energy, specifically to the manufacture, sale, installation and maintenance of wind turbines. The company has plants located in Denmark, Germany, India, Italy, Romania, the United Kingdom, Spain, Sweden, Norway, Australia, China and the United States.

Expropriated Party

Ana María De la Encarnación

1 The Concept of the Expropriated Party

Under every legal system, the expropriated is the one who is part of a compulsory purchase procedure, being deprived of one or more of his/her assets. This former owner of the expropriated property is entitled to prompt, effective and adequate compensation granted in the due procedure.

2 The Expropriation

2.1 *The Compulsory Purchase of Private Assets*

The word expropriation comes from the Latin. The word 'ex' means 'out of' and 'proprius' means 'owner'. It describes a procedure, granted by the law-maker, by which the acquiring authority (state, government, etc.) may require a private individual (landowner) or a legal entity (corporation) to transfer the ownership of a private asset, based on the public utility purpose previously established and by means of an adequate and timely indemnity (compensation). This property will be used for the public benefit.

In addition to the term expropriation, expressions such as 'compulsory purchase', 'dispossession', 'taking', 'privation' or 'deprivation' are also used,[1] all describing

[1] In the USA it is commonly known as the 'eminent domain', which, according to Black's Law Dictionary is the inherent power of a governmental entity to take privately owned property and convert it to public use, subject to reasonable compensation for the taking.

A. M. De la Encarnación (✉)
Administrative School of Law, University of Valencia, Valencia, Spain
e-mail: ana.maria.encarnacion@uv.es

A. Bartolini et al. (eds.), *Dictionary of Statuses within EU Law*,
https://doi.org/10.1007/978-3-030-00554-2_32

the severest interference in private property. It represents one type of transfer of ownership right, forced by the State, meaning the legal termination of ownership for the individual holder and the beginning of that for the acquiring authority.

Even though the requirements established by every legal system may be different, the essence of this forced acquisition is essentially similar: the acquiring authorities purchase the private property of a landowner under perfectly legitimate circumstances, namely the acquisition must be in the public interest, must take place under the due process of law, should be accompanied by adequate compensation and not being discriminatory (State laws must forbid discrimination between people on the basis of race, colour, sex, nationality, ethnicity, religion, class or any other status).

2.2 *Expropriation Under EU Law*

Regarding expropriation, although there is no rule in EU law that directly regulates it (García De Enterría 1990, p. 24), the Treaty on the Functioning of the European Union, along with court decisions, delineates EU jurisdiction to regulate expropriation. Section 215 of the Treaty establishes the accountability of the European authorities and their servants (contractual and non-contractual liability) in the performance of their duties. This responsibility shall be applicable in accordance with the general principles common to the laws of the member states. The latter expression (*principles in common*) can be understood as containing a general principle that also includes the guarantee of the principle of responsibility that also supports the expropriation.

Since it is a question of fundamental rights, the position of the Convention for the Protection of Human Rights and Fundamental Freedoms is more explicit thanks to the First Protocol to the convention, drafted in Paris on 20 March 1952. According to section 1 of this Protocol: 'Every natural or legal person is entitled to the peaceful enjoyment of his possessions. No one shall be deprived of his possessions except in the public interest and subject to the conditions provided for by law and by the general principles of international law'.

The text is absolutely unequivocal in its intention, but there are some interpretive problems that have been solved by the European Court of Human Rights (ECHR). As established by the ECHR, the abovementioned section includes, along with property, the legal regime of expropriation, establishing the guarantees that every expropriation implies, such as the confluence of the public interest (James, 1986) and the payment of the due compensation (Sporrong, 1984; The Holy Monasteries, 1994). Despite the ECHR deferring to the discretion of the member states to determine the public interest of the expropriation unless it is 'manifestly without reasonable foundation', this court has given a broad definition about the notion of public interest: 'pursuance of legitimate social, economic or other policies'. This procedure entitles the previous existence of individual rights, the idea of private ownership of land and the power to take land compulsorily. These two previous requirements are established by a great number of countries in the European Union (including Spain and the United Kingdom).

Thus, there are certain general EU standards (*ius commune*) for the expropriation of private property that shall be applicable to regulate expropriations in Europe, but it is the national legislation of each member state that must establish the specific expropriation procedure in their respective territories, in accordance with those standards. Those requirements, established under section 1 of Protocol I are accepted as the *ius commune* of the expropriation. Therefore, every national law must contain adequate safeguards to ensure that expropriations do not occur arbitrarily or for invalid reasons. In practice, most states establish the right to property and general conditions for expropriation in their constitutions, enacting comprehensive legislation that defines expropriation procedures, designates relevant authorities, elaborates on the meaning of public purpose or public interest and specifies the manner of compensation.

3 The Parties in the Expropriation Procedure

In general, the expropriation procedure is made up of two parties: the acquiring authority and the expropriated party. However, some European legal systems (such as the Spanish one) regulate the existence of a third party, which is known as a beneficiary.

3.1 The Acquiring Authority

The acquiring authority is the body which acquires land compulsorily and is required to pay compensation for that land (Barnes 2014, p. 560).

Expropriation action must issue from an appropriate authority and comply with adequately accessible and sufficiently precise domestic legal provisions (Lithgow, 1986). The power to expropriate is reserved for public authorities.

In Spain, this power is only given to the so-called Territorial Administration, that is the State, the Regions and the Local Authorities (sec. 2.1 of the Spanish Expropriation Act, 1954). This power implies/involves the authority to fully develop the expropriation, establishing the boundaries and conditions of public utility and social interest that support the sacrifice of the right of property proclaimed in section 33 of the Spanish Constitution. Consequently, neither individuals nor non-territorial public (e.g. public companies) can ever have powers to expropriate, being at most, beneficiaries of the expropriation. This is because only the former institutions represent the general and abstract purposes of the Spanish Public Administration.

Under the UK legal system, Parliament authorises the taking of land, for the 'public good', giving compulsory purchase powers (sec. 97 of the Housing Act, 1957). Many authorities which exercise these powers are local authorities (e.g. municipalities, sec. 120–124 Local Government Act 1972) or providers of utility services (formerly statutory undertakers) (Plimmer 2008, p. 145). Parliament achieves the compulsory acquisition of land by, effectively, preventing the land owner from withdrawing from the transaction with the acquiring authority.

3.2 *The Expropriated Party*

3.2.1 The Property Owner

The expropriated is the owner or holder of the right subject to expropriation, that is, either movable or immovable assets or properties, because expropriation is directly related to the notion of ownership of land). Section 1 of the protocol refers to the term 'possession'. This concept has an autonomous meaning, which is independent from the formal classification in domestic law. It is often argued that the concept is very broadly interpreted in the court's case-law because it not only includes the right of ownership but also a whole range of pecuniary rights such as rights arising from shares, patents, arbitration award, established entitlement to a pension, entitlement to a rent and even rights arising from running of a business (Grgiæ et al. 2009, p. 7). In consequence, the exercise of the expropriation power requires the previous determination of who is the owner of the rights to be compulsorily purchased. In this sense, the expropriated party shall be whoever appears as the owner in public records.

The awarding of compulsory purchase powers does not alter the legal ownership of the assets or rights to be expropriated until those powers are exercised by the acquiring authority. However, once the expropriation has been completed, the ownership of the asset or the right will be effectively transferred to the acquiring authority.

Given that the expropriated status is granted by the ownership of a property, both natural (private individuals) and legal persons (legal entities) (Agrotexim, 1995) can have such status. In principle, even though it depends on the requirements established by each member state, there are no exempt subjects to the expropriation. It would be a different matter to establish exceptions related to the rights or assets to be expropriated.

The expropriated party intervenes in the procedure fundamentally aimed at supporting the loss of his property and, in exchange, at achieving a timely and adequate compensation. Compensation is, therefore, required in terms of expropriation but only exceptional circumstances may justify the absence of this payment; otherwise the right to property would be largely 'illusory and ineffective' (Jahn, 1999).

With regard to the amount of compensation, it should be proportionate, that is, an amount reasonably related to the value of the property should be paid (Akkus, 1992; Stran Greek Refineries, 1987) according to the market value because it reflects the community's perception of value rather than the owner's (Scordino, 1997).

Finally, despite not having the status of expropriated party, there may be more people or legal entities directly or indirectly affected by the expropriation. The property to be expropriated can have an *ius in rem (real right in land)*, that is, a right of lease, use, easement, usufruct, emphyteusis or even a mortgage. The holders of these rights must also be compensated since the expropriation should be carried out over a property free of charges.

3.2.2 The Expropriation Procedure

The expropriation requires a concrete and formal procedure in order to guarantee the fundamental right to property, protecting a person against unjustified interference by the State in the peaceful enjoyment of his or her possessions (Grgiæ et al. 2009, pp. 10–11). Consequently, any state would be liable for a *de facto* expropriation in case of avoiding the due procedure (Papamichalopoulos, 1993; Brumărescu, 1995; Pressos Compania Naviera SA, 1991).

According to the expropriation procedure and in order to satisfy the above-mentioned international standards of due process, member state laws must contain fair and proper procedural safeguards against arbitrary or unjust deprivation of property (Hentrich, 1994) in order to protect the expropriated party interests. These safeguards include that the expropriated must be provided with timely notice of the expropriation decision, with its justifications, and an opportunity to challenge the expropriation before a neutral party (Kingsbury et al. 2005, pp. 45–46).

Under the UK legal system, this notice is called a Notice to Treat, which effectively commits both parties, the acquiring authority and the landowner, to the sale of the land. In Spain, the acquiring authority must issue the Administrative Measure establishing the public utility of the right or asset to be expropriated. This Administrative Measure must be published and notified to the expropriated party. This measure can be challenged.

As mentioned before, one of the few things the expropriated party is entitled to do during the procedure is to decide the amount of compensation to be paid for the loss of his assets. In general, both parties can try to reach an agreement about the value of the asset or right. If so, the expropriation would terminate in a prompt and satisfying way for both parties, Otherwise, the acquiring authority and the expropriated party should try to approach positions in order to fix the value of the private rights or assets. In Spain, the Expropriation Act (1954) establishes that the first party to suggest a quantity is the expropriated party and the acquiring authority could agree with this assessment or suggest a different one to the other party. If the expropriated party rejects the offer made by the acquiring authority, the compensation will be fixed by the Expropriation Board, and administrative, non-judicial body (sec. 31). Once the board has ruled, the parties can challenge the amount of compensation before the courts.

3.3 *The Beneficiary of the Expropriation*

As seen before, expropriation is only permitted in order to achieve a public interest. Though member states are entitled to interpret the words 'public interest' differently, it generally signifies that the property, once put to the intended use, will benefit the community or country generally. There are no particular individual or concrete groups taking advantage of the expropriation. For instance, national security, economic growth and social justice usually qualify as public interest.

As long as the State can decide the interpretation of this requirement, Spain has a unique and special expropriation system, since the expropriation relationship is not always settled between two parties. Occasionally, a third party called a beneficiary, appears, representing the public or social interest for whose realisation it is authorised not to expropriate (because it is not entitled to have the power to expropriate), but to urge the acquiring authority to exercise its powers to compulsorily acquire the private property or right.

References

Barnes, M. (2014). *The law of compulsory purchase and compensation*. Oxford: Hart Publishing.

García De Enterría, E. (1990). Las garantías de la expropiación según el Derecho Europeo. *Documentación Administrativa, 222*, 23–40.

Grgiæ, A., Mataga, Z., Longar, M., & Vilfan, A. (2009). Council of Europe, the right to property under the European Convention on Human Rights. A guide to the implementation of the European Convention on Human Rights and its protocols. In *Human Rights Handbooks*, 10. Retrieved from http://www.supremecourt.ge/files/upload-file/pdf/article5eng.pdf

Kingsbury, B., Krisch, N., & Stewart, R. B. (2005). The emergence of global administrative law. *Law and Contemporary Problems, 68*(15), 45–46.

Plimmer, F. (2008). Compulsory purchase and compensation: An overview of the system in England and Wales. *Nordic Journal of Surveying and Real Estate Research, Special Series*, (3), 144–164.

Family Member

Valentina Colcelli

1 Introduction

The EU is interested in the status of family member, not only in terms of the realisation of the freedom of movement of persons, but also to fulfil its internal market objective by removing obstacles to the realisation of this objective (Policastro 2011, p. 177).

European Union law and the case law developed by the Court of Justice emphasise family relations and have enhanced them as a basis for the effectiveness of citizens' freedom of movement (Á De Sotomayor 2011, p. 263).

In order to understand the notion of family member status that is accepted today by the European Union, it is necessary to make reference to the principles and rules of the country of origin that establish the criteria for defining individual status as well as the status of family member.

As matter of fact, through the *Dassonville* and *Cassis de Dijon* judgments, the European Court of Justice prohibited any directly discriminatory national measures, and later it prohibited indirectly discriminatory national measures in the Member State of destination with regard to the movement of goods, so all measures having an effect equivalent to quantitative restrictions on trade between Member States were prohibited (Mangas Martín and Liñan Nogueras 2010).

These historic rulings require recourse to mutual recognition in the legal systems of the Member States, by introducing an assessment of the compatibility of state measures—even those measures that are indirectly applicable—with the principle of the free movement of goods.

During this period, the same principle was extended by the case law to freedom of establishment (C-55/94) and freedom of movement of workers (C-415/93) (in respect of professional qualifications, banking, insurance and financial services),

V. Colcelli (✉)
National Research Council, IFAC Institute, Sesto Fiorentino, Firenze, Italy
e-mail: valentina.colcelli@cnr.it

A. Bartolini et al. (eds.), *Dictionary of Statuses within EU Law*,
https://doi.org/10.1007/978-3-030-00554-2_33

with a broader meaning regarding the principle of mutual recognition, the freedom of movement of persons and the right of establishment.

With reference to an individual and his/her qualities, as embodied in the concept of status, it has been stressed that the so-called principle of origin acts more broadly with respect to jurisprudential positions relating to goods and professions. With regard to persons and family status, the Court of Justice's own case law (C-67/91 and C-268/91) does not impose any restrictions, in the same way as in the area of the free movement of goods. In the latter case, there is, in fact, an obligation to comply with European production and marketing regulations with regard to both the state of origin and the state of destination.

The status of the person, as well as that of the professional or of goods, is regulated by the rules of the country of origin, and then the person, professional or goods circulates freely within the Union (Snell 2003, p. 325). Therefore, the state of origin has the competence to regulate the status of the person, the professional or the goods, and the state of destination has to accept this ruling since equivalence between the rules is presumed. A state of destination that wished to oppose the recognition of the status of the professional or the goods, but not that of the person, would have to prove that the rules of the state of origin were not appropriate to the relevant mandatory requirements (Rossolillo 2002). The situation is different regarding the status of family member.

2 Defining 'Family Member'

The feeling of the European Union regarding the status of family member is defined in Directive 2004/38/EC and the *Reed* judgment (C-59/85) (although, in this case, reference was made to the previous legislation on the reunification of family members and workers, Reg. 1612/1968), and shows a broader application of the concept of family member than that used by the Court of Justice itself, if the problem is the effectiveness of the protection of rights and the guarantee of fundamental rights (Sanz Caballero 2006, p. 29).

Originally, the European Community took family members into consideration in order to reach its economic objectives. The interference in family law by the EU legislator was justified to guarantee the freedom of movement of persons, especially initially in this field, by favouring the family through the family reunion system. The family is a 'paradigmatic model of freedom of movement by way of derivative instruments' (Coussirat-Coustère 2000, p. 281).

The Court of Justice, in its judgment in *Commission* v *Kingdom of Spain* of 14 April 2005 No 157/03, recalls that the Community legislature has recognised the importance of ensuring the protection of the family life of citizens of the Member States in order to remove obstacles to the exercise of the fundamental freedoms guaranteed by the Treaty (C-60/00 and C-459/99).

Today, the right of movement and residence of the family member of a European citizen is regulated by Directive 2004/38/EC. EU law and case law address issues relating to the care of family members and, in regard to free movement, effectively govern these issues.

Directive 2004/38/EC defines a 'family member' as '(a) the spouse; (b) the partner with whom the Union citizen has contracted a registered partnership, on the basis of the legislation of an [EU/EEA] Member State, if the legislation of the host Member State treats registered partnerships as equivalent to marriage and in accordance with the conditions laid down in the relevant legislation of the host Member State; (c) the direct descendants who are under the age of 21 or are dependants and those of the spouse or partner as defined in point (b); (d) the dependent direct relatives in the ascending line and those of the spouse or partner as defined in point (b)'. Directive 2004/38/EC codified much of the Court's case law and earlier residency Directives.

The notion of the family member has particular relevance in connection with the right of asylum, the expulsion of immigrants, family reunification, and other aspects, because the lives of individuals are connected with the mission of the EU legal system.

If status is a prerequisite for an individual to enjoy a right within the Union, the pre-conditions of one of the Member States for the enjoyment of EU rights cannot be affected by where the subject is. This follows from the principle of equality for European citizens.

According to EU law regarding the free circulation of citizens, the status of the person circulates with the person himself/herself. For instance, it could happen that, if a Member State's legal system permits the legal recognition of a child by a same-sex couple, that legal recognition must be realised in a Member State that does not have the same permissive legislation. The same applies to the status of a registered partnership as equivalent to marriage in accordance with the conditions laid down in the relevant legislation of a person's own Member State, even if this situation is not recognised in the host Member State (which was the case in Italy, for example, until the promulgation of law n. 76 of 20 May 2016 on the recognition of civil unions, even between persons of the same sex).

The principle that a person's status is uniquely defined should therefore apply to civil statuses, as well as to the status of a person as defined in his/her Member State of origin. This is because this status and the pre-conditions for the determination depend on the existence and enjoyment of benefits and rights established in the EU, whether for admission and residence or for other benefits, such as pay and pensions or for taking care of a child.

This conclusion reflects the judgment of the Court of First Instance (Case T-69) which said that the criterion for determining the condition of a dependent child is the emotional commitment to satisfy in whole or in part the essential needs of the child, in particular with regard to housing, food, clothing, education, care and medical expenses. A divorce, or the granting of the custody of a child to a spouse who is not officially the child's parent, does not negate the condition of being a dependent child.

As matter of fact, the notion of the unified status of a family member is already operational in secondary legislation in a way that is directly related to EU officials.

In this context, the definition is applied, for example, to the independent concept of the family and especially to parent–child relationships. On this subject, under the EU laws for the employees of EU institutions, for example, such employees are eligible for a family allowance for dependent children as well as a pension for orphans (see Articles 1 and 2 of Annex VII to the Staff Regulations, EEC/EAEC Council: Regulation No 31 (EEC), 11 (EAEC), laying down the Staff Regulations of Officials and the Conditions of Employment of Other Servants of the European Economic Community and the European Atomic Energy Community).

3 Public Documents of an Act of Civil Status as a Formal Obstacle to the Recognition of a Parental Relationship

Starting from the idea that the status of family member, as defined by a person's original Member State, cannot change if—when a person exercises his/her right to move freely—that status is not present in the host Member State's legal system, public documents cannot be an formal obstacle to free circulation, according to Regulation (EU) 2016/1191 of the European Parliament and of the Council of 6 July 2016 on promoting the free movement of citizens by simplifying the requirements for presenting certain public documents in the European Union and amending Regulation (EU) No 1024/2012.

The EU has a legal basis for defining individual status (see Articles 21(2) and 114(1) TFEU), but the real problem arises because of administrative obstacles. This is acknowledged in the Stockholm Programme, which was adopted by the European Council in December 2009: 'Certain formalities for the legalisation of documents also represent an obstacle or an excessive burden. Given the possibilities offered by the use of new technologies, including digital signatures, the Union should consider abolishing all formalities for the legalisation of documents between Member States. Where appropriate, thought should be given to the possibility of creating, in the long term, authentic European documents.'

A civil registry and its documentation do not have secondary importance, but it should be borne in mind that the principle of a unique status has to be applicable to an act of civil status, and this should not be an obstacle to free circulation. As one relevant example, it is impossible in the Italian civil registry to register a new parental right, whether paternal or maternal, that is not grounded on traditional Italian legal principles. The historic facts of birth, death, marriage, divorce, etc. precede their bureaucratic registration, and bureaucratic registration cannot affect respect for family life, and the right to marry and have a family, as fundamental EU rights.

According to the *Dafeki* judgment (Case C-336/94), in fact, the judgment of equivalence is made on the basis of an act of civil status. The case of *García Avello* is likewise noteworthy: in this judgment, the obligation to recognise a person's status seems to arise from the status of the person (linked to the right to a name) that pertains in the person's country of origin (paragraphs 31 and 45).

It should be recalled how the Court of Justice established matters in the judgment in the *Dafeki* case. In the absence of legislation to harmonize the matter, with reference to the value of an extraterritorial certificate of civil status given by one country, the administration and the courts of the Member State of destination or residence of the citizen have an obligation to abide by the documents of civil status issued by the country of origin, aside from the mere recognition of the probative value of those documents, as submitted, or of the recognition of the validity of the act. This is inherent to the concept of European citizenship and close to the principle of freedom of movement and the freedom to acquire personal and family status in each Member State.

At the same time, non-registration does not give any formal/documentary evidence of individual legal status that could have an influence on, or be used or presupposed for, the operationalisation of EU law or the clarification of its aims.

EU law has an impact on the 'traditional' legal status of individuals (i.e., parents, children, family members of workers, partners, and wives/husbands), and it also creates a new individual legal status, taking into account the notion of the family and its members that is relevant for the application of the right of free circulation.

4 Free Circulation of Citizens; Parental Responsibility in Relation to the Meaning of Family Member

At the moment, the European legal system does not have a composite formulation for how EU law affects the person and how it can change the traditional categories of individual status according to time and place, and nor does it demonstrate how to examine the evidence of what EU law has been at a particular time.

Such a formulation could establish the principles of the European law on persons. It would be able to provide coherence to the various legislative and case law solutions in the EU.

EU law and the EU legal system have an indirect influence on the 'pedocentric' (Cippitani 2013, p. 119) relationship between parents and children; even though this regulatory area is not part of the EU harmonisation process, it extends the analysis to the relevance or irrelevance of the sexual orientation of the parent when considering the children's rights.

The right of the free circulation of citizens also has effects on parental responsibility, the presumption of paternity, and declaratory actions and the disowning of paternity. Many aspects of children's lives are not properly within the competence of the EU, but the free market has generated unwanted side effects for children. In 2000, the European Community adopted a Regulation on jurisdiction, recognition, and enforcement in matrimonial matters and matters of parental responsibility for children of both spouses (Brussels II—Regulation (EC) No 1347/2000). The rule adopted by the EU in 2003 (Brussels II bis—Council Regulation (EC) No 2201/2003) extended the scope of Brussels II to all decisions on parental responsibility (which was an improvement on Brussels II), and included provisions on jurisdiction and the return of the child in cases of child abduction. These regulations have had not only procedural effects but also substantive effects on, for example, the notion of parental responsibility.

For example, an Italian Court of Cassation Judgment has examined the notion of the child and *kafalah* in the light of Directive 2004/38/EC. For the Court of Cassation, Italian Legislative Decree No 286 of 1998 is not applicable to the right to family unity, as it is designed exclusively for applications for the family reunification of non-EU citizens. However, Legislative Decree No 30 of 2007, which implements Directive 2004/38/EC on the right of EU citizens and their families to move and reside freely within the territory of the Member States, is considered applicable, even with respect to third countries citizens. By a well-articulated argument, the Court ruled that the term 'family' can be deduced, under this new system of regulation, to cover a child in *kafalah* (having been adopted/under guarantee) (Harkrisnowo et al. 2016).

For the application of the rules on the child as a member of a family, the notion formulated in European Union law must also be taken into account.

Ultimately, it must be remembered that: "the notion of direct relatives in the descending and ascending lines extends to adoptive relationships or minors in custody of a permanent legal guardian. Foster children and foster parents who have temporary custody may have rights under the Directive, depending upon the strength of the ties in the particular case."[1] As a matter of fact, in implementing the Directive, Member States must always act in the best interests of the child, in accordance with the United Nations Convention on the Rights of the Child of 20 November 1989.

5 Conclusion

The status of family member, according to the decisions of the European Union Court of Justice, reflects the fact that the protection of the rights of family members is based not on the formal unity of the family, but on the protection of vulnerable people in need of solidarity, bearing the duties and responsibilities of those who hold family status. The main EU law in this field is Directive 2004/38/EC on the right of citizens of the Union and their family members to move and reside freely within the territories of the Member States.

The status of the family member should be defined taking into consideration the principle of mutual recognition, the freedom of movement of persons and the right of the establishment, as evaluated with a broader meaning and applied in accordance with the non-discrimination principle enshrined in Article 21 of the EU

[1] Communication from the Commission to the European Parliament and the Council on guidance for better transposition and application of Directive 2004/38/EC on the right of citizens of the Union and their family members to move and reside freely within the territory of the Member States. COM/2009/0313.

Charter of Fundamental Rights, in particular. In this framework we can interpret the following persons to have the status of family member: spouses by marriages validly contracted anywhere in the world; partners with whom an EU citizen has a de facto durable relationship; family members in direct line (as direct relatives in the descending and ascending lines extends to adoptive relationships or minors in custody of a permanent legal guardian); foster children and foster parents who have temporary custody; and family members who are dependent as result of a factual situation characterised by the fact that material support for that family member is provided by the EU citizen or by his spouse/partner (Communication from the Commission to the European Parliament and the Council (COM(2009) 313) on guidance for better transposition and application of Directive 2004/38/EC on the right of citizens of the Union and their family members to move and reside freely within the territory of the Member States). A person's status as a family member is therefore defined by that person's own original Member State, and it cannot change if—in exercising his/her right to move freely—that status is not present in the host Member State's legal system. No public document or act of registration can be a formal obstacle to the free circulation of a member of a family.

References

Á De Sotomayor, L. D. (2011). La libre circulación de personas tras el Tratado de Lisboa. *Rev del Ministerio de Trabajo e Inmigración, 92*, 257–282.

Cippitani, R. (2013). Riforma dello status e fonti comunitarie. In R. Cippitani & S. Stefanelli (Eds.), *La Parificazione degli status di filiazione* (pp. 119–152). Roma: ISEG Srl.

Coussirat-Coustère, V. (2000). Famille et CEDH. In R. Ryssdal & P. Mahoney (Eds.), *Protection des droits de l'homme: la perspective européenne. Mélanges à la mémoire de Rolv Ryssdal* (pp. 281–307). München: Carl Heymanns.

Harkrisnowo, H., Juwana, H., & Oppusunggu, Y. U. (Eds.), (2016). *Law and justice in a globalized world.* Proceedings of the Asia-Pacific Research Conference in Social Sciences and Humanities, Depok, Indonesia. Topics in Law and Justice. November 7–9. London: Routledge.

Mangas Martín, A., & Liñan Nogueras, D. J. (2010). *Instituciones y Derecho de la Unión Europea.* Madrid: Tecnos.

Policastro, P. (2011). Diginidad de la persona y los principios constitucionales en la época de la globalización. *Persona y derecho, 64*, 175–206.

Rossolillo, G. (2002). *Muto riconoscimento e tecniche conflittuali.* Padova: Ed. Cedam.

Sanz Caballero, S. (2006). *La familia en perspectiva internacional y europea.* Valencia: Editorial Tirant lo Blanc.

Snell, J. (2003). Who's got the power? Free movement and allocation of competences in EC law. *Yearbook of European Law, 22*, 323–335.

Farmer

Viola Prifti

1 Introduction

The aim of this chapter is to define the legal status of farmers under European Union law. The legal status defines the set of rights, obligations, powers, or restrictions as defined by the EU *acquis*, i.e., laws and court decisions that constitute the body of EU law. The Treaty on the Functioning of the European Union, one of the primary EU treaties, provides for common rules that apply to farming activities under Articles 38–44 of Title III, "Agriculture and Fisheries". These articles provide neither a definition of farmer nor of her/his rights and obligations. The objective of Title III is to establish rules and objectives for the realization of a common agricultural policy (CAP), taking into account its importance for the economy as well as agricultural specificities between EU countries. The purpose of the CAP is to institute a common market that helps produce safe and sufficient quantities of food, avoid food crisis, create jobs, and maintain welfare. This purpose should be understood in its context.

The CAP was first created in 1962 (EU 2012) in order to tackle food shortages after World War II (D.P.E. 1945). Through CAP subsidies, farmers could renovate their farms and obtain better seeds and equipment. Guaranteed minimum prices for agricultural commodities helped farmers produce more at a lower price even if the demand for their products did not change. This led to surplus and food waste in 1970, and the EC started to introduce quotas in the 1980s to align the production with the market demand (EU 2016).[1] In addition to regulating the quantity of farm produce, the CAP regulates the safety and quality of production standards with rigorous plant and animal health controls as well as the sustainability of EU farming

[1] Milk quotas were an important part of the CAP reform for 30 years before they were abolished in April 2015. For more, see European Union (2016), p. 113.

V. Prifti (✉)
Right and Science Jean Monnet Centre of Excellence, University of Perugia, Perugia, Italy

A. Bartolini et al. (eds.), *Dictionary of Statuses within EU Law*,
https://doi.org/10.1007/978-3-030-00554-2_34

in order to preserve biodiversity through an efficient use of natural resources.[2] As a result of the CAP, farmers now are obligated to maintain permanent pastures, diversify crops, produce less intensively, develop renewable energies, use by-products and residues, and change livestock diets. The cost of these activities is subsidized by the CAP in order to remunerate farmers for their activities that benefit society as a whole. These activities change the role of the farmer from a simple terrain worker to a more active worker or entrepreneur who makes use of traditional and modern knowledge produced in scientific laboratories to advance common goals. This means that the rights and obligations of EU farmers have changed in parallel with the development of science and modern economic precepts. The following pages explain these changes and the role of EU *acquis* in shaping the status of farmers.

2 The Definition of Farmer

Article 4 of EU Regulation No. 1307/2013[3] defines the farmer as "a natural or legal person, or a group of natural or legal persons, regardless of the legal status granted to such group and its members by national law, whose holding is situated within the territorial scope of the Treaties, as defined in Article 52 TEU in conjunction with Articles 349 and 355 TFEU, and who exercises an agricultural activity". From the wording of this provision, it is clear that the legal status of "farmer" under national law is not relevant for the applicability of EU legislation. National laws may provide for different rights and obligations. Italy and France, for instance, have similar understandings of "agricultural activities" as biological cycles that involve plants, animals, or fish, but the legal provisions are contained in different legal instruments[4] that provide for different rights and obligations. One example is bankruptcy law. Although Italian law applies some provisions of bankruptcy law to farmers,[5] French legislation regulates bankruptcy for farming activities more comprehensively.[6]

[2] This concept was coined at the United Nations Conference on Environment and Development in 1992 in Rio de Janeiro. For more, see http://www.un.org/geninfo/bp/enviro.html. Accessed 5 October 2017.

[3] Commission Delegated Regulation (EU) No. 639/2014 of 11 March 2014, supplementing Regulation (EU) No. 1307/2013 of the European Parliament and of the Council, establishing rules for direct payments to farmers under support schemes within the framework of the common agricultural policy and amending Annex X to that regulation.

[4] For Italy, see Article 2135 of the civil code. For France, see L. 311-1 of the Code Rural et de la Pêche Maritime, version consolidée au 7 Octobre 2017, available at https://www.legifrance.gouv.fr/affichCode.do?idArticle=LEGIARTI000029593397&idSectionTA=LEGISCTA000006152225&cidTexte=LEGITEXT000006071367&dateTexte=20171011. Accessed 11 October 2017. For an understanding of agricultural activities in France, refer also to Ministère de l'agriculture, de l'agroalimentaire et de la forêt (2015), pp. 15–18.

[5] Legge falimentare del 1942, d.l. 6 July 2011, n. 98 convertito con modificazioni in l. 15 July 2011, n. 111. http://www.altalex.com/documents/news/2016/10/19/fallimento.

[6] L. 351-1 Code Rural. For an analysis, see Guadagno (2012).

These differences in national law are irrelevant in regard to the application of EU law. In order to achieve the benefits and goals of a common market, however, it is important to have a common definition at the EU level.

Under EU law, farmers are either individuals or groups of individuals who exercise an "agricultural activity" in the territory of the European Union. The meaning of "agricultural activity" can be derived from Article 2 a) of EC Regulation No. 1166/2008 of the European Parliament and of the Council,[7] which clarifies that "'agricultural holding' or 'holding' means a single unit, both technically and economically, which has a single management and which undertakes agricultural activities listed in Annex I within the economic territory of the European Union, either as its primary or secondary activity". Annex I relies on NACE coding (Nomenclature Statistique des Activités Économiques dans la Communauté Européenne)[8] to identify activities of growing crops, plant propagation, animal propagation, mixed farming, and support activities to agriculture.[9] Not all farmers have the abilities and financial capacities to engage in all of these activities. Moreover, some farmers may own land or animals, while others may work under a contract. Farming can be a professional activity or a hobby. Rights and obligations vary according to farms' size and activity.

For the purpose of defining the term "farmer", it is also important to refer to the concept of "active farmer" defined in Article 9 of EU Regulation No. 1307/2013. The rationale of this provision is to reward only those who engage in significant agricultural activities. The regulation does not explain when an activity is "significant", but member states can determine its meaning in line with the regulation and the specificity of their agricultural systems. Some examples of insignificant activities for agricultural purposes are found in Article 9.2 of the regulation: airport, railway service, waterworks, real estate service, sports ground, or recreation facility. Those who operate such activities are not considered "active farmers" unless they comply with the criteria for direct payments laid down in Articles 9–15. The provision on "active farmer" became compulsory in 2015, but the commission has proposed to make the clause on "active farmer" optional.[10]

[7] Regulation (EC) No. 1166/2008 of the European Parliament and of the Council of 19 November 2008, on farm structure surveys and the survey on agricultural production methods and repealing Council Regulation (EEC) No. 571/88. Official Journal of the European Union, L 321/14 of 1 December 2008.

[8] For an explanation, see http://ec.europa.eu/eurostat/statistics-explained/index.php/Glossary:Statistical_classification_of_economic_activities_in_the_European_Community_(NACE). Accessed 10 October 2017.

[9] For a thorough understanding of the activities that fall under the concept, see the Eurostat Glossary at http://ec.europa.eu/eurostat/statistics-explained/index.php/Glossary:Agricultural_holding. Accessed 10 October 2017.

[10] See "Parliamentary Questions", 26 October 2016, available at http://www.europarl.europa.eu/sides/getDoc.do?pubRef=-//EP//TEXT+WQ+E-2016-008032+0+DOC+XML+V0//EN&language=en. Accessed 10 October 2017. See also the answer dated 14 December 2016, available at http://www.europarl.europa.eu/sides/getAllAnswers.do?reference=E-2016-008032&language=EN. Accessed 10 October 2017.

3 Farmers' Rights and Obligations Under EU Law

Given the multifaceted nature of the agricultural sector, several EU institutions play a role in shaping the legal status of farmers[11] through instruments such as directives, regulations, decisions, opinions, priorities, communications, etc. As mentioned in the previous section, rights and obligations of EU farmers differ based on the farm size and activity. The Eurostat reports on agriculture can help us better understand these issues.[12] The 2016 report distinguishes between small and large farms, explaining that small farms have always been a cornerstone of agricultural activity in the EU, but there is "no fixed definition as to what constitutes a 'small' or a 'large' farm." However, the report relies on two main criteria to define farm size: standard output and utilised agricultural area.[13] EU legislative bodies have taken account of these differences and have provided for rules that directly or indirectly influence the status of small and large farms as well as that of farmers based on age and gender. For example, regulations and decisions of the European Parliament and of the Council have harmonized rules on subsidies for farmers.[14] In order to face the problems of an aging farming population, special measures favour young farmers directly, through subsidies and access to credit, or indirectly, by supporting early retirement.[15] The Court of Justice of the European Union (CJEU) has also intervened to eliminate discrimination by gender. In case C-401/11, EU judges decided that member states must observe the principle of equal treatment between women and men when they grant early retirement support to elderly farmers.

Other important laws and decisions that influence the status of farmers are those on plant variety protection, which have redefined the status and concept of the farmer. Since the dawn of agriculture, farmers have been free to exchange, sow, and re-sow seeds. This practice changed when intellectual property (IP) laws started to protect the biotechnological inventions embedded in the plant. Patents and plant breeder's rights are the most important forms of IP laws in this field (Prifti 2015). While patent rights extend to plant seeds as long as they contain the protected biotechnological information, plant breeder's rights set limitations on the type and

[11] See "Agriculture", available at https://europa.eu/european-union/topics/agriculture_en. Accessed 12 October 2017.

[12] The last Eurostat report is from 2016. For previous statistics, see http://ec.europa.eu/eurostat/statistics-explained/index.php/Agricultural_production_-_crops. Accessed 10 October 2017.

[13] For an understanding of these terms, see page 64–65 of the Eurostat report.

[14] For a list of the relevant regulations, see http://eur-lex.europa.eu/search.html?textScope0=ti-te&qid=1507278641583&DTS_DOM=EU_LAW&type=advanced&lang=en&andText0=farmers&SUBDOM_INIT=LEGISLATION&DTS_SUBDOM=LEGISLATION. Accessed 10 October 2017.

[15] Some EU initiatives in these areas are a pilot project on exchange programs for young farmers, available at https://ec.europa.eu/agriculture/external-studies/young-farmers_en, and the European Council of Young Farmers, available at http://www.ceja.eu/about/. Accessed 10 October 2017.

quantity of seed farmers can save.[16] The CJUE has strengthened these obligations by authorizing right holders to request information from a farmer when the farmer makes use of the option to save and use protected seed.[17] On one hand, IP provisions grant more rights to farmers by prohibiting third parties from using the products of their work, but on the other hand, they impose more obligations when farmers need to use protected seed.

Rights are often accompanied by duties. For example, the right to receive financial support is subject to farmers' obligations to comply with animal health welfare, food safety, and environmental measures.[18] Further obligations are those on organic farming.[19] Member states have some flexibility when complying with rights and duties imposed at the EU level. This is the case for genetically modified organisms, for which states have the option to restrict or prohibit cultivation.[20] This flexibility appears necessary in order to take into account the diversity of agriculture and domestic interests.

4 The Influence of the European Integration on Farmers' Status

The CAP policy has created rights and obligations for farmers in support of the objective to integrate European countries in a common market for agriculture. Regulations 1184/2006[21] and 1234/2007,[22] for example, establish rules on trade and

[16] See Article 14 of the Council Regulation (EC) No. 2100/94 of 27 July 1994, on European Community plant variety rights, and Commission Regulation (EC) No. 1768/95 of 24 July 1995, implementing rules on the agricultural exemption provided for in Article 14 (3) of Council Regulation (EC) No. 2100/94 on European Community plant variety rights.

[17] Case C-305/00, Christian Schulin and Saatgut-Treuhandverwaltungsgesellschaft mbH, Press Release No. 32/02, 10 April 2003, available at https://curia.europa.eu/jcms/upload/docs/application/pdf/2009-03/cp0332en.pdf. Accessed 12 October 2017.

[18] See, for example, commission delegated regulation (EU) 2017/1155 of 15 February 2017, available at http://eur-lex.europa.eu/legal-content/EN/TXT/PDF/?uri=CELEX:32017R1155&from=EN. Accessed 10 October 2017. The new rules will enter into force in 2018.

[19] Council Regulation (EC) No. 834/2007, 28 June 2007, on organic production and labelling of organic products and repealing Regulation (EEC) No. 2092/91, available at http://eur-lex.europa.eu/LexUriServ/LexUriServ.do?uri=OJ:L:2007:189:0001:0023:EN:PDF. Accessed 10 October 2017.

[20] Directive (EU) 2015/412 of the European Parliament and of the Council, 11 March 2015, amending Directive 2001/18/EC as regards the possibility for the Member States to restrict or prohibit the cultivation of genetically modified organisms (GMOs) in their territory. Text with EEA relevance available at http://eur-lex.europa.eu/legal-content/EN/TXT/?uri=celex%3A32015L0412. Accessed 10 October 2017.

[21] Council Regulation (EC) No. 1184/2006, 24 July 2006, applying certain rules of competition to the production of, and trade in, agricultural products (codified version), available at http://eur-lex.europa.eu/legal-content/EN/ALL/?uri=CELEX%3A32006R1184. Accessed 10 October 2017.

[22] Council Regulation (EC) No. 1234/2007, 22 October 2007, establishing a common organisation of agricultural markets and on specific provisions for certain agricultural products (Single CMO

on common agricultural markets, which apply and favour farmers' undertakings and associations of undertakings between member states. EU legislation combined with the expansion of the common market may have contributed to a decline in the numbers of small and very small farms and an increasing trend of medium and large farms.[23] However, EU farming remains a family activity.[24] The process of integration in agriculture is also connected with global markets that reflect food demand. Farmers that produce for foreign markets have additional obligations to comply with export rules.[25] The agricultural policies of foreign countries' and pre-accession states in Central and Eastern Europe, specifically, are also influenced by the CAP.[26] It should be noted that the process of EU integration has harmonized areas functional to a common market by taking into account the particularities of agriculture and domestic policies.

5 The Function of the Farmer: From the Field to the Market

The main function of farming is to provide food. The process of industrialization and recent technological advancement in biological fields have enriched this function. Now the farmer is not only a field worker or provider of raw materials, but she can also specialize in different points of the agricultural value chain. The agricultural value chain refers to a variety of "actors and activities that bring a basic agricultural product from production in the field to final consumption, where at each stage value is added to the product" (FAO 2010). This concept also embraces activities that are not directly related to farming, such as packaging, storage, marketing, transportation, and distribution. In recent years, there has also been an emphasis on the role of the farmer in sustainability and preservation of ecosystems.

Regulation), available at http://eur-lex.europa.eu/LexUriServ/LexUriServ.do?uri=OJ:L:2007:299:0001:0149:EN:PDF. Accessed 10 October 2017.

[23] For the purpose of the Eurostat study, farms are differentiated as follows based on their standard output: Very small farms: < EUR 2000; Small farms: EUR 2000 – < EUR 8000; Medium-sized farms: EUR 8000 – < EUR 25,000; Large farms: EUR 25,000 – < EUR 100,000; Very large farms: ≥ EUR 100,000. Based on their utilised agricultural area: Very small farms: < 2 ha; Small farms: 2 ha – < 20 ha; Medium-sized farms: 20 ha – < 100 ha; Large farms: ≥ 100 ha.

[24] As the Eurostat report explains, approximately three-quarters (76.5%) of EU-28's agricultural labour force in 2013 was provided by family members. For more, see page 41 of the Eurostat report.

[25] For import and export rules in the EU, see https://ec.europa.eu/agriculture/organic/eu-policy/eu-rules-on-trade/import-export_en. Accessed 10 October 2017.

[26] See the pre-accession agricultural instrument (SAPARD), available at http://eur-lex.europa.eu/legal-content/EN/TXT/?uri=legissum:l60023. Accessed 10 October 2017.

6 Conclusions

The rights and duties of farmers under EU law have been developed in concomitance with technological progress and economic policies. While technology has contributed to a better understanding and improvement of farming techniques, EU economic goals have pushed towards market expansion. Consequently, EU law has adapted the rights and duties of farmers in line with these developments and at the same time has allowed for flexibility at the national level. Agriculture, indeed, is strongly correlated with the culture and traditions of farming practices in a particular area. Therefore, the rights and duties for EU farmers differ based on domestic needs, but they all aim at the realization of food security in the EU common market.

References

D. P. E. (1945). Food for Post-War Europe: Shortage of world supplies. *Bulletin of International News, 22*(11), 465–474. *JSTOR*, www.jstor.org/stable/25643818

European Union. (2012). *The common agricultural policy: A story to be continued.* Retrieved October 4, 2017, from http://ec.europa.eu/agriculture/50-years-of-cap/files/history/history_book_lr_en.pdf

European Union. (2016). *Agricultural, forestry and fishery statistics*. Retrieved October 5, 2017, from http://ec.europa.eu/eurostat/documents/3217494/7777899/KS-FK-16-001-EN-N.pdf/cae3c56f-53e2-404a-9e9e-fb5f57ab49e3

FAO. (2010). *Agricultural value chain development: threat or opportunity for women's employment?* Gender and Rural Employment Policy Brief no. 4. Retrieved October 10, 2017, from http://www.fao.org/docrep/013/i2008e/i2008e04.pdf

Guadagno, E. (2012). Fallimento e Impresa Agricola: un percorso legislativo tormentato. Il caso italiano e quello francese. *Diritto e Giurisprudenza Agraria, Alimentare e dell'Ambiente*, no. 5.

Ministère de l'agriculture, de l'agroalimentaire et de la forêt, Conseil général de l'alimentation, de l'agriculture et des espaces ruraux (CGAAER). (2015).

Prifti, V. (2015). *The breeder's exception to patent rights. Analysis of compliance with article 30 of the TRIPS agreement*. Cham: Springer International.

Rapport relatif à l'accueil social sur les exploitations agricoles et l'affiliation au régime agricole, Rapport no. 14141. Retrieved October 11, 2017, from http://agriculture.gouv.fr/sites/minagri/files/cgaaer_14141_2015_rapport.pdf

Former EU Citizen

Joakim Nergelius

1 Introduction and Background

The idea of the EU citizenship was introduced into EU law through the Maastricht Treaty, 25 years ago.[1] The rules on this topic, including rules on non-discrimination, are now to be found in Arts. 18 to 25 of the so-called Functional Treaty (TFEU). Certain important rules are also to be found in TEU, the Treaty on European Union, as well as in the Charter of Fundamental Rights (CFR), which is now an integrated part of the Lisbon Treaty.

However, formal regulation is one thing. It is probably of greater importance, in order to understand the growth of the concept, to understand the legal development, through the case-law of the European Court of Justice (ECJ).[2] In this respect, the *Martinez Sala*[3] case of 1998 is one of the cornerstones of the early jurisprudence of the ECJ. Mrs Martinez Sala was a Spanish citizen who had resided in Germany since 1998, and the German authorities refused to grant her certain social benefits that were provided to German nationals (namely a child-raising allowance) on the grounds that she had neither German nationality nor a residence entitlement or permit. She had had such permits until 1984 (when they were replaced by documents certifying that she had applied for an extension). The decision of the German authorities was considered to be a violation of EU law. The case finally reached the ECJ, who concluded that the case fell within the scope of the EC Treaty and that the

[1] The Maastricht Treaty was adopted in December 1991 and entered into force on 1 November 1993 after it had been ratified by all the then 12 Member States. For a full historical account, see Kadelbach (2005, pp. 455 ff.).

[2] For an overview of this jurisprudence, see Wollenschläger (2011, p. 2, fn. 5).

[3] C-85/96, Martinez Sala, ECR 1998 I p. 2691.

J. Nergelius (✉)
Department of Law, University of Örebro, Örebro, Sweden
e-mail: Joakim.nergelius@oru.se

A. Bartolini et al. (eds.), *Dictionary of Statuses within EU Law*,
https://doi.org/10.1007/978-3-030-00554-2_35

national legislation that had been applied constituted a clear case of direct discrimination based on nationality (Art. 18 TFEU). Thus, a connection between EU citizenship and non-discrimination was established.

This case was then followed by other important judgments that stated, for instance, that the status of EU citizenship 'is destined to be the fundamental status of nationals of the Member States'[4] and also, in the well-known *Baumbast* case (which concerned a Colombian woman who was married to a German citizen and was living in the UK (and wanting to stay there permanently with their children while he worked abroad)) that the former Art. 18 of the EC Treaty (now Art. 21 TFEU) has direct effect, meaning that it can be invoked before the national courts and other public authorities in the Member States.[5] At the same time, the fact that Member States are not always obliged to pay social benefits to EU citizens residing there was clarified by the important *Dano* case of 2014.[6]

Another important judgment was rendered in 2008, in the well-known *Metock* case, which was very controversial politically (at least in some Member States).[7] Although the case actually consists of four cases joined together, the issue in all four of the cases concerned the right of an EU citizen to live in another Member State with a spouse who was a non-EU national, in a situation where the spouse had no prior lawful residence anywhere in the EU.[8] Here, in contrast to its earlier jurisprudence,[9] the ECJ found that Directive 2004/38/EC (on citizenship) prevents there being national legislation in a Member State according to which a non-EU citizen who is married to an EU citizen living in a Member State other than his or her own 'home state' (the state where he or she is a citizen) must have resided lawfully in another Member State before arriving in the Member State where he or she may want to settle down with the spouse (of 'EU nationality'). This applies regardless of when or where the marriage took place.

The ECJ stressed that securing the possibility for EU citizens to lead a normal family life was central to realizing and protecting the free movement of EU citizens between the Member States.[10]

In these cases, we can also clearly see how the protection of the family (cf. Art. 8 ECHR) takes a value of its own, emphasizing and strengthening the value of EU citizenship in situations where the outcome of the case, if the citizenship had deter-

[4] C-184/99 Rudy Grzelczyk, ECR 2002 I p. 6153 (para. 31).

[5] C-413/99, Baumbast, ECR 2002 I p. 7091.

[6] C-333/13, Dano v Jobcenter Leipzig, EU:C:2014:341.

[7] See, on this case, Costello (2009), Currie (2009) and The Court of Justice in the limelight – again (2008).

[8] In these four cases, C-127/08, ECR 2008 I P. 6241, two British nationals, one German citizen and one Polish citizen all wished to live and work in Ireland with spouses who had been refused asylum in the EU, which serves to underline the controversial nature of the case, as well as the multinational dimension that the rules on EU citizenship may bring into play in specific cases.

[9] In particular *Akrich*, C-109/01, ECR 2003 I p. 9607.

[10] See para. 62 of the judgment. See also Jacqueson (2010).

mined certain rights, would otherwise have been less evident.[11] This tendency was also clear in the latest very crucial judgment in this area, in the *Ruiz-Zambrano* case of 2011.[12]

This case, which is perhaps the most dramatic that there has been so far in terms of revealing the profound human rights dimension of EU citizens' rights, concerned a Colombian couple, Mr and Mrs Ruiz-Zambrano, who had lived in Belgium as political refugees, with a child, since 2000. While living there, Mrs Ruiz-Zambrano gave birth to a second child in 2003 and then to a third in 2005. The Belgian authorities wanted to expel them, since their reasons for being considered as refugees were not deemed to be sufficient, but it turned out that while Colombia does not recognize children born abroad as citizens of Colombia, unless the parents make a special request for this, children who are born in Belgium are automatically considered as Belgian citizens.

In its judgment, the ECJ also took into account the fact that Mr and Mrs Ruiz-Zambrano and their children had never left Belgium. However, as indicated in some of the previous judgments mentioned above, this lack of exercise of free movement and the rights that may then follow (cf. Art. 21(1) TFEU) was not considered to prevent the application of the concept of citizenship, to the surprise of some Member States who had intervened in the case on the side of the Belgian government. On the contrary, as Mr Ruiz-Zambrano argued, the children, being Belgian citizens, were also automatically considered as EU citizens, in spite of the fact that they had never left Belgium. This was considered as part of the 'core' of the right to citizenship, but what was undoubtedly even more surprising was that, having regard to the protection of family life in Art. 8, as well as Art. 3 of Protocol 4 ECHR, the parents and in fact all the family members were also considered to be EU citizens. In this specific case this means that they were entitled to stay and reside in Belgium (or move to some other Member State, of course).[13] The judgment also shows how the concept may affect the lives of citizens of third nations, particularly in family situations.[14]

2 The Current Regulation of EU Citizenship

It follows from Art. 9 TEU and Art. 20 TFEU that EU citizenship complements national citizenship without replacing it, which is of course entirely logical. Still, the introduction of the concept of EU citizenship within the EU Treaty may be said to symbolize or encapsulate a move away from purely economic integration towards

[11] See also the *Garcia Avello* case, C-148/02, ECR 2003 I p. 11613.

[12] C-34/09, Judgment 8 March 2011.

[13] See paras. 40–45 of the judgment.

[14] This has also been said with regard to a subsequent judgment, given in May 2011, in the case of *McCarthy*. It has sometimes been suggested that this case implies that the consequences of EU citizenship must now be seen as more limited. C-434/09, McCarthy v Secretary of State for the Home Department, Judgment 5 May 2011, ECR 2011 I p. 3375.

a more all-encompassing union of peoples, with a focus on promoting important human and cultural values too.[15]

Of greater practical importance, however, are the rules in Arts. 18–25 TFEU. First, then, we have the general non-discrimination rule in Art. 18. This is now supported by Art. 19, which empowers the EU to enact further appropriate measures in order to combat any kind of discrimination. Citizenship as such is then mentioned in Art. 20, which mentions, when talking about the specific rights that it entails, the right to move freely and reside within the territories of the Member States, as well as the rights to vote in elections for the EU Parliament, to be elected to the EU Parliament and also to vote in municipal elections (although not national ones) in the state where the citizen resides, on the same conditions as the nation's own citizens.[16] The right to consular protection in a third country, outside the EU, by official representatives of EU nations other than the person's own home state is also included (see Art. 20(c), as well as Art. 23 TFEU and Art. 46 CFR).

Art. 21 TFEU, then, which is perhaps the most practically important rule in view of the jurisprudence mentioned above, lays down the basic right to move and reside freely in the EU. As we have seen, this right may be seen as an extension of the original right to free movement for economically active persons, and now encompasses the right to be accompanied by family members even if they are nationals of a third country, which is of course a significant change. More detailed rules on many of the practical issues involved in relation to the application of the citizenship rules are also to be found in the important EU Directive 2004/38/EC. Further provisions to strengthen the rights that follow from EU citizenship may be brought in, according to Art. 25 TFEU, although this requires unanimity in the Council and subsequent approval by the Member States.

However, in view of the frequent recent treaty changes, new legal acts and case-law within this area, a few important limitations may also be drawn. Though this development represents one of the most important changes in EU law in recent years, we must nevertheless be aware that the rights emanating from EU citizenship are not unlimited.

First of all, it follows from Art. 9 TEU and Art. 20 TFEU that every person who is a national of a Member State is also an EU citizen. In this regard, no Member State may call into question a classification made by another Member State,[17] but it must also be observed that EU law has no specific opinion concerning national legislation in this area, which thus may differ considerably between the 27 or 28 states. Member States, such as, for instance, the UK with its rather complicated citizenship rules (which are mainly the result of its colonial past[18]), may even be allowed to classify which of its nationals are to be considered as national citizens and thus also EU citizens.[19] At the same time, however, it should be underlined that

[15] Rosas and Armati (2012), pp. 128 ff.

[16] See also, in this respect, Art. 22 TFEU and Arts. 39–40 CFR.

[17] C-369/90, Micheletti, ECR 1992 I p. 4239.

[18] See e.g. C-192/99, Kaur, ECR 2001 p. 1237.

[19] See the *Kaur* case.

no Member State may deny the status of EU citizen to a person who has been duly classified as such by another Member State.[20] This means, to sum it up, that all EU citizens are also citizens of a Member State, while the reverse is normally, but not necessarily always, the case.[21]

An important thing to keep in mind is that citizenship, once gained, should normally be valid and it should be impossible for the state to take it away. At least one exception to this rule may, however, be noted, namely when a person has obtained citizenship on false grounds, by misleading the authorities. That was what happened in 2010 in the important case of *Rottmann*.[22] The ECJ here found it to be reasonable that a person who had acquired German citizenship on false grounds, and thereby lost his original Austrian citizenship, would, as a consequence, lose his German citizenship, thus becoming stateless and no longer an EU citizen. 'A decision withdrawing naturalisation because of deception corresponds to a reason relating to the public interest'.[23] Even in that situation, however, the consequences for the person in question and possibly his family members must be taken into account (see para. 56 of the judgment).

There are quite a few conclusions to be drawn from this case. Obviously, it shows that someone who loses his or her national citizenship of an EU Member State, for one reason or another, may also lose his or her EU citizenship. Thus, in other words, there is no automatic right to maintain an acquired status as an EU citizen.

At the same time, issues like the ones occurring in the *Rottmann* case should also have repercussions in the EU Member States, although they may be quite different, depending on the circumstances. In Sweden, the constitutional protection of citizenship in Chap. 2, Art. 7 of the Instrument of Government (IG, the Regeringsformen of 1974, which is the main constitutional Act), was severely strengthened by a judgment of the Supreme Court in April 2014. In this case, a person who had been wrongly deprived of his Swedish citizenship was awarded financial compensation of 100,000 SEK, since his treatment was deemed to be unconstitutional.[24] Another similar case was decided by the Supreme Court in March 2018, with a similar result.[25]

The forthcoming, or at least likely, Brexit situation raises the question of the legal position of those UK citizens who are not also citizens of another EU country. At the time of writing, in September 2018, it is, in fact, completely impossible to answer this question, since we do not know what the future relationship between the EU and the UK will be. However, it is clear that if, or when, the UK really leaves

[20] See C-369/90, Micheletti, ECR 1992 I p. 4239, as well as (and in particular) C-200/02, Zhu and Chen, ECR 2004 I p. 9925.

[21] Rosas and Armati (2012), pp. 133 ff.

[22] C-135/08, ECLI:EU:C:2010:104.

[23] Para. 51 of the judgment.

[24] NJA 2014 p. 323. In this case, the claimant had a British mother and Swedish father. When his parents divorced, it turned out during a trial that his father was not, after all, his biological father. As a consequence, the Swedish authorities wrongly deprived him of his Swedish citizenship.

[25] Judgment 5 March 2018, Case T 2480-17, NJA 2018, p. 103.

the EU, these persons will no longer be EU citizens, regardless of what kind of relationship this will then be. Art. 20 TFEU makes it very clear that EU citizenship only exists for citizens of EU Member States. Thus, citizens of the EEA states of Iceland, Liechtenstein and Norway are not EU citizens, and should the UK in the end opt for what is called the Norwegian position, UK citizens will enjoy free movement in all its famous four aspects, but not EU citizenship. With the British borders being more closed than that UK citizens will not enjoy the four freedoms either—a solution with which most of them are likely to be unhappy.[26]

It follows from Directive 2004/38/EC that every EU citizen has an unconditional right to stay, live and reside in other EU Member States for no less than 3 months.[27] Once that period has expired, economically non-active citizens who wish to stay longer must, according to Art. 7(1)(b) of the Directive, have 'sufficient resources for themselves and their family members not to become a burden on the social assistance system of the host state during their period of residence'. In other words, the right to stay in another EU state for longer than 3 months depends on certain economic criteria being met,[28] as was also stressed in the 2014 *Dano* case mentioned above, but on the other hand it must be noted that every EU citizen who has resided legally in a host Member State for a period of 5 years receives a permanent right to residence (Art. 16 of the Directive), which is another example of the dynamic character of the citizenship rules. In the same way, EU citizens who have once used their right to move to another Member State may, should they be disadvantaged when returning to their home states or moving to a third EU state, invoke the right to treatment that is equal to that of other nationals or residents who have not exercised their right to free movement.[29] Furthermore, it follows from the case-law of the ECJ that an EU citizen who travels from a third country to a Member State other than his 'own' may rely on his rights as an EU citizen even if he has in fact never visited his country of nationality.[30]

---

[26] A factor that may be revealing here, and that has to be solved before the real negotiations on the future relationship between the UK and the EU can start, concerns the control of the border between Ireland and Northern Ireland (which, as we know, is a part of the UK). Since neither the UK nor Ireland wants to reintroduce the border controls that were abolished in 1998, a possible solution may be to give Northern Ireland a special kind of EEA status. However, Scotland is then likely immediately to ask for a similar status, which will make things difficult for the UK government. Given these facts, UK may after all have to accept a kind of Norwegian solution, but this is of course purely speculative. – It may also be mentioned in this respect that as of 5 April 2018, a so-called citizen's initiative aiming at letting UK citizens keeping their EU citizenship after Brexit (ECI(2017)000005) was far from receiving the required one million signatures that will, under Article 11 of the EU Treaty, force the EU Commission to analyse whether a legislative initiative should be made. The deadline for achieving this number of signataires is 2 May, 2018.

[27] Having this in mind, the legality of actions taken by French and Swedish authorities against gypsy people from Romania in the summer of 2010 must be called into question.

[28] It may be noted, however, that these rules do not apply to students.

[29] See e.g. C-365/02, Lindfors, ECR 2004 I p. 7183.

[30] See C-138/02, Collins, ECR 2004 I p. 2703.

To sum up this analysis, we find that EU citizenship today entails a general right to move around, live and reside in all the EU Member States, with the notable exception, or rather limitation, that once a period of 3 months has expired, and until the person in question has managed to stay in another Member State for 5 years, he may be refused permission to stay unless he is able to support himself economically. It is also worth noting that each Member State may establish its own rules concerning who is a national citizen—and that the national legislation does in fact differ widely, from generous legislation such as that of Belgium to restrictive and varied legislation like in the UK—but that, on the other hand, once a person has been recognized as a national citizen in one Member State, he is also at the same time an EU citizen in all 27 Member States. Hence this is, in the words of the ECJ in the *Grzelczyk* case, 'the fundamental status of nationals of the Member States'.[31] However, once a person loses his national citizenship in an EU Member State, he may also lose his status as an EU citizen. And for citizens in a state that chooses to leave the EU under Art. 50 TEU, there seems to be no hope at all of maintaining their EU citizenship.

References

Costello, C. (2009). Metock: Free movement and 'normal family life in the Union. *Common Market Law Review, 46*, 587–622.

Currie, S. (2009). Accelerated justice or a step too far? Residence rights of non-EU family members and the Court's ruling in Metock. *European Law Review, 34*, 310–326.

Jacqueson, C. (2010). *Metock* as a shock? The struggle between rights and sovereignty. In H. Koch, K. Hagel-Sörensen, U. Haltern, & J. H. H. Weiler (Eds.), *Europe – The new legal realism, essays in honour of Hjalte Rasmussen* (pp. 277–296). Copenhagen: DJOF Publishing.

Kadelbach, S. (2005). Union citizenship. In A. Von Bogdandy & J. Bast (Eds.), *Principles of European constitutional law* (pp. 453–499). Oxford: Hart Publishing.

Rosas, A., & Armati, L. (2012). *EU constitutional law – An introduction* (2nd ed.). Oxford: Hart Publishing.

The Court of Justice in the Limelight – Again. (2008). Editorial Comment. *Common Market Law Review, 45*(6), 1571–1579.

Wollenschläger, F. (2011). A new fundamental freedom beyond market integration: Union citizenship and its dynamics for shifting the economic paradigm of European integration. *European Law Journal, 17*, 1–34.

[31] C-184/99, ECR 2001 P. 6193, para. 31. See also Joined Cases C-482/01 and 493/01, Orfanopoulos and Oliveiri, ECR 2004 I p. 5257, para. 64.

Gender Victim of Gender-Based Violence

Beatriz Belando Garín

1 Introduction

The concept of a female victim of gender violence is complex, because behind it there are different legal concepts and diverse legal responses among the different Member States.

Violence against women was recognized by the United Nations as a violation of fundamental rights in 1993 in Resolution 48/104, 20th December 1993. This stated, on the ending of violence against women, as follows: 'Gender violence is (…) or is likely to result in, physical, sexual or psychological harm or suffering to women, including threats of such acts, coercion or arbitrary deprivation of liberty, whether occurring in public or in private life. (…) it groups all the forms of violence that are exerted by men onto women according to their gender role: sexual violence, trafficking of women, sexual exploitation, genital mutilation, etc. regardless of the type of interpersonal relationship that the aggressor and victim have, which may be sentimental, work, family, or non-existent'.

Recently, the Council of Europe's Convention on preventing and combating violence against women and domestic violence (the Istanbul Convention), which was adopted in 2011, defined, in Article 3, violence against women as follows: 'a violation of human rights and a form of discrimination against women and shall mean all acts of gender-based violence that result in, or are likely to result in, physical, sexual, psychological or economic harm or suffering to women, including threats of such acts, coercion or arbitrary deprivation of liberty, whether occurring in public or in private life'.

B. Belando Garín (✉)
Faculty of Law, Department of Administrative Law, University of València, Valencia, Spain
e-mail: beatriz.belando@uv.es

A. Bartolini et al. (eds.), *Dictionary of Statuses within EU Law*,
https://doi.org/10.1007/978-3-030-00554-2_36

The European Union has not adopted its own concept of a victim of gender violence, but its recognition of gender-based violence as a violation of human rights has led to the issuing of different legal instruments that *de facto* imply an common approach in the different Member States to the treatment of women who suffer this type of violence.

2 The Impact of European Law on the Protection of Victims of Gender-Based Violence

The Directive on the European Protection Order 2011/99/EU is part of the European 'victims package' initiative that was launched by the Commission in May 2011. It consists of two regulations on the protection of victims of crime, with particular attention being paid to victims of gender-based violence. The first of these regulations is Regulation (EU) No 606/2013, of the European Parliament and of the Council, 12 June 2013 on mutual recognition of protection measures in civil matters. This Regulation complements the recently approved European Protection Order, which refers to criminal matters.

The European Protection Order guarantees victims of crimes such as violence, harassment, terrorism or human trafficking the same level of protection from their aggressors throughout the entire European Union. The other initiative is Directive 2012/29/EU, which establishes minimum standards on the rights of, and support and protection for, victims of crime. This Directive means that individuals can assert the same basic rights and have confidence in the justice system wherever they may be in the European Union, and regardless of whether the crime was committed in Spain or in any other country. The victim must be recognized and treated with respect and sensitivity on the basis of her needs, and she must receive information about her role, her rights in the justice system and the evolution of the proceedings.

Directive 2011/99/EU on the protection of victims of crime has undoubtedly been one of the main tools that the European Union has used to protect its citizens against criminal behaviour, therefore consolidating a European area of security and freedom. In the case of the protection of women who suffer gender-based violence, the purpose for which Directive 2011/99/EU was originally intended, the new rule, creating a European protection order (EPO) for women who suffer this type of violence, will allow the extension of their national protection status beyond national borders. This recognizes that violence is a cross-border phenomenon and therefore requires a legal response of the same nature. The complexity of the practical application of this measure extends to all the agents who are called on to apply it: police forces, judges, lawyers, social services and victim support centres. However, this cannot lead to inactivity on the part of the Member States, which is in any case not possible given the binding nature of this kind of European standard.

The Directive considers the problems for public administrations in managing this measure, given that it means recognizing as victims of gender violence women from other countries who want to access the assistance and protection systems of the country in which they are living.

3 The Need for Administrative Coordination Across Europe

Coordination involves implementing a set of factors for a specific purpose. Coordination is unavoidable in the area in which we find ourselves, given that the variety of actions, as well as groups and bodies involved in the protection of victims, could lead to the adoption of decisions with contradictory effects. It is, precisely, the unity of action and the subsequent avoidance of contradictory results that is the strong idea that inspires coordination.

For this reason, the European protection order (EPO) poses an important challenge of administrative coordination, by obliging not only the entities and bodies (judicial, social services, and police) in the country of origin of the victim, but also the individuals and equivalent groups in the state of reception of the woman to act in an orderly manner. This implies, among other things, that a joint database must be implemented, incorporating not only the protection orders that are covered by Directive 2011/99/EU but also orders issued by other authorities whose cross-border perception is based on the regulation for the mutual recognition of civil protection measures. In this sense, the Spanish example, where multiple administrations (state, autonomous and local) are involved, can serve as an example for the introduction of a similar model at the European level.

4 Proposals for the Framework of the European Protection Order

Taking into account the Spanish experience, two proposals can be made in relation to the coordination that will be required by the implementation of the European protection order.

4.1 The Need for a National Authority

One of the main obstacles that will be faced in practice by the EPO will be the difficulty of identifying the judicial body to which the OEP must be transmitted. That is why the need for a central national authority to coordinate and manage the issue and execution of all orders has already been raised, so that the status of the procedures for modifying and cancelling an OEP can be monitored. This also links to Article 4.1 of the Directive, which establishes the possibility that the Member States might create authorities of this sort. Nevertheless, these central authorities should not limit themselves to this procedural aspect: it would be advisable if they also became the centres for information relating to the different assistance and support centres for the victims as well as detailed information on the rights that assist them.

It should be remembered that Directive 2012/29/EU, 25th October, which establishes minimum standards on the rights of, and support and protection for, victims of crime, includes in its 62 articles a specific mention of the need to create meeting points or assistance that victims can access and where they can obtain comprehensive services. In the case of Spain, this service is provided by the government delegation where the different actions to protect against gender violence are coordinated.

In the case of European protection orders, it is necessary to create a national authority not only to centralize the orders but also to provide clear information about the support and prevention resources of the Member State.

4.2 Establishment of a European Protocol for Action

The drawing up of protocols has undoubtedly been essential in the success of the Spanish protection legislation. One of the proposals for an adequate mechanism for the European protection order in cases of gender violence is undoubtedly the implementation of such protocols at a European level. The protocols establish common standards of action, which undoubtedly facilitate women's understanding of the protection that will be offered in the country of destination, as well as facilitating the work of all the agents involved. The proper working of the protocols requires, in any case, the designation of national coordination authorities, which ensures the correct application of the protocols and allows deficiencies in their implementation to be corrected. Ultimately, it is even possible that, together with the national authorities, a European office can be created to centralize all this information and make proposals for improvement.

5 Extent of the Protection

5.1 The Implications of the European Protection Order for Assistance

The application of the European protection order implies a recognition that this judicial instrument serves as a document proving that there is a situation of violence and allowing access to the social assistance provided by the Member State for its nationals. This point is undoubtedly crucial, and has recently been highlighted in the Report of the European Parliament with recommendations to the Commission on combating violence against women of 31 January 2014 (PE 522.850v02-00), in which the Member States are urged (in Recommendation 2) to: 'ensure that specialised shelters (conceived both as first contact assistance and as safe and empowering space for women) are available and equip them with facilities and properly trained staff, offering places for at least 1 woman per 10,000 inhabitants'.

Certainly, the most complete system of assistance offered to women suffering gender-based violence exists in Spain, which provides integrated social protection as a right of the victim (Article 19 Ley Orgánica 1/2004). Along with this broadly configured right to social assistance, we find the right to an economic benefit called social assistance (Article 27 Ley Orgánica 1/2004 and Regulation 1452/2005), which is made as a single aid payment. This broad list of subsidies is completed in turn with other indirect subsidies such as priority in access to housing for official protection or to public residences for the elderly (Article 28 Ley Orgánica 1/2004), etc.

5.2 *Entitlements in a Situation of Gender Violence*

The issue of a European order allows a woman to have access to healthcare that has been designated for her. In the Spanish case this will involve a modification of Article 23 of Ley Orgánica 1/2004, which only entitles a woman to this healthcare if there is an order of protection under Article 554 ter Criminal Procedural Law (LECrim), in exceptional cases, a report by the Public Prosecutor. Therefore, nothing has been foreseen in the case of the issuance of a European order, although in an attempt to save the situation we can understand that, in accordance with Article 9 of the Directive 2011/99/EU, once a European order has been received it will be replaced by a national protection order, which, in Spain for example, would be an order of protection under Article 554 ter LECrim.

In short, the Directive establishes an obligation to convert the OEP into an equivalent measure provided in the Member State's legal system; in our case, this will be an order of protection under Article 554 ter LECrim. This is complex, given that there is no legal uniformity on the protection against gender violence in the European context, but it implies, in any case, that the EPO establishes the requirement for the translation into the national equivalent (a restraining order, for example) The lack of prior harmonization of the rights that are covered by the OEP has been highlighted. However, it cannot *de facto* paralyse the effectiveness of such an important tool for women who suffer violence. In this way, the access to the welfare protection system occurs indirectly through the conversion of the original document (the OEP) into a national entitlement (a protection order).

5.3 *The Need for Legal Residence*

A state may find legal residence to be an obstacle to gaining access to social benefits. In many Member States, access by victims of gender violence to certain protections requires them to be nationals or to have legal residence.

Beyond the national sphere, some Member States (Germany, for example) have made political moves to exclude individuals who are not nationals of a Member State from certain social benefits, so the situation can be complicated. The ECJ on 11 November 2014 (case C-333/13) contributed negatively by endorsing these restrictive policies, limiting the scope of Directive 2004/38/EC of the European Parliament and the Council of 29 April 2004 concerning the right of citizens of the Union and their family members to move and reside freely within the territory of the Member States.

The judgment came in response to questions raised by the social court of Leipzig in relation to a dispute between, on the one hand, two Romanian nationals, Mrs. Dano and her son, and, on the other, the Leipzig Jobcenter, which refused them certain insurance benefits that were reserved in Germany for job seekers. The judgment sought to limit the scope of Directive 2004/38/EC and to determine whether it was possible to exclude claimants from the basic German insurance benefits. The Court noted that, according to the Directive, the host Member State is not obliged to grant social assistance benefits during the first 3 months of residence. When the period is longer than 3 months but less than 5 months (as it was in the present case), the Directive restricts the right of residence for people who do not exercise an economic activity to those who have sufficient resources. Thus, the regulation tries to prevent Union citizens who are not engaged in economic activity from using the benefits system of the host Member State to guarantee their subsistence. Therefore, a Member State should have the option of denying social benefits to citizens of the Union who do not carry out an economic activity and who exercise their freedom of movement for the sole purpose of receiving social assistance from another Member State when they do not have enough resources to opt for the right of residence; in this regard, the right must be examined on a case-by-case basis.

Although the goal is to avoid so-called ‘benefits tourism’, the truth is that this case might have important consequences in the area of our analysis. The author’s conclusion is that the specific circumstances of the victim should exclude the application of the limitations derived from this jurisprudential interpretation.

6 Conclusion

Directive 2011/99/EU has generated enormous expectations about the protection that women who suffer violence can receive in the European space, preventing them from having to begin a new process to access the protection of the European country in which they choose to live. The measure is based on a recognition of the judicial decisions of other countries, but it has been adopted without harmonizing the criminal categories that give it substance and without establishing a European protection network. For this reason, the final outcome will depend on the will and capacity of the states to design and implement an organic and legal structure that responds to the explicit needs that are derived from the European protection order. This is not just about trying to bring legal systems closer, but also about designing common structures that allow protection for women and their children that is at least equivalent to the protection they enjoyed in their country of origin.

In short, the status of a victim of gender violence has undergone colossal change, and uniformity has been introduced by the different measures adopted at European level, but the process has not been completed.

Human Embryo

Roberto Cippitani

1 Definition of a 'Human Embryo' in European Legal Sources

As argued by the *Warnock Report* (written by a panel of experts appointed by the English government in 1984), the term 'human embryo' may be variously defined.

This variability is particularly evident when one considers European legislation (for an overview, see Palazzo 2013).

Opinion No. 12 of 23 November 1998, issued by the European Group on Ethics in Science and New Technologies (hereinafter the 'EGE') at the request of the European Commission, concerning 'Ethical aspects of research involving the use of human embryo in the context of the 5th Framework Programme', explains that in many European states (especially those that are members of the EU) there is no legal definition of 'embryo' (this is the case in Belgium, Denmark, Finland, France, Greece, Ireland, Italy, Luxembourg, Netherlands, Portugal and Sweden) (para. 1.17).

On the other hand, among those Member States that define the term 'embryo' in their legislation, the existing definitions vary considerably from one country to another.

As a matter of fact, in Austrian law the word 'embryo' is not defined, and the term 'developable cells' is used and is defined as inseminated ova and cells developed from them; German law defines an embryo as a 'fertilised human egg cell capable of development, from the moment of fusion of the pronuclei'; Spanish law makes a distinction between the 'pre-embryo' (the group of cells resulting from the fertilisation of an ovum until the implantation and formation of the primitive

R. Cippitani (✉)
Department of Medicine, Università degli Studi di Perugia, Perugia, Italy
e-mail: roberto.cippitani@unipg.it

A. Bartolini et al. (eds.), *Dictionary of Statuses within EU Law*,
https://doi.org/10.1007/978-3-030-00554-2_37

streak – 14 days),[1] the 'embryo' (the process of forming organs which continues for about two and a half months) and the 'foetus' (from two and a half months on); and British law defines an embryo as a 'live embryo where fertilisation is complete (i.e. completion is when a two cell zygote appears), including an egg in the process of fertilisation'.[2]

As observed by Advocate General Bot in the Opinion[3] in the *Brüstle* case (see para. 66–70),[4] with respect to the definition of the term 'human embryo' the European national legislation may be grouped into two categories: 'the first considering that the human embryo exists from fertilisation and the second taking the view that it is from the time when the fertilised ovum has been transplanted into the endometrium' (para. 66).

Examples of the first approach may be seen in Article 3 of the *Kunstliku viljastamise ja embrüokaitse seadus* (Law on Artificial Insemination and Embryo Protection) of Estonia, which provides that an embryo is the foetus in its early stage of development, from the time of fertilisation; in the German law that sets out that an embryo is a fertilised human ovum capable of development, and any cell removed from a 'totipotent' embryo that is able to divide and develop into an individual; and in the United Kingdom, where section 1(1)(b) of the Human Fertilisation and Embryology Act 1990, as amended by the Human Fertilisation and Embryology Act 2008, states that references to an embryo include an egg that is in the process of fertilisation or is undergoing any other process capable of resulting in an embryo.

On the other hand, in other Member States such as Spain or Sweden, the human embryo is regarded as such from the time the ovum is transplanted into the uterus.

In Spain, pursuant to Article 3(l) of Ley 14/2007 *de Investigación Biomédica* of 3 July 2007, the embryo is defined according to the stage of its development, commencing from the time the fertilised oocyte lies in the woman's uterus until organogenesis begins to occur and ending 56 days after fertilisation, except days when development might have stopped.

According to Advocate General Bot (see para. 99 of the Opinion) most Member States take the view that pluripotent stem cells are not human embryos.

Under German law, for example, this follows directly from the distinction between pluripotent cells and totipotent cells. Thus, under Paragraph 8(1) of the *Embryonenschutzgesetz* ('ESchG'), the human embryo also includes any 'totipotent' cell removed from an embryo.

---

[1] See Article 1(2) of Ley 14/2006 *sobre técnicas de reproducción humana asistada* of 26 May 2006.

[2] On the other hand, the above-mentioned *Warnock Report* takes into consideration the embryonic stage of the 6 weeks immediately following fertilisation, 'which usually corresponds with the first 8 weeks of gestation counted from the first day of the woman's last menstrual period' (para. 1.4).

[3] Opinion delivered on 10 March 2011, ECLI:EU:C:2011:138.

[4] Court of Justice, judgment of 18 October 2011, *Brüstle* v *Greenpeace e.V.*, C-34/10, ECR 2011 p. I-9821, ECLI:EU:C:2011:669.

Section 1(1) of the United Kingdom Human Fertilisation and Embryology Act 1990 provides that stem cells obtained from a human embryo at the blastocyst stage are not included within the concept of a human embryo, in particular because they are incapable of further development.[5]

Within that framework, the Court of Justice provides a definition of 'human embryo', in the above-mentioned *Brüstle* judgment. This was needed in order to establish the legal meaning of Article 6, para. 1, of the Directive 98/44/EC of the European Parliament and of the Council of 6 July 1998 on the Legal Protection of biotechnological inventions, which states that 'Inventions shall be considered unpatentable where their commercial exploitation would be contrary to public order or morality', and, in particular, refers to the prohibition of the 'uses of human embryos for industrial or commercial purposes' (Article 6, para. 2(c)).[6]

The Court of Justice argues that 'although, the definition of human embryo is a very sensitive social issue in many Member States, marked by their multiple traditions and value systems, the Court is not called upon, by the present order for reference, to broach questions of a medical or ethical nature, but must restrict itself to a legal interpretation of the relevant provisions of the Directive (see, to that effect, Case C-506/06 *Mayr* [2008] ECR I-1017, paragraph 38)' (para. 30).

According to the Court, 'The context and aim of the Directive thus show that the European Union legislature intended to exclude any possibility of patentability where respect for human dignity could thereby be affected. It follows that the concept of 'human embryo' within the meaning of Article 6(2)(c) of the Directive must be understood in a wide sense' (para. 34).

Therefore, within that wide sense, 'any human ovum after fertilisation, any non-fertilised human ovum into which the cell nucleus from a mature human cell has been transplanted and any non-fertilised human ovum whose division and further development have been stimulated by parthenogenesis constitute a "human embryo" within the meaning of Article 6(2)(c) of the Directive' (para. 38).

In the case of non-fertilised human ova, the Court affirms that: 'Although those organisms have not, strictly speaking, been the object of fertilisation, due to the effect of the technique used to obtain them they are, as is apparent from the written observations presented to the Court, capable of commencing the process of development of a human being just as an embryo created by fertilisation of an ovum can do so' (para. 36).

The Court of Justice also left open the qualification as an embryo of 'stem cells obtained from a human embryo at the blastocyst stage', depending on whether they are capable of commencing the process of development of a human being, on the basis of scientific developments (para. 37).

[5] See also, in the Czech Republic, Article 2(d) of the *Zákon o výzkumu na lidských embryonálních kmenových buňkách* (Law on Stem Cell Research, 227/2006 Sb.).

[6] See Morgese (2012) for a commentary on the *Brüstle* judgment.

2 The Special Status of the 'Human Embryo' and the Necessity for Its Protection

Scholars from several viewpoints argue that a specific moral status has to be recognised for a human embryo (see Baertschi 2008; for a criticism, see Devolder and Jhon 2007).

According to Opinion No. 12 of the EGE, European legislation varies with respect to the 'personhood' of the human embryo and with respect to the answer to the question of when human life begins.[7]

Two main views exist about the status of the embryo and thus about the legal protection afforded to it in scientific research:

(a) human embryos are not considered as human beings and consequently are less worthy of protection than human beings; and
(b) human embryos have the same moral status as human beings and consequently are equally worthy of protection.

The Warnock Report stated: 'the embryo of the human species ought to have a special status and that no one should undertake research on human embryos the purposes of which could be achieved by the use of other animals or in some other way. The status of the embryo is a matter of fundamental principle which should be enshrined in legislation. We recommend that the embryo of the human species should be afforded some protection in law' (para. 11.17).

The first specific legislation regarding research on embryos was the above-mentioned Spanish Law of 1988. This legislation permitted, for the first time, research on the 'pre-embryo' (see the definition given above). Since then, several other pieces of legislation have come into force, with different approaches to embryo research.

Within the legal sources of the Council of Europe, the Convention of Oviedo[8] does not contain a definition of embryo. In any event, Article 18.1 of the Convention provides that 'where the law allows research on embryos in vitro, it shall ensure adequate protection of the embryo'.

The necessity for protection is also affirmed under para. 2.2 of Opinion No. 12 of the EGE, which states that: 'The human embryo, whatever the moral or legal status conferred upon it in the different European cultures and ethical approaches, deserves legal protection'. Even if taking into account the continuity of human life, this protection ought to be reinforced as the embryo and the foetus develop.

---

[7] EGE, 'Ethical aspects of research involving human embryo in the context of the 5th Framework Programme', Opinion No. 12, 23 November 1998, para. 1.13 ff.

[8] Convention for the Protection of Human Rights and Dignity of the Human Being with regard to the Application of Biology and Medicine: Convention on Human Rights and Biomedicine (ETS No 164,) opened for signature on 4 April 1997 in Oviedo.

3 Principles and Rules for Protection of the Human Embryo

Because of the special status of the human embryo, rules to protect it are provided by the legal sources.

Despite the differences in European legislation, some common principles are applicable to activities involving human embryos, especially in the fields of medicine and research (see Opinion No. 15 of 2000 of the EGE, 'Ethical aspects of human stem cell research and use', para. 2.2; see also para. 1.26 of the EGE Opinion No. 12).

In particular, the European sources refer to the principle of respect for human dignity.

Dignity is a pivotal principle of European law, as demonstrated in the constitutional sources (see, for example, the preamble of the EU Charter).[9]

As Advocate General Christine Stix-Hackl argues in her opinion (submitted on 18 March 2004) in the *Omega* case,[10] '"Human dignity" is an expression of the respect and value to be attributed to each human being on account of his or her humanity' (para. 75).

A human embryo may be considered as an expression of humanity, even if this does not necessarily lead to the embryo being considered as a person.[11] Thus in research and medical activities, the dignity of the embryo must be respected (Andorno 2013, p. 132; Mathieu 1999).

The humanity of the embryo has, as a corollary, respect for human life (EGE Opinion No. 12, para. 2.10) from the beginning and therefore from the embryonic stage (see para. 1.26 of EGE Opinion No. 12).

The respect for human life from the earliest stages of its development inspires some constitutional norms such as those provided by Article 3, para. 2, (b) to (d), of the EU Charter, which prohibits:

- eugenic practices, in particular those aimed at the selection of persons;
- making the human body and its parts as such a source of financial gain; and
- the reproductive cloning of human beings.

Furthermore, respect for human life implies other limitations such as those considered in EGE Opinion No.12 (para. 1.21):

- a time limit for the use of human embryos—including the carrying out of research activities; this is generally only allowed until 14 days after fertilisation;

---

[9] With respect to the concept of dignity in the EU Charter, see, among others, Jones (2012); for dignity in bioethics, see Andorno (2009).

[10] ECJ judgment 14 October 2004, C-36/02, *Omega Spielhallen- und Automatenaufstellungs-GmbH* v *Oberbürgermeisterin der Bundesstadt Bonn*, ECR 2004, I-p. I-9609.

[11] The European Court of Human Rights affirmed, in its judgment in *Evans* v *United Kingdom*, that a human embryo has no legal personality, but the same Court, in its judgement in the *Parrillo* case (see note 13 below) seems to agree with the Italian Law no. 40/2004, which, in Article 1, considers the human embryo as a person. On the case law on Italian Law no. 40/2004, see Cippitani (2017).

- the prohibition of the genetic modification of normal pre-implanted embryos;
- the prohibition of the creation of human–animal hybrids;
- the prohibition on replacing ‘in vivo’ embryos that have previously been used for research; and
- the need to obtain the consent of each person whose gametes were used to bring about the creation of an embryo.

According to the institutional sources, any activity concerning a human embryo must respect individual autonomy, entailing the giving of informed consent by the woman or the couple concerned (see Article 3, para. 2(a) of the EU Charter), respect for privacy and the confidentiality of personal data (see Article 8 of the EU Charter).

Furthermore, activities related to an embryo have to comply with other principles, such as proportionality, which allow the use of embryos only if necessary and only if no alternative, more acceptable, methods are available.

The Opinions of the EGE also refer to the precautionary principle, in order to take into consideration the potential long-term consequences of stem cell research and use for individuals and society.

4 Research on Embryos

The necessity to protect human embryos should be balanced with other fundamental interests such as human health (Article 35 EU Charter) and freedom of scientific research (Article 13 EU Charter).

As matter of fact, Opinion No. 12 of the EGE, when considering the protection of the human embryo, at the same time reminds its readers of the need to observe the principles of justice and of beneficence, in particular with respect to the improvement and protection of health. The relief of human suffering should be taken into consideration, and then the need to guarantee the quality and safety of medical treatment.

On the other hand, Opinions Nos. 12 and 15 of the EGE underline the importance of ensuring freedom of research. This in particularly required in order to protect people’s health (see the *Warnock Report*, para. 11.8).

Research on human embryos is a controversial issue, and there are differing views as to whether or not research on human embryos ‘in vitro’ is morally acceptable (EGE Opinion No. 12 para. 2.6).[12]

According to the European Court of Human Rights (hereinafter referred to as the ‘ECtHR’) in the *Parrillo* judgment,[13] a broad margin of discretion should be given

[12] The EC Working Group on Human Embryos and Research, set up by the European Commission, states, in its first Report (1992,3), that ‘(t)hese views are fundamentally different and it is difficult to see how, at these extremes, the differences can be reconciled’. On ethical issues concerning embryo research, see Andorno (2013), *passim*, and in particular pp. 134 ff.; Solter et al. (2003).

[13] See ECtHR, Grand Chamber, judgment of 27 August 2015, *Parrillo* v *Italy* (Application no. 46470/11) (see the commentaries of D’amico (2015), Poli (2015) and Conti (2015)).

to the national legislation because the matter of the donation of embryos is a delicate ethical issue, and one for which there is no consensus within the legislation of the states of the Council of Europe: 17 states out of the 50 members allow research on embryonic human cell lines; certain states (Andorra, Latvia, Croatia and Malta) expressly prohibit any research on embryonic cells; and some other states (Slovakia, Germany, Austria and Italy) allow research on cells imported from abroad. The other states have no specific legislation concerning the use of human embryos for research.

Therefore, the Court confirmed that states have the power 'to enact restrictive legislation where the destruction of human embryos is at stake, having regard, inter alia, to the ethical and moral questions inherent in the concept of the beginning of human life and the plurality of existing views on the subject among the different Member States' (para. 180).

The Court of Strasbourg also referred to several European legal sources (issued by both the Council of Europe and the European Union) that establish limits on the research on human embryos in order to 'temper excesses in this area' (para. 182). An example of such a source is Article 18 of the Convention of Oviedo, which requires adequate protection of the embryo subject to research and forbids the creation of human embryos for research purposes.

Opinion No. 12 (para. 2.7) of the EGE states that to prohibit the destruction of an embryo may be equivalent to forbidding all kinds of research. In order to respect the freedom of research, which is also a very sensitive field, scientific activities 'should not a priori exclude human embryo research which is the object of different ethical choices in different countries but that this funding should, nevertheless, only be granted under the strict conditions' represented by the principles referred to above (para. 2.8)

In particular, EU legal sources concerning funding for scientific activities try to find an equilibrium between freedom of research and the discretion of the state to protect human embryos.

According to Recital no. 31 and Article 19, para. 4, of Regulation (EU) No 1291/2013 of the European Parliament and of the Council of 11 December 2013 establishing the Programme 'Horizon 2020', a project may not be funded by the European Union if the research activities are forbidden in all Member States, and a project may only be funded in a Member State where such activities are allowed.

However, in accordance with the freedom of circulation of researchers, researchers and research bodies from countries prohibiting research on human embryos may participate in projects funded by the European Union, and carry out their scientific research where this is allowed.

In compliance with the European principles (see para. 3 above), Article 19, para. 3 of Regulation (EU) No 1291/2013 does not allow research in the following cases: (a) research activity aiming at human cloning for reproductive purposes[14]; (b) research activity intended to modify the genetic heritage of human beings which

[14] See also the Additional Protocol to the Convention of Oviedo, on the Prohibition of Cloning Human Beings, of 1998.

could make such changes heritable; and (c) research activities intended to create human embryos solely for the purpose of research or for the purpose of stem cell procurement, including by means of somatic cell nuclear transfer.

The Commission is committed to verifying compliance with the principles and the rules protecting human embryos in research, both in the evaluation of proposals and in ethics checks during the lifetime of a research project.[15]

References

Andorno, R. (2009). Human dignity and human rights as a common ground for a global bioethics. *Journal of Medicine and Philosophy, 34*, 223–240.

Andorno, R. (2013). *Principles of international biolaw. Seeking common ground at the intersection of bioethics and human rights*. Brussels: Bruylant.

Baertschi, B. (2008). The question of the embryo's moral status. *Bioethica Forum, 1*(2), 76–80.

Cippitani, R. (2017). The 'curious case' of Italian Law no. 40 of 2004: How the dialogue between judges is modifying the legislation on medically-assisted reproduction. *Rights and Science*, 23–42.

Devolder, K., & Jhon, H. (2007). The ambiguity of the embryo: Ethical inconsistency in the human embryonic stem cell debate. *Metaphilosophy, 38*(2–3), 153–169.

Jones, J. (2012). Human dignity in the EU Charter of Fundamental Rights and its interpretation before the European Court of Justice. *Liverpool Law Review, 33*(3), 281–300.

Mathieu, B. (1999). La Recherche sur l'Embryon au Regard des Droits Fondamentaux Constitutionnels. *Recueil Dalloz, 41*, 451–456.

Morgese, G. (2012). La recente giurisprudenza della Corte di giustizia dell'Unione Europea sulla protezione giuridica delle invenzioni biotecnologiche: le pronunzie Monsanto technology e Brüstle. *Rivista di Diritto Agrario, 1*, 3–32.

Palazzo, A. (2013). *La filiazione*. Milan: Giuffrè.

Solter, D., Beyleveld, D., Friele, M. B., Holówka, J., Lilie, H., Lovell-Badge, R., et al. (2003). *Embryo research in pluralistic Europe*. Berlin, Heidelberg: Springer-Verlag.

[15] See the Declarations of the Commission (Framework Programme), 2013/C 373/02.

Human Resource in Science and Technology

Roberto Cippitani

1 Definition of HRST

The phrase 'Human Resources in Science and Technology' (HRST) has been coined in the 'Canberra Manual'[1] of the Organisation for Economic Cooperation and Development (OECD) in order to identify and to measure for statistical purposes the special skilled labour force required by the rapid change and new challenges that are emerging in science and technology (see para. 1.1).

According to the Manual, HRST may refer to 'human resources actually or potentially devoted to the systematic generation, advancement, diffusion and application of scientific and technological knowledge' (para. 1.3).

This definition includes researchers, that is to say, 'professionals engaged in the conception or creation of new knowledge, products, processes, methods and systems and also in the management of the projects concerned'.[2]

According to EU sources, the definition of 'researcher' is very broad, and covers 'professional activities related equally to "basic research", "strategic research", "applied research", experimental development and "transfer of knowledge" including innovation and advisory capacities, depending upon whether the discovery or acquisition of knowledge is aimed at a particular application (either in industry or for social purposes) or not'.[3]

[1] OECD, 'The measurement of scientific and technological activities. Manual on the measurement of human resources devoted to S&T: "Canberra Manual"', Paris, 1995.

[2] OECD, 'Guidelines for Collecting and Reporting Data on Research and Experimental Development: Frascati Manual', 2015, para. 5.35.

[3] European Commission, 'Researchers in the ERA: One profession, multiple careers', COM (2003) 436 of 18 July 2003, para. 2.

R. Cippitani (✉)
Department of Medicine, Università degli Studi di Perugia, Perugia, Italy
e-mail: roberto.cippitani@unipg.it

A. Bartolini et al. (eds.), *Dictionary of Statuses within EU Law*,
https://doi.org/10.1007/978-3-030-00554-2_38

Therefore, it is not only theoretical or academic research activities that are taken into consideration, but also 'any activity directly or indirectly related to R&D including the management of knowledge and intellectual property rights, the exploitation of research results or scientific journalism as an integral part of a career in R&D'.

On the one hand, HRST is a set of professionals that does not just include researchers. The identification of this category is not easy: 'Two main systems can be used to identify HRST: by occupation (people employed in Science and Technology activities – hereinafter referred to as 'R&S'- at the appropriate level), and by qualification (people with the formal education which fits them to be so employed).'

On the other hand, Eurostat considers to be classed as HRST those persons who fulfil one or the other of the following conditions: (a) having successfully completed education at the third level; or (b) not being formally qualified as above, but being employed in an S&T occupation where these qualifications are normally required.[4]

The statistical agency of the EU therefore includes within the class of HRST, under point (b) above, Groups 2 (Professionals) and 3 (Technicians and Associate Professionals) of the ISCO-08 classification, which deals with S&T.

In particular, professionals 'increase the existing stock of knowledge; apply scientific or artistic concepts and theories; teach about the foregoing in a systematic manner; or engage in any combination of these activities'.

The tasks of such professionals usually include: conducting analysis and research and developing concepts, theories and operational methods; advising on or applying existing knowledge related to physical sciences, mathematics, engineering and technology, life sciences, medical and health services, social sciences and humanities; teaching the theory and practice of one or more disciplines at different educational levels; teaching and educating persons with learning difficulties or special needs; providing various business, legal and social services; creating and performing works of art; providing spiritual guidance; and preparing scientific papers and reports. The supervision of other workers may be included among these tasks.

In particular, among Group 2, one can find the following professionals: science and engineering professionals (physical and earth science professionals; mathematicians, actuaries and statisticians; life science professionals; engineering professionals; electrotechnology engineers; architects, planners, surveyors and designers); health professionals; teaching professionals (university and higher education teachers; vocational education teachers; secondary education teachers; primary school and early childhood teachers; other teaching professionals); business and administration professionals; information and communications technology professionals; and legal, social and cultural professionals.

[4] See: Glossary: Human resources in science and technology (HRST), available at: http://ec.europa.eu/eurostat/statistics-explained/index.php/Thematic_glossaries.

2 Intra-European Mobility of HRST

Researchers and, in general, HRST represent an important share of employees within Europe (totalling 2.46 million, and representing the 1.11% of all people in employment, according to Eurostat), which is one of the largest shares across the world (for example, China has 1.74 million researchers, who represent 0.23% of all people in employment; however, in the USA and in Japan, even if the number of researchers is lower, the share of all people in employment is near to 1.5%).

In the last 20 years, the phenomenon of the mobility of researchers and other HRST has dramatically increased because of the EU integration process and specific actions put in place by the EU, such as the Framework Programmes and, in particular, the Marie Skłodowska Curie actions, which are specifically focused on the mobility of researchers.

More than for other jobs, the transnational circulation of researchers and HRST is necessary for the growth of the economy and society, as well as for the development of careers (see the Recommendation on the European Charter for Researchers and on a Code of Conduct for the Recruitment of Researchers: Commission, 2005).

According to the relevant EU sources (Inzelt, A.), the total of non-national HRST who are citizens of an EU27 country increased from 229,000 in 2000 to 376,000 in 2006, implying an annual growth rate of 8.6%. Their share in HRST has increased overall from 2.2% in 2000 to 2.9% in 2006.

The same trend shows that the increase in mobility is higher for extra-EU HRST than for intra-EU HRST: the total extra-EU HRST increased from 524,000 to 854,000 (an increase of 8.5% per annum), proving the attractiveness of the European research system.

The trans-European mobility of HRST is several times (at least three times) the mobility of the whole population (EU15 < 1%; EU27 < 0.5%; source: OECD, Economic Review—European Union, 2012).

3 Freedom of Knowledge

EU sources recognise that researchers and HRST have a particular position, introducing a specific understanding of the EU freedoms.

Free movement of persons within the EU (Article 26, para. 2, Treaty on Functioning of the European Union, hereinafter referred to as 'TFEU') has been the major success of the integration process.

In the first stage, a community market was established, and this then became a legal system not only regulating relationships between states but also recognising rights of natural persons and legal entities (ECJ, *Van Gend en Loos* v *Administratie der Belastingen*).

Under the pressure of the actual circulation of European people, the freedoms granted by the internal market have begun to regulate several non-economic aspects of people's lives, such as education and training, the recognition of diplomas, social and healthcare schemes, pension rules, etc.

Furthermore, the freedom of movement has led to the protection of human rights (see the *Stauder* judgment of the ECJ of 1969, and, today, the EU Charter of Fundamental Rights and Article 6 of Treaty on European Union, hereinafter referred to as 'TEU').

The 'freedoms' recognised by the EU Treaties have led to the development of social and political rights and to the national legal systems becoming more open.

As a result of the integrated system (at a European and a national level) of judicial protection, EU citizens have become the principal guardians of EU law (Weiler 2003).

The set of rights (Álvarez Ledesma and Cippitani 2013) that was laid down during the integration process has represented the basis for the introduction, by the Treaty of Maastricht, of the notion of 'citizenship of the European Union' (see Article 9 TEU and Article 17 Charter of EU).

This concept deeply changes the old national identity that was built, in just a couple of centuries, on 'fictitious ethnicities' (Balibar and Wallerstein 2007; Thiesse 1999).

The new citizenship is based on mobility, diversity, complexity and openness. A new identity for European citizens, among whom Erasmus students are the paradigm (Rifkin 2005), is emerging from the opportunities and problems that arose from free circulation (Balibar 2001).

Recently, a new form of freedom of circulation, linked to science and technology, has been identified.

Among other objectives, the EU Treaties aim to establish the 'ERA', where 'knowledge' derives from the cross fertilisation of three activities[5]: research (the production of knowledge), education (the main instrument for sharing knowledge), and innovation (which turns research and education into development). The relationship between these activities is called the 'knowledge triangle'.[6]

Within the ERA, researchers, scientific knowledge and technology (Article 179, para. 1, TFEU), and students and teachers (Article 165, para. 2, TFEU; see Cippitani and Gatt 2009) can circulate freely.

Therefore, EU legal sources identified 'freedom of knowledge' as the 'fifth freedom'.[7] This particular application of the EU freedoms is a crucial instrument for both economic and social development.[8]

---

[5] European Commission, Communication to the Spring European Council, 'Working together for growth and jobs – A new start for the Lisbon Strategy', COM(2005) 24 final, 2 February 2005, para. 3.3.

[6] European Commission, 'Building the ERA of knowledge for growth', COM(2005) 118 final, 6 April 2005.

[7] European Commission, Communication, 'Better careers and more mobility: A European partnership for researchers', COM(2008) 317 final.

[8] European Commission, Communication to the Spring European Council, 'Working together for growth and jobs', n. 5.

4 The Fifth Freedom As a New Set of Supranational Rights and Obligations

Legal texts show that the EU legal system at this time of a knowledge-based society is based on the main result of European integration: the internal market.

Indeed, this internal market is not an exclusively economic concept.

However, the idea of knowledge can move the EU legal system forwards.

There are several aspects of integration based on knowledge that cannot be reduced to the idea of an internal market: research, education and innovation cannot always be conceived as the production of goods and services, and so the EU legal sources take into consideration aspects of knowledge that cannot be related to economic interests (e.g. ethical issues).

EU rules do not just create a market of new products with particular characteristics (indeed, the products can be used at the same time by many users; can be translated into symbols; can be infinitely reproduced; and so on).

Within the legal system of a knowledge-based society, there are not only products that are the objects of patrimonial rights.

The case of the concept of 'information' seems to be clear enough. EU law considers information to be either a right of the parties to economic relationships (in relation to consumers, workers, shareholders, etc.), or a fundamental right of persons (see Article 11 EU Charter). In addition, the power to gather information (personal, genetic or economic) may also violate fundamental rights (e.g. the rules concerning privacy).

Furthermore, the freedom of researchers and other HRST is not only a right, but a necessity. Europe as a knowledge-based society will not be built if researchers, students, teachers and entrepreneurs coming from different Member States do not actually collaborate (Article 165, para. 2, and Article 180(d), TFEU).

This need for the real exchange of persons involved in research and educational activities was born only when the Treaties took into consideration the movement of workers and enterprises.

The Court of Justice interpreted those freedoms as being granted also to students[9] and teachers,[10] and considered a reciprocity rule for the recognition of diplomas to be illegal.[11] Those judgments provided the legal basis for the first edition of the Erasmus programme.[12]

[9] Moreover see the following judgments: ECJ 13 Feb. 1985, Case 293/83, *Gravier* v *Ville de Liège*, [1985] ECR p. 593; ECJ 2 Feb. 1988, Case 24/86, *Blaizot* v *Université de Liège and others*, [1988] ECR p. 379.

[10] ECJ 3 Jul. 1986, Case 66/85, *Lawrie-Blum*, [1986] ECR p. 2121, para. 19; ECJ 26 Feb. 1992, Case C-3/90, *Bernini*, [1992] ECR p. I-1071; ECJ 17 Mar. 2005, Case C-109/04, *Kranemann*, [2005] ECR p. I-2421, paras. 15 and 16.

[11] ECJ 25 Jul. 1991, Case C-58/90, *Commission* v *Italy*, [1991] ECR p. I-4193.

[12] Decision of the Council of 15 June 1987, for the period 1990–1994.

Therefore, as stated above, it is crucial today to make the fifth freedom effective by deleting the residual bureaucratic and administrative obstacles (Springtime European Council of 2002, Presidency Conclusion para. 33).

Indeed, many documents of the Commission request the Member States to eliminate rules and practices which *de facto* limit the movement of researchers (such as closed systems of recruitment; lack of recognition of mobility in careers in recruitment process; model contracts, taxes and social charges which are often not appropriate for persons who are moving about).[13]

EU case law considers to be illegal all discrimination against researchers and lecturers coming from other Member States.[14]

Research, education and training, once an expression only of 'national identity', now have to be considered in a European dimension. 'National interests' cannot be a reason to derogate from the freedoms granted by the EU Treaties.[15]

Furthermore, EU programmes support legal entities that adopt regulations, contracts and other instruments in order to improve the circulation of persons involved in research and educational activities.[16]

Steps are also needed to make EU research and educational systems attractive abroad. In order to do so, the institutions have adopted legal texts such as the Directive on a specific procedure for admitting third-country nationals for the purposes of scientific research (Directive 2005/71/EC of Council of the 12 October 2005). Domestic laws on immigration should take these steps into consideration.

5 Contents of the Freedom of Knowledge

In addition to freedom of circulation, EU sources identify several rights concerning people involved in activities related to knowledge (its production, sharing and transfer).

[13]European Commission, 'Communication, Better careers and more mobility', n. 7; European Commission, 'Reviewing Community innovation policy in a changing world', COM(2009) 442 final, 2 September 2009.

[14]e.g.: ECJ 17 Jul. 2008, Case C-94/07, *Raccanelli*, [2008] ECR p. I-5939, relating to the social scheme applicable to PhD students; ECJ, 30 Nov. 2000, Case C-195/98, *Österreichischer Gewerkschaftsbund*, [2000] ECR p. I-10497; ECJ, 26 Jun. 2001, Case C-212/99, *Commission* v *Italy*, [2001] ECR p. I-4923; ECJ, 2 Aug. 1993, Cases C-259/91, C-331/91 and C-332/91, *Pilar Allué and Carmel Mary Coonan and others* v *Universita degli Studi di Venezia and Universita degli Studi di Parma*, [1993] ECR p. I-04309.

[15]e.g.: ECJ 2 Jul. 1996, Case C-473/93, *Commission* v *Luxemburg*, [1996] ECR p. I-03207; ECJ 2 Jul. 1996, Case C-290/94, *Commission* v *Greece*, [1996] ECR p. I-3285). For instance, those interests cannot be invoked to reserve a job in a public research body for citizens of a particular Member State (see ECJ 16 Jun. 1987, Case 225/85, *Commission* v *Italy*, [1987] ECR p. 2625).

[16]European Commission, Communication of the Commission to the Spring European Council, 'Working together for growth and jobs', n. 5.

In many cases such rights are set out in relation to 'researchers'. However, as mentioned above, because of the broad definition of researcher, as well as the favourable approach of EU law towards all HRST, it is possible to extend the rights of the researchers to all professionals dealing with research, training and education, and innovation.

Therefore, in accordance with the European Charter of Researchers,[17] HRTS have specific rights, such as: (a) recognition of their professional qualifications at every stage of their career (in particular at the beginning); (b) a right not to be discriminated against in any way on the basis of their gender, age, ethnic, national or social origin, religion or belief, sexual orientation, language, disability, political opinion, or social or economic condition; (c) a favourable work environment; (d) stability and permanence of employment; (e) the enjoyment of fair and attractive conditions and salaries; (f) gender balance; (g) career development; (h) a recognition of the value of mobility to them (geographical, intersectoral, inter- and transdisciplinary and virtual); (i) access to research training and continuous development; (j) access to careers advice; (k) access to their intellectual property rights; (l) teaching; (m) systems for assessing their professional performance; (n) appropriate procedures to make complaints/appeals; (o) participation in decision-making bodies; and (p) transparent and adequate recruitment processes.[18]

6 Limitations of Academic Freedom and Research

On the other hand, since the freedom qualifies as a 'right', it is also necessary to consider the limits to the freedom.

Academic freedom, and in particular the freedom of research, in the same way and even more than other rights arising from modern constitutions, is understood to play a function within society (Crisafulli 1956, p. 70; Pototschnig 1971).

Since it is an individual right, academic freedom cannot be considered as absolute and, therefore, it is subject to legislative limitations (see the Italian *Corte costituzionale*, judgment 4 June 1958, n. 36).

Therefore, researchers and HRST in general have several obligations arising from their function within society. The European Charter of Researchers particularly points out the following:

(a) professional responsibility, in particular avoiding professional misconduct, plagiarism, and breach of intellectual property rights; (b) familiarity with the strategic goals governing their research environment and funding mechanisms; (c) knowledge of the applicable law and regulations; (d) accountability for their activities, in particular with respect to the use of taxpayers' money; (e) observation of good prac-

[17] The two documents are annexes to the Recommendation 2005/251/CE of 11 March 2005. See https://euraxess.ec.europa.eu/jobs/charter/european-charter.

[18] Code of Conduct for the Recruitment of Researchers enclosed to Recommendation 2005/251/CE of 11 March 2005.

tice in research; (f) dissemination of the results of research; (g) public engagement in order to improve the public's understanding of science; and (h) continuing professional development, through the regular updating of skills and competencies.

Above all, among the duties of the researchers and HRST, one can find respect for 'ethical principles', that is to say, legal provisions and other kinds of rules (e.g. those established by case law, codes of practice, or the opinions of ethics committees) that have the scope to protect fundamental interests that may be affected by techno-science, such as human dignity and human rights, the environment, the well-being of animals, and security (see also the entry 'Ethics Advisor on Research Projects' by Cippitani in this Dictionary).

References

Álvarez Ledesma, M. I., & Cippitani, R. (Eds.). (2013). *Diccionario analítico de Derechos humanos e integración jurídica*. Rome: ISEG.

Balibar, E. (2001). *Nous, citoyens d'Europe? Les frontières, l'état, le people*. Paris: la Découverte.

Balibar, E., & Wallerstein, I. (2007). *Race nation classe. Les identités ambigües*. Paris: la Découverte.

Cippitani, R., & Gatt, S. (2009). Legal developments and problems of the Bologna process within the European higher education area and European integration. *Higher Education in Europe, 34*, 385–397.

Crisafulli, V. (1956). La scuola nella Costituzione. *Rivista trimestrale diritto pubblico*, 54 ff.

Inzelt, A. *Analysis of researchers' mobility in the context of the European Research Area*. Retrieved from https://ec.europa.eu/research/evaluations/pdf/archive/fp7-evidence-base/experts_analysis/a.%20inzelt_-_researchers%27_mobility.pdf

Pototschnig, U. (1971). Insegnamento (libertà di). In *Enciclopedia del diritto* (Vol. XXI). Milan: Giuffrè.

Rifkin, J. (2005). *The European dream. How the Europe's vision of the future is quietly eclipsing the American dream*. New York: Tarcher.

Thiesse, A. M. (1999). *La Création des identité nationales. Europe XVIII-XX siècle*. Paris: Seuil.

Weiler, J. H. H. (2003). *La costituzione dell'Europa*. Bologna: Il Mulino.

Immigrant and Emigrant

Mario Savino

1 Emigrant

For over 40 years, reference to the concept of "emigration" has surfaced in acts of Community law, which were enacted to support the free circulation of workers from one Member State to another,[1] or to selectively address root causes of emigration from less-developed European areas.[2] More recently, a broader understanding of the concept of "emigration" (from third countries) has emerged in the context of European Union ("EU" or "Union") external actions of assistance. For instance, a cooperation programme of financial and technical aid was established in 2004, with the aim of facilitating "the contribution of migrants to the social and economic development of communities in their country of origin" through remittances and microcredit programmes.[3]

It is evident that these programmes are intended to affect migration control by the clause that makes them "particularly, but not exclusively, intended for those third countries actively engaged in preparing or implementing a readmission agreement (…) with the European Community."[4] The same logic has affected the

[1] First Council Directive for the implementation of Article ("Art.") 67 of the Treaty of 1 July 1960 and Second Council Directive 63/21/EEC of 18 December 1962. See also Art. 1 of Council Decision 74/327/EEC of 27 June 1974 on action by the European Social Fund for migrant workers.

[2] See Council Regulation (EEC) No 1820/80 of 24 June 1980 for the stimulation of agricultural development in the less-favoured areas of the west of Ireland.

[3] Art. 2(2)(c) of Regulation (EC) No 491/2004 of 10 March 2004 establishing a programme for financial and technical assistance to third countries in the areas of migration and asylum (AENEAS).

[4] Art. 1(2) of Regulation (EC) No 491/2004.

M. Savino (✉)
Department DISTU University of Tuscia, Viterbo, Italy
e-mail: mario.savino@unitus.it

A. Bartolini et al. (eds.), *Dictionary of Statuses within EU Law*,
https://doi.org/10.1007/978-3-030-00554-2_39

development of Euro-Mediterranean relations during the last 15 years. Measures enacted to address root causes of emigration from African countries (typically, actions oriented toward "improving living conditions, creating jobs, and income generating activities and developing training in areas from which emigrants come")[5] have been adopted to pursue the overarching European objective to curb immigration.

Apart from this generic reference to emigration, the legal notion of "emigrant" appears in EU law only for statistical purposes. According to Regulation (EC) No 862/2007—establishing common rules for the collection and compilation of Community statistics on immigration to and emigration from Member States—"emigrant" means "a person undertaking an emigration," which, in turn, is "the action by which a person, having previously been usually resident in the territory of a Member State, ceases to have his or her usual residence in that Member State for a period that is, or is expected to be, of at least 12 months."[6] As evidenced by this regulation's limited scope, EU law attaches no set of rights and duties to the emigrant condition. The above definition has merely a descriptive value.

2 Immigrant: A Negative and Fragmented Status

Immigration is a field that touches upon sensitive prerogatives of sovereign States, which retain an exclusive power to admit and exclude foreign nationals from their territory (Perruchoud 2012). The status of European citizenship has severely limited that power with regard to nationals of other Member States. "[A]n area of freedom, security and justice without internal frontiers, in which the free movement of persons is ensured," (TEU Art. 3) is the main privilege that the EU offers its citizens (Barnard 2017; Condinanzi et al. 2008).

Immigration from third countries is based on a different legal paradigm. In the areas of freedom, security, and justice, the Union holds a shared competence (TFEU Art. 4). Accordingly, the EU can develop, in addition to a common policy on asylum (TFEU Art. 78), "a common immigration policy aimed at ensuring, at all stages, the efficient management of migration flows, fair treatment of third-country nationals residing legally in Member States, and the prevention of, and enhanced measures to combat, illegal immigration and trafficking in human beings" (TFEU Art. 79(1)). In the exercise of this competence, however, the Union can "not affect the right of Member States to determine volumes of admission of third-country nationals coming from third countries to their territory in order to seek work, whether employed or self-employed" (TFEU Art. 79(4)).

[5] Art. 65(a) of Council Decision 2004/635/EC of 21 April 2004.

[6] Arts. 2(1)(c) and (g) of Regulation (EC) No 862/2007 of 11 July 2007 on Community statistics on migration and international protection.

Just like international law, EU law provides no general regime on the legal treatment of the immigrant as such. It establishes only minimum harmonization requirements for the entry and the residence of specific categories of migrants, such as family members of immigrants,[7] long-term residents,[8] trafficked persons,[9] non-European students and researchers,[10] seasonal,[11] and highly-qualified workers.[12] Moreover, migrants fleeing conflict and persecution may obtain "special" asylum status, and qualify as beneficiaries of international protection or subsidiary protection (Hailbronner and Thym 2016; Peers 2016, 2017).[13]

Therefore, under UE law, there is no unitary "immigrant" status as such. The set of rights held by each category is determined by the entry and residence status of third-country nationals in the host Member State. Rather than a legal status, the legal concept of the immigrant is a complex notion; it is a patchwork composed of many national and supranational rules, which define the legal treatment of each migrant category (Weissbrodt 2008). While immigrant rights vary dramatically, there is one unifying element across the Union: the immigrant is *not* a European citizen. Accordingly, the term "immigrant" includes any third-country national who is present, legally or illegally, in the territory of a Member State.

The same approach helps to determine the rights that European citizens enjoy, to the exclusion of immigrants. In addition to the right to move and reside freely within EU territory, European citizens enjoy political rights (the right to vote and to stand as candidates in elections to the European Parliament and in municipal elections in the Member State of residence) and other ancillary rights, including the right to diplomatic protection (TFEU Art. 20). The following paragraphs focus on the legal divide between the European citizens and third-country nationals with regard to their rights of entry and residence and the limitations imposed on them.

3 The National Foundation of Immigrants' Rights of Entry and Residence

Pursuant to Article 45 of the Charter of Fundamental Rights of the European Union ("EU Charter"), European citizens hold "the right to move and reside freely within the territory of the Member States," while nationals of third countries may or may not be granted the same right. In principle, third-country nationals enjoy the right to freely move and reside only within the territory of the Member State in which they

[7] Council Directive 2003/86/EC of 22 September 2003.

[8] Council Directive 2003/109/EC of 25 November 2003.

[9] Council Directive 2004/81/EC of 29 April 2004.

[10] Directive (EU) 2016/801 of 11 May 2016.

[11] Directive 2014/36/EU of 26 February 2014.

[12] Council Directive 2009/50/EC of 25 May 2009 (Blue Card Directive).

[13] Directive 2011/95/EU of 13 December 2011.

are legally present. They can enter and stay in the territory of a Member State, provided that they fulfil all the conditions established by domestic legislation on immigration. Unless a person belongs to a protected category (e.g. asylum seeker), EU Member States retain the power to select, admit, or exclude a non-citizen from their territory.

The European Court of Justice's case law clarifies some implications of this general provision. Long before the introduction of European citizenship in 1992, the right of free movement was granted to workers and their family members by primary and secondary sources of EC law.[14] In the 1970s, the Court of Justice inferred from those provisions that "the right of nationals of a Member State to enter the territory of another Member State and reside there for the purposes intended by the treaty (…) is a right conferred directly by the Treaty" and is, thus, "acquired independently of the issue of a residence permit by the competent authority of a Member State."[15] Such permits, thus, have a merely *declarative* nature. Accordingly, Member States have an obligation to issue the required permit to any entitled EU citizen who can prove his or her right to stay. Moreover, EU law details the conditions governing the right of European citizens and their families to enter and reside within the territory of Member States.[16] The law offers broad protections to EU citizens and "the mere failure (…) to complete the legal formalities concerning access, movement and residence of aliens does not justify a decision ordering expulsion."[17]

Therefore, the fundamental nature of EU citizens' freedom of circulation within the Union significantly restricts Member States' power. Member States, in fact, are prohibited from "creating" a right of entry and residence; establishing the conditions for the enjoyment of the same right, as an EU directive leaves them almost no discretion; and expelling a European citizen in the case of his or her irregular presence.

For third-country immigrants the paradigm is reversed, as State interests have priority over individual freedoms. Even when the State has the power to admit some categories of immigrants (e.g. refugees, family members) it is constrained by international or EU law. Obtaining the required visa or domestic permit is not a mere legal formality, but is necessary to prevent expulsion. Moreover, immigrants' basic rights are established at the domestic level; EU law intervenes only under certain circumstances, such as establishing the rights of long-term residents and family members of EU citizens.

A further difference concerns the movement of legal immigrants from the Member State that admitted them to a second State (secondary movement). Union citizens can move freely within the EU, and their right to remain in another Member State for more than 3 months depends on whether they meet basic requirements,

[14] Art. 48 EEC Treaty and Council Directives 64/220/EEC, 68/360/CEE and 1973/148/CEE.

[15] Court of Justice, *Royer*, Case 48-75, 8 April 1976, §§ 32-33.

[16] Directive 2004/38/EC of 29 April 2004.

[17] Court of Justice, *Royer*, § 38.

such as the availability of sufficient resources.[18] Third-country nationals, meanwhile, are severely restricted in their movement due to their State-based status. If they want to move to a second Member State for longer than three months, they must go through the normal immigration procedures. As a rule, they may apply for a residence permit in a second Member State only after they have acquired long-term residence status in the first Member State. This normally occurs after they have remained within the first Member State for at least five years, provided that other conditions are met,[19] and unless more favorable conditions apply.[20]

Whereas the right of European citizens to enter and stay in the territory of a Member State has its direct and autonomous foundation in EU law, immigrants' rights of entry and residence are based, and hence depend, on national law and the decision of the authorities of the receiving Member State. Member States are obliged to recognise a pre-existing fundamental right afforded to EU citizens, without significant margins of discretion left to them. With regard to immigrants, Member States retain discretion with regard to both the criteria of admission and their enforcement (Savino 2012).

4 The Restrictions on Immigrants' Rights of Entry and Residence

The rights of European citizens and third-country nationals are further differentiated by the respective freedom of, or limitations on, movement, and the public interest justifying these differences. European citizens' freedom of movement can be constrained only under limited circumstances, such as public policy, public security, or public health. These grounds are listed in the Treaties and specified in secondary EU law.[21] As the Court of Justice has clarified, "This restriction must be regarded *not as a condition precedent to the acquisition of the right* of entry and residence *but as providing the possibility*, in individual cases where there is sufficient justification, *of imposing restrictions on the exercise* of a right derived directly from the Treaty."[22]

In line with this premise, limitations on freedom of movement in the EC/EU in the name of "public order" have been restrictively interpreted by the Court of Justice (Néraudau-d'Unieville 2006). Accordingly, a Member State may limit the free movement of a Union citizen in the name of public policy or public security only if the following three conditions are satisfied. First, public order cannot be understood

[18] Art. 7 of Directive 2004/38/EC.

[19] Arts. 14–15 of Directive 2003/109/EC.

[20] Highly skilled workers who have obtained a Blue Card in a first Member State may be allowed to move to a second Member State after eighteen months (Art. 18 of Directive 2009/50/EC).

[21] Arts. 45(2), 52 and 202 TFEU and Article 1 of Directive 2004/38/EC.

[22] Court of Justice, *Regina v Stanislaus Pieck*, Case 157/79, 3 July 1980, § 8 (emphasis added).

as an "ideal" concept, which refers to the preservation of (national) identity and values. Rather, it must be based "exclusively on the personal conduct of the individual concerned," which is (restrictively) defined in "material" terms, as "a genuine, present and sufficiently serious threat affecting one of the fundamental interests of society."[23] Second, measures taken on public order grounds must "comply with the principle of proportionality," which rules out any automatic expulsion based previous criminal convictions, as well as any measure based on "considerations of general prevention."[24] Third, a threat to public order requires more than a mere "perturbation of the social order inherent in any infringement of the law,"[25] and hence it cannot be understood as a "normative" concept. It follows that when a European citizen violates a legal provision (for instance, the conditions for legal entry) in the host Member State, he or she can be subject to a proportionate sanction, but not to expulsion, as European citizens can only be returned to their home country on the grounds of public policy and public security, as interpreted by the Court of Justice.[26]

In the field of immigration, by contrast, the default rule is that the individual right *depends* on its compatibility with the public interest priorities set by the Member State in question. The right of immigrants to enter and remain in the territory of a Member State follows the assessment of the relevant public interests. Those interests do not constitute a limit placed on a preexisting right, but rather a condition for obtaining that right (Savino 2012).

The protections against interference from public authority and the freedom of movement enjoyed by European citizens are not afforded to third-country nationals. To begin with, EU law does not establish public interest justifications for third-country nationals to enter and stay within Member States. Domestic legislatures enjoy broad discretion in this respect, and may restrict immigrants' rights on several grounds, from public order to public health, and from protection of the internal economy and job market to international relations.

Moreover, the notion of public order or public policy is elaborated at domestic level. Unless strict constitutional scrutiny is enforced, "public order" may well assume an "ideal" meaning and, thus, expand the public interest limit to the detriment of aliens' freedoms, despite some recent attempts of the Court of Justice to export this (restrictive) "material" definition to the realm of immigration.[27]

Also, the relevance of the proportionality principle is uncertain and elusive. Although proportionality is a general principle of European and national administrative law, it is randomly applied to the rights in question, which do not have constitutional backing. This is why, for instance, some domestic constitutional courts defer to legislative provisions establishing mandatory expulsion of third-country nationals convicted of a crime, leaving no discretion for the administrative authority (Savino 2016).

---

[23] Art. 27(2) of Directive 2004/38/EC.

[24] Art. 27(2) of Directive 2004/38/EC.

[25] Court of Justice, Case 30/77, *Bouchereau*, 27 October 1977, § 35.

[26] Arts. 27–33 of Directive 2004/38/EC.

[27] Court of Justice, *Z. Zh.*, Case C-554/13, 11 June 2015.

Finally, immigrants' rights of entry and residence are prone to the overarching public interest related to border control (Dubin 2012). This public interest is both national, as it entails the observance of immigration rules established by the Member State, and supranational: when State borders correspond to the external borders of the Union, it also involves the enforcement of the Schengen border code.[28] EU law, thus, strengthens it.

It follows that, while European citizens cannot be expelled for illegally entering or staying in another Member State, and cannot be subjected to administrative detention for the purpose of removal, the opposite is true with regard to third-country nationals. The lack of prescribed authorization makes the presence of immigrants in the territory of a Member States illegal and thus exposes them to expulsion, since "Member States shall issue a return decision to any third-country national staying illegally on their territory."[29] Moreover, when the expelled immigrant does not depart voluntarily, repatriation to the country of origin requires the adoption of coercive means. Under such circumstances, Member States may keep the third-country national in detention for up to 18 months in order to prepare their return and to carry out the removal process.[30]

The fragmented human condition of persons migrating in the Union is, thus, crossed by a major dividing line, which marks a crucial distinction between regular immigrants and irregular ones. In principle, all the fundamental rights, recognized as such in the EU Charter, can be enjoyed by any person in the European territory and, hence, also by immigrants. Nonetheless, since those rights can be constrained in the name of various public interests, including the control of national and Union borders, the illegality of their presence significantly affects the enjoyment of fundamental rights of the persons who immigrate irregularly in the Union.

References

Barnard, C. (2017). Free movement of natural persons and citizenship. In C. Barnard & S. Peers (Eds.), *European Union law (Ch. 13)*. Oxford: Oxford University Press.

Condinanzi, M., Lang, A., & Nascimbene, B. (2008). *Citizenship of the Union and free movement of persons*. Leiden: Martinus Nijhoff Publishers.

Dubin, L. (Ed.). (2012). *La légalité de la lutte contre l'immigration irrégulière par l'Union européenne*. Bruxelles: Bruylant.

Hailbronner, K., & Thym, D. (2016). *EU immigration and asylum law: A commentary*. Oxford: Hart.

Néraudau-d'Unieville, E. (2006). *Ordre public et droits des étrangers en Europe*. Brussels: Bruylant.

Peers, S. (2016). *EU justice and home affairs law. Vol. I: EU immigration and asylum law*. Oxford: Oxford University Press.

[28] Articles 5–14 of Regulation (EU) 2016/399 (Schengen Borders Code).

[29] Art. 6(1) of Directive 2008/115/EC of 16 December 2008 (Return Directive).

[30] Art. 15 of Directive 2008/115/EC.

Peers, S. (2017). Immigration and asylum. In C. Barnard & S. Peers (Eds.), *European Union law (Ch. 26)*. Oxford: Oxford University Press.

Perruchoud, R. (2012). State sovereignty and freedom of movement. In B. Opeskin, R. Perruchoud, & J. Redpath-Cross (Eds.), *Foundations of international migration law (Ch. 5)*. Cambridge: Cambridge University Press.

Savino, M. (2012). *Le libertà degli altri. La regolazione amministrativa dei flussi migratori*. Milano: Giuffrè.

Savino, M. (2016). The right to stay as a fundamental freedom? The demise of automatic expulsion in Europe. *Transnational Legal Theory, 7*(1), 70–94.

Weissbrodt, D. (2008). *The human rights of non-citizens*. Oxford: Oxford University Press.

Individual Genetic Status

Hedley Christ

1 Introduction

At Recital 34 Regulation 2016/679, genetic data is given as 'that personal data relating to the inherited or acquired genetic characteristics of a natural person which result from the analysis of a biological sample from the natural person in question, in particular chromosomal, deoxyribonucleic acid (DNA) or ribonucleic acid (RNA) analysis, or from the analysis of another element enabling equivalent information to be obtained'. Prior to this Regulation, the need for the control of genetic data of individuals, had already, an international perspective,[1] reflected in the OECD's 1981 Guidelines on the Protection of Personal Privacy and Transborder Flows of Personal Data.[2] In 1985, the Ministers of the OECD adopted a Declaration on Transborder Data Flows, which promoted access to data and information, transparency, common approaches and to consider their implications.[3] In particular, the OECD in 2004, held a workshop on Human Research Databases (HGRDs)—Issues of Privacy and Security. This workshop concluded that *inter alia*; such databases are valuable tools which have immense possibilities for medicine; however, there is a need to be clear as to whether genetic information should be treated as distinct from other forms of

[1] The nature of research and medical application using these databases cannot be defined by a country's nationals; their application is and must be international. Diseases, for example, are rarely confined by geographical borders. Many international organizations have stated the need for an international approach, we cannot rely therefore on national laws to govern these databases particularly when we consider the conflict between an individual's informational privacy and the disclosure which may be necessary for the public health of nation States.

[2] The intention of these guidelines was to harmonize national privacy legislation and provide a framework for facilitating international flows of data.

[3] Other Guidelines have sought harmonization on security systems and cryptography policies.

H. Christ (✉)
Law Department, Brighton Business School, Brighton, UK
e-mail: H.Christ@brighton.ac.uk

A. Bartolini et al. (eds.), *Dictionary of Statuses within EU Law*,
https://doi.org/10.1007/978-3-030-00554-2_40

personal information. Furthermore, that individuals should enjoy privacy rights over their genetic information, and that there should be trust in the development, management, and governance of these databases. The workshop concluded that the OECD should develop principles of best practice for the governance of health, and thereby genetic databases. However, these guidelines of best practice were never developed.

The reason for the lack of development in the governance of genetic databases lies in its complexity. In part the OECD acknowledges: 'The protection of individuals' genetic information relies on a combination of health-related confidentiality, and/or personal data protection laws. Many countries also provide constitutional protection or human rights legislation which incorporate, even if obliquely, genetic information of the individual. In general, however, no specific law which distinguishes the processing of genetic data from other personal or sensitive information, has yet been provided, particularly within an international framework. Yet genetic data is perceived as being special because it reveals important information about both an individual and his/her family and can have a significant impact on an individual's life, including his or her reproductive choices.[4]

Genetic databases will also play a significant role in public health management. Gostin et al. (1996) notes that the development of public health information has produced a vast reservoir of information on health status giving States a means of surveillance (Gostin et al. 1996). Public health investigation for disease, and now genetic and protein databases enable the public health systems to identify health problems, both for the individual and society, inform the public, intervene, and influence funding decisions. There is, therefore, a potential conflict between an individual's informational privacy[5] (Richards 2006) and the disclosure and access to genetic and protein data for surveillance on public health issues. The antithesis of privacy, therefore, is surveillance, that is, the need to monitor the genetic health status of national, regional, and transnational movement[6] of genetic populations. This type of surveillance may be a constitutive element of a State organization. In fact, all societies formulate privacy as a balance between the individual demand for

[4]Article 14 of the Universal Declaration on Human Genetic Data requires States should endeavour to protect the privacy of individuals and the confidentiality of human genetic data linked to an identifiable person, a family or, when appropriate, a group, in accordance with domestic law consistent with the international law of human rights.

[5]Richards (2006) notes 'Privacy is a particularly troubling term to use in the database context. On the one hand, virtually all scholars agree that privacy is a concept that has eluded definition, on the other hand, privacy has come to be associated with a wide variety of meanings in addition to control over personal data, including residential solitude, rights to self-definition, freedom from government surveillance, and fundamental rights to make autonomous decisions about one's body'.

[6]The Council of Europe Treaty (Treaty 180) Convention for the Protection of Individuals with Regards to the Automatic Processing of Personal Data, Article 12 states, a party shall not for the sole purpose of the protection of privacy, prohibit or subject to special authorization, transborder data flows of personal data to the territory of another party. Article 18 of the Universal Declaration on Human Genetic Data requires 'States should regulate, in accordance with their domestic law and international agreements, the cross-border flows of human genetic data, human proteomic data and biological samples so as to foster international medical and scientific cooperation and ensure fair access to this data.'

informational privacy within organizations, both public and private, and demand for personal information. There can, therefore, seem to be a conflict between what is seen as an erosion of privacy and the need for social safeguards.

2 Governance of Genetic Databases and International Approach

The laws on privacy typically provide procedural rules without tackling the substantive issues concerning the processing of personal data, especially if the data is to be used for surveillance as well as medical research and practice. This conflict between an individual's informational privacy and the disclosure and access to genetic data is further complicated by the introduction of intellectual property and the possibility of a commercial application of these databases. In its final report the OECD's Working Group on Biological Information notes 'The actual holding of biological material already leads to the control of the access to related information and, in practice, also to the control of any possible invention that could derive from those materials. In this perspective the problem of intellectual property of biological information is also connected to this problem of ownership of the media where that information is stored.' Bovenberg (2000) noted 'The database right in a DNA database would almost undoubtedly represent valuable intellectual property especially with the uncertainty that still surrounds DNA sequence patenting. The database right allows its holders to prevent extraction or reutilization of substantial parts of the database (Bovenberg 2000). In fact, the right may pertain in perpetuity given that it can be rolled over following any substantial investment. Such modifications include the routine business of DNA databases: extractions, deletions, and amendments.' It has been suggested that privacy should be seen as a property right in which the commercial exploitation of one's own information is one way of giving individuals choice. Schwartz (1999) proposes a theory of "constitutive privacy" which views privacy as a right to control the use of one's personal data (Schwartz 1999).

It is clear that the governance of genetic databases requires an international approach which can resolve, or at least articulate, the issues of informational privacy, surveillance, both for society and the individual, and intellectual property and why genetic databases, which hold data and information on individuals, are different from other types of personal data and information. This is particularly relevant when rights are given to data subjects to first, see that data and information, and second, make corrections or deletions of their genetic data and information if inaccurate, obsolete or incomplete. How will data subjects be able to access that right on genetic/proteomic data, that is, on DNA and protein structures and sequences and scientific annotations of the sequences without themselves being a molecular biologist? How useful is a fair information principle on data and information which, by its very nature, cannot be known to the majority of individuals who contribute their genetic and protein sequences? Can the privacy paradigm be adapted to the scientific reality of genetic/protein databases? How can governments use genetic/protein databases in their capacity of public health guardians if these databases are useful for public health surveillance and how can data controllers use their intellectual property rights? How will an adapted privacy paradigm include State surveillance and intellectual property rights?

3 Regulation (EU) No 2016/679 and Its Impact Upon the Collecting Genetic Data

It is clear that Regulation 2016/679 will impact upon these organisations which collect genetic data. More so in that, such collected genetic data will almost certainly be processed by other organisations interested in using genetic data in their own research. However, the regulation does not seem to go beyond that of which, the data controller has not already been subject to. The data controller must obtain the consent from the individual, providing the sample for the processing of their genetic data, and for specific purposes. However, Recital 33 states that it is often not possible to fully identify the purpose of personal data for scientific research purposes, at the time of data collection. Data subjects, therefore, should be able to give their consent to certain areas of scientific endeavour.[7]

The regulation, however, does not consider the nature of consent which, needs to be thought of as informed consent, because, it is with informed consent that we may balance the nature of the individual with the health of the population. In General Comment number 14 to the European Convention on Human Rights, it states 'the right to health is closely related to and dependent upon, the realisation of other human rights'. Thus, rights in patient care are not only individual rights but also universal rights. In providing informed consent the genetic donor obtains the right to seek, receive and impart information and ideas concerning health issues. Under the European Convention on Human Rights and Biomedicines,[8] patients' rights are balanced against those of the providers of health care. Individual rights of patients, therefore, are circumscribed by the individual responsibility to contribute information to promote societal good. In the World Health Organisation's Alma-Ata Declaration, Article 4, there is an understanding of the universal access and patient participation in health care and public health decision-making.[9] The European

[7]The nature of children, however, is different and requires the consent of a parent or custodian, Article 4 & 7 regulation 2016/679.

[8]The notion of informed consent is given at Article 5 in that the person shall beforehand be given appropriate information as to the purpose and nature of the intervention, as well as, on its consequences.

[9]This should include: Principles—how the patient would be treated in respect of the information they provided, reasons for the research; Norms—standards of behaviour defined in terms of rights and obligations; Rules—specific prescriptions and proscriptions, what could be done with patients' genetic data, and their sample would be anonymized, how could the DNA be linked to the patient if needed, and Decision-Making Processes—practice for making and implementing collective choice, who would be able to gain access to the data.

Convention on Human Rights and Biomedicine, at Article 17(2) states 'The research has the aim of contributing through significant improvement in the scientific understanding of the individual's condition, disease or disorder to the ultimate attainment of results capable of conferring benefit to the person concerned or to other persons in the same age category or afflicted with the same disease or disorder or having the same condition'.[10] Privacy must be understood in terms of purposes that transcend that of the individual benefit, without denying the importance of individual consent.

4 Conclusions

How then stands the notion of the Genetic Individual? It is clear from the Universal Declaration on Human Genome and Human Rights that the human genome underlies the fundamental unity of all members of the human family, as well as the recognition of their inherent dignity and diversity. In a symbolic sense, it is the heritage of humanity.[11] That everyone has a right to respect for their dignity and for their rights regardless of their genetic characteristics, and that dignity makes it imperative not to reduce individuals to their genetic characteristics and to respect their uniqueness and diversity.[12] That the human genome contains potentialities that are expressed differently according to each individual's natural and social environment, including the individual's state of health, living conditions, nutrition and education[13] which thereby renders them unique. However, it also states that the human genome in its natural state shall not give rise to financial gains[14] a situation which, if improvements in human health are to be achieved, cannot hold true. The genetic status of the individual cannot therefore, be an individual one. The genetic status is universal and belongs to all humanity. Regulation 2016/679 fails to establish this, because in trying to protect the privacy of an individual's genetic data it fails to understand the value of genetic research, or at least its potential. True, the individual, who provides the genetic data, must be protected from discrimination and any use of the data not prescribed by the purposes of its collection and processing. This conflict is

[10] This is derived from the Universal Declaration on the Human Genome and Human Rights at Article 5 'research, treatment or diagnosis affecting an individual's genome shall be undertaken only after rigorous and prior assessment of the potential risks and benefits pertaining thereto and in accordance with any other requirement of national law…Research which does not have an expected direct health benefit may only be undertaken by way of exception, with the utmost restraint, exposing the person only to a minimal risk and minimal burden and if the research is intended to contribute to the health benefit of other persons in the same age category or with the same genetic condition, subject to the conditions prescribed by law, and provided such research is compatible with the protection of the individual's human rights'.

[11] Article 1.

[12] Article 2.

[13] Article 3.

[14] Article 4.

confounded by the introduction of intellectual property, practically from patents and database rights. The issue of intellectual property rights is particularly important because not only does the private sector rely on such rights to recoup costs but also, because many public sector bodies, are now under a directive from their governments to consider at all times the commercial application of their research. The issue of governance becomes of central importance when we consider how individuals can control the data held on them. Without the necessary scientific training, individuals are unable to consider whether the genetic or proteomic data held on them is correct or not. It is crucial therefore that we identify an approach to the governance of these genetic databases that will be able to consider these and other issues, within an international framework. Clearly, therefore, under Regulation 2016/679 there is an individual genetic status; a data subject who has control over the genetic information held and possessed on them, no matter how difficult that may be in practice. But it must not be forgotten that, along with certain rights comes responsibilities.

References

Bovenberg, J. A. (2000). Should companies set-up databases in Europe? *Nature Biotechnology, 18*, 907–909.

Gostin, L. O., Lazzarini, Z., & Neslund, V. S. (1996). The public health information infrastructure: A national review of the law on health information privacy. *JAMA, 275*, 1921–1927.

Richards, N. M. (2006). The information privacy law project. *Georgetown Law Journal, 94*, 1087–1140.

Schwartz, P. (1999). Privacy and democracy in cyberspace. *Vanderbilt Law Review, 52*, 1609–1702.

Internet Entrepreneur

Federica Marabini

1 Introduction

According to a definition available on Wikipedia,[1] an 'internet entrepreneur' is an 'entrepreneur, an owner, founder or manager of an Internet based business undertaking who makes money through risk [or] initiative'.

The main question this paper seeks to analyse, according to the available literature and other relevant sources, as well as national and European Union (EU) instruments is: Does the digital world open up new entrepreneurial opportunities for people from all types of backgrounds? Furthermore, this paper aims to analyse how a business can be developed through new technology and within the internet environment and remain compatible with the entrepreneur regulations; for example, if the internet entrepreneur is submitted to a special or different regulation compared to the 'usual' concept of entrepreneur, or if it is an usual entrepreneur and the 'internet', 'web' or 'digital' environment acts only as distinctive feature.

To reach these purposes, it is necessary to understand who an entrepreneur is, given that the term 'entrepreneur' is one of those terms that is marked by intellectual confusion and not likely to and unique definitions. The meaning of the term 'entrepreneur' has, indeed, different connotations.

[1] https://en.wikipedia.org/wiki/List_of_Internet_entrepreneurs.

F. Marabini (✉)
Department of Law, University of Perugia, Perugia, Italy
e-mail: federica.marabini@unipg.it

A. Bartolini et al. (eds.), *Dictionary of Statuses within EU Law*,
https://doi.org/10.1007/978-3-030-00554-2_41

2 The Term of Entrepreneur: Looking for a Definition

It is very difficult to define the meaning of the term 'entrepreneur' and to identify who is an entrepreneur, based on different languages. According to the relevant content of analysis, this term may acquire different meanings or different senses (Jonsson 2017).

The term entrepreneur, derived from the French term 'entreprendre', which means to take action, to begin, 'to do something' or 'to undertake'. If translated in Italian, the term means 'imprenditore',[2] namely, 'businessman', 'businesswomen', 'business owner' or 'contractor'.

When looking on dictionaries, it is possible to find different definitions for the term entrepreneur, such as: (1) 'a person who sets up a business or businesses, taking on financial risks in the hope of profit' (online Oxford Dictionary, dictionary entry: entrepreneur); (2) 'one who organizes, manages and assumes the risk of a business or enterprise' (on-line Merriam-Webster Dictionary, dictionary entry: entrepreneur); (3) someone who 'exercises initiative by organizing a venture to take benefit of an opportunity and, as the decision maker, decides what, how, and how much of a good or service will be produced' (online Business Dictionary dictionary entry: entrepreneur).

The term entrepreneur is used in the context of business and economic activities only in the eighteenth century by Richard Cantillon (Cantillon 1755, 2010; Cantillon et al. 1959; Say 1827), for whom, in the original formulation, entrepreneur means a person who bears uncertainty and risk.

It is so clear that there is no single way of defining an entrepreneur.

In general terms, we can conclude that an entrepreneur is someone who organises and manages a business and assumes the complete risk of the initiative and management of the business giving their personal guarantee and taking personal decisions and liabilities.

The act of being an entrepreneur is defined as entrepreneurship (Yetisen et al. 2015). Although there is no official definition of entrepreneurship, Onuoha (2007) defines entrepreneurship as 'the practice of starting new organizations or revitalizing mature organizations, particularly new businesses generally in response to identified opportunities' (Timmons 1994).[3]

---

[2]According to Article 2082 of the Italian Civil Code, an 'imprenditore' is someone who professionally carries out an organised economic activity for the purpose of producing or exchanging goods or services. Furthermore, in the Italian Civil Code, Article 2083 defines the small entrepreneur and Article 2135 defines the agricultural entrepreneur.

[3]The definition of entrepreneurship, generally accepted by authors, evolved from work done at Harvard Business School by Timmons (1994): 'Entrepreneurship is the process of creating or seizing an opportunity and pursuing it regardless of the resources currently controlled.

3 The New Business Models: Internet Entrepreneur

One of the most common themes in Joseph A. Schumpeter's writings (Schumpeter 1939, 1950, 1954, 2004) was the role of innovation ('new combinations') and entrepreneurship in economic growth. In Schumpeter's account, it is the enterpreneur who create innovation. And innovation is not only invention (McCraw 2010). Schumpeter coined the phrase 'creative destruction' (Schumpeter 1950; McCraw 2010; Reinert and Reinert 2006) as follows: the 'process of industrial mutation, that incessantly revolutionizes the economic structure from within, incessantly destroying the old one, incessantly creating a new one'. This occurs when innovation deconstructs long-standing arrangements and frees resources to be deployed elsewhere. The theory of Schumpeter (1939, 1950, 2004) can be transposed to the innovative business world (Grebel 2007) based on the Internet in view of the opportunities offered by the Internet and by the new technologies; entrepreneurs and the Internet actively highlight new profit opportunities that did not previously exist.

The internet environment and the new technologies led an innovative revolution (Porter and Stern 1999). In both social and economic organisations and have provided the opportunity for a new business and entrepreneurs models and for a large number of web-based tools that facilitate the business.

Starting from the general definition of entrepreneur, as recalled above, an internet entrepreneur is an entrepreneur, an owner or a leader of an internet-based business enterprise (prevalently start-up)[4] who makes money through creating innovative customer value, taking risk, and turning problems to opportunities.

[4]A start-up 'is an *entrepreneurial venture* which is typically a newly emerged, *fast-growing business* that aims to meet a marketplace need by developing a viable *business model* around an *innovative* product, service, *process* or a platform. A start-up is usually a *company* designed to *effectively develop and validate* a *scalable business model*' (Definition by Wikipedia). The Start-up procedure ('procedural cycle for a start-up that can be considered complete when a company is fully operational to develop its economic activities' (http://ec.europa.eu/growth/smes/promoting-entrepreneurship/advice-opportunities/start-up-procedures_en) taken up by the 2006 Council (http://europa.eu/rapid/press-release_DOC-06-1). The EU Commission as a part of the strategy to make a deeper and fairer single market, has promoted various initiatives for startup as for example: the Startup and Scaleup initiative that aims at improving the conditions for startups to scaleup, create more jobs and enhance Europe's competitiveness (Communication from the Commission to the European Parliament, the Council, The European Economic and Socila Committee and the Committee of the Regions Europe's next leaders: the Start-up and Scale-up Initiative; COM/2016/0733 final). The main proposals of the Startup and Scale up initiative are: to remove barriers for startups to scaleup in the Single Market; to create better opportunities for partnership, commercial opportunities and skills; to facilitate the access to finance. See also: the Small Business Act (Communication from the Commission to the Council, the European Parliament, the European Economic and Social Committee and the Committee of the Regions—"Think Small First"—A "Small Business Act" for Europe—SEC (2008)2101—SEC (2008)2102; COM/2008/0394 final) invites EU countries to simplify and reduce the administrative burden on businesses and to improve the quality of legislation; a dedicated expert group of start-up coordinators was established to monitor the progress made by EU countries. Start-up procedures are also discussed by National SME Envoys set up in 2011 as part of the review of the Small Business Act; the Entrepreneurship

Therefore, the biggest difference between the standard entrepreneur and the internet entrepreneur is that the latter leverages the Internet to generate business, profit and income, while the former type of entrepreneur's core focus is not web driven. This does not mean that a non-internet-based business avoids the use of the Internet. It just means that its business is not solely focused on the Internet. Therefore, an internet entrepreneur or a 'digital entrepreneur' is someone that find in the digital environment both the instrument and the market for its own business (Zaccone 2016), whether it's a physical merchandising business or a play on innovative modern services.

Within the Internet, it is possible to find different forms of business from e-commerce (electronic commerce or EC), affiliate marketing, contextual advertising and mobile banking to new methods of merchandising online, social media advertising or business communication as blogger, vlogger influencer, instagrammer and a numerous other e-innovations that give rise to new kinds of business models as well as reinvented old tried-and-true models.

To analyse how and if the digital technology perspective would build on the existing entrepreneurship theories and regulations, it is necessary to analyse some of the various forms of the business make in or through the Internet.

4 Merchandising on the Internet: E-commerce

E-commerce[5] is the activity to buy and sell goods and services, or transmitting funds or data, over an electronic network, primarily the Internet.[6] The e-commerce business includes any merchandising business owner from those with extensive online stores and huge websites to those trading through an online shopping platform (e.g., eBay, which is a 'dotcomgiftshop', other than a matchup dotcom). The Internet is the key component in this type of business. The Internet and internet-based companies, so-called 'dotcom' (the most common type of Internet start-up company) companies (e.g., Amazon),[7] creates a revolution similar to Schumpeter's theory

Action Plan (Communication from the Commission to the European Parliament, the Council, the European Economic and Social Committee and the Committee of Regions Entrepreneurship 2020 Action Plan Reigniting the entrepreneurial spirit in Europe, COM/2012/0795 final) promotes digital and web start-ups.

[5] The term 'E-preneur' (which derives from the term e-commerce), namely, someone that runs their businesses entirely on the Internet. An e-preneur rarely has official, physical business premises, but instead, tend to operate from home offices. They may also rent a warehouse or storage premises for stock. E-preneurs are quite often also solopreneurs (i.e., a business person who operates entirely on their own and without support from others).

[6] https://searchcio.techtarget.com/definition/e-commerce.

[7] Dotcom companies are so-named because of the URL '.com', which stands for commercial (i.e., the 'dot' means 'point'), such as www.Amazon.com. Amazon is a titan of e-commerce, logistics, payments, hardware, data storage and media. The most known dotcom companies are also eBay, Hotmail, Flickr, GeoCities, PayPal, Skype, MySpace, Writely, YouTube and Facebook.

(Schumpeter 1950) in both a social and economic organisation; the old economy companies that could not adapt in time to take advantage of the new technology are in danger to disappear or lose profits. The 'dotcom' companies, especially, create business by selling products or offering services through an online shopping platform, and the product lines are available through internet-based mechanisms, including normal products of other and several media outlets.

In any type of e-commerce business, the 'actors' shall keep the requirements, provided for in the legal framework of their own country, to become an entrepreneur and shall conform its business to the regulation, the legal aspects and the rules of e-commerce transactions to sell products or services online.[8] Therefore, it is clear that this type of business can be done only by someone who owns legal requirements and respects all the regulations provided for the e-commerce business. With the Digital Single Market strategy, adopted by the European Commission (EC) since 2015, the European Union (EU) aims to define an appropriate e-commerce framework and prevent unfair discrimination against consumers and businesses when they try to access content or buy goods and services online within the EU.[9]

5 Marketing Business on the Internet: The Pay-Per-Click Marketing (PPC Advertising)

The greatest example of the implementation of the entrepreneurial processes and outcomes on the Internet, as well as the way of dealing business based on the new digital technologies, is offered by the internet advertising model named 'pay-per-click' (PPC), also known as cost-per-click (CPC), in which users bid on keywords and pay for each click on their advertisements. PPC is commonly associated with search engines (e.g., Google AdWords and Microsoft Bing Ads) or social networks, such as Facebook, Twitter, LinkedIn and Instagram or digital platform such us Amazon. Google is one of the most important businesses in the new economy, and it is a well-known 'digital entrepreneur' (i.e., a digital business). One of its main products is its internet-based search engine. Google is a search engine based on the PageRank technique that sorts search results, specialised in internet-related services

[8] The website must clearly notify users of a series of important aspects: pre-contractual and post-contractual information, withdrawal period, use of cookies, data protection, etc.

[9] The Digital Single Market includes 16 specific initiatives which have been delivered by the EC till January 2017 aiming to ensure access to online activities for individuals and businesses, shape the environment for digital networks and services and stimulate, under conditions of fair competition, consumer and data protection, removing geo-blocking and copyright issues, a new wave of innovative European start-ups with growth potential. As part of the EC's Digital Single Market strategy and its plan to boost e-commerce, the EC adopted the new Regulation (EU) 2017/2394 of the European Parliament and of the Council of 12 December 2017 on cooperation between national authorities responsible for the enforcement of consumer protection laws and repealing Regulation (EC) No 2006/2004; *OJ L 345, 27.12.2017, pp. 1–26.*

and products, which include online advertising technologies, search engine, cloud computing and software. Google AdWords is the single most popular PPC advertising system in the world. The AdWords platform enables businesses to create ads that appear on Google's search engine and other Google properties. When a search is initiated, Google digs into the pool of AdWords advertisers and chooses a set of winners to appear in the ad space on its search results page. The 'winners' are chosen based on a combination of factors, including the relevance and quality of their keywords and ad performance, as well as the size of their keyword offers.

The PPC advertising model is open to abuse through click fraud (Jansen 2007). Some international trade associations and trade groups involved in online media (i.e. Google, Facebook, Microsoft, the Interactive Advertising Bureau—IAB), formed the Coalition for Better Ads to develop and implement new global standards for ads, creating the Better Ads Experience Program to improve the online experience of users. On February 15, 2018 Google has made the ad-blocker on Chrome to block ads which do not comply with the Better Ads Standards provided for by the Coalition for Better Ads.

The EC released a Statement of Objections to Google for an alleged abuse of its dominant position in web searches and online advertising, "alleging the company has abused its dominant position in the markets for general internet search services in the European Economic Area (EEA) by systematically favouring its own comparison shopping product in its general search results pages"[10] (Marabini 2015) the EC on 27 June 2017 has fined Google issuing a ruling according to antitrust law.[11]

6 Innovative Business: Marketing Strategies

The Internet has enabled digital businesses to create new internet 'figures', such as: an infopreneur, blogger, vlogger, Twitterpreneur and influencer. Not all people that become one of these new internet 'figures' can be considered an entrepreneur or individuals who are able to change their hobby in a business to make money with their website. The term 'infopreneur',[12] which is a portmanteau of the terms

---

[10] European Commission—Press release of April 15, 2015. Antitrust: Commission sends Statement of Objections to Google on comparison shopping service; opens separate formal investigation on Android (http://europa.eu/rapid/press-release_IP-15-4780_en.htm).

[11] The EC ruled that Google abused its market dominance as a search engine by giving an illegal advantage to another Google product, its comparison shopping service. The EC also ruled that Google abused this market dominance by giving its own comparison shopping service an illegal advantage. It gave prominent placement in its search results only to its own comparison shopping service, whilst demoting rival services. It stifled competition on the merits in comparable shopping markets. European Commission—Press release of June 27m 2017. Antitrust: Commission fines Google €2.42 billion for abusing dominance as search engine by giving illegal advantage to own comparison shopping service (http://europa.eu/rapid/press-release_IP-17-1784_en.htm).

[12] The word 'preneur' is considered as a neologism or a *libfix*, identifying people that exercise particular economic activities, such as: (1) a *mompreneur* (i.e., a stay-at-home mom, who runs a

information and entrepreneur, was coined in the 1980s by Weitzen (1987). The infopreneur is an entrepreneur who turns information into a revenue stream. This can be in the form of books, courses, lectures or consulting in both the online and offline space. Infopreneurs changed the idea of entrepreneurship allowing to set up a business without having to hire staffs or equipment or to invest relevant capital. Sites like WordPress, YouTube and Facebook show that anyone can share information and supply it in a free matter. A 'Twitterpreneur' is someone who makes their business, mostly or entirely, through the social platform, Twitter. It could also be someone whose business relies largely on Twitter for its income. Many entrepreneurs use social media as a standing stone on which to build their customer base and to increase their market and industry authority. A 'blogger' (i.e., a synonym of weblogger) is a person who creates and posts to a blog. A blog, or a weblog, is a personal online journal that is frequently updated and intended for general public consumption. Blogs are defined by their format: a series of entries posted to a single page in reverse-chronological order. Topics are various and can include food, beauty, life style, work, commentary on the Internet and other social issues and links to other sites chosen by the author, especially those that support a point being made on a post. A '*vlogger*' is someone who film themselves talking to a camera whilst doing all sorts of stuff and then put the film up on content-sharing sites, such as YouTube. There are different types of vloggers and different types of vlogs. One of the most popular types of vloggers are the beauty vloggers. An 'influencer' is someone who has the power to influence the perception of others or gets them to do something different.

It is necessary to specify that a dedicated and uniform regulation governing all the possible activities done by these new internet 'figures' does not exist, as well as an absence of uniform requirements for them to make a business.

The best way for a blogger or an influencer to do a business is by advertising to market a company's products and services. Thus, a digital company may use the power of social media (e.g., Facebook, YouTube and Twitter) to directly market their products and use the power of a blogger, influencer or celebrity to directly or indirectly connect with customers, push advertising and establish brand images.

Companies may develop marketing strategies that stretch across platforms. They could form expensive partnerships with celebrities or other brands to help position their products. Celebrity marketing is a tactic that features a famous person offering an endorsement of a product. That famous person might be an actor, musician, ath-

business from home); (2) a *youngpreneur* (i.e., someone who starts a business while they are still in education, either full time or part time); (3) an *ideapreneur* (i.e., somebody who likes to generate new and innovative ideas—whether it is for business or other purposes—and to help realise those ideas; (4) an *innerpreneur* (i.e., someone who is basically an entrepreneur but who is working for the sole purpose of personal growth and development rather than for the purpose of trying to grow a specific business venture; (5) a *freepreneur* (i.e., someone who only uses free or very low-cost methods of setting up and running a business; (6) a *megapreneur* (i.e., also referred to as a *superpreneur* and is essentially a celebrity or superstar of the entrepreneurial world; and (7) a *wingpreneur* (i.e., someone who provides something essential to a start-up business—albeit funding, support, knowledge, skills, etc.—but takes a backseat in the overall running of a business.

lete or a cartoon character. They do not need to be international superstars; they only need to be familiar to the target audience. This is a direct form to market the products, specifically called 'celebrity endorsements', based on an agreement between the company and the celebrity, allowing the company to use image, photo and name of the celebrity (intellectual property rights). In such cases, the consumers know the celebrity is getting paid to promote a particular product.

In a similar way, the companies could use the blogger or influencer paying them to do advertising. The companies often look for someone with a lot of followers (e.g., an Instagram influencer or a digital influencer)[13] and pay them to advertise a product wearing products or posting contents of the blog page.[14] This type of internet advertising techniques, adopted by the blogger, is named 'sponsored posts' (i.e., native advertising), which consists of content in line with the blog's overall subject area and mentions a specific product in a natural context. The vendor, in turn, pays the blogger for the mention. The advertising is based on the power of the blogger to influence the followers.

The blogger may also use the technique of product placement[15] (i.e., embedded marketing), namely, a marketing technique in which references to specific brands or products are incorporated into another work (e.g., a film, text or television program), with a specific intent to promote said products. The blogger may use such technique, for example, in 'text link ads', in which ads are not served based on the content of a blogger's page but rather based on specific text within the posts of a blog.

These types of commercial advertising techniques are equally a direct sponsorship and advertisement. Thus, it is necessary that the blogger, vlogger or influencer add a specific disclaimer about advertising in the video or content of the blog (i.e. "this video includes product placement which is indicated by […]").[16] The text must

---

[13] These terms were coined when the audience of the bloggers started to shift away from the blogs and, instead, started following the bloggers predominantly on Instagram.

[14] See for example the techniques of: Online marketing by a brand, where a brand collaborates with a vlogger and makes a video blog ("vlog") about the brand and/or its products and this video is uploaded to the brand's own channels and then shared by the brand on their own social media channels; "Advertorial" vlogs where the whole video is in the usual style of the vlogger but the content is controlled by the brand and the vlogger has been paid (not necessarily with money).

[15] A product might be used as a 'prop' along with messages that have been controlled by the advertiser within a vlog that is largely editorial. For example a vlogger might create a make-up tutorial where the vlogger features a specific set of brushes.

[16] See for example regulation provided for in: the Advertising Codes, written by the Committees of Advertising Practice (CAP) and applied by Advertising Standards Authority (ASA) the UK's independent regulator of advertising across all media (https://www.asa.org.uk/). A key rule under the CAP Code is that if the content is controlled by the marketer, not the vlogger, and is written in exchange for payment, then it is an advertisement feature and must be labelled as such (rule 2.4); the art. 7 of Code of Marketing Communication Self-Regulation Italy (63rd edition effective March 8th, 2017; http://www.iap.it/digital-chart/endorsement/vlogger/): "Marketing communication must be clearly distinguishable as such. In the media and in the marketing communication when news and other editorial matter are presented to the public, it should be ensured that the marketing communication is readily distinguishable as such".

clarify that content is sponsored, or that a product placement arrangement is in place.

The relationship between blogger or vlogger and producer company are frequently based on an agreement, in which the blogger does not need particular legal requirements nor required to be an entrepreneur. In certain countries it is not necessary to create a business entity for this scope; for example, in Italy, it can be sufficient to have a Value-Added Tax (VAT) registration number,[17] even if normally the agreement between blogger and produce is signed by intermediaries or agent (usual establish in a formal entity of company) acting as representative mandatory of the blogger. The mandatory signs the agreement, takes the remuneration and issues the invoice.

Is summary, notwithstanding the different ads techniques by blogger or vlogger recalled above, it is possible to conclude that a 'commercial advertising'—subject to the relative regulation—is any citation of a brand or a product showed in a video of a vlogger or in the post of a blogger or in a content of the blog when the "message" is shared by the producer that controls the content. This means that it's unlikely that a specific label such as "ad" will be necessary appear on the blog or video. Differently if a producer sends to a vlogger items for free without any control of the content (or any conditions attached) and the vlogger can choose to include or not these items in a vlog, the public relation activity done by blogger not need to be labelled as an advertorial, even if, in general, the consumers should be advised whether a vlogger has an incentive (financial or otherwise) to talk about a product.

The blogger can also show AdSense and other ads on their blog—for example: (1) 'contextual ads' (part of the keyword advertising), which are typical PPC ads that are delivered based on the content of the blog page where the ads will be displayed (e.g., Google AdSense and Kontera). In traditional contextual advertising, automated systems display ads related to the content of the site based on keyword targeting; (2) 'impression-based ads',[18] which are ads that pay bloggers based on the number of times the ad appears on the blog; (3) 'affiliate ads', which are ads where bloggers are given a choice of programs to provide links to products and paid when someone purchases the advertised product (e.g., Amazon Associates and eBay Affiliates are popular affiliate advertising programs); and (4) 'direct ads', which are ads where the bloggers offer an option for visitors to purchase advertising space on their blogs; (5) "vlogger's video about their own product", where the sole content of a vlog is a promotion of the vlogger's own merchandise. The vlogger is responsible for claims made about the product; (6) "Editorial video referring to vlogger's products" as for example, when vlogger, during an otherwise editorial video a gaming

[17] Whoever providing goods and services across international borders, or shipping products abroad to an overseas warehouse or fulfillment center, providing digital services to other businesses and consumers, or a host of other scenarios, likely have a VAT because this type of business has both legal and tax implications.

[18] "Impressions" are when an advertisement or any other form of digital media renders on a user's screen. Impressions are not action-based and are merely defined by a user potentially seeing the advertisement.

vlogger, say "I'm currently using the new headphones I've just released; you can purchase them through the link below".

In such cases, bloggers need a business licence and an entity (i.e. company to be created according to the national law for establishment), and bloggers need to respect other legal and fiscal requirements provided for in different countries included the regulation about commercial advertising[19] as well as the regulation of unfair commercial practices in business-to-consumer transactions.[20]

7 Conclusion

In the communication of the EC, 'A Digital Single Market Strategy for Europe',[21] it is pointed out that:

The global economy is rapidly becoming digital.

The Internet and digital technologies are transforming the lives we lead, the way we work—as individuals, in business, and in our communities as they become more integrated across all sectors of our economy and society.

A key aim of the Digital Single Market Strategy is to establish a supportive investment climate for digital networks, research and innovative business.

---

[19] See the European Advertising Standards Alliance (EASA), that is the coordinating body for advertising self-regulatory organisations within Europe, and seeks to promote responsible advertising. It does this by providing guidance to its members on how to go about advertising self-regulation for the benefit of both businesses and consumers: the 'Digital Marketing Communication Best Practice Recommendation', the 'Best Practice Recommendation on Online Behavioural Advertising' and the 'Framework Interactive Advertising Bureau Europe' (http://www.edaa.eu; http://www.easa-alliance.org); see in Italy the regulation provides for the 'Istituto dell'Autodisciplina Pubblicitaria' (IAP) in the *Code of Marketing Communication Self-Regulation Italy 63rd edition effective March 8th, 2017.*

[20] EU Unfair Commercial Practices Directive' 2005/29/E of 11 May 2005 concerning unfair business-to-consumer commercial practices in the internal market and amending Council Directive 84/450/EEC, Directives 97/7/EC, 98/27/EC and 2002/65/EC of the European Parliament and of the Council and Regulation (EC) No 2006/2004 of the European Parliament and of the Council, OJ L 149, 22; EU Regulation n. 2017/2394 of the European Parliament and of the Council of 12 December 2017 on cooperation between national authorities responsible for the enforcement of consumer protection laws and repealing Regulation (EC) No 2006/2004 (Text with EEA relevance); *OJ L 345, 27.12.2017*; Commission Staff Working document guidance on the implementation/application of Directive 2005/29/EC Accompanying the document Communication from the Commission of the European Parliament, the Council, the European Economic and Social Committee and the Committee of the Regions a comprehensive approach to stimulating cross-border e-Commerce for Europe's citizens and businesses; SWD/2016/0163 final (https://eur-lex.europa.eu/legal-content/EN/TXT/?uri=CELEX%3A52016SC0163); European Parliament Draft opinion 2018/2008(INI) 2018/2008(INI); PR\1147015IT.docx-PE618.324v01-00 (http://www.europarl.europa.eu/meetdocs/2014_2019/plmrep/COMMITTEES/IMCO/PR/2018/03-21/1147015IT.pdf).

[21] Brussels, 6.5.2015, COM (2015) 192 final.

In this context, the Internet and new technologies have a relevant role, and the legal framework applied on the new business offered by the Internet could not be in step with the innovative development of a business framework, even if the internet entrepreneur, right now, is not submitted to a special or different regulation compared to the 'usual' concept of entrepreneur, acting the 'internet', 'web' or 'digital' environment as distinctive feature.

Notably, the internet entrepreneur cannot be categorised in a single way, given the diversity of the various subject that could be classified under the terms 'internet entrepreneur' or 'digital entrepreneur': a usual entrepreneur acting on the Internet or anyone that act through the Internet. In the latter case (i.e., anyone acting through the Internet), the actor could be an entrepreneur or not. According to the different types of activities performed on the Internet, it is possible (i.e., ex post by the regulator and ex ante by the 'actors' of the business) to find the relative regulation to be applied.

Looking at the diversity of the businesses and traders on the Internet, as well as the development of innovation, it is perhaps more correct to talk about the 'internet business' rather than the internet entrepreneur according that the meaning of the term business is: "the activity of making one's living or making money by producing or buying and selling goods or services"[22] as long as "an organizational entity and legal entity made up of an association of people, be they natural, legal, or a mixture of both who share a common purpose and unite in order to focus their various talents and organize their collectively available skills or resources to achieve specific declared goals and are involved in the provision of goods and services to consumers.[23]

References

American Heritage Dictionary. Retrieved from https://ahdictionary.com/

Business Dictionary. Retrieved from http://www.businessdictionary.com/definition/entrepreneur.html

Cambridge Business Law Academy. Retrieved from http://cblaedu.com/en/business/

Cantillon, R. (1755). *Essai sur la nature du commerce en general: edited with an English translation and other material by Henry Higgs, C.B. Reissued for The Royal Economic Society*. London: Frank Cass and Co., Ltd.

Cantillon, R. (2010). *An essay on economic theory: An English translation of Richard Cantillon's Essai sur la Nature du Commerce en Général* (C. Saucier, Trans.). Auburn: Ludwig von Mises Institute.

Cantillon, R., Higgs, H., & Jevons, W. S. (1959). *Essai sur la nature du commerce in général (An essay on economic theory)*. London: Frank Cass and Co., Ltd.

[22] Definition by Wikipedia recalling American Heritage Dictionary, Longman Business English Dictionary, Longman Dictionary of Contemporary English, and Oxford Dictionaries.

[23] Definition by Cambridge Business Law and Academy voice business—http://cblaedu.com/en/business.

Grebel, T. (2007). Neo-Schumpeterian perspectives in entrepreneurship research. In H. Hanusch & A. Pyka (Eds.), *Elgar companion to Neo-Schumpeterian economics* (pp. 147–158). Cheltenham, United Kingdom: Edward Elgar.
Jansen, B. J. (2007). Click fraud. *Computer, 40*(7), 85–86.
Jonsson, P. O. (2017). On the term "entrepreneur" and the conceptualization of entrepreneurship in the literature of classical economics. *International Journal of English Linguistics, 7*(6), 16.
Longman Business English Dictionary. Retrieved from https://www.ldoceonline.com/spellcheck/english/?q=businss
Marabini, F. (2015). *La funambolica posizione di Google tra antitrust e "patent war"*. Assago, Milan: Wolters Kluwer.
McCraw, T. K. (2010). *Prophet of Innovation: Joseph Schumpeter and creative destruction.* Cambridge: Harward University Press.
Merriam Webster Dictionary. Retrieved from https://www.merriam-webster.com/dictionary/dictionary
Onuoha, G. (2007). Entrepreneurship. *AIST International Journal, 10*, 20–32.
Oxford Dictionary. Retrieved from https://en.oxforddictionaries.com/
Porter, M. E., & Stern, S. (1999). *The new challenge to America's prosperity: Findings from the innovation index.* Washington, DC: Council on Competitiveness. Retrieved from http://www.hbs.edu/faculty/Publication%20Files/Downloads_Porter_index1_el_be68d54c-4990-45da-88c0-ee754c99ffdb.pdf
Reinert, H., & Reinert, E. S. (2006). *Creative destruction in economics: Nietzsche, Sombart, Schumpeter.* Berlin, Heidelberg: Springer Science+Business Media, LLC.
Say, J. B. (1827). *A treatise on political economy; or the production, distribution and consumption of wealth.* Philadelphia: John Grigg.
Schumpeter, J. A. (1939). *Business cycles: A theoretical, historical, and statistical analysis of the capitalist process* (Vol. 2). New York: McGraw-Hill.
Schumpeter, J. A. (1950). *Capitalism, socialism and democracy* (3rd ed.). London: Allen and Unwin.
Schumpeter, J. A. (1954). *History of economic analysis*. New York: Oxford University Press.
Schumpeter, J. A. (2004). *The theory of economic development: An inquiry into profits, capitals, credit, interest, and the business cycle* (10th ed.). News Brunswick, NJ: Transaction.
Timmons. (1994). *New venture creation: Entrepreneurship for the 21st century* (4th ed.). Burr Ridge, IL: Irwin Press.
Weitzen, H. S. (1987). *Infopreneurs: Turning data into dollars*. New York: John Wiley & Sons.
Yetisen, A. K., Volpatti, L. R., Coskun, A. F., Cho, S., Kamrani, E., Butt, H., et al. (2015). Entrepreneurship. *Lab on a Chip, 15*(18), 3638–3660.
Zaccone, E. (2016). *Digital entrepreneur: Principles, practices and skills for their startup*. Milan, Italy: Franco Angeli.

Inventor

Marc Mimler

1 Introduction

Patent rights constitute the most important regulatory measure affecting the status of inventors. Inventors are entitled to the grant of the patent on their invention after registration[1] providing their holders with significant economic rights.[2] National patent laws of EU Member States have historically regulated and shaped the status of the inventor to a large extent. Some form of harmonisation of the substantial national patent laws within EU member states has been achieved outside the EU's framework by the European Patent Convention (EPC). The EU's influence on patent law has been limited when compared to trade mark and design law (Bently and Sherman 2014, p. 389) to certain areas of patent law, such as that in relation to biotechnological inventions. Eventually, the UPP which is currently being implemented may increase the EU's involvement in the field of patents.

2 The European Patent System

Patent law within EU member states which regulates the status of inventors, such as questions of inventorship and employee inventions are still largely based on national law. However, some form of convergence of national patent laws occurred outside

[1] Article 60 (1) EPC.

[2] In addition, some jurisdictions provide inventor with protection through utility models or petty patents.

M. Mimler (✉)
Centre for Intellectual Property Policy & Management (CIPPM), Bournemouth University, Poole, UK
e-mail: mmimler@bournemouth.ac.uk

A. Bartolini et al. (eds.), *Dictionary of Statuses within EU Law*,
https://doi.org/10.1007/978-3-030-00554-2_42

the EU framework. The most important measure is the EPC which is an intergovernmental treaty and as such open to non-EU Member states.[3] It created the European Patent Office (EPO) which provides inventors with the possibility to receive a bundle of national patents with a single application. The UPP may eventually provide for patent rights under the EU framework.

2.1 *Evolution of the European Patent System*

The European patent system can be traced back to initiatives in the late 1940ies (Wadlow 2010, p. 143). The Council of Europe spearheaded these early attempts of harmonisation with the "Longchambon plan" which foresaw the creation of a European patent office granting European Certificates of Inventions. This plan can be regarded as the blueprint of the EPC of 1973 (Arnold 2013, p. 26) whose aim was to enable industry to secure patent protection across national boundaries, hence reducing cost. The EPC system uses a central granting office applying common rules on patentability. Once granted, the patent holder would enjoy protection in EPC states designated in the application.[4] The enforcement of such patents would be subject to the applicable national law.[5] The relevance of the EPC for harmonising patent law in Europe is increased since its substantive provisions on patentability have been applied in many national patent laws of EPC states. As to the harmonising efforts of the EU and its predecessors: Several attempts to provide for unitary patent rights have failed. The first version of a Community Patent Convention 1975 (CPC1975) never came into force due to the failure of some countries to ratify it[6] (Krieger 1988, pp. 145–146). Later attempts to revive the project, such as the CPC 1989,[7] also failed.

---

[3] Though all EU member states are Contracting states of the EPC. Switzerland, Norway and Turkey are, for instance, contracting states of the EPC.

[4] See Articles 64(1), 79 EPC.

[5] Subsection (3) of Article 65 states *expressis verbis* that "[a]ny infringement of a European patent shall be dealt with by national law." However, an opposition proceeding however may be launched after the grant of the patent before the EPO.

[6] However, the substantive provisions of the Community Patent Convention with regards to post-grant phase of patents, such as the rules on infringement were adopted in many national patent laws of EU member states.

[7] This was an amended version of the CPC 1975 and was envisaged as an international agreement and was signed on 15.12 1989 again in Luxembourg, 1989 89/695/EEC, OJ EEC L 401, 30.12.1989, 1–27. Similarly to the CPC 1975 this Agreement failed to enter into force.

2.2 The Patent with Unitary Effect

The current European patent framework has apparent deficiencies due to parallel litigation to enforce EPO bundle patents in multiple jurisdictions which increases costs and the possibility of national courts diverging in their findings of infringement of identical patents granted by the EPO[8] (Fisher 2007, pp. 246 ff.). The CPC 1975 aimed at addressing this but would have not resolved the issue of adjudicating EPO patents designating non-EU states. The European Patent Litigation Agreement (EPLA) elaborated under the auspices of the EPO would have allowed the participation of non-EU states and was favoured by many patent practitioners due to the court system it proposed[9] (Ullrich 2012, p. 53). Its adoption was, however, not possible since EU member states would not have the competence to conclude such an agreement (Ellyne 2014, p. 60). In order to eliminate the deadlock caused largely due to the language regime of prospective patents of the EU,[10] the Council of the EU authorized enhanced cooperation with respect to the creation of unitary patent protection which resulted in the UPP.[11] Spain and Italy initially sued against the decision to apply enhanced collaboration but the CJEU dismissed the case.[12]

The UPP includes 3 legislative measures: 2 EU Regulations (one creating the patent with unitary effect[13] and another on the translation regime[14]) and one international agreement between the participating Member States on a centralized court system (UPC Agreement).[15] Patents with unitary effect would be granted by the EPO.[16] The court system entails a court of first instance with national- , regional- and a central division(s) and would oversee litigation over the validity and infringement of patents with unitary effect and of national European Patents of such EU Member States that are part of the UPP. Oddly, the substantive provisions on patent infringement and exceptions thereof have been placed within the Agreement on the

[8] The prime example for this are the so-called "Epilady" cases.

[9] EPLA foresaw "the establishment of a highly specialized, semi-centralized European Patent Court having exclusive jurisdiction over litigation concerning the revocation and the infringement of the European bundle patent".

[10] A consensus was established to generally apply the three official languages of the EPO—English, French and German.

[11] Council Decision 2011/167/EU of 10 March 2011 authorising enhanced cooperation in the area of the creation of unitary patent protection (OJ 2011 L 76, p. 53).

[12] Joined Cases C-274/11 and C-295/11 Spain and Italy v Council. Italy eventually ratified the Agreement on the Unified Patent Court.

[13] Regulation (EU) No 1257/2012 of the European Parliament and of the Council of 17 December 2012 implementing enhanced cooperation in the area of the creation of unitary patent protection (UP Regulation).

[14] Council Regulation (EU) No 1260/2012 of 17 December 2012 implementing enhanced cooperation in the area of the creation of unitary patent protection with regard to the applicable translation arrangements.

[15] Agreement on a Unified Patent Court, <https://www.unified-patent-court.org/sites/default/files/upc-agreement.pdf.>

[16] UP Regulation, Recital 5.

court system (Ellyne 2014, pp. 64–65) and not within the Regulation where they initially were placed. This was aimed to curtail the CJEU's influence on substantial patent law and is most probably based on the scepticism of some EU member states and practitioners towards the role of the CJEU (Pagenberg 2012, p. 587) on the highly technical subject matter of patent law. The full implementation of the Unitary Patent Package is currently stalled since the necessary ratifications of the UPC Agreement are lacking.[17] Brexit (McDonagh and Mimler 2017, p. 176) and a Constitutional complaint before the German Federal Constitutional Court currently stall the ratification of the UP Agreement and the implementation of the UPP.[18]

3 EU Law Regarding Patents

3.1 Biotech Directive

The Biotech Directive[19] is presently the only legislative measure by the EU that covers substantive patent law. It covers areas, such as patentability, the scope of protection of biotechnological patents, excluded subject matter and cross-licensing which makes it important for the status of inventors. It aims at resolving the divergent approaches towards the patenting of biotechnology to assist this field of technology.[20] The Directive's substantive provisions were adopted within the EPC framework[21] in order to avoid discrepancies between the law of the EPC and that of EU Member States. The Directive is particularly relevant to the status of inventors as it enabled the patenting of genetic material by declaring biological material as being a patentable invention where the material is isolated from its natural environment or produced by means of a technical process even if it previously occurred in nature.[22]

The morality exclusions within Article 6 of the Directive produced the most controversial case law of the CJEU in the field of patents. The patent in suit in the *Brüstle* case[23] involved isolated and purified neural precursor cells produced from human embryonic stem cells (HECSs) for treating damaged organs. The patent was challenged based on the provisions which declared uses of human embryos for

---

[17] Article 89 UPC Agreement.

[18] Kluwer Patent Blog (2017) German complaint against Unified Patent Court Agreement: deadline for submitting views is end of October. http://patentblog.kluweriplaw.com/2017/09/12/german-complaint-unified-patent-court-agreement-deadline-submitting-views-end-october/. Accessed 15 Jan 2018.

[19] Directive 98/44/EC for Biotechnological Inventions (1998).

[20] European Commission (1988) A European Patent Law for Biotechnology. http://europa.eu/rapid/press-release_P-88-111_en.htm. Accessed 15 Jan 2018.

[21] Administrative Council Decision, OJ EPO 7/1999, pp. 437–440.

[22] Article 3(2) Biotech Directive.

[23] *Oliver Brüstle v Greenpeace eV* (C-34/10) [2012] 1 C.M.L.R. 41.

industrial or commercial purposes as unpatentable. The referring court sought the CJEU's clarification, *inter alia*, on what constitutes an "embryo". The CJEU provided a broad interpretation of the term embryo which would include "any human ovum after fertilisation." In addition, non-fertilised human ova "into which the cell nucleus from a mature human cell" were transplanted or such stimulated by parthenogenesis would be considered as embryos. The decision was criticised (Bonadio 2012, p. 93) for its wide implications for stem cell research in Europe, its autonomous interpretation creating a fictional consensus of what is considered an embryo and its questionable conformity with the TRIPS Agreement (Nordberg and Minssen 2016, p. 144). In a later decision, the CJEU appears to have narrowed its approach with regards to non-fertilized ova.[24] But the question remained whether the CJEU, as a generalist court with the primary function of safeguarding the interpretation and application of EU law,[25] would be a suitable forum for adjudicating highly technical patent disputes (Pagenberg 2012, p. 587).

3.2 Supplementary Protection Measures

The EU's first field of activity related to the term of protection for patents (Bently and Sherman 2014, p. 389). The patent term of 20 years was deemed to be insufficient for products requiring regulatory approval, particularly pharmaceutical products. Before being placed on the market, medicinal and plant protection products require either national or EU marketing authorisation. In order to compensate for the delays that may occur, the European legislator provided 2 Regulations[26] which created supplementary protection certificates (SPCs) for medicinal and plant protection products. The recitals of the Regulations state that both product groups warrant "favourable rules" which would provide for sufficient protection to encourage research in Europe.[27] Rather than extending the term of patents, the European legislator created a *sui generis* system distinct from patents in order to avoid a conflict with the maximum term of a patent of 20 years as stipulated in Article 63 EPC.[28] SPCs take effect at the end of the term for the patent and can extend the effect of the basic patent for up to 5 years.[29]

[24] Case C-364/13 *International Stem Cell Corporation v. Comptroller General of Patents*.

[25] Article 19(1) TEU.

[26] Regulation (EC) No 469/2009 of the European Parliament and of the Council of 6 May 2009 concerning the supplementary protection certificate for medicinal products and Regulation (EC) No 1610/96 of the European Parliament and of the Council of 23 July 1996 concerning the creation of a supplementary protection certificate for plant protection products.

[27] Regulation (EC) No 469/2009, Recital 3; Regulation (EC) No 1610/96, Recital 3.

[28] Article 63 EPC was subsequently amended in order to take account of SPCs.

[29] Regulation (EC) No 469/2009, Article 13; Regulation (EC) No 1610/96, Article 13.

3.3 Enforcement Directive

Another field where EU law affected the status of the inventor is the enforcement of patents. The Enforcement Directive,[30] which was adopted in 2004, had the aim to target counterfeiting and piracy, in particular actions on a large scale, industrial level (Massa and Strowel 2004, p. 244). To address this, the internal market logic was applied again: Recital 9 of the Directive states that the different frameworks of IP enforcement would "lead to a weakening of the substantive law on intellectual property and to a fragmentation of the internal market in this field." The Directive requires EU Member States to provide for certain enforcement measures, such as measures for preserving evidence, precautionary measures, injunctive relief and damages.

4 Trade Secrets

Finally, a related field of law to patents influencing the statues of inventors are trade secrets. Inventions are often valuable information which some inventors keep secret rather than seek patent registration. Commercially valuable trade secrets are an important asset of many firms and the protection of trade secrets plays "an important role in protecting the returns to innovation." (Baker and Mackenzie 2013, p. 2). In order to overcome the diverging approaches of trade secret protection within EU member states, the EU has recently adopted the Trade Secrets Directive in 2016.[31] The Directive does not specify the role of inventors but defines the holder of a trade secret as a legal or natural person having control over the trade secret.[32] This definition does not provide clarification as to the position of the inventor as the "creator," e.g. whether he or she will be a joint holder of such information of the trade secret. This arguably remains to be determined by national laws; hence the direct impact of the Directive on the status of inventors is limited.

5 Conclusion

The EU has had limited direct effect on the status of inventors since national patent laws already forged the status of inventors to a large extent before the European legislator sought to regulate within this field. Where the EU legislator acted, the legislative changes were generally aimed at expanding the scope of protection, enhancing

[30] Directive 2004/48/EC of the European Parliament and of the Council of 29 April 2004 on the enforcement of intellectual property rights.

[31] Directive (EU) 2016/943 of the European Parliament and of the Council of 8 June 2016 on the protection of undisclosed know-how and business information (trade secrets) against their unlawful acquisition, use and disclosure (Trade Secrets Directive).

[32] Article 2(2) Trade Secrets Directive.

enforcement measures, extending the rights or supplementing them in form of trade secrets. These measures were based on the goal to eliminate distortions within the internal market. This overarching goal may have led to some commentators to criticise the value of the CJEU in the highly technical field of patents. In addition, the EU legislator is aiming at further harmonising patent law within the Union. This task has to resolve the complex issue of integrating the current European patent landscape. These activities directly affect the inventor who is also the right holder of the patent. But even where this is not the case, patent law and its legal reflex affect the status of inventors indirectly by aiming to promote innovative activities.

References

Arnold, R. (2013). An overview of European harmonization measures in intellectual property law. In A. Ohly & J. Pila (Eds.), *The Europeanization of intellectual property law*. Oxford: Oxford University Press.

Baker and Mackenzie. (2013). *Study on trade secrets and confidential business information in the internal market*. MARKT/2010/20/D, p. 2. Retrieved January 15, 2018, from http://eur-lex.europa.eu/legal-content/EN/TXT/HTML/?uri=CELEX:32016L0943&from=EN

Bently, L., & Sherman, B. (2014). *Intellectual property law* (4th ed.). Oxford: Oxford University Press.

Bonadio, E. (2012). Stem cells industry and beyond: What is the aftermath of Brüstle? *European Journal of Risk Regulation, 3*, 93–97.

Ellyne, E. (2014). European unitary patent: Are we there yet? *Queen Mary Journal of Intellectual Property, 4*, 57–79.

Fisher, M. (2007). *Fundamentals of patent law - Interpretation and scope of protection*. Oxford: Hart Publishing.

Kluwer Patent Blog. (2017). *German complaint against Unified Patent Court Agreement: Deadline for submitting views is end of October*. Retrieved January 15, 2018, from http://patentblog.kluweriplaw.com/2017/09/12/german-complaint-unified-patent-court-agreement-deadlinesubmitting-views-end-october/

Krieger, A. (1988). The Luxembourg Convention on the Community Patent – A challenge and a duty. *International Review of Intellectual Property and Competition Law, 19*, 143–157.

Massa, C.-H., & Strowel, A. (2004). The scope of the proposed IP Enforcement Directive: Torn between the desire to harmonise remedies and the need to combat piracy. *EIPR, 26*, 244–253.

McDonagh, L., & Mimler, M. (2017). Intellectual property law and Brexit: A retreat or a reaffirmation of jurisdiction? In M. Dougan (Ed.), *The UK after Brexit – Legal and policy challenges*. Cambridge: Intersentia.

Nordberg, A., & Minssen, T. (2016). A ray of hope for European stem cell patents or out of the smog into the fog? An analysis of recent European Case Law and how it compares to the US. *International Review of Intellectual Property and Competition Law, 47*, 138–177.

Pagenberg, J. (2012). Die EU-Patentrechtsreform – zurück auf Los? *Gewerblicher Rechtsschutz und Urheberrecht, 6*, 582–589.

Ullrich, H. (2012). Harmonizing Patent Law: The Untameable Patent Union. *Max Planck Institute for Intellectual Property and Competition Law Research Paper*, 12-03. Available at SSRN. Retrieved March 12, 2018, from http://papers.ssrn.com/sol3/papers.cfm?abstract_id=2027920

Wadlow, C. (2010). Strasbourg, the forgotten patent convention, and the origins of the European patent jurisdiction. *International Review of Intellectual Property and Competition Law, 41*, 124–149.

Jean Monnet Chairholder

Carlos Francisco Molina del Pozo and Covadonga Reyes Assiego

1 Introduction and Genesis

Professors who are Jean Monnet Chairholders have several differences from other professors.

Such title derives from one of the so-called "founding fathers" who was also the architect of the process of European integration, Jean Monnet (1888–1889). He was the driving figure behind the establishment of the European Coal and Steel Community (ECSC). In 1950, he had already sketched out a basic idea of what the European Economic Community (EEC) would become a few years later.

These scholars carry out their activities, both teaching and research, in the field of European issues through Chairs awarded by the European Commission within the framework of what began as the Jean Monnet Action and later became the Jean Monnet Programme.

The teaching position is characterised by the scholar's speciality and requires a full or very significant commitment of working time to addressing the diversity and plurality of subjects concerning the wider context of the European Union. Since 1990, when the first call for Jean Monnet Chairs was launched, during the period (3 years) of the funding granted to each Chair awarded to a professor of a specific university, a series of specific activities are carried out and marked by the programme defined by the projects that the candidates must submit to become Chairholders.

Likewise, in the early calls for proposals, the agreement between the corresponding university where the candidate for the Chair will carry out his or her functions and the European Commission included the commitment of the hosting university to continue to finance, for an additional 4 years, the actions carried out by the Jean Monnet Professor, which were previously provided and properly planned.

C. F. Molina del Pozo (✉) · C. Reyes Assiego
Department of Law, Universidad de Alcalá de Henares, Alcalá de Henares, Spain
e-mail: carlosf.molina@uah.es

A. Bartolini et al. (eds.), *Dictionary of Statuses within EU Law*,
https://doi.org/10.1007/978-3-030-00554-2_43

Therefore, at the beginning of the so-called Jean Monnet Action, the Jean Monnet Programme implied an obligation for the co-financing of the activities of the Chair, which were initially funded only by the Commission and, after the end of the first 3 years, were entirely funded by the specific university concerned in each case for a further period of 3 or 4 years.

Today, there is no longer such an obligation on the university, but, in any case, as we will see, the Jean Monnet Chairholders can continue to carry out their academic activities using the prestigious Jean Monnet label.

As a matter of fact, Jean Monnet Chairs, awarded through the corresponding annual world-wide competitions, may continue to develop their activities as such, without any time limit, even after the end of the agreement signed at the beginning of the programme. However, at that point, they no longer have any financial support, which must be obtained by the Chairholders to continue their work and activities.

The Chairholder can only be a single person who already holds the status of professor or researcher in a university and who fulfils the necessary requirement of a minimum of 90 teaching hours per academic year, always on subjects related to the process of European integration. Other hours may be spent in the participation in congresses, seminars and other academic activities.

As mentioned above, in order to become Jean Monnet Chairholders, these scholars must complete a genuinely competitive selection process called annually by the European Commission, which takes place through the Education, Audiovisual and Culture Executive Agency (EACEA). The applicants are highly specialised professors and/or researchers who must meet the minimum requirements or standards of the competition. In this sense, the Jean Monnet Chair is not limited to promoting courses that enrich knowledge about the European Union, but also has many other objectives worthy of mention. Research is also supported through the programming of activities that are not limited to merely theoretical aspects but are extended to the development and implementation of actions aimed at achieving dissemination, communication and training, always—as we have said—within the rich subject of European integration.

Acquiring the title of Jean Monnet Professor implies that the professor has previously achieved and has been proven to have a commendable professional career, with a large number of hours dedicated to teaching about subjects related to the European Union. In this sense, it can be said that, for the European Commission, it is very important that these scholars are in the labour market: It is not unknown that a large number of people are completely unaware of what the European Union can contribute, as a phenomenon of our society, to the economy and to politics. Above all, we feel it is extremely important not to ignore what the European Union implies in the field and in the context of the Member States' legal systems. Thus, it could be argued that Jean Monnet Professors should have a vast knowledge and preparation, because these professionals will be the guiding thread between their students, usually young people, and the institutions, bodies, offices and agencies of the European Union.

As stated above, these teaching positions are specialised in studies on the European Union, whether from a legal, economic, historical or political point of view, and are open to university professors, regardless of their rank on the university teaching scale. They have a series of objectives, the most important of which is probably to teach and disseminate everything related to the process of European integration. However, there are also a number of other objectives that are at least as relevant and equally important.

In particular, the main activities carried out by the Jean Monnet Chairholder are the following:

- The improvement of the teaching of European Union studies by establishing the most appropriate programme. The aim is to increase students' knowledge of the European Union's functions through courses given by these teachers. It is extremely important in a knowledge-based society for the younger generations know about the means available to them which can be provided by the European Union.
- Research on everything related to the European Union must be carried out, supervised and controlled by these specialised teachers at the various levels of education. The responsibility for these research projects must lie with real experts in the field.
- Advising and training future generations of teachers and researchers, and providing specialised guidance to future professionals working on European issues. Teaching about how to search for reliable and truthful information is also vital in a highly globalised society where not all information is sufficiently proven and where good teachers representing the Union can teach these methods for the acquisition of knowledge.

But the enumeration of all the activities mentioned above, which can be considered as discretionary objectives, does not seem to be sufficient to define the position of a Jean Monnet Professor. In this sense, we believe that, in order to limit this search, it is also necessary to mention the set of activities (imperatives) to be carried out by the aforementioned professors, assuming a dichotomy between teachers. Thus, for example, it is a pleasant surprise to see that teachers can carry out activities and give lessons to students from other branches of knowledge. In other words, the Jean Monnet Chairholder can give classes to students in architecture, medicine, pharmacy, engineering, etc., so that these students can obtain training and information on the process of European integration in all its facets. This can be of the greatest use to them in the further development of their future professional lives.

There is, in fact, a somewhat mistaken concept of an education promoted by the European Union, as it is not only jurists who must understand what the European Union means for society. Rather, it is open to all the orientations and specialities of science. In fact, all branches of labour are susceptible to being involved, to a greater or lesser extent, because of the legislative changes that take place in their respective environments and are caused by the normal mechanisms of the functioning of a supranational organisation such as the Union. This highlights the enormous importance of bringing all citizens closer to the various matters that affect its scope.

2 Obligations

The following are among the many other obligations of a Jean Monnet Professor:

- They should pursue the publication of books and scientific articles in specialised journals and in the university press in order to achieve greater dissemination of the contents, during the period in which they benefit from the Chair, which covers part of the publication costs and, in various cases, the translation costs. Some of these publications necessarily must deal with the European Union or the integration process, which means that there must be a minimum reference to the activities related to the Chair. The Jean Monnet Professor is also required to produce publications including information or the divulgation of content on the European Union.
- They should carry out initiatives in favour of political innovation. This will be done by stimulating the development of policies and testing to enable the public authorities to act with remarkable effectiveness. A Jean Monnet Professor should also support European policy instruments, thus facilitating transparency and the recognition of competences and qualifications. The ultimate aim of these policies is to promote assurance, learning, skills and advice.
- They should organise events of all kinds (conferences, seminars, workshops, etc.) with policy makers at the local (e.g. mayors and councillors may participate here), regional and national levels, involving structured civil society groups and schools. In order to work towards the goals of regional integration, the visibility and importance of the events organised could be beneficial. To this end, it is helpful to count on the presence and participation of various political positions, which consolidate their image and make them closer to society.
- They must disseminate and share the results of their activities through the organisation of events, whose modalities we have already mentioned, but which are adapted to the public to which they are addressed in each specific case, to the general public and to representatives of civil society. The possible discoveries made by a Jean Monnet Chairholder can become, in the future, a very useful teaching tool for other teachers, hence the importance of disseminating information about their discoveries.
- They should collaborate and network with other Jean Monnet Chairs and coordinators of modules, centres of excellence and institutions supported by the European Commission, within or outside the Jean Monnet Programme. A networked society now has greater access to information, which teachers use to disseminate their knowledge to a greater number of people located in different parts of the world.

Jean Monnet Chairholders cannot limit their activity to conventional teaching, but are expected to offer different resources or open educational media and to integrate open education activities. The aim of these methods is to increase the flexibility and accessibility of quality education. It is not enough to be content with old-fashioned teaching: Technology offers new ways of teaching and locations where didactic activities can easily be developed. The medium of telematics greatly favours dynamics and teaching.

- There are also Jean Monnet teaching modules and various Jean Monnet Associations which are responsible for providing spaces for teaching specialised in the knowledge of the European Union, as it is sometimes difficult to find the ideal place to carry out activities. As a result, locations where scholars can hold conferences, lectures, study days, seminars, round tables, etc. are easily accessible.
- Support for the Associations: These specialised professors are supported by the European Union through the Jean Monnet Programme itself and by the European Associations which, at the level of each member country and even of third countries, are spread throughout the continents and are made up of scholars who study the phenomenon of European integration. On various occasions, these professors will need facilities to enable them to go to other universities, publish in magazines, organise seminars, etc.
- It is also enriching for the academic world for broad debates in the scientific world to be enhanced. To this end, there are computer or online scenarios such as Jean Monnet Networks or Jean Monnet Projects. Through these platforms, Jean Monnet Professors can initiate and carry out debates in the academic field with the aim of enriching and improving knowledge on matters of European integration.

3 Criteria for the Award of the Jean Monnet Chairs

The legal entities which can apply in order to host a Jean Monnet Chair include the following: Any higher education institution (HEI), regardless of the country in which the institution is located. HEIs from the EU must have obtained the Higher Erasmus Charter (ECHE). HEIs of partner countries are not subject to this requirement. It is important to remember that applications from individuals are not accepted.

The Jean Monnet Chairholders must be members of the staff of the applicant institution and must be university professors. Visiting or adjunct professors are not eligible for these Chairs. This requirement can be replaced by an age-related one, since, as stated earlier, in order to apply for the Jean Monnet Chair, it is absolutely necessary to have a remarkable curriculum vitae and to demonstrate the dedication of many years to the study of the subject of European integration in such a way that a high degree of qualification in the field has been achieved. Finally, as already indicated, the Chair's period of activity lasts 3 years. However, if the teachers continue to carry out their own tasks for more years than initially planned in the project of action within the framework of the Chair, and they are able to finance the different activities that they organise, then they may continue to use the name of the Jean Monnet Chair for the development of their work on European integration. Furthermore, the scholars are entitled to hold the title of Jean Monnet Professor in the performance of their duties in the context of the university in which they hold the position of professor, belonging to the various bodies of teaching staff, in accordance with the internal regulations of their country. In any case, the application containing the project of each teacher applying for the competition must be submitted to the Education, Audiovisual and Culture Executive Agency, whose headquarters is in Brussels.

The purpose of the Jean Monnet Chairs is not limited simply to their direct circle of influence or activity, but also to disseminating and making use of the results of the tasks and actions carried out and organised beyond the parties directly involved. In order to achieve this impact, the holders of the Chair must include within their activities the offer of educational resources in accordance with technological progress. Creativity can thus be developed and expanded, and can reach out to a wider range of stakeholders.

The Chairholders are also obliged to update their working tools and some of their publications online in a timely manner using the Erasmus + platform, where all the known information on the various activities carried out by the numerous Jean Monnet Chairs that are active and distributed throughout the world can be found.

4 Form of the Grant

The maximum possible funding is 50,000 euros, with a ceiling of 75% of the total cost of the Jean Monnet Chair.

In order to make it possible to award grants for Jean Monnet activities, a system based on a combination of scales of unit costs and funding at a fixed rate is applied that is determined on the basis of the calculation of the national hourly cost of education.

- Unit cost of teaching: This is the national unit cost of teaching calculated per hour, D.1, multiplied by the number of teaching hours of the Jean Monnet Chair.
- Funding: A maximum of 10% is added to the unit cost for a Jean Monnet Chair. This maximum percentage takes into account the additional academic activities included in a Chair, such as personnel costs, travel and subsistence, dissemination costs, teaching materials, etc. As mentioned earlier, it is possible that the European Commission and the various European associations of a national nature in the field of studies on European integration (ECSA) could provide support for the activities of a Jean Monnet Professor.

The final grant is thus obtained by applying the maximum funding from the European Union, which is 75% of the total amount calculated, and respecting the ceiling set for a Jean Monnet Chair (EUR 50,000). It is not possible to finance anything in excess of this figure, thus implying possible private or third-party financing. If you wish to carry out activities that exceed the indicated amount, only interested third parties with available capital can make this possible by contributing toward implementing the corresponding project or projects that a Jean Monnet Professor intends to carry out in the context of his or her Chair.

5 Call for Proposal 2017/2018

For this year, 2018, the publication of the calls for proposals took place on 25 October 2017; the deadline for submission was 22 February 2018 (12 a.m., Brussels time).

The evaluation period is 5 months, i.e. the allocation of the place is not immediate. The applicants must wait until July 2018, so there are still a few months until the results are known. Beginning on 1 September (which coincides with the beginning of the academic year), the aspiring professors, selected in the open competition within which they submitted their various projects to be carried out in their respective universities, will be able teach their courses and perform the programmed activities with the title of Jean Monnet Professor.

6 Conclusion

Consequently, and after all that we have said and considered about the figure and status of Jean Monnet Chairholder, we can conclude that Jean Monnet Professors can indeed be of great use to European society as advisers of several institutions of the European Union. Their advanced and privileged skills on the functioning of the European Union make them a broad and exclusive source of knowledge within the labour market. Generally speaking, as we indicated at the beginning of this paper, what most interests Jean Monnet professors is the knowledge of the process of European integration. It is an ambitious process that continues to be an objective which the Union wishes to achieve and exploit in all its breadth. At the same time, it represents a paradigmatic mirror through which many other and varied integration processes that are taking place or are being attempted at the global level can be seen.

Journalist

Belén Andrés Segovia

1 The Advent of the New Radio and Television

In European Comparative Law, new communication formulas that combine the management of public services with private services are beginning to be observed. Evidence of this is the English Law of 1954, which was pronounced upon the public broadcaster of the *British Broadcasting Corporation* (hereinafter BBC), together with another entity of public origin, the *Independent Broadcasting Authority* (hereinafter IBA). The objective of both organisations was to carry out the execution of television programmes produced by public companies that, at the same time, were financed through commercial advertising by private entities. This revolution in the world of communication would take up to 30 years to grow after its approval by the different member states of continental Europe.

The first reason for 'liberalisation' in this venue is represented by the dissemination of the contents through the cable network and by the diffusion of the contents through the cable network. The options that were provided in relation to the privatisation were several. The first one is referred to the mode of transmission. Among the countries that adopted this form of communication were Switzerland, Denmark, France and Great Britain, where they used thousands of meters of cable in order to guarantee the liberalisation of radio and television (i.e., terrestrial and cable). Secondly, there were territories that only applied this formula to radio broadcasts, such as Sweden. Thirdly, other countries, such as Norway and the Netherlands, applied this method for radio and television: broadcasted only by cable.

Regarding the level of diffusion, only the first list of private broadcasts used the propagation of private broadcasts via local channels, while in the others favoured the possibility of promoting private initiatives at a national level, such as: France,

B. Andrés Segovia (✉)
Dpto. Derecho Administrativo y Procesal, Universitat de Valencia Campus de Tarongers, Valencia, Spain
e-mail: Belen.Andres@uv.es

A. Bartolini et al. (eds.), *Dictionary of Statuses within EU Law*,
https://doi.org/10.1007/978-3-030-00554-2_44

Germany, Great Britain and Italy. The emergence of private television channels in Spain, with a view to the European Union (EU)—promoted by the jurisprudence and materialised *de facto* by the legislator after the approval of La Ley 46/1983 on the 26th of December, regulating the third television channel—was initially produced within a basic regulatory framework that allowed private entities to access the communications market, as long as they obtained the concession title, which was appropriate to the administrative procedure. This measure of an administrative nature is presumed because the radio spectrum is unlimited; therefore, the free establishment of a channel without prior control could not be allowed.

However, we reaffirm the idea of 'apparent' because the jurisprudential and normative responses should not be made to wait. This fact evidenced the problems that the EU audiovisual sector suffered, which could be summarised in the following three ways. Firstly, there is a clear *normative dispersion*. The existence of a multiplicity of laws that regulated the different facets of the audiovisual causes a *legal insecurity* among those who are part of the sector. That fact is evidenced by the large number of juxtaposed laws, which made up the audiovisual regulatory framework until 2010. Secondly, there is an *absence of a harmonic audiovisual model*. The existing laws in this period, regarding the audiovisual sector, took the opportunity. In other words, it becomes the answer given by the legislator for new technological advances, which in many cases were more dynamic than regulatory. Thirdly, there is *a lack of system between the legislation, caused by technological advances*. The continuous innovations have arisen from responding to new innovation has led to the approval of various audiovisual laws in a disorderly manner.

In some cases, some texts have been repealed in favour of others, which try to introduce new legislation but do not match the existing audiovisual landscape; therefore it becomes difficult to interpret them. This supposes that sometimes it has been necessary to resort to doctrinal opinions with the purpose of supplying the deficiencies that the constant evolution has reflected in the normative framework. The evidence of this is provided by the audiovisual services that broadcast their content through the cable. Consequently, the regulatory excess that is displayed in a disorderly manner may imply a violation of the principle of effective judicial protection of the different radio and television operators, since the judicial branch does not have clear references for clear parameters to proceed and protect the rights of the different agents.

2 Legislative Recasting of the Audiovisual Media Service Directive

The insufficiency of a clear regulatory framework results in the three questions that have been raised, which will find a response by the legislator—through which the harmonisation of *economy* and *technique* is allowed—and become decisive in order to understand the current audiovisual situation.

From the EU, it was specified, on the one hand, the need to regulate an audiovisual framework in which the new communicative methods had emerged from the *technique*. The new communicative methods had not yet adopted a clear legislature due to their characteristics, or they had not been considered as a means of audiovisual communication—for example, videogames. On the other hand, the need to confront the economic analysis of the new audiovisual reality results in a very meticulous task; in fact, it is observed how the new means of communication are crossing borders and sometimes arouses the interest of several territories. However, in many cases, the curiosity of several of them may occur.

In order to respond to these two premises, the Directive of audiovisual communication services proposes a new audiovisual legal framework, in which not only radio and television will be included but also a number of other existing mediums will be able to expand and venture towards other means of social communication. According to Section 23 of the Directive of audiovisual communication services, 'the term "audiovisual" should refer to moving images, accompanied or not by sound'. Moreover, audiovisual is a *numerus apertus* concept that implies that it can be extended to new formats, such as: videogames, the online press, television, radio and the Internet, as well as other media that acquire the digital format.

3 The New Digital Scene: The Technological Convergence and the Breaking of the Correspondence Between Media and Services

So far, we have dealt with the problems that arose from the exercise of freedom of speech and information, in terms of the different media used or those that can be defined as social or conventional media (e.g., the press, radio and television). In order to give an account of this communicative and social reality, very diffuse terms have been used, such as the conversion of the 'old media', which now come together alongside the 'new media' (i.e., media that provide us with the technological development). It is for this reason that we can only consider as a preliminary point the fact that has been raised from innovation and the consequent phenomenon of technological convergence, which allows the use of a medium in order to proceed to the diffusion of a variety of services.

This definition, which was unthinkable prior to the Directive on communication services, has broken the existing relationship between media and services: a relationship that had been traditionally conceived and one that set up the regulation systems of the media, according to the support that was carrying it. For its part and in particular, innovation has led the phenomenon we call technological convergence to a transformation of the audiovisual scene, represented by the relationship between media and services, which has marked the crisis of the traditional idea of media infrastructure and set its current regulatory framework as a 'Media Law'. This theory is the consequence of the sum that composes strategic planning of standards in the sector, in a few, in order to gradually change the right of the convergence of the media, in which, the role of the Internet is preponderant if we pay attention to a previous visualisation with general character, of the audiovisual scene and with partial character, the current legislation.

The convergence presumed in these aspects is the result of the disintegration of different technologies. In the communicative scene, new technological combinations have arisen, thus, inviting us to be bold in the way in which electronic media is regulated. Computers and digital media have been integrated with broadcasting and television systems understood in their traditional sense. All of this is a consequence of the Internet becoming available in television sets, as well as computers and handheld devices; thus, in essence, the distinctions between broadcasting and cyberspace have been blurred.

4 Definition of the Internet as a New Audiovisual Structure

The approval of the Communication Services Directive allows us to further delimit the area of action of those considered as new media. In doing so, we could classify the Internet as a new form of media, which would reinforce our reasoning as of why we should interpret the Internet as a medium of audiovisual communication—based on the following five reasons.

The first reason is that the Internet is a service of an economic nature. The Internet service is a profit-making service. We could reason that the different web links and private Internet services consist of the sharing or distribution of certain contents that users consume, despite being outside the area of the Directive; thus, it is an additional part of the audiovisual content. We cannot include, in this sense, the search engines because their purpose is not to offer a global vision of the contents but simply ways of investigation. What really motivates its interpretation is that the Internet has skills in radio and television matters and subsumes them; thus, in doing so, its provision shares economic interests.

The second reason is the existence of an editorial responsibility. The service is subject to an effective supervision and control system that allows the selection of programmes during the exploration of diverse content. However, there is a point-to-point transmission. In other words, we can find on the Internet a catalogue of contents resulting from the liberalisation of the service, which allows us the access to multiple channels through the same network. It is at this last point, where editorial responsibility acquires a certain importance—as it refers to a specific investigation in order to observe—on whom the duty of effective control falls: the time of transmission of the message or the origin or opportunity of the content offered. In this sense, from the EU, control techniques of this content are established through independent authorities of regulation of State origin and new directives that regulate the way to proceed before rights are violated on the Internet.

The third reason is that we must address to main point. The idea of service that is inherent in the media does not cover the accidental and marginal concept of audiovisual content. In order to be considered in this category, they must be on the platform with assiduous and changing character since, otherwise, they may be considered as mere advertising sites.

The fourth reason hinges on the fact that we must address the programmes' broadcast. That is to say, the Internet must transmit a set of moving images, with or without sound, which constitutes an individual element within an schedule or an established catalogue by the publisher and whose form and content are comparable to those of television broadcasts. This technique is intuited as prescriptive but insufficient, since it must be completed with information that constitutes *entertaining and educating the viewer*. From the Internet, it is relevant to combine the technique with the content.

The final reason why we should interpret the Internet as a medium of audiovisual communication is subject to the fact that we must address the existence of a receiver, without whom the communication would not be possible. A closed circle of communication, where the existence of a recipient of the message is not perceived, would have no place as a means of communication. It is for this reason that the idea that on the Internet the public, in general, can become a potential consumer of the contents that are broadcast is valued. The existence of these five premises, together with the arguments previously made, make us understand that the Internet is a means of communication. Such determination is very relevant because it allows us to observe the broad regulatory legal framework that is proper to this sector. Without such framework the Internet would become a legal jungle, where its users would be left unprotected in any external illicit attack, which could easily shake today's society [See in particular, Carotti (2016), pp. 24–30].

5 Conclusion

In the past, the possibility of imparting information to a mass audience has been to a greater extent the privilege that was given to those who participated in the media, such as: the press, radio and television. The traditional media, thus, enjoy certain privileges that we announced at the beginning of this chapter, which, to a certain extent, help to observe the correct use of discourse but are also subject to greater duties and responsibilities. However, the impact of this development on their rights to freedom of expression is far from being fully explored. In the exercise of the search for the balance between freedom of expression on the Internet and traditional media, it has been conceptualised by Oster (2017) in the following terms.

5.1 Conflicting Interests

The content of the message that the sender wishes to transmit will be considered in order to guarantee its origin. If the intention is the violation of rights (e.g., honour, privacy and self-image), the appropriate measures should be adopted in order to guarantee the cessation of said publications on the net. When this data is issued through the network, we must consider, from the perspective of the EU Law, the Regulation (EU) 2016/679 of the European Parliament and of the Council, of 07 April 2016, regarding the protection of individuals with regard to the processing of personal data and the free circulation of this data and by which Directive 95/46/EC (hereinafter General Data Protection Regulation) is repealed.

This norm has been built on the basis of a few technical certainties that the new digital era brings. Consequently, it is determined to regulate an uncertain technological future, so the large number of indeterminate legal concepts that are foreseen in its text are intended to adjust to the various scenarios that advances may make; thus, it provides the maximum possible flexibility in its regulation. This also creates a legal uncertainty that has its basis in self-regulation as an alternative to legislation and previous unforeseen circumstances. This principle collides with the bases that show what is not regulated and what is not prohibited.

Consequently, there is a legal uncertainty that is shown in favour of the technical innovations that are happening. In this way, given the obvious impossibility of foreseeing specific guidelines based on the dynamic technological evolution, the legislator has foreseen a *numerus apertus* of possible regulated equipment through self-regulation. Finally, from criminal law, this branch of law also has the support of the community law through Directive (EU) 2016/680 of the European Parliament and of the Council of 27 April 2016 on the protection of individuals with regard to the processing of personal data by the regulating authorities for the purposes of prevention, investigation, detection or prosecution of criminal offenses or the execution of criminal sanctions and the free movement of such data.

5.2 Internet Users vs. Journalists

The expression through the Internet does not convert its author nor does it presume the professional status of the information. That is why they are not automatically granted the privileges of journalists when they provide their information through traditional media. This category will be presumed only for individuals or non-journalistic organisations that publish issues of public interest and follow the rules of diligence when collecting and disseminating information and ideas, that is, in accordance with the principle of the guarantee of truthful information.

5.3 *Versatility*

The new communicative scenario establishes the need to legislate, above all, uncertainty and complexity. This idea is based on versatility. That is to say, the need to adapt the emerging legal regulations that have caused the regulation of gender violence through the new technologies that are increasing will have to overco3rrme the different obstacles of the technique since the legal fact is almost obsolete and moving towards new regulatory needs.

To summarise, the meaning that is extrapolated from the understanding of the Internet as a new communicative formula is nourished by its own logic and semantics, which is different from what is conventionally granted to the press, television and radio. This vision can provoke two reactions, either the constitution of a new ideology or, when applicable, the modification of certain existing points of view. Consequently, the freedom of expression of ideas and information through the Internet should no longer be understood in absolute terms, as was the case with the rest of the media, since it is a support in itself. However, we must also pay attention to, as we have emphasised, the implications that this new reality has for the legal order in order to respond to the different conflicts that have arisen and prevent further violations of rights.

References

Carotti, B. (2016). Il sistema di Governo di Internet. In S. Cassese (Ed.), *Saggi di Diritto amministrativo* (pp. 24–30). Milano: Giuffrè.

Oster, J. (2017). *European and international media law*. Cambridge, UK: Cambridge University Press.

Landowner

Ana María De la Encarnación

1 Concept

A proprietor is an owner (a natural or legal person) who has the right to possess, use and convey something; a person in whom one or more interests are vested. This is directly related to the right to property.

2 The Right to Property Under the EU Law

According to Black's Law Dictionary, property is the right to possess, use and enjoy a determinate thing, either a tract of land or a chattel.

European Union Law recognises and protects the right to private property as a fundamental one.

Section 2 of the Declaration of the Rights of Man and of the Citizen (1789) placed the right to property in the privileged group of the natural and imprescriptible rights of man (Barcelona Llop 2011). However, in spite of the fact that section 17 of the Declaration remarked that the right to property was inviolable and sacred, its deprivation was, nevertheless, admitted, "*lorsque la nécessité publique, légalement constatée, l'exige evidemment, et sous la condition d'une juste et préalable indemnité*". From then on, conceptions about property rights have undergone an important development. However, the guarantee of this right to property and the possibility of its deprivation, which is necessarily subject to certain conditions and requirements, go hand in hand in every fundamental text.

A. M. De la Encarnación (✉)
Administrative School of Law, University of Valencia, Valencia, Spain
e-mail: ana.maria.encarnacion@uv.es

A. Bartolini et al. (eds.), *Dictionary of Statuses within EU Law*,
https://doi.org/10.1007/978-3-030-00554-2_45

Nevertheless, it was not until the First Protocol to the European Convention on Human Rights that the right to property was incorporated (section 1) into the catalogue of the convention (Barnes 1996, p. 125). Latterly, the Charter of Fundamental Rights of the European Union (2009) strengthens the protection of the fundamental rights, whose Article 17 has expressly established the right to property in the EU.

Hence, despite the absence of a codified and legally binding catalogue of fundamental rights under the so-called Primary EU Law, and the apparent exclusion of community interference over private property (Art. 295 of the Treaty establishing the European Community), one can witness the slow development of certain aspects of the right of private property under the EU legal system over the last decades. One of the main causes refers to the case law of the Court of Justice of the European Communities by means of the flexible interpretation of the abovementioned section 295, but above all, thanks to the consideration of the right to property as a general principle of the EU (Stauder 1969).

Consequently, the EU must respect, in the public intervention on citizens' property, the content of the right to property as interpreted by the European Court of Human Rights (ECHR) and recognised in the European Convention on Human Rights and in the national constitutions. In fact, the constitutions of the member states are based on the same basis as the European Convention: social function, subordination to the general interest, respect for the principle of proportionality, guarantees for the expropriation, etc.

2.1 Section 1 of the First Protocol to the European Convention on Human Rights

Section 1 of this Protocol provides that every natural or legal person is entitled to the peaceful enjoyment of his/her possessions. No one shall be deprived of his/her possessions except in the public interest and subject to the conditions provided for by law and by the general principles of international law. The preceding provisions shall not, however, in any way impair the right of a state to enforce such laws as it deems necessary to control the use of property in accordance with the general interest or to secure the payment of taxes or other contributions or penalties. Thanks to this recognition of private property, every ownership is protected against any arbitrary type of expropriation or deprivation of property.

As can be seen, section 1 uses the word 'possession' rather than property. Possession has been widely defined in the decisions of the ECHR. It includes all acquired rights, including immaterial rights, an interest in land, such as the entitlement to rent and the benefit of a restrictive covenant (S. v The United Kingdom, 1984).

The purpose of section 1 was first spelt out in the Marckx judgement (Marckx 1979), which declared that 'by recognising that everyone has the right to the peaceful enjoyment of his possessions, Article 1 is in substance guaranteeing the right of property'. This *obiter dictum* makes it possible to extend the section's scope to guaranteeing the right to property *per se*, and not simply protecting owners against arbitrary confiscation, which was the focus of the *travaux préparatoires* and of the Commission's first decisions (Sermett 1998).

The conditions for application of section 1 were later defined in the principal decision of the ECHR, *Sporrong and Lönnroth v. Sweden* (1984) judgement. The Court said that section 1 contains three distinct rules related to interferences with the right to property. The first rule, which is of a general nature, enounces the principle of peaceful enjoyment of property; it is set out in the first sentence of the first paragraph. The second rule covers deprivation of possessions and subjects it to certain conditions; it appears in the second sentence of the same paragraph. The third rule recognises that the states are entitled, amongst other things, to control the use of property in accordance with the general interest, by enforcing such laws as they deem necessary for the purpose; it is contained in the second paragraph (James 1986; Allan 1984; The Holy Monasteries 1994). The second and third rules need to be interpreted in the light of the first rule (Lithgow 1981).

Therefore, in order to confirm whether an action is contrary to what is established in section 1 of the Protocol, it is required to determine the factual assumption regarding where it should be included (Barnes 1996, p. 127). The European Court of Justice distinguishes between two different interventions on this right:

On one side, the *delimitation* of its content without a right to be compensated. The case law of the Court of Justice establishes that the right to property does not entail an absolute prerogative to his/her owner, because due to the so-called social function its exercise may be restricted or limited, provided that such limitations effectively meet the general interest pursued by the EU, and without providing an excessive and intolerable intervention that harms the very essence of the right to property (Booker Aquaculture 2003). On the other side is the deprivation of the domain and the required compensation (Utrilla Fernández-Bermejo 2010).

Therefore, when it comes to an interference that constitutes a complete deprivation of the right, we are facing a compensable expropriation. However, if it is a state intervention that constitutes a mere delimitation of the exercise of the right, then it is a called 'control of the use of property'; then, it is not compensable (Agosi 1986).

Nevertheless, these types of interference with property must be subject to certain principles, namely, lawfulness (Carss-Frisk 2001, p. 8), public interest and proportionality. Regarding the legality of the interference, this requisite is expressly stated in the first paragraph of section 1 of the abovementioned Protocol, where it is established that a deprivation of property must be subject to the conditions provided for by law. Even though this principle of legality is indeed inherent in the European Convention on Human Rights as a whole, it must be complied with whichever of the three rules of section 1 applies.

In terms of the public interest, the ECHR leaves it to the states to determine the meaning of the so-called 'public interest', since the State is more familiar with the potential characteristics of its system, applicable regimes, political and social conditions.

The principle of proportionality implies that the individual human rights holder must not be burdened excessively. This means that any measure against the right to property must also be proportionate; it is necessary to consider whether any interference with property strikes a fair balance between the protection of the right to property and the requirement of the general interest. Such a fair balance will not have been struck where the individual property owner is made to bear 'an individual and excessive burden' (Sporrong 1984).

2.2 The Expropriation of Property (Section 1.1 of the First Protocol)

Expropriation is the procedure, granted by the law-maker, by means of which the acquiring authority (state, government, etc.) may require a private individual (landowner) or a legal entity (corporation) to transfer the ownership of a private asset, based on the public utility purpose previously established and by means of an adequate and timely indemnity (compensation). This property will be used for the public benefit. This measure is a complete deprivation of property, which produces the loss of the right to its holder; therefore, temporary dispossession cannot be regarded as deprivation, but constitutes control of the use of property, as established in Handyside.

As provided under section 1 of the First Protocol, the deprivation (expropriation) of private property is lawful, provided that it is carried out for reasons of general interest, by means of compensation and in accordance with due process,[1] in the public interest and the individual human rights holder must not be burdened excessively (principle of proportionality). In this regard, state parties to the convention enjoy a certain margin of appreciation, only limited by a reasonableness test. The margin of appreciation gives states a certain degree of freedom as to how to comply with their obligations under the ECHR. While this approach is less invasive towards the states which are obliged under the European Convention, this freedom of course is not unproblematic in that it offers states the possibility to limit the scope of the human rights already guaranteed by the convention. However, this margin of appreciation is not an absolute norm. In fact, there is an alternative to the wide margin of appreciation afforded by the convention organs to the member states. Actually, a fundamentally opposite approach to interpreting the convention exists, which has likewise been endorsed by the ECHR and the old Commission—the notion of autonomous concepts. Rather than arguing that existing differences of opinion between the member states would require giving the states a wide margin of appreciation, the convention organs have often taken the opportunity to provide for the definition of certain terms within the context of the convention by establishing the so-called 'autonomous concepts' (Letsas 2004). Autonomous concepts were cre-

[1] See the entry 'Expropriated party' in this book.

ated first by the Commission and are still used by the Court 'to prevent contracting states from circumventing the convention guarantees'.

It is upon the ECHR to declare if the duties, restrictions or burdens that, by virtue of the so-called social function established by the states constitute a deprivation of the right to property, in the light of section 1 of the Protocol and, consequently, if there is a duty to compensate this burden. In *James (1986)*, the ECHR concluded that the taking of property in the public interest without payment of compensation is treated as justifiable only in exceptional circumstances. As far as section 1 is concerned, the protection of the right to property would be largely 'illusory and ineffective in the absence of any equivalent principle. Clearly, compensation terms are material to the assessment whether the contested legislation respects a fair balance between the various interests at stake and, notably, whether it does not impose a disproportionate burden on the applicant (…)'.

2.3 Control of the Use of Property (Section 1.2 of the First Protocol)

The third rule (in the second paragraph of section 1 of the First Protocol) applies when an interference with property is intended or is part of a legislative scheme whose purpose is to control the use of property (Sporrong 1984; Pine Valley 1991; Mellacher 1989). The European Convention institutions have sought to ensure that any interference with property rights pursues the general or public interest. States also that control concerns the use of property. In practice, it may also concern the right to dispose of property. Thus, the Commission has decided that restrictions on freedom of contract in respect of tenancies can constitute control of the use of property (Carss-Frisk 2001, p. 25). A measure falls within this rule if its main aim is for the State to control the use of property, be it in the general interest (Grgiæ et al. 2007, p. 5).

Therefore, when there is an interference on the right to property of a citizen, which cannot be qualified as an expropriation since it does not produce a complete deprivation of the right, it will be a mere intervention over the property, in which its delimitation will be carried out. In *Handyside (1976)*, the authorities seized the applicant's book because it contained obscene images. Since the book had been seized only temporarily, the measure did not involve a deprivation of property, but instead fell to be examined under the third rule of section 1 of the First Protocol.

References

Barcelona Llop, J. (2011). Privación de la propiedad y expropiación forzosa en el sistema del Convenio Europeo de Derechos Humanos. *Revista de Administración Pública, 185*, 49–87.

Barnes, J. (1996). La jurisprudencia del Tribunal Europeo de Derechos Humanos sobre la propiedad privada. In E. Guichot Reina & J. Barnés (Eds.), *Propiedad, expropiación y responsabilidad: la garantía indemnizatoria en el Derecho europeo y comparado: Unión Europea, Convenio Europeo de Derechos Humanos, España, Alemania, Francia, Italia* (pp. 124–150). Madrid: Tecnos.

Carss-Frisk, M. (2001). Council of Europe, The right to property. A guide to the implementation of Article 1 of Protocol No. 1 to the European Convention on Human Rights. In *Human Rights Handbooks* (Vol. 4, p. 6 ff). Retrieved June 30, 2018, from https://rm.coe.int/168007ff4a

Grgiæ, A., Mataga, Z., Longar, M., & Vilfan, A. (2007). Council of Europe, The right to property under the European Convention on Human Rights. A guide to the implementation of the European Convention on Human Rights and its protocols. *Human Rights Handbooks*, 10. Retrieved June 30, 2018, from https://rm.coe.int/168007ff55

Letsas, G. (2004). The truth in autonomous concepts: How to interpret the ECHR. *European Journal of International Law, 15*(2), 279–305.

Sermett, L. (1998). The European Convention on Human Rights and property rights. *Human Rights Files, 11*, 7–55.

Utrilla Fernández-Bermejo, D. (2010). La garantía patrimonial ante actos normativos lícitos en Derecho Comunitario: entre la responsabilidad patrimonial objetiva y el derecho de propiedad. *Revista de Administración Pública, 181*, 219–235.

Lawyer

Reyes Marzal Raga

1 Introduction

EU law does not establish a harmonized concept of a lawyer, and the scope of the concept comes from the internal legislation of each Member State, which establishes not only the academic training leading to the corresponding qualification but also the set of attributes that the legal system confers on lawyers in that state. However, in line with the principle of freedom of movement of persons and services between the Member States (hereinafter referred to as MS), which is one of the objectives of the EU, there is a harmonized regulation regarding the exercise of the profession of a lawyer when it takes place in a Member State (hereinafter referred to as the other Member State) other than that in which the professional qualification has been obtained.

Freedom of establishment requires it to be possible to participate in a stable and continuous way in the economic life of a host MS. This implies that nationals of an MS have the right to exercise a profession, whether they are employed or self-employed, in any other MS.

The EU regulatory framework is established under Directive 77/249/EEC (March 22). This Directive is meant to facilitate the effective exercise by lawyers of the principle of freedom to provide services. It was the first Directive to recognize the status of a lawyer, and allowed the provision of legal services in another MS, although not permanently. Afterwards, Directive 98/5/EC (February 16) aimed to facilitate the permanent practice of the law in another MS.

Another legal provision related to this matter is Directive 89/48/EEC (December 21), which deals with the general system for the recognition of higher education qualifications of more than three years that certify the right to practise a profession.

R. Marzal Raga (✉)
Administrative Law Department, University of Valencia, Valencia, Spain
e-mail: Reyes.Marzal@uv.es

A. Bartolini et al. (eds.), *Dictionary of Statuses within EU Law*,
https://doi.org/10.1007/978-3-030-00554-2_46

In accordance with this provision, an MS may recognize a degree for the exercise of certain professions, although it may require complementary measures (e.g. an internship) when this requirement does not exist in the state of origin or when the conditions for access to the profession are well known to be different.

This regulatory framework has been challenged before the CJEU, which has stated that it is in accordance with the fundamental principles of the EU.

2 The Status of a Lawyer as a Provider of Professional Legal Services

Directive 77/249/EEC, mentioned above, defines a 'lawyer' as any person entitled to exercise professional activities under the name established by his own state. The recognized names in some of the MS are the following: Belgium: *avocat/advocaat*; Denmark: *advokat*; Federal Republic of Germany: *Rechtsanwalt*; France: *avocat*; Ireland: *barrister, solicitor*; Italy: *avvocato*; Luxembourg: *avocat-avoué*; the Netherlands: *advocat*; the United Kingdom: *barrister, solicitor*. The correspondence between these designations has been extended to those countries that joined the EU after 1977, such as Spain (where lawyers are known as *abogados-abogadas*), or Portugal (*advogados*).

2.1 Access Requirements to the Legal Profession

The EU lawmaker wanted the Member States themselves to establish the name and content of the profession of a lawyer. Thus, MS have a wide discretion to define the scope of this concept by establishing the requirements for access to the legal profession and the changes to these over time, and to determine the scope of the competences that a lawyer can practise in that state.

For example, in Spain only those who have an academic degree in law, who professionally defend third parties in all kinds of procedures and who give legal advice (section 542, Ley Organica del Poder Judicial) are considered to be lawyers. However, lawyers are also required to join the Spanish bar association (Colegio de Abogados), provided that all the due requirements are fulfilled, devoting themselves to professional legal advice, mediation and the defence of the public or private legal interests of others (section 9.1, Real Decreto 658/2001 (June 22), approving the General Statute of Spanish Advocacy).

In France, lawyers are also required to join the appropriate bar association, in accordance with law n° 71-1130 (December 31). In addition, they must have had legal training in a university (a Master's degree in law) and have passed an exam (*certificat d'aptitude à la profession d'avocat*, CAPA) organized by the relevant body (usually the *Instituts d'études judiciaires des universités*). However, there are some exceptions: those holding a PhD in law are not required to pass the *certificat d'aptitude* exam. In addition, it is compulsory to undertake continuous training throughout one's professional life as a lawyer.

In Germany, the qualification to practise as a lawyer (*Rechtsanwalt*) requires the lawyer to pass different and very difficult tests, according to the *Bundesrechtsanwaltsordnung* (BRAO) or General Statute of the Law, and the lawyer is also obliged to undertake continuous training. In some *Länder* (Nordrhein-Westfalen, Bremen, Berlin) a lawyer can also be authorized to practice as a notary if they qualify as a notary-solicitor or *Anwaltsnotar*.

The MS are therefore entitled to establish the requirements for the access to and exercise of the profession of a lawyer, determining the concept of a lawyer. An example of the problem that this definition may give rise to can be found in the CJEU judgment issued in response to a request for a preliminary ruling presented by the *Symvoulio tis Epikrateias* (Greece) on July 17, 2017 (C-431/17). This judgment declared that an MS legislator was entitled to prohibit the registration of a Church of Greece monk as a lawyer in the records of the competent authority of an MS other than that in which the monk acquired his qualification. In accordance with national law, the monk could not join the bar association because, as a result of the special conditions applying to him, he did not comply with certain essential requisites for the practise of the legal profession.

However, it is not an abusive practice for a national of one MS to move to another MS to acquire a professional qualification as a lawyer, as long as he or she passes the necessary exams and returns to his or her own state to practise as a lawyer with the professional qualification obtained in the other MS (*Torresi*, C- 58/13 and 58/14, EU:C:2014:2088).

2.2 The Professional Competences of the Lawyer

Since there is no harmonization of professional competences, each MS will establish the activities that its lawyers can perform, so that the content of the professional activity may be different in each of the EU states.

The notion of 'the activity of a lawyer' encompasses not only the legal services typically provided by lawyers, such as the giving of legal advice or the representation and defence of a client before a court, but also other types of activities. Directive 77/249/EEC recognises a distinction between the legal services usually provided by lawyers, such as the giving of legal advice or the representation and defence of clients before the courts, and other activities such as the authentication of signatures, which, even though they may be performed by lawyers in some MS, can only be exercised by notaries in other MS, such as Spain (CJEU, 9 March 2017, Leopoldine Gertraud Piringer, C342/15, EU:C:2017:196).

Therefore, it is not contrary to the principle of freedom to provide services in the EU that an MS establishes the scope of the professional activity of a lawyer, and even exceptions on the grounds of public order or public health and safety, expressly referred to in Articles 51, 52 and 62 TFEU, may be allowed. Limitations may be justified provided they are not applied in a discriminatory manner, they are made for overriding reasons of general interest (Judgment of 28 January 2016, Laezza, C-375/14, EU:C:2016:60), and they are appropriate to guarantee the achievement of the objective pursued and do not go beyond what is necessary to achieve it (Judgment of 17 March 2011, Penarroja Fa, C-372/09 and C-373/09, EU:C:2011:156).

In addition, an MS regulation reserving different powers to different types of lawyer, such as the regulations in the United Kingdom and Ireland, is not contrary to EU law. These countries recognize the existence of different categories of lawyers, namely barristers and solicitors, who, in accordance with their national law, have exclusive competence to deal with certain legal instruments in the field of real estate law, while this competence belongs to notaries or the courts in other MS.

3 The Influence of EU Law on the Services of Professional Lawyers

The exercise of the profession of a lawyer requires the possession of a professional qualification, and enrolment in the appropriate legal body. EU law allows the harmonization of national legislation for the exercise of such professional activity, establishing a distinction between the permanent right to practice in an MS with an academic degree obtained in another state (Sect. 3.1 below), the right to practice for a fixed period of time using a qualification obtained in another state in order to be able to integrate into the latter (Sect. 3.2), and the possibility of the recognition of the qualification of the state of origin to obtain the title of lawyer in the host state (Sect. 3.3).

3.1 Permanent Practice of the Profession of a Lawyer in a Member State with a Professional Qualification from the State of Origin

EU law has achieved harmonization in the regulation of the requirements for practising as a lawyer, bringing to an end the inequalities and obstacles to the free movement of people and services.

Directive 98/5/EC establishes a unique requirement: due registration before the competent authority of the host MS. Any EU lawyer can practise his legal activities in any EU state, using his legal qualification. The only requirement is that he must submit to the competent authority of the host Member State a certification of registration received from the competent authority of the MS of origin. In these cases, the same professional activities can be carried out as could be carried out by a lawyer who is qualified as such in the host state, including giving advice on the national law of the host state. Directive 98/5/EC even permits the exercise of these rights by a group, when one or more lawyers belonging to a group in their country of origin wish to continue their activity as members of their group in the host country.

In all cases, lawyers must respect the professional and ethical rules of the host country, even if they are still subject to those of their country of origin, and will be subject to the disciplinary procedures of the host country (CJEU, 19 January 1988, Gullung As. 292/86).

3.2 *The Integration of a Lawyer Who Is Qualified in His Country of Origin Into the Profession of the Host State*

In accordance with Directive 98/5/EC, lawyers with professional qualifications obtained in their state of origin can be integrated into the profession of the host MS after completing a period of professional practice in the host MS. This is a different situation from that mentioned above because, in this case, lawyers with a qualification in the state of origin, after working for a period of 3 years as a lawyer, can obtain the professional qualification of the host state. This is an easier method of integration than the one established under Directive 89/48/EC and the special system of Directives concerning the recognition of professional qualifications.

3.3 *The Recognition of a Lawyer's Academic Degree Obtained in Another Member State Through the System of the Recognition of Professional Qualifications*

A lawyer in an EU Member State may request the recognition of his professional qualification obtained from another MS for the purpose of being recognized as a lawyer in the host state. This possibility is recognized in both Directives 2005/36/EC and Directive 2006/100/EC, which deal with the recognition of professional qualifications.

The lawyer is required to have joined the bar association of the state of origin. The CJEU (Judgment, February 3, 2011 (C-359/09), Fővárosi Ítélőtábla of the Republic of Hungary) has said that neither Directive 89/48/EEC nor Directive 98/5/EC go against the obligation 'registry with the Bar Association of the host Member State'. Both Directives 89/48 and 98/5 complement each other, offering European lawyers two possibilities to exercise his legal activities in a host MS with the professional qualification of this MS. The recognition of the academic degree from the state of origin requires an exam to be passed, although the host state may also require an internship period, plus joining the appropriate bar association.

4 Adaptation of the Directives to the Fundamental Principles of EU Law

4.1 Adaptation to the General Principle of Free Movement of People and Provision of Services

The provisions of Directive 98/5/EC are intended to facilitate the permanent practising as a lawyer in an MS other than that in which the academic degree was obtained, and seek to avoid obstacles to the free movement of persons and services, which is an essential objective of the EU.

According to the case law of the Court of Justice, the right of freedom to provide services (Art. 56 TFEU) that is given to nationals of an MS and, therefore, to citizens of the EU, includes the freedom to provide services 'passively'. In other words, there is freedom for the recipients of services to travel to another MS in order to make use of the services, without being hindered by restrictions (Judgment, September 24, 2013, Demirkan, C 221/11, EU:C:2013:583). It follows that Directive 77/249, having as its object the facilitation of the effective exercise by lawyers of the freedom to provide services, must be interpreted to mean that it is applicable both in the typical case of the lawyer who moves to provide his services in an MS other than that in which he is established, and in the case where there is no transfer of the professional, that is to say, when the recipient of the service travels from his MS of residence to another MS to benefit from the services provided by a lawyer established in the latter. However, it is contrary to the freedom of movement and provision of services by lawyers for national regulations to make the registration of a lawyer with a professional title from another MS subject to a prior check of language skills (Judgments September 19, 2006, Wilson, C-506/04, and Commission against Luxembourg, C-193/05), or to force these lawyers to present a certificate every year showing they are registered with the competent authority of their MS of origin (Judgment of 19 February September 2006, Commission against Luxembourg, C-193/05). However, Directive 98/5 does not preclude national legislation imposing an obligation to be a member of an entity such as the bar association in order to practise law as a qualified lawyer in the host MS.

4.2 Adaptation to the General Principle of Equality

It has been suggested that there is a lack of harmonization in Directive 98/5/EC, because there is a difference there between lawyers who exercise their profession in their country of origin and those who do so using a qualification from the host MS. The CJEU (Judgment of November 7, 2000 (Luxembourg/Parliament and Council, C-168/98, EU:C:2000:598)) has ruled that there is no discrimination in relation to practising as a lawyer, because someone with a professional qualification from his country of origin is subject to certain prohibitions, and certain obligations may also be imposed on him in relation to representation and defence procedures. Thus, the host MS may, from the scope of activity of the migrant lawyer who practises using his professional qualification from his state of origin, exclude the possibility of preparing instruments that qualify for the administration of the assets of someone who has died or related to the creation or transfer of real estate rights (Art. 5.2 Directive 98/5/EC).

Section 56 TFEU not only requires the elimination of any discrimination based on nationality to the detriment of the service provider established in another MS, but also removes any restriction on the freedom to provide services, even though the restriction applies without distinction to national service providers and those of the other Member States, if such a restriction may prevent a provider established in another MS from providing services similar to those that he can lawfully provide in that other MS (judgments of 18 July 2013, Citroën Belux, C-265/12, EU:C:2013:498, and of June 11, 2015, Berlington Hungary and others, C-98/14, EU:C:2015:386).

4.3 *Consumers' Rights*

The CJEU does not allow Directive 98/5/EC to infringe on consumers' rights or the proper administration of justice, to the extent that migrant lawyers who are practising under the professional qualification from their country of origin are obliged to do so under that qualification, so that the consumer is informed that the professional entrusted with the defence of their interests has not obtained their training in the host MS.

5 Conclusions

The process of European integration has not modified the traditional legal definition of the concept of lawyer, which is determined by the internal legislation of each EU country. There is still substantial divergence, both substantive and procedural, between the different legal systems. However, there is largely consensus in the requirement for prior legal studies (a Master's degree in law or equivalent), for passing an entrance exam and for joining the relevant bar association.

MS also retain a wide right to impose restrictions on the conditions under which a lawyer can practise in their territory (e.g. the reservation of the notarial function to notaries), although these restrictions cannot be discriminatory, and therefore contrary to EU law, and should be applied to every lawyer registered in the state, whether or not they have obtained their professional qualification in that state.

2. Practising as a lawyer has acquired a new range as a consequence of the integration in the EU, since the freedom of movement and provision of services guarantees the right of lawyers to practise in any EU Member State provided they possess a professional qualification issued in their country of origin. The freedom to provide

'passive' services (the freedom for recipients of services to travel to another MS in order to make use of the services) is protected and cannot be hindered by restrictions.

3. EU harmonization in relation to the practice of the profession of a lawyer ensures uniformity in the provision of professional activity. Administrative structures have been created, such as the Council of Lawyers of Europe (1960), an international non-profit association acting as a link between national bar associations and the EU. There is also the possibility of obtaining a European lawyer's ID.

LGBTIQ People

Francesco Bilotta

1 Introduction

The acronym LGBTIQ indicates different realities with a common history of exclusion and stigma against which people who call themselves lesbians, gays, bisexuals, transsexuals, intersexuals and queer/questioning have fought a battle for social recognition and legal protection (Slootmaeckers et al. 2016, pp. 7–8). This acronym refers simultaneously to sexual orientation (LGB), gender identity (T) and to the condition of a person who, due to a variation in sexual development from an anatomical, chromosomal, gonadal and/or hormonal point of view, has a biology that cannot be taken into consideration with reference to male/female binarism (I).

Finally, the Q sometimes refers to the term *queer*, which is used to overcome the "categorisations" related to the sexual sphere, gender and sexual orientation; sometimes, it refers to the term *questioning*, describing those whose self-discovery and experimentation with respect to their orientation and/or gender identity is under development. More and more, in place of the Q, there is the sign "+", which flags any other individual characteristic, not just those referring to the sexual sphere.

People belonging to each of these categories are part of socially excluded groups, created over time by the stratification of the social and legal rules that produce discrimination. It should be noted that these characteristics could be considered in connection with each other, in an intersectional logic (Taylor et al. 2010).

From a legal point of view, the characteristics mentioned (or their combination) produce different problems. For instance, the issue of access to marriage is very different if we consider it from the perspective of homosexual persons or from the perspective of trans people. Until a few years ago, homosexuals did not have the opportunity to see their relationships recognised by law. In 12 EU Member States, same-sex couples can now enter marriage, and in many other EU Member States,

F. Bilotta (✉)
Department of Legal Sciences, University of Udine, Udine, Italy
e-mail: francesco.bilotta@uniud.it

A. Bartolini et al. (eds.), *Dictionary of Statuses within EU Law*,
https://doi.org/10.1007/978-3-030-00554-2_47

they can be recognised as registered couples. After the transition, trans people, if they are heterosexual, do not have problems in marrying, except in those countries where the transition is not recognised by the registry office. In these countries, the trans persons suffer a double injury in their sexual sphere: in consideration of their own gender identity, they cannot legally live in the gender they have chosen; in consideration of their sexual orientation, they cannot marry, because they should marry a person who is legally of their same-sex (ECtHR, *Goodwin v. The United Kingdom*, no. 17488/90, Grand Chamber, 27 March 1996).

2 Is LGBTIQ Status Conceivable?

Defining sexual orientation, gender identity or the variation of sexual development "statuses" depends on our conception of status. Properly, the status is the set of rights and duties that qualify the juridical sphere of a person by virtue of a particular relationship with a social group (e.g. the family) or with society as a whole (e.g. the State). We also find the definition of "hidden" or "indirect" status. In this case, a personal characteristic (e.g. sexual orientation) or a person's life choices (e.g. founding a family outside of marriage) become relevant to the law, not to assigning the rights and duties that bind the person to a specific social group (Colcelli 2013), but occasionally to recognising some protections and sometimes even rights, or to providing special rules that allow to those with certain characteristics to acquire the status in the proper sense (e.g. the status of spouse, or the status of refugee or the status of worker for homosexual persons). Thus, sexual orientation, gender identity or a variation of sexual development could be considered, at most, "hidden" or "indirect" statuses.

A legal policy consideration could lead us to the same conclusion. One of the purposes of the liberation movements is to make personal characteristics irrelevant with regard to the assignment of rights and duties. If these characteristics even became a status in the proper sense, a special right would be created, which would be a legal segregation (Bilotta 2005).

3 LGBTI Issues and Legal History

For the first time, the Treaty of Amsterdam (1997) made explicit reference to sexual orientation with the provision of art. 6a. Subsequently, art. 10 TFEU (after the Lisbon Treaty, 2007) specified the relevant risk factors for the definition of European policies, including sexual orientation. Furthermore, art. 19 TFEU entrusts to the Council the task of taking measures to combat discrimination, including that based on sexual orientation. This competence was used with the adoption of Council Directive 2000/78/EC (*Employment Equality Directive*). A general prohibition of discrimination based on sexual orientation is provided by art. 21 of the Charter of Nice.

Several resolutions of the EU Parliament have addressed this personal characteristic. Lastly, the Resolution on the EU Roadmap against homophobia and discrimination on the grounds of sexual orientation and gender identity, adopted in 2013 (based on *Lunacek Report*, P7_TA(2014) 0062, 4 February 2014), should be mentioned.

According to the latest Report of the Fundamental Rights Agency in 2014, 13 States have extended the Racial Equality Directive to include sexual orientation covering all areas of life, while seven EU Member States still limit protection against discrimination based on sexual orientation to the employment field (FRA 2015, p. 7).

In these rules, sexual orientation is not considered a status in the proper sense, but a personal characteristic that must be taken into account to avoid less favourable treatment with the aim of protecting the dignity and equality of individuals. We must remember that the Equal Treatment Directive proposed by the European Commission in 2008 is still under negotiation (COM(2008) 426 final, 2 July 2008). This proposal extends the prohibition against discrimination based on sexual orientation to all areas of life.

In the aforementioned legal acts, there is no reference to intersex persons, due to the low social visibility of intersex people. Rethinking the traditional notions of maleness and femaleness was the first true step in changing the situation. In 2013, the "working definitions" laid down by the EU Council stated that those notions are culturally established (Council of the European Union 2013, p. 4). Furthermore, it should be remembered that the European Parliament's Lunacek Report recommended that the EU Commission, the EU Member States and the relevant agencies should address the current lack of knowledge, research and pertinent legislation on the human rights of intersex people (EU Parliament (2014), *Report on the EU Roadmap against homophobia and discrimination on grounds of sexual orientation and gender identity* (2013/2183(INI)), Plenary sitting, No. A7-0009/2014, 7 January 2014, (para. G. iv). Not long ago, on 12 October 2017, the Council of Europe Parliamentary Assembly (35th Sitting) adopted Resolution 2191 (2017) *Promoting the human rights of and eliminating discrimination against intersex people.*

Gender identity has also acquired a progressive legal relevance. The Court of Justice has always brought this condition back to "sex", as a personal characteristic protected by law. Subsequently, Directive 2006/54 (5 July 2006, recital 3), Directive 2011/95/EU (13 December 2011, art. 10(1)(d) and Directive 2012/29/EU (25 October 2012, recital 9) have mentioned gender identity.

4 Evolution of EU Law Concerning LGBTIQ Issues

It is not possible to analyse the development of EU law on LGBTIQ people using a unitary approach. In the areas of EU competence—and not even in all of them—relevance has been given to sexual orientation and gender identity, while no act has yet been issued on the condition of intersex people.

The most important provision from the point of view of status—apart from art. 21—is undoubtedly art. 9 of the Charter of Nice (Right to Marry and Right to Found a Family), which makes the status of spouse and family member gender neutral. Thus, same-sex couples can be recognised when EU acts have to be implemented by judges at the national level, even in those countries that do not allow gay and lesbian people to marry and to found a family.

The first Court of Justice judgement concerning the characteristics of the person analysed in this paragraph was about gender identity. In *P. v. S. and Cornwall City Council* (CJEU, C-13/94, 1996), a trans person was fired when she announced her decision to begin the transition process. The relevant status is that of a worker. Despite the absence of any legal reference to gender identity in EU law at that time, the Court considered the layoff discriminatory on the ground of the applicant's sex.

Over time, the EU Court of Justice has established that the instruments implementing the principle of equal treatment between men and women should be interpreted broadly to cover discrimination on the grounds of an intended or actual reassignment of gender (FRA 2015, 28; CJEU, C-117/01, *K.B. v. National Health Service Pensions Agency*, 2004; CJEU, C-423/04, *Richards v. Secretary of State for Work and Pensions*, 2004).

Other cases have taken into consideration the status of a worker in connection with the status of a family member, with reference to the sexual orientation or gender identity of the applicant. In *Grant v. South-West Trains Ltd*, for the first time, the Court of Justice took into consideration the request of a woman who complained of discriminatory treatment because her partner was a woman compared to her co-workers, who were engaged in heterosexual *de facto* partnerships (CJEU, C-249/96, 1998). The Court held that there was no discrimination because the comparison could not be made with straight men, but rather with gay men engaged in a *de facto* relationship. Because the latter were treated in the same way as lesbian women, i.e. they were given no benefit (reduction on transport prices), then there was no discrimination. It is evident that this case dealt with indirect discrimination. At that time, the Court was satisfied to note that sexual orientation was not a personal condition protected by the European legal system.

Similar conclusions were reached in the case *D. and Kingdom of Sweden, v. Council of the European Union,* although the case was about a registered cohabitation and not about a *de facto* relationship (Joined Cases C-122/99 and C-125/99, 31 May 2001). It is important to underline that the Court took note of the great variety of rules that are applied to family relations in the different EU Member States. Nevertheless, the Court continued to hold that the situation of workers in a registered union is not comparable to the condition of their married (hetero) co-workers, focusing all attention on sexual orientation and not on the effects that sexual orientation has on the family member's status.

Remarkable progress has been made since then. The rule of law of the Court is not to admit any differences in the treatment of spouses and registered partners who are in situations comparable to spouses (CJEU, C-267/12, *Frédéric Hay v. Crédit agricole mutuel de Charente-Maritime et des Deux-Sèvres*, 12 December 2013; C-147/08, *Romer v. City of Hamburg*, 11 May 2011; C-267/06, *Tadao Maruko v.*

Versorgungsanstalt der deutschen Bühnen, 1 April 2008). This is the result of two simultaneous phenomena: 1. the growing number of European Union countries recognising the right of same-sex couples to marry or found a family through an alternative institution to marriage; 2. the existence of art. 9 of the Nice Charter, which prevents discrimination against same-sex couples.

5 European Integration for LGBTIQ People

Even if the European law is strictly limited by the respect for the States' competences, it must be emphasised that (a) the provision of sexual orientation in the Treaties and the Nice Charter and (b) the protection of gender identity as an aspect of the personality together with sex generate a virtuous circle for the protection of LGBTIQ people. In fact, the governments of the EU Member States are urged to pay attention to the needs of LGBTIQ people, even when national public opinion is not very inclined to deal with certain issues. Furthermore, national judges (even in the absence of national laws) must apply European acts without any discrimination against LGBTIQ people, and they are influenced by the judgements of the EU Court of Justice in interpreting those acts (Martinico 2004).

The Fundamental Rights Agency has long been observing and analysing the legal treatment that EU Member States reserve for LGBTIQ people, even in those areas that are not strictly within the EU competence. In its periodic reports, the Agency provides comparative data regarding the EU Member States. The circulation of information on the trends in the different countries, and above all, the dissemination of information on good practices for the protection of LGBTIQ people should push the EU Member States to homogenise their national legal systems.

With regard to trans people, the last Report underlines two aspects: 1. there is a slow trend towards making legal gender recognition available to children (starting at age 16); 2. the majority of EU Member States still require trans persons to be single (or to divorce) to have their gender legally recognised. However, with regard to the conjugal status, the introduction of marriage for same-sex couples has made this requirement irrelevant in some Member States (FRA 2015, p. 7).

On this point, Italy is an exception. Although same-sex marriage is not foreseen, trans persons are no longer obliged to divorce to ask the registry office to rectify their data. According to sentence n. 170/2014 of the Italian Constitutional Court, the will to remain married must be respected. Furthermore, according to Italian law n. 76/2016, in this case, marriage becomes a civil union (article 1, 27° co.).

This legal provision would not exist in Italy without the judicial battle before the Constitutional Court and the Court of Cassation, which has increased public awareness of the legal treatment of married trans people (Cass. civ. it., 21 aprile 2015, n. 8097). In these cases, the ruling of the European Court of Human Rights in the case *Hämäläinen v. Finland* (ECtHR, No. 37359/09, Grand Chamber, 16 July 2014) and the EU Parliament Resolutions were crucial.

Thanks to the EU directives, the definition of "family member," which includes same-sex couples, triggers an expansive mechanism at the national level. In fact, the Member States must also take account of this extended definition in areas not covered by European law to respect the coherence of the national legal system and the principle of equality.

Lastly, the inclusion of gender identity and sexual orientation in the definition of a "particular social group" under Directive 2011/95/EU made it possible to give relevance to persecution based on sexual orientation and gender identity as grounds for international protection, changing the conditions for the recognition of the status for refugees or for persons eligible for subsidiary protection (FRA 2015, p. 11).

6 The Actual Function of LGBTIQ People's Condition in the EU Context

The goal of a fully inclusive European society for LGBTIQ people faces two obstacles: the first at the European level, because the relevance of these personal characteristics is not extended to all areas of EU competence; the second at the national level, because, despite the efforts to harmonise the national legal systems, not all the EU Member States are adapting their laws, and if they do, they are only introducing rules in the areas they are urged to do so by the EU. This situation frequently gives rise to conflicts between the European and national laws. The existence of such a contrast is by no means a negative aspect, because any contrast between rules of law requires an effort to overcome it. We can consider EU law an incentive for all the Member States to provide more protection for LGBTIQ people. This happens according to two different dynamics: 1. European acts encourage legal practitioners to consider the condition of LGBTIQ people relevant to the law, even beyond the specific field in which European acts are introduced; 2. the movement of citizens among the EU Member States involves the circulation of traditional statuses, so the condition of LGBTIQ people—when it is relevant in the country of origin—becomes relevant (directly or indirectly) in the destination country, although the latter does not protect LGBTIQ people.

The recent case involving Romania is an example (CJEU, C-673/16, *Coman et al. v. Inspectoratul General pentru Imigrări et al.*, case in progress). The case concerns the relevance for Romanian law of the marital status acquired abroad of a Romanian citizen and a third-country citizen. The denial of a long-term residence permit for family reasons to the couple, two men, gave rise to a judicial proceeding up to the Constitutional Court, which turned to the EU Court of Justice to ascertain the correct interpretation of the Romanian law in light of the EU directives.

What happened in Italy is even more eloquent. After a Court decision (Tribunal of Reggio Emilia, decision 13 February 2012), the Italian Ministry of the Interior informed some police headquarters (Questure) that they must recognise the long-term residence cards for family reasons of all same-sex spouses of Italian citizens, although (a) the marriage had been celebrated abroad; (b) the same-sex marriage had no other effects in Italy.

7 Conclusion

Being an LGBTIQ person is not a prerequisite for acquiring a legal status, because it no longer assigns rights or new duties to those who carry these characteristics. The proper status (parent, spouse, worker, consumer and so on) can be chosen, while it is not possible to choose whether or not to have a certain sexual orientation or a certain gender identity. It is a condition that pertains to the deepest essence of the person, and as such, cannot be the prerequisite for any duty (the original EtCHR definition of sexual orientation was "*an essentially private manifestation of human personality*", see *Dudgeon v. The United Kingdom*, No. 7525/76, 22 October 1981, § 60).

The relevance of some personal characteristics in European law tends to pursue a goal: to prevent subjects from being treated differently because of their disadvantaged social and/or physical condition, unless this different treatment is not functional to include the persons in their social context. On the contrary, the legal relevance of the status determines a different legal treatment of a certain subject. For this reason, the law regulates very precisely the relations between certain subjects and the context in which they live (family, work, society as a whole), establishing not only mutual rights and duties, but also the actions related to these rights and duties.

The law does not create new rights or new duties for LGBTIQ people, but creates the conditions to overcome the obstacles to accessing the rights and duties that are normally connected to the statuses that everyone can acquire.

References

Bilotta, F. (2005). Diritto e omosessualità. In P. Cendon (Ed.), *I diritti della persona. Tutela civile, penale e amministrativa (I)* (pp. 375–397). Torino: Utet.

Colcelli, V. (2013). Status en el derecho de la Unión Europea. In M. I. Álvarez Ledesma & R. Cippitani (Coord.), *Diccionario analítico de derechos humanos e integración jurídica* (pp. 653–659). Roma-Perugia-México: ISEG.

Council of the European Union. (2013). *Guidelines to promote and protect the enjoyment of all human rights by lesbian, gay, bisexual, transgender and intersex (LGBT) persons.* Luxembourg: Foreign Affairs Council Meeting.

FRA – European Union Agency for Fundamental Rights. (2015). *Protection against discrimination on grounds of sexual orientation, gender identity and sex characteristics in the EU, Comparative legal analysis, update 2015.* Luxembourg: Publications Office of the European Union.

Martinico, G. (2004). Le sentenze interpretative della Corte di giustizia come forme di produzione normativa. *Rivista di diritto costituzionale*, 249–282.

Slootmaeckers, K., Touquet, H., & Vermeersch, P. (Eds.). (2016). *The EU enlargement and gay politics: The impact of eastern enlargement on rights, activism and prejudice*. London: Palgrave McMillan.

Taylor, Y., Hines, S., & Casey, M. (Eds.). (2010). *Theorizing intersectionality and sexuality*. London: Palgrave McMillan.

Member of the European Parliament

Dunja Duić

1 Introduction

The European Parliament (EP) is one of the EU institutions listed under Art. 13 TEU. The listing order is not arbitrary, and the fact that the EP is the first of the institutions listed under Art. 13 TEU emphasizes the importance of the only EU institution to which members are elected through direct universal suffrage. The Lisbon Treaty regulates members of the European Parliament (MEPs) in several provisions, with the important ones being mentioned below. Primarily, Art. 14 TEU regulates the competences of the EP, the composition of the EP and elections for the EP. Additionally, Articles 223–234 TFEU regulate the EP. Finally, aside from primary law, as regards the determination of the individual status of MEPs, relevant acts include the Statute for Members of the European Parliament (Decision 2005/684/EC), the Code of Conduct for Members of the European Parliament (2012), and the Rules of Procedure (2017).

All the Treaty provisions and statutory documents mentioned above will be reviewed in this chapter, with the aim of analysing the relationships between the EP and an MEP in the light of the law relating to the European integration process and the unitary definition of the legal status of an MEP under EU law, as well as providing an overview of how this individual status has changed during the European integration process. This chapter will attempt to answer the following questions: What role did EU law play in developing the individual status of MEPs, and does the status of an MEP have a new function because of the Lisbon Treaty?

D. Duić (✉)
Faculty of Law Osijek, Josip Juraj Strossmayer University of Osijek, Osijek, Croatia
e-mail: dduic@pravos.hr

A. Bartolini et al. (eds.), *Dictionary of Statuses within EU Law*,
https://doi.org/10.1007/978-3-030-00554-2_48

2 The European Parliament and MEPs During the European Integration Process

The European Parliament originated in the Common Assembly of the European Coal and Steel Community (ECSC), which held its first session on 10 September 1952. The Common Assembly comprised 78 members appointed from the national parliaments of the Member States. It was a consultative assembly with no legislative power. After the establishment of the European Atomic Energy Community (Euratom) and the European Economic Community (EEC), the Common Assembly covered all three communities. An assembly of 142 members appointed from the national parliaments of the Member States was convened for the first time on 19 March 1958 as the 'European Parliamentary Assembly', and this became the 'European Parliament' in 1962. The EEC and Euratom Treaties granted some decision-making powers to the Common Assembly, but they implied that the Common Assembly would issue opinions on proposals for Community acts and send them to the Council, meaning that at this point of the European integration process the European Parliament had only consultative powers (Kreppel 2002, pp. 52–60; Mangiameli 2013, p. 589).

On the basis of the Decision and the Act on European elections by direct universal suffrage that was signed in Brussels on 20 September 1976 and entered into force in 1978, the first members of the European Parliament were elected on 7 and 10 June 1979. The first elections were held several years after the first enlargement, and the enlargement is the crucial element for the number of MEPs. As early as 1973 (the year of the first enlargement), the number of MEPs was increased to 198. In the second enlargement, 24 Greek MEPs were added. In 1986, the year of the third enlargement, the number of MEPs increased from 434 to 518. Following German unification, the number rose from 518 to 567, and after the fourth EU enlargement the number of MEPs increased to 626. The Intergovernmental Conference of Nice set the maximum number of MEPs at 732. Once Bulgaria and Romania had joined the Union, the number of MEPs after the 2009 elections was 736 (Chalmers et al. 2011, pp. 81–82). The Treaty of Lisbon prescribed a maximum number of 751 MEPs: 'The European Parliament shall be composed of representatives of the Union's citizens. They shall not exceed seven hundred and fifty in number, plus the President. Representation of citizens shall be degressively proportional, with a minimum threshold of six members per Member State. No Member State shall be allocated more than ninety-six seats' (Art. 14(2) TEU). With the accession of Croatia on 1 July 2013, the number of MEPs was temporarily raised to 766, but after the 2014 elections the total number of seats was again reduced to 751. We can expect the number of MEPs to decrease (by 73 MEPs) following the withdrawal of the United Kingdom from the EU.

The first extension of the Parliament's competence was the introduction of budgetary powers under the Treaty of Luxembourg (22 April 1970) and the Treaty of Brussels (22 July 1975). Further, the 1986 Single European Act enhanced the EP's powers in some legislative areas (through the introduction of the cooperation procedure), and by giving the EP the power of assent on accession and association treaties (Arts. 192, 251, 252, 310 EC). The Maastricht Treaty introduced the procedure for co-decisions with the Council in some areas, and extended the cooperation procedure to other areas of legislation (Corbett et al. 2016, pp. 52–64). The Treaty of Amsterdam and Nice extended the co-decision procedure to most areas of legislation, making the EP a co-legislator next to the Council (Arts. 251, 252 EC). Moreover, the EP was granted control and nomination powers over the Commission: it could pass a motion of censure on the activities of the Commission (Art. 201 EC) and nominate the president of the Commission who was proposed by the Council and approved by the members of the Commission (Art. 214 EC).

The Treaty of Lisbon extended the ordinary legislative procedure (the co-decision procedure) to most legislative areas, with the EP thereby becoming an equal co-legislator with the Council. We may conclude that today the EP is fully exercising the powers given to it in Art. 14 TEU: 'The European Parliament shall, jointly with the Council, exercise legislative and budgetary functions. It shall exercise functions of political control and consultation as laid down in the Treaties. It shall elect the President of the Commission' (Craig and De Burca 2011, pp. 51–57; Mangiameli 2013, pp. 594–599).

3 Legal Regulation of the Individual Status of a Member of the European Parliament

The answer to the question of who is a member of the European Parliament, or what is the composition of the EP, is prescribed in the Treaty, Art. 14(2) TEU: 'The European Parliament shall be composed of representatives of the Union's citizens'. This is a shift from the previous Treaty provision, which stipulated that MEPs are representatives of the peoples of the states. Supported by Art. 20 TFEU, which regulates EU citizenship, this regulation is generally in line with CJEU jurisprudence, and demonstrates that MEP status has a new function within the regulation of the Lisbon Treaty, as it means that MEPs should be representatives of the citizens of the Union in unity without differentiation. Although this was the initial idea of the legislator, it is the present author's opinion and the accepted view in the literature that MEPs are still representatives of the peoples of the Member States (German Federal Constitutional Court, 2 BvE 2/08, para. 284; Piris 2010, p. 115).

As stated previously, MEPs have been directly elected since 1979. The election of MEPs is regulated under Art. 14(3) TEU: 'The members of the European Parliament shall be elected for a term of five years by direct universal suffrage in a free and secret ballot', and by Art. 20(2)(b) TFEU: 'Citizens of the Union shall enjoy, inter alia: the right to vote and to stand as candidates in elections to the European Parliament and in municipal elections in their Member State of residence, under the same conditions as nationals of that State'. Building on the discussions in the literature, we can say that EP elections focus essentially on national questions rather than European issues, and that there has been a disproportional turnout in elections in comparison to national elections. This is true especially if one considers that the EP has increased its powers since 1979 and yet turnout has continued to decline since the first elections in 1979 (Blondel et al. 1998; Corbett et al. 2016, pp. 52–53; Katz and Wessels 1999). However, we must emphasize the shift in regulation, as a result of which, under the Lisbon Treaty, the EP is composed no longer of 'representatives of the peoples of the States' (Art. 189 EC) but of 'representatives of the Union's citizens' (Art. 14(2) TEU). This change must be considered as important for the determination of the individual status of an MEP. However, it is up to the MEPs to stand behind this new Treaty stipulation by focusing more on EU issues during the elections and especially during the time of their mandate in the EP.

In accordance with Art. 223(3) TFEU, the Parliament enjoys autonomy from other institutions in determining the duties of MEPs: 'The European Parliament, acting by means of regulations on its own initiative in accordance with a special legislative procedure after seeking an opinion from the Commission and with the consent of the Council, shall lay down the regulations and general conditions governing the performance of the duties of its Members'. Moreover, internal organization rules (Rules of Procedure) for the Parliament are adopted by a majority of its members (Art. 232 TFEU).

Aside from the Treaty provisions analysed above that regulate the legal status of MEPs, there are three significant documents that provide a unitary definition of the legal status of MEPs and determine their duties and how their duties are to be performed under EU law: the Statute for Members of the European Parliament (Decision 2005/684/EC), the Code of Conduct for Members of the European Parliament (2012), and the Rules of Procedure (2017). The Statute lays down the regulations and general conditions governing how members of the European Parliament are to perform their duties (Art. 1, Decision 2005/684/EC). Article 1 of the Statute takes the concept of 'member' and makes it clear that the Statute does not deal with members' rights and obligations, but covers the rules and general conditions applicable to the exercise of their mandate (Preamble (3) Decision 2005/684/EC). Article 2 of the Statute is of great importance for the unitary definition of the legal status of MEPs, because the freedom and independence of MEPs, which are prescribed in Article 2, are not mentioned in any of the provisions of primary law. Moreover, according to Art. 3(1) of the Statute, members of the European Parliament are obliged to vote on an individual and personal basis, and must not be bound by any instructions or receive a binding mandate. Nonetheless, most MEPs belong to political groups and are put under pressure to follow opinions that are accepted in the group (Corbett et al. 2016, p. 66).

The Code of Conduct sets out the guiding principles for MEPs, stating that they are to act in the public interest and conduct their work with disinterest, integrity, openness, diligence, honesty, accountability and respect for the European Parliament's reputation (Art. 1, Code of Conduct). The Code sets out the main duties of MEPs that are essential for their freedom and independence. It defines conflicts of interest and how MEPs should address them, and obliges MEPs to submit a detailed declaration of their financial interests.

The Rules of Procedure (RoP) lay down internal organizational rules for the EP, and, among these, the rules in Chapter 1 are dedicated to MEPs: Rule 1—European Parliament, Rule 2—Independent mandate, Rule 3—Verification of credentials, Rule 4—Term of office of Members, Rule 5—Privileges and immunities, Rule 6—Waiver of immunity, Rule 7—Defence of privileges and immunity, Rule 8—Urgent action by the President to assert immunity, Rule 9—Procedures on immunity, Rule 11—Members' financial interests and standards of conduct, Rule 12—Internal investigations conducted by the European Anti-Fraud Office (OLAF), and Rule 13—Observers. First, the Rules of Procedure establish that MEPs shall exercise their mandate freely and independently, shall not be bound by any instructions and shall not receive a binding mandate (Rule 2, RoP). Moreover, according to Rule 5 MEPs enjoy privileges and immunities. It is up to Parliament to ensure the independence of its members in the performance of their duties. Parliamentary immunity is not a Member's personal privilege but a guarantee of the independence of Parliament as a whole, and of its Members.

4 Conclusion

We can conclude that EU law has played a significant role in developing the individual status of a member of the European Parliament. However, MEP elections are still strongly influenced by national parties. Although MEPs in the EP belong to political groups in their home countries, they are still members of national parties, and this strongly influences their individual status. Nonetheless, we must consider EU law as the most significant in the determination, definition and development of the individual status of a member of the European Parliament.

The status and function of an MEP has changed as a result of the Lisbon Treaty. Today the EP is fully exercising its powers: its legislative functions, budgetary functions and functions of political control and consultation, as laid down in the Treaties. We can conclude that the Lisbon Treaty has increased the importance of MEPs in the EU legal system, and, what is more, the concept of an MEP has changed as a result of the Lisbon Treaty, since MEPs should be representatives of Union citizens as a whole without differentiation. However, in practice, because of the crisis in the identity of the Union, MEPs have not yet embraced this pro-integration change in their status, and it could be said that although they are exercising their newly increased powers, they still act as representatives of the peoples of the states.

Conclusively, building on all the documents and Treaty provisions that we have analysed, we offer a definition of MEPs: Members of the European Parliament are representatives of the Union's citizens who are elected for a term of 5 years by direct universal suffrage and are not bound by any instructions. They act in the public interest and exercise their mandate freely and independently.

References

Blondel, J., Sinnott, R., & Svenson, P. (1998). *People and parliament in the European Union: Participation, democracy and legitimacy*. Oxford: Clarendon Press.

Chalmers, D., Davies, G., & Monti, G. (2011). *European Union law: Cases and materials*. Cambridge: Cambridge University Press.

Corbett, R., Jacobs, F., & Neville, D. (2016). *The European Parliament* (9th ed.). London: John Harper Publishing.

Craig, P. P., & De Burca, G. (2011). *EU law: Text, cases and materials*. Oxford: Oxford University Press.

Katz, R., & Wessels, B. (Eds.). (1999). *The European Parliament, national parliaments and European integration*. Oxford: Oxford University Press.

Kreppel, A. (2002). *The European Parliament and supranational party system: A study in institutional development*. Cambridge: Cambridge University Press.

Mangiameli, S. (2013). The European Parliament. In H.-J. Blanke & S. Mangiameli (Eds.), *The Treaty on European Union (TEU)* (pp. 587–614). Berlin: Springer Verlag.

Piris, J.-C. (2010). *The Lisbon Treaty. A legal and political analysis*. Cambridge: Cambridge University Press.

Musician

Reyes Marzal Raga

1 Introduction

European Union law uses the word 'musician' to refer to professional artists who work in orchestras and other publicly owned musical groups. The legal sources on which we have relied to establish this definition are basically jurisprudential and are, in particular, the resolutions issued by the CJEU in order to solve the labour law problems derived from the performance of professional services by musicians in different musical groups under public ownership. However, the term musician fits within the broader concept of artist, for which the European Parliament issued a Resolution of 7 June 2007, on the social status of artists. The idea that underpins the concept of musician can also be found in the legislation referring to copyright, although the term used by European law is not 'a musician' but 'a performer', in accordance with Directive 2014/26/EU concerning the collective management of copyright and related rights and the granting of multi-territorial licences of rights in musical works for online use in the internal market.

2 The Status of the Musician as an Artist

In 1961, the Rome International Convention on the Protection of Performers, Producers of Phonograms and Broadcasting Organizations was adopted; in addition to giving an express acknowledgement of performers' intellectual property rights in their creations, it reflected the need to set working conditions. Later, within the European Union, the European Parliament issued its Resolution of 7 June 2007, on

R. Marzal Raga (✉)
Administrative Law Department, University of Valencia, Valencia, Spain
e-mail: Reyes.Marzal@uv.es

A. Bartolini et al. (eds.), *Dictionary of Statuses within EU Law*,
https://doi.org/10.1007/978-3-030-00554-2_49

the social status of artists, according to which Member States are asked to develop a legal and institutional framework, taking into account the atypical nature of the different artistic professions, to include social protection measures related to social security, health insurance, the recognition of specific diseases, retirement, and direct and indirect taxation.

The different countries of the EU have collected together some aspects of this in the Social Statute; these are mainly aimed at establishing the professional status of an artist in order to regulate issues related to the artist's status as a worker such as social benefits and the social security scheme, to which these workers must submit.

2.1 The Regulatory Framework in Spain

2.1.1 The Musician as a Member of a Public Orchestra or Musical Group

In general, the professional activity of musicians in orchestras and musical groups gives them the status of public employees (officials or other personnel), since these groups are mostly considered to be public entities. The general norms contained in Real Decreto Legislativo 5/2015, of October 30, which approves the revised text of the Estatuto Básico del Empleado Público, apply to this professional activity.

2.1.2 The Professional Musician as a Worker in a Special Employment Relationship

A professional musician can also be considered as a salaried worker. Royal Decree 1435/1985, of 1 August, regulates the special employment law relationship between an organizer of public shows or businessman and someone who voluntarily dedicates themselves to the performance of an artistic activity on account of and within the scope of that organization and under the direction of the organizer. The decree establishes the rules on capacity to enter into a contract, the form of the contract, trial periods, the duration and modalities of the contract, the rights and duties of the parties, remuneration, working hours, and breaks and holidays, among other issues. In respect of other areas not regulated by this provision, the Statute of Workers and other labour standards of general application are applied, insofar as they are compatible with the nature of the work of artists in public performances.

The public social security system takes into consideration some particular aspects of the employment relationship, such as the discontinuity and flexibility of employment or the fixing of remuneration for each day that is worked. In addition, the intermittent nature of this activity has certain special consequences for entitlement to social security benefits, such as rules related to the calculation of the days that are counted towards the benefit, as well as the adaptation of the calculation of the regulatory bases of some benefits that are calculated on the basis of the last 12 months, the direct payment of benefits and the rules applying at the moment the benefit is requested.

2.1.3 The Professional Musician as a Self-Employed Artist

When the musician is not subject to a special employment relationship, he will be governed by the social protection rules established for self-employed workers, so he must join the Social Security Scheme, although Law 31/2015, of September 9 modifies and updates the legislation on self-employment, and enables the worker to benefit from a partial contribution, ranging from the abolition of the fee for being self-employed, if the individual's income is lower than the minimum inter-professional salary (SMI) through a progressively higher fee when the individual's income is higher, as well as a contribution based on real income that, in the case of non-income, allowing the musician to keep his/her status joined to the Social Security Scheme.

However, the term 'musician' does not appear in the sections on tax on economic activities, although the headings 'Performers on musical instruments' and 'Other activities related to music' do appear.

2.1.4 The Proposal for Approval of the Status of Artists

At present, a proposal related to the status of artists has been put before the Commission of Culture of the Spanish Parliament, with the aim of improving the working conditions of these workers, who include musicians. In essence, the main proposals refer to the recognition that the activity is not performed continuously and that the services are provided for a limited period of time. The intent is to define a set of rights for intermittent workers using a new social security model, with a fiscal regime that does not penalize the intermittent nature of the provision of services, and the creation of a strong union model.

With regard to social protection, the suggested reforms take the French system as a model, and are based on the intermittent nature of the services that are provided. It is proposed that artists who have been hired for a certain number of hours in a given period can access this scheme. Specifically, artists would have to work for 507 hours in the 319 days prior to the end of the contract. The reforms also establish the need to meet specific requirements, by taking into consideration such things as: (a) overtime—penalizing the use of overtime and controlling how it is performed; (b) the training received within the intermittent working, as well as the training provided; (c) the periods between work performed under the same contract that have to be accounted for as assimilated to the registration to the Social Security Scheme, although they do not generate entitlement to the benefit until the period exceeds 21 days; and (d) the hours devoted to specific training and recognized by the system for intermittent working.

2.2 *The Regulatory Framework in France*

2.2.1 The Musician as an Artist in a Performance

According to Article L. 762-1 of the Labour Code, 'performers include the lyric artist, the dramatic artist, the choreographic artist, the variety artist, the musician, the singer, the so-called "complementary artist" (those who help the main artist), the orchestral conductor, the arranger-orchestrator and, for the material execution of his artistic conception, the conductor'.

2.2.2 The Professional Musician as a Worker. The Presumption of a Salary

The professional musician considers himself to be a salaried worker when he is in a situation of legal subordination to his employer. According to the Cour de cassation judgment in the *Société Générale* case of November 13, 1996: 'le lien de subordination est caractérisé par l'exécution d'un travail sous l'autorité d'un employeur qui a le pouvoir de donner des ordres et des directives, d'en contrôler l'exécution et de sanctionner les manquements de son subordonné; que le travail au sein d'un service organisé peut constituer un indice du lien de subordination lorsque l'employeur détermine unilatéralement les conditions d'exécution du travail''.

There is a legal presumption that a musician is an employee, in accordance with Article L. 762-1 of the Labour Code, according to which "Every contract by virtue of which an individual or legal entity guarantees, in exchange for remuneration, the performance of an artist is presumed to be a work contract if the performer does not perform the activity covered by this contract under conditions that imply registration in the commercial register". This presumption is independent of the method and amount of the remuneration, and of the description given to the contract by the parties, and it is not destroyed by proof that the artist retains freedom of expression in his art, or owns all or part of the material used or that he himself uses one or more people to assist him, as long as he personally participates in the show.

2.2.3 The So-called "Intermittent Performing Artists"

Among other unusual features, French law defines a regime for intermittent salaried employees (intermittent performers). This applies to an artist who, in the course of any particular period, has a succession of fixed-term contracts, being employed by others and having several employers, alternating with periods of inactivity. In these cases, Circulaire n° 2016-08, of 27 January 2016, applicable to intermittent workers, artists or technicians contains, in terms of specific unemployment protection (allocation d'aide au retour à l'emploi, ARE), some provisions that are very beneficial for artists. In particular, it is aware of the importance of the artist maintaining and renewing their personal skills, and it also considers the artist's participation in training courses carried out between two working contracts, regarding this as a period similar to a working period for the purpose of receiving unemployment benefit. French artists enjoy an unemployment insurance scheme that guarantees the continuity of their income under their conditions of irregular employment, providing coverage of 8 months at a minimum wage to those who obtain 507 hours of performing work within the 304 days preceding the end of a contract, for technicians, and the preceding 309 days in the case of artists.

3 The Musician as a Performing Worker in European Jurisprudence

3.1 The Status of Salaried Worker

Taking into account the nature of the artistic performance undertaken by a musician, one of the problems that arises is whether the musician is a salaried worker or an independent economic operator.

The CJEU judgment of December 4, 2014, delivered in case C 413/13, in resolution of the preliminary ruling request submitted by the Gerechtshofte's Gravenhage (Netherlands) in the case between FNV Kunsten Informatie in Media and Staat der Nederlanden (ECLI: EU: C: 2014: 2411) stated, in relation to the work of substitute musicians in an orchestra, that, for the purposes of EU law, the concept of worker must be defined according to objective criteria. These criteria include whether the individual acts under the direction of an employer, in particular with regard to his freedom to determine his schedule, his place of work and the content of his work; and whether he participates in the commercial risks of the entrepreneur and is integrated into the company during the period of the employment relationship and, in this way, becomes part of the same economic unit. From that perspective, the Court of Justice stated that the qualification of 'self-employed provider' under national law does not exclude the possibility that the same person qualifies as a 'worker' for the purposes of Union law if his independence is only fictitious and disguises what is, to all intents and purposes, an employment relationship (see also the *Allonby* judgment, C 256/01, EU: C: 2004: 18, paragraph 71).

The CJEU has also established that there is a difference between the performances of a soloist, which have a very strong personal character and are linked to the fame of the soloist, and the performances of choirs or chamber music ensembles. Applying this distinction, the CJEU has concluded that, for the purposes of exemption from VAT for certain activities of general interest, the expression 'other recognized cultural bodies' contained in Council Directive 77/388/EEC of 17 May 1977 (sixth Directive on the harmonization of the laws of the Member States relating to turnover taxes) does not exclude soloists acting in an individual capacity (judgment of 3 April 2003, Case C-144/00).

3.2 *Stability in Employment*

Although the nature of the artistic work that musicians perform requires the successive use of fixed-term employment contracts concluded with temporary workers in the entertainment industry, it is contrary to European law for employers to misuse successive employment contracts of fixed duration, unless they can justify this by the existence of 'objective reasons' (CJEU 26 February 2015, *European Commission/ Grand Duchy of Luxembourg*, Case C-238/14, ECLI: EU: C: 2015: 128).

Although for many artists successive temporary contracts may be justified by objective reasons, this general rule is not applicable to the group as a whole, as when, for example, the employer hires the permanent members of an orchestra and the basic staff of a theatre company or a television station, on a stable basis. The CJEU did not deny the fact that the Luxembourg legislation allows for flexibility in the temporary hiring of artists and guarantees social protection for temporary workers because of the intermittent nature of their contractual benefits, but it stated that, in this specific case, the national legislation did not conform to the purposes of the European legislation, insofar as it does not allow the existence of specific circumstances that feature the activity in question to be demonstrated and therefore, allow them to justify in this particular context the successive use of fixed-term work contracts. The conclusion of the CJEU is clear: 'to allow a Member State to invoke an objective such as flexibility arising from the use of fixed-term employment contracts' in order to exempt it from the obligation to justify the objective reasons for fixed-term contracts would go against one of the objectives pursued by the Framework Agreement, stability in employment, conceived as a fundamental element of worker protection, and could also significantly reduce the categories of people who can benefit from the protective measures established in clause 5 of the Framework Agreement.

3.3 *Free Movement of Working Musicians and Equal Treatment in Access to Employment*

Access to employment for workers in the Member States of the European Union cannot be limited by reason of nationality, since the free movement of workers, which is one of the constituent pillars of the European Union, would then be violated. This is shown by the ECJ judgment of July 2, 1996, in Case C-290/94, Commission/Greece, referring to the decision of the Athens opera to refuse to hire a German musician because of his nationality. The government alleged that the Athens opera musicians and municipal orchestras are part of the Greek public service, and therefore Greek nationality is required to access these jobs. The CJEU stated that a Member State cannot, in general, impose a nationality requirement for any jobs in the music and artistic sectors without exceeding the limits of the exception provided in Article 48(4) of the Treaty. The principles of free movement of workers and equal treatment in access to employment require the sectors in question to be open to nationals of other Member States, with the application of the nationality requirement limited exclusively to access to jobs that actually involve direct or indirect participation in the exercise of public power and in functions that have the purpose of safeguarding the general interests of the state or other public entities.

3.4 Recognition of Previous Service in Other State Orchestras

The CJEU recognized that Community law does not cover the discriminatory treatment of migrant workers, when it resolved the complaint of a private individual, of Greek nationality, who worked from April 1986 onwards as a musician in the Thessaloniki Orchestra, which was a legal entity under public law, but was bound by a contract governed by private law. The interested party had previously worked in the Municipal Orchestra of Nice (France) for 5 years, and complained at the refusal of the Greek authorities to take into account, for the purposes of his classification on the salary scale and the granting of his seniority level, the 5 years that he had worked in France. If he had worked for that same period in a municipal orchestra in Greece, he would have been granted the seniority level. In its judgment of March 12, 1998 (Case C-187/96), the CJEU stated that the Hellenic Republic had failed to comply with its obligations under Community law and, in particular, with the provisions of Article 48 of the EC Treaty and Article 7(1) of Regulation No 1612/68, by excluding, in its regulations and administrative practice, the possibility of considering, for the purpose of granting the seniority level and ranking on the scale salary of employees of the Greek public administration, services rendered in the public administration of another Member State just because the said services had not been rendered in the national public administration.

4 Conclusions

The process of European integration has modified the legal definition of the musician as an artist. The Member States, in accordance with the Resolution of the European Parliament of 7 June 2007, must approve a social status for artists in which the particular features of this type of workers are addressed.

The regime for the social protection of musicians in their capacity as professional artists depends on their legal relationship with their employer. When it comes to public orchestras or musical groups, these follow the rules of the public sector of the country. In any other case, the regime depends on the individual's status as a salaried or independent worker.

The legal status of musicians as entertainment workers has been altered by the rulings of the CJEU, which has recognized the status as a salaried worker, the right to stability in employment, the recognition of previous service in other state orchestras and the guarantee of the free circulation of working musicians and equal treatment in access to employment.

References

Informes sobre el Estatuto del Artista, el Autor/Creador y el Trabajador de la Cultura, Fundación SGAE, 2017. Retrieved from http://sgae.es/es-ES/SitePages/EstaPasandoDetalleActualidad.aspx?i=365&s=2

La protection sociale des artistes, Centre de Sécurité Sociale des Travailleurs Migrants (CSSTM), July 2000. Retrieved December, 2017, from www.cleiss.fr/pdf/etude_artistes.pdf

The status of artists in Europe, Culture and Education Study, Policy Department Structural and Cohesion Policies, Directorate General Internal Policies of the Union. IP/B/CULT/ST/2005-89, November 2006. Retrieved December, 2017, from https://www.andea.fr/doc_root/ressources/enquetes-et-rapports/51b5afb01bb8d_The_status_of_artists_in_EU.pdf

Party to Contracts

Roberto Cippitani

1 The Position of the Parties to a Contract Within Traditional Civil Law

Within traditional private law, contracts are the main legal instruments to exchange patrimonial elements, mainly obligations and property rights (Savigny 1886), from one subject to another (Caprioli 2008; Halperin 1992).

That task arises from the dispositions of the continental Civil Codes, such as the French *Code Civil*, which sets out that '*Le contrat est une convention par laquelle une ou plusieurs personnes s'obligent, envers une ou plusieurs autres, à donner, à faire ou à ne pas faire quelques chose*' (see also Article 1321, Italian *Codice Civile* and Article 1254, Spanish *Código Civil*).

The subjects involved in patrimonial exchanges, which are carried out through contracts, are called "parties" (see Article 1321 *Codice civile*).

The position of the parties within the contract is characterised by certain features.

Each party is expected to have interests different from those of the other party: e.g., within the sale, the seller wants to obtain a price, while the buyer seeks the availability of the goods. The difference of the interests is an expression of the individual "egoism" which is considered to be the foundation of traditional civil law (Jhering 1972, p. 47).

On the other hand, the opposing interests of the parties must lead to a patrimonial balance, as a result of the exchange, which is expressed by several concepts, depending on the specific legal system, such as: '*corrispettività*' and '*onerosità*' in the Italian Codice Civile; '*bilateralité*' and '*onerosité*' under the French Law; and the bilateral contract in accordance with the common law.

R. Cippitani (✉)
Department of Medicine, Università degli Studi di Perugia, Perugia, Italy
e-mail: roberto.cippitani@unipg.it

A. Bartolini et al. (eds.), *Dictionary of Statuses within EU Law*,
https://doi.org/10.1007/978-3-030-00554-2_50

The traditional civil law relationships are based on the rule of patrimonial equilibrium, i.e., each modification (increasing or decreasing) of the patrimony of a party should be justified by a patrimonial movement from the opposite direction.

Furthermore, the parties to a contract are considered to be formally equal, although they have different functions within the same contract. They are 'decontextualized', meaning that the traditional Civil Codes do not distinguish the parties on the ground of their respective economic, political, etc., positions.

The abstraction from the context is also accompanied by an abstraction from the specific purposes of the parties entering into a contract (Savigny 1886, p. 370). Only the aim of the abstract typology of the contract, as established by the legal system, is relevant.

De-contextualisation and abstraction comply with the necessity that private law had to be neutral to achieve, in legal terms, the idea of equality between persons that was affirmed, in philosophical terms, by the Enlightenment (see Weber 1922).

The traditional civil law refers exclusively to the parties directly involved in the contract, and it has no effect with respect to third subjects.

2 Contracts in the Age of Constitutions and European Integration

During the nineteenth and twentieth centuries, the social and ideological context of private law changed substantially.

Particularly after the first half of the twentieth century, the construction of the traditional private law was put into crisis as a result of two phenomena: constitutionalisation and European integration.

Constitutions consider the fundamental rights of natural persons to be the centre of the legal system. The realisation and protection of fundamental rights has become the priority of the State (Pérez Luño 1991, p. 19) and the new justification of its political powers (Rawls 1980, pp. 4–7).

The State acquired a 'social' character (e.g., Article 1 of the French Constitution of 1958; Article 20, para. 1, of the German *Grundgesetz*; Article 1, para. 3, Romanian Constitution; Article 2, Constitution of Slovenia).

The protection of individual rights is also guaranteed at the international level (Bobbio 1984) through the establishment of a 'global constitutionalism' (Espinoza de los Monteros Sánchez 2010) which constitutes the development of the national constitutions (Pernice 1999; Häberle 2002; Cardone 2011).

Several international conventions have been stipulated to protect the rights of human beings, such as the Charter of the United Nations of 1945 and, in Europe, the European Convention on Human Rights of 1950 promoted by Council of Europe.

The legal systems shaped by the constitutions are no longer focused only on the regulation of patrimonial issues (Perlingeri 1983; see Carbonnier 2004, p. 97, referring to solidarity in private relationships).

In addition, the fundamental rights recognised and protected by the constitutions are applied both to vertical relationships (those between citizens and public authorities) and horizontal relationships (i.e., those between individuals).

Particular attention has been focused on the constitutional interpretation of contract law (Cédras 2003) and not only with respect to work contracts, which constitute the first field of application of fundamental rights to contractual relationships (see, for example, Article L120-2 of the French Code du travail).[1]

Above all, another event has changed the destiny of Europe, and, as far as it is relevant, the idea of private law, especially contract law.

Furthermore, in the 1950s of the last century, the process of European integration undermined the idea that private law only referred to domestic private relationships.

The process of European integration, since its early period, has established a community "market", i.e., an area without borders in which the free movement of persons, goods, services and capital is recognised and protected as a fundamental right.

This market is not merely an economic context, but a legal system, as recognised by the Court of Justice since the 1960s of the previous century in the *Van Gend en Loos*[2] and *Costa v Enel* judgements.[3]

According to the legal sources and documents of the EU institutions, civil matters are the cornerstone of the construction of the European legal system (see Chapter VII of the Presidency Conclusions of the Tampere European Council 15 and 16 October 1999).

In particular, the European legal integration process has had an impact on the traditional notions concerning contracts.

This has occurred through legislative interventions (directly regulating matters such as contracts between professionals and consumers, contracts between enterprises, public procurements, etc.) and non-legislative actions (through the elaboration of common principles such as those provided in the Draft of the Common Frame of Reference, hereinafter referred to as "DCFR"; for an overview, see among others, Clive 2008; Fuchs 2008).

European Union law also includes among its objectives the protection of human rights, as argued by the Court of Justice since its early case-law[4] and as is currently stated by the Charter of Fundamental Rights (hereinafter referred to as the "EU Charter") and the reference to the European Convention on Human Rights and the case-law of the European Court of Strasbourg (see Article 6 TEU).

[1] See, for example, the judgements of the *Cour de Cassation*, Soc., 13 March 2001, in Bull. 2001, V, no 87, p. 66; Soc., 28 May 2003, no 02-40.273, concerning the unfairness of the dismissal in case of violation of fundamental rights.

[2] ECJ, 5 February 1963, 26-62, *Van Gend en Loos/Administratie der Belastingen*, ECR, 1963, p. 3.

[3] ECJ, 15 July 1964, 6/64, *Flaminio Costa/E.N.E.L.*, ECR 1964, p. 1141.

[4] See ECJ, 12 November 1969, *Stauder/Stadt Ulm*, 29/69, ECR, 1969, 419.

3 The Impact of the Context in the Discipline of Contracts and in the Position of the Parties

The legal discipline of contracts which has arisen from constitutionalisation and European integration has dramatically changed with respect to the tradition which was at the base of the Civil Codes.

In particular, that process has affected the traditional ideas concerning the parties to the contracts.

3.1 Substantial Equality of the Parties

From a first viewpoint, the legislation and the legal literature have recognised that the parties cannot be considered to be equal in any case.

Thus, the weaker party must be protected with respect to the party which (for patrimonial or other reasons) is in a situation of advantage.

For example, this approach is used in *Berliner Verkehrsbetriebe* (BVG) in the judgement of 19 October 1993, which, although private autonomy is recognised by the German constitution, stated the possibility for the judge, in the presence of contracts involving a serious imbalance, to investigate the existence of disparities between the contractual force of parties and to rebalance the disparities.

At the supranational level, the Court of Justice, in the *Courage* judgement, pointed out that a party may be in a situation of "serious inferiority" due to the conclusion of a contract that can severely limit its contractual freedom.[5]

A case that is particularly interesting under EU law is the protection of the parties whose interests may be affected because they have less information than other parties.

A right to be informed is provided under Article 11 of the EU Charter. Several EU directives and other legal sources foresee the obligation to provide information in pre-contractual phases as well as during the implementation of the contract (see, for example, Directive 97/5/EC on cross-border bank transfers; Directive 2000/31/EC, the 'Directive on electronic commerce'; Directive 87/344/EEC on the legal protection in the insurance sector; Directive 90/314/EEC on package travel; Directive 92/96/EEC, etc.).

3.2 Collaboration

As mentioned above, under traditional private law, which was exclusively focused on patrimonial issues, the main instrument to ensure the movement of assets was represented by the exchange between the parties.

[5] ECJ, judg. 20 September 2001, C-453/99, *Courage y Crehan*, ECR 2001 p. I-6297.

Marginally, the civil codes deal with contracts without exchange (among the exceptions, see the Italian Civil Code, which contains a few provisions relating to contracts "*plurisoggettivi con comunione di scopo*", Articles 1420, 1446, 1459, 1466).

On the contrary, EU legal sources and the practice in recent years make many references to contracts governing collaboration between the parties.

In particular, EU legal documents consider agreements establishing collaboration between legal entities, such as universities, undertakings, public bodies and other entities for research initiatives, education and training.

The EU legal sources not only provide new typologies of legal entities, arising from associative agreements in addition to those established by national legislation, such as the European Economic Interest Group (Council Regulation (EEC) No 2137/85 of 25 July 1985) or the *Societas Europaea* (Council Regulation (EC) No 2157/2001 of 8 October 2001 on the Statute for a European company) and the European Cooperative Society (see the Council Regulation (EC) No 1435/2003 of 22 July 2003 on the Statute for a European Cooperative Society).

Moreover, the European documents also take into consideration collaborative agreements which do not establish new legal entities.

These agreements may be referred to with different names: Consortium Agreements (see, for example, Article 2, no. 4, Regulation (UE) 1291 of the European Parliament and the Council of 11 December 2013, establishing the Programme Horizon 2020) or Grouping of economic operators which submit tenders under public contracts (see Article 19, para. 2, Directive 24/2014/EU).

Other examples of collaborative contracts are "grant agreements", which are different from contracts "with pecuniary interests", because they establish a collaboration between a funding body (such as the European Commission) and beneficiaries (see in this Dictionary, the entry "Recipient of EU Programmes").

3.3 *Non-patrimonial Interests*

Also, in private relationships, the parties not only have to satisfy their patrimonial interests, but must also respect fundamental rights.

For example, the German Constitutional Court (*Bundesverfassungsgericht*) in the case *Parabolantenne*, interpreting § 242 of the BGB in light of § 5 (1) Basic Law, guarantying the freedom of information, affirmed the illegitimacy, in a rent contract, of a refusal of the lessor to allow the installation of a satellite antenna by the tenant.[6]

Another example is provided by EU law, according to which the grants provided by the European Commission must satisfy interests such as the protection of the environment and the equality between women and men.[7]

[6] BVerfG 9 February 1994, BVerfGE 90, 27 (Parabolantenne).

[7] ECJ, judg, 15 January 1998, C-44/96, *Mannesmann Anlagenbau Austria AG et oth./Strohal Rotationsdruck GesmbH*, ECR. 1998, p. I-00073.

In particular, contractual relationships must protect human dignity, which is the indispensable core of all fundamental rights, arising from the "primacy" of individuals in modern legal systems (see, e.g., the preamble of the EU Charter and Article 16 French Civil Code) (see, among others, Jones 2012).

As highlighted by Advocate General Christine Stix-Hackl in her comments (submitted on 18 March 2004) concerning the "*Omega*" case,[8] "'Human dignity' is an expression of the respect and value to be attributed to each human being on account of his or her humanity. It concerns the protection of and respect for the essence or nature of the human being per se – that is to say, the 'substance' of mankind" (para. 75).

In accordance with Article 1 of the EU Charter (see also Section 1 of German Grundgesetz), dignity must not only be respected, but also must be protected by States and by international and supranational organisations (Sanz Caballero 2013).[9]

For that reason, public bodies must intervene in cases in which a private relationship may affect human dignity or other fundamental rights, as affirmed within the abovementioned *Omega* judgement.

The autonomy of the parties to the contract cannot justify a violation of fundamental human rights, a stance also recognised by the Human Rights Committee of the International Covenant on Civil and Political Rights of the United Nations in respect to a ban by French authorities of the activity known as "dwarf throwing" (Wilkinson 2003, p. 42; Millns 1996).[10]

The change of perspective with respect to traditional private law is particularly evident in the DCFR (Cherednychenko 2010, p. 42; see also Colombi Ciacchi 2006, p. 167; Hesselink 2003, p. 119), as can be seen even in its first articles. In fact, Article I.-1:102 provides that the rules contained in the DCFR should be interpreted and applied in light of the fundamental rights and fundamental freedoms.

3.4 Public Parties and the Purpose of Implementing Public Policies

Today, the contract is among the main instruments for the implementation of public policies aimed at protecting personal and collective interests (Alpa 1996; Lipari 1987).

---

[8] ECJ, judg. 14 October 2004, C-36/02, *Omega Spielhallen- und Automatenaufstellungs-GmbH/ Oberbürgermeisterin der Bundesstadt Bonn*, ECR 2004, I-p. I-9609.

[9] See also the case-law of the Court of Justice of the European Union affirming the need for the States to respect the fundamental rights, such as: ECJ, judg, 24 March 1994, C-2/92, *Bostock*, ECR 1994, p. I-955, para. 16; ECJ, judg. 13 April 2000, C-292/97, *Karlsson et oth.*, ECR 2000, p. I-2737, para. 37; ECJ 12 December 2002, C-442/00, *Rodríguez Caballero*, ECR 2002, p. I-11915, para. 30.

[10] See Communication No. 854/1999: France. 26/07/2002. CCPR/C/75/D/854/1999, especially para. 7.4.

For example, at the supranational level, according to the White Paper on *European Governance*, the EU should adopt "a less top-down approach and complementing its policy tools more effectively with non-legislative instruments".[11]

In fields concerning fundamental interests (e.g., privacy, experimentation activities involving humans and animals), the relevant legislation usually provides for the establishment of several types of codes of conduct (Galgano 2001) and agreements that complete or implement supranational or national policy (Zagreblesky 1992).

Education provides another example: Documents concerning the Bologna Process and the policy of the EU consider agreements between universities establishing joint degrees and recognising training periods to be the main instruments for the implementation of educational policies, (Cippitani and Gatt 2009).

Collaboration agreements between local authorities and other private and public legal entities are expected to establish the principle of subsidiarity and the cohesion policy (e.g., Article 174 of the TFEU).[12] The main means for the implementation of policies of economic, social and territorial cohesion may be the Structural and Cohesion Funds (Armstrong 1995; Barro and Sala-I-Martin 1991; De La Fuente and Domenéch 1999; López-Bazo et al. 1999). One area in which such collaboration is very significant is that of cross-border cooperation, which is enabled by liaisons between the local authorities of different states, especially in relation to border territories (Perkmann 2003).[13]

4 Contracts and Legal System

Within European law, the contract continues to play the role assigned to it within the national systems, but it has been inserted into a new legal framework and has purposes other than its traditional ones.

A contract is no longer an isolated area which governs the relationship between the parties regardless of the context.

On the one hand, within EU law, a growing number of integrative interventions to protect the fundamental rights and the weaker party (which is the case in the discipline concerning consumers or protecting SMEs) can be observed. On the other hand, the law considers various effects of the agreement on several other subjects, in addition to the parties to the contract (see the entire discipline of competition).

Party autonomy cannot be understood simply as the intention of the parties to achieve the direct effects recognised by the legal system (as Windscheid argued in para. 69 of his *Lehrbuch des Pandektenrechts*, dealing with the concept of "negotium").

Thus, EU law considers the legal subjects and their relationships based on a global approach which is no longer restricted to the perspective of the parties.

---

[11] European Commission, *European Governance*, COM (2001) 428 final/2, of 5 August 2001, p. 4.

[12] See para. 1.3., White Paper of the Committee of European Regions on Multilevel Governance, 'Building Europe in partnership' of 17 June 2009.

[13] See Council of Europe, *Practical Guide to Transfrontier Co-operation*, 2006.

This change can be observed in contract law. In the past, contracts were governed by principles such as private autonomy and the relativity of the effects (as mentioned above, contracts only have effects on the parties) (Irti 2003, pp. 41 ff.).

Within EU law, a different approach is applicable. Contracts are considered from the viewpoint of the whole system. In other words, contracts are considered from the collective perspective, and therefore they are expected to protect some fundamental interests such as freedom of movement, gender equality, consumer protection, competition rules, etc. The EU legal system provides several instruments to respond in instances in which a contract violates these interests, thus breaking the sovereignty of the will of the parties. Those instruments of reaction are applied in every type of agreement, even if they are without consideration[14] or "binding in honour only".[15] The competition rules, for instance, shall be applicable to gentlemen's agreements[16] and other non-binding agreements.[17]

The global function of contracts and in particular their function to protect the funadamental interest can also be seen in the consequences for breaches of the obligations arising from the contract. For example, the Article II.-7: 301 DCFR also states that 'a contract is void to the extent that: (a) it infringes a principle recognised as fundamental in the laws of the Member States of the European Union; and (b) nullity is required to give effect to that principle'.

References

Alpa, G. (1996). Autodisciplina e codice di condotta. In P. Zatti (Ed.), *Le fonti di autodisciplina* (p. 3 ff). Padova: Cedam.

Armstrong, H. W. (1995). Convergence among regions of the European Union 1950–1990. *Papers in Regional Science, 74*(2), 143–152.

Barro, R. J., & Sala-I-Martin, X. (1991). Convergence across states and regions. *Brookings Papers on Economic Activity, 2*, 107–182.

Bobbio, N. (1984). *Il problema della guerra e le vie della pace*. Bologna: Il Mulino.

Caprioli, S. (2008). *Il Codice civile. Struttura e vicende*. Milano: Giuffrè.

Carbonnier, J. (2004). *Droit civil* (Vol. I). Paris: PUF.

Cardone, A. (2011). Diritti fondamentali (tutela multilivello dei). In *Enciclopedia del diritto. Annali, IV*. Milano: Giuffrè.

Cédras, M. J. (2003). Le solidarisme contractuel en doctrine et devant la Cour de cassation. In www.courdecassation.fr

Cherednychenko, O. (2010). Fundamental rights, policy issues and the draft common frame of reference for European private law. *European Review of Contract Law, 6*(1), 39–65.

[14] ETFI, 10 July 1991, T-76/89, *Independent Television Publication Limited/Commission*, ECR 1991, p. II-575.

[15] ECJ, 17 September 2002, *Town and County Factors*, C-498/99, ECR 2002, p. I-7173.

[16] ECJ, 15 July 1970, *Chemiefarma/Commission*, 41/69, ECR1970, p. 661; Id. 29 October 1980, *Heintz van Landewyck Sarl e altri/Commission*, from 209/78 to 215/78 e 218/78, ECR, 1980, p. 3125.

[17] See, for example, the case *Polypropylene* (European Commission, 23 April 1986, *Polypropylene*, in O.J., 1986, L 230/1).

Cippitani, R., & Gatt, S. (2009). Legal developments and problems of the Bologna process within the European Higher Education Area and European Integration. *Higher Education in Europe, 34*(3), 385–397.
Clive, E. (2008). An introduction to the academic draft common frame of reference. *Era Forum, 9*, S13–S31.
Colombi Ciacchi, A. (2006). The constitutionalization of European contract law: Judicial convergence and social justice. *European Review of Contract Law, 2*(2). Available at SSRN: https://ssrn.com/abstract=2013063
De La Fuente, A., & Domenéch, R. (1999). The redistributive effects of the EU budget: An analysis and some reflections on the Agenda 2000 negotiations. *CERP Discussion Paper, 2113*.
Espinoza de los Monteros Sánchez, J. E. (2010). Contitucionalismo global. In *Diccionario Histórico Judicial de México, Ideas e Instituciones* (Vol. I). México: Suprema Corte de Justicia de la Nación de México.
Fuchs, A. (2008). A plea a Europe-wide discussion of draft common frame of reference. *Era Forum, 9*, S1–S6.
Galgano, F. (2001). *Lex mercatoria*. Bologna: Il Mulino.
Häberle, P. (2002). Dallo Stato nazionale all'Unione europea: evoluzioni dello Stato costituzionale. *Diritto pubblico comparato europeo*, 460 ff.
Halperin, J. L. (1992). *L'impossible Code Civil*. Paris: PUF.
Hesselink, M. (2003). The horizontal effect of social rights in European contract law. In M. Hesselink et al. (Eds.), *Privaatrecht tussen autonomie en solidariteit*. Den Haag: Boom Juridische Uitgevers.
Irti, N. (2003). *L'ordine giuridico del mercato*. Roma-Bari: Laterza.
Jhering, R. (1972). *Lo scopo del diritto* (M. G. Losano, Trans.). Turin: Einaudi.
Jones, J. (2012). Human dignity in the EU charter of fundamental rights and its interpretation before the European Court of Justice. *Liverpool Law Review, 33*, 281–300.
Lipari, N. (1987). La formazione negoziale del diritto. *Rivista di diritto civile*, 307 ff.
López-Bazo, E., Vayá, E., Mora, A. J., & Suriñac, J. (1999). Regional economic dynamics and convergence in the European Union. *Annals of Regional Science, 33*, 257–370.
Millns, S. (1996). Dwarf-throwing and human dignity: A French perspective. *Journal of Social Welfare and Family Law, 18*(3), 375 ff.
Pérez Luño, A. E. (1991). *Los derechos fundamentals*. Madrid: Tecnos.
Perkmann, M. (2003). Cross border regions in Europe. Significance and drivers of regional cross-border cooperation. *European Urban and Regional Studies, 10*, 153–171.
Perlingeri, P. (1983). Depatrimonializzazione e diritto civile. *Rassegna diritto civile*, 1 ff.
Pernice, I. (1999). Multilevel constitutionalism and the Treaty of Amsterdam: European constitution-making revisited? *Common Market Law Review, 36*(4), 703–750.
Rawls, J. (1980). *A theory of justice*. Cambridge, MA: The Belknap Press of Harvard University.
Sanz Caballero, S. (2013). Obligaciones positivas del Estado. In M. I. Álvarez Ledesma & R. Cippitani (Eds.), *Diccionario analítico de Derechos humanos e integración juridical* (pp. 466–474). Roma-Perugia-México: ISEG.
Savigny, F. K. (1886). *Il sistema del diritto romano attuale* (Scialoja, Trans.) (Vol. I). Turin: UTET.
Weber, M. (1922). *Wirtschaft und Gesellschaft*. Tübingen: Mohr.
Wilkinson, S. (2003). *Bodies for sale: Ethics and exploitation in the human body trade*. London: Routledge.
Zagreblesky, G. (1992). *Il diritto mite*. Torino: Einaudi.

Passenger

Eugenio Olmedo-Peralta

1 Transportation Policy Within the Goals of the EU

The creation of a single area in the European Union requires the removal of frontiers and barriers to the free movement of persons, to enable the establishment of the four economic freedoms: free movement of goods, services, labour and capital. To achieve this, it is crucial that an appropriate transportation policy is implemented in the EU and that a complete and harmonized catalogue of rights for passengers within the European territory is provided. Freedom of movement is recognized as a right of European citizenship by Article 3.2 TEU, which states that the Union will offer its citizens an area of freedom, security and justice without internal borders, with the free movement of persons being ensured in conjunction with appropriate measures with respect to external border controls, asylum, immigration and the prevention and combating of crime.

From a legal point of view, freedom of movement can only be practically achieved if the rights of passengers are harmonized within the territories of the different Member States. The process of the regulation of passengers' rights has gone through different stages. At first, transportation was considered as a strategic industry for the European economy and the fulfilment of the European project, and thus this sector was strictly regulated and, in most cases, transport activities were excluded from the general regulations.[1] Once the legal basis for the construction of the industry was set, European institutions paid more attention to the regulation of

[1] For example, until Council Regulation (EC) No 1/2003 of 16 December 2002 on the implementation of the rules on competition laid down in Articles 81 and 82 of the Treaty, air transport had its own competition rules. Consider, for instance, Council Regulations (EEC) No 3975/87 and 3976/87.

E. Olmedo-Peralta (✉)
University of Málaga, Málaga, Spain
e-mail: olmedo@uma.es

A. Bartolini et al. (eds.), *Dictionary of Statuses within EU Law*,
https://doi.org/10.1007/978-3-030-00554-2_51

passengers' rights. Some of these rights had already been dealt with in international conventions, but the effectiveness of the conventions depended on whether they were ratified by every single Member State. Regarding the transport of passengers by air, it is important to consider the Convention for the Unification of Certain Rules relating to International Carriage by Air (the Warsaw Convention 1929, and the Protocols of The Hague 1955 and Guatemala 1971) and the Convention for the Unification of Certain Rules for International Carriage by Air (Montreal 1999). The transport of passengers by sea was covered by the Athens Convention relating to the Carriage of Passengers and their Luggage by Sea (PAL, 1974). For the transport of passengers over land, the Uniform Rules concerning the Contract of International Carriage of Passengers by Rail (CIV)—Appendix to COTIF 1980, Convention concerning International Carriage by Rail—dealt with rail transport, whilst road transport was covered by the Convention on the Contract for the International Carriage of Passengers and Luggage by Road (CVR, Geneva, 1973).

At the beginning, the regulation of the rights of passengers in the European Union was different for different means of transport. The Regulations considered the particular nature of the means of transport, and the values that needed special protection. However, currently, and with the latest versions of these Regulations, a tendency to inter-modal unification can be seen, and the rights of passengers are now mostly governed by the same Regulation, regardless of the particular means of transport to which they relate.

2 The Notion of the Passenger in the Different Means of Transport

European Regulations do not define the concept of a passenger. The reader may think that the concept of a passenger is pretty clear: it is a person who is transported from one place to another using a vehicle. Normally the right to be transported is documented with a bill, a fare or a transport ticket. Nevertheless, some particular considerations must be added to pin this concept down.

First, the passenger is a party to a contract of carriage. By means of this contract, the carrier assumes the obligation to transport the passenger and his luggage from one point to another using the specified vehicle, complying with safety and security rules and in return for payment. On the one hand, this implies that members of the crew are not considered to be passengers, as their movement takes place as a consequence of a contract of employment with the carrier, not as a result of a voluntary contract of carriage. On the other hand, a contract of carriage is always for payment, regardless of how this remuneration is made. This implies the need to distinguish cases of totally free transport—for example, free riders or people who are freely transported on the basis of friendship—and cases where there is indirect compensation—when the passenger receives a free ride as a consequence of some other contractual link, such as a loyalty programme, company agreement, etc. People in the first cases are not considered to be passengers, as they do not fulfil the payment requirement; people in the second cases are passengers, as payment is made—even though it comes from another relationship.

Another interesting problem that comes from the given definition is that the regulation of the contract of carriage is binary, in the sense that it covers the transportation of passengers or of goods, but not the carriage of other 'objects' such as animals. For this reason, the literature normally considers that the general regulations regarding the transport of goods apply to the transport of animals, even when taking into account their needs for special treatment, or they are considered as luggage when they come with a passenger. It is clear overall that the transportation of luggage is covered by the single contract for the transport of a passenger, and that it does not imply any independent contract.

Obviously, there are important differences in how the service to transport passengers is provided for the different means of transport. Security and safety reasons require that the service is provided in a particular way, and, in many cases, this implies a need to recognize particular rights for passengers. For this reason, the regulations covering the different means of transport tend to solve the particular problems that arise from the transport by air, sea and inland waterways and land (road or rail). The determination of liabilities and the safety and security obligations of the carrier also vary.

2.1 *Air Transport*

The transport of passengers by air is mostly regulated in the EU by means of Regulation (EC) No 261/2004 establishing common rules on compensation and assistance to passengers in the event of denied boarding and of cancellation or long delay of flights, and Regulation (EC) No 889/2002 amending Council Regulation (EC) No 2027/97 on air carrier liability in the event of accidents. Besides these, Regulation (EC) 1107/2006 considers the rights of disabled persons and persons with reduced mobility when they are travelling by air.

2.2 *Transport by Sea*

The transport of passengers by sea is covered by Regulation (EU) No 1177/2010 of the European Parliament and of the Council of 24 November 2010 concerning the rights of passengers when travelling by sea and inland waterways, which amends Regulation (EC) No 2006/2004, and by Regulation (EC) No 392/2009 of the European Parliament and of the Council of 23 April 2009 on the liability of carriers of passengers by sea in the event of accidents (Berlingieri 2011; Olmedo Peralta 2014b). The first establishes the catalogue of rights for passengers on a ship, whilst the second performs the compulsory implementation of the rules of the Athens

Convention for all maritime transport in the EU (Comenale Pinto 2006; Olmedo Peralta 2014a; Petit Lavall 2013).

2.3 *Transport by Land: Rail, Bus and Coach*

Land transport of passengers was the final means of transport for which the European authorities decided to create a comprehensive catalogue of rights for passengers. Transport by rail is covered by Regulation (EC) No 1371/2007 of the European Parliament and of the Council on rail passengers' rights and obligations,[2] and Regulation (EU) No 181/2011, concerning the rights of passengers in bus and coach transport, covers the rights of passengers on this kind of vehicle.

3 Fundamental Rights Granted in the EU to All Kinds of Passengers

The Regulations mentioned above show a certain tendency to the unification of the regulation of passengers' rights across all the different means of transport (González Cabrera 2013). The European authorities have expressly stated this objective and considered its benefits.[3] Throughout the Regulations, some fundamental rights for passengers in the EU can be seen. These include the principle of non-discrimination between passengers, the right to access and assistance for disabled passengers and passengers with reduced mobility, the right to get complete information about the performance of the transport,[4] the right to choose to cancel a trip because of disruption, and the right to reroute and rebook a trip in the event that a journey cannot be concluded. Passengers also have fundamental rights to get assistance in the event of long delays, and to claim compensation in cases of cancellations or delays. Finally, regulations on the transport of passengers pay special attention to the liability of the carrier—and its limitation—as well as to the establishment of mechanisms for the easy handling of complaints that may arise for any kind of breach of contract or liability; these mechanisms are indispensable in the effective enforcement of rights.

---

[2] At the time this chapter is being written, there is a Proposal for a new Regulation that will recast the rights and obligations of rail passengers. See COM/2007/0548 final – 2017/0237 (COD).

[3] See Communication from the Commission to the European Parliament and the Council, A European vision for Passengers: Communication on Passenger Rights in all transport modes [COM/2011/0898 final].

[4] In particular, details of the identity of the carrier, and information about the creation of the so-called blacklist of air carriers. See Regulation (EC) No 2111/2005 on the list of air carriers subject to an operating ban within the EU and the identity of operating air carriers.

4 Related Concepts Covering Special Situations

4.1 Travellers

A concept that is different from, but related to, that of a passenger in the European Regulations is that of a 'traveller'. According to Article 3(6) of Directive 2015/2302/EU of the European Parliament and of the Council of 25 November 2015 on package travel and linked travel arrangements, a 'traveller' means any person who is seeking to conclude a contract, or is entitled to travel on the basis of a concluded contract, that lies within the scope of this Directive (a package travel contract or linked travel arrangements). In Article 2.2.c), the same Directive forbids professionals from being considered as passengers, excluding from its jurisdiction those packages and linked travel arrangements purchased on the basis of a general agreement for the arrangement of business travel between a trader and another natural or legal person who is acting on purposes relating to his trade, business, craft or profession. To the extent of the regulations on package travel, travellers are considered to be consumers.

4.2 Disabled Passengers and Passengers with Reduced Mobility (PRM)

Following the United Nations Convention on the Rights of Persons with Disabilities (CRPD 2006), European Regulations regarding the transport of passengers have included special provisions to grant the right to effective transport to a person with reduced mobility or with a disability. These provisions are included within the general catalogue of rights given in the Regulations on sea and land transport, and in a special norm—Regulation (EC) No 1107/2006, on the rights of disabled persons and persons with reduced mobility when travelling by air—for passengers on an aircraft. This latter Regulation defines in its Article 2(a) a 'disabled person' or a 'person with reduced mobility' as any person whose mobility when using transport is reduced due to any physical disability (sensory or locomotor, permanent or temporary), intellectual disability or impairment, or any other cause of disability, or age, and whose situation needs appropriate attention and the adaptation, to his or her particular needs, of the service made available to all passengers. The recognition of special rights for this kind of passenger is crucial for ensuring the fundamental right to mobility within the European area that is granted by the Treaties (Benavides Velasco 2013, 2015).

4.3 Unruly Passengers

In some cases, and especially regarding some means of transport, the behaviour of one passenger on the vehicle may jeopardize the security of all the passengers on the vehicle. The gravity of these acts is greater in vehicles such as aircraft or ships, where the captain has to exercise his authority by taking the necessary measures to ensure the security of all passengers. This situation of the so-called *unruly passenger*—someone who does not follow the instructions of the captain and the crew—has been addressed in certain international regulations, such as the Tokyo Convention on Offences and Certain Other Acts Committed on Board Aircraft 1963, and its amendment in the Montreal Protocol 2014 (Márquez Lobillo 2013).

4.4 Passengers in the Sharing Economy: Carpooling and Carsharing

The very notion of passenger has evolved in recent years because of the great success of electronic platforms in the sharing economy, such as *Uber*, *Lyft*, *Cabify* and *Blablacar*. The sharing economy removes the radical distinction between the provider of the services and the user, creating the figure of the 'prosumer', a person who may at one and the same time—regarding the collaborative transport—be the carrier and the passenger. For transport by land using collaborative vehicles, we can distinguish cases of carpooling—in which the passenger only contracts for one seat in a shared car—and carsharing—consisting of the sharing of the same vehicle by different subjects.

References

Benavides Velasco, P. (2013). Los derechos de los pasajeros con discapacidad o movilidad reducida en el transporte aéreo. In P. Lavall, M. Sanz, & R. Castells (Eds.), *La nueva ordenación del Mercado de Transporte* (pp. 473–487). Madrid: Marcial Pons.

Benavides Velasco, P. (2015). Obligaciones de información y asistencia en el transporte aéreo de personas con movilidad reducida. In G. Lebrón (Ed.), *La responsabilidad del transportista aéreo y la protección de los pasajeros* (pp. 221–254). Madrid: Marcial Pons.

Berlingieri, F. (2011). The Athens Convention on the carriage of passengers and their luggage by sea and the European Parliament Regulation (EC) No. 392/2009. *Il Diritto Marittimo, IV*, 1125–1140.

Comenale Pinto, M. (2006). Il trasporto marittimo di passeggeri: disciplina attuale e prospettive. *Diritto del Turismo, 2*, 110.

González Cabrera, I. (2013). Retraso, cancelación y denegación de embarque: un análisis comparado de su tratamiento en el Derecho de la navegación marítima y aérea. *Revista de Derecho del Transporte, 11*, 81–114.

Márquez Lobillo, P. (2013). La modernización del convenio de Tokio para la inclusion del 'unruly passenger'. In P. Lavall, M. Sanz, & R. Castells (Eds.), *La nueva ordenación del Mercado de Transporte* (pp. 595–615). Madrid: Marcial Pons.

Olmedo Peralta, E. (2014a). *Régimen jurídico del transporte marítimo de pasajeros: contratos de pasaje y crucero*. Madrid: Marcial Pons.

Olmedo Peralta, E. (2014b). New requirements and risk distribution for the liability of carriers of passengers by sea in the event of accidents under Regulation (EC) No 392/2009. *European Transport Law, III*, 247–270.

Petit Lavall, M. V. (2013). El Reglamento (UE) núm. 1177/2010 y la protección de los pasajeros que viajan por mar. *Revista de Derecho del Transporte, 12*, 11–29.

Patient

Melania D'Angelosante

1 Introduction: The Role of the EU in the Health Fields According to the EU Treaties

This study aims to analyse whether it is possible to argue the existence of a status of 'patient' in the EU framework and, if it exists, what its prerogatives (i.e. rights and duties) are and how it is being conditioned by contemporary EU law. In this perspective, it is necessary, first of all, to focus on the role of the EU in the fields of health and healthcare according to the Treaties of the European Union ("EU Treaties").

As regards this issue, taking into account a combined analysis of TEU Articles 2, 3 and 6,[1] one of the goals of the EU is achieving substantive equality among its citizens, so individual status should be restricted to assigned values which constitute a necessary precondition for the operation of EU law. This is also confirmed by the ECHR[2] Article 14, which forbids any form of discrimination based on citizenship.[3]

[1] To be more precise, Article 2 declares that the Union is founded on the values of respect for human dignity, freedom, democracy, equality, the rule of law and human rights, and that these values are common to the Member States in a society in which pluralism, nondiscrimination, tolerance, justice, solidarity and equality between women and men prevail. Article 3 lists the following among the aims of the EU: well-being, sustainable development, social market economy, full employment, social progress, and combating social exclusion and discrimination. Finally, Article 6 establishes that the Union recognises the rights, freedoms and principles set out in the Charter of Fundamental Rights of the European Union, which has the same legal value as the EU Treaties.

[2] European Convention on Human Rights, adopted by the Member States of the Council of Europe.

[3] Both the ECJ and ECoHR tried to check the existence of reasonableness in those sources of law, which established, for instance, some limits to social rights on the basis of national citizenship, see

M. D'Angelosante (✉)
Department of Legal and Social Sciences, G. d'Annunzio of Chieti-Pescara University, Pescara, Italy
e-mail: melania.dangelosante@unich.it

A. Bartolini et al. (eds.), *Dictionary of Statuses within EU Law*,
https://doi.org/10.1007/978-3-030-00554-2_52

In this framework, the TFEU establishes: the duty of the EU to take into account, in defining and implementing its policies, a high level of protection of human health[4] and the duty of the EU and Member States to have as their objectives improving employment, living and working conditions (including their harmonisation), and proper social protection.[5] Furthermore, the EU has: direct powers related to the establishment and management of the freedom of movement of persons as one of the tools for the establishment and management of the internal market[6]; powers aimed at supporting and complementing the activities of the Member States in the field of social policies[7]; powers aimed at the completion of national policies and the fostering of cooperation between them in the health field.[8]

This simple picture clarifies that the EU has direct and strong powers as regards the management of the internal market and economic development but indirect and weak powers as regards social policies (including health policies).

This is also confirmed by what the EChFR[9] establishes as regards healthcare, that "*everyone has the right of access to preventive health care and […] to benefit from medical treatment under the conditions established by national laws and practices*", though "*a high level of human health protection shall be ensured in the definition and implementation of all Union policies*".[10]

However, focusing only on social policies from a general point of view, one may argue that they have a double role: directly meeting certain essential needs of the population, but also indirectly increasing economic development.[11] Moreover, the funding of social rights, the access to them and the free movement of EU citizens are strictly intertwined and may increase a certain form of competition among the Member States. In fact, on the one hand, the discipline of rights in each of them can influence the movement of persons throughout Europe, and, on the other hand, the

---

ECJ Case C-209/03 *Bidar* [2005]; ECoHR Application P-46368/06 *Zeïbek v. Greece* [2009]; ECoHR Application P-5335/05 *Ponomaryovi v. Bulgaria* [2011].

[4]Article 9. As regards this issue, since the beginning of the new millennium, the ECJ has declared that the protection of health should prevail over economic development, see ECJ Case C-236/01 *Monsanto Agricoltura s.p.a. v. President of Council of Ministries* [2003]: this seems to imply, among others, the application of the precautionary principle.

[5]Article 151.

[6]Articles 45–48.

[7]Articles 151–161.

[8]Article 168.

[9]EU Charter of Fundamental Rights, which has the same legal value as the EU Treaties according to TEU Article 6, but is essentially aimed just at making the national fundamental rights more visible.

[10]Article 35.

[11]For instance, as regards healthcare, because "access to high-quality […] services can reduce health inequalities, social exclusion and poverty, key objectives of the Europe 2020 strategy", Eurofound (2014). In fact, from a wider ranging perspective, access to high-quality 'services of general interest' (among which healthcare is a key-service) is an important aspect of social protection, contributing to 'inclusive growth', a main objective of the Europe 2020 Strategy (EU Commission, 2010).

movement of persons throughout Europe can influence the social spending of the hosting State and the State to which the moving person belongs. From this perspective, the role of the EU in social policies could be increased (and in fact it has already increased in the past and perhaps it will also increase in the future) on the basis of the second dimension of the above-mentioned double role of these policies. Thus, due to these elements, the ESM[12] has realistically been based mainly on: (1) the enlargement of community policies beyond the original core of the economic and monetary union since the European Single Act and the Maastricht Treaty; and (2) the formulation, since the beginning of the new millennium, of the theory[13] that social services can be considered, under certain conditions, services of general economic interest subject to the rules of the Treaties regarding competition (unless the application of these rules hinders the particular task assigned to them).[14]

None of the sources above, however, refer to the concept of *patient* or use this word, though it is possible to argue that most of the policies regarding health imply this notion.

2 How the EU Treaties Have Been Implemented in the Health Fields

In the implementation of the picture emerging from the EU Treaties, however, the notion of *patient* emerges more frequently and explicitly.

In fact, since the 1980s, the ECJ has been declaring measures making the free movement of services between the Member States more difficult than the provision of the same services in each Member State in contrast with the principle of free movement of services in the EU,[15] unless there are reasons of financial sustainability of the national system.[16] As a consequence, according to some more recent decisions of the ECJ, if the NHS to which the patient belongs does not guarantee him a

[12] European social model.

[13] Coming from the ECJ and European Commission.

[14] See COM (2006), 2006/177, of the EC Commission, *Implementing the Community Lisbon programme: Social services of general interest in the European Union*; COM (2006), SEC 1195/4, of the EC Commission, *Consultation on a community action in the field of healthcare services*; COM (2007), 2007/725, of the EC Commission, *Accompanying the Communication on "A single market for 21st century Europe"—Services of general interest, including social services of general interest: a new European commitment*; Sorace (2010, pp. 1 ss.); Merusi (2010, pp. 313 ss.); Civitarese Matteucci (2009, pp. 179 ss.); Gobbato (2005, pp. 797 ss.). For further discussion on the themes developed in this chapter, see: Antoniazzi (2004); Carboni (2016); Chenal (2010); Da Costa and Borges (2011); Guazzarotti (2016); Henry and Chauviere (2011); Hervey (2002); Hetzel (2012); Kaczorowska (2006); Kilpatrick and De Witte (2014); O'Cinneide (2013); Repetto (2013); Streeck (2000).

[15] At present established in TFEU Article 56.

[16] See ECJ Case C-238/82 *Duphar Bv et al.* [1984]; ECJ Case C-204/90 *Bachmann v. Belgium* [1992]; ECJ Case C-158/96 *Kohll v. Union des caisses de maladie* [1998].

set of healthcare services covered by public financing of quantity and kind at least corresponding to those existing in other Member States, together with the duty of obtaining, when this correspondence exists, an authorization as a precondition of the reimbursement, it represents a hindrance to the free movement of services, as it seems to discourage the mobility of patients in the EU because of deficiencies regarding the healthcare services covered by public financing in the State of affiliation. In fact, if the healthcare service that the patient wishes to receive from another Member State is not listed among those covered by public financing in the State to which he belongs, he cannot ask for the reimbursement of the service in the State of affiliation.[17] On the contrary, the authorization or reimbursement can be denied, without compromising the free movement of services, if that healthcare can be delivered by the State of affiliation at a time and under conditions which are compatible with the degree of the illness.[18]

Following this case law, which is essentially focused on the management of the internal market *via* the free movement of services, the EC/U legislator adopted Regulation 2004/883/EC (whose implementation procedure is established by Regulation 2009/987/EC) on the coordination of social security systems, and Directive 2011/24/EU on the application of patients' rights regarding cross-border healthcare. However, while in the former the word *patient* is not used, since the text refers to *persons* needing healthcare (and Regulation 2009/987/EC uses the word *patient* just once in the Preamble), the latter is formally focused on the *patient*, which is defined as "*any natural person who seeks to receive or receives healthcare in a Member State*" (Article 3).[19]

The first difference between the *regulation-system* and the *directive-system* is that, while the former regards—among other social services—both *urgent and scheduled cross-border healthcare*, the latter regards just *scheduled cross-border healthcare*.

Moreover, the regulation allows EU citizens in possession of the European Health Insurance Card to benefit from healthcare in a Member State different from that to which they belong—and according to the organisational requirements existing in this State, without paying anything (except tickets if existing in the host State) since the spending is directly covered by the State of affiliation. Thus, the regulation establishes a *direct assistance scheme*, and does not generally cover private healthcare. It is possible to benefit from this scheme, even for specialized or hospital care—or for scheduled cross-border healthcare—if the following conditions exist: the healthcare system to which the patient belongs has authorised the mobility; the

[17] See ECJ Case C-211/08 *Commission v. Spain* [2010]; ECJ Case C-368/98 *Vanbraekel* [2001]; ECJ Case C-255/09 *European Commission v. Portuguese Republic* [2011].

[18] See ECJ Case C-157/99 *Smits v. Peerbooms* [2001].

[19] This action has been also accompanied by many not binding, and even important, sources of law: see, among others, COM (2006), SEC 1195/4, 26 September 2006, *Consultation on a community action in the field of healthcare services*.

healthcare service concerned cannot be provided in the State to which the patient belongs under conditions which are compatible with the degree of the illness.[20]

On the contrary, the directive[21] establishes an *indirect assistance scheme* and regards, as stated above, just the *scheduled cross-border healthcare*. According to the directive, in fact, the healthcare services delivered in the host State have to be paid, usually, directly by the patient.[22] The patient, in turn, can ask for reimbursement from the State of affiliation if the care concerned belongs to that which is covered by public funding in his national healthcare system, observing the limits on the cost of the service in this system. Moreover, for some care, the patient needs the authorisation of the State of affiliation (which cannot be denied if in the same State the healthcare service concerned cannot be provided at a time which is compatible with the degree of the illness).[23]

One of the implementing tools for the scheme set up by the directive consists of the so-called ERNs[24] between healthcare providers and centres of expertise in the Member States, to be developed, according to the directive itself, by the Member States with the support of the Commission. Following the directive, according to Commission Delegated Decision 2014/286/EU, the first ERN was launched in 2017.[25] In this framework, Annex II to the delegated decision is worthy of mention as regards, among others, some of the conditions established for applicants who want to become members of a network, for instance, measures aimed at ensuring respect of "the patients' rights", "such as the right to informed consent; the right to information concerning their own health; the right to access to their medical records; the right to privacy; the right to complain and the right to obtain compensation, the

[20] The first framework legislation on this issue, i.e. Regulation 1971/1408/EEC, on the application of social security schemes to employed persons and their families moving within the Community, just regards these recipients and establishes, in the field of healthcare, the right of the employed person to receive: (1) *immediate care* during a stay in the territory of another Member State, (2) *scheduled care in kind* from the State where he stays or resides with funds covered by the NHS to which he belongs, and (3) *benefits in cash for healthcare* covered by his NHS, expendable in the State where he stays or resides. Both the benefits to which rights (2) and (3) above refer are conditional, as a general rule, on the authorisation of the NHS to which the employed person belongs. These measures have been adopted pursuing the aim of the abolition of any discrimination based on nationality between workers of the Member States (at present enshrined in TFEU Articles 45 and 46).

[21] Adopted in light of the approximation of laws on the internal market and policies in the field of public health according to TFEU Articles 114 and 168.

[22] However, the directive also mentions the possibility of a direct payment by the State of affiliation.

[23] The directive also establishes the mutual recognition of prescriptions for a medicinal product or device issued in the Member States—if the medical product or device is authorised to be marketed in the territory of one of them—unless the special conditions allowing restrictions to recognition exist.

[24] European Reference Networks.

[25] Involving more than 900 highly specialised healthcare units from over 300 hospitals in 26 EU countries, with the aim of facilitating the discussion on complex or rare diseases, even concentrating knowledge and resources.

right to be empowered and to participate", even indirectly, in the management and organisational strategies of the applicant provider. Other conditions dealing with the patients' rights include the duty of the applicant provider to "ensure feedback on patient experience and the active evaluation of patient experience", "transparency", "a patient safety programme or plan", "clinical guidelines", and the use of "the best knowledge and evidence-based health [...] treatments".

The right of patients to be informed is also established in other sources regarding medicines, which refer moreover to the participation of patients' groups[26] and to the need for medicines to be more efficacious, safer, higher in quality, more available and affordable.[27] From a narrower point of view, sometimes a particular kind of protection, including the right to information, emerges as regards certain categories of patients.[28]

In more recent years, however, the ongoing crisis has affected both the economic sector and the European integration process, as Brexit shows. In this framework, the role of the EU partly changed and is still changing. This role also changed and is still changing as regards the relationship between the EU and the States' sovereignty. To sum up, the issues stemming from this picture are, first of all, the fact that the decrease of the States' sovereignty may endanger the sustainability of the national welfare systems, and, second, the fact that the present condition of the EU integration process could make the national dimension inappropriate to meet certain social needs.

The EU is partly facing the dual dimensions (the financial dimension and that related to the EU integration process) of the crisis by improving the ESM[29] via the so-called Strategy based on the adoption of the EPSR, which was proclaimed by the EU Council, Parliament and Commission on November 2017 and is addressed to the Member States of the Euro Area,[30] though also the other Member States can ask to be part of the Pillar.

The main goals of the Pillar, as mentioned in its preamble, are: addressing the consequences of the financial crisis, since economic and social progress are intertwined; building a more inclusive and sustainable growth model, for the same reasons; and introducing a guide aimed at fostering the other goals. The principles enshrined in the Pillar concern both the EU citizens and third-country nationals with legal residence in the EU countries.

---

[26] In order to ensure that patient needs are duly taken into account.

[27] See EC Council Resolution of 2 December 2003 on *pharmaceuticals and public health challenges—focusing on the patients*; EC Council Recommendation of 9 June 2009 on *patient safety, including the prevention and control of healthcare-associated infections* (as regards patient safety, the recommendation itself clarifies that it consists of the "freedom, for a patient, from unnecessary harm or potential harm associated with healthcare"); Directive 1993/42/CE concerning medical devices.

[28] See EEC Council Resolution of 16 June 1986, concerning *the protection of dialysis patients by minimising the exposure to aluminium*.

[29] Instrumental to increasing economic development, *supra*.

[30] Since, according to its preamble, a stronger focus on social performance is particularly important to strengthen the Economic and Monetary Union.

However, the same Pillar limits itself, declaring that: (1) it does not prevent Member States from establishing more ambitious social standard; (2) it respects the organization of the Member States and their right to define the fundamental principles of their social security systems and to manage their financial systems; (3) it does not restrict rights and principles as already recognized by Union, international, and national law; and (4) requires dedicated measures to be adopted at the appropriate level to make legally enforceable the principles and rights it enshrines.

In this framework, it gives both the EU and Member States[31] the duty to implement the principles and rights it establishes respectively at the EU and national levels.

As regards the contents, they may be distinguished on the basis of a general and special perspective. According to the former, the Pillar focuses on the confirmation of some of the rights already present in the Union *aquis* and the establishment of new principles addressing the challenges of the new millennium. According to the special perspective, it enshrines 20 principles/rights, divided into three chapters: the third of these chapters, named *Social protection and inclusion*, mentions, among others, the right to healthcare (Article 16, according to which "*everyone has the right to timely access to affordable, preventive and curative health care of good quality*"), and long term care (Article 18, according to which "*everyone has the right to affordable long-term care services of good quality, in particular home-care and community-based services*").

However, the reading of the Pillar allows us to highlight some of its further and implied limitations: first of all, despite its preamble, in the wording of the 20 principles/rights we usually find expressions such as *have/has the right*, *shall*, and *must be*, while just twice we find the expression *should*; moreover, just four times does this wording refer to national policies, autonomy and rules. Second, despite the wording of the 20 principles/rights, their content is too general to allow the checking of their violation and no sanction is established or suggested for the violation: thus, the Pillar seems mainly aimed just at making some principles/rights more visible and at giving the same visibility to new principles/rights. Finally, the main limit to the further improvement of the ESM via the Pillar seems to reside in the relationship between its main substantive goal and the tools at its disposal to achieve it: in fact, while the Pillar tends to ensure the achievement of a certain common standard by the national welfare systems, this achievement is under the exclusive financial responsibility of the Member States, since the Pillar does not deal with the financial aspects and the EU does not have the power to levy taxes[32] to support the achievement of this common standard.

[31] Within their competences in accordance with the principles of subsidiarity and proportionality.

[32] Common fiscal policy.

3 Concluding Remarks

Different issues emerge from the study as regards the existence of a status of *patient* and its meaning in the contemporary EU law.

First, as regards *the existence of a concept of patient as an individual status in the EU framework*, it is necessary to distinguish between primary EU law, on the one hand, and secondary EU law and case law, on the other.

The first dimension does not include any legal basis for the status of patient, which, at least, may be considered implied in EU powers aimed at fostering a high level of human health and at the completion of national policies and the fostering of cooperation between Member States in the health field.

On the contrary, if we focus on the second dimension, we can find that, since the new millennium, first the ECJ and second the legislator began to refer to the *patient* (as an individual having his own status different from that of the *citizen* or *person*).

Second, as regards *the meaning of this status, whether it is focused on the creation of new privileges undermining the goal of achieving substantive equality between EU citizens or on its use as a necessary precondition for the operation of EU law*, we can find that the second option seems to be supported by the following considerations.

The ECJ case law began to consider the status of 'patient' in the light of the management of the internal market, *i.e.* with the aim of guaranteeing the free movement of healthcare services and their users (the patients). Following this case law, the EC legislature adopted: Regulation 2004/883/EC (where the word *patient* is not used, since it refers to *persons* needing healthcare) and Regulation 2009/987/EC (where the word *patient* is used just once in the Preamble) on the coordination of social security systems; and Directive 2011/24/EU on the application of patients' rights in cross-border healthcare. The directive is even formally focused on the *patient*, who is defined as "*any natural person who seeks to receive or receives healthcare in a Member State*". Both the Regulations and the Directive seem mainly oriented to the same perspective adopted by the case law, though the directive also contains seeds for the further development of the status of patient over this dimension. In fact, one of the implementing tools for the scheme set up by the directive consists of the so-called ERNs, the first of which was launched according to Commission Delegated Decision 2014/286/EU, whose Annex II establishes, among the other conditions for the membership of the network, the putting into place of measures aimed at ensuring the respect of "the patients' rights" mentioned in paragraph 2 above. Before this, some patients' rights have been taken into account just by several not binding sources of law or directives regarding medicines or few categories, such as dialysis patients (*supra*, par. 2).

In more recent years, the eruption of the economic crisis has strengthened the EU social policies (including health), since the improvement of social benefits is considered instrumental to the increase in economic development. We refer to the strategy based on the EPSR, which, however, besides not mentioning the (status of) patient,[33] shows the limitations we have already enshrined in paragraph 2 above.

Third, as regards the existence of a *unitary definition of the legal status of the patient over that constructed by a particular Member State's legal system*, the peculiarity of the EU approach, which distinguishes it from the approach of each Member State, is the consideration of the patient mainly as a user of certain services to be managed in the light of their free movement. Beside this, the notion of the patient as an individual who is also the recipient of certain rights emerges explicitly just in some sectorial sources of law.[34] Furthermore, it refers to entitlements that, due to their contents[35] seem to be traceable to the common traditions of the Member States. This is similar to the role of the EPSR, when it confirms some of the rights already present in the Union *aquis*, and to the role of the EUChFR, when it uses the concept of everyone (implying that of the patient) having the right of access to preventive health care and to benefit from medical treatment under the conditions established by national laws and practices.

References

Antoniazzi, S. (2004). Sistema sanitario nazionale e principio comunitario di libera prestazione di servizi: la scelta dell'utente per prestazioni mediche erogate in un diverso paese membro, subordinata alla necessaria autorizzazione amministrativa dello stato membro di appartenenza per il rimborso delle spese sostenute. *Riv, it. Dir. Pubb. Comunit., 2*, 603 ff.

Carboni, G. (2016). La mobilità nel diritto dell'Unione europea. *DPCE, 1*, 13 ff.

Chenal, R. (2010). Il diritto alla salute e la Convenzione europea dei diritti dell'uomo. In R. Cavallo Perin, L. Lenti, G. Racca, & A. Rossi (Eds.), *I diritti sociali come diritti della personalità* (p. 75 ss). Napoli: Esi.

Civitarese Matteucci, S. (2009). Servizi sanitari, mercato e "modello sociale europeo". *MCR, 1*, 179 ff.

Da Costa, D., & Borges, L. (2011). Making sense of human rights in the context of European Union health-care policy: Individualist and communitarian views. *International Journal of Law in Context, VII*(3), 335 ff.

Eurofound. (2014). *Access to healthcare in times of crisis*. Luxembourg: Publications Office of the European Union.

Gobbato, S. (2005). Diritto comunitario della concorrenza e servizi di interesse generale di carattere sociale. Note a margine della recente giurisprudenza della Corte di giustizia. *Dir. Un. Eur., 4*, 797 ff.

Guazzarotti, A. (2016). Giurisprudenza CEDU e giurisprudenza costituzionale sui diritti sociali a confronto. http://www.gruppodipisa.it

[33] Though it may be considered implied in the concept of "*everyone*" having "*the right to timely access to affordable, preventive and curative health care of good quality*", like the EChFR Article 35.

[34] For instance, in the fields of medicines, dialysis patients or membership of the ERNs.

[35] Information, participation, access, privacy, complaining, minimized exposure to risks.

Henry, J., & Chauviere, M. (2011). Quel statut pour les services sociaux dans l'union européenne? Arguments pour des services sociaux non économiques d'intérêt général. *Revue du droit sanitaire et social, 6*, 1043 ff.
Hervey, T. K. (2002). Mapping the contours of European Union health law and policy. *European Public Law, 8*, 69 ff.
Hetzel, R. L. (2012). *The great recession: Market failure or policy failure?* Cambridge: Cambridge University Press.
Kaczorowska, A. (2006). A review of the creation by the European Court of Justice of the right to effective and speedy medical treatment and its outcomes. *European Law Journal, 12*(3), 365 ff.
Kilpatrick, C., & De Witte, B. (2014). *Social rights in times of crisis in the eurozone: The role of fundamental rights' challenges*. Firenze: European University Institute.
Merusi, F. (2010). Lo schema della regolazione dei servizi di interesse economico generale. *Dir. amm., 2*, 313 ff.
O'Cinneide, C. (2013). Legal accountability and social justice. In N. Bamforth & P. Leyland (Eds.), *Accountability in the contemporary constitution*. Oxford: Oxford University Press.
Repetto, G. (2013). "Non di sola CEDU…" – La fecondazione assistita e il diritto alla salute in Italia e in Europa. *Dir. pubb., 1*, 131 ff.
Sorace, D. (2010). I servizi "pubblici" economici nell'ordinamento nazionale ed europeo, alla fine del primo decennio del XXI secolo. *Dir. amm., 1*, 1 ff.
Streeck, W. (2000). Il modello sociale europeo: dalla ridistribuzione alla solidarietà competitiva. *Stato e Mercato, 1*, 3 ff.

Policemen

Mary Muscat

1 The Evolution of European Policing

European legal instruments have been speaking of 'police officers' rather than specifying the gender of the same. European policing, however, is not the sole remit of police officers; there is the wider context of law enforcers having policing duties that would encompass other agencies having police powers. In fact, the Council Framework Decision 2006/960/JHA on the exchange of police information, in its definition (art. 2) speaks of the 'competent law enforcement authority' within the MS which includes 'a national police, customs or other authority that is authorised by national law to detect, prevent and investigate offences or criminal activities and to exercise authority and take coercive measures in the context of such activities.' Regulation (EU) 2015/2219 outlining the Cepol mandate defines law enforcement officials as 'staff of police, customs and other relevant services, as defined by individual MS, that are responsible for, and staff of Union bodies that have tasks relating to… the prevention of and fight against serious crime affecting two or more MS, terrorism and forms of crime that affect a common interest covered by a Union policy; or crisis management and public order, in particular international policing of major events.'

At the national institutional level, the police officer has assumed new roles specifically created to foster European police cooperation, namely the 'liaison officer' within agencies such as Europol, the 'correspondent' within Cepol, and the member of the 'joint investigation team' (JIT). The definition of 'liasion officer', according to Council Decision 2003/170/JHA,[1] is "a representative of one of the Member States, posted abroad by a law enforcement agency to one or more third countries or

[1] https://eur-lex.europa.eu/legal-content/EN/TXT/HTML/?uri=CELEX:32003D0170&from=EN.

M. Muscat (✉)
Civil Law Department, Faculty of Laws, University of Malta, Msida, Malta
e-mail: mary.muscat@um.edu.mt

A. Bartolini et al. (eds.), *Dictionary of Statuses within EU Law*,
https://doi.org/10.1007/978-3-030-00554-2_53

to international organisations to establish and maintain contacts with the authorities in those countries or organisations with a view to contributing to preventing or investigating criminal offences."

Specialised programmes such as OLAF (fraud investigation) and Daphne (victims of violence), the harmonization of laws such as human trafficking, child sexual abuse, sexual exploitation and child pornography, and specific tools apart from the JITs such as the European Investigation Order (EIO), the European Arrest Warrant (EAW) and the European Protection Order (EPO) have been developed since Nadelmann (1993) had famously predicted that European policing has only one avenue to follow—'Americanization', in view of the Drug Enforcement Agency and the Federal Bureau of Investigation models, as well as the police technological advances developed within the US. Twenty-five years later, EU policing formed its own model of police cooperation away from federalisation and the single agency having enforcement powers largely given the various legal traditions, sovereignty and jurisdictions of the ever-increasing number of MS (Hoffman 2008, Collantes Celandor 2009, Cools et al. 2010, Haggenmüller 2013, Leonard and Kaunert 2016, Devroe et al. 2017). This could only exist within the European context in sharp contrast to the United States being a single, homogeneous country, or even in contrast with Interpol, since the EU has its own 'semi-autonomous security fields' (Devroe et al. 2017). Not only that, but the authors identify the 'variegated historical experiences of European countries' that form the base of 'the local reality of policing' and therefore the 'continued importance of national policing strategies'.

Bigo (2000) identifies diplomacy between the MS as a crucial attribute that shaped European police cooperation, an element that would prevent the shaping of a process such as Americanization, with trail blazers such as the TREVI and Pompidou groups during the 90s. Authors such as Killingray (1997), Mazower (1997), Barth and Cvetkovski (2015), Gekas (2017) and O'Reilly (2018), to mention a few researchers of colonial police histories, have shown over and over again that the experience of a shared model of policing that has been exported to parts of the empire, helped foster a policing experience and identity that enriched the European experience, through better or worse through cross-fertilisation of experiences. 'Empire knowledge', or the accumulation and exchange of experience of governors and principal civil servants serving the empire who moved from colony to colony to carry out their assignments was another factor that was a precursor to cooperation rather than Americanization.

Even the Europeanisation of policing debate has moved on since the early 90s (Benyon 1994, Benyon et al. 1993, Anderson et al. 1995, Sheptycki 2000, Haberfeld and Cerrah 2008, Hoffman 2008, Bowling and Sheptycki 2012). Anderson et al. (1995) had expressed caution at using the term since it implied the existence of 'European crime', which could either mean crimes directed against the European institutions or crime that could only occur within Europe. This was far from the case; the Europeanisation being debated had two models it could either emulate or aspire to: Interpol and the American federal agencies such as the FBI, and DEA. There was never really a need to have a supranational police agency, the equivalent of the European Court in terms of justice. The formation of EUROPOL was quite a 'culture shock' (Anderson et al. 1995) especially for Interpol, of which incidentally, all 27 MS of the EU are currently members. But with the Justice and Home Affairs (JHA) pillar and subsequent JHA programmes the gaps that prevented cooperation started to be bridged with the acknowledgment and tribute to existing police structures. With the benefit of hindsight, the academic and political debates on Europeanisation in the early 90s contributed to the efforts made at harmonizing practices throughout the MS.

Apart from the JHA programmes, the routes leading to the present status were multiple, including legislation and judgments of the European Court of Human Rights. In terms of legislation, for instance, data protection measures governing the exchange of police data facilitated the eventual development of systems such as the Schengen Information System (SIS), the Supplementary Information Request at the National Entries (SIRENE), the Visa Information System (VIS), the Secure Information Exchange Network Application (SIENA) and the Eurodac fingerprint database. As for European Court of Human Rights (ECrtHR) judgments, standards in policing were set through cases such as Salduz v Turkey (2008),[2] where the Salduz principle finally paved the way through the last bastions of policing that did not yet allow the presence of a lawyer either before and/or during police interrogations, or the availability of legal assistance during police detention.

At the EU level the "policeman's" role took on another role hitherto not envisaged at the national level unless there was a colonial situation in place—state-building, as in the European Union Police Mission (EUPM) in Bosnia and Herzegovina. Policing experience has also been exchanged and has been the catalyst for the formation of new institutions such as the Eurogendfor, which is based specifically on the gendarmerie model of policing and has followed along the lines of the UN's UNPOL and peace-keeping missions.

Incidentally, both the non-armed police and the gendarme models are equally represented within the EU, in the sense that there is no preference for one model over the other as occurred in the colonial policing models, as was the case with the British Empire in particular with relation to the Irish versus the Metropolitan police models imposed in the colonies, often with repressive and tragic effects. This is another characteristic of police cooperation in the EU: democratically promoting what already exists in the MS without having recourse to re-inventing the European policing wheel. Not only that, but there is a sense of equality and respect for the diversities of policing and no singular model has been imposed over existing state institutions. To do that would be anathema to the very idea of cooperation. Perhaps Europe has learnt its historical lessons from colonial policing.

---

[2] Salduz v. Turkey [GC] - 36391/02 Judgment 27.11.2008: https://hudoc.echr.coe.int/eng#{"fulltext":["salduz"],"documentcollectionid2":["GRANDCHAMBER","CHAMBER"],"itemid":["001-89893"]}.

2 New Policing Tools

The main tools enhancing and streamlining police procedure and infrastructure are summarised as follows (in descending chronological order):

Instrument	Subject	Procedures introduced
Directive (EU) 2016/800	Procedural safeguards for children who are suspects or accused persons in criminal proceedings	Determination of the age of the child; children should receive information about general aspects of the conduct of the proceedings; where a child is deprived of liberty, the Letter of Rights is provided; to be assisted by a lawyer without undue delay; the right to be accompanied by the holder of parental responsibility during other stages of the proceedings at which they are present, such as during police questioning; the right to an individual assessment to identify their specific needs in terms of protection, education, training and social integration.
Directive (EU) 2016/681	Use of passenger name record (PNR)	Establishing a single designated passenger information unit ('PIU') in the relevant MS, retention periods of data as appropriate
Directive (EU) 2016/680	Processing of data protection (police and judicial cooperation)	Introduces role of Data Protection Officer, registration of police info databases, and establishes giving notice to data subject of breach of data within 72 h of such breach
Directive (EU) 2016/343	Strengthening of certain aspects of the presumption of innocence and of the right to be present at the trial in criminal proceedings	Aims to foster effective trust of MS' criminal justice systems and to facilitate mutual recognition of decisions in criminal matters; right to remain silent; right not to incriminate oneself which should not prevent authorities from taking the necessary evidence including biological samples; abstain from presenting suspects or accused persons in court or in public while wearing prison clothes; abstain from presenting suspects or accused persons as being guilty, in court or in public, through the use of measures of physical restraint, such as handcuffs, glass boxes, cages and leg irons, unless the use of such measures is required for case-specific reasons; appropriate ways of presenting info to the media re-suspect; prosecution, but also judges and competent courts are charged with seeking both inculpatory and exculpatory evidence. Right to fair trial and to be present for the same

(continued)

Instrument	Subject	Procedures introduced
Directive 2014/41/ EU	The European Investigation Order (in criminal matters)	Investigation in real time, continuously and over a certain timeframe; covert investigations included; cover any investigative measure except for the setting up of a joint investigation team; may be transmitted via the European Judicial Network (EJN); parameters in place such as time limits, transmission of evidence between MS, legal challenges to the evidence gathered, video and telephone conferencing
Regulation (EU) No 1052/2013	Eurosur	European Border Surveillance System: establishing a National Coordination Centre (NCC) for the exchange of info with Frontex
Regulation (EU) No 604/2013	Eurodac	Sets up the EU asylum fingerprint database; time limits for inputting data as well as time limits for the retention of such data in the system
Directive 2013/48/ EU	Right of access to a lawyer in criminal proceedings, EAW proceedings and deprivation of liberty	Right to lawyer of persons detained by the police including children; introduction of the procedure of Letter of Rights
Directive 2012/29/ EU	Minimum standards on the rights, support and protection of victims of crime (the 'Budapest roadmap')	Acknowledgement of complaint to be given to the victim, info about reimbursement for injuries; info re-release or escape of offender; specialist support and legal protection for vulnerable victims; free translation of documents if victim's language is different; right to be informed of prosecutor's case management
Directive 2012/13/ EU	The right to information in criminal proceedings	Disclosure proceedings—right of access to the materials of the case, Letter of Rights, right to information about the case; training for law enforcement officials
Directive 2011/99/ EU	European Protection Order	Mutual recognition of protection measures in criminal matters between MS; does not include witness protection programmes; treatment of protection to be swift; if withdrawn by issuing State the executing State can introduce protection measures according to national law if the need exists
Regulation (EC) No 1071/2009	ERRU	Establishing and interconnecting national registers in the European Register for Road Undertakings system
Council Framework Decision 2009/315/ JHA	Extraction of info from the criminal record between MS	The electronic exchange of extracts of information about convictions between the central authorities
Regulation (EC) No 767/2008	The Visa Information System (VIS)	Categories of data covered: alphanumeric, photographic, fingerprint, links to other available applications

(continued)

Instrument	Subject	Procedures introduced
Council Decision 2008/617/JHA	The improvement of cooperation between the special intervention units of the MS of the EU in crisis situations	Assistance in providing the requesting MS with equipment and/or expertise and/or of carrying out actions on the territory of that MS, using weapons if so required
Council Decision 2008/616/JHA	Cross-border cooperation in combating terrorism and cross-border crime	Ensuring the availability of the systems of automated searching or comparison of DNA data, dactyloscopic data and vehicle registration data to be made accessible 24/7
Council Recommendation 2007/562/EC	Sharing of information on terrorist kidnappings	Refers to sharing of info such as hostage taker's background, mediator services
Council Decision 2007/533/JHA	Law enforcement cooperation	Allowing competent authorities to create and consult alerts on missing persons and on persons or objects related to criminal offences
Directive 2006/126/EC	European rules on driving licences	New driving licence categories, harmonization of driving licence documents; establishment of a network for the exchange of driving licence information (RESPER)
Council Decision 2004/919/EC	Tackling vehicle crime with cross-border implications	Drive to increase use of European Vehicle and Driving Licence Information System (EUCARIS)
Council Decision 2002/348/JHA	Security in connection with football matches with an international dimension	Establishment of a national football information point and related procedure
Council Decision 2003/335/JHA	The investigation and prosecution of genocide, crimes against humanity and war crimes	To facilitate investigation and prosecution of such crimes through coordination and periodic meetings
Council Decision 2003/170/JHA	The common use of liaison officers posted abroad by the law enforcement agencies of the MS	To regulate questions relating to the fight against serious cross-border crime
Framework Decision 2002/584/JHA	European arrest warrant proceedings (EAW)	Mutual recognition of arrest warrants
Council Framework 2002/465/JHA	Joint investigation teams	Model JIT agreement
Regulation (EC) No 1987/2006	Border control cooperation	The SIS enables border guards and visa issuing and migration authorities to enter and consult alerts on third-country nationals for refusing their entry into or stay in the Schengen Area
Regulation (EC) No 1986/2006	Cooperation on vehicle registration	Vehicle registration services may consult the SIS to check the legal status of the vehicles presented to them for registration. They only have access to SIS alerts on vehicles, registration certificates and number plates

3 Conclusion

The table above can be supplemented further with related instruments depending on the remit of the police powers and duties of the MS. For instance, borders can be manned by police officers rather than border guards in certain MS. The table can include other programmes and police-related networks such as crime prevention; it is by no means exhaustive. But the 28 instruments listed above are indicative of how far European policing has moved. At the basis of this lies the EU's Area of Freedom, Security, and Justice (AFSJ) fortified slowly over the two decades by programmes such as Tampere, The Hague, Stockholm, and the Ypres strategic guidelines. In a sense, the lure of police technology that was central to the idea of Americanization in the early 90s materialised through an exercise of diplomacy and cooperation that manifested as a combination of EU legal procedures and police technology especially in terms of the specialised databases and networks.

References

Anderson, M., den Boer, M., Cullen, P., Gilmore, W., Raab, C., & Walker, N. (1995). *Policing the European Union*. Oxford: Clarendon Press.

Barth, V., & Cvetkovski, R. (Eds.). (2015). *Imperial co-operation and transfer, 1870–1930. Empires and encounters*. London: Bloomsbury.

Benyon, J. (1994). Policing the European Union: The changing basis of cooperation on law enforcement. *International Affairs, 70*(3), 497–517.

Benyon, J., Turnbull, L., Willis, A., Woodward, R., & Beck, A. (1993). *Police co-operation in Europe: An investigation*. Leicester: University of Leicester.

Bigo, D. (2000). Liaison officers in Europe: New officers in the European security field. In J. W. E. Sheptycki (Ed.), *Issues in transnational policing* (p. 67 ff). London: Routledge.

Bowling, B., & Sheptycki, J. (2012). *Global policing*. London: Sage.

Collantes Celandor, G. (2009). Becoming 'European' through police reform: A successful strategy in Bosnia and Herzegovina? *Crime Law Social Change, 51*, 231–242. https://doi.org/10.1007/s10611-008-9157-x

Cools, M., De Kimpe, S., Dormaels, A., Easton, M., Enhus, E., Ponsaers, P., et al. (Eds.). (2010). *Police, policing, policy and the city in Europe*. Den Haag: Eleven International Publishing.

Devroe, E., Edwards, A., & Ponsaers, P. (Eds.). (2017). *Policing European metropolises. The politics of security in city-regions*. London: Routledge.

Gekas, S. (2017). *Xenocracy. State, class and colonialism in the Ionian Islands, 1815–1864*. New York: Berghahn Books.

Haberfeld, M. R., & Cerrah, I. (Eds.). (2008). *Comparative policing. The struggle for democratization*. Thousand Oaks, CA: Sage.

Haggenmüller, S. (2013). The principle of proportionality and the European Arrest Warrant. *Oñati Socio-Legal Series, 3*(1), 95–106.

Hoffman, H. (2008). Mapping the European administrative space. *West European Politics, 31*(4), 662–676.

Killingray, D. (1997). Securing the British Empire: Policing and colonial order, 1922–1969. In M. Mazower (Ed.), *The policing of politics in the twentieth century. Historical perspectives*. (p. 167 ff. Providence, RI: Berghahn Books.

Leonard, S., & Kaunert, C. (2016). Beyond Stockholm: In search of a strategy for the European Union's area of freedom, security, and justice. *European Politics and Society, 17*(2), 143–149.
Mazower, M. (Ed.). (1997). *The policing of politics in the twentieth century. Historical perspectives*. Providence, RI: Berghahn Books.
O'Reilly, C. (Ed.). (2018). *Colonial policing and the transnational legacy. The global dynamics of policing across the Lusophone community*. London: Routledge.
Sheptycki, J. W. E. (Ed.). (2000). *Issues in transnational policing*. London: Routledge.

Pollution Victim

Fabio Anile

1 Introduction

From the very outset, the issue of protecting individuals from harm caused by pollution in the environment has been made harder by the complexity of the definition of the "environment", which is also taken as including "the right to a healthy environment" and the related issue of "environmental damage".

First and foremost, addressing the question of safeguarding people affected by harm to the environment requires the existence of a legal definition of the "environment". This term refers not only to the *biological environment* as defined by the science of ecology, but also implies a diverse set of political, social and philosophical factors entailing environmental protection through the protection of animals, the reduction of pollution, the promotion of renewable energy sources and sustainable development, the safeguarding of natural resources and ecosystems, and the promotion of protected natural areas. What emerges from this intermingling of values and interests is clearly the importance of people, in other words, the fact that people are "part of the environment". Therefore, when we demand the right to a healthy environment, we are essentially seeking to affirm our right to life, health, safety and the right to enjoy our own habitat. In this regard, the term "environment" is emblematic, as it actually means "what lies around us". The very notion of the "environment" becomes all the more complex as it implies the safeguarding of multiple value-based requirements. Unquestionably, one of the most problematic aspects is how to quantify damage (Cordini 2016). In other words, should it be chiefly based on harm to human health and to the environment in general, or on distinct, specific environmental interests? This is a difficult issue because these are questions implying the valuation of particularly delicate aspects (attributing liability, financial evaluation of damage, burden of proof, insurance against risks, access to legal judgements and

F. Anile (✉)
Ordine degli avvocati di Roma, Rome, Italy

A. Bartolini et al. (eds.), *Dictionary of Statuses within EU Law*,
https://doi.org/10.1007/978-3-030-00554-2_54

standing to initiate legal proceedings) which largely arise as a consequence of discrepancies in the national legal systems, and within a European Union framework, the contentious decision regarding and doubtful possibility of using a liability model based on a wider, unitary concept of environmental protection (Acts of I International Forum, 1989).[1]

2 The History of EU Regulations

In regulatory terms, we should start by considering that, originally, the EEC treaty, like the previous European Convention, contained no reference whatsoever to the environment. However, as time passed, the institutions, and indirectly, the Court of Justice, could not avoid taking an interest in the environment due to points of contact with the construction of the single European market. Thanks to what is known as the severability clause contained in article 235 TEEC (now article 352 TFEU), the European institutions could take the initiative with regard to areas outside their remit provided that they contributed to achieving Treaty aims.[2] Only in 1987, when the Single European Act was passed, was a chapter specifically included within the EEC treaty which dealt with the environment. Thus, from that time on, actions undertaken by European Union institutions on the environment rested on a solid regulatory foundation, initiating what became a veritable environmental policy. The key aims of this policy are now set in general terms by article 2, paragraph 3 TEU, as amended by the Lisbon Treaty,[3] which states: "*The Union shall establish an internal market. It shall work for the sustainable development of Europe based on balanced economic growth and price stability, a highly competitive social market economy, aiming at full employment and social progress, and a high level of protection and improvement of the quality of the environment. It shall promote scientific and technological advance*".

Specifically, and chiefly in the last few years, a strong emphasis has been placed on the above-mentioned principle of sustainable development and on the need to ensure a high level of environmental protection, as is moreover enshrined in article 37 of the European Union's Charter of Fundamental Rights introduced in 2016.[4] Both these issues have underpinned discussions on intergenerational responsibility

[1] With regard to this area, see Acts of I International Forum (1989) Istituto Poligrafico dello Stato, Rome, 1990 (by the Italian Ministry of the Environment).

[2] The first time the concept of the environment was developed in Europe dates back to the directive on the Environmental Impact Assessment (Directive 85/337/CE), wherein article 3 circumscribed "*... the environment to all natural and cultural resources in a correct balance between physical factors (ground, water, air, climate), the landscape and culture*".

[3] The Lisbon Treaty, which amended the Treaty on the European Union and the Treaty establishing the European Community, was signed in Lisbon on 13 December 2017 and was included in the Official Gazette of European Union C-306 on 17 December 2007.

[4] The European Union Charter of Fundamental Rights (2016/C 202/02), included in the Official Gazette of European Union of C 202/389 on 7 June 2016.

and, for this reason, have a bearing on the realisation of a fundamental right to live in a healthy environment.

3 (Continued) The Directive 2004/35/EC on Environmental Liability Governing the Prevention and Remedying of Environmental Damage

With regard to regulations, the latest important measure is **directive 2004/35/EC** on environmental liability governing prevention and remedying of damage (known as the environmental liability directive or "ELD")[5] in which certain guidelines already stated in the White Book of 2000 are invoked, and the central role played by the "polluters pay" principle is acknowledged, as expressly invoked by article 174 of the Treaty, alongside the principles of precaution and prevention.

The 2004/35/EC directive doubtless has other merits, such as having defined the legally significant environmental harm threshold, which is not equivalent to any environmental alteration, but to the "*measurable negative change to a natural resource or the measurable deterioration in a service of a natural resource which may happen directly or indirectly* (article 2, paragraph 2). These natural resources, which were compulsorily listed, are *protected natural species and habitats, water and land.*[6] Nevertheless, this directive does not yet appear to be sufficiently capable, given the affirmation of the actual right to a healthy environment, of offering identical forms of protection to private parties whose interests (first and foremost, health) have been harmed by environmental damage.

Pursuant to article 12 of directive 35/2004/EC (Request for action), natural persons and legal entities "*having sufficient interest in the environmental decision-making process*" or "*who are or could be affected by environmental harm*" have legal standing only to present observations to the relevant authorities relating to any case of environmental damage or imminent threats of environmental damage coming to their attention and to ask the relevant authorities to intervene in accordance with the directive.

The measure therefore concerns all non-governmental organisations promoting the protection of the environment, as well as individuals, and culminates in an instrument designed to spur the Public Body to consider and assess the facts and

---

[5] Directive passed by the European Union and Council on 21 April 2004, CEE/35/2004 on environmental liability with regard to prevention and remedying environmental damage in the Official Gazette of European Union. L143 on 30 April 2004.

[6] In this regard, it is nevertheless worth pointing out that with regard to the environmental contexts of water and land, the European Union regulatory framework shows a fundamental diversity of approach. It is *ecocentric* in the case of water, where importance is given to "its ecological, chemical and/or quantitative state and ecological potential", but *anthropocentric* in the case of land, where instead, importance is given to the "significant risk of harmful effects, including indirect effects, on human health". In this regard, see Anile (2007).

observations made by these parties. Nevertheless, "*the elements constituting the 'sufficient interest' and 'breach of a right' are determined by the member states*". Consequently, access to this right and the manner in which the right is exercised are likely to be regulated in different ways depending on the related legal system.[7]

Specifically, with regard to the protection of a person harmed by environmental damage, the European Union regulatory framework is expressly uncoupled from legal liability, as is shown by *recital* numbers 11 and 13, and specifically, number 14, which importantly notes: "*This directive does not apply to cases of personal injury, damage to private property or financial loss and does not prejudice any right concerning these types of damage*".[8] In accordance with these preliminary considerations, article 3, paragraph 3 therefore excludes damage to health or physical safety and damage to private property from the purview of the European Union directive. When a person's right "*to be indemnified following environmental damage or an imminent threat of such damage*" is at stake, the European Union legislature requires that reference be made to "*the relevant national legislation*".

The matter is currently of great interest to the European Union institutions, as shown by the recent opinion issued by the Commission for the Environment, Public Health and Food Safety on 20 June 2017 (within the framework of the process of verifying the application of the aforementioned directive 2004/5/EC),[9] which was partially incorporated into the resolution passed by the European Parliament on 26 October 2017,[10] in which the Commission is asked to assess whether it is necessary to include legal liability for harm caused to human health and to the environment (point 31) in the ELD.

4 Case Law

When the environment came under the purview of the Court of Justice, the environment and fundamental rights finally intersected. This occurred in 1991, when the Court stated that "*air quality standards are adopted in order to protect human*

[7] In the case of the Italian legislation (article 310), for example, those with legal standing may bring an action against inertia by the Ministry of the Environment and/or against acts and measures adopted by this Ministry which are illegitimate, in addition to an action to seek damages caused by any delay in ministerial intervention. Optionally, if the applicants are not satisfied, they are entitled to appeal against the decision or ministerial inertia.

[8] Recital numbers 11 and 13 state, respectively: "*The aim of this directive is to prevent and remedy environmental damage and it does not relate to rights to traditional compensation for damage recognised by relevant international agreements governing liability*" and "*Not all forms of environmental damage can be remedied through liability*", *which* "*... is therefore not a suitable instrument for dealing with pollution on a general, widespread basis in cases where it is not possible to connect adverse environmental effects with acts or omissions by certain parties*".

[9] http://www.europarl.europa.eu/sides/getDoc.do?pubRef=-//EP//TEXT+REPORT+A8-2017-0297+0+DOC+XML+V0//IT#title3.

[10] http://www.europarl.europa.eu/sides/getDoc.do?type=TA&reference=P8-TA-2017-0414&language=IT&ring=A8-2017-0297.

health" (*Commission v. Germany*, 1991). Consequently, as the ruling states, individuals must be guaranteed standing to seek redress before a national court in order to ensure that these standards are met.[11] This ruling by the Court seemed to herald the recognition of the right to demand clean/healthy air or water of all those who are victims of air or water pollution. And yet, legal theory at the time, just like environmental organisations and private citizens, underestimated the potential inherent in this dictum, and as a consequence, it was ultimately "essentially ignored" (Feliziani 2012a, p. 6).[12]

The subsequent case law debate ultimately protected human health without, however, openly emphasising its connection with the environment, concentrating instead on compliance with procedural rights, in other words, the right to access a legal system and environmental information, in addition to the right to take part in decision-making proceedings relating to environmental impact (Kramer 2016; Lee 2008).[13]

In other words, the case law decisions by the European Court of Justice on the environment show that the primary goal is to ascertain whether there have been significant omissions in the process leading to the balancing of values by the state, rather than to enshrine the fundamental nature of the right to live in a healthy environment. Within this context, there has been no shortage of rulings by the European Court of Justice stigmatising situations entailing environmental deterioration likely to adversely affect people's health. This is the case in the decision handed down by the Court of Justice in 2010, which, despite finding the Italian state guilty of breaching articles 4 and 5 of directive 2006/12/EC for poor management of the waste disposal emergency in Campania, it recognised the connection between the poor handling of waste and health hazards and those living in the areas affected by the crisis. It thereby took into due account the rationale underlying directive 2006/12 EC, extending its purview to the right of every person to live in healthy conditions rather than limiting it to merely protecting the environment (*Commission v. Italy*, 2012; Feliziani 2012b).[14]

[11] ECJ 30 May 1991, *Commission v. Germany*, C-361/88.

[12] Feliziani (2012a).

[13] Kramer (2016). Similarly, see Lee (2008), pp. 131–138, where one can read: *"Provisions for public participation in decision-making have become something of a conventional feature of environmental legislation over recent years, perhaps best marked at EU level by the moves to implement the Aarhus Convention. Public participation is now a thoroughly mainstream part of discussion of good environmental governance, even if the objectives of participation are more controversial, and achieving meaningful participation in practice remains challenging"*.

[14] ECJ, IV, 4 March 2010, *Commission v. Italy*, C-297/08. In this regard see also Feliziani (2012b). The duty of Member States to guarantee the right to a healthy environment: A consideration of European Commission v. Italy (C-297/08). *Journal of Environmental Law, 24*(3).

5 Conclusions

The contents of these pages show that it is possible to formulate several considerations regarding the current state of the matter at hand. Although in procedural terms, environmental law has attained a good level of "legal quality", there still tends to be an imbalance when it comes to identifying, at the European level, the fundamental right to live in a healthy environment.

However, the situation is in a constant state of flux and is not at an arrival point. Although the treaties still lack a rule which expressly acknowledges the right to a healthy environment, there are "clues" contributing to the establishment of this right. Not only does article 191 TFEU refer *expressis verbis* to the protection of human health,[15] but also an increasingly conspicuous series of second level laws governing the environment include the protection of people's health amongst their aims. These sources are increasingly influencing the European Court of Justice's case law decisions, which are moving toward the establishment of people's right to a healthy environment.

References

Anile, F. (2007). *Danno ambientale: le nuove norme. Disciplina per la tutela risarcitoria e il raccordo con il sistema delle bonifiche* [Environmental damage: The new rules. The regulatory framework for damages and the connection with the system for seeking redress]. Milano: Edizioni Ambiente (MI).

Cordini, G. (2016). Il danno Ambientale e la comunità internazionale: profili di diritto comparato. In *Diritti Umani e Ambiente* [Environmental damage and the international community: Aspects of comparative law. In Human Rights and the Environment], by Antonio Augusto Cançado Trindade and César Barros Leal (pp. 25–42). Fortaleza Catalogação na Publicação Bibliotecária: Perpétua Socorro Tavares Guimarães.

Feliziani, C. (2012a). *Il diritto fondamentale all'ambiente salubre nella recente giurisprudenza della corte di giustizia della Corte EDU in materia di rifiuti. Analisi di due approcci differenti* [The fundamental right to a healthy environment in recent case law decisions by the ECHR governing waste. Analysis of two different approaches]. Milano: Giuffrè Editore.

Feliziani, C. (2012b). The duty of Member States to guarantee the right to a healthy environment: A consideration of European Commission v. Italy (C-297/08). *Journal of Environmental Law, 24*(3), 535–546. Oxford Academic.

Kramer, L. (2016). *In EU environmental law*. London: Sweet & Maxwell.

Lee, M. (2008). The environmental implications of the Lisbon Treaty. In *Environmental law review* (pp. 131–138). London: Sage Publishing.

[15] Article 191 TFEU (*previously* article 174 TCEE) states: "*The Union's environmental policy contributes to achieving the following aims: 1) safeguarding, protecting and improving environmental quality; ii) protection of human health; (...)*".

Project Manager

Donata Franzi

1 Introduction

Being able to simplify complex situations and having the ability to communicate with people have been identified as the two main features of a project manager.

The first time such features were, to a certain extent, codified was in the 1940s in the USA during the Manhattan project,[1] the programme managing the creation of the atomic bomb, in order to speed up the end of the Second World War.

Until that moment, project management was characterised by strong parcelization of work without a clear understanding of the connections and definition of responsibilities along the work chain; in the production line, each line manager was responsible for his or her own piece of work and no overall view of the process or the final product was required. Indeed, knowledge sharing was not allowed in a system characterised by *over the fence management* of complex projects (Kerzner 2017, p. 40) and rigid division of the work to be done.

Complex projects, such as the Manhattan one, required more than over the fence management. It was not just a case of reaching the final outcome but how to obtain successful results considering the multiple actors involved (scientists, entrepreneurs, contractors, army) and resources (financial and human) needed.

The two characteristics mentioned at the beginning of this article, being able to simplify complex situations and having the ability to communicate with people, summarise the main aspects of the two people that were in charge of managing both

[1]The Manhattan project as a case study in project management:

https://www.nqicorp.com/en/2017/07/11/the-manhattan-project-project-management-during-difficult-times/

http://projectmanagementhistory.com/The_Manhattan_Project.html.

D. Franzi (✉)
Direzione Ricerca Trasferimento Tecnologico e Terza Missione, Università degli Studi di Modena e Reggio Emilia, Modena, Italy
e-mail: donata.franzi@unimore.it

A. Bartolini et al. (eds.), *Dictionary of Statuses within EU Law*,
https://doi.org/10.1007/978-3-030-00554-2_55

resources and people's interactions during one of the most complex, expensive, and destructive projects in the history of the world. The two people in charge were Colonel General Leslie R. Groves[2] and Robert Oppenheimer. The Colonel was known for his optimistic personality, and Oppenheimer for his soft skills and ability to manage people.

Soft skills and positive thinking are not the sole characteristics a project manager must have. Project management is successfully performed using various techniques and tools; when properly used, these allow a project manager to reach their main objective: successful and outcome-oriented interactions among different subjects within a project.

Again, the Manhattan project is a clear example of how projects may be positively conducted:

- distribution of the work to be done in tasks using specific objectives and different teams;
- decentralisation of decision making powers at task-level, identifying which individuals are to lead specific tasks to coordinate people both at task level and in relation to the project leader;
- identification of complementary activities to be developed simultaneously. In the Manhattan project case, for example, this was the case of conducting research, development, and production phases simultaneously rather than doing it step-by-step because of time constraints (the Second World War urged an end!).
- Use of tools like the Complex Network Diagram, Programme Evaluation Review Technique (PERT) Diagrams, the Critical Path Method, and the Gantt chart.

This introduction notes some aspects that need to be further developed, such as project management methodologies and tools, as well as a project manager's features, skills and, to some extent, virtues.

2 Project Management Methodology

With regard to methods, managing projects like those supported by the European commission and its agencies are characterised by increasingly integrated approaches based on a clear set of performance indicators, provisions for monitoring activities, shared reporting templates, and guidelines common to all beneficiaries of the grant, as well as risk mitigation strategies.

Usually, when unexpected issues and problems arise during work execution, there is a shortage of financial resources, the expected results are often late, and the time planning of activities is not respected. This means that something went wrong in the project design phase. These issues not only relate to the definition of a management strategy of a project; problems like those quoted above show that the man-

[2]Also known for his strong managing aptitude. Additionally, he worked on managing major projects, such as the construction of the Pentagon (1941–1943).

agement strategy was not conceived in conjunction with the strategic objectives that the project aims to achieve. The financial resources scheduled for the action then prove to be overestimated or underestimated for objectives that may not be clearly measurable, realistic, nor achievable.

3 Project Management Tools

Objectively Verifiable Indicators describe the project's objectives in operationally measurable terms. Non-SMART objectives[3] show that activities and resources scheduled for a project have not been properly estimated.

A clear assessment of the problems or challenges deriving from a specific situation is pivotal to the proper definition of

- needed activities,
- required resources,
- time necessary for the action execution.

An experienced project manager must never forget that results need to be achieved in a specific time frame with limited available resources.

Thus, at first, numerous project management tools are already made available during the project design phase when a clear assessment of the problem is to be addressed, as well as a thorough consideration of what one may achieve with his or her own resources and with additional funds provided by the donor during a specific time frame.

Today, some project management tools used in European programmes may be helpful. These tools are required by several donors such as the European Commission and its agencies to implement policies through funding initiatives (like research, education, environment, and development cooperation), pursuing the objective of an ever-closer Union.

The PERT Diagram and the Gantt chart are expressly required within project proposal templates provided by the European Commission and European funding agencies, which each have fully adopted criteria of the project cycle management.[4]

As shown by initiatives like the Manhattan project and the Polaris Project (1958),[5] a visual illustration of the interlinkage among activities during the project's

[3] *Regarding to the objective, it is supposed to be measurable (either quantitatively or qualitatively); available at an acceptable cost; relevant to the information needs of managers; time-bound – so we know when we can expect the objective/target to be achieved* (The first guide to the project cycle management for European funding initiatives came in 2004 from the former EuropeAid Cooperation Office of the European Commission (https://ec.europa.eu/europeaid/aid-delivery-methods-project-cycle-management-guidelines-vol-1_en, p. 81).

[4] The first guide to the project cycle management for European funding initiatives came in 2004 from the former EuropeAid Cooperation Office of the European Commission (https://ec.europa.eu/europeaid/aid-delivery-methods-project-cycle-management-guidelines-vol-1_en).

[5] http://projectmanagementhistory.com/Program_Evaluation_Review_Technique_(PERT).html.

lifetime through the PERT diagram, as well as establishing relations with moments in which criticalities are expected to emerge through Critical Path Analysis, is pivotal for a project's successful implementation. Critical Path Analysis and Critical Path Method (CPM) are both aimed at identifying the "critical paths" of a project through complex algorithms.

Considering that many project managers are asked to manage a project already conceived by someone else, a large part of the work may come during the project execution phase.

Although objectives are related to activities in the design phase, during the executing phase results (milestones and deliverables) need to be achieved through the action plan.

In the execution moment, project managers need to prove that they are capable of the following:

- running the Executing Kick-off Meeting;
- distributing information on contractual arrangements established with the donor;
- identifying the main characteristics of the Communications Management Plan and be able to work closely with the project communications manager at the beginning of the task;
- support the project Coordinator performing Quality Assurance (QA) activities as defined in the Quality Management Plan to ensure that the project adheres to the agreed quality standards;
- if not defined, write down a project Quality Management Plan!
- Supporting the coordination of the project's work, people, and resources, and resolving conflicts and issues;
- helping project participants to produce the project's deliverables in accordance with the project's plans;
- hand over the deliverables as described in the Deliverables Acceptance Plan.

Project managers today usually make reference to the word Agile in order to identify those methods in which *requirements and solutions evolve through collaboration between self-organising, cross-functional teams.*

The four values comprising the Agile Manifesto are:

1. Individuals and interactions over processes and tools.
2. Working solutions over comprehensive documentation.
3. Stakeholder collaboration over contract negotiation.
4. Responding to change over following a plan.

This implies the following aspects that people working on projects frequently forget:

To be treated with respect, be provided with suitable working conditions/environment to perform the job, being informed about the business context, and make decisions in a timely manner.

Respect the commitments involved, both within the team and at the overall project and organisational scope.

Actively participate in the planning and estimation of activities, commit to delivering within the quality and organisational standards.

To facilitate a continuous learning environment.[6]

4 Project Manager: More Than Filling in a Budget!

Usually people working as project managers are asked to fill in numbers on a budget sheet without being actively involved in a project's structure or actions design. Since managing a *complex reality with limited resources and strong time constraints* (so-called projects!) implies several capabilities (technical and soft skills), let's have a look at how a project manager may be defined.

In the PM^2 project management methodology guide,[7] project managers are defined as follows:

> A project role appointed by the Project Steering Committee to manage the project's daily progress, to deliver the outputs within the agreed constraints. The Project Manager manages the Project Core Team on a daily basis (PM^2, Glossary page. 138).

A number of personal and professional virtues of a project manager are described below, among others:

- The virtue of humour is described as the mean between boorishness and buffoonery;
- The virtue of calmness refers to the management of anger. It is the mean between spirited and irritability;
- Broadly speaking, the virtues of fairness, friendliness, generosity, and honesty, which each respond to good personal communication skills;
- The virtue of leadership;
- The virtues of prudence, judgment, temperance, and honour, which can be found in results-oriented people.

(*PM^2, page. 125–126*)

IPMA ICB (2015)[8] distinguishes between people, practice, and perspective competences: people or how a project manager interacts with the people around her; the practice of managing projects, programmes, and portfolios; perspectives about the context within which the initiative is run.

In terms of a manager's aptitude and skills, the IPMA ICB focuses on those already mentioned by PM^2: self-management, personal integrity, and reliability; personal communication skills, being capable of leadership and teamwork; having the right mind-set to get things done (p. 62 IPMA ICB).

---

[6] PM^2 Project Management Methodology Guide Open Edition, p. 110, ed. 2017.

[7] https://ec.europa.eu/isa2/solutions/open-pm2_en, 2017 edition.

[8] IPMA ICB—Individual Competence Baseline®, ICB version 4.0, 2015.

To summarise, there are at least ten characteristics of a good project manager[9]:

- Inspirational view: a project manager knows how to inspire a shared vision; the project is OUR project; the project's main objective is OUR mission;
- Ability to communicate at different levels: in the best case, a project manager is an *influencer* but in most cases a good project manager is someone able to maintain good relationships at different levels (project partners, stakeholders, technical experts, and auditors, etc);
- Capable of establishing a shared modus operandi (supporting the people involved in the project's execution with tools, guidelines, and helpful templates and, where possible, never asking workers to accept redundancy);
- A good project manager is a leader too: *a great project manager sets the tone for the project and provides a clear vision of the team's objectives*[10]*;*
- Capable of making decisions under time and resource constraints;
- Being well organised;
- Being able to delegate and share the task's jobs and identify task leaders;
- Capable of identifying solutions to problems valorising their own and their partners' resources and expertise;
- Always being prepared or being aware of their own limits;
- Always being available to collaborate despite contentions. A good project manager should be aware of debates; these are inextricably related to working in a group.

References

European Commission. (2004). *The first guide to the project cycle management for European funding initiatives came in 2004 from the former EuropeAid Cooperation Office of the European Commission.* https://ec.europa.eu/europeaid/aid-delivery-methods-project-cycle-management-guidelines-vol-1_en

European Commission. (2017). PM2 Project Management Methodology Guide Open Edition. https://doi.org/10.2799/957700

International Project Management Association (IPMA). (2015). Individual Competence Baseline®, ICB version 4.0. http://products.ipma.world/wp-content/uploads/2016/03/IPMA_ICB_4_0_WEB.pdf

Kerzner, H. R. (2017). *Project Management: A systems approach to planning, scheduling, and controlling* (12th ed.). Hoboken, NJ: Miley.

[9] https://www.knowledgehut.com/blog/project-management/10-characteristics-of-a-good-project-manager.

[10] See footnote 9.

Provider and User of Genetic Resources

Valentina Colcelli

1 Introduction and Legal Framework

The status of a provider and that of a user of genetic resources are laid down in international treaties, in particularly in the Convention on Biological Diversity (CBD), the Nagoya Protocol (NP) and the International Treaty on Plant Genetic Resources for Food and Agriculture (ITPGRFA). Otherwise, a provider and a user are defined by EU law.

The objectives of the CBD are 'the conservation of biological diversity, the sustainable use of its components and the fair and equitable sharing of the benefits arising out of the utilization of genetic resources, including by appropriate access to genetic resources and by appropriate transfer of relevant technologies' (Art. 1). The NP is one of the CBD protocols. The NP relates to access to genetic resources and the traditional knowledge associated with genetic resources and complies with Art. 15 of the CBD, which concerns the fair and equitable sharing of the benefits (monetary and non-monetary) arising from the utilization and commercialization of genetic resources (Posey 1993, p. 287). Such benefits should accrue to the holders of genetic resources and traditional knowledge in the countries and particularly in the indigenous and local communities from where the genetic resources were obtained. However, the NP gives priority in relation to genetic resources to specialized instruments if they are limited and qualified (Godt 2015, p. 319). This is the case of the ITPGRFA, just in relation to the genetic resources covered and for the purposes of this specialized instrument (Art. 4(4) NP).

Talking of the ITPGRFA, its aim is 'the conservation and sustainable use of plant genetic resources for food and agriculture and the fair and equitable sharing of the benefits arising out of their use, in harmony with the CBD, for sustainable agriculture

V. Colcelli (✉)
National Research Council, IFAC Institute, 50019, Via Madonna del Piano 10,
Sesto Fiorentino, Firenze, Italy
e-mail: valentina.colcelli@cnr.it

A. Bartolini et al. (eds.), *Dictionary of Statuses within EU Law*,
https://doi.org/10.1007/978-3-030-00554-2_56

and food security' (Art. 1). Access to genetic resources and the fair and equitable sharing of benefits (ABS) is developed according to the relationship described above among the international treaties. Access to and transactions in genetic resources are governed by a multilateral system for ABS if a country, on the basis of its own national priorities and decisions, provides special treatment for the ITPGRFA or other specialized instruments for ABS (Perron and Phillips 2013, p. 53). Otherwise, access to and exchange of genetic resources is governed by the CBD/NP bilateral approach (essentially requiring prior informed consent (PIC) and mutually agreed terms (MAT)). This is relevant because, so far, the ITPGRFA has 128 parties and the CBD 194. A number of CBD parties are therefore not members or parties of the ITPGRFA.

In 2011, the European Commission (EC) adopted an EU biodiversity strategy extending to the year 2020, aimed at halting the loss of biodiversity and ecosystem services by 2020 (Colcelli 2017). This document is an integral part of the Europe 2020 strategy and the 7th Environmental Action Programme. However, it was only during 2014 that the EU introduced measures for users under the NP. Within the EU, the NP was spelt out in Regulations (EU) No 511/2014 and 2015/1866, through which the mechanisms for establishing access and benefit-sharing are laid down. These Regulations describe the means by which access to genetic resources and the benefit of their utilization and commercialization may be shared, where 'genetic resources' means genetic material of actual or potential value, and 'genetic material' means any material of plant, animal, microbial or other origin containing functional units of heredity (Art. 2 Regulation (EU) No 511/2014).

At the moment of writing this chapter, only 12 of the EU Member States have signed the NP.[1] The application of the ABS system to all the Member States is therefore assured by the Regulations (EU) No 511/2014 and 2015/1866.

In this multilevel framework, we can define what 'provider' and 'user' mean.

2 Provider and Sovereign Rights of States Over Their Natural Resources

The provider is the person who 'has the authority to grant access to genetic resources or traditional knowledge associated with genetic resources and who should be involved in the negotiation of mutually agreed terms with potential users'.[2] According to Recital 21 of Regulation (EU) No 511/2014, users should use due diligence to ascertain whether 'genetic resources have been accessed in accordance with applicable legal or regulatory requirements and to ensure that, where relevant, benefits are fairly and equitably shared'. As a matter of fact, Art. 15 of the CBD recognizes 'the sovereign rights of States, the authority to determine access to

[1] http://sdg.iisd.org/news/three-african-countries-eu-and-12-member-states-sign-abs-protocol/.

[2] http://ec.europa.eu/environment/nature/biodiversity/international/abs/pdf/Glossary%20for%20Europa.pdf.

genetic resources rests with the national governments and is subject to national legislation. (…)'. So, each State: shall endeavour to create conditions to facilitate access to genetic resources for environmentally sound uses by other Contracting Parties and not to impose restrictions that run counter to the objectives [of the CBD]. (art. 15 CBD).

The sovereign rights of states in relation to the legal status of genetic resources include property regimes (Sandberg 2007, p. 615), administrative law and legislation for the protection of natural areas and/or plant and animal species.

According to the choices made by a state, the ways in which resources are covered by national and regional law range from public ownership to a system where the rights over genetic resources follow the private property rights over the land.

Even in case of public ownership over genetic resources, a national government will typically delegate the authority to grant prior informed consent to a sub-national (e.g. regional authority) or non-state entity (e.g. a reference collection).[3]

Regulation (EU) No 511/2014 identifies a set of criteria, using the identity of the area (country, region, etc.) from which the genetic material used for developing new varieties comes. These criteria reflect the enforcement of legal rights, the rate of entrepreneurship, and the structure of the higher education system, etc. of the partner countries of the NP.

Ownership of genetic resources in (…) European countries is generally derived from the ownership of biological resources and/or land, which is defined either by the Constitution or the civil code. This means that when genetic resources occur in *in situ* conditions and are not (indirectly) covered by specific legal rules (….), landowners can manage their biological resources as they see fit, and reap the potential benefits arising from their use. (…) Only Norway (….) specifically indicates that genetic resources are considered a common resource belonging to society as a whole, even if that does not preclude the application of (intellectual) property law and other relevant legislation. In most countries, the ownership of land or of an organism extends to the fruits and the products generated by it. Once the fruit or the product is collected or extracted, thus becoming movable property, a different property regime may apply. (…) Some countries provide exceptions to these ownership rules for specific cases. As such, in Greece, for trees located at boundaries of immovable properties a separate ownership is established. In Norway, private ownership over biological material may end when this material stops being excludable. (…). In (…) European countries, ownership and use of biological resources is limited in some way by nature conservation laws or by legislation on protected species, protected areas, forests and/or marine environments, some of which have a European origin. The level of protection can be contingent upon the type of resources, with several countries ranking their protected fauna and flora according to their protection level (Coolsaet 2015, p. 366).

[3] http://ec.europa.eu/environment/nature/biodiversity/international/abs/pdf/Glossary%20for%20Europa.pdf.

3 Due Diligence by the Users in Their Activities Linked to Genetic Resources

By 'users', Regulation (EU) No 511/2014 means the natural/legal persons that utilize genetic resources or the traditional knowledge associated with genetic resources.

A broad range of users and suppliers in the Union, including academic, university and non-commercial researchers and companies from different sectors of industry, use genetic resources for research, development and commercialisation purposes. Some also use traditional knowledge associated with genetic resources (Reg. (EU) No 511/2014, Recital 3).

Users must exercise due diligence in their activities that are linked to genetic resources. Art. 3 of Regulation (EU) No 511/2014 includes terms and conditions for this utilization, as well as subsequent applications and the commercialization of genetic resources. Articles 4 and 5 of the Regulation, respectively, address 'obligations of users', and monitoring and checking user compliance.

In the context of ABS, due diligence means doing one's very best to establish which access and benefit-sharing conditions apply to the genetic resources one wishes to access, and taking care to meet those conditions (Colcelli 2018).

Users therefore exercise due diligence in their activities linked to genetic resources prior to obtaining: internationally-recognised certificates of compliance as evidence that the genetic resources covered were legally accessed and that mutually agreed terms were established for the user and the utilisation specified therein (Recital 21 Reg. (EU) No 511/2014).

The national authorities should also accept the certificates.

The requirements for meeting the standard are very much dependent on the circumstances.

Activities such as the transfer and keeping of genetic resources, and for food and agriculture not contained under Annex I of the ITPGRFA, require an internationally recognized certificate of compliance (Art. 4 Reg. (EU) No 511/2014). Under Art. 4(4) Regulation (EU) No 511/2014, users are considered to have exercised due diligence in accordance with Article 4(3) if they have acquired PGRFA in a country that is party to the NP.

Users obtaining a genetic resource from a collection included in the register of collections within the EU shall be considered to have exercised their obligation of due diligence (Recital 9 Reg. (EU) No 2015/1866).

If internationally-recognized certificates of compliance are not present, the user has to comply with the *minimum* information required by Art. 17(4) of the NP, as specified in Art. 4(3)(b) of Regulation (EU) No 511/2014. Where no international certificate exists, documents and information have to be verified by the users (Art. 4 Reg. (EU) No 511/2014).

According to Art. 17 mentioned above, and Regulation (EU) No 511/2014, Art. 4(3), where no internationally-recognized certificate of compliance is available, the following documents are required:

(i) the date and place of access of the genetic resources or of the traditional knowledge associated with genetic resources;
(ii) a description of the genetic resources or of the traditional knowledge associated with genetic resources that were utilized;
(iii) the source from which the genetic resources or traditional knowledge associated with genetic resources were directly obtained, as well as the subsequent users of the genetic resources or traditional knowledge associated with genetic resources;
(iv) the presence or absence of rights and obligations relating to access and benefit-sharing, including rights and obligations regarding subsequent applications and commercialization;
(v) access permits, where applicable; and
(vi) mutually agreed terms, including benefit-sharing arrangements, where applicable.

4 Provider and User As Contracting Parties on Mutually Agreed Terms

Regulation (EU) No 511/2014 requires MAT and PIC to establish the terms for benefit-sharing with the provider of the genetic resources or the traditional knowledge associated with the genetic resources. Regulation (EU) No 511/2014 links the 'general principles of law' to one of the most visible areas of intersection between EU law and ethical choice, in the light of maintaining the EU legal system (Vezzani 2007, p. 305). The mutually agreed terms and contracts covered by Art. 3 Regulation (EU) No 511/2014 are correlated with distributive justice and the principle of solidarity (Cippitani 2011), which underpin the entire EU legal system (Colcelli 2015).

These kinds of contracts must set out specific conditions for the fair and equitable sharing of the benefits arising from the utilization of genetic resources or the traditional knowledge associated with genetic resources.

First, the contractual arrangements should guarantee the effectiveness of legal contracts and technology transfer agreements once the biotech research activity is completed. Second, they have to contribute to developing the potential market value of new varieties (Von Kries and Winter 2015, p. 125).

Measurement of the returns—mainly monetary returns—from commercializing innovation will be crucial for identifying a fair price at which the new varieties could be sold, with particular attention to local communities. One of these criteria is a provision for sharing benefits with the provider of the genetic resources or of the traditional knowledge in the contract made for the utilization, subsequent application and commercialization of products derived from the genetic resources or traditional knowledge associated with them. It is possible to fulfil the goal of Regulation (EU) No 511/2014 through the jurisdictional control of contracts for the utilization, subsequent application and commercialization of genetic resources and the traditional knowledge linked with them; in the European Union's internal market, this requires the fair and equitable sharing of the benefits arising from the utilization of genetic resources and traditional knowledge.

5 User's Due Diligence

As described above, Art. 4 of Regulation (EU) No 511/2014 explains how users must comply and perform 'due diligence'. Among these provisions, a due diligence declaration is required (only) for genetic resources, or traditional knowledge associated with genetic resources, obtained from a party to the NP that has established relevant access and benefit-sharing legislation or regulatory requirements pursuant to Art. 6(1) and Art. 7 of Regulation (EU) No 511/2014. In the EU legal framework, through the system called Declare,[4] users request access to the system, submit due diligence declarations and review submitted declarations. Through the Declare system, the competent authority of the EU Member State approves new submitting organizations and submitted declarations, and transmits data to the Access and Benefit-sharing Clearing-house (ABSCH), the platform for exchanging information on ABS and a key tool for facilitating the implementation of the NP (Colcelli 2017).

Recital 25 of Regulation (EU) No 511/2014 affirms that one suitable point for such a declaration is when research funds are received, and that another is at the final stage of utilization. The stage of the final development of a product can be identified with legal certainty as having been completed at the time when either market approval or authorization is sought, or when a notification required prior to placing for the first time on the Union market is made or, where neither market approval or authorization nor a notification is required, at the time of placing for the first time on the Union market.

6 Conclusion

EU law recognizes the status of a provider and a user, defining rights but also duties. These statuses are identified by international treaties (the CBD, NP and ITPGRFA). In the EU legal system, they are defined by Regulation (EU) No 511/2014, which sets out compliance measures on ABS for users under the NP arising from the utilization in the Union. In whole Union, compliance with the ABS system is ensured by Regulations (EU) No 511/2014 and 2015/1866, because of the fact that only 12 of the EU Member States have signed the NP. Before 2011, the moment at which the EC adopted an EU biodiversity strategy, there was no definition of the above-mentioned concepts. The EU biodiversity strategy implements the EU's

[4]Log-in with ECAS (http://ec.europa.eu/europeaid/funding/about-grants/how-apply-grant/applicant-registration-pador/ecas-registration_en).

commitments under the CBD. Regulation (EU) No 511/2014 expressly defines who is a 'user'. To define a provider, one needs to look at the definition borrowed from international law.

A 'provider' is the natural/legal person who 'has the authority to grant access to genetic resources or traditional knowledge associated with genetic resources and who should be involved in the negotiation of mutually agreed terms with potential users'. On the other hand, 'users' are natural/legal persons who utilize genetic resources or the traditional knowledge associated with genetic resources. Users, such as academic, university and non-commercial researchers and companies from different sectors of industry, can use genetic resources for research, development and commercialization purposes only if they comply with the ABS due diligence obligation and with the declaration system, according to Regulations (EU) No 511/2014 and 2015/1866. In the EU framework, non-compliance with the ABS system therefore means:

- A negative impact on the development of any project funded by an EU programme in the framework of the ethical and legal issues of the project (Recital 25 Regulation (EU) No 511/2014 /Art. 5 Regulation (EU) No 2015/1866): the grant may be reduced (Articles 34.4 and 43 Grant Agreement H2020) or the participation of the beneficiary may be terminated (Articles 34.4 and 50 Grant Agreement H2020).
- No legitimization of possible plant patents granted if they were derived from genetic resources and traditional knowledge associated with genetic resources (see EU Directive 98/44/EC).
- No placement of products derived from genetic resources or traditional knowledge associated with genetic resources in the Union market.
- Liability for the user's failure to act with the ABS due diligence obligation.

References

Cippitani, R. (2011). *La solidarietà giuridica tra pubblico e privato*. Rome: Iseg srl.

Colcelli, V. (2015). The solidarity principle in new EU Member States. In C. Perugini & F. Pompei (Eds.), *Inequalities during and after transition in Central and Eastern Europe* (pp. 247–265). Basingstoke: Palgrave.

Colcelli, V. (2017). Research activity and the principle of solidarity in the EU legal framework for biodiversity. *Rights and Science*, 43–54.

Colcelli, V. (2018). Information on access and benefit sharing regarding the utilisation of genetic resources under the European Union legal regulation. In R. Arnold, R. Cippitani, & V. Colcelli (Eds.), *Genetic information and individual rights. Law & Science - Book (1)* (pp. 80–96). Regensburg: Universität Regensburg.

Coolsaet, B. (2015). Comparing access and benefit-sharing in Europe. In B. Coolsaet, F. Batur, A. Broggiato, J. Pitseys, & T. Dedeurwaerdere (Eds.), *Implementing the Nagoya Protocol. Comparing access and benefit-sharing regimes in Europe* (p. 366). Leiden: Brill.

Godt, G. (2015). The multi-level implementation of the Nagoya Protocol in the European Union. In B. Coolsaet, F. Batur, A. Broggiato, J. Pitseys, & T. Dedeurwaerdere (Eds.), *Implementing the Nagoya Protocol. Comparing access and benefit-sharing regimes in Europe*. Leiden: Brill.

Perron, F., & Phillips, F.-K. (2013). *The interface between the Nagoya Protocol on ABS and the ITPGRFA at the international level. Potential issues for consideration in supporting mutually supportive implementation at the national level.* FNI Report 1/2011. Lysaker: Fridtjof Nansen Institute.

Posey, D. A. (1993). Intellectual property rights and just compensation for indigenous knowledge, Amazonia and Siberia: Legal aspects of the preservation of the environment and development in the last open spaces. *Anthropology Today, 6*(4), 287.

Sandberg, A. (2007). Property rights and ecosystem properties. *Land Use Policy, 24*, 613–623.

Vezzani, S. (2007). Il Primo Protocollo alla Convezione europea dei diritti umani e la tutela della proprietà intellettuale di popoli indigeni e comunità locali. *Diritti Umani e Diritto Internazionale, 1*, 305–342.

Von Kries, C., & Winter, G. (2015). Defining commercial and non-commercial research and development under the Nagoya Protocol and in other context. In E. Chege Kamau, G. Winter, & P. T. Stoll (Eds.), *Research and development on genetic resources. Public domain approaches in implementing the Nagoya Protocol* (pp. 125–147). London: Routledge.

Public Body

Andrea Maltoni

1 Introduction

In the last two decades the organizational system of the EU has become more integrated at the European and national levels. As is well known, the system is composed not only of the European administration but also of national public authorities.

The Treaty of Lisbon introduced Article 298 of the Treaty on the Functioning of the European Union (TFEU), which states at para. 1 that '*In carrying out their missions, the institutions, bodies, offices and agencies of the Union shall have the support of an open, efficient and independent European administration*'. This provision confirms that the European Union has, on the one hand, a direct organization (which is inferred from the term 'bodies'), and, on the other hand, an indirect organization.

However, it may be observed that this Article does not contain a general definition of a public body.

The absence of that definition is closely related both to the fact that the national law of each Member State describes a wide variety of public bodies and to the principle of decision-making autonomy (see Article 4, para. 2 TEU),[1] (Diés Picazo 2004, p. 866; Chiti 2011, p. 262) which means, as stated in the Preamble of the Charter of Fundamental Rights of the European Union, that the Union respects '*the*

[1] Article 4, para. 2, TEU provides that: '*The Union shall respect the equality of Member States before the Treaties as well as their national identities, inherent in their fundamental structures, political and constitutional, inclusive of regional and local self-government. It shall respect their essential State functions, including ensuring the territorial integrity of the State, maintaining law and order and safeguarding national security. In particular, national security remains the sole responsibility of each Member State*'.

A. Maltoni (✉)
Department of Economics and Management, University of Ferrara, Ferrara, Italy
e-mail: andrea.maltoni@unife.it

A. Bartolini et al. (eds.), *Dictionary of Statuses within EU Law*,
https://doi.org/10.1007/978-3-030-00554-2_57

national identities of the Member States and the organisation of their public authorities at national, regional and local levels'.

It must be noted that in European law (legislation and case law), there is no possibility of finding a unitary legal definition of a public body: there are in fact several definitions, which different from sector to sector, and they are directly related to the specific purposes of the applicable law.

Therefore, as will be outlined in this chapter, as a result of European law each definition of 'public body' has a 'functional' character. Consequently, the term 'public body' may be considered as a general term, with definitions that depend on the scope of the sectoral legislation, and, in most cases, the definition includes both public authorities and bodies governed by private law.

The main aspects in which the definition of a public body ought to be considered relevant are the following: the extent to which European Directives have a direct effect, in terms of the bodies that are compelled to enforce them; according to the European Directives, the identity of the 'contracting authorities' that are under a duty to award public contracts in the internal market; the extent to which the definition of a public authority may authorize the national legislators to impose restrictions on the freedom of movement for workers; and the extent to which advantages granted to an undertaking by a body must be considered as state aid.

In addition, it might be observed that Directive 2003/4/EC, which implements the Aarhus Convention, gives citizens and businesses the right of access to environmental information in the possession of public authorities without making it necessary for them to state their reasons.

2 Directives Having a Direct Effect and the Bodies That Are Under a Duty to Exercise a Special Power

In accordance with the settled law of the European Court of Justice, a Directive cannot of itself impose obligations on an individual and cannot therefore be relied upon as such against an individual.[2] The same European judges have also held that provisions of a Directive that are unconditional and sufficiently precise may be relied upon by individuals on whom those provisions confer rights, not only against a Member State and all the organs of its administration, such as decentralized authorities,[3] but also against organizations or bodies that are subject to the authority or control of the state or that possess special powers beyond those which result from the normal rules applicable to relationships between individuals.[4] Furthermore, the

[2] See ECJ, Case C-152/84, Marshall, 26/2/1986, para. 48; ECJ, Case C-91/92, Faccini Dori, 14/07/1994, para. 20; ECJ, Case C-397/01 to C-403/01, Pfeiffer and Others, 05/10/2004, para. 108; ECJ, Case C-441/14, DI, 19/04/2016, para. 30.

[3] See, to that effect, ECJ, Case C-103/88, Costanzo, 22/06/1989, para. 31.

[4] See ECJ, Case C-188/89, Foster and Others, 12/07/1990, para. 18; ECJ, Case C-253/96 to C-258/96, Kampelmann and Others, 04/12/1997, para. 46.

Court of Justice has recently held that such organizations or bodies can be distinguished from individuals and must be treated as comparable to the state because they are legal persons governed by public law and are 'part of the state' in the broad sense, or because they are subject to the authority or control of a public body, or because they have been required by such a body to perform a task in the public interest and have been given, for that purpose, special powers. In other words, a body or an organization—even one governed by private law—to which a Member State has delegated the performance of a task in the public interest and which possesses for that purpose special powers beyond those that result from the normal rules applicable to relationships between individuals, is a body against which an individual may rely on the provisions of a Directive that have direct effect.[5]

In conclusion, in order to establish whether the provisions of a Directive that are capable of having direct effect may be relied on against a private law body, what is relevant, in the opinion of the Court, is not the fact that the body is governed by private law, but the fact that a Member State has conferred a task in the public interest on that body, which means that the body is under a duty to exercise a special power.

3 Bodies That Perform Activities as 'Contracting Authorities' Under Directives 2014/23-24-25/EU

In accordance with the European Directives 2014/23-24-25/EU, the definition of 'contracting authorities' is not restricted to those bodies that, under the law of a Member State, act as public authorities, but includes bodies governed by public law, which means '*bodies that have all of the following characteristics: (a) they are established for the specific purpose of meeting needs in the general interest, not having an industrial or commercial character; (b) they have legal personality; and (c) they are financed, for the most part, by the State, regional or local authorities, or by other bodies governed by public law; or are subject to management supervision by those authorities or bodies; or have an administrative, managerial or supervisory board, more than half of whose members are appointed by the State, regional or local authorities, or by other bodies governed by public law*'.[6]

This means that even a body or an organization that is governed by private law might fall within the scope of the definition in Directive 2014/24/EU of a body governed by public law.

Furthermore, as stated in the judgment of the Court of Justice in Case 31/87, in order to give full effect to the principle of freedom of movement, the term 'contracting authority' must be interpreted in functional terms,[7] which means that, if the

[5] See ECJ, Case C-413/15, Elaine Farrell, 10/10/2017, paras. 34–35.

[6] See Article 6, para. 4 of Directive 2014/23/EU, Article 2, para. 4 of Directive 2014/24/EU, and Article 3, para. 4 of Directive 2014/25/EU.

[7] See ECJ, Case 31/87, Beentjes v State of the Netherlands, 20/09/1988, para. 11.

entity is established to meet needs in the general interest not having an industrial or commercial character, no distinction should be drawn by reference to the legal form of the provisions setting up the entity and specifying the needs that it is to meet.[8]

Moreover, the status of a body governed by public law is not dependent on the relative importance, within its business as a whole, of the meeting of needs in the general interest not having an industrial or commercial character, because it is immaterial if commercial activities may be carried out by a separate legal person forming part of the same group or concern.[9]

The above mentioned Directives also define a public undertaking[10] as a 'contracting entity', and contain a definition of other contracting authorities, such as entities '*which pursue one of the activities referred to in Annex II and award a concession for the pursuit of one of those activities*'[11] and entities '*which: (a) are contracting authorities or public undertakings and which pursue one of the activities referred to in Articles 8 to 14; (b) when they are not contracting authorities or public undertakings, have as one of their activities any of the activities referred to in Articles 8 to 14, or any combination thereof and operate on the basis of special or exclusive rights granted by a competent authority of a Member State*' (see Article 4, para. 1 of Directive 2014/25/EU).

In conclusion, the status of a body governed by public law is connected to the activity exercised by that body—which must meet all the characteristics mentioned in the Articles of Directives 2014/23-24-25/EU—and not to the importance of that activity, which may be relative to that body.

[8] See ECJ, Case C-360/96, Gemeente Arnhem and Gemeente Rheden/BFI Holding BV, 10/11/1998, para. 62.

[9] See ECJ, Case C-360/96, Gemeente Arnhem and Gemeente Rheden/BFI Holding BV, 10/11/1998, para. 56.

[10] See Article 7, para. 4 of the Directive mentioned above, which defines a 'public undertaking' as '*any undertaking over which the contracting authorities may exercise, directly or indirectly, a dominant influence by virtue of their ownership thereof, their financial participation therein, or the rules which govern it. A dominant influence on the part of the contracting authorities shall be presumed in any of the following cases, in which those authorities, directly or indirectly: (a) hold the majority of the undertaking's subscribed capital; (b) control the majority of the votes attaching to shares issued by the undertaking; (c) can appoint more than half of the undertaking's administrative, management or supervisory body*'.

[11] See Article 7, para. 1 of Directive 2014/23/EU. The 'contracting entities' mentioned above are: "*(a) State, regional or local authorities, bodies governed by public law or associations formed by one or more such authorities or one or more such bodies governed by public law; (b) public undertakings as defined in paragraph 4 of this Article; (c) entities other than those referred to in points (a) and (b) of this paragraph, but which operate on the basis of special or exclusive rights, granted for the exercise of one of the activities referred to in Annex II*'.

4 Freedom of Movement for Workers and the Related Definition of a Public Administration

Freedom of movement for workers, as established by Article 45 TFEU, requires Member States to abolish any discrimination based on nationality between workers in regards to employment, remuneration and other conditions of work and employment.[12]

An explicit derogation from the principle laid down in Article 45 TFEU—comparable to the one that is applied, under Articles 62 and 51 TFEU, to the freedom to provide services[13]—is provided in Article 45(4) TFEU, which states that the provisions of the same article '*shall not apply to employment in the public service*'. The extent of this exception to the fundamental principle that workers in the European Union should enjoy freedom of movement, which has to be interpreted strictly, has been made more specific over the years by the Court of Justice.

In a number of rulings, some of them not recent,[14] the EU judges have recognized, in particular, that access to civil servants' and public employees' posts may be restricted to nationals.

The domestic law may restrict the application of the nationality condition to only those posts that actually involve direct or indirect participation in the exercise of the powers conferred by public law and/or duties designed to safeguard the general interests of the state or of other public authorities, thus presuming, on the part of those occupying those positions, the existence of a special relationship of allegiance to the state and reciprocity of rights and duties that form the foundation of the bond of nationality.[15]

It follows that, without prejudice to the rule of equal treatment in access to employment, Member States can refuse to engage a worker on the grounds of his/her

---

[12] See also Directive 2004/38/CE on the right of citizens of the Union and their family members to move and reside freely within the territory of the Member States; Regulation (EU) No 492/2011 on freedom of movement for workers within the Union; Regulation (EC) No 883/2004 on the coordination of social security system and Regulation (EC) No 987/2009 laying down the procedure for implementing Regulation (EC) No 883/2004.

[13] See ECJ, Case C-2/74, Reyners, 21/06/1974, para. 14, 15; ECJ, Case C-42/92, Thijssen, 13/07/1993; ECJ, Case C-272/91, Commission of the European Communities v Italian Republic, 26/04/1994, paras. 6–13; ECJ, Case C-114/97, Commission of the European Communities v Spain, 29/10/1998, paras. 34–48; ECJ, Case C-355/98, Commission of the European Communities v Kingdom of Belgium, 09/03/2000, paras. 27–34.

[14] See ECJ Case C-149/79, Commission of the European Communities v Kingdom of Belgium, 17/12/1980, paras. 7–11; ECJ Case C-225/85 Commission of the European Communities v Italian Republic, 16/06/1987, paras. 7–14.

[15] See ECJ Case C-33/88, Pillar Alluè and Carme Mary Coonan v Università degli Studi di Venezia, 30/05/1989, para. 21; ECJ Case C-4/91, Bleis, 27/11/1991, paras. 6–8; ECJ Case C-173/94, Commission of the European Communities v Kingdom of Belgium, 2/07/1996, paras. 17–21; ECJ Case C-473/93, Commission of the European Communities v Grand Duchy of Luxembourg, 2/07/1996, paras. 25–50; ECJ Case C-290/94, Commission of the European Communities v Hellenic Republic, 2/7/1996, paras. 34–39.

nationality when the post involved has all the characteristics indicated (for instance, participation in the exercise of powers conferred by public law and duties designed to safeguard the general interest).

As a consequence of that delineation of the notion of the civil service, a rather restricted definition of public administration has been outlined.

According to the case law of the Court of Justice, the exception in Article 45(4) TFEU does not cover posts in bodies responsible for administering commercial services, in public health care services, in state education and in research for non-military purposes conducted in public establishments. The application of a nationality condition can be relevant in the defence, public order, external relations and monetary policy fields (Cassese 1997, pp. 88 ff.).

It can be added that, while in Italy there is no correspondence between the legal status of public workers and the restriction on the principle of freedom of movement, in other European countries the legal status of public employees depends on the legal framework of the specific activity of the public service; this is the case in France and Spain, where the legal position of public workers is related to the type of activity carried out by the office in which they are employed (Pioggia 2006. pp. 256 ff.).

5 Public Bodies and State Aid

In accordance with Article 107 TFEU, '*any aid granted by a Member State or through State resources in any form whatsoever which distorts or threatens to distort competition by favouring certain undertakings or the production of certain goods shall, in so far as it affects trade between Member States, be incompatible with the internal market*'.

First of all, it should be noted that this provision only contains a definition of aid that is incompatible with the internal market.

Furthermore, it ought to be pointed out that the phrase '*aid granted by a Member State*' includes not only state and central government aid, but also aid given by regions and local authorities.

Thirdly, it has to be taken into consideration that the phrase '*through State resources in any form whatsoever*' suggests a fairly broad concept of state aid. In fact, as the case law has acknowledged, '*only advantages granted directly or indirectly through State resources are to be considered aid within the meaning of Article 92(1) EC.*[16] *The distinction made in that provision between "aid granted by a Member State" and aid granted "through State resources" does not signify that all advantages granted by a State, whether financed through State resources or not, constitute aid, but is intended merely to bring within that definition both advantages*

[16] See what is now Article 107, para. 1, TFEU.

which are granted directly by the State and those granted by a public or private body designated or established by the State'.[17]

This means that, to some extent, it is not only the legal status of a body that must be considered, but also whether the state or the central, regional or local government exercises a dominant influence over an undertaking. In this regard, the European Commission, referring to the Directive of 25 June 1980 on the transparency of financial relations between Member States and public undertakings (80/723/EEC), clarified that '*public authorities may exercise a dominant influence on the behaviour of public undertakings not only where they are the proprietor or have a majority participation but also by virtue of powers they hold in management or supervisory bodies as a result either of the rules governing the undertaking or of the manner in which the shareholdings are distributed*'.[18]

In conclusion, even advantages granted by a public or private body that is under the dominant influence of a public authority should be considered as state aid within the meaning of Article 107 TFEU.

6 Conclusions

The primacy of European law and its *effet utile* has meant that, even if only in some sectors, the European definition of a public body has replaced the national one (this is the case, for instance, in the public procurement area).

The 'functional' definition of a public body has affected national laws for a number of reasons.

The 'functional' character of the definition of a public body, as stated by European law, has influenced national legislators, so that they dedicate more attention (and in some cases exclusive attention) to the kind of activity involved and the particular legal regime, with the consequence that the legal status (public or private) of the body does not matter.

From this perspective, it may be noted that private bodies are also, in some cases, legally entitled to exercise public powers, and, in other cases, public authorities are allowed by the law to confer public powers on private bodies.

In these cases, the activities and acts performed by these private bodies, in exercising public powers, are similar, in their legal regime, to the same activities and

[17] See ECJ, Case C-379/98 Preussen Elektra, 13/03/2001, para. 58; ECFI, joined cases T-228/99 and T-233/99 Westdeutsche Landesbank Girozentrale and Land Nordrhein-Westfalen v Commission, 06/03/2003, para. 179; ECFI, Case T-95/03 Asociación de Estaciones de Servicio de Madrid and Federación Catalana de Estaciones de Servicio v Commission, 12/12/2006, para. 104.

[18] See, in particular, Article 2 of that Directive, according to which 'A *dominant influence on the part of the public authorities shall be presumed when these authorities, directly or indirectly in relation to an undertaking: (a) hold the major part of the undertaking's subscribed capital; or (b) control the majority of the votes attaching to shares issued by the undertaking; or (c) can appoint more than half of the members of the undertaking's administrative, managerial or supervisory body*'.

acts performed by public authorities. This implies that the protection of the subjective legal positions of citizens and economic operators in relation to these actions is equal to the protection they can get from public authorities exercising the same powers.

Finally, the 'functional' notion of a public body, as examined above, has led national legislators, even outside the field of application of European law, more commonly to define public bodies—where there are institutions that are not public authorities—differently from sector to sector or differently in their specific legal scope. This trend has resulted in the extension to private bodies (especially companies that are under the dominant influence of public authorities) of the rules and the principles normally applied to a public authority.

References

Cassese, S. (1997). Stato-nazione e funzione pubblica. *Giornale di diritto amministrativo*, 88.

Chiti, M. P. (2011). *Diritto amministrativo europeo*. Milan: Giuffré.

Diés Picazo, L. M. (2004). Il principio di autonomia istituzionale degli Stati membri dell'Unione Europea. *Quaderni costituzionali*, (4), 865–867.

Pioggia, A. (2006). La Corte costituzionale e il modello italiano di impiego alle dipendenze delle amministrazioni pubbliche. In G. Della Cananea & M. Dugato (Eds.), *Diritto amministrativo e Corte costituzionale* (pp. 255–340). Naples: Edizioni scientifiche italiane.

Public Officer

Barbara Gagliardi

1 The Status of Public Officers in National Law and the EU Legal System

The EU legal system has taken on a significance for the status of public officers that goes well beyond the limits established by the concept of 'employment in the public service' outlined by the Treaty (Art. 45(4) TFEU).

The restrictive interpretation established for this concept has extended the right of free movement of workers to most jobs belonging to the public sphere in many national legal systems. As a result, the nationality restriction—which has marked the European legal culture since the formation of modern nation states—has been overcome and it has thus become necessary to make adjustments capable of implementing the principle of non-discrimination, which is a corollary of freedom of movement, in the public service.

Nevertheless, there does not appear to be any 'hostility' in this obligation of openness with regard to the traditional definition of public officer that is common to European (and especially continental) legal culture.

More specifically, for the definition of the status of a public officer—and the choice between a public or private law model—reference continues to be made to national legal systems, in what can be summarized as a relationship of ongoing 'indifference' between the two systems.

This does not mean that the Union, and more generally European law, is incapable of influencing the rights and obligations related to this status.

B. Gagliardi (✉)
Department of Law, University of Turin, Torino, Italy
e-mail: barbara.gagliardi@unito.it

A. Bartolini et al. (eds.), *Dictionary of Statuses within EU Law*,
https://doi.org/10.1007/978-3-030-00554-2_58

2 The Concept of 'Employment in the Public Service' in EU Law

The EU legal system refers explicitly to 'employment in the public service' in order to exclude this from the scope of the freedom of movement for workers (Art. 45(4) TFEU). This exclusion pays tribute to a legal tradition that is a prime expression of national sovereignty (Sendín García 2005) and therefore of the identity 'inherent in the fundamental structures, political and constitutional' of the Member States (Art. 4 TEU).

The restriction on nationality for access to public employment has assumed a function of identity and consolidation for state organizations in European national legal systems (Maravall 1972). Introduced in the modern era alongside mandatory military conscription, it served to reinforce the bond of citizenship by expressing identification with the state organization grounded in the related obligation of loyalty for public officers.

Alongside the 'professionalization' of public administrations (Weber 1980), the restriction in favour of nationals distinguishes the European administrative organization model, assuming primary importance in the national unification process. The right to equal access to public office is considered a political right: participation in the community of membership and in the organization, allowing its perpetuation (Costa 2005).

A peculiar notion of public service employment has developed over time in the European legal order. This does not match the notion that is specific to national laws, but instead has a more restrictive meaning (Gagliardi 2012; Ziller 2010).

As a result, the restriction on nationality has gradually been overcome: in fact, only employment involving the 'exercise of official authority' can be reserved for nationals (Art. 51 TFEU); this means activities 'which involve a direct or indirect participation in the exercise of powers conferred by public law and duties designed to safeguard the general interests of the State or of other public authorities'.

This restriction is justified because these positions require a 'special relationship of allegiance to the State and reciprocity of rights and duties, which form the foundation of the bond of nationality'.[1]

The same perimeter for positions characterized by official authority is interpreted restrictively: activities that cannot alter the powers of assessment and decision of public authorities, or that are merely 'auxiliary and preparatory',[2] such as those of expert translators with respect to the judicial function, cannot be regarded as 'connected with the exercise of official authority'.[3] Furthermore, 'certification' func-

---

[1] Communication from the Commission, 11.12.2002, *Free movement of workers: achieving the full benefits and potential*, COM(2002) 694 fin; Commission action in respect of the application of Article 48(4) of the EEC Treaty, 18.03.1988, 88/C72/02, *Freedom of movement of workers and access to employment in the public service of the Member States*. See also: ECJ, 31.05. 2001, C-283/99, *Commission v Italian Republic*.

[2] ECJ, 22.10.2009, C-438/08, *Commission v Republic of Portugal*.

[3] ECJ, 6.10.2015, C-298/14, *Brouillard*; ECJ, 17.03.2011, C-372/09, C-373/09, *Peñarroja Fa*.

tions without authoritative powers do not constitute activities connected with official authority because they cannot express a will attributable to public administration—this applies, for example, to notaries.[4] Thus, positions in which the exercise of an activity of a 'technical and financial management nature' is prevalent, and in which the exercise of functions of authority occurs solely 'occasionally or in exceptional circumstances', are excluded.[5]

Therefore, a national law violates the EU legal system, so that the national courts must set it aside, where access for European citizens is excluded in a generalized way for positions at the summit of the administration, with no assessment of the tasks exercised in the particular case.[6]

The result is a concept of official authority that is subject to gradual erosion, consistent with the evolution of the Union legal order that increasingly requires the exercise of administrative functions—including those of an authoritative nature—in a relationship of continuity between national and European institutions (Cavallo Perin 2017; Ziller 2014).

All public administration employment that does not fall within this perimeter must be open to EU citizens, with full equality of treatment in access to the position and career development.

The result is the full integration of European workers in the field of public services (education, health, and local public utilities)[7] and administrations having technical legitimacy. By contrast, positions in the police force, army, judiciary, and diplomatic service, etc. remain restricted to nationals.

3 A 'Trivialization' of Public Employment?

The approach of the EU legal system is intended to concentrate on the type of tasks performed, regardless of the status of public or private law applicable to the employment relationship. For this reason, it has sometimes been seen as a threat to national legal traditions.

---

[4] ECJ, 24.05.2011, C-47/08, *Commission v Kingdom of Belgium*, C-50/08, *Commission v French Republic*, C-53/08, *Commission v Republic of Austria.*

[5] ECJ, 10.09.2014, C-270/13, *Haralambidis;* ECJ, 10.12.2009, C-460/08, *Commission v Hellenic Republic*; ECJ, 11.09.2008, C-447/07, *Commission v Italian Republic*; ECJ, 30.09.2003, C-405/01, *Colegio de Oficiales de la Marina Mercante Española*; ECJ, 30.09.2003, C-47/02, *Anker.*

[6] Recently, see Italian Council of State, sez. VI, 24.07.2017, n. 3666.

[7] ECJ, 2.07.1996, C-473/93, *Commission v Grand Duchy of Luxembourg*; ECJ, 2.07.1996, C-173/94, *Commission of the European Communities v Kingdom of Belgium;* ECJ, 2.07.1996, C-290/94, *Commission v Hellenic Republic*; ECJ, 1.12.1993, C-37/93, *Commission v Kingdom of Belgium;* ECJ, 2.08.1993, C-259/91, C-331/91, C-332/91, *Allué*; ECJ, 27.11.1991, C-4/91, *Bleis*; ECJ, 30.05.1989, C-33/88, *Allué*; ECJ, 16.06.1987, C-225/85, *Commission v. Italian Republic;* ECJ, 3.06.1986, C-307/84, *Commission v French Republic;* ECJ, 3.06.1986, C-66/85, *Lawrie-Blum.*

More specifically, this approach has been considered incompatible with the 'career systems' that hitherto dominated the continental European legal systems, in which employment relationships in public administrations are subject to special disciplines under public law, inspired by common constitutional principles (an obligation of loyalty, exclusivity of service, access based on merit and impartiality, liability of officers, etc.).

The attention to the type of tasks performed, which has been imposed by the EU concept of 'official authority', appeared to contradict a model of administration in which access is understood as being 'for life' regardless of the duties associated with the post (Aubin 2010). Hence, it was considered that there might be a contradiction with the principle by which access to public employment determines the assignment of a 'rank' that corresponds to multiple positions, at the discretion of the administration (in France the '*principe de séparation du grade de l'emploi*').

Moreover, EU law has been invoked to justify the stabilization of 'precarious' forms of public employment,[8] by reason of the principle whereby contracts of an indefinite duration are 'the general form of employment relationship between employers and workers',[9] sometimes even through the introduction of specific private law contractual regimes in systems that are otherwise based on public law (Melleray 2006).[10]

Thus, it was considered that EU institutions wished—more or less on purpose—to promote an overthrow of the specialization of public employment, leading to a 'smoothing' of employment relationships and thereby trivializing national legal traditions (Bourdon 2005).

4 The Relationship of 'Indifference' Between European and National Law

It cannot be denied that European legal systems (both EU law and the European Convention of Human Rights) have influenced national legal systems in defining the rights and obligations of public officers.

This derives mainly from an ongoing indifference to the distinction between employment relationships falling under public law and those falling under private law, according to a concept of 'worker' that embraces anyone who pursues gainful activity 'for and under the direction of another person in return for which he receives remuneration',[11] regardless of the public or private nature of the employer and the laws applicable to the relationship.

---

[8] In Italy: l. 13.07.2015, n. 187. See also: Italian Const. Court, 15.06.2016, n. 187; ECJ, 26.11.2014, C-22/13, C-61/13, C-62/13, C-63/13, C-418/13, *Mascolo*.

[9] Framework Agreement on Fixed-term Work, annexed to Dir. 1999/70/EC of 28.06.1999.

[10] In France: loi n° 2005-843 du 26.07.2005.

[11] ECJ, 19.07.2017, C-143/16, *Abercrombie & Fitch Italia Srl*; ECJ, 11.09.2008, C-228/07, *Petersen*.

Overcoming the restriction on nationality for access to public employment implies that European public officers are guaranteed treatment that is free of direct or indirect discrimination, and prohibits any provision that would constitute an obstacle to the freedom of movement or would even simply discourage its exercise (Art. 45(2), TFEU).

While not asserting a right of access to the civil service, EU law does mould its requirements in the name of the fundamental right of movement. A consequence of this is the illegality of linguistic[12] or residence[13] requirements that appear disproportionate and therefore discriminatory (Ziller 2010).

The principle of equal treatment also implies that there is an obligation to recognize the equivalence of national diplomas and professional experience that can be considered to complement university education (Consito 2012).[14]

More generally, all European social law is imposed on public administrations, with a number of limitations to protect the rights of workers (De Becker 2016).

Thus, anti-discrimination laws have established the obligation to avoid requirements relating to maximum age[15] or gender (even indirectly, in relation to physical requirements, e.g. height),[16] for access, career path[17] and retirement in a public employment relationship.[18]

The ECHR—which establishes the 'general principles of the Union's law' (Art. 6 TEU)—applies a similar perspective in recognizing the rights of public workers.

Disputes concerning public employment are comparable to those concerning private work as regards the right to a fair trial (Art. 6 European Convention on Human Rights): public officers may apply to the courts within a reasonable time and be assured of a right of response, and of the neutrality and independence of the judiciary.[19]

The right to respect for private life and freedom of expression (Art. 8 and Art. 10 European Convention on Human Rights) may be invoked to limit the power to dismiss a public employee.[20]

The right to form and join a trade union (Art. 11 European Convention on Human Rights) contradicts rules that radically exclude it for all public servants or even only

[12] ECJ, 5.2.2015, C-317/14, *Commission v Kingdom of Belgium*; ECJ, 6.6.2000, C-281/98, *Angonese*.

[13] ECJ, 26.10.2006, C-192/05, *Tas-Hagen*; ECJ, 22.5.2008, C-499/06, *Nerkowska;* ECJ, 10.9.2009, C-269/07, *Commission v Federal Republic of Germany*.

[14] ECJ, 9.09.2003, C-285/01, *Burbaud*; ECJ, 6.10.2015, C-298/14, *Brouillard.*

[15] ECJ, 15.11.2016, C-258/15, *Salaberria Sorondo*; ECJ, 13.11.2014, C-416/13,*Vital Perez.*

[16] ECJ, 18.10.2017, C-409/16, *Ypourgos Esoterikon*; ECJ, 30.9.2004, C-319/03, *Briheche*; ECJ, 11.1.2000, C-285/98, *Kreil*; ECJ, 30.6.1988, C-318/86, *Commission v French Republic.*

[17] ECJ, 7.09.2017, C-174/16, *H.*

[18] ECJ, 6.11.2012, C-286/12, *Commission v Republic of Hungary*; ECJ, 21.07.2011, C-159/10, C-160/10, *Fuchs*; ECJ, 18.11.2010, C-250/09, C-268/09, *Georgiev*.

[19] ECHR, 19.09.2017, *Regner v the Czech Republic*; ECHR, 17.10.2017, *Tel v Turkey*; ECHR, 23.06.2016, *Baka c. Hungary*; ECHR, 19.4.2007,*Vilho Eskelinen v Finland.*

[20] ECHR, 23.06.2016, *Baka v Hungary*; ECHR, 26.09.1995, *Vogt v Germany*; ECHR, 7.09.2016, *Şahin Kuş v Turkey.*

for certain categories (the police force, the armed forces). The right of such workers to strike may be restricted,[21] at most, but they may not be prevented from organizing trade unions or other associations representing the interests of people in the same category.[22]

The 'culture of rights' that marks the European approach permits a penetrating examination of the public administration's discretionary assessments relating to labour relations, even where they are founded in the special disciplines of public law and are typical expressions of an authoritative power (e.g. access to employment, disciplinary powers).

Limitations on the rights of public officers are admissible only if they can be justified under the principle of proportionality, for which it is not sufficient to demonstrate a link to the public interest: the limit must also be proportional to the aim pursued and there must be no suitable alternative measures (Galetta 2014).

5 The Insurmountable Special Status of Public Officer

Even in EU law, however, an affirmation of public workers' rights does not require the distinction between private and public work to be eliminated.

Indeed, there is plenty of evidence of a European tribute to the specific 'culture' of public officers (Gagliardi 2017), which is affirmed in 'constitutional traditions common to the Member States' (Art. 6 TEU).

These require specific obligations for public officers, which are rooted in the idea of service to the community (Cavallo Perin 2009; Jean-Pierre 1999): thus, public officers have an obligation of loyalty to the established power,[23] and an obligation of impartiality or neutrality.[24]

Under national constitutions, public officers have special rights that guarantee the effectiveness of their obligations: impartiality and neutrality are protected by the right to employment permanence (Cassese 2007),[25] as well as by the right to expect 'protection' by the administration and 'meritocratic equality' in access to employment and career progression (Cassese and Pellew 1987; Ziller 1988).[26]

---

[21] ECHR, 21.04.2015, *Junta Rectora del Ertzainen Nazional Elkartasuna (ER.N.E.) v Spain*; ECHR, 6.11.2009, *Yapi-Yol Sen v Turkey*.

[22] ECHR, 2.10.2014, *Matelly v France*; ECHR, 26.5.2015, *Altun v Turkey*; ECHR, 24.3.2015, *Sezer v Turkey*.

[23] See Art. 33.4, Basic Law for the Federal Republic of Germany; Art. 54.2, Italian Const; Art. 103.1, Constitution of Hellenic Republic.

[24] See Art. 153 Polish Const.; Art. 1, French Const. 1958; Art. 269.1, Portuguese Const.; Arts. 97–98, Italian Const.

[25] See Art. 103.4, Constitution of Hellenic Republic.

[26] See Art. VI, Déclaration des droits de l'homme et du citoyen (1789); Art. 23 Spanish Const.; Art. 33.1, Basic Law for the Federal Republic of Germany; Art. 33 Lithuanian Const.; Art. 70 Hungarian Const.; Art. 3, Const. of the Netherlands; Art. 60, Polish Const.

The ability of EU law to take account of such an administrative culture—and its specific national features—is an element of integration (Cavallo Perin 2017) that leads to the definition of a status of public officer that is also relevant for the EU system (Oberdoff 2014), beyond the derogation from the freedom of movement.

Thus, in the review of the implementation of the EU Directive on fixed-term work, a recognition of the principle of competitive exams allowed differentiation in the treatment of private and public workers. EU law is not violated where, in the case of the unlawful renewal of a contract, public sector workers are protected on the basis only of simple compensation for damages (instead of the automatic conversion of the relationship).[27]

Moreover, the protection of legitimate neutrality in the public service supersedes the limitation on freedom of religion with the banning of the Islamic veil: this is even more true when the principle of neutrality is a principle to which the national law 'attaches greater weight'.[28]

The obligation of loyalty to power allows a restrictive interpretation of the right to respect for private life, legitimizing the dismissal of an official who had previously worked with the political police in a former Communist country.[29]

Therefore, a consideration of national legal systems reveals and strengthens the outlines of the special nature—or extraordinariness—of public employment relationships, which could be regarded as expressing the special status of the public officer, founded on a common European culture of public administration.

References

Aubin, E. (2010). Les catégories du droit de la fonction publique. In J.-B. Auby (Ed.), *L'Influence du droit européen sur les catégories du droit public* (pp. 721–738). Paris: LGDJ.

Bourdon, J. (2005). Vers une banalisation du droit de la fonction publique? Actualité Juridique Fonctions Publiques. *AJFP, 6*, 284–288.

Cassese, S. (2007). *L'ideale di una buona amministrazione*. Naples: Editoriale Scientifica.

Cassese, S., & Pellew, J. (Eds.). (1987). *Le système du mérite - The merit system*. Brussels: Institut International des Sciences Administratives.

Cavallo Perin, R. (2009). L'etica pubblica come contenuto di un diritto degli amministrati alla correttezza dei funzionari. In F. Merloni & R. Cavallo Perin (Eds.), *Al servizio della nazione, Etica e statuto dei funzionari Pubblici* (pp. 147–161). Milan: Franco Angeli.

Cavallo Perin, R. (2017). L'organizzazione delle pubbliche amministrazioni e l'integrazione europea. In R. Cavallo Perin, A. Police, & F. Saitta (Eds.), *L'organizzazione delle pubbliche amministrazioni tra stato nazionale e integrazione europea* (pp. 3–36). Florence: Firenze University Press.

Consito, M. (2012). *L'immigrazione intellettuale. Verso un mercato unico dei servizi intellettuali*. Naples: Jovene.

[27] However, some sort of effective sanction is required: ECJ, 12.09.2013, C-50/2013 *Papalia*; ECJ, 1.10.2010, C-3/10, *Affatato*.

[28] ECHR, 26.11.2015, *Ebrahimian v France*; ECHR, 4.12.2008, *Dogru v France*; ECHR, 24.01.2006, *Kurtulmus v Turkey*; ECHR, 10.11.2005, *Leyla Sahin v Turkey*.

[29] ECHR, 21.10.2014-21.01.2015, *Naidin v Romania*.

Costa, P. (2005). *Cittadinanza*. Rome-Bari: Laterza.

De Becker, A. (2016). La situation juridique des fonctionnaires et du personnel contractuel dans le secteur public en Belgique: quelle unité dans la diversité. In J. P. Dunand, P. Mahon, & S. Perrenoud (Eds.), *Le droit de la relation de travail à la croisée des chemins* (pp. 328–348). Geneva-Zurich-Bâle: Schulthess.

Gagliardi, B. (2012). *La libera circolazione dei cittadini europei e il pubblico concorso*. Naples: Jovene.

Gagliardi, B. (2017). 'Al servizio dell'integrazione': il funzionario pubblico europeo. In R. Cavallo Perin, A. Police, & F. Saitta (Eds.), *L'organizzazione delle pubbliche amministrazioni tra stato nazionale e integrazione europea* (pp. 555–578). Florence: Firenze University Press.

Galetta, D. U. (2014). Le principe de proportionnalité. In J.-B. Auby & J. Dutheil de la Rochère (Eds.), *Traité de droit administratif européen* (2nd ed., pp. 501–537). Brussels: Bruylant.

Jean-Pierre, D. (1999). *L'éthique du fonctionnaire civil: son contrôle dans les jurisprudences administrative et constitutionnnelle françaises*. Paris: LGDJ.

Maravall, J. A. (1972). Le origini dello Stato moderno. In E. Rotelli & P. Schiera (Eds.), *Lo Stato moderno. Dal Medioevo all'età moderna* (Vol. I, pp. 69–90). Bologna: il Mulino.

Melleray, F. (2006). Les reformes contemporaines de la fonction publique remettent-elles en cause le compromis de 1946? *Revue du Droit Public (RDP), 1*, 185–200.

Oberdoff, H. (2014). L'influence du droit de l'Union européenne sur la fonction publique française. In J.-B. Auby & J. D. de la Rochère (Eds.), *Traité de droit administratif européen* (2nd ed., pp. 1261–1280). Brussels: Bruylant.

Sendín García, M. A. (2005). *La libre circulación de empleados públicos en la Unión europea*. Salamanca: Ratio Legis.

Weber, M. (1980). *Economia e società*, vol. IV. (F. Casabianca & G. Giordano, Trans.) Milan: Edizioni di Comunità. (Original work published 1922–1956).

Ziller, J. (1988). *Egalité et mérite, L'accès à la fonction publique dans les Etats de la Communauté européenne*. Brussels: Bruylant.

Ziller, J. (2010). *Free movement of European Union citizens and employment in the public sector. Report for the European Commission*. Brussels: European Commission.

Ziller, J. (2014). Les concepts d'administration directe, d'administration indirecte et de co-administration et les fondements du droits administrative européen. In J.-B. Auby & J. D. de la Rochère (Eds.), *Traité de droit administratif européen* (2nd ed., pp. 327–400). Brussels: Bruylant.

Recipient of EU Programmes

Roberto Cippitani

1 Public Financing

The phenomenon of public funding has a long history[1] and has been interesting to scholars for at least a couple of centuries.[2]

However, an important system of public financing has developed only over the second half of the last century (Serrani 1971).

Particularly after the Second World War, the State began to dispense considerable resources to fulfil many collective tasks (Corso 1990).

According to international organisations, annual public funds are more than $1 billion, or about 4% of the world's GDP.[3]

Public funding can be considered as an expression of the teleological nature of the modern State, which, in accordance with the constitutions and international treaties, pursues objectives related to social welfare and solidarity (Cippitani 2010, pp. 182 ff.; Pericu 1967, p. 31).

Noberto Bobbio argued that public funding shows the transformation of the nineteenth century 'administrative state' into the present 'Rule of law' that intervenes in areas previously left exclusively to the relations between individuals (Bobbio 1977, p. 106).

[1] See, in Rome, the *Leges frumentariae* (Law establishing the free distribution of grain), among which the first was the *Lex Sempronia frumentaria* of 123 B.C., proposed by Caius Grachus (Perelli 1993, p. 168 f.).

[2] Among the first to deal with public funding from a scientific perspective, see Napolitan jurist Giacinto Dragonetti in his *Trattato delle virtù e de' premj* published in 1766.

[3] WTO, *Rapport sur le commerce mondial 2006. Analyse des liens entre les subventions, le commerce et l'OMC*, p. 306, in: www.wto.org/French/res_f/booksp_f/anrep_f/world_trade_report06_f.pdf.

R. Cippitani (✉)
Department of Medicine, Università degli Studi di Perugia, Perugia, Italy
e-mail: roberto.cippitani@unipg.it

A. Bartolini et al. (eds.), *Dictionary of Statuses within EU Law*,
https://doi.org/10.1007/978-3-030-00554-2_59

Mainly through funding, the State has abandoned authoritarian forms as a normal means of government, moving to forms of collaboration with individuals and voluntary involvement.

Public funds have become the main instrument of contemporary State action, especially in the economic sphere, but not solely in that sphere (Benadusi 1966).

In particular, over the last 50 years, the sector has been enriched by funding granted in the framework of international cooperation.

The international funding organisations are numerous and cover a wide range of fields: just think of the UN agencies, the World Bank, NATO and cultural and scientific organisations such as CERN, ESA, and the Council of Europe.

2 Public Funding of the European Union

Since the 1950s of the last century, European Union (hereinafter also referred to as 'EU') funding has become very important in Europe (see among others, Castaldi 1998, pp. 95 ff.). With respect to the programmes concerning specific fields, see Either (1993), Frazer (1995), Guzzetti (1995), Mullin (2001) and Pépin (2006).

The first kind of funding was for research in the field of nuclear energy, which was created in the years immediately following the signature of the Euratom Treaty.

During the 1960s, programmes were also financed in the fields of competence originally provided for by the Treaties (the agricultural sector; the Structural Funds in the field of cohesion policy; the first programmes in the field of vocational training).

From the 1970s onwards, as a result of the Paris Summit of October 1972, funding from the Institutions was launched in areas not yet under the responsibility of the Communities, such as research (in fields other than nuclear research) and education (with the establishment of the first generation of programmes such as Erasmus, Petra, Comett, Eurotecnet, Fuerza, Lingua, Tempus, Youth for Europe).

After the Single European Act and the Maastricht Treaty formally recognised EU's competences in areas such as the environment, research, and education, the use of Community funds, in terms of resources and better organisation, was further improved.

In addition to promoting the integration of Europe, funding has been the main instrument for the enlargement and openness of the European Union.

Actions (such as Tempus and Phare) were used in the 1980s and 1990s to prepare new countries for accession to the Union.

Even today, EU funds are at the centre of international cooperation with Latin America, Asia, the Mediterranean, the Middle East and Africa.

Over the last 20 years, they have been reflected in EU policy strategies, from the White Paper on Growth, Competitiveness and Employment of the Delors Commission (1993), to the 'Lisbon Strategy' of 2000, to the current strategy contained in the Europe 2020 document, and to strategic objectives such as the creation of a European

Research and Innovation Area, the Bologna process and the implementation of a knowledge-based economy.

All these documents include funding (e.g., research and development framework programmes, education and training programmes, structural funds, international cooperation programmes) among the Union's main instruments of action.

3 The 'Programmes' of the European Union

Many words are used, each with different meanings, to speak about public funding, such as subsidies, grants, contributions, prizes, etc. (Galasso 1980).

This heterogeneity means that it is very difficult to provide an exact definition of the phenomenon of public funding. In this respect, more than in other areas of legal science, there has been great difficulty in reaching an agreement on the terms used.

Particularly interesting is the case of the European Union, which over a few decades, as mentioned above, has developed a specific discipline for its 'programmes'.

The programmes are in fact the subject of very detailed legislation, which consists of the specific legal sources with which these programmes are adopted.

In addition, EU programmes are governed by a general discipline which, today, is mainly made up of Regulation (EU, Euratom) No 966/2012 of the European Parliament and of the Council of 25 October 2012 on the financial rules applicable to the general budget of the Union and the Commission Delegated Regulation (EU) No 1268/2012 of 29 October 2012 on the rules of application of Regulation (EU, Euratom) No 966/2012 of the European Parliament and of the Council.

Those legal sources constitute a detailed and organic regulation, which has few comparisons with national regulations or with the rules adopted by international bodies.

Under European Union law, a programme 'means any activity, set of activities or other initiative which the relevant basic instrument or budgetary authorisation requires the Commission to implement for the benefit of one or more categories of specific beneficiaries, by committing expenditure'.[4]

The elements of the definition can be applied to many forms of action in which the Commission (or other EU institution or body, hereinafter referred to as 'funding authorities'), on the basis of the principle of legality (the presence of a 'basis act' of EU law, see Article 2, let. d) Regulation 966/2012), bears costs in favour of individuals and other legal entities, more correctly called 'recipients' (Article 2, let. i), Regulation 966/2012).

[4] See the definition set out by Council Regulation (EC) No 58/2003 of 19 December 2002 laying down the statute for executive agencies to be entrusted with certain tasks in the management of Community programmes. See also Cippitani (2013, pp. 22 ff.).

4 Forms of Legal Relationship Between Financing Institutions and Beneficiaries

Programmes may be implemented in several ways, and this has led to the establishment of differences in both the procedure for choosing the recipients and the legal relationships with the funding authorities.

The categories of those legal relations regulated by EU law may be classified as 'financial instruments', 'public contracts', 'grants' and other forms of funding.

(a) Financial Instruments The legal basis for some EU programmes provides for the implementation of 'financial instruments', which are defined as 'financial support provided on a complementary basis from the budget in order to address one or more specific policy objectives of the Union' (Articles 2, let. p), Regulation 966/2012; see the discipline provided under Article 139 ff. of the abovementioned Financial Regulation).

In particular, a loan is defined as an 'agreement which obliges the lender to make available to the borrower an agreed sum of money for an agreed period of time and under which the borrower is obliged to repay that amount within the agreed time' (Article 2, let. k), Regulation 966/2012).

Other financial operations in the form of guarantees ('written commitment to assume responsibility for all or part of a third party's debt or obligation or for the successful performance by that third party of its obligations if an event occurs which triggers such guarantee, such as a loan default', see let. l), Article 2 mentioned above), equity investments ('provision of capital to a firm, invested directly or indirectly in return for total or partial ownership of that firm and where the equity investor may assume some management control of the firm and may share the firm's profits', see let. m), risk-sharing instruments ('financial instrument which allows for the sharing of a defined risk between two or more entities, where appropriate in exchange for an agreed remuneration', see let. o) Article 2).

The financial instruments are put in place by the European Investment Bank (see Article 308 ff. The Treaty on the Functioning of the European Union, hereinafter 'TFEU') and the European Investment Fund.

(b) Public Procurements According to EU law, the programmes may be implemented even by means of 'public contracts', i.e., on the basis of Regulation 966/2012: 'contracts for pecuniary interest concluded in writing between one or more economic operators and one or more contracting authorities (…), in order to obtain, against payment of a price paid in whole or in part from the budget, the supply of movable or immovable assets, the execution of works or the provision of services'.

Therefore, EU funding authorities may use public contracts when, in applying the programme, they have to purchase movable or immovable property, a supply, a work or a service.

(c) Grants Grants are one of the more well-known legal techniques used to implement programmes.

Under EU law, Article 121 of Regulation 966/2012 states: 'Grants are direct financial contributions, by way of donation, from the budget in order to finance any of the following:

(a) an action intended to help achieve a Union policy objective;
(b) the functioning of a body which pursues an aim of general Union interest or has an objective forming part of, and supporting, a Union policy ("operating grants")'.[5]

Grants, therefore, are characterised by the fact that the funding institution participates, with a financial contribution, to the realisation of a project proposed by one or more beneficiaries, through the provision of an amount of money.

(d) Other Funding Techniques But, in practice, there are many more techniques for public funding. For example, there are 'prizes' (i.e., 'a financial contribution given as a reward following a contest', see let. j), Article 2 Regulation 966/2012, see also Article 138) or the constitution of legal entities in order to implement a programme, such as Joint Undertakings for carrying out research activities under Article 187 TFEU.

5 Requirements of the Recipients

In order to participate in the procedure of selection and eventually receive the funding, the recipients must comply with some general requirements: (a) legal subjectivity; (b) location; (c) honourability; (d) capacity to carry out the activities.

Furthermore, the basic act of the programme may provide other specific requirements, for example, in the case of public procurement, the recipient should be qualified under EU law as an "economic operator" (see Article 101, para. 1, Regulation 966/2012); within Erasmus+, some actions only fund higher education institutions (for example, the Jean Monnet Chairs), and similarly, for some programmes, the projects can be submitted only by Small- and Medium-sized Enterprises (SMEs), etc.

(a) Legal Subjectivity First, the recipient must be a natural person or a legal entity.

[5]This type of grant therefore covers part of the body's management costs and is not linked to the implementation of a specific project. Operating grants are those specially directed to bodies established by EU law, such as: (a) the College of Europe (Bruges and Natolin Campus); (b) the European University Institute in Florence; (c) the European Institute of Public Administration in Maastricht; (d) the Academy of European Law in Trier; (e) the European Agency for the Development of Special Needs Education in Middelfart; (f) the International Centre for European Training (CIFE) in Nice (Article 36(2) of Decision 1720/2006).

A legal entity may be a legal person, that is to say, an entity characterised by a legal personality (normally this occurs when the legal entity is patrimonially autonomous with respect to its members) according to EU, national or international law.

However, legal subjects without a legal personality are also eligible as recipients, "provided that their representatives have the capacity to undertake legal obligations on behalf of the entity" (see Article 131, para. 2, Regulation 966/2012 concerning the beneficiaries of grants).

(b) Location The recipient normally must be established in a Member State of the European Union or in Countries associated with the EU.

The possibility for legal entities from other Third Countries to participate must be provided by the basic act of the programme.

(c) Honourability The legal entities are not entitled to participate in an EU programme when they (or the persons who act on behalf of the legal entity) are in situations such as: having been found guilty of some criminal offences concerning their professional conduct, e.g., fraud; failing to comply with certain obligations such as the payment of social security contributions; or having been subject to insolvency proceedings.

In particular, the cases of exclusion are provided by dispositions such as Articles 106, para. 1, 107, 108, 109 and 131, para. 4, Regulations 966/2012.

(d) Capacity to Carry Out the Activities Provided by the Programme According to Article 131, para. 3, Regulation 966/2012, the beneficiary must "demonstrate his or her financial and operational capacity to carry out the proposed action or work programme". The financial capacity implies the possession of the necessary economic resources (in addition to the funding); the operational capacity means the availability of the skills and instruments requested to achieve the aims of the project.

Analogous capacity is provided for other kind of recipients, such as Article 110, para. 3, which is the Financial Regulation for the economic operators participating in public contracts.

6 Obligations of the Recipients

Generally speaking, the recipients of the EU Programmes, including those from Third Countries, must comply with the applicable national legislation, but also with European Union law. In particular, recipients must comply with human rights requirements (see the reference to the European Convention on Human Rights, contained in article 6 EU Treaty), the bioethical rules (as laid down in the Charter of Fundamental Rights of the European Union), gender equality, competition and state aid rules, and so on (see, for example, Court of Justice, 15 January 1998, C-44/96, Mannesmann Anlagenbau Austria and others)/Strohal Rotationsdruck, [1998] ECR I-120.

More specifically, the recipients must comply with the dispositions provided by the agreements with the funding authorities and by the basic act of the programmes, such as the following:

6.1 The Main Obligation to Perform the Activity

The recipients are obliged to carry out the project in the case of grants; to provide service, supply or work within the public contract; and to put in place the activities established in the case of the financial instruments.

If there are two or more recipients in the same agreement with the funding authority, they assume a joint and several liability.

6.2 Other Obligations

In addition to the obligation to carry out the planned activity, the recipients are subject to additional obligations.

(i) Providing information on various aspects of the implementation of the activities;
(ii) Avoiding conflicts of interest, which are defined as any situation "where the impartial and objective exercise of the functions of a financial actor or other person… is compromised for reasons involving family, emotional life, political or national affinity, economic interest or any other shared interest with a recipient" (cf. art. 57, par. 2, Regulation 966/2012). There is, of course, a conflict when this interest runs counter to the EU interest in implementing the project and respecting the financial rules.
(iii) Publication and dissemination of information. The recipients must state in any communication or publication relating to the project that he has received EU funding.
(iv) Confidentiality, i.e., to keep confidential all documents, information and other material directly related to the subject matter of the agreement which have been duly classified as confidential and the dissemination of which may cause damage to the other parties.
(v) The obligation to report on the technical and financial implementation of the activity.
(vi) Obligations with respect to third parties, such as employees (e.g., compliance with security and social schemes and with security conditions); subcontractors and other providers of services and goods (e.g., the implementation of rules of transparency in their selection); other third parties collaborating with the recipients, etc.

(vii) Other obligations. Some recipients have additional obligations such as those of the "coordinator", i.e., the recipient who acts as an intermediary between the funding authority and the other recipients. Other obligations may be provided for a specific typology of funding.

7 Rights of the Recipients

Subject to the compliance with the abovementioned obligations, the recipients are entitled to receive the contribution, price or other kind of performance provided for under the agreement and the basic act.

They also have the other rights provided by the specific programme or technique of funding, such as ownership or access to the results of the actions established by the grant agreements.

Furthermore, the recipients have the right for the funding authorities to act in compliance with rules and principles such as the 'principles of sound financial management' (Article 317 TFEU) and the principles of 'good administration' (Article 41 EU Charter of Fundamental Rights), which implies the obligation to hear the persons and give reasons for their decisions (see also Article 296 TFEU).

References

Benadusi, L. (1966). Attività di finanziamento pubblico: aspetti costituzionali ed amministrativi. *Riv. trim. dir. pubbl.*, 890 ff.

Bobbio, N. (1977). *Dalla struttura alla funzione*. Milan: Edizioni di Comunità.

Castaldi, G. (1998). *Sovvenzioni, incentivi e finanziamenti pubblici, Dig. disc. priv., Sez. comm.* (Vol. XV). Turin: UTET.

Cippitani, R. (2010). *La solidarietà giuridica tra pubblico e privato*. Rome-Perugia: ISEG.

Cippitani, R. (2013). *La sovvenzione come rapporto giuridico*. Rome-Perugia: ISEG.

Corso, G. (1990). Lo Stato come dispensatore di beni. Criteri di distribuzione, tecniche giuridiche ed effetti. *Soc. dir., 1–2*, 109 ff.

Either, D. (1993). La réforme des fonds structurels de la Communauté Européenne: de l'Acte Unique à l'après-Maastricht. *Revue Internationale des Sciences Administratives*, 232 ff.

Frazer, T. (1995). The new structural funds, state aids and interventions on the single market. *European Law Review*, 3 ff.

Galasso, A. (1980). Finanziamenti pubblici. In *Noviss. Dig. it., App* (Vol. III, p. 764 ff). Turin: UTET.

Guzzetti, L. (1995). *A brief history of European Union research policy*. Luxembourg-Bruxelles: Office for Official Publications of the European Communities.

Mullin, J. (2001). Évolution des modes de financement de la recherche (1960–2000). *Revue internationale des sciences sociales, 2*(168), 269 ff.

Pépin, L. (2006). *Histoire de la coopération européenne dans le domaine de l'éducation et de la formation*. Luxembourg-Bruxelles: Office for Official Publications of the European Communities.

Perelli, L. (1993). *I Gracchi*. Rome: Salerno Editrice.

Pericu, G. (1967). *Le sovvenzioni come strumento di azione amministrativa* (Vol. I). Milan: Giuffrè.

Serrani, D. (1971). *Lo Stato finanziatore*. Milano: Franco Angeli.

Refugee

Nevila Saja and Sebastian Seefried

1 Introduction

The definition of refugees in Germany and their rights given by law have undergone major changes in recent decades. One of the consequences of the Second World War was the vast number of refugees it produced in Europe and other parts of the world. Nearly every country was confronted with this issue. As a result of this development, numerous countries agreed on the necessity to create a common definition of refugees. Until then, a common definition had not existed. However, the agreement of the definition on the attributes of refugees was only the first step; the compromise of the rights of refugees and their duties needed to be transferred into national law to come into force. At the same time, Europe began to establish institutions to closely examine and challenge potentially new aggressive actions between national countries. Thus, on the one hand Europe tried to create common standards when dealing with asylum seekers and refugees; on the other hand, the individual countries had to transfer these agreements into their national law. Both developments have led to changes in German national law in recent years.

N. Saja (✉)
Faculty of Law, University of Regensburg, Regensburg, Germany

S. Seefried
Ludwig-Maximilians-Universität München, Historisches Seminar, Elitestudiengang Osteuropastudien, München, Germany

A. Bartolini et al. (eds.), *Dictionary of Statuses within EU Law*,
https://doi.org/10.1007/978-3-030-00554-2_60

2 Convention Relating to the Status of Refugees

The Convention, signed by Germany in 1954, is the foundation upon which the definition of refugees was built. Thereby, the Convention and later the Protocol do not just include the right of asylum, they define them. The Convention standardises the Law of Asylum among the states, which are signatories of the Convention and/or the Protocol. The definition of a Refugee is,

> a person who owing to a well-founded fear of being persecuted for reasons of race, religion, nationality, membership of a particular social group or political opinion, is outside the country of his nationality and is unable or, owing to such fear, is unwilling to avail himself of the protection of that country; or who, not having a nationality and being outside the country of his former habitual residence as a result of such events, is unable or, owing to such fear, is unwilling to return to it.[1]

The Convention was a consequence of the Second World War. Nations around the world had to struggle for the first time with vast numbers of persons not living in their home countries. Furthermore, as the time before the Second World War had shown, agreements between single states could not solve such problems. Nevertheless, the declaration of refugees was not solely connected to persons suffering from war.

Reasons which have since become relevant, like natural catastrophes or poor economic conditions, are not included as acceptable reasons.

The Convention includes more than just the rights of refugees; countries' responsibilities are also a key section. The Convention is built on Article 14 of the "Universal Declaration of Human Rights" (UDHR). The article contains the right to seek asylum in another country for each person. "This right may not be invoked in the case of prosecutions genuinely arising from non-political crimes or from acts contrary to the purposes and principles of the United Nations".[2]

The Convention was a product of the post-war era. Millions of people became homeless after the war or were forced to leave their home countries. Despite this situation, there was no definition between the countries as to who was considered to be a refugee and the rights this status entailed.

3 European Union

The basic definition of a refugee in the European Union (EU) is contained within the Convention. However, the EU has made further steps in terms of harmonising the standards and rules between the individual states in the Union.

The first agreements about the range field of refugees and asylum were made in the beginnings of the EU, in the Treaties of Rome in 1957. Although the chief aim

[1] Article 1, Convention Relating to the Status of Refugees, 1951.

[2] Article 14, Universal Declaration of Human Rights, 1948.

of the Treaties of Rome was the economic growth and mobility of European workers between European states, some milestones were reached with regards to the common rules for migration. Further steps were made in 1980, when individual states began to cooperate more when discussing refugees and their safety.

It was not until late 1990s that most of the progress was made in terms of which countries were responsible for asylum seekers. The implementation of the Schengen Agreement brought new questions about handling asylum in Europe. Politicians from different countries agreed that single state solutions would not be effective.

Schengen I was followed by Schengen II and closer cooperation between the single states. The rules related to asylum were indeed not included in this agreement; they were made between European countries and not by the EU. One of the most well-known agreements was the Dublin Regulation. This regulation included the question of which country was responsible for the procedures of granting the right of asylum in the EU. The Dublin regulations aimed to prevent refugees being sent from country to country. The main principle of the regulations is the one-state-only principle, which means that a person could only ask for asylum in one European state. Generally, this is the state which they first entered.

The regulation was often criticised, and not just by Germany. One major point of criticism was that central European states could not be reached without crossing other European states. Moreover, the handling of the regulation itself was strongly criticised. Non-governmental organisations and the United Nations High Commissioner for Refugees (UNHCR) stated that while the responsibilities had been regulated to a large extent, common standards had not been implemented thus far.

In the late 1990s, the Treaty of Amsterdam was pivotal in critically changing the politics of most European States. Up until then, asylum and migration had fallen under the domestic jurisdiction of individual states. It was seen as a genuine national function to determine the law of migration and asylum. Additionally, this aspect had always been connected to the question of safety.

With the Treaty of Amsterdam, many powers were transferred from the national states to the EU; this was also the case for Germany, a signatory of the treaty. Now, the law sector that previously dealt with asylum and its related fields was transferred to the first pillar of the European Community.

Thereafter, asylum law and the handling of refugees became a supranational question, including existing laws and rules like the Schengen Treaty. Another step was taken with the Treaty of Nice; after 2003, the European Parliament had equal rights in asylum law. Subsequently, both the parliament and the European Commission had to agree on a law before it could enter into force. With Qualification Directive 2004/83/EC in 2004,[3] previously reached agreements on this topic were put into law. The EU, and subsequently Germany, set out minimum standards in asylum for refugees and stateless persons which were then integrated into domestic law.

[3] Council Directive 2004/83/EC of 29 April 2004, Official Journal L 304, 30/09/2004 P. 0012–0023.

The Treaty of Amsterdam established the foundations of asylum politics and how to deal with refugees. In the year after the ratification of the Treaty, the European states came together to discuss the contents of the common asylum standards.

The following programme was named after Tampere in Finland; during the preparation of the programme, guidelines had been constructed. The contract's design related to both the "Convention relating to the Status of Refugees", as well as the "UDHR".

Aside from the commitment to the Convention and the UDHR, the European Council paved the way to the introduction of the Charter of Fundamental Rights of the EU.[4] The European Community created, therefore, the Convention on the Future of Europe in 2001, the actual aim of which was to create a European Constitution. The charter would thus become part of the constitution. After the European Constitution was rejected in 2005, the charter alone remained and was put into law.

The aim of the programme was "the creation of an area of freedom, security and justice in the EU",[5] where asylum and migration would be of particular importance. The Tampere Programme was subdivided into four areas, which each dealt with different aspects of asylum: partnership with states of origin, a common European asylum system, fair treatment of third country nationals and management of migration flows.

The first area was created to minimise state emigration; to this purpose, EU poverty should be combated within the states and living standards raised. Through improving the conditions in the states, people should have no reason to leave their home countries and emigrate elsewhere. However, emigration could not be eradicated by these measures alone.

To regulate asylum in the EU, it was necessary to create common standards and one system for its members; the EU and its member states thereby "attach to absolute respect of the right to seek asylum".[6] The basis for the common standards was the Convention relating to the Status of Refugees. Furthermore, international organisations like the UNHCR were consulted and bound during the progress. The aim was to create workable standards in the EU and to quickly determine which states were responsible for an asylum seeker. Moreover, "the approximation of rules on the recognition and content of the refugee status"[7] was a focal point of discussion within this area.

The long-term aims had been to create common rules and standards for asylum in the EU. Persons seeking asylum must have the same conditions and rules in all member states in the EU. Nevertheless, Great Britain, Ireland and Denmark did not take part in the programme. The programme also forced the establishment of "the system for the identification of asylum seekers"[8] to avoid misuse of asylum in the

---

[4] Tampere European Council 15 and 16 October 1999, Presidency Conclusions, http://www.europarl.europa.eu/summits/tam_en.htm.

[5] Tampere (1999).

[6] Tampere (1999).

[7] Tampere (1999).

[8] Tampere (1999).

EU. The aims have still not been fully realised and, given the circumstances of asylum politics in many countries in the EU, it does not seem like they will be reached in the near future. The programme ran for 5 years until it was succeeded by the Hague Programme. During the time of the Tampere Programme, several directives were enacted.

In 2003, the Dublin Convention was replaced by the Dublin II Regulation.[9] There were not many changes to the first Convention; its focus still lies on which country is responsible for granting asylum. In most cases, it is the EU state that was first entered by a refugee. The Regulation also seeks to provide fair processes during the asylum procedure. On the other hand, the Dublin Regulation led to stricter control of the EU's borders; as a result, the states on the EU's external borders tried to avoid large numbers of asylum seekers. Through EURODAC and FADO, systems were implemented to avoid one person seeking asylum in multiple countries.

The Hague Programme in 2004 expanded on the Tampere Programme; however, an asylum system for all EU member states was still the main aim. Despite the preexisting aims of the programme, the focus was now on terrorism. After 9/11 and Madrid 2004, safety became a leading role in asylum questionnaires. Both terrorist attacks and the fight against human trafficking at the borders led to the founding of the "European Border and Coast Guard Agency".[10] The EU's member states started to cooperate more closely against illegal immigration. Meanwhile, the main aim of a single system for asylum in the EU remained elusive.

The Hague Programme was followed by the Stockholm Programme in 2010 and the Post Stockholm Programme in 2014. The focus of these programmes shifted to questions of safety. Nevertheless, the aims of previous programmes remained. The Stockholm Programme added one new aspect of migration. There was now also an attempt to find and harmonise a legal way of migration into the EU.[11]

To implement the single topics of the different programmes, two measures were taken. The first one was to create a legal framework. With that in mind, the first directives were created and put into law; the framework consisted of the Dublin Regulation and the Council Directives. The directives were 2003/9/EC,[12] 2004/83/EC[13] and 2005/85/EC[14]; these combined with the 5-year-programmes should lead to equal standards and an equal asylum policy in the EU.

---

[9] Council Regulation (EC) No. 343/2003.

[10] Council Regulation (EC) No. 2007/2004.

[11] EUR-Lex-j10036-EN, https://eur-lex.europa.eu/legal-content/EN/TXT/?uri=LEGISSUM:jl0036.

[12] Council Directive 2003/9/EC of 27 January 2003 laying down minimum standards for the reception of asylum seekers, Official Journal L 031, 06/02/2003 P. 0018–0025.

[13] Council Directive 2004/83/EC of 29 April 2004 on minimum standards for the qualification and status of third country nationals or stateless persons as refugees or as persons who otherwise need international protection and the content of the protection granted, Official Journal of the European Union, L 304/12.

[14] Council Directive 2005/85/EC of 1 December 2005 on minimum standards on procedures in Member States for granting and withdrawing refugee status, Official Journal of the European Union, L 326/13.

The aim was to achieve better standards throughout the EU. However, Germany slowed down the negotiations, particularly with regards to the question on the definition of refugees. During this time, there was an in-depth discussion about a new German immigration law. The previous law included different residence permit titles which had become complicated. The multiple options bound to different conditions were not easy to understand, even for experts. Therefore, until a new formulation of the law in Germany was agreed, they did not want to commit to a European law. The effect of the new directives led to minimum standards for refugees in the EU. The definition of a refugee was no longer just a matter for national states.

In Germany, the biggest changes took place in the early 2000s when a new asylum and immigration law was implemented. The discussions about the new law were long-lasting and controversial. At the end of 2004, Germany agreed on the formulation of Directive 2004/83/EC. The directive was even put into law before the new German asylum and immigration law. This new formulation in Germany brought many changes; for example, the number of residency titles was limited to two. Thereafter, there was only a distinction between 'Aufenthalserlaubnis'[15] and 'Niederlassungserlaubnis'[16] in Germany. Some groups were excluded from the regulations, like highly qualified persons or some family members.

Changes were also made with regards to the definition of refugees and the right to asylum. The new law now referred to the Convention relating to the Status of Refugees which is named in the first sentence of the article.[17] Until then, German law did not explicitly refer to the Convention relating to the Status of Refugees, which led to legal disagreements due to the fact that Germany had signed the convention.[18] With the new formulation, Article 1 of the Convention was not transferred to German domestic law word-for-word. However, the naming of it in the first sentence of the German Asylum law document brought more judicial guarantee. Another new policy was that, from then onwards, an actor did not have to be a governmental worker. Germany, unlike other countries, combined chasing, leading to flight to governmental acting.[19] The definition of the German legislation led to increased clarity around this issue. The legislation also completed preliminary work in acting before Directive 2004/83/EC was adopted to national law[20]; the directive

[15] An Aufenthaltserlaubnis is a temporary residence permit and is given for 3 years, bounded to a purpose regulated through law (§ 7-8, AufenthG).

[16] A Niederlassungserlaubnis is a permanent residence permit (§9 AufenthG).

[17] See §3, 1 AsylG and BGBl. 1953 II S. 559, 560, https://www.bgbl.de/xaver/bgbl/start.xav?start=//*%5B@attr_id=%27bgbl253019.pdf%27%5D#__bgbl__%2F%2F*%5B%40attr_id%3D%27bgbl253019.pdf%27%5D__1525095561304.

[18] See Duchrow (2004), p. 339.

[19] Until that time, German courts argued that a chasing had to come from a governmental actor. Even in court decisions of the Bundesverwaltungsgericht, this view was confirmed. For example, see BVerwGE 95, 42.

[20] See Duchrow (2004), p. 340.

was transferred into national law in 2007.[21] It was the first time that the status as a refugee was adopted by German law as a unique attribute.

In 2013, the new formulation of the directive, now 2011/95/EU,[22] had been adopted by German law. The changes were mostly the regulation of the German law. The definition of a refugee did not change. A critical part of the directive, which had been adopted to German law, was the qualification for subsidiary protection. This had not existed in German law until that time. This gives people who do not fulfil all the attributes of a refugee as defined by the Geneva Convention a guarantee of protection; people could not be sent back to their home country if they feared serious harm, such as the death penalty or execution. Aside from the threat of a governmental actor, an individual could also be prevented from adequate medical supply in another country from deportation; this could be due to serious health risks that result from a lack of medical care.[23]

German law makes a distinction between a refugee and a person who has the right of asylum. A person entitled to asylum also has to have the attributes of a refugee. A person who is a refugee is not automatically entitled to asylum. The distinction lies in the different reference of the law. The definition of a refugee is connected to the Geneva Convention and includes the chase of governmental bodies as non-governmental groups.[24] The entitlement of asylum is only given for political reasons. In normal cases, the chasing has to come from a governmental body.[25] Exceptions include when the state and its organisations could not guarantee the safety of its habitants. Asylum is only granted when a person has not acted against the Dublin Regulation. Nevertheless, both groups receive the same residency permit if they are accepted.

4 Conclusion

The definition of a refugee in Germany had been the same for the past six decades. Since the ratification of the Convention relating to the Status of Refugees in the early 1950s, the definition was binding for Germany. The changes made after the Second World War had mostly been in the field of regulations of national law. The development was closely related to the acting of the EU and its former organisations. German law was adapted according to European directives and international

[21] See Gesetz zur Umsetzung aufenthalts- und asylrechtlicher Richtlinien der Europäischen Union, BGBl. I S. 1970.

[22] Directive 2011/95/EU of the European Parliament and of the on standards for the qualification of third-country nationals or stateless persons as beneficiaries of international protection, for a uniform status for refugees or for persons eligible for subsidiary protection, and for the content of the protection granted (recast) of 13 December 2011, Official Journal of the European Union, L 337/9.

[23] See § 60, 7 AufenthG.

[24] See § 3 AsylG.

[25] See § 16a GG.

agreements; nonetheless, Germany acted independently for as long as possible. At the beginning of the twenty-first century, it was Germany who delayed the formulation of the EU directive. Germany did not strictly act according to the directives; however, it did impose restrictions on other countries, such as the prohibition of banishing European countries due to a perceived lack of standards. Overall, however, the definition and handling of refugees remained close to the development made in the 1950s.

References

Bundesgesetzblatt Teil II 1953 Nr. 19 vom 24.11.1953 Komplette Ausgabe. https://www.bgbl.de/xaver/bgbl/start.xav?start=//*%5B@attr_id=%27bgbl253019.pdf%27%5D#__bgbl__%2F%2F*%5B%40attr_id%3D%27bgbl253019.pdf%27%5D__1525095561304

Duchrow, J. (2004). Flüchtlingsrecht und Zuwanderungsgesetz unter Berücksichtigung der sog. Qualifikationsrichtlinie. *ZAR, 10*.

Presidency Conclusions. (1999). Tampere European Council 15 and 16 October 1999. http://www.europarl.europa.eu/summits/tam_en.htm

Religious Believer

Caterina Drigo

1 Preliminary Remarks

Analysis of EU law, international provisions, and CJEU and ECtHR case law demonstrates a landscape that moves from the promotion and defence of religious believers' fundamental rights, starting from the right to manifest one's personal belief or religion and not to be discriminated against on the ground of belonging to a certain religion (see, *ex multis*, Bielefledt et al. 2016; Mock & Demuro 2010; Requejo & Ungureanu 2014; Ferrari & Pastorelli 2012).

For the purpose of this work, a 'religious *believer*' is an individual who has a personal religious belief, considered in its external dimension, in its external manifestations, while a religious *person* is an individual who has a personal religious belief, considered in its internal dimension (see, *infra*, '*The legal status of religious person*'). Consequently, this work considers only the so-called *forum externum* of the freedom of religion, which includes the freedom to manifest religion or belief in worship, proselytising, teaching, practice and observance.

Conversely, this work does not address the topic of the problematic definition of the concept of 'religion' or of 'religious denomination' (for this, see, *infra*, '*The legal status of religious person*')—neither their connection with the public authority nor with the controversial issue of Islamic political parties.

C. Drigo (✉)
School of Law, Alma Mater Studiorum University of Bologna, Bologna, Italy
e-mail: caterina.drigo@unibo.it

A. Bartolini et al. (eds.), *Dictionary of Statuses within EU Law*,
https://doi.org/10.1007/978-3-030-00554-2_61

2 Religious Freedom and Status of Religious Believer Through International and European Perspectives

Although European interest in the religious dimension and rights connected to it dates back to the 1960s and has resulted in the adoption of several specific provisions, the Lisbon Treaty modified the Preamble of the TEU, valuing the religious element and connecting it to cultural and humanist 'inheritance of Europe, from which have developed the universal values of the inviolable and inalienable rights of the human person, freedom, democracy equality and the rule of law'. Another significant reference can be found in art. 17 TFEU regarding religious and non-confessional organisations and creating the normative basis for a European constitutional law of religions (Häberle 2009, pp. 513 ff.).

Within Europe and internationally, freedom of thought, conscience, religion and belief are distinguished by the freedom to manifest religion or belief.

Article 10 CFREU protects the 'right to freedom of thought, conscience and religion', including the 'freedom to change religion or belief and freedom, either alone or in community with others and in public or in private, to manifest religion or belief, in worship, teaching, practice and observance' (para. 1) and represents one of the pillars of modern democratic and pluralist societies.

In its possible manifestations and multiple declinations, religious freedom is also protected by several international documents (see, *infra*, '*The legal status of religious person*' and, for a broad perspective, see Bielefledt et al. 2016; Taylor 2005, pp. 339 ff.).

Art. 10 CFREU clearly evokes the contents of art. 9 ECHR and, in accordance with art. 52 (para. 3) CFREU, it has the same meaning and scope (Guazzaroti 2012, pp. 370 ff.; Groppi 2010, pp. 64 ff.) and art. 18 UDHR of 1948.

Moreover, the ICCPR of 1966 (art. 18), the Human Rights Committee's *General Comment n. 22*, and other international documents, both generally and regarding specific categories of people (such as women, vulnerable persons, child, and migrants) expressly protect the multiple declination of the *forum externum* of the religious freedom (see, *infra*, '*The legal status of religious person*', § 2). In particular, *General Comment n. 22* specifies that the *forum externum* of freedom of religion 'encompasses a broad range of acts', and indeed:

The concept of worship extends to ritual and ceremonial acts giving direct expression to belief, as well as various practices integral to such acts, including the building of places of worship, the use of ritual formulae and objects, the display of symbols, and the observance of holidays and days of rest.

The observance and practice of religion or belief may include not only ceremonial acts but also such customs as the observance of dietary regulations, the wearing of distinctive clothing or head coverings, participation in rituals associated with certain stages of life, and the use of a particular language customarily spoken by a group .... [T]he practice and teaching of religion or belief includes acts integral to the conduct by religious groups of their basic affairs, such as the freedom to choose their religious leaders, priests and teachers, the freedom to establish seminaries or religious schools and the freedom to prepare and distribute religious texts or publications.

The main difference between the *forum internum* and the *forum externum* of religious freedom is that the second can be subjected to specific limitations imposed by the States (Fawcett 1987, p. 238; Shouppe 2013, pp. 855 ff.).

Freedom to manifest one's religion or beliefs may be 'subject only to such limitations as are prescribed by law and are necessary to protect goods such as public safety, order, health, or morals or the fundamental rights and freedoms of others' (art. 18, para. 3, ICCPR). Art. 9, para. 2, ECHR adds that these limitations shall be 'necessary in a democratic society'.

For the purposes of this work, the contents of art. 10 CFREU shall be linked to arts. 21 and 22 CFREU. According to the first (art. 21, para. 1), all discrimination is prohibited based on any ground, including religion or belief. According to the second (art. 22), 'cultural, religious and linguistic diversity' must be respected. In particular, this last provision protects not only diversity of religions *strictu sensu* considered, but also multiple aspects of the cultural matrix existing within European society (Geiger et al. 2015; Celotto 2010, p. 134; Grillo et al. 2009).

The provisions of art. 21 CFREU shall be also coordinated with art. 18 TFEU (art. 12 TEC), 19 TFEU (art. 13 TEC), and art. 14 ECHR, all of which are dedicated to combatting discrimination in all its forms (Favilli 2008, p. 80). Additionally, several EU legal provisions (mostly Directives), protect various aspects connected to religious believers (for example, Directive 2000/78/EC, which also considered direct and indirect discrimination based on religion or Directive 93/119/EC of 1993 on the protection of animals at the time of slaughter or killing).

Legal provisions and practices dedicated to the protection of religious freedom and defining the status of a religious believer can also be considered a direct expression of the principle of human dignity, as stated in art. 1 CFREU (Loretan 2016).

3 Jurisprudential Path: Rights of the Religious Believer Through the Prism of Case Law

3.1 Nature and Content of the Freedom of Religion with Reference to Religious External Manifestations

In the famous leading case *Kokkinakis v. Greece* (25.5.1993, § 31), the ECtHR defined the freedom of thought, conscience and religion, 'enshrined in Article 9', as 'one of the foundations of a "democratic society" within the meaning of the Convention'. The Court, although recognising that 'religious freedom is primarily a matter of individual conscience', stated that 'it also implies an external dimension' and includes 'freedom to "manifest [one's] religion"'. A freedom that 'is not only exercisable in community with others, "in public" and within the circle of those whose faith one shares, but can also be asserted "alone" and "in private"' (*Kokkinakis*, cit. *supra*, § 31, and similarly, *Leyla Şahin v. Turkey*, [GC], 10.11.2005, § 105).

In particular, the ECtHR recognises both the right to preach and proselytise and the freedom of religious worship, which also includes the right to provide, open and maintain places or buildings devoted to religious worship.

The external dimension of religious freedom is not absolute: 'since the manifestation by one person of his/her religious belief may have an impact on others', art. 9, para. 2, ECHR allows States to impose some limits on the right to manifest one's religion, but those limits must be justified only in light of its prescriptions. So, 'any limitation placed on a person's freedom to manifest religion or belief must be prescribed by law and necessary in a democratic society in pursuit of one or more of the legitimate aims set out therein' (*Eweida and Others v. the United Kingdom*, ECtHR, 27.5.2013, § 80).

It must be stressed that not 'every act which is in some way inspired, motivated or influenced' by religious beliefs 'constitutes a "manifestation" of' that belief: 'In order to count as a "manifestation" within the meaning of Article 9, the act in question must be intimately linked to the religion or belief' (*Eweida and Others*, cit., *supra*, § 82, but see *Skugar and Others v. Russia*, ECtHR, 3.12.2009, and *Arrowsmith v. the United Kingdom*, Commission's report 12.10.1978, Decisions and Reports 19, p. 5; *Zaoui v. Switzerland*, ECtHR, 18.1.2001).

However, art. 9 ECHR neither protects every action inspired or motivated by a religious purpose nor always assures the right to behave in the public sphere in the ways dictated or inspired by one's religion or beliefs (*Kalaç v. Turkey*, ECtHR, 1.7.1997).

According to the ECtHR, 'the existence of a sufficiently close and direct nexus between the act and the underlying belief must be determined on the facts of each case. In particular, there is no requirement on the applicant to establish that he or she acted in fulfilment of a duty mandated by the religion in question' (*Eweida*, cit., *supra*, § 82, and, *ex multis*, *Cha'are Shalom Ve Tsedek v. France*, [GC], 27.6.2000, §§ 73–74; *Leyla Şahin*, cit. *supra*, §§ 78 and 105;, §; *Skugar*, cit. *supra*).

Save exceptional hypothesis (see ECtHR, *Skugar*, cit. *supra*), or where a law that establishes a privilege or a special exemption for members of a given religious community comes into question (for example, in the employment field (see *Kosteski v. Former Yugoslav Republic of Macedonia*, ECtHR, 13.4.2006, § 39)), the domestic authorities are not justified in casting doubt on the sincerity of beliefs and their manifestations, and the ECtHR tends to dismiss objections on this point (see, for example, *S.A.S. v. France*, ECtHR, [GC], 1.7.2014, § 56 or *Vartic v. Romania*, n. 2, ECtHR, 17.12.2013, § 469).

3.2 *Religious Symbols or Clothing*

Although the ECtHR recognises that 'a healthy democratic society needs to tolerate and sustain pluralism and diversity' (*Eweida*, cit. *supra*, § 94), its case law highlights the fact that the right to wear religious symbols or clothing is not absolute and must be balanced with the legitimate interest of other natural and legal persons. In this field, the case law diverges into three areas: (a) the public spaces, (b) the workplace, and (c) schools and universities.

3.2.1 Religious Symbols or Clothing in the Public Sphere

The use of religious symbols in the public sphere is quite controversial because several potential opposing interests are at stake. As the ECtHR recognises a wide margin of appreciation to the States, it tends to legitimate the bans meted out and justified on a legislative ground; if not, a violation of art. 9 ECHR is found (see *Ahmet Arslan and Others v. Turkey*, ECtHR, 23.2.2010).

Quite recently, the ECtHR has been faced with cases related to religious freedom in the context of states wishing to maintain secularism. It has placed particular weight on the State's stated aim of preventing disorder and protecting the rights and freedoms of others.

In this regard, a good example of the legal reasoning of the Court is the case *S.A.S. v. France* (ECtHR, [GC], 1.7.2014). Deciding on the legitimacy of the French ban on the wearing in public of clothing that covers the face, the ECtHR ruled that, since 'the face plays an important role in social interaction', the ban 'falls within the powers of the State to secure the conditions whereby individuals can live together in their diversity', respecting the 'set of values of an open democratic society' (*S.A.S.*, cit. *supra*, §§ 114–122). So, 'a State may find it essential to give particular weight in this connection to the interaction between individuals and may consider this to be adversely affected by the fact that some conceal their faces in public places' (*S.A.S.*, cit. *supra*, § 141, *Belcacemi and Oussar v. Belgium*, ECtHR, 11.7.2017, and *Dakir v. Belgium*, ECtHR, 11.7.2017).

3.2.2 Religious Symbols or Clothing at Workplace

The issue of religious symbols and clothing is also controversial in regard to their use in the workplace. When the ECtHR has occasion to rule on this issue, it tends to recognise that 'this is a field where the domestic authorities must be allowed a wide margin of appreciation' (*Eweida*, cit. *supra*, § 99). So, in general, the Court admits that a commercial company can legitimately impose a dress code on its employees that imposes a restriction on wearing religious symbols in order to project a specific commercial image (*Eweida*, cit. *supra*, § 94).

Similarly, hospitals have the power to lay down their own rules on clothing to protect the health and safety of their patients and medical staff (*Eweida*, cit. *supra*, and *Ebrahimian v. France*, ECtHR, 26.11.2015).

Nevertheless, these interests, however legitimate, are not absolute and must always be weighed, case by case, against the individual's right to manifest one's religion or belief, and any restriction cannot have the effect of discriminating against certain categories of individuals, especially women.

Recently, the CJEU had occasion to rule on this issue and delivered its first judgments on discrimination on the grounds of religion in *Achbita v. G4S Secure Solutions* (CJEU C-157/15, 14 March 2017) and in *Asma Bougnaoui and ADDH v. Micropole SA* (CJEU, C-188/15, 14 March 2017). According to the judges, a rule restricting religious symbols or attire can only be seen to be appropriate when it is part of a neutral policy that is genuinely pursued in a consistent and systematic manner.

3.2.3 Religious Symbols or Clothing in State Schools and Educational Institutions

In view of the diversity of the approaches taken by national authorities on the issue and in relation to the cases of wearing religious symbols and clothing in State schools and educational institutions, the ECtHR has always recognised to the States a wide margin of appreciation. Indeed, according to the Court, it is impossible to discern a uniform conception of the significance of religion throughout Europe, and the meaning or impact of the public expression of a religious belief will differ according to time and context (see, *ex multis*, *Leyla Şahin*, cit. *supra*, *Otto-Preminger-Institut v. Austria*, ECtHR 20.9.1994, or *Dahlab v. Switzerland*, ECtHR, 15.2.2001). Consequently, '[w]here questions concerning the relationship between State and religion are at stake, on which opinion in a democratic society may reasonably differ widely, the role of the national decision-making body must be given special importance' (*Leyla Şahin* cit. *supra,* §109, but see *Cha'are Shalom Ve Tsedek*, cit. *supra*, § 84, or *Wingrove v. the United Kingdom*, ECtHR, 25.11.1996, § 58).

In particular, with reference to the right of teachers to wear religious symbols or clothing, the ECtHR appears aware that it is very difficult to assess the impact that a powerful external symbol (such as a headscarf) may have on the freedom of conscience and religion of very young children. The ECtHR, in weighing the right of a teacher to manifest her religion against the need to protect pupils by preserving religious harmony, stated that, 'having regard, above all, to the age of the children for whom a person that wish to wear some religious symbols is responsible as a representative of the State, the domestic authorities did not exceed their margin of appreciation if they do not allow the wearing of headscarves, since it appears both to have a proselytizing effect and hard to square with the principle of gender equality' (*Dahlab v. Swizterland*, 15.2.2001, § 2).

3.3 *Religious Freedom of Parents and Educational Rights of Children*

Another controversial issue is how to balance the religious freedom and beliefs of parents and the educational rights of children.

If the ECtHR recognises that art. 9 ECHR protects individuals against religious indoctrination of the State (*Angeleni v. Sweeden*, Commission Decision, 3.12.1986, DR 51, p. 41), at the same time, it does not consider every parental request to be legitimate, since the ECtHR also values the right to a proper integration and a fair instruction of children.

A good example of the reasoning of the ECtHR can be found in a quite recent case, *Osmanoğlu and Kocabaş v. Switzerland* (10.01.2017), brought by Muslim parents who wanted their young daughters to be exempted from swim lessons in a mixed-gender class. The ECtHR, after having recognised that 'school plays a special role in the process of social integration', especially where 'children of foreign origin are concerned', considered that 'an exemption from certain lessons is justified only in very exceptional circumstances, in well-defined conditions and having regard to equality of treatment for all religious groups'. Indeed, 'the children's interest in an all-round education, facilitating their successful social integration according to local customs and mores, takes precedence over the parents' wish' (*Osmanoğlu and Kocabaş*, cit. *supra*, §§ 96–97). This case also appears to be significant because the ECtHR and the applicants were arguing based on opposing conceptions of integration and discrimination.

The right of parents to have upheld their right 'to ensure the education and teaching of their children in conformity with their own religious and philosophical convictions' is also guaranteed by art. 2 of Protocol No. 1 ECHR, which is, in principle, the *lex specialis* in relation to art. 9 ECHR (*Lautsi and Others v. Italy*, [GC], 18.3.2011, or *Folgerø and Others v. Norway*, [GC], 29.6.2007).

3.4 *Further Dimension of Religious Believers' Rights*

The protections of ECHR and CFREU also extend to health issues and the observance of dietary law. With reference to the first, in a case of refusal of blood transfusion because of religious beliefs, the ECtHR ruled that a free refusal (a refusal not expressed by minors) is a matter of personal autonomy, so it is protected by art. 9 ECHR and by the principle of self-determination (*Jehovah's Witnesses of Moscow and Others v. Russia*, 10.6.2010).

With reference to the second, the Court stated that the observance of dietary laws dictated by a religion or a philosophical system is a 'practice' which is protected by art. 9 ECHR (*Cha'are Shalom Ve Tsedek*, cit. *supra*, *Jakóbsky v. Poland*, 7.12.2010, and *Vartic v. Romania*, n. 2., cit. *supra*), even if it does not extend to every activity, and so, for example, it does not include the right to participate personally in the performance of ritual slaughter and the subsequent certification process (*Cha'are Shalom Ve Tsedek*, cit. *supra*, § 82).

4 Conclusions

Analysis carried out above highlights how, at the European level, the protection of the *forum externum* of religious freedom covers the majority of the ECtHR's decisions on freedom of religion.

Several decisions, both of the ECtHR and the CJEU have been controversial. The protection of the *forum externum* of religious freedoms or beliefs, especially in the field of religious symbols and clothing, shows all its slipperiness if one considers that even in some cultural contexts, particularly the Islamic one, there is no agreement on symbols and situations to be considered acceptable or legitimate. This shows the extreme difficulty of adopting a model of integration that can be said to be free from axes of tension or critical profiles (Drigo 2017, pp. 335 ff.)

The path to reach effective protection of religious freedom, especially in consideration of the principle of equality and freedom, is far from being complete.

The challenges posed by the multicultural dimension of the European territory, with the different normative strategies brought about in different States, impose continuing reflection on the theme of religious freedom and its limits.

The European landscape shows us in all its seriousness how critical issues are not resolved by simply legitimising any behaviour, regardless of potential violations of the set of fundamental values, or, conversely, limiting to the maximum the external expressions of religiosity.

We would not avoid difficulties and clashes that firstly are of cultural origin, and not strictly religious, and any simplistic reading is to be rejected categorically.

Although the pragmatic approaches of the CJEU or of the ECtHR, which compress or extend the margin of appreciation of the States depending on the context, the European States are faced with the heroic task of identifying the real point of equilibrium between opposing interests.

The tragic terroristic events that have occurred in recent years show us that 'the European model of strict separation between state and religion and the claim, sometimes connected to this model, that religion should be ignored in public space' begins 'to waver', and it is therefore necessary to reflect carefully on the concept of secularism to which we adhere (Cantaro and Losurdo 2014, p. 591).

To oscillate between assimilationist practices and relativistic attitudes could have as an epilogue the spread of unequal situations that are potentially harmful only for a particular category of individual, the women. Such individuals often—even if not always—are confined to a subordinate role by some religious rules, and this is dangerous, as well as harmful, for the protection of those fundamental rights which the European States claim to be guarantors.

References

Bielefledt, H., Ghanea, N., & Wiener, M. (2016). *Freedom of religion or belief: An international law commentary*. Oxford: Oxford University Press.

Cantaro, A., & Losurdo, F. (2014). "Secolarizzazione" e "desecolarizzazione" negli ordinamenti giuridici islamici. *Diritto Pubblico Comparato ed Europeo, 2*, 581 ff.

Celotto, A. (2010). Article 22, cultural, religious and linguistic diversity. In W. B. T. Mock & G. Demuro (Eds.), *Human rights in Europe, commentary of the Charter of Fundamental Rights of the European Union* (pp. 134–140). Durham: Carolina Academic Press.

Drigo, C. (2017). Traiettorie di una convivenza difficile. Spunti di riflessione a partire dalla c.d. questione Burkini. *Percorsi costituzionali, 1*, 333–353.

Favilli, C. (2008). *La non discriminazione nell'Unione Europea*. Bologna: il Mulino.

Fawcett, J. E. S. (1987). *The application of the European Convention on Human Rights*. Oxford: Oxford University Press.

Ferrari, S., & Pastorelli, S. (Eds.). (2012). *Religion in public spaces: A European perspective*. Farnham: Ashgate.

Geiger, R., Khan, D. E., & Kotzur, M. (Eds.). (2015). *European Union treaties: A commentary*. Munich: Hart.

Grillo, R., Ballard, R., Ferrari, A., Hoekema, A. J., Maussen, M., & Shah, P. (Eds.). (2009). *Legal practice and cultural diversity*. Farnham: Ashgate.

Groppi, T. (2010). Article 10. Freedom of thought, conscience and religion. In W. B. T. Mock & G. Demuro (Eds.), *Human rights in Europe: Commentary of the Charter of Fundamental Rights of the European Union* (pp. 64–71). Durham, NC: Carolina Academic Press.

Guazzaroti, A. (2012). Art. 9: Libertà di pensiero, coscienza e religione. In S. Bartole, P. De Sena, & V. Zagrebelsky (Eds.), *Commentario breve alla Convenzione europea per la salvaguardia dei diritti dell'uomo e delle libertà fondamentali* (pp. 370–397). Padova: Cedam.

Häberle, P. (2009). *Europäische verfassungslehre*. Germany: Nomos.

Loretan, A. (2016). La libertà religiosa ha il suo fondamento nella dignità umana. In E. Camassa (Ed.), *Democrazie e Religioni* (pp. 19–24). Napoli: Editoriale Scientifica.

Mock, W. B. T., & Demuro, G. (Eds.). (2010). *Human rights in Europe: Commentary of the Charter of Fundamental Rights of the European Union*. Durham, NC: Carolina Academic Press.

Requejo, F., & Ungureanu, C. (Eds.). (2014). *Democracy, law and religious pluralism in Europe*. New York: Routledge.

Shouppe, J. P. (2013). Libertà di religione, multiculturalismo e laicità dello Stato. In P. Gianniti (Ed.), *I diritti fondamentali nell'Unione europea: La Carta di Nizza dopo il Trattato di Lisbona, Commentario del codice civile e codici collegati Scialoja-Branca-Galgano* (pp. 855–906). Bologna: Zanichelli.

Taylor, P. M. (2005). *Freedom of religion: UN and European human rights law and practice*. Cambridge, UK: Cambridge University Press.

Religious Person

Caterina Drigo

1 Introduction

Analysis of EU law, international provisions, and case law from the CJEU and ECtHR shows an articulated landscape that moves from the promotion and the defence of religious persons' fundamental rights, beginning with non-discrimination on the ground of belonging to a certain religion. In this perspective, European and international institutional actors and judges have played a central role in favour of implementing anti-discrimination legislation, enforcing personal and religious beliefs and human dignity (see, *ex multis*, Fawcett 1987, Ferrari and Pastorelli 2012, Mock and Demuro 2010; Requejo and Ungureanu 2014).

For the purpose of this work, a religious *person* is an individual who has a personal religious belief, considered in its internal dimension, while a religious *believer* is an individual who has a personal religious belief, considered in its external dimension, in its external manifestations (see, *infra, Religious believer*). Consequently, this work considers only the so-called *forum internum* of the freedom of religion: freedom of religion as granting to the religious person the right to adopt, change, or renounce a religion or belief; the freedom from any coercion; the right to observe holidays and a day of rest; and the right not to be discriminated against based on religion or religious beliefs.

Moreover, this work introduces the problematic definition of the concept of 'religion' or of 'religious denominations' from the jurisprudential perspective (for a theoretical point of view see *ex multis*, Shouppe 2013, pp. 873–875). Related to this issue, the Human Rights Committee's *General Comment n. 22* specifies that '[t]he terms "belief" and "religion" are to be broadly construed', so that international protection is not limited, in its application, 'to traditional religions or to religions and beliefs with institutional characteristics or practices analogous to those of traditional

C. Drigo (✉)
School of Law, Alma Mater Studiorum University of Bologna, Bologna, Italy
e-mail: caterina.drigo@unibo.it

A. Bartolini et al. (eds.), *Dictionary of Statuses within EU Law*,
https://doi.org/10.1007/978-3-030-00554-2_62

religions' (par. 2). If this vague definition of religion has the merit of expanding the range of protected situations, it also has a negative implication in that some groups of a sectarian nature could abuse the guarantees provided for the protection of religious freedom.

Finally, this work could not address the issue of religions and religious denominations and their connection with the pubic authority or with the controversial issue of Islamic political parties.

2 Freedom of Religion, Status of Religious Persons, and Non-discrimination Through International and European Perspectives

Although European interest in the religious dimension and rights dates back to the sixties and has resulted in the adoption of several provisions (mostly Directives) characterised by a specific nature and contents, the Lisbon Treaty modified the Preamble of the TEU, valorising the religious element and connecting it to cultural and humanist 'inheritance of Europe, from which have developed the universal values of the inviolable and inalienable rights of the human person, freedom, democracy equality and the rule of law'. Another significant reference can be found in art. 17 TFEU regarding religious and non-confessional organisations creating the normative basis for a European constitutional law of religions (Häberle 2009, pp. 513 ff.).

Moreover, art. 10 of the CFREU protects the 'right to freedom of thought, conscience and religion', including the 'freedom to change religion or belief and freedom, either alone or in community with others and in public or in private, to manifest religion or belief, in worship, teaching, practice and observance' (para. 1) and represents one of the pillars of modern democratic and pluralist societies.

This legal provision clearly evokes the contents of art. 9 of the ECHR (Guazzaroti 2012, pp. 370 ff.; Groppi 2010, pp. 64 ff.) and art. 18 of the UDHR of 1948.

In its possible manifestations and multiple declinations, religious freedom is also protected by the ICCPR of 1966 (art. 18) and in the Human Rights Committee's *General Comment n. 22*. One can look elsewhere for similar legislation protecting religious freedom, including: *Declaration on the Elimination of All Forms of Intolerance and of Discrimination Based on Religion or Belief* proclaimed by General Assembly Resolution 36/55 of 25 November 1981; art. 4 of the *Declaration of Fundamental Rights and Freedoms* adopted by the European Parliament with the Resolution of 12 April 1989; the *EU Guidelines on the Promotion and Protection of Freedom of Religion or Belief* approved by the Council of the European Union at the end of the Council meeting of 24 June 2013; and *Council Conclusions on Freedom of Religion or Belief* of 16 November 2009.

In the international landscape, freedom of religion is also protected with reference to specific categories of people, such as women, vulnerable persons, child, migrants, and others (for a broad perspective, see Bielefledt et al. 2016; Taylor 2005, pp. 339 ff.).

Within Europe and internationally freedom of thought, conscience, religion, or belief is distinguished by the freedom to manifest religion or belief. In the first case, one should not be restricted by any limitations whatsoever on the freedom of thought and conscience, nor in the freedom of having or adopting a religion or belief of one's choice, nor one can be compelled to reveal his thoughts or adherence to a religion or belief. On the contrary, with reference to the freedom to manifest religion or belief, some limitation can be imposed by the States (see, *infra, "The legal status of religious believer*").

It is opportune to stress that there is a significant difference between the protection of freedom of religion provided by the ECHR and the ICCPR. According to the ICCPR is not possible, neither in exceptional cases, to derogate the duty to guarantee religious freedom (act. 4.2 of the *Pact*), while, according to art. 15 ECHR, art. 9 ECHR is included among the provisions of the Convention that, in exceptional cases, such as war or other danger that threatens the life of the Nation, could be derogated by the States.

On the contrary, there is a significant consonance among art. 9 ECHR and art. 10 CFREU, even if only the CFREU expressly mentions the right of conscientious objection.

The rights delineated across different pieces of legislation are substantially similar: the right guaranteed in art. 10, para. 1 CFREU corresponds with the right guaranteed in art. 9 ECHR and, in accordance with art. 52 (para. 3) CFREU, it has the same meaning and scope.

Moreover, the right to conscientious objection, guaranteed in art. 10, para. 2, refers to national constitutional traditions and to the development of State legislation on this issue.

For the purposes of this work, the contents of art. 10 CFREU shall be linked to arts. 21 and 22 CFREU. According to the first, (art. 21, para. 1), any discrimination is prohibited based on any ground such as, among others, religion or belief. While, according to the second (art. 22), 'cultural, religious and linguistic diversity' shall be respected. In particular, this last provision protects not only diversity of religions *strictu sensu* considered, but also multiple aspects of the cultural matrix existing within European society (Geiger et al. 2015; Celotto 2010, p. 134; Grillo et al. 2009).

The provisions of art. 21 of the *European Charter* shall be also coordinated with art. 18 TFEU (art. 12 TEC), 19 TFEU (art. 13 TEC), and art. 14 ECHR, all of which are dedicated to combatting discrimination (Favilli 2008, p. 80). Additionally, several EU legal provisions (mostly Directives), tend to protect various aspects connected to religious persons (for example, directive 2000/78/EC, which considered also direct and indirect discrimination based on religious reasons).

Legal provisions and practices dedicated to the protection of religious freedom and defining the status of a religious person can also be considered a direct expression of the principle of human dignity, as stated in art. 1 CFREU (Loretan 2016).

3 Jurisprudential Path: Rights of Religious Person Through the Prism of Case Law

3.1 Nature and Content of the Freedom of Religion

In the famous leading case *Kokkinakis v. Greece* (25.5.1993, §31), the ECtHR defined the freedom of thought, conscience, and religion 'enshrined in Article 9', as 'one of the foundations of a "democratic society" within the meaning of the Convention'. According to the judges, the 'religious dimension' is 'one of the most vital elements that go to make up the identity of believers and their conception of life', and 'it is also a precious asset for atheists, agnostics, sceptics and the unconcerned. The pluralism indissociable from a democratic society, which has been dearly won over the centuries, depends on it'.

The direct result of this would be the prohibition from limiting the enjoyment of the *forum internum* of religious freedom. Accordingly, the State has a narrow margin of appreciation and must advance serious and compelling reasons for an interference with the choices that people may make in pursuance of the religious standard of behaviour within the sphere of their personal autonomy. An interference may be justified in light of art. 9, para. 2, if their choices are incompatible with the key principles underlying the ECHR (but, for more details see *infra*, "*The legal status of religious believer*").

The freedom of religion protected under art. 9 ECHR shall be interpreted to also include its negative dimension, such as the right not to have or to choose any religion (*Darby v. Sweden*, European Commission of Human Rights and then ECtHR, 23.10.1990; but more clearly *Kokkinakis v. Greece*, cit. *supra*; or *Buscarini et al. v. San Marino*, ECtHR [GC], 18.2.1999).

Another declination of this freedom is the recognition of an individual's right not to be obliged to manifest his or her beliefs because a contrasting interpretation could lead to discrimination (*Sinan Işık v. Turkey*, ECtHR, 2.2.2010, where the Court struck down a provision imposing indication of one's religion in ID Card). Similar considerations have been made with reference to the text of the oath in court (*Alexandridis v. Greece*, ECtHR, 21.2.2008; but see also *Buscarini*, cit. *supra*) or in relation to the right not to reveal his or her religious opinions and the controversial issue of ecclesiastical taxes (*Wasmuth v. Germany*, ECtHR, 17.2.2011).

Moreover, the ECtHR has held on many occasions that the imposition of administrative or criminal sanctions for the manifestation of religious beliefs or the exercise of the right to freedom of religion is an illegitimate interference on the rights guaranteed by art. 9, para. 1 ECHR (*Nolan v. Russia*, 12.2.2009, § 61; but also *Serif v. Greece* of 1999; *Larissis et al. v. Greece*, 24.2.1998; *Kokkinakis*, cit., *supra*). Consequently, these kind of provisions would be in conflict with ECHR and an expulsion of an individual based only on the hostility for his or her belonging to a certain religion would be illegitimate (*Nolan v. Russia*, cit., *supra*).

Even prior to the enactment of the CFREU, at the European level the freedom of religion, in its internal dimension, has been widely protected (see, *supra*).

Since the end of the sixties the fundamental importance of religious freedom has been recognised, and the CJEU considered that the legal provisions adopted at European level should conform to it. For example, the CJEU stated that the European institutions, in appointing public competitions, must avoid fixing dates that can discriminate against individuals belonging to certain religions if the person concerned provides notice of this fact within the time required (see: *Vivien Prais v. Council of the European Communities*, C-130/75, 27.10.1976).

Moreover, several decisions have been pronounced regarding a weekly day of rest. In particular, the CJEU overturned the rule providing Sunday as the weekly day of rest. According to the Court, this is a decision to be left to the appreciation of the Member States, in consideration of their cultural, ethnic, and religious diversity (see: *UK and Ireland v. Council*, C-84/94, 12.11.1996; but also *Torfaen Borough Council*, C-145/88, 23.11.1989).

3.2 The Controversial Definition of 'Religion' or 'Belief'. General Jurisprudential Paths

As introduced above, the definition of 'religion' or 'religious denominations' is particularly problematic. Until now, both the ECtHR and the CJEU have avoided providing a juridical definition of religion, favouring the freedom of all religious denominations, including those that do not enjoy the same social acceptance as the 'great religions' ('new' religions, such as Scientology, are also protected; see *Church of Scientology Moscow v. Russia*, ECtHR, 5.4.2007).

In several cases, the ECtHR has clearly pointed out that the State's legal provision cannot prescribe in narrow terms what constitutes a 'religion' or a 'belief'. These notions, indeed, are to be considered as guaranteeing every inner dimension; a religion or a belief is considered something essentially personal and subjective (see: *The Moscow Branch of the Salvation Army v. Russia*, 5.10.2006; *Metropolitan Church of Bessarabia et al. v. Moldova*, 13.12.2001; *Hasan and Chaush v. Bulgaria* [GC], 26.10.2000). Consequently, those concepts protect also 'atheists, agnostics, sceptics and the unconcerned', those who choose 'to hold or not to hold religious beliefs', and 'to practise or not to practise' any religion (*S.A.S. v. France* [GC], 1.7.2014, § 124; but see also *İzzettin Doğan et al. v. Turkey* [GC], 26.4.2016).

Recently, what actually constitutes a 'religion' or 'belief' qualifying for protection has been a matter of a decision concerning the manifestation of religion at work, as seen in the case *Eweida et al. v. UK*, ECtHR,15.1.2013 (on this case see also *infra "The legal status of religious believer"*).

3.3 Freedom of Religion and Protection Against Discrimination

It is interesting to compare the EU system and the ECHR's system with reference to the protection against discrimination on the basis of religion or belief.

In the majority of cases in which the ECtHR ascertains that a violation of the freedom of religion has occurred, the possible further considerations on the discriminatory nature of the contested measures are considered absorbed by the violation of art. 9 ECHR (*ex multis*: *Biserica Adevărat Ortodoxă din Moldova et al. v. Moldova*, 27.2.2007; *Jehovah's Witnesses of Moscow et al. v. Russia*, 10.6.2010; *Vojnity v. Hungary*, 12.2.2013).

With reference to ill treatment that private individuals can inflict against a religious person, the ECtHR attributes to the States the duty to take all reasonable steps to unmask any religious motives, and to establish whether religious hatred or prejudice could have played a role in the events at issue (*Milanović v. Serbia*, 14.12.2010).

However, it shall be noted that the ECtHR resolves most of the issues of discrimination based on religion using the argument of neutrality of law, according to which religious freedom does not confer the right to be exempted from a general or neutral discipline (for a partially divergent conclusion, see *Thlimmenos v. Greece* [GC], 6.4.2000).

In any case, the ECtHR respects the States' enactments if the rules they have approved are based on objective and reasonable justification. If not, the legal provision can be recognised as discriminatory on the ground of religion (see *O'Donoghue et al. v. UK*, 14.12.2010; *İzzettin Doğan et al. v. Turkey* [GC], 26.4.2016).

Analysis of ECtHR case law suggests that the Court tends to carry out a rigorous scrutiny of proportionality only in relation to so-called 'direct discrimination', leaving vague decision-making tools regarding so-called 'indirect discrimination' (see: *D.H. et al. v. Czech Republic*, 13.11.2007).

With reference to this last issue, in the EU landscape the screen represented by the neutrality of the law could be overcome by amplifying the hermeneutical potential of the concept of indirect discrimination and its related hermeneutical tools.

In 2017, several years after the adoption of Directive 2000/78 EC, the CJEU applied its first sentences on religious discrimination in *Samira Achbita and Centrum voor gelijkheid van kansen en voor racismebestrijding v. G4S Secure Solutions NV*, C-157/15, 14.3.2017 and *Asma Bougnaoui and Association de défense des droits de l'homme (ADDH) v. Micropole SA*, C-188/15, on the same day.

These decisions are controversial because there do not seem to be easily identifiable constitutional traditions common among the Member States that can support European judicial intervention. On the contrary, diversified positions appear to exist. In making its decisions, the Court of Justice appears to have accepted a model of secularism in line with only with some European countries and not with others (Drigo 2017, pp. 333 ff; Olivito 2017, pp. 1 ff).

4 Conclusions

The analysis carried out above highlights how, at the European level, there is a strong protection with reference to the *forum internum* of religious freedom.

Not only has the CJEU's and ECtHR's jurisprudence played a central role in favour of implementing anti-discrimination legislation, but also EU institutional actors have coordinated and monitored the implementation of fundamental rights of religious persons at the European level, in addition to implementing the exchange of good practices among Member States.

From the point of view of concrete enforcement, since 2010 the European Commission has adopted a specific strategy with the purpose of monitoring and ensuring the effective implementation of the rights and freedoms enshrined in the CFREU.

This strategy developed around three main objectives: (a) to guarantee that the rights and principles of the *Charter* are correctly taken into account at every step of the legislative process; (b) to improve EU citizens' understanding of fundamental rights protection within the EU; and (c) to monitor the progress of the *Charter*'s application through annual reports regarding religious freedom.

In particular, those annual reports monitor progress in areas where the EU has power to act, showing how the CFREU has been taken into account, especially when new EU legislation is proposed.

Additionally, the EU is cooperating with international organisations on freedom of religion or belief, in particular, strengthening its cooperation with the Office of the UN High Commissioner for Human Rights and the UN Special Rapporteur on freedom of religion or belief or with the Council of Europe. Moreover, possible new outcomes, in terms of implementation of the level of protection, could derive from the access of the EU to the ECHR.

Although these are important results, the path to reach totally effective protection of religious freedom, especially in consideration for the principle of equality and freedom, is far from being complete.

The challenges posed by the multicultural dimension of the European territory, with the different normative strategies brought about in different States, impose continuing reflection on the theme of religious freedom and its limits, also in order to prevent that only the judges have the burden of identifying the balancing point between potentially opposing rights and needs.

References

Bielefledt, H., Ghanea, N., & Wiener, M. (2016). *Freedom of religion or belief. An international law commentary*. Oxford, UK: Oxford University Press.

Celotto, A. (2010). Article 22, cultural, religious and linguistic diversity. In W. B. T. Mock & G. Demuro (Eds.), *Human rights in Europe, commentary of the charter of fundamental rights of the European Union* (pp. 134–140). Durham: Carolina Academic Press.

Drigo, C. (2017). Traiettorie di una convivenza difficile. Spunti di riflessione a partire dalla c.d. questione Burkini. *Percorsi costituzionali, 1*, 333–353.

Favilli, C. (2008). *La non discriminazione nell'Unione Europea*. Bologna: il Mulino.

Fawcett, J. E. S. (1987). *The application of the European Convention on Human Rights*. Oxford, UK: Oxford University Press.

Ferrari, S., & Pastorelli, S. (Eds.). (2012). *Religion in public spaces. A European perspective*. Farnham, UK: Ashgate.

Geiger, R., Khan, D. E., & Kotzur, M. (Eds.). (2015). *European Union treaties, a commentary*. Munich: Hart.

Grillo, R., Ballard, R., Ferrari, A., Hoekema, A. J., Maussen, M., & Shah, P. (Eds.). (2009). *Legal practice and cultural diversity*. Farnham, UK: Ashgate.

Groppi, T. (2010). Article 10. Freedom of thought, conscience and religion. In W. B. T. Mock & G. Demuro (Eds.), *Human rights in Europe. Commentary of the charter of fundamental rights of the European Union* (pp. 64–71). Durham: Carolina Academic Press.

Guazzaroti, A. (2012). Art. 9. Libertà di pensiero, coscienza e religione. In S. Bartole, P. De Sena, & V. Zagrebelsky (Eds.), *Commentario breve alla Convenzione europea per la salvaguardia dei diritti dell'uomo e delle libertà fondamentali* (pp. 370–397). Padova: Cedam.

Häberle, P. (2009). *Europäische verfassungslehre*. Germany: Nomos.

Loretan, A. (2016). La libertà religiosa ha il suo fondamento nella dignità umana. In E. Camassa (Ed.), *Democrazie e Religioni* (pp. 19–24). Napoli: Editoriale Scientifica.

Mock, W. B. T., & Demuro, G. (Eds.). (2010). *Human rights in Europe. Commentary of the charter of fundamental rights of the European Union*. Durham: Carolina Academic Press.

Olivito, E. (07.04.2017). La Corte di giustizia non si "svela": Discriminazioni indirette e neutralità religiosa nei luoghi di lavoro. Il cliente (non) ha sempre ragione!, *Diritticomparati.it*. Retrieved from www.diritticomparati.it

Requejo, F., & Ungureanu, C. (Eds.). (2014). *Democracy, law and religious pluralism in Europe*. New York: Routledge.

Shouppe, J. P. (2013). Libertà di religione, multiculturalismo e laicità dello Stato. In P. Gianniti (Ed.), *I diritti fondamentali nell'Unione europea. La Carta di Nizza dopo il Trattato di Lisbona, Commentario del codice civile e codici collegati Scialoja-Branca-Galgano* (pp. 855–906). Bologna: Zanichelli.

Taylor, P. M. (2005). *Freedom of religion: UN and European human rights law and practice*. Cambridge, UK: Cambridge University Press.

Research Volunteer

Yolanda Gómez Sánchez

1 Introduction

A growing number of investigations, studies and clinical trials, ever more diverse in their scope and nature, at both a national and an international level, have quantitatively and qualitatively increased the complexity of the relationships between the different agents (personal and/or institutional) involved in scientific studies. In clinical trials involving human participation these relationships acquire distinctive characteristics and the protection of the fundamental rights of those involved is a paramount concern.

This paper will provide an analysis of the legal position of those individuals who voluntarily participate in clinical trials. At the outset it must be stressed that there is an unavoidable need to have the participation of patients and healthy volunteers, given that there are no scientifically viable alternatives to such participation in the research field. Therefore, legislation must balance the legal rights of those involved and, in all cases, protect and uphold the fundamental rights of volunteers who freely participate in such scientific investigations. This paper will refer exclusively to the regulation of participation in clinical trials, although much of what is outlined in what follows is equally applicable to biomedical research in general.

2 The Concept of the Research Volunteer

We can define a clinical trial volunteer as any human individual, healthy or sick, old or young, of either sex and any condition, who voluntarily (through their own agency or through a representative) agrees to participate in a clinical trial that

Y. Gómez Sánchez (✉)
Faculty of Law, Universidad Nacional de Educación a Distancia (UNED), Madrid, Spain
e-mail: ygomez@der.uned.es

A. Bartolini et al. (eds.), *Dictionary of Statuses within EU Law*,
https://doi.org/10.1007/978-3-030-00554-2_63

involves the performance of invasive acts upon their person of some level of intensity (Gómez Sánchez 2013).

The collaboration of patients and healthy volunteers alike in clinical trials contributes to the advancement of biomedical science and the protection of the health of the entire population, although it also presents legal conflicts that must be addressed by appropriate legislation so that both the fundamental rights of the participants (Gómez Sánchez 2011a) and the free exercise of the fundamental right to undertake scientific research are upheld and protected Gómez Sánchez (2009).

Article 13 of the *Charter of Fundamental Rights of the European Union* (hereinafter referred to as the Charter) states that: 'The arts and scientific research shall be free of constraint', thereby affirming that, in Europe, scientific research is a true fundamental right. Article 15 of the *Convention on Biomedicine and Human Rights* also recognizes the freedom of scientific research within the framework of respect for human rights. Thus, scientific research is a fundamental freedom that contributes to progress in society but, like any fundamental right, its content and scope must be weighed against other fundamental rights as recognized both in European Union law and the domestic legislation of the Member States.

Volunteers who participate in clinical trials have fundamental rights, and should not be treated as mere sources of biological material or passive recipients of scientific investigation (Flear 2016). This requirement has been enshrined in the legislation of the European Union, specifically in Article 3(2) of the Charter, which recognizes the right to integrity with respect to biomedical applications and upholds the free and informed consent of all participants; it specifically outlaws eugenic practices and trade for profit in human bodies or parts, as well as imposing a prohibition on the reproductive cloning of human beings. In addition, Article 35 of the Charter expressly recognizes the right to health protection, stating that: 'Everyone has the right of access to preventive health care and the right to benefit from medical treatment under the conditions established by national laws and practices. A high level of human health protection shall be ensured in the definition and implementation of all Union policies and activities.'

Although each Member State lays down its own health policies, there are common values throughout the entire European Union, including the universal right to a high-level public health service and equitable access to quality health care, rights that clinical trials help to achieve (Gómez Sánchez 2011b).

Together with the Charter, Regulation (EU) No 536/2014 of the European Parliament and of the Council of 16 April 2014 on clinical trials of medicinal products for human use, repealing Directive 2001/20/EC (hereinafter, the Regulation), in Recital (1), establishes that: 'In a clinical trial the rights, safety, dignity and well-being of subjects should be protected, and the data generated should be reliable and robust'. Recital (1) continues by affirming that: 'The interests of the subjects should always take priority over all other interests'.

In line with the above, Article 3 of Regulation states that 'A clinical trial may be conducted only if: (a) the rights, safety, dignity and well-being of subjects are protected and prevail over all other interests; and (b) it is designed to generate reliable and robust data'.

The Regulation also confirms that fundamental rights and the principles recognized in the Charter must be respected. These are: human dignity, and the integrity of the person (Article 3); the rights of the minor (Article 24); respect for private and family life (Article 7); the protection of personal data (Article 8); and the freedom of the arts and sciences (Article 13). Member States must apply the Regulation in conformity with those rights and principles. In line with these affirmations, the Regulation follows the precedents set down by the Council of Europe, especially in the *Biomedicine and Human Rights Convention* of 4 April 1997 (Preamble, Articles 1 and 2) and in the *Additional Protocol to this Convention on transplantation of organs and tissues of human origin* passed in Strasbourg on 24 January 2002 (Article 1).

3 Classes of Research Volunteers

Clinical trials can involve all types of person: adults and minors, individuals with full capacity, and individuals with limited or insufficient capacity to grant a valid expression of intention. In each case, these participants can be healthy patients or volunteers. Each of these groups and, if applicable, each individual subject must be treated according to their circumstances in such a way that their human dignity and fundamental rights are effectively protected in all cases and that there is full compliance with the guarantees inherent in good scientific practice.

Regulation (EU) 536/2014 (Chapter V), which refers to the protection of subjects and informed consent, lists eight conditions that must be met in order for a clinical trial involving human beings to be approved (Article 28). These conditions are as follows:

(a) the anticipated benefits to the subjects or to public health justify the foreseeable risks and inconveniences, and compliance with this condition is constantly monitored;
(b) the subjects, or, where a subject is not able to give informed consent, his or her legally designated representative, have been informed in the way required by Article 29. Participants should receive clear and precise information as to whether or not the clinical trial can potentially generate therapeutic benefits for the participants themselves. This avoids the *therapeutic misconception* that misleads a participant into failing to differentiate correctly between clinical practice and research, in a way that tends to give rise to the idea, for example, that mere participation in a clinical trial will bring about a direct therapeutic benefit—which is not always the case—and consequently may give rise to an erroneous assessment of the risks of participation in the said clinical process and thereby frustrate their expectations concerning it;
(c) the subjects, or, where a subject is not able to give informed consent, his or her legally designated representative, have given their informed consent in the way required by Article 29(1), (7) and (8); any subject, or, where the subject is not

able to give informed consent, his or her legally designated representative, may, without any resulting detriment and without having to provide any justification, withdraw from the clinical trial at any time by revoking his or her informed consent. Without prejudice to Directive 95/46/EC, the withdrawal of the informed consent shall not affect the activities already carried out and the use of data obtained based on informed consent before such consent was withdrawn.

(d) the rights of the subjects to physical and mental integrity, to privacy and to the protection of the data concerning them in accordance with Directive 95/46/EC are safeguarded; in this regard, Article 28(2) of the Regulation allows specific consent to be requested from the volunteer, or his/her representative if he/she is a minor or lacks capacity, for the use of his/her personal data exclusively for scientific purposes outside the protocol of the clinical trial (Gómez Sánchez 2006);

(e) the clinical trial has been designed to involve as little pain, discomfort, fear and any other foreseeable risk as possible for the subjects, and both the risk threshold and the degree of distress are specifically defined in the protocol and are constantly monitored; the more or less invasive nature of the procedure, the risks and implications for the health and well-being of the participant, and any repercussions for the normal conduct of the subject's life (frequency and duration of their participation and recovery time after their participation) should be taken into consideration (Article 6).

(f) the medical care provided to the subjects is the responsibility of an appropriately qualified medical doctor or, where appropriate, a qualified dental practitioner;

(g) the subject, or, where the subject is not able to give informed consent, his or her legally designated representative, has been provided with the contact details of an entity that will provide further information in case of need; and

(h) no undue influence, including that of a financial nature, is exerted on subjects to participate in the clinical trial.

Regulation 536/2014 imposes additional conditions when participants belong to especially vulnerable groups, and also allows Member States to adopt even stricter requirements in such cases. The Regulation considers vulnerable groups to include the disabled, minors, pregnant or breastfeeding women, and other specific groups to which the Regulation refers in general (Gennet et al. 2015).

3.1 *Persons Incapable of Giving Consent*

In relation to subjects who lack the capacity to give consent, Article 10(2) of the Regulation establishes that specific attention will be given to the evaluation of the request for authorization of a clinical trial, on the basis of the experience of the disease in question and the patient population concerned, or after taking advice on clinical, ethical and psycho-social questions in the field of the relevant disease and the patient population concerned.

Article 31 establishes certain conditions, additional to those set forth in the general case in Article 28, that must be satisfied to carry out a clinical trial in the case of subjects who lack capacity and who have not given, or have not refused to give, informed consent prior to the onset of their lack of capacity. In addition, Member States can establish other more protective measures by improving the European protection standard.

3.2 *Minors*

The legislation of the European Union and that of the Member States does not impose a total exclusion of minors from participation in clinical trials, and it insists that they should participate especially if there is a direct benefit for them. However, many clinical trials will not improve the health of the children who participate but the health of other children in the future, and it is therefore reasonable that, with adequate protective measures, minors should be allowed to participate in clinical trials. This is regulated under Article 32 of the Regulation in accordance with the provisions of Articles 6, 16 and 17 of the *Convention on Human Rights and Biomedicine*. These additional protective measures are as follows:

(a) the informed consent of the minor's legally designated representative has been obtained and the minor has received information about his/her participation, in a manner that is adapted to their age and mental maturity, from researchers or members of the research team with training or experience in dealing with minors. Both European legislation and that of the Member States provides that minors who can form an opinion and evaluate the information given to them must give their consent alongside the consent of their designated legal representative (Recital 32 and Article 29(8)). In any case, the minor's consent can only be obtained with the consent of their legal representative. Given that consent by the representative supplements the lack of full capacity of the minor, if, during the clinical trial, the minor reaches the legal age to give informed consent as defined in the law of the Member State concerned, his or her express informed consent must be obtained before he or she can continue to participate in the said clinical trial (Article 32(3) of the Regulation);

(b) the explicit wish of a minor to refuse to participate in, or to withdraw from, the clinical trial at any time, is respected by the investigator;

(c) no incentives or financial inducements are given to the subject or to his or her legally designated representative, except for compensation for expenses and loss of earnings directly related to participation in the clinical trial;

The researcher must therefore adopt all measures necessary to avoid any situation that could give rise to undue influence in the process of selection and acceptance of the participants in the research;

(d) the purpose of the clinical trial is to investigate treatment for a health issue that only occurs in minors and the data so obtained is useful for them, or the trial can only be carried out on minors; and

(e) there are scientific reasons to expect the clinical trial to produce a direct benefit for the minor concerned or some benefit for the population represented by that minor, provided that the risks and benefits of the trial are adequately assessed. The research must not involve disproportionate risks or discomforts in relation to the proposed scientific objectives.

Article 10(1) of the Regulation establishes—as does Article 10(2) for persons who lack capacity—that where the subjects are minors, specific consideration must be given to the assessment of the application for authorization of the clinical trial on the basis of paediatric expertise or after taking advice on clinical, ethical and psycho-social problems in the field of paediatrics.

3.3 Pregnant or Breastfeeding Women

Like persons lacking the capacity to consent and minors, pregnant or lactating women can only participate in clinical trials if specific protective measures are adopted, especially if the trial does not generate potential benefits for them or for their future children (Recital 34). In accordance with this, Article 10(3) of the Regulation determines, in a similar fashion to the case of minors and persons lacking the capacity to give consent, that, in these cases, specific consideration must be given to the assessment of the application for authorization of the clinical trial and with expert advice as to the relevant condition and the population represented by the subject concerned.

Article 33 of the Regulation establishes that, if there is no potential benefit for the woman or her future child, the possibility of carrying out the trial on non-pregnant women or women who are not breastfeeding should be assessed, and it should be established whether the clinical trial poses a minimal risk to, and imposes a minimal burden on, the pregnant or breastfeeding woman concerned, and her embryo, foetus or child after birth. In any case, any negative impact on the health of the child should be avoided and the woman should not receive any incentive or economic reward.

3.4 Other Vulnerable Groups

Other groups that may require specific protection are also highlighted. These include persons performing compulsory military service, persons deprived of their liberty, persons who, as the result of a judicial decision, cannot participate in studies or clinical trials, and individuals who, because of their age, disability or state of health, are dependent on others. In all these cases, the Regulation allows Member States to adopt additional protective measures (Recital 35), and, as set forth in Article 34, expressly allows the Member States to have in force supplementary provisions in relation to persons who are performing compulsory military service, persons deprived of their liberty, persons who, following a judicial decision, cannot participate in clinical trials, or persons residing in health care institutions. In addition, Article 10(4) establishes that, in these cases, special attention must be given to the evaluation of the request for authorization of the clinical trial, on the basis of specialized knowledge of the group represented by the test subjects in question, and specific consideration must be given to the assessment of the application for authorization of the clinical trial using expert advice as to the population represented by the subjects concerned.

4 Conclusions

As stated at the beginning of this article, the participation of patients and healthy volunteers in clinical trials is currently a necessity as part of the scientific process by which medicines are validated. However, this need cannot permit the dignity and rights of those participating in these scientific studies to go unprotected. The law must adequately respond to these challenges and assess the rights at stake and benefits involved by applying the principle that the interests of the human individual take priority over the interests of science and society. In this context, only appropriate statutory regulation that upholds and protects the rights of individuals and their participation in clinical trials can be acceptable.

Contemporary European Union legislation covering scientific research in particular is still wanting, although Regulation 536/2014, which is referred to throughout this article, represents an important advance in the standardization of the specific regulations governing clinical trials. The principles and rights contained in this Regulation lay down a minimum standard for the protection of participants, and incorporate additional measures in relation to vulnerable groups such as persons who lack the capacity to consent, minors, prospective or lactating mothers, and other vulnerable groups in the population.

This welcome Regulation, in addition, allows Member States to enact domestic legislation with more restrictive measures and/or to establish additional requirements, thereby allowing the Member States themselves to improve the standard of protection established under the Regulation.

References

Flear, M. L. (2016). The EU clinical trials regulation: Key priorities, purposes and aims and the implications for public health. *Journal of Medical Ethics, 42*(3), 192–198.

Gennet, E., Andorno, R., & Elger, B. (2015). Does the new EU regulation on clinical trials adequately protect vulnerable research participants? *Health Policy, 119*, 925–931.

Gómez Sánchez, Y. (2006). La protección de datos genéticos: nuevos derechos para nuevas biotecnologías. *Revista Española de Protección de Datos, 1*, 61–91.

Gómez Sánchez, Y. (2009). La libertad de creación y producción científica: especial referencia a la ley de investigación biomédica. *Revista de Derecho Político, 75–76*, 489–516.
Gómez Sánchez, Y. (2011a). Dignidad y autodeterminación física como fundamento del estatuto del paciente. *Acta Bioethica, 17*(1), 37–46.
Gómez Sánchez, Y. (2011b). El derecho a la salud: un nuevo derecho de libertad. In S. Delgado Bueno & F. Bandrés Moya (Eds.), *Tratado de medicina legal y Ciencias Forenses. Derecho Sanitario y Medicina Legal del Trabajo*. Barcelona: Bosch.
Gómez Sánchez, Y. (2013). Reflexiones sobre la participación de voluntarios en la investigación. In *Desafíos para los derechos de la persona ante el siglo XXI/Sfide per i Diritti della persona dinanzi al XXI secolo: Vita e Scienza/Challenges of individual rights in the XXI Century: Life and Science* (pp. 259–274). Navarra: Thomson Reuters/Aranzadi.

Researcher

Carlos Francisco Molina del Pozo and Roxana Balaur

1 Introduction

We can affirm that, since its creation, the European Union has always been at the forefront of innovation. The first treaties (the Treaty of Paris, by which the ECSC was established, and the Treaty of Rome, which created the EURATOM) included a strategy associated with research within their respective community policies. Currently, Article 179 of the Treaty on the Functioning of the European Union (TFEU) establishes two main objectives to be achieved within the framework of research policy; on the one hand, the strengthening of technological development and, on the other hand, the promotion of international competitiveness for European projects. Implementing and achieving the outlined objectives is carried out by effecting programmes and action plans that bring about more specific objectives and goals. Accordingly, in 2000 the European Research Area (ERA) was created, which can be defined as a knowledge space where both national and European research integrates based on the circulation, exchange and financing of research projects.

It is clear that innovation and research policies, alongside common field objectives, is the key to technological developments that enable these policies to dynamically respond to society's challenges, impacting the world as a whole. However, research is not an impersonal science, and it is not a mere concept to be developed; its practical uses are expressed through the work carried out by researchers (Molina Del Pozo 2017).

C. F. Molina del Pozo (✉) · R. Balaur
Department of Law, Universidad de Alcalá de Henares, Alcalá de Henares, Spain
e-mail: carlosf.molina@uah.es

A. Bartolini et al. (eds.), *Dictionary of Statuses within EU Law*,
https://doi.org/10.1007/978-3-030-00554-2_64

2 The Role of the Researcher

The definition of a researcher can be found in the Council Resolution of November 10, 2003: "[…] professionals who work in the conception or creation of knowledge, products, processes, methods and systems of a novel nature and in the management of corresponding projects". In this sense, the importance of developing new technologies and conducting scientific research seems to be clear; however, their participation within society is much more extensive.

First of all, we have to identify researchers within society; subjects can be both public and private. In addition, they can be individual people or foundations, associations or entities. It is important to note that all subjects, regardless of the research project or its level (national or European), must respect the provisions set forth in the European Charter for Researchers and in the Code of Conduct.

When referring to researchers, we begin from the incontrovertible idea that they are highly qualified professionals. In the formation of research projects, researchers draw upon their extensive knowledge base and attempt to develop a new idea. Recognising that researching is a type of "work", we can also see that researchers are effectively employees during the course of their project. It is important to note that research has its own "labour market" and, as in any other sector, it is possible to assess its impact on society, not only from the point of view of the contributions of successful research projects, but also during the project itself.

Within the European Union, the Commission is responsible for promoting job opportunities in the research market; it manages projects, giving researchers a portal to contact likeminded professionals in the hope of collaborating for a project. The Commission offers financial support through the Horizon 2020 Program, as well as granting scholarships; its most paradigmatic examples are Sklodowska-Curie Actions. Since 2005, the Commission has held the "European Night of the Researchers", involving more than 340 European cities. The meeting aims to bring the work of researchers closer to citizens in order to make them aware of the importance of research in society.

3 Types or Researchers

The needs of society are unquestionably varied and are continuously evolving. Researchers, therefore, must have a clear idea of what they intend to achieve in their project and, depending on the scope of their research and objective, will have to observe a series of strict formalities.

Likewise, it is also important to consider the differences between scientific and technological research. Science makes reference to the creation of new knowledge and aims to "responder y entender la naturaleza y la sociedad"("respond and understand nature and society") (Tamayo 2007). Technology, on the other hand, studies processes in order to provide solutions for the different and varied problems that arise in society as a whole. Therefore, we can conclude that a scientific researcher will outline a hypothesis responding to "what" to do, while a technological will focus on "how" to do it. The method used by researchers during their project will depend on the type of research they are undertaking, which may be as varied as the objectives that they intend to achieve. In light of previous considerations, it is necessary to highlight that scientific investigations will essentially focus on data collection, observing social phenomena and its variations or will develop theories based on existing principles. To contrast, technological research will focus on the application of theories. The two types of research represent the pillars of innovation; thanks to their existence, society has drastically evolved over the past two centuries.

In particular, human experimentation is an essential and enormously vast field as research. Indeed, these investigations usually investigate biomedical solutions, disease treatments and cures and introduce new developments in the pharmaceutical industry. In our opinion, the requirements that these professionals must observe seem to be particularly strict, so much so that they must base their research on three inescapable ethical principles: autonomy, beneficence and justice. With regard to autonomy, it refers to the ability of human beings to deliberate and make themselves autonomously and voluntarily available for research. The principle of beneficence—or of non-maleficence—is the maximisation of benefits and the minimisation of damage and requires that the benefits achieved overcome the risks. As for justice, although it is a broad term, it must be understood in this context as the obligation to treat each person according to what is considered to be morally correct.

All previous considerations lead us to the conclusion that the researcher has an absolute freedom to move and to manage and orient their study in any direction; however, it should be specified that, although it is true that the researcher must prioritise their attention on the identification and analysis of the research objectives, they must not lose sight of the system of ethical and legal standards that have been set forth and govern the behavioural standards of society.

4 The Mobility of Researchers

It is widely acknowledged that a large number of researchers tend to move in order to develop their activities and studies; this mobility in researchers promotes the exchange of knowledge and experiences in researchers across the globe.

Additionally, it is evident that within the European Union researcher cooperation, whether public or private, is fostered. Special attention is devoted to complying with EU principles and, in particular, to equal opportunities and non-discrimination. Therefore, it seems logical that researchers take advantage of the opportunities arising in this field, either in training or employment in a member state, and benefit from whatever financial support they are able to obtain within the European Union, whether that be economic aid or scholarships.

As mentioned above, the Marie Curie actions are one of the best and most complete opportunities for researchers in the specific field. The scholarships included within this action "are addressed to researchers of all the levels of experience, independently of their nationality and covering all fields of scientific and technological investigation".

The European Union recognises research is of vital importance to society and ensures researchers are able to move both within and outside its territory. These displacements are expected greatly advantage both the European Union itself and for all its member states.

In relation to researchers, mobility allows them to acquire experience in a different environment, with the opportunity to freely access systems or technologies that are not yet sufficiently developed in their respective home countries, contributing to the researcher's personal growth.

The main advantage of mobility opportunity for researchers in the European Union is the promotion and enhancement of the existence of the ERA. From the member states' point of view, the aforementioned displacements reduce the existing problem of the so-called "brain drain", and assist in achieving the territorial distribution of experienced researchers, and avoiding a concentration of researchers in a single country. This phenomenon may be caused by a country taking advantage of the research. To contrast, it would be possible to increase the population of these professionals in less advantaged countries with fewer resources. Among the entities devoting their activities to research or promoting the turnout of researchers, universities are among the main institutions supporting the mobility of researchers, both through their teaching staff and by encouraging and fostering, through numerous actions and programmes, the mobility of students who may later become professional researchers in other centres.

5 Researchers from Third Countries

In the previous section, we referred to the mobility of European researchers within the ERA; in this section, we provide an overview of researchers from third (non-European) countries who move to a member states to work on a research project.

The European Union undoubtedly receives research personnel from third countries and it intends, increasingly, to establish itself as an attractive space for research and innovation in order to improve its overall competitiveness and to achieve one of the ERA's key objectives: the creation of an open labour market "for researchers from the Union and from third countries".

In order to facilitate this exchange, the European Union has—through directives such as Directive (EU) 2016/801[5]—the entry and residence conditions of third country nationals for research purposes.

The measures adopted in the aforementioned directive allow researchers and, where appropriate, of members of their family, to reside in the European Union for periods of more than 90 days, reducing the procedures for the exercise of their profession. For example, if a researcher moves to a member states and is received by a research entity, they will not need to apply for a work permit as long as they have a hosting agreement. These measures also allows a researcher residing in a member state to enter and remain in other member states if they are required to for research purposes; these are called "seconds".

One of the most important actions that the EU undertakes is carrying out and financing international exchanges of research personnel. This is called *Research and Innovation Personnel Exchange*, and it allows contacts between academic bodies, such as universities and research centres, as well as non-academic organisations, such as companies, around the world. These are short-term exchange projects, funded for between 1 month and 4 years, which require the participation of at least three partners belonging to three different countries (under the condition that two of them, at least, are citizens of the European Union). The selection procedure uses open and transparent calls so that all associations that fulfil the registration requirements are able to submit their application.

6 The Responsibility of Researchers Towards Society

The importance of research and, therefore, of researchers is crucial for society as a whole but in the performance of their activity these professionals must comply with a series of obligations. These obligations and responsibilities, which are set forth in the European Charter for Researchers, are varied. This paper prioritises two outstanding duties of researchers towards society: the rendering of accounts and the dissemination of results.

Although a researcher can be employed to perform a job, their duties are not only towards their employer; the researcher works for society as a whole, acting as an intermediary between reality and citizens and carrying out authentic social commitments. The researcher must, therefore, work diligently, using reliable sources and respecting the moral and ethical principles of society.

In the dissemination of results, also known as scientific dissemination, the scope of responsibility is easier. If knowledge does not involve scientific dissemination, it would not be able to solve societal problems; consequently, it is absolutely necessary that research results are publicly available, either for free or through commercial channels. This contributes to the knowledge of citizens and enables other researchers to use existing research to further their own. The results of research are, therefore, extremely valuable to society.

Today, more people are showing an interest in a career in research, it is true that the dissemination of results from studies carried out both in the European Union and internationally encourages many young people to pursue a promising alternative to the usual job opportunities existing in our society.

Reference

Molina Del Pozo, C. F. (2017). *La responsabilidad del investigador en la Unión Europea, Rights and Science, Juri-dileyc*. Retrieved December 7, 2017, from https://global.juri-dileyc.com/la-responsabilidad-del-investigador-en-la-union-europea/

Sex Worker

Cristina Benlloch Domènech and Juan Alberto Tormos Pérez

1 Introduction

This paper analyses the category known as sex workers and investigate how they are conditioned by European Union (EU) law. First, a sociological analysis of sex workers is undertaken in order to understand the difficulty of regulating this phenomenon. Once the general sociological framework is established, we analyse the legal concept of sex workers and how EU law conditions them; as discussed, this largely depends on the different regulatory models in existence in individual member states. Following this, we consider how EU law can effect a change in the definition of sex workers.

2 Sociological Aspects of the Definition of a Sex Worker

It is not possible to approach the concept of a sex worker without referring to the accompanying sociological approach. This concept, like other regulated concepts, is not exempt from social controversy, and the position assumed by the legislator is not exempt from this. Prostitution, from the point of view of sociology, is the exchange of sexual favours in return for monetary retribution (Giddens 2010).

From a cultural point of view, studies warn that, in one way or another, this concept has existed in social contexts throughout history. While it is true that there are both male and female prostitutes, most sex workers are women, so much so that the

C. Benlloch Domènech (✉)
Sociology and Social Work Department, Faculty of Social Sciences, Law and Communication, Valladolid University, Segovia, Spain

J. A. Tormos Pérez
Work Law Department, Faculty of Law, University of Valencia, Valencia, Spain

A. Bartolini et al. (eds.), *Dictionary of Statuses within EU Law*,
https://doi.org/10.1007/978-3-030-00554-2_65

number of male sex workers is only a few, and that many male prostitutes focus on a male clientele (Giddens 2010). However, around this "aseptic" definition, there are different social positions taken on prostitution; these positions are confronted by social collectives and the feminist movement.

Those who consider it to be just consider it to a simple profession tend to focus on the legalisation of the phenomenon and implementing greater safety measures for the group of men and women who practice this trade. Some groups go as far as to affirm that practicing prostitution is a form of empowerment; others are of the opinion that its prohibition is not a solution because an activity that is so ingrained in society cannot be eradicated. It was estimated that in 2014 in Spain, 39% of men had paid for sex, while in the Netherlands this figure was 20% (Source Institute National of Statistics).

On the other hand, those who consider female prostitutes to be victims, in any case, speak of women being prostituted and oppose any type of legalisation. In addition, they affirm that in the contexts in which the exercise of prostitution is allowed, there is no decrease in the number of trafficking or delinquency crimes that seem to go hand in hand with prostitution (Daich 2012).

Nevertheless, as Bernstein (2005) reflected, there are always cultural and institutional forces behind the regulation of normalized (touristic and business) and problematised (street sex) commercial sex.

These views are likely to remain after legal decisions on prostitution and sex work. This is one of the reasons why it seems difficult for the EU to reach a consensus on legislation beyond what can be done to prosecute trafficking, given the opposing views, especially because the models applied to the legislation on sex work never seem to solve the problems it intended to solve. Moreover, Agustín (2008) questioned the law's relevance to the commercial sex market; however, legal power is able to support the hegemonic power dynamic. There exists a gap between formal theoretical law and its practical implementation, and so the law does matter in the end (Scoular 2010, pp. 13–14; p. 22).

3 Legal Aspects of the Definition of Sex Worker in the EU

After reviewing numerous datasets investigating sex work from a sociological point of view, it is necessary to analyse the main elements that shape a sex worker on a legal level; that is, how this category is regulated in the EU.

From a legal standpoint, the regulation of prostitution—"the direct exchange of sexual services for money or other utilities" derived from legislation and case law (Danna 2013, p. 6)—where we frame the category of sex worker is a matter that does not belong to the EU competences; it is limited by EU treaties (Sarrión Esteve 2017, p. 47).

Although there is a preoccupation within the EU with prostitution, particularly street prostitution, antithetical regulations are implemented in each member state (Hubbard 2008) in the absence of a single model.

In this sense, the legal regulation of the concept of sex workers has great disparities in the different member states of the EU, depending on the legal approach that each country has chosen to apply in order to regulate this issue.

The varied regulatory approaches existing in the different countries of the EU can be grouped into three models according to their permissiveness with the practice of prostitution and their recognition of sex workers. These models are the abolitionist model, the legalising model and the regulationist model. Of course, neat classifications are usually problematic due to gaps between political and social aims, followed by the legislation and the final model implemented (Phoenix 2009; Scoular 2010). Moreover, there are always paradoxical and relevant empirical similarities in the different regulatory approaches to sexual work (Scoular 2010).

3.1 The Abolitionist Model

The abolitionist model is the most restrictive, as it does not recognise the provision of sexual services by sex workers as a lawful practice and therefore does not consider there to be sex workers as such. This model seeks to prosecute the providers of sexual services, and is characterised by prosecuting and punishing the recipients or buyers of these services, of whom the model considers an essential element for such illicit activity to occur. With this, the intention is to completely abolish prostitution, considering it a practice intrinsically linked to criminality and sexual exploitation, mainly of women.

This is the prevailing model in the majority of Nordic countries, with the most important exponent being the long-standing regulations in Sweden. In 1998, Sweden was a pioneering country in prohibiting prostitution with the Act, which prohibited the purchase of sexual services and came into force on 1 January 1999. The initiative came from the Swedish Feminist movement, who concluded that prostitution was a "patriarchal tool of oppression" (Ekberg 2004, p. 1191); the act was therefore an instrument to achieve gender equality (Scoular 2010, p. 17). This legislation criminalises all forms of prostitution, considering it to be a form of violence against women that is incompatible with the principle of equality between males and females; this is why it focuses on sanctions for those purchasing sexual services, who can face penalties of up to 1 year in prison. On the other hand, in 2016, and after a parliamentary debate that spanned years, France also approved a law criminalising the clients of prostitutes, implementing fines for persons requesting such services, in line with the abolitionist model established in Sweden, which considers prostitutes to be victims. In the abolitionist model, therefore, the client is punished, but not the prostitute, who is considered a victim, and not a sex worker.

3.2 The Legalising Model

Taking a totally contrary approach, other countries have adopted the legalising model (also called the regulatory model), which consists of expressly regulating the practice of prostitution as a free activity, implying that prostitutes should be considered to be sex workers who freely carry out an economic activity within their sexual freedoms, and with important consequences regarding the recognition of a series of rights and guarantees for them: inclusion in social security protection mechanisms like any other employee, and access to health protection measures. The idea that underlies this legalising model is the possibility of improving control over cases of sexual exploitation and being able to fight against organised crime while guaranteeing social rights and health protection measures for those sex workers who provide prostitution services freely and voluntarily.

The paradigmatic and pioneer country in this case is the Netherlands, who in the year 2000 legalised prostitution, allowing the provision of sexual services by sex workers in different spaces; however, this is under strict conditions and regulations and is controlled by the municipal authorities. The legalisation replaced the regulated tolerance of the previous legal system (Scoular 2010, p. 20).

The free exercise of prostitution allows prostitutes to become sex workers, who are usually self-employed, enabling them to be subject to all tax and social security regulations. Sex workers are also subject to various provisions regarding health protection; this system aims to more effectively combat sexual exploitation and human trafficking networks. The regulation prohibits minors from engaging in this activity and requires health authorities to conduct health checks on sex workers, especially in the prevention of sexually transmitted diseases.

3.3 The Regulationist Model

The third model, which can be seen as an intermediate approach, is the regulationist model (also called the prohibitionist model), where the practice of prostitution is legally prohibited, but there are various legal gaps and even situations of tolerance in the exercise of prostitution under certain conditions. An example of such a model would be Spain, where the Penal Code prohibits prostitution and sexual exploitation, with prostitution understood as being that which is forced. Besides this, there is a legal void regarding the practice of voluntary prostitution, and when conducting the practice in a public space, multiple municipal ordinances that regulate and restrict this practice are to be observed. However, the practice of prostitution is widely tolerated in Spain, which generates situations of a lack of protection for sex workers who are not recognised as such. Despite this, some verdicts have ruled in recognition of the employment relationship between sex workers and their employer or, in other cases, their status as self-employed workers, with consequences such as the recognition of labour rights and their inclusion in the social security system (González del Río 2013; Panizo 2015).

3.4 Sex Work from an EU Law Perspective

Within this disparity of models, the EU has not yet regulated prostitution due to a lack of competencies in the matter, as stated previously, due to the principle of conferral (Sarrión Esteve 2017, p. 47). Nevertheless, it is true that the scope of EU law is not exclusively confined to EU competencies; member states, in their exercise of national powers, should respect EU law when there is an overlap of laws (Sarrión Esteve 2013, 2015).

In fact, there have been remarkable pronouncements by EU institutions. On the one hand, and from the point of view of jurisprudence, we have to mention the European Court of Justice (ECJ) which, in a judgement on the 20 November 2001 (Aldona Malgorzata Jany and others, C-268/99, ECLI:EU:C:2001:616), recognised prostitution as an economic activity carried out independently or on a freelance basis, thus leaving the door open to the formal recognition of this activity, without prejudicing the existing regulations across other member states within their competency framework. Therefore, under this perspective EU law doctrine conceives prostitution as a commercial activity (Martí 2014) in which, if it is carried out in a free and independent manner, a service is provided in return for remuneration.

All this is of special relevance and interest for EU regulation because if sex work is considered to be a business activity, that is, an activity of an economic nature, then the people who perform these activities will be beneficiaries of the economic freedoms recognised by EU law; if sex work is a service like any other, the providers of such a service will benefit from the freedom to provide services among the member states that is recognised by EU law.

In fact, the ECJ recently had the opportunity to solve a case related to the authorisation of a window prostitution business in the Netherlands regarding the free services Directive (2006/123). In this case, the ECJ controlled the negative municipal decision regarding the authorisation of a window prostitution business—by renting out rooms in shifts—in the Netherlands because the municipality specified that the service provider needed to be able to communicate with the service recipient, in this case the sexual workers, having shared language. The ECJ considered it to be a condition which did not go beyond what is necessary to achieve a legitimate objective (ECJ Judgement of 1 October 2015, Harsem, joined cases C-340 and 341-14, ECLI:EU:C:2015:641, 77).

In 2004, on the other hand, the European Parliament passed a resolution on sexual exploitation and prostitution and its impact on gender equality, and although this was not legally binding, it adopted an approach contrary to the ECJ ruling of 2001. In this, a less permissive approach was adopted, linking all forms of prostitution to sexual exploitation and with a clear gender impact, which urged member states to evaluate their preventative policies to include the possibility of punishing service recipients.

Therefore, this resolution, although it does not have any binding legal status, leaves the door open for member states to adopt restrictive regulations regarding sex work; however, this remains in the hands of member states.

4 Conclusions

EU law does not clearly regulate the sex work trade, as it is a matter outside its competencies. However, the EU has adopted decisions that, in some ways, condition the conception of this category in a manner that respects the plurality of regulatory frameworks currently existing across member states. In this sense, the jurisprudence of the ECJ has determined sex work is a commercial activity susceptible to being exercised freely and voluntarily, deriving from this the possibility that sex workers can benefit from the economic freedoms that the treaties reflect. However, the aforementioned resolution of the European Parliament recalls the strong gender impact of this type of work and its close connection with the networks of sexual exploitation and human trafficking, and therefore recommends that member states adopt measures that take into account the protection of women's rights.

References

Agustín, L. (2008). Sex and the limits of enlightenment: The irrationality of legal regimes to control prostitution. *Sexuality Research & Social Policy, 5*(4), 73–86.

Danna, D. (2013). *Report on prostitution laws in the European Union*. Retrieved January 27, 2018, from http://lastradainternational.org/lsidocs/3048-EU-prostitution-laws.pdf

Daich, D. (2012). ¿Abolicionismo o reglamentarismo?: Aportes de la antropología feminista para el debate local sobre la prostitución. *Runa, 33*(1), 71–84.

Ekberg, G. (2004). The Swedish law that prohibits the purchase of sexual services. *Violence Against Women, 10*(10), 1187–1218.

Giddens, A. (2010). *Sociología*. Madrid: Alianza.

González del Río, J. M. (2013). *El ejercicio de la prostitución y el derecho del trabajo*. Granada: Comares.

Hubbard, P. (2008). Regulating sex work in the EU: Prostitute women and the new spaces of exclusion. *A Journal of Feminist Geography, 15*(2).

Martí, A. (2014). El trabajo sexual en Europa. *El Jurista*. Retrieved January 27, 2018, from http://www.eljurista.eu/2014/05/15/el-treball-sexual-a-europa

Panizo, J. A. (2015). *¿El ejercicio de la prostitución puede dar lugar a la inclusión en la seguridad social?* Madrid: Centro de Estudios Financieros CEF – Laboral Social.

Phoenix, J. (2009). *Regulating sex for sale: Prostitution, policy reform and the UK*. Portland: The Policy Press.

Sarrión Esteve, J. (2013). *El Tribunal de Justicia de Luxemburgo como garante de los derechos fundamentales*. Madrid: Dykinson.

Sarrión Esteve, J. (2015). *Actual trends and challenges of the constitutional fundamental rights and principles in the ECJ case law from the perspective of multilevel constitutionalism*. Retrieved January 27, 2018, from SSRN: https://ssrn.com/abstract=2656394

Sarrión Esteve, J. (2017). *Lecciones Fundamentales de Derecho de la Unión Europea*. Valencia: Tirant lo Blanch.

Scoular, J. (2010). What's law got to do with it? How and why law matters in the regulation of sex work. *Journal of Law and Society, 37*(1), 12–39.

Soldier

Riccardo Ursi

1 Citizens in Uniform

Civil and political rights form an extensive body of rights and fundamental freedoms which should be enjoyed by all members of society, including those who serve in the armed forces. Along the spectrum stretching from the position where soldiers and citizens have identical rights and duties (civilian soldiers) to one in which the armed forces are kept quite separate from civilian society (militarised soldiers), most States are somewhere in the middle (Rowe 2007, p. 8 ff).

What is the legal meaning of the phrase "citizens in uniform"? One theory is that it grounds the army within society so as to prevent it from being seen as a tool to be used by the sovereign or the government to oppress the civilian population, or indeed, to act as a hedge against military interventionism. If the army sees itself as being composed merely of civilians in uniform, it is unlikely to take such action against fellow citizens. This theory assumes that the civilian population is homogenous and that soldiers themselves see all citizens as equally worthy of such protection. It also assumes that the army will not be used as a substitute police force in quelling disorder. Where it is used in this way, the theory's proponents may be superficially satisfied by the argument that the soldier's powers in acting for this purpose are no greater than those of a civilian, and indeed less than those of a police officer (Skinner 2000, p. 266). Although rules of engagement are drawn up on this basis, the reality is often quite different. The State frequently provides soldiers with weapons designed for "war fighting" to try and maintain order. Whilst citizens may have a limited duty to preserve peace, the soldier deployed for this purpose must put his duties as a soldier above those he must accept as a civilian.

In conclusion, the concept of "citizens in uniform" indicates that armed forces personnel are entitled to all of the same rights and freedoms as regular citizens and

R. Ursi (✉)
Department of Law, University of Palermo, Palermo, Italy
e-mail: riccardo.ursi@unipa.it

A. Bartolini et al. (eds.), *Dictionary of Statuses within EU Law*,
https://doi.org/10.1007/978-3-030-00554-2_66

that these rights can only be restricted as prescribed by law, in a proportionate manner, and with a legitimate aim.

2 Armed Forces and Democratic Constitutions

At present, the role of armed forces in Europe is defined by constitutional documents. They are inherently entitled to use force, and they are entrusted with essential duties upon which the very existence of the State is dependent, such as defending the realm and protecting citizens in the event of armed conflicts. In addition, they are responsible for safeguarding the constitutional framework of the State and specific tasks in the event of emergencies and natural disasters.

The majority of constitutions establish not only fundamental rights but also the limits that may be imposed on those rights in situations such as emergencies and international conflicts. In addition, they codify how authority and powers are divided among constitutional bodies in the spheres of national defence and security. Finally, constitutions determine how and whether the individual rights of members of the armed forces should be restricted due to their status (Nolte and Krieger 2003, p. 29). Furthermore, constitutional regulations normally provide specific details of the effects and importance of international treaties, bearing in mind that international cooperation plays a significant part in the role of the armed forces, both in the form of strategic defence and security alliances (such as NATO) and in the numerous peace enforcement and peacekeeping missions during conflicts.

Alongside the rules regarding the upholding and protection of the fundamental rights of members of the armed forces, there are others that prevent them from fully participating in local and national political life in order to ensure that the armed forces have a neutral role in the specific national frame of reference. There is a notable tendency in liberal democracies to consider members of the armed forces "citizens in uniform", thereby officially acknowledging their full civil rights and only putting in place—and legally defining—the restrictions that are strictly necessary to ensure that the entire organisation remains completely non-political. In this respect, it is always important to note whether or not there is a military justice system that is separate from the main justice system and used to preside over crimes committed by members of the armed forces.

Democratic control of the armed forces in accordance with constitutional criteria is mainly guaranteed through compliance with the principle of legality, the principle animating the fundamental regulations of the military system have been adopted by Parliament. This set of regulations establishes the forms, recruitment methods and legal status of military personnel. The presence of these regulations is one of the distinguishing features of modern democracies. It makes the military system fully subordinate to constitutional powers and establishes legislative regulation over the activities of the organisation that are completely integrated with the rest of the framework of the State.

3 Restrictions of Fundamental Rights for Military Personnel

When restrictions on fundamental rights are indispensable for the efficient running of an organisation or they are motivated by national security requirements, they must be defined and provided for by law, in keeping with constitutional principles. Moreover, the restrictions must comply with the international commitments and pledges made by States in order to prevent abuses. In this respect, The European Convention on Human Rights not only states that everyone has the inviolable right to respect for their private and family lives; freedoms of thought, conscience and religion; freedom of expression; and freedom of assembly and association (Articles 8–11) but also establishes that there may be restrictions to these rights as long as they are "prescribed by law and are necessary in a democratic society in the interests of national security or public safety, for the prevention of disorder or crime, for the protection of health or morals or for the protection of the rights and freedoms of others".

3.1 Restrictions to Freedom of Expression

Members of the armed forces can exercise their right to freedom of expression in many ways, and they should be able to do so as long as it does not affect their ability to perform all of their duties effectively. It is possible for restrictions to be imposed on the forms of communication that are open to military personnel and what they can and cannot actually say, but any limitations of this kind must be proportionate.

Members of the armed forces must be taught to show discretion and exercise their right to freedom of expression in a responsible manner. Whenever they voice their opinions in social, public or political spheres, they must display sound judgement. At the same time, it is essential to distinguish between the two sides of members of the armed forces, private individuals and representatives of the State, and establish in which capacity they are acting. If the circumstances make it apparent that a servicemember is speaking or writing as a private individual rather than in an official capacity, no disclaimers are required. The fact that they are "citizens in uniform" means that they can even use their freedom of speech to criticise the armed forces. This actually helps to give both the military and the State as a whole a reputation of being more trustworthy, open and accountable.

On the other hand, prior authorisation from superior officers or the relevant authorities is necessary for anyone who wishes to make statements in an official capacity. Members of the armed forces can draw on their experience to make contributions to trade magazines and publications of all kinds. However, they must always get permission beforehand if they wish to divulge classified information or details of official matters, regardless of whether they are communicating in a public or a private setting.

Article 10 of the ECHR protects the right to freedom of expression. In 1997, the ECtHR acknowledged that military personnel are free to express their views, recognising that "Article 10 does not stop at the gates of army barracks" (*Grigoriades v. Greece* 121/1996/740/939). The Court has also acknowledged that soldiers are free to voice concerns about their own rights or about working in dangerous conditions. However, this right does not apply when one is divulging military secrets and information concerning national security. The armed forces may restrict such forms of communication (*Hadjianastassiou v. Greece*, 16 December 1992).

3.2 Restrictions to Freedom of Association

In addition, legal restrictions on exercising the right to form and join trade unions can be imposed on members of both the police and the armed forces.

The International Labour Organization's Freedom of Association and Protection of the Right to Organise Convention confirms the commitment by States to implementing the provisions contained therein, which aim to guarantee that public authorities allow freedom of association.

Article 2 states that "Workers and employers, without distinction whatsoever, shall have the right to establish and, subject only to the rules of the organisation concerned, to join organisations of their own choosing without previous authorisation", while Article 9 establishes that "[t]he extent to which the guarantees provided for in this Convention shall apply to the armed forces and the police shall be determined by national laws or regulations", and that "[i]n accordance with the principle set forth in paragraph 8 of Article 19 of the Constitution of the International Labour Organisation the ratification of this Convention by any Member shall not be deemed to affect any existing law, award, custom or agreement in virtue of which members of the armed forces or the police enjoy any right guaranteed by this Convention".

The Council of Europe has expressed its opinion a number of times on the right to freedom of association for members of the armed forces.

With Resolution 903 in 1988, it stated that members of the armed forces should be considered "citizens in uniform" who should not be isolated from democratic society and who "must experience, at first hand, the democracy which they are protecting", then called on all Member States "to grant professional members of the armed forces of all ranks the right, under normal circumstances, to establish, join and actively participate in specific associations formed to protect their professional interests within the framework of democratic institutions". Subsequently, in Recommendation 1572 (2002), the Council of Europe noted the reluctance of Member States to promote the civic right of members of the Armed Forces to freedom of association, which was not recognised at all or was subject to severe limitations on the conditions governing it. In addition, due to the conversion in several Member States from a conscription system to a purely professional system, members of the armed forces increasingly will be seen as regular employees who should be fully eligible to exercise the employee rights established by the European

Convention on Human Rights. In particular, while they are performing the duties associated with their service, they should have the right to join and actively participate in associations that have been created to safeguard their professional interests within the bounds of democratic institutions. Consequently, the Assembly called on the governments of Member States to allow servicemembers to take part in representative associations with the right to negotiate about issues relating to pay and working conditions and to reduce the restrictions that were in place regarding the right to freedom of association for military personnel.

A similar appeal was made in Recommendation 1742 (2006), in which the Parliamentary Assembly of the Council of Europe noted that "despite its repeated requests to Member States, the situation of members of the armed forces in some States vis-à-vis the rights which they enjoy under the European Convention on Human Rights and the case law of the European Court of Human Rights is far from satisfactory" and urgently demanded real, efficient protection of the human rights of servicemembers. Subsequently, the Committee of Ministers presented Recommendation 4 (2010) on "human rights of members of the armed forces". The Recommendation invites governments of Member States to "ensure that the principles set out in [its] appendix are complied with in national legislation and practice relating to members of the armed forces". Governments are also invited to "ensure, by appropriate means and action, a wide dissemination of the recommendation among […] members of the armed forces with a view to raising awareness of the human rights and fundamental freedoms of members of the armed forces, and to providing training aimed at increasing their knowledge of human rights" (regulations are contained in particular on Section K).

In the explanatory appendix, the Council of Europe states that while some States restrict the right to freedom of association in order to ensure total military neutrality, the general principle is nonetheless that "members of the armed forces should enjoy these rights" and that "it favours the idea that all citizens, including members of the armed forces, enjoy the same political rights". Accordingly, the reasons why rights are restricted should be reviewed by governments on a regular basis, and the restrictions should be lifted if they are no longer justified.

Although it is not an international act in the strictest sense of the term, it is nevertheless worthwhile to contemplate the Handbook on Human Rights and Fundamental Freedoms of Armed Forces Personnel, which was published in 2008 by the Organization for Security and Co-operation in Europe (OSCE) Office for Democratic Institutions and Human Rights and the Geneva Centre for the Democratic Control of Armed Forces (DCAF). With reference to the European Convention on Human Rights, "it seeks to contribute to the effective implementation of existing standards by presenting a number of models, or best practices, from within the OSCE region that demonstrate how military structures can successfully integrate human rights and fundamental freedoms". The Handbook made a number of recommendations to Member States in order to promote best practices in terms of human rights for military personnel. In particular, with regard to the right to freedom of association: "States should permit all members of the armed forces to join either a professional association or a trade union representing their interests; these associations or unions should enjoy the right to be consulted in discussions concerning conditions of service for members of the armed forces; disciplinary action or victimisation of individual members of the armed forces for participation in the activities of such professional associations or trade unions should be prohibited; any restrictions on freedom of association (for example, with regard to industrial action) should be: prescribed by law, proportionate to legitimate State interests recognised in human rights treaties, and also be non-discriminatory."

Analysis of the acts and documents mentioned above establishes the cornerstones of this interpretative framework, within which fall the two parts of Article 11 of the European Convention on Human Rights.

In cases brought before it, the European Court of Human Rights in Strasbourg has linked Article 11 with other articles of the ECHR that seek to guarantee diversity of opinions in a democratic society. Recognition of the right to freedom of assembly and association is deemed an essential prerequisite for effective implementation of the broader right to freedom of expression provided for by Article 10. The way in which its execution is ensured and overseen by authorities "reveal[s] the state of democracy in the country concerned". (*Ezelin v. France* on 26 April 1991 and *Chassagnou et al. v. France* on 29 April 1999).

Freedom of association is strictly correlated with trade union freedom, which should be considered "one form or a special aspect of freedom of association" and, even more prominently, accomplishes the objectives of democracy that freedom of association on the whole facilitates, thus enabling effective permeation between social and economic rights and between civil and political rights.

As for the obligations of States resulting from Article 11, in the judgement in the *Ouranio Toxo v. Greece* case in 2005, the judges in Strasbourg specified that they cannot be limited to mere negative duties performed by the State (not interfering). There are also positive duties that aim to ensure genuine freedom of association, which nonetheless does not have universal, boundless scope. Like other provisions of the ECHR, it can be limited in order to achieve the aims identified in part 2 of Article 11.

Traditionally, the second sentence of Article 11 is considered as a separate ground for restrictions on the exercise of the right to freedom of association by members of armed forces, the police and the administration of the State.

In two more recent cases from 2 October 2014 (*Matelly v. France* and *ADEFDROMIL v. France*), the Court had to decide on the right of military personnel to freedom of association. Although the Court had already examined cases involving trade union freedom within the police and the civil service, it was the first time that the Court had considered the specific situation of the armed forces.

Essentially, the restrictions that can be imposed on members of the armed forces must be construed strictly and they must only govern how rights are *exercised*, without affecting the actual essence of the right to form associations. Consequently, the Court cannot accept restrictions that are detrimental to the vital characteristics of trade union freedom—such as the right to join trade unions—because it would mean that the freedom had no substance or significance (Van Hiel 2016).

In terms of the way in which professional associations of military personnel act and express themselves, trade union freedom can be limited and restricted quite significantly but it cannot be totally banned, because measures of that kind would be disproportionate, unnecessary and in contravention of the European Convention on Human Rights.

References

Nolte, G., & Krieger, H. (2003). Comparison on European military law systems. In G. Nolte (Ed.), *European military law system* (pp. 22–175). Berlin: De Gruyter Recht.

Rowe, P. (2007). The soldier as a citizen in uniform: A reappraisal. *New Zealand Armed Forces Law Review, 1*, 7–25.

Skinner, S. (2000). Citizen in uniform: Public defence, reasonableness and human rights. *Public Law, 2*, 266–281.

Van Hiel, I. (2016). Blanket ban on the right of military personnel to form and join a trade union violates Article 11 ECHR. Retrieved June 22, 2018, from https://strasbourgobservers.com/2014/11/06/blanket-ban-on-the-right-of-military-personnel-to-form-and-join-a-trade-union-violates-article-11-echr/

Sportsperson

Giulia Mannucci

1 Introduction

Following the Lisbon Treaty, sport was included among the EU competences for coordination and support. According to Article 165 TFEU, 'The Union shall contribute to the promotion of European sporting issues, while taking account of the specific nature of sport, its structures based on voluntary activity and its social and educational function'. This provision acknowledges the social dimension of sport, meaning its social cohesion and educational functions (Weatherill 2012) Nevertheless, since the 1970s the European Union has contributed to the development of the economic and professional status of a sportsperson. In particular, the European Court of Justice, by approaching sport in its economic dimension (i.e. as an economically recognizable activity), has contributed to defining the status of a sportsperson (Bastianon and Nascimbene 2005; Tognon 2009, p. 4). As we will see below, this definition by the European Court has had a significant impact, both on the organization of sport (at an international and a national level) and on the legal systems of the individual Member States.

This contribution moves on from the traditional definition of a sportsperson to analyse how the European Court of Justice has reshaped that definition in the mentioned three respects: free movement of sporting workers, free competition and judicial protection.

G. Mannucci (✉)
University of Florence – Department of Legal Studies, Firenze, Italy
e-mail: giulia.mannucci@unifi.it

A. Bartolini et al. (eds.), *Dictionary of Statuses within EU Law*,
https://doi.org/10.1007/978-3-030-00554-2_67

2 The Traditional Definition of a Sportsperson

The traditional definition of a sportsperson is affected by the idea of the relationship between the state and the institutional sports setting (Ferrara 2007).

For instance, in the Italian debate on the rights and duties of the sportsperson it is often assumed that a sports organization constitutes a genuine legal order, autonomous from the state legal order. Accordingly, some scholars exclude the sports system from the application of the common rules governing the general legal order, and argue in favour of the application of special rules that best reflect the peculiarities of the sports phenomenon.

The underlying idea is the following: the peculiar needs of the sports world allow (or, in some ways, impose) a large number of exceptions to the common rules. This leads to a tension between conflicting values, as emerges from the debate on judicial review in this sector. In this context, the debate involves whether state courts should have the competence to hear claims concerning sport: for some scholars, impartiality and the guarantee of due process require the maximum extension of such competence; for other scholars, the need for specialization and efficiency can only be satisfied by sports judges (even if their impartiality cannot be fully guaranteed, as they are nominated by—or at least related to—sporting federations).

Therefore, the legal status of a sportsperson that has been set over the years has been conditioned by this particular vision: the sportsperson ended up being understood as a subject having rights and duties that are crucially relevant to the sporting order, as a direct result of his affiliation to a particular federation. It is, in fact, through his or her affiliation to a federation that the sportsperson enjoys rights and undertakes obligations, thus 'binding' himself or herself to the federation rules.

Against that backdrop, European Union law has significantly contributed to the emergence of a 'new' legal status for sportspersons, meaning that the application of supranational law has taken away the special nature of the sports system. As we will see below, the Court of Justice of the European Union (the CJEU) has, in fact, identified several general rules that apply to athletes. As a result, it has significantly reduced the relevance of the 'sporting exemption' (Bastianon and Nascimbene 2005, pp. 249–251).

3 The Freedom of Movement of Athletes

The first seminal judgments of the Court of Justice on the status of a sportsperson date back to the mid-1970s and concern the freedom of movement of European athletes. These two cases (CJEU, 12 December 1974, C-36/74, *Walrave and Koch* and CJEU, 14 July 1976, C-13/76, *Donà/Mantero*) set out some key principles that significantly influenced the subsequent case law.

First, the Court acknowledged that sport, even if at the time it did not fall within the direct competences of the European Community, is subject to European law insofar as it is an economic activity. The Court of Justice rejected the idea that sporting law belongs to a separate organizational and regulatory system and escapes the application of European law. Moreover, the Court recognized that Article 2 of the Treaty provided a sufficient legal basis for the competence of European institutions in the field: because of its economic dimension, the sport sector is a relevant part of the common market (which, by then, was emerging) and, for that reason, it cannot escape the application of European law.

This key principle has a significant consequence: when a sporting activity is related to a remunerated job (through either employment or self-employment), it interferes with—and is subject to—the rules on free movement of workers. Accordingly, when a sporting activity is an expression of an economically relevant activity, the sportsperson must be treated as a worker comparable to other Community workers and, therefore, the same rules must be applied to him as to other workers. For instance, European law does not allow any discrimination based on nationality. The fact that sports federations (which regulate the matter in question) are private associations and not public authorities cannot shield them: all the actors in sport, be they private or public in nature, are required to comply with European law. Otherwise, 'the abolition as between Member States of obstacles to freedom of movement for persons and to freedom to provide services, which are fundamental objectives of the Community contained in Article 3(c) of the Treaty, would be compromised if the abolition of barriers of national origin could be neutralized by obstacles resulting from the exercise of their legal autonomy by associations or organizations which do not come under public law' (C-36/74, para. 18).

Nevertheless, the Court of Justice acknowledged the existence of an exception to this general rule: the principle of non-discrimination based on nationality does not apply to sporting activities when the discrimination is necessary to ensure the proper conduct of the competition. Take, for instance, the right to select only athletes from a particular country to represent that country in Olympic competitions or in competitions conceived as a challenge between athletes (or teams) of different nationalities. In such cases, an unconditional application of the rules on free movement would undermine the spirit of competition. On this point, the Court stated that 'this restriction on the scope of the provisions in question must however remain limited to its proper objective', and said that it cannot be invoked to exclude an entire sport from the application of the Treaty (C-13/76, paras. 14–15). The purpose of the exception is to reconcile two different needs: on the one hand, the need to promote a uniform application of European law; on the other hand, the need for autonomy invoked by the sports organizations.

Over the years, the Court of Justice has repeatedly come back to the question of the applicability to sport of the rules on freedom of movement, and has thus refined the principles laid down in the *Walrave* and *Donà* rulings.

The most important judgment was given in the well-known *Bosman* case (15 December 1995, C-415/93), where, by extending the scope of the rules on freedom of movement, the CJEU ruled out long-term practices of the sports system (Weatherill 1996, p. 991).

The first of these was the so-called 'transfer allowance', a clause that was then contained in football players' contracts, according to which 'a professional footballer who is a national of one Member State may not, on the expiry of his contract with a club, be employed by a club of another Member State unless the latter club has paid to the former a transfer, training or development fee' (C-415/93, para. 68). The aim of the clause is to 'compensate' the first club for the costs that it had incurred to raise and train the football player. According to the Court of Justice, such a contractual clause is contrary to the European rules on freedom of movement, insofar as it may limit the ability of the player to provide his own services (Coccia 1994, p. 356).

Moreover, the Luxembourg Court held that the '3+2 rule' was incompatible with EC law. This rule, adopted by the Union of European Football Associations (UEFA), allowed 'each national association to limit to three the number of foreign players whom a club may field in any first division match in their national championships, plus two players who have played in the country of the relevant national association for an uninterrupted period of five years, including three years as a junior' (C-415/93, para. 27), the same limitation also applying to UEFA competitions. In UEFA's view, this rule would encourage the growth of traineeships, pushing football clubs to invest in young people. However, according to the Court of Justice, it caused unlawful discrimination based on nationality (Bastianon and Nascimbene 2005, pp. 260–261; Kranz 1999, p. 431).

Sporting organizations perceived the *Bosman* decision to represent undue interference by the European Union, which did not respect the autonomy, values and overall balance on which the sports system was founded (Manzella 1996, p. 409).

Nonetheless, in the years that followed the *Bosman* decision, the Court of Justice further extended the applicability of the rules on freedom of movement to the sporting world, holding that nationality restrictions are not allowed even when they concern non-EU workers coming from third countries that have cooperation or partnership agreements with the EU (see, for instance, CJEU, 12 April 2005, C-265/03, *Simutenkov*). In this and other related cases, the application of the rules on freedom of movement concerned not the entry but the working conditions of third-country athletes in the European labour market: once they have been admitted as workers into the Community, they are entitled to enjoy the same treatment as Community workers with regard to working conditions, remuneration and dismissal (C-265/03, para. 37).

To sum up, the Court of Justice, in its attempt to subject sporting organizations to European rules (i.e. in the pursuit of the Community interest), has reshaped the status of a sportsperson using the tools offered by the freedom of movement regime (Duval 2016, pp. 81–83). Every worker, including sportspersons, must be free to work in other Member States, irrespective of his or her nationality. As long as a sporting activity has economic relevance, it cannot be excluded from the application of European law (Parrish 2016, p. 187), and any derogations must be limited to their specific object and be proportionate to their purpose (CJEU, 16 March 2010, C-325/08, *Olympique Lyonnais SASP/Olivier Bernard and Newcastle*).

4 Competition

The realm of competition is the second area in which the Court of Justice has contributed to a redefinition of the status of sportspersons.

In the earliest case law mentioned above (*Walrave*, *Donà* and *Bosman*), the Court had been asked to rule on the compatibility of sports rules with European competition law, but it always declined to do so. The first case in which the Court accepted the request to deal with the issue was that of *Piau* (TFI, 25 January 2005, T-193/02; on this judgment, see Waelbroeck and Ibáñez Colomo 2006), but the most relevant ruling arrives in the *Meca-Medina* case. Two swimmers had been disqualified by their international membership federation (the *Fédération internationale de natation*—FINA) for doping offences. According to the athletes, the FINA regulation identifying the tolerance threshold for the drug level in the blood was contrary to the principle of proportionality because the criteria were too rigid, limiting the ability of athletes to compete freely in their work, contrary to Articles 81 and 82 of the EC Treaty.

The EC Tribunal of first instance reaffirmed the traditional 'sports-centred' approach. Initially, it acknowledged the distinction between purely sporting rules and other rules applicable to sportspeople: the first kind, 'having nothing to do with economic activity', are outside the reach of EC law and are thus exempt from the scrutiny of the Court of Justice. It then held that anti-doping rules are purely sporting rules, on the grounds that they do 'not pursue any economic objective'. Those rules are, rather, intended both 'to preserve (…) the spirit of fair play, without which sport, be it amateur or professional, is no longer sport', and 'to safeguard the health of athletes', with the consequence that 'the prohibition of doping, as a particular expression of the requirement of fair play, forms part of the cardinal rule of sport' (TFI, 30 September 2004, T-313/02, paras. 41 and 44).

The Court of Justice, by contrast, rejected the assumption of the Tribunal that purely sporting rules (such as anti-doping rules) are, in principle, exempted from the scope of European law. Even though anti-doping rules create a purely sporting regime, they cannot be considered *per se* to be exempt from compliance with EC competition law. Instead, a case-by-case assessment is necessary: 'the mere fact that a rule is purely sporting in nature does not have the effect of removing from the scope of the Treaty the person engaging in the activity governed by that rule or the body which has laid it down', and therefore the restrictions on free competition imposed by anti-doping rules 'must be limited to what is necessary to ensure the proper conduct of competitive sport' (CJEU, 18 July 2006, C-519/04P, paras. 27 and 47). This ruling, therefore, blurs the distinction between purely sporting rules and other (economically relevant) sporting rules by resorting to a case-by-case assessment (Weatherill 2006, p. 645): there are no sporting rules exempt as such from compliance with Community antitrust law, because a concrete assessment of their impact is always required (Colucci 2006, pp. 29–31).

This line of jurisprudence adds another 'de-specializing' layer to the status of a sportsperson. Insofar as he or she performs an economically relevant activity, the athlete enjoys the rights (and must respect the duties) arising from the European rules on competition law (Pijetlovic 2016).

5 Judicial Review

A third contribution of the Court of Justice to the development of the status of a sportsperson concerns legal protection. This aspect does not, of course, stand alone, but, rather, is connected to those already mentioned. If, and to the extent that, a sporting activity falls within the scope of European law, this involves the justiciability of claims that are based on that law. This touches upon one of the most sensitive aspects of the autonomy of the sports system: whether, and to what extent, common courts may intervene in and decide on sports disputes. This issue has deep dogmatic roots, as it is related to the recurring tensions that arise between state legal orders and the sports system when the former intervene in the realm of the latter: the intervention of the common courts is perceived by sports associations as an unwarranted invasion. However, as the CJEU case law shows, the need to protect the overarching European norms and principles often prevails over the demands of the sports system for autonomy and self-regulation.

6 Conclusions

The analysis undertaken above shows how deeply the traditional status of a sportsperson has been affected by the case law of the European Court of Justice. Indeed, the supranational Court has identified a number of rights and obligations that must apply to sport activities, particularly in the areas of freedom of movement, freedom of competition and judicial protection.

This case law also significantly affects the vision of the organized sports system as being 'special': by identifying a series of rights and duties of a sportsperson, the Court of Justice has crucially contributed to the rejection of the idea that sports activities, because of their peculiarities, are in principle exempt from the scope of European Union law (Clarich 1996). Those peculiarities, to the extent that they correspond to specific legitimate needs of the sports system, may justify some exceptions to the application of European law, but any such derogations must be limited to their specific object and be proportionate to the purpose to be achieved (Gardiner and Welch 2016).

References

Bastianon, S., & Nascimbene, B. (2005). Lo sport e il diritto comunitario. In E. Greppi & M. Vellano (Eds.), *Il diritto internazionale dello sport* (pp. 247–297). Turin: Giappichelli.
Clarich, M. (1996). La sentenza Bosman: verso il tramonto degli ordinamenti giuridici sportivi? *Rivista italiana di diritto pubblico comunitario*, (3–4), 613–628.
Coccia, M. (1994). L'indennità di trasferimento e la libera circolazione dei calciatori professionisti nell'Unione Europea. *Rivista di diritto sportivo*, 350–363.
Colucci, M. (2006). L'autonomia e la specificità dello sport nell'Unione Europea. *Rivista di diritto ed economia dello sport*, (2), 15–33.
Duval, A. (2016). The FIFA regulations on the status and transfer of players: Transnational law-making in the shadow of Bosman. In A. Duval & B. Van Rompuy (Eds.), *The legacy of Bosman* (pp. 81–116). The Hague: Asser Press.
Ferrara, L. (2007). L'ordinamento sportivo: meno e più della libertà privata. *Diritto pubblico*, (1), 1–31.
Gardiner, S., & Welch, R. (2016). Nationality based playing quotas and the international transfer system post-Bosman. In A. Duval & B. Van Rompuy (Eds.), *The legacy of Bosman* (pp. 51–80). The Hague: Asser Press.
Kranz, A. O. (1999). The Bosman case: The relationship between European Union law and the transfer system in European football. *Columbia Journal of European Law, 5*(3), 431–459.
Manzella, A. (1996). L'Europa e lo sport: un difficile dialogo dopo "Bosman"? *Rivista di diritto sportivo*, 409–415.
Parrish, R. (2016). The European social dialogue: A new mode of governance for European football? In A. Duval & B. Van Rompuy (Eds.), *The legacy of Bosman* (pp. 187–211). The Hague: Asser Press.
Pijetlovic, K. (2016). EU competition law and organisational rules. In A. Duval & B. Van Rompuy (Eds.), *The legacy of Bosman* (pp. 117–151). The Hague: Asser Press.
Tognon, J. (2009). Unione Europea e sport: evoluzioni e sviluppi di un rapporto "particolare". In J. Tognon (Ed.), *Diritto comunitario dello sport* (pp. 3–41). Turin: Giappichelli.
Waelbroeck, D., & Ibáñez Colomo, P. (2006). Case law. *Common Market Law Review, 43*(6), 1743–1756.
Weatherill, S. (1996). Case law. *Common Market Law Review, 33*(5), 991–1033.
Weatherill, S. (2006). Anti-doping revisited – The demise of the rule of 'purely sporting interest'? *European Competition Law Review, 27*(12), 645–657.
Weatherill, S. (2012). EU sports law: The effect of the Lisbon Treaty. In A. Biondi & P. Eeckhout (Eds.), *EU law after Lisbon* (pp. 403–419). Oxford: Oxford University Press.

Statutory Auditor

Antonio Chiappalupi

1 International and Historical Background

The word audit is Latin in origin. "*Audire*" means to hear. According to Matthews (2006, p. 6), in Britain, the term audit dates back to medieval times when "*the auditor on landed estates literally heard the accounts read out and checked on the lord's behalf that his stewart had not been negligent or fraudulent*".

The meaning of the term audit, as well as its application and role in society, are strictly linked to the development of the economic and business environment (from local, international, to global markets) as well as to the applicable legislation which has evolved through the years. The statutory audit has developed at different moments among the European countries.

As described by Ajao et al. (2016), the evolution of the audit can be divided into five stages.

1.1 Stage 1: Before 1840

Evidence traces audit activity back to the medieval period. According to Pontani (2015), we can recall the *Domesday Book* in England, which is related to one of the first control systems for inventory. In the late medieval times, in Italy, France and England, the first control activities started to be formalised. In England, the city of London records that it has undergone audits since 1200. In 1314, the first office to audit official accounts was established in England: the so-called "*Auditor of the Receipt of the Exchequer*" (Pontani 2015). Other developments were made during this period in various European countries. However, we must wait until the end of

A. Chiappalupi (✉)
Basel, Switzerland

A. Bartolini et al. (eds.), *Dictionary of Statuses within EU Law*,
https://doi.org/10.1007/978-3-030-00554-2_68

the eighteenth century to see the first *Office for Auditing Public Accounts* created in England.

In this period, the primary role and objective of the auditor was to detect fraud. Auditors inspected accounts in a detailed manner without applying sampling techniques (Ajao et al. 2016).

1.2 Stage 2: 1840–1920

The effects of the Industrial Revolution transformed the environment, industries and business activities, thus creating the need for audits. In fact, as explained by Lee (1988, cited in Matthews 2006, pp. 6–7), "*developments in the economic structure of civilizations caused audit needs. Industrialization created the need for financing. This created, in turn, the need for incorporation. And this created the need for financial reporting of audited information*". In 1844, the Joint Stock Companies Act was established in the U.K. The Act foresaw the appointment of auditors to check the financial statements of companies. The statutory audit became mandatory in England only with the Companies Act, 1862, which stated: "*…Once at the least in every year the accounts of the company shall be examined, and the correctness of the balance sheet ascertained, by one or more auditors…*". In France, for example, the accounting audit became mandatory in 1863, followed by Belgium (1873). In Germany, the process was delayed compared to the Anglo-Saxon world, as the statutory audit became mandatory only in 1889 and was fully established in 1930 (Evans 2003). With the British Companies Act of 1908, specific and detailed provisions were set in regard to the auditor's appointment, fee, powers and duties.

1.3 Stage 3: 1920–1960

Statutory audit activity became more and more formalised in various European countries until the advent of the European Economic Community (EEC) in 1957 and the participation of Great Britain in 1973. According to Pontani (2015), Great Britain played a crucial role in Europe regarding audit techniques and methods: The country was involved in several different socio-economic experiences and participation in the international market to greater dimensions. Larger companies came into play in different industries with a clear separation of ownership and management. Internal control functions began to be important, and auditors started to be relied upon (Ajao et al. 2016). The concept of materiality, together with sampling techniques, was introduced. Different sources of information were gathered at this stage from the auditor: internal and external documentary evidence, as well as physical observations (Porter et al. 2005).

1.4 Stage 4: 1960–1990

This period is very important as the Eight Council Directive n. 253 of 10 April 1984 was established and was focused on the approval of persons carrying out statutory audits. The Directive states the requirements and qualifications needed by an auditor to be able to practice the activity, as well as to meet the objectives of independence and honourability. This period is also characterised by the development and presence of the big audit firms, operating internationally. The audit activities switched from detailed transaction reviews to company system reviews. This means that, given the increased complexity of company operations (due to size, markets and businesses), the auditor reviewed the internal control system and assessed and documented its reliability (Ajao et al. 2016).

1.5 Stage 5: 1990 to Date

This stage is characterised by the further development and adoption of a risk-based audit approach, the usage of computer-based audit tools, as well as data analytics techniques. The auditor's activity has switched from the mere review of accounts and testing to consulting services. In fact, audit duties are not only referred to the reliability of financial statements but also to provide "*value adding services*" (Lee and Ali 2008, p. 1). Further, recent decades have been characterised by legal reforms and new audit requirements to ensure the reliability of company financial disclosures in response to company scandals stemming from misstatements and fraud; we might recall the Enron case in 2001 (the overstatement of profits to hide losses), WorldCom in 2002 (the overstatement of income) and the Parmalat scandal in Italy (Treasury Today 2006). In response to those incidents, the new Sarbanes-Oxley Act was established in 2002 in the U.S., new requirements were provided in the Companies Act in 2004 in U.K., and the EC 8th Company Law Directive was revised (Competition Commission 2013).

The Directive represents the major legal basis for the statutory audit in Europe.

2 EU Applicable Legislation on the Statutory Audit: Definition, Role, Position and Liabilities

2.1 EU Applicable Legislation: Introduction

The Eight Council Directive n. 253 of 10 April 1984 can be considered to be the most important step with regard to the statutory audit in the European Union. In fact, although the regulation did not provide specific standards for auditing financial statements, it stated the criteria for the approval of the statutory auditors, such as their qualifications, independence and honourability. The Directive was meant to be implemented by all the member states by January 1990. Specifically, according to Soltani (2007, p. 161), the lack of clarity, particularly with regard to the requirement of independence, "*has led to inevitable differences in national legislations, and in some cases, to an absence of legislative backing*". The way that companies are audited and the standards to be followed were considered with the Communication from the Commission to the Parliament proposed in 2003 on "Reinforcing the statutory audit in the EU" (European Commission 2003). The proposal passed in September 2005. The new Directive includes the application of international standards as well as external quality assurance and strengthened the principle of auditor independence among the European member states through the establishment of the Audit Committee (Soltani 2007). Other topics such as auditor liability, education and training, and transparency were also considered in the so-called "*modernised and principles-based 8th Directive*" as named in the aforementioned Communication from the Commission under paragraph 2.1.

The current applicable EU legislation for the statutory audit is Directive 2014/56 (hereinafter referred to as the "Directive"), which amends Directive 2006/43/EC on *statutory audits of annual accounts and consolidated accounts*, and Regulation 537/2014 on *specific requirements regarding statutory audit of public-interest entities* (hereinafter referred to as the "Regulation").

With the Directive, auditor independence has been reinforced, and the role of the audit committee has been strengthened. In fact, according to KPMG (2016), and with regard to Public Interest Companies (hereinafter referred to as "PIEs"), the auditors need to rotate on a regular basis. Several Non-Audit Services (so-called "NAS") have been forbidden from being provided to the audited entities (e.g.: specific tax services such as the preparation of tax forms, payroll taxes, custom duties). Further, the audit committee must be composed by at least one expert in accounting/auditing, and it is responsible for managing the tender process for the external auditor's appointment (KPMG 2018).

In order to strengthen the cooperation between the European countries, the Committee of European Auditing Oversight Body (CEAOB) was established in 2016 with the aim of reinforcing the proper application of EU legislation in the countries (European Commission 2018).

2.2 *Definition and Role of the Statutory Auditor*

According to art. 2, point 1 of the Directive, statutory audit

> means an audit of annual financial statements or consolidated financial statements in so far as:
>
> (a) required by Union law;
> (b) required by national law as regards small undertakings;

(c) voluntarily carried out at the request of small undertakings which meets national legal requirements that are equivalent to those for an audit under point (b), where national legislation defines such audits as statutory audits.

According to Bragg (2017), the audit of annual financial statements examines a set of reports such as the balance sheet, income statement, statement of cash flow and supplementary notes of a company. The role of a statutory audit is to certify that those statements represent in a fair manner the financials, performance and cash flow of the audited entity and that they are free from material errors, so that stakeholders can rely on the reported information (Bragg 2017). According to the international accounting standards, a misstatement is considered to be material if it affects the economic decisions made by the relevant stakeholders. According to the International Accounting Standard n. 1, the term "fair presentation" refers to "*the faithful representation of the effects of transactions, other events and conditions in accordance with the definitions and recognition criteria for assets, liabilities, income and expenses*" (European Commission 2011). In doing so, as described by the European Commission, the auditor's role helps the markets to function in an ordered and transparent environment, thus increasing the reliability of the financial information disclosed to the relevant stakeholders.

The results of the audit review are documented in a report which states the auditor's opinion about the financial statements. Both the Directive and the Regulation provide specific and detailed provisions on the content of the audit report. The content of the auditor's report is different if it is related to an audited entity in general than if it is related to PIEs. In the first case, as described in article 28 (2)(f) of the Directive, the audit report must include a statement "*on any material uncertainty relating to events or conditions that may cast significant doubt about the entity's ability to continue as a going concern*" (KPMG 2018). For PIEs, according to art. 10 (2)(c) of the Regulation, the audit report needs to "*provide, in support of the audit opinion, the following: (i) a description of the most significant assessed risks of material misstatement, including assessed risks of material misstatement due to fraud, (ii) a summary of the auditor's response to those risks, and (iii) where relevant, key observations arising with respect to those risks*" (KPMG 2018).

2.3 Position (Qualifications and Requirements) and Liability of the Statutory Auditor Within the European Union

The position and liability of the statutory auditor were already discussed in the Green Paper of 24 July 1996: "*The role, the position and the liability of the statutory auditor within the European Union*" (European Commission 1996).

According to the current Directive, a statutory auditor is any person that meets the criteria set out in arts. 4, 6, 10 and 12. Specifically, the conditions are:

a) Good repute, which, if compromised, shall cause the withdrawal of the auditor.
b) Qualifications, which comprise the university degree, training and final examination foreseen by the member state concerned. The Directive provides a list of

subjects regarding the examination tests, as well as the eligibility criteria for exemptions.

c) Practical training, which consists of at least 3 years of training in accounting and auditing duties. At least two thirds of the 3 years should be completed under the supervision of a qualified statutory auditor.
d) Continuing education, which foresees that auditors are subject to continuous learning to ensure that their knowledge and skills are up to date. The failure of the auditor to participate in those learning programmes may imply a sanction as per art. 30 of the Directive.
e) Public Registration, which is mandatory for any auditor in any member state to be eligible to carry out his activity.

A qualified auditor who would like to practice the activity in another member state, according to the Directive, might need to undergo a "*compensation measure*" imposed by the hosting state. This is considered necessary to ensure the high quality of the statutory audit activity with the required knowledge of the local applicable legislation as well as fiscal and social matters.

When carrying out the review, the auditor must comply with the International Standards on Auditing (ISAs) as well as the standards foreseen by the IFAC (International Federation of Accountants) with regard to audit practice, independence and internal quality controls (ISQC).

The auditor must be independent from the audited entity and this is crucial for a thorough assessment (Cargou and Dekker 2010). The new revised Directive of 2014 gives considerable attention to the topic of auditor independence and, in turn, to the audit committee to further strengthen this concept. According to Schmid and Werstermark (2016), the auditor shall be independent from the audited entity and should not participate in any decision-making process. In case of any threats to their independence, auditors must refrain or resign from carrying out the audit engagement.

With reference to auditor sanctions, art. 30 of the Directive states that "*member States shall ensure that there are effective systems of investigations and sanctions to detect, correct and prevent inadequate execution of the statutory audit*." Specifically, the Directive sets forth specific provisions that need to be taken into account by the competent authorities of the member states when reporting and effectively applying the sanctions.

Auditors' liability is mentioned in the subsequent art. 31, which was not amended by the new Directive. As of today, the Directive proposes a cap on auditors' liability. However, there is no full harmonised regime for auditors' liability so far within the EU (Dufour et al. 2014).

3 Role of Audits Within EU Programmes

A specific note needs to be made with regard to the audit activity for EU financing programmes.

European funding has been increasing and has played an important role in the research and development of the Union, as well as in the cooperation with third countries.

The grant agreement signed between the beneficiary and the European Commission includes the terms and conditions of the funding. The agreement includes, among other things, the criteria for the eligibility of costs.

The beneficiary must provide, within the agreed deadline, a certificate on the financial statement performed by an external auditor (i.e.: "*Independent Report of Factual Findings on costs declared...*" under a specific programme name), (European Commission 2017). The auditor is appointed by the beneficiary, and an agreement between the two parties needs to be formalised in accordance with the template provided by the European Commission (i.e.: "*Terms of Reference for an Independent Report of Factual Findings on costs declared under a Grant Agreement financed under the programme...*"), hereinafter referred to as a "ToR". The template provides a full set of criteria for the requirements of the auditor. In fact, according to art. 1.2 of the ToR, the auditor must:

a) Be qualified to perform statutory audits as per Directive 2006/43/EC or other applicable national legislation legitimating the auditor to perform such activity.
b) Be independent from the beneficiary and not involved in the preparation of the financial statements.
c) Plan the work to perform the procedures as required by the ToR and report according to the specific format.
d) Support the report issued with the respective evidence.
e) Submit the report to the beneficiary.

Further, the ToR specifies the applicable standards that the auditor needs to observe and meet. In particular, it recalls the *International Standard on Related Services ('ISRS') 4400* and the *Code of Ethics for Professional Accountants* issued by the International Ethics Standards Board for Accountants (IESBA).

According to the grant agreement provided by the European Commission, the auditor must avoid any conflicts of interest with the beneficiary. The content of the report of factual findings (hereinafter referred to as the "Report") must comply with the format enclosed in the ToR. The activity of the auditor is limited to performing the agreed upon procedures and verifying their compliance with the terms and conditions of the contracts and respective standards. The auditor must report the result of the review for each procedure: Confirmed ("C"); Exception ("E"); or Not Applicable ("NA").

The Report is sent to the European Commission together with the financial statement prepared by the beneficiary and other sets of technical reports disclosing the status of the project.

According to art. 20.8 of the grant agreement, in the case of non-compliance of one of the reports, the EC might suspend the payment of the grant and apply other measures such as: rejection of costs, reduction of the granted amount, recovery of undue amounts, or administrative sanctions based on arts. 106 and 131(4) of the Financial Regulation No 966/2012. The EC might also require compensation for the damage caused in relation to the unsuccessful or uncompliant results of the implementation of the agreement by the beneficiary.

References

Ajao, O. S., Olamide, J. O., & Temitope, A. A. (2016). *Evolution and development of auditing*. Ilishan Remo Ogun: Babcock University.

Bragg, S. (2017). *Financial statement audit*. Accounting Tools. Retrieved from https://www.accountingtools.com/articles/what-is-a-financial-statement-audit.html

Cargou, C., & Dekker, P. (2010). *Guidance on the 8th EU Company Law Directive. Monitoring the effectiveness of internal control, internal audit and risk management systems*. Brussels: FERMA/ECIIA.

Companies Act. (1862). *Regulations for management of a company limited by shares*. Retrieved June 21, 2018, from https://assets.publishing.service.gov.uk/government/uploads/system/uploads/attachment_data/file/386497/comm7Aug1862CoAct1862_P1.pdf

Competition Commission. (2013). *Audit market investigation. Development of the statutory financial audit*. Competition Commission. Retrieved June 21, 2018, from https://assets.publishing.service.gov.uk/media/5329db4140f0b60a76000016/development_of_the_statutory_financial_audit.pdf

Dufour, A., Eddoo, N., & Felix, G. (2014). *Liability of statutory auditors as well as tax and legal counsels in Europe*. Retrieved June 21, 2018, from http://www.acc.com/legalresources/quick-counsel/liability-of-statutory-auditors.cfm?makepdf=1

European Commission. (1996). Green Paper: "*The role, the position and the liability of the statutory auditor within the European Union*" (pp. 19–27). Official Journal C 321 of 28.10.1996. Retrieved June 21, 2018.

European Commission. (2003). *Communication from the Commission to the Council and the European Parliament*. Reinforcing the statutory audit in the EU, COM (2003) 286 final. Brussels: European Commission.

European Commission. (2011). *International Accounting Standard 1 – Presentation of financial statements*. Retrieved June 21, 2018, from http://ec.europa.eu/internal_market/accounting/docs/consolidated/ias1_en.pdf

European Commission. (2017). *H2020 programme. Multi beneficiary: General model grant agreement*. Retrieved June 21, 2018, from http://ec.europa.eu/research/participants/data/ref/h2020/mga/gga/h2020-mga-gga-multi_en.pdf

European Commission. (2018). *Auditing of companies financial statement*. Retrieved June 21, 2018, from https://ec.europa.eu/info/business-economy-euro/company-reporting-and-auditing/auditing-companies-financial-statements_en

Evans, L. (2003). Auditing and audit firms in Germany before 1931. *Accounting Historians Journal, 30*(2), 1.

KPMG. (2016). *EU Audit reform: The impact on the role and responsibilities of audit committees*. Retrieved from https://home.kpmg.com/content/dam/kpmg/pdf/2016/04/aci-audit-reform-impact.pdf

KPMG. (2018). *European Union audit legislation: Frequently asked questions*. KPMG International. Retrieved June 21, 2018, from https://assets.kpmg.com/content/dam/kpmg/xx/pdf/2017/07/shedding-light-on-eu-audit-legislation.pdf

Lee, T., & Ali, A. M. (2008). The evolution of auditing: An analysis of the historical development. *Journal of Modern Accounting and Auditing, 4*(12), 1–8.

Matthews, D. (2006). *A history of auditing: The changing audit process in Britain from the nineteenth century to the present day*. New York: Routledge.

Pontani, F. (2015). *La Revisione Contabile nel Mondo Occidentale Dal Medioevo all'Età Contemporanea*. Pavia: Pavia University Press.
Porter, B., Simon, J., & Hatherly, D. (2005). *Principles of external auditing*. Chichester: John Wiley & Sons.
Schmid, C., & Werstermark, H. (2016). *Legal opinion on the regulation of audit and audit supervision in the European Union, Germany and France*. Lausanne: Institut Suisse de droit comparè.
Soltani, B. (2007). *Auditing: An international approach*. Harlow: Pearson Education.
Treasury Today. (2006). *The 8th EU Directive*. Treasury Today. Retrieved from http://treasurytoday.com/2006/06/the-8th-eu-directive

Further Readinngs

Council Chamber, Whitehall. (1918). *Report of the Committee upon the amendment of the law under Companies Acts, 1908 to 1917*. Whitehall: Darling and Son, Limited.
Wells, H. (2018). *Research handbook on the history of corporate and company law*. Cheltenham: Edward Elgar Publishing Limited.

Student

Enrico Carloni

1 Introduction

'Student' status is deeply linked to the influence exerted on national systems by supranational law and by the law of the European Union (EU). This, in particular, in the sense of the affirmation of a status that is linked to the human person and regardless of nationality, is significant in the face of a fundamental social right. Also, in the sense of the progressive extension of the rights connected to the central core linked to the access of education, being a 'student' requires, in fact, the recognition of a set of rights that sometimes go beyond the relationship with educational institutions.

Another important element is the impact of the European influence on the overall conformation of education systems and, in particular, higher and university education. The need to favour student mobility, which is the main driving force behind the European approach to the subject, entails a tendency towards homogenisation of the education systems, albeit, through 'soft law' processes and with agreements that also see the states protagonists.

This paper analyses the set of rights that currently make up the status of a student in Europe, showing the influence of international rules, the principles enshrined in the European Court of Human Rights (ECHR) and the influence of European treaty law and secondary legislation. Thus, a picture emerges, which is above all the action of the jurisprudence of the courts—in particular, the Court of Justice of the European Union (the Court) and ECHR (collectively referred to as 'the Courts')—to guide the still fragmented but significant construction of a European right to education.

E. Carloni (✉)
Department of Political Science, University of Perugia, Perugia, Italy
e-mail: enrico.carloni@unipg.it

A. Bartolini et al. (eds.), *Dictionary of Statuses within EU Law*,
https://doi.org/10.1007/978-3-030-00554-2_69

2 The Influence of the European System

As with other issues relating to the overall issue of human rights and citizenship, the European student status includes a set of legal situations that are closely intertwined with the recognised rights of individual Member States of the EU. Thus, in preliminary terms, it is necessary to clarify that the legal status of the student consists of a plurality of legal situations, which directly concern access to education (i.e., the so-called 'right to education') and access to a series of facilitations and provisions that make effective the use of the right to education.

They are excluded from a reflection aimed at investigating the status of the 'student' other issues that are also relevant in the construction of the educational system and, therefore, only indirectly address the student, such as the right to set up schools (e.g., with confessional content or in any case with a cultural orientation different from that of public schools), the right to teaching, the autonomy of scholastic and university institutions and the freedom of science and teaching.

In the context of the student status, situations in each case fall considerably different; above all, in relation to the degree of study (and in this field the distinction between basic and compulsory education, higher education, university education) and the type of training (i.e., either school or vocational).

The construction of student status encompasses a series of different issues, but all converge in making possible, on equal and non-discriminatory conditions, the exercise of the right to education within the EU.

3 Protection of the Right to Education at the International Level

A starting point in the reconstruction of the content recognised as a 'student' is given by Article 26 of the Universal Declaration of Human Rights (the Universal Declaration). The incipit of Article 26 is that 'everyone has the right to education'. Moreover, the Universal Declaration represents the legal and political basis of subsequent law acts, such as for education in Article 13 of the International Covenant on Economic, Social and Cultural Rights (1966).

The UN Convention on the Rights of the Child (1989) is also of considerable importance in this context. Article 28 of UN Convention on the Rights of the Child has an essential content that repeats substantially what was already stated in the Universal Declaration and the International Covenant mentioned above: universal access to primary education, obligatory and gratuitousness and equal opportunities in access to secondary education.

In this sense, this right is inseparably linked to the principle of non-discrimination. In Article 2, UN Convention on the Rights of the Child it is established that all the rights enshrined in the UN Convention, including the right to education, must be guaranteed to all children without any discrimination.

However, the right to education is ensured by a series of benefits that are not limited to access to educational institutions only, and it is in this set of performance rights that 'envelop' the intangible core of the right to education that some elements of differentiation can be found that vary between students of the same state, European students, third-country students and asylum seekers.

4 The Rights Provided by the ECHR

The European Convention for the Protection of Human Rights and Fundamental Freedoms (the European Convention) moves on a plan that is not only under international law but also under European law because of the reference made to it in the Treaty on European Union (TEU) (Article 6, para. 2 and 3). This dual value makes the ECHR's forecasts particularly penetrating, thanks to the application made by the European Union Court of Justice and the EU system.

This first period of Article 2 of the Additional Protocol to the ECHR (i.e., 'No person shall be denied the right to education') establishes a right to education as a human right to all persons subject to the jurisdiction of each State, as guaranteed by virtue of Article 1 of the European Convention.

Despite the negative formulation, the provision is certainly suitable to establish a fundamental right. In addition to being entitled 'Right to education', the provision uses the term 'right', and presents a structure of the provision that is similar to that of Articles 2–4, § 1 and 7 of the European Convention ('*Nul ne peut*') and provisions that consecrate the fundamental values of the democratic societies.

In substantial terms, the first sentence of Article 2 of the European Convention consequently gives everyone a right of access to the schools existing at a given time in the Contracting States. Around this essential content, which is not prejudicial to national regulations, an overall status of the student is constructed, which only exceptionally can admit, in the further spheres, differentiation margins.

In essence, in a general article dominated by the first period, the prohibition on 'denying the right to education' implies, for the Contracting States, the duty to grant access to anyone under their jurisdiction, to existing school facilities, as well as the right to be officially recognised as having been completed (case *Kjeldsen and others Busk, Madsen* and *Pedersen v Denmark* (1976) 1 EHRR 711; case *Belgian Linguistic* case (No. 2) (1968) 1 EHRR 252).

5 The Right to Education in the Charter of Rights

Under EU law, Article 14 of the Charter of Fundamental Rights of the EU (the Charter of Rights) guarantees every person the right to education and access to 'vocational and continuing training, which includes free access to compulsory education'.

In general terms, the provision contained in the Charter of Rights establishes an evolutionary path that has led to the progressive emergence and autonomy of the right to education (like other social and fundamental rights). From the previously recognised centrality to the 'economic' perspective, this in particular in terms of freedom of movement and the right not to be discriminated on the basis of nationality. This conceptual framework is superseded by the solemn affirmation of the law but continues to find expression in the competences reserved to the Member States and to the limited role that the EU has in the field of education.

In any case, starting from the Treaty of Maastricht (the Maastricht TEU), we are witnessing an evolutionary path aimed at building a European right to education by virtue of EU law: this was achieved thanks to the introduction of specific powers for the EU in the field of education and the creation of European citizenship.

Despite this, the contents of the student status result predominantly descended from the work of the Courts. In particular, thanks to the Court, provisions of the Treaty (TEU) have been interpreted in the sense of the affirmation of the rights to free movement and non-discrimination of European citizens on the basis of their status as citizens (and, by extension, of students) irrespective of their position as workers.

On this basis, as mentioned above, the responsibility for education and training continues to fall essentially on the Member States. We have seen the definition of the common status of students in Europe, but it matured in fragmentary terms thanks to the Courts' action.

Access to educational institutions does not exhaust the student status, which embraces a series of different situations that concern the student, his family and even matters outside the enjoyment of the school.

In its essential core, the right—although fundamental—is not an absolute right; however, the limits must be foreseeable for the people involved and must pursue a legitimate aim. Thus, in particular, disciplinary measures are permitted, including suspension or expulsion from a teaching establishment, provided that such measures meet the conditions for the permissible limits. To assess whether these forms of exclusion from education involve the denial of the right to education will be considered factors, such as procedural safeguards, the duration of exclusion, attempts to reintegrate and the adequacy of the proposed alternative education (case Ali; case Catan and others).

An implication of the affirmation that educational institutions must be accessible to everyone, without discrimination, is the particular protection granted to students with disabilities. In fact, the Court has also stated that the integration of children with disabilities into ordinary schools should be the norm (case European Action of the Disabled), and the teaching in special schools should be the exception (case Mental Disability Advocacy Center—MDAC). At any way, Member States have to respect the principle of adaptability of education: 'measures to respond to their special needs' (case MDAC).

6 Equality and Differentiation in the Enjoyment of the Right to Education of Foreign Students in the EU

Generally, children of third-country nationals can access state education under the same conditions, while they are not necessarily entitled to enjoy the associated benefits, such as maintenance allowances.

The rights to education of the children of asylum seekers are even weaker: these persons have the right to access the education system of the host State on 'similar' conditions but not necessarily under the same conditions that apply to the citizens of that country (Reception Conditions Directive). Under international law, equal access to education for the children of migrants is recognised by the Convention on the protection of the rights of migrant workers and members of their families (Article 30).

For European citizens, the right to education is part of the rights that make up European citizenship: a condition that normally involves the ineligibility of differentiated treatments among the citizens of the Member States and brings with it, however, spaces reduced differentiation even with reference to third-country nationals.

The Court has interpreted the provisions of the Treaty on the subject of vocational training by determining rights for European students who are on the move. In particular, the Court stated (case Grzelczyk) that European citizenship entails for the citizen-student the right not to be denied on the basis of nationality, a treatment otherwise recognized to the citizens of the Member State.

It is worth mentioning that the Treaty prohibits discrimination on the basis of nationality, and it does not allow direct discrimination (that is, made openly on the basis of nationality or a feature inextricably linked to it), except for the derogations explicitly provided for in the Treaty and interpreted in a way that is very strict by the Court. The hypothesis of indirect discrimination also derives from the prohibition of the Treaty, which occurs when the criteria applied are separable from nationality, but the effect is, however, disproportionate to the detriment of foreign citizens, as in the case of the residence requirement. In these cases, the measure is not radically excluded, but burdens the State to show that the different treatment is based on objective reasons that prescind from nationality and is proportionate and necessary.

These principles find applications on different aspects of the right to education. A specific case of certain interest to the Court, for example, is that of tuition fees, even in the presence of loans or exchanges that help to support them. In general, the benefits to qualify for the right to education must be recognised in non-discriminatory terms in relation to nationals of the Member States (Case Casagrande; case Bernini).

7 The Other Rights Related to Student Status

In the host Member State, the student is eligible for a series of benefits that are related to his status but do not directly relate to the enjoyment of the right to education. These are often services that, although not part of the education service, are often normally relevant in terms of the actual enjoyment of the 'main' right (e.g., for public transport or the availability of accommodation).

These aspects, which belong to a broader concept of the right to education (which can also be defined as the right to study), have found first attention at the European level with reference to the benefits granted to migrant workers and their families. With European citizenship, the question is put in more general terms for all citizens of the EU, regardless of their status as workers, and especially for students. Thus, the principle is fully applied with regard to access to public transport at a reduced price, which cannot be denied to students on grounds of nationality.

In regards to the use of 'maintenance' grants (that is to say, not already to reimburse the costs of education but to contribute to the life costs of the student), we find only a partial application of the principle of non-discrimination. In a ruling, the Court ruled that stock exchanges and maintenance loans also fell within the scope of the Treaty; provided, however, that the relationship between the foreign citizen and the Member State is not only related to the status of a student (Directive 2004/38/EC).

A right that is obviously linked to the status of a student is that of residence. In fact, it is clear that in order to be able to fully enjoy their student status they must be able to reside in the host country. As students of the EU, European citizens and their families have the right to move and reside anywhere in the EU (Directive 2004/38/EC; case Raulin).

Another issue that is linked to the right to education is that of linguistic requirements. In this case, the obligation to prove adequate knowledge of the language of the host country is a possibility left to the Member States, provided that the requisites are proportionate. Therefore, the linguistic competence must be requested in sufficient terms compared to the specific needs, but do not go beyond what is necessary (case Angonese).

One last question related to student status is that of recognition of qualifications. In fact, a specific aspect that concerns, albeit indirectly, the status of a student is that of the right to the certification of the studies carried out and, when it comes to another State (or return to the State of origin), it has the legitimate expectation that this title is recognised. This is an element not secondary from the perspective of the effective guarantee of the right to mobility of students and workers. However, this requirement is confronted with the typical characteristics of each educational system and its variety.

8 European Policies for Student Mobility

The status of the European student depends, only to a limited extent, on secondary legislation and, in particular, on the action of the European Commission (the Commission), which has also been promoting mobility in learning for decades. In particular, it should be noted that the Commission has been promoting, also as a Partner, the 'Bologna Process': an agreement through which the aim was to create a common standard in European high school education.

As part of the 'Europe 2020' strategy, which emphasises learning mobility as a tool to increase the skills of individuals and the EU as a whole, one of the 'flagship initiatives' is that of 'Youth in the move', aimed at increasing the international attractiveness of higher education institutions and raising the quality of all levels of education (e.g., giving young people the opportunity to spend part of their educational path in another Member State).

In particular, in order to facilitate the procedures for the recognition of qualifications, the Commission has also developed several instruments to be used: (1) the 'European Qualifications Framework', which is a system that links the qualifications of different countries to a common European reference framework; (2) the 'Diploma Supplement', which is a document attached to a degree or a diploma with a description of the content and level of studies completed by the student; (3) the 'European Credit Accumulation and Transfer System' (ECTS), which is a system that enables students to collect credits for learning in higher education, based on the learning outcomes and workload of a determined course.

9 Conclusions

The evolution of the right to education as a fundamental right, only exceptionally susceptible to differentiated treatments on the basis of nationality, appears at first glance to be coherent and without contradictions. The sense of evolution clearly goes towards expanding the set of positions that constitute the student status and the homogenisation of the guarantee level, regardless of the student's nationality.

If we shift the view from the individual's right to the system as a whole, however, the picture changes and important contradictions emerge in the evolution of national systems in the European scenario. The reference is, in particular, to the centrality recognised in the Euro-Unit system to economic stability and the balance of public budgets, even with the detriment of the effective capacity of national systems to provide adequate guarantees to fundamental rights.

This, in countries characterised by economic crisis and a high level of indebtedness, produces a new EU social question (de Witte 2013), especially in European areas where the economic-monetary union enters a 'collision course' with the welfare state, which is still entrusted to the responsibility of the national states (Giubboni 2017; Joerges 2011).

In our specific field, a sub-financing of the education system, which inevitably links a reduction in the substantial content of rights, largely ignores nationality. The European law of the crisis shows, in essence, the limits of a jurisprudential approach with respect to a guarantee requirement that demands an answer through policies and adequate investments on the education system as a whole.

References

de Witte, F. (2013). EU law, politics, and the social question. *German Law Journal, 14*(5), 591–612.
Giubboni, S. (2017). Stato sociale e integrazione europea: Una rivisitazione teorica. *Quaderni fiorentini per la storia del pensiero giuridico moderna, 46*(1), 553–586.
Joerges, C. (2011). Will the welfare state survive European integration? On the exhaustion of the legal conceptualisations of the integration project from the foundational period and the search for a new paradigm. *European Journal of Social Law, 2011*(1), 4–19.

Subsidiary Status

David Edward Zammit

1 Introduction

Subsidiary status is a new status which has developed within EU law as an alternative to refugee status for: 'a person who is facing a risk of serious harm in his country of origin and is unable to enjoy the protection of that home country' (Jakuleviciene 2010). This paper explores the way subsidiary status has been constructed in EU law as a way to grant asylum to such persons and explores the implications of this particular approach on the scope and content of subsidiary status. With reference to the Maltese experience, it is shown how while this status initially replaced the pre-existing THP 'Temporary Humanitarian Protection Status', it is often practically assimilated to it, while THP has also been revived, as an inferior form of protection creating dependency.

2 Subsidiary Status in the Qualification Directive

Subsidiary Status was introduced into EU law through the 'Qualification Directive', technically known as Council Directive 2004/83/EC of 29 April 2004; as subsequently 'recast' on the 13th December 2011 by Directive 2011/95/EU; henceforth 'the Directive'. The Directive seeks to harmonise EU law in order to: 'ensure that Member States apply common criteria for the identification of persons genuinely in need of international protection, and, on the other hand, to ensure that a minimum level of benefits is available for these persons in all Member States' (Gil-Bazo 2006).

The Directive represents an attempt at 'minimal harmonisation', which leaves Member States free to offer higher levels of protection should they wish. It seeks to

D. E. Zammit (✉)
Faculty of Laws, University of Malta, Msida, Malta
e-mail: david.zammit@um.edu.mt

A. Bartolini et al. (eds.), *Dictionary of Statuses within EU Law*,
https://doi.org/10.1007/978-3-030-00554-2_70

achieve its objectives mainly through the creation of two EU law statuses: (1) refugee status; meant for those who qualify as refugees under the Refugee Convention[1] and (2) subsidiary status; meant for persons who would not qualify as refugees under this Convention, but who are nonetheless protected from *refoulement* by international human rights law and who fall within the scope of this Directive.

Subsidiary status seeks to cater, through one broadly defined status-category, for a range of protection statuses which, prior to the entry into force of the Directive, had been developed separately by various Member States. These statuses would be granted to applicants who, while not qualifying for recognition as refugees, could not be *refouled* in terms of the obligations these states had assumed under international human rights treaties. Here it is important to keep in mind that Member States always retain a discretion to grant protection to new categories of vulnerable persons who do not qualify either for refugee or subsidiary status. This discretion is based upon the minimal harmonisation aimed at by the Directive; which means that Member States may still grant asylum on humanitarian grounds to some persons who do not even qualify for subsidiary status. Furthermore, the scope of subsidiary status is defined in the Directive such that it does not include all the persons entitled to protection in terms of the relevant human rights treaties; indicating that Member States are obliged, in regard to such persons who do not qualify either for refugee or subsidiary status, to grant protection on a different basis (Gil-Bazo 2006).

3 Subsidiary Status as a Substitute for Asylum

Prior to transposing the Directive, the asylum laws of EU Member States were based upon the Refugee Convention and echoed the prevailing position at international law, that: 'as the United Nations High Commission for Refugees (UNHCR) has insisted, refugee status is not a status that is granted by states; it is rather simply recognized by them' (Hathaway and Foster 2014). Since at international law the right to grant or refuse asylum remains a prerogative of the State (Edwards 2005), the Directive was innovative as it: 'constitutes the first legally binding instrument in Europe of supranational scope that imposes an obligation on states to grant asylum to refugees and other persons in need of protection' (Gil-Bazo 2006). At the same time, the way in which this duty to grant asylum was worded in the Directive is problematic precisely because instead of referring to asylum, the Directive refers to refugee or subsidiary *status*. This wording is:

> unfortunate, as a person is a refugee within the meaning of the 1951 Convention as soon as he fulfils the criteria contained in the definition –regardless of whether his refugee status has been formally determined-something that the Directive itself recognizes. As UNHCR has pointed out, 'the Qualification Directive appears to use the term "refugee status" to

---

[1]The Convention relating to the Status of Refugees (adopted 28 July 1951, entered into force 22 April 1954) 189 UNTS 137 (Refugee Convention) art 33 and Protocol relating to the Status of Refugees (adopted 31 January 1967, entered into force 4 October 1967) 606 UNTS 267, art 2.

mean the set of rights, benefits and obligations that flow from the recognition of a person as a refugee. This second meaning is, in UNHCR'S view, better described by the use of the word "asylum"'. A similar analysis can be made of the protection granted to other persons in need of protection, who don't meet the criteria for the recognition of refugee status. (Gil-Bazo 2006, p. 8).

It is thus clear that the Directive conflates asylum with the granting of refugee or subsidiary *statuses* (Gil-Bazo 2015). In the process it moves away from the orthodox meaning of refugee status within the Refugee Convention as a status which is acquired by fulfilling the criteria of the international definition of refugees, regardless of whether it is *recognized* by the state or not. This new understanding of refugee status introduced by the Directive makes this status appear to be something which it is in the discretion of the Governments of Member States to *grant or withhold;* which is not the case according to the Refugee Convention. It also means that the preferred way by which asylum could be granted according to the Directive to persons who qualify because they could not be refouled according to international human rights law, could only be through the creation of yet another separate and distinct 'subsidiary' *status*. Since this new status is 'subsidiary', there is a tendency—which appears to have no basis in international refugee or human rights law—to consider this status as inferior to refugee status leading to a status-based differentiation between weaker and stronger forms of asylum which reduces the protection afforded to persons possessing the former status.

4 The Restricted Scope of Subsidiary Status

In terms of the Directive, subsidiary status is granted to persons who face a real risk of suffering serious harm if forcibly removed from EU territory. The definition of 'serious harm' encompasses:

1) The death penalty or execution (Art.15(a)); 2) Torture or inhuman or degrading treatment or punishment of the applicant in the country of origin (Art.15(b)); 3) Serious threat to a civilian's life by reason of indiscriminate violence in situations of international or internal armed conflict (Art. 15(c)). (Jakuleviciene 2010)

This codifies the obligations of Member States not to refoule persons at risk which emerge from various international human rights instruments, notably the European Convention on Human Rights, the Convention against Torture and the Charter of Fundamental Rights of the European Union. At the same time, there are various persons at risk of serious violations of their human rights who cannot be forcibly removed from EU territory under international human rights treaties to which Member States are signatory and who do not qualify for subsidiary status. EU nationals, for example, may not apply for subsidiary status because Article 2e) of the Directive only targets third country nationals (TCNs) or stateless persons. Furthermore this category of persons includes persons who were denied status under the Qualification Directive but cannot be returned according to international human rights treaties such as the Convention against Torture and individual asylum seekers who are the victims of 'systematic or generalized violence and human rights violations.' (Jakuleviciene 2010)

Over and above the inherent discretion which states possess to grant asylum on a humanitarian basis to deserving applicants, there is thus a category of persons who do not qualify either for refugee or subsidiary status but who nevertheless cannot be refouled according to international human rights law. Keeping in mind that the Directive is meant to bring about a minimal harmonization in this field and does not abrogate Member States' duties under international human rights treaties they signed, this should not per se be a problem. However the equation established by the Directive between refugee/subsidiary *status* and asylum in EU law has rendered the position of persons who are legally entitled to asylum but nevertheless lack a recognized legal status, extremely problematic in practice. Such persons risk having their entitlement to asylum completely ignored and even if they are not refouled, they may be effectively condemned to a marginal existence, without meaningful recognition or asylum in the Member State which is hosting them.

The principal solution developed by particular Member States to resolve the problematic position of this category of asylum seekers has been to develop new forms of (non-harmonised) protection-statuses at a national level. These statuses can be granted to persons who fall within this category in order to clarify their legal positionality and entitlements. However this is problematic because, apart from fomenting the proliferation of new national statuses leading to 'conceptual confusion' (Haddad 2004) and flatly contradicting the harmonizing aim of the Directive, these new statuses are generally of a humanitarian kind and: 'the situations that these people face must be clearly distinguished from the situations of people applying for asylum on purely compassionate grounds' (Jakuleviciene 2010).

5 'Reduced Rights' as the Content of Subsidiary Status

Since EU law has effectively replaced the unitary concept of asylum with the binary dichotomy of refugee or subsidiary status, it is not surprising that the actual rights which form the content of subsidiary status should be not only distinct from, but also less than those associated with refugee status (Battjes 2007). In 2011 the Recast Directive, which made both statuses part of a broader category of 'beneficiaries of international protection, managed to reduce but not to eliminate this disparity between the rights granted to subsidiary status holders and those of refugee status holders. The content of subsidiary status currently reflects this disparity in that it allows:

5.1 Discriminatory Access to Family Reunification

While Family Reunification is made available to refugees according to the Family Reunification Directive, also known as Council Directive 2003/86/EC of 22 September 2003 on the right to family reunification, Article 3(2)(c) of this Directive specifically excludes holders of Subsidiary Protection from its scope. This has permitted particular Member States to impose particularly stringent requirements, such as requiring a two year period of residency before subsidiary status holders are allowed to accede to family reunification in the German case (Laubach 2016). This disparity appears to lack an objective justification, since: 'the humanitarian protection needs of persons benefiting from subsidiary protection do not differ from those of refugees' (Ecre-Elena 2016). Moreover it appears to violate the principles of equality and non-discrimination enshrined in the EU Charter and the European Convention of Human Rights (Ecre-Elena 2016).

5.2 Discrimination in the Duration of Residence Permits

While Refugees are entitled to receive a renewable residence permit which is valid for at least three years, Subsidiary Protection status recipients 'will receive a renewable residence permit which must be valid for at least one year and, in case of renewal, for at least two years' (ECRE 2013). Again this is a distinction which does not appear to be 'objectively justifiable' (ECRE 2013), since the protection needs of Subsidiary Status holders do not appear to substantially differ from those of Refugees (ECRE 2013).

5.3 Discrimination in Social Welfare Entitlement

The Recast Qualification Directive states that refugee and subsidiary status holders are both in principle entitled to the same social assistance as is provided to its nationals by the hosting Member State. Yet this Directive nevertheless allows Member States to 'limit social assistance granted to beneficiaries of subsidiary protection status to core benefits' (Gil-Bazo 2006).

Various attempts have been made by scholars to find an objective basis for this discriminatory treatment of subsidiary status recipients. Hemme Batjes dedicated an important article to this question (Battjes 2007). After observing that, in terms of these Directives, subsidiary status holders are generally entitled to the same kind of asylum as refugee status holders, he observes that when these Directives were drafted it was expected that subsidiary protection would be utilised in cases of mass influxes and/or that it would be a temporary measure to cater for protection needs shorter in duration than refugee status. In practice, the ways in which the Directive are interpreted and applied by Member-States ensures that Subsidiary Status is not available to cater for situations of mass influx and that recipients are persons who require precisely the same kind of long-term protection given to Refugee status holders. He concludes:

> A balance of interests of the refugee and the host state resulted in the set of refugee benefits in the Refugee Convention and (with slight alterations) in the Qualification Directive. Exactly the same interests are at stake when defining the benefits for subsidiary protection beneficiaries (Battjes 2007).

The 'reduced rights' which characterize subsidiary status in relation to refugee status thus appear to lack an objective legal justification and to have developed on the basis of: (1) the conceptual replacement of asylum by status and (2) the consequent distinction between 'subsidiary' and 'refugee' statuses resulting from the EU's Qualification Directive.

6 Subsidiary Status in Malta

Until 2008 only one kind of intermediate protection status from refugee status existed in Maltese law. This was 'Humanitarian Protection', colloquially known as 'Temporary Humanitarian Protection' or THP; which according to Maltese law: 'constituted special leave to remain in Malta for those persons who did not qualify for Refugee status but could not be returned safely to their country of origin' (European Migration Network 2009). Beyond this, the scope of Humanitarian Protection was at the complete discretion of the Refugee Commissioner who would grant this status both to persons who would subsequently qualify for subsidiary status and to those whom he considered deserved this status on a humanitarian basis (European Migration Network 2009; Zammit 2016). The content of Humanitarian Protection was not legally defined and thus unspecified benefits might or might not be granted at the complete discretion of the Refugee Commissioner (Zammit 2016).

In 2008, the Qualification Directive was transposed into Maltese law, with the result that 52% of the total applicants for asylum were granted Subsidiary status by the Refugee Commissioner; reflecting the situation previously where, in 2007, for example, 65% of applicants were granted Humanitarian Protection (Zammit 2016). To a certain extent, Subsidiary Status simply replaced Humanitarian Protection. However, there are important differences in the scope and content of Subsidiary Status.

Maltese law now reflects the Recast Qualifications Directive, both in terms of the persons entitled to receive subsidiary status and its content. This has created difficulties in granting asylum to persons who deserve protection while not qualifying for subsidiary or refugee status. The solution has been to create other forms of inferior status, on an extra-legal basis, which reflect the previously existing Humanitarian Protection in being national statuses granted and renewed at the complete discretion of the Refugee Commissioner and giving access to an opaque set of benefits instead of legally enforceable rights. These problematic un-harmonised statuses include Temporary Humanitarian Protection (THP), Provisional Humanitarian Protection and Temporary Humanitarian Protection New (THPN) (Zammit 2016).[2] By contrast, Subsidiary Status holders now have access to various legally defined rights instead of benefits. However the flip-side is that the Maltese state has transposed the Directive very restrictively and has not granted any access to family reunification to Subsidiary Status holders. Moreover, Maltese law has restricted their access to social welfare and medical care to undefined 'core benefits and care' (Zammit 2016). In so doing it has also assimilated Subsidiary Protection Status holders to recipients of Humanitarian Protection. In this field the latter, like the former, only have access to opaque 'benefits' instead of legally enforceable rights.

7 Conclusion

This paper has argued, also by referring to the Maltese experience, that while the introduction of Subsidiary Status has helped to harmonise and enhance protection for persons falling within the scope of the Recast Qualifications Directive, it has negatively impacted on those who do not. Moreover, holders of this status are generally treated as second-class refugees and important rights continue to be denied to them by states which have restrictively transposed the Directive.

References

Battjes, H. (2007). Subsidiary protection and reduced rights. In K. Zwaan (Ed.), *Qualification Directive. Central themes, problem issues and practice in selected member states* (pp. 49–59). Nijmegen: Wolf Legal Publishers.

Edwards, A. (2005). Human rights, refugees, and the right 'to enjoy' asylum. *International Journal of Refugee Law, 17*(2), 293–330.

European Council on Refugees and Exiles. (2013). ECRE Information Note on the Directive 2011/95/EU of the European Parliament and of the Council of 13 December 2011 on standards for the qualification of third-country nationals or stateless persons as beneficiaries of international protection, for a uniform status for refugees or for persons eligible for subsidiary protection, and for the content of the protection granted (recast). Retrieved June 28, 2018, from http://www.refworld.org/docid/551922ae4.html

European Legal Network on Asylum (ELENA). (2016). Information note on family reunification for beneficiaries of international protection in Europe. Retrieved June 28, 2018, from http://www.ecre.org/information-note-on-family-reunification-for-beneficiaries-of-international-protectionin-europe/

European Migration Network. (2009). The practice in Malta concerning the granting of non-EU harmonised protection statuses: EMN National Report. Retrieved June 28, 2018,

[2] 'In 2014 Temporary Humanitarian Protection status was awarded to 165 applicants (Zammit 2016).

from https://homeaffairs.gov.mt/en/MHAS-Information/EMN/Documents/EMN%20Non-Harmonised%20forms%20of%20protection%20report%20-%20MT%20.pdf

Gil-Bazo, M. (2006). *Refugee Status, subsidiary protection, and the right to be granted asylum under EC law* (Research paper No. 136). UNHCR, November 2006.

Gil-Bazo, M. (2015). Asylum as a general principle of international law. *International Journal of Refugee Law, 27*(1), 3–28.

Haddad, E. (2004). 'Who is (not) a Refugee?'. EUI Working Paper SPS NO. 2004/6. Retrieved June 28, 2018, from http://cadmus.eui.eu/bitstream/id/1769/sps2004-06.pdf/

Hathaway, J. C., & Foster, M. (2014). *The law of refugee status* (2nd ed.). Cambridge: Cambridge University Press.

Jakuleviciene, J. (2010). Is there a need for an extension of subsidiary protection in the European Union Qualification Directive? *Jurisprudence, 2*(120), 215–232.

Laubach, B. (2016). Subsidiary protection instead of full refugee status complicates family reunification' in *Legal Dialogue,* 24th November 2016. Retrieved June 28, 2018, from https://legal-dialogue.org/subsidiary-protection-instead-full-refugee-status-complicates-family-reunification

Zammit, D. E. (2016). Vernacularising asylum law in Malta. In V. Colcelli & R. Arnold (Eds.), *Europeanization through Private Law Instruments, Series Entwicklung Im Europaischen Recht (Book 6).* Regensburg: Schnell & Steiner.

Taxpayer

Rafael Sanz-Gómez

1 Introduction

The aim of this paper is to analyse how the status of a taxpayer is being conditioned by contemporary EU law. Taxes have been levied since ancient times, but the concept of tax is, of course, a product of its historical evolution. Liberal, bourgeois revolutions linked the statuses of taxpayer and citizen, as can be seen in the motto 'no taxation without representation'. The welfare state created a double vertical relationship, between taxpayers and the state, and between the state and welfare beneficiaries, which is the concrete result of a communitarian principle which is implemented by the state (Santos 2002, p. 47).

The EU does not levy taxes directly (EU resources come from the Member States), and taxation as such is not an EU competence. Nevertheless, the Member States' taxing powers are limited by several parts of the Treaties, such as the tax provisions of Articles 110 to 113 of the Treaty on the Functioning of the European Union (hereinafter, TFEU) regarding indirect taxes, the provisions regarding freedoms of movement, and the state aid regime. Also, according to Articles 113 and 115 TFEU, the Council can enact secondary EU legislation regarding taxation only to the extent that this is necessary to ensure the establishment and the operation of the internal market and to avoid distortion of competition.

R. Sanz-Gómez (✉)
Department of Business Law, Universidad Nacional de Educación a Distancia, Madrid, Spain
e-mail: rafaelsanz@der.uned.es

A. Bartolini et al. (eds.), *Dictionary of Statuses within EU Law*,
https://doi.org/10.1007/978-3-030-00554-2_71

2 National Definitions of a Taxpayer and the Elements of These Definitions

A taxpayer is any person who is liable to tax. General definitions in national or international law are deliberately broad or are just implicit. Each Member State (hereinafter, MS) considers different criteria when designating an individual as a taxpayer. However, as they share a common legal culture, most of the elements concerning the meaning of taxpayer do not change from one country to another. In many MS, a taxpayer is a (tax) debtor,[1] but sometimes this definition overlaps with that of a taxable person or of other persons who have to pay tax on behalf of a taxpayer.[2] A taxpayer can also be described as one of the primary subjects of the legal relationship for tax, the other being the tax administration.[3] Finally, some countries focus on the link between the taxpayer and an activity of the taxpayer, the taxable event.[4] Definitions of the taxpayer for each tax rely on the identification and definition of a taxable event, which is a specific manifestation of the person's ability to pay. The ability to pay principle requires that a taxpayer's burden is fixed according to his or her economic capacity to bear that burden.

The condition of being a taxpayer is traditionally explained as a consequence of a state's power to tax, or the consequence of an obligation to contribute to the tax revenues in order to cover the expenses of the state and ensure its sustainability. A designation as a taxpayer demands a link with the taxing state, usually based on residence or source (or, more rarely, citizenship). The international consensus is that the state of residence is entitled to impose full tax liability, which implies the taxation of the taxpayer's global income. On the other hand, the source state only taxes specific goods or activities under its jurisdiction.

[1] Some examples would be Austria, the Czech Republic, Estonia, Lithuania, Luxembourg, Poland and Portugal.

[2] For example, Germany describes a *Steuerpflichtiger* (which is equivalent to a taxpayer, according to the translation provided by the Language Service of the Federal Ministry of Finance) as 'any person who owes a tax, is liable for a tax, or is obliged to withhold and remit to revenue authorities a tax which is due on behalf of a third party, as well as other obligations' (section 33 of the *Abgabenordnung*, the Fiscal Code of Germany). Also, the Guidelines for a Model for a European Taxpayers' Code—a soft law document published by the European Commission—use 'taxpayer' to mean any person who takes part in tax-related interactions with the administration.

[3] This is specifically the case under Croatian law, but is also the theoretical framework in countries such as Spain or Italy.

[4] In Spain, a taxpayer is a taxable person who performs a taxable event. Other examples are Latvia and, partially, Poland and Slovenia.

3 Definitions of Taxpayer Under EU Positive Law

The word 'taxpayer' appears only once in the Treaties. Article 65 TFEU states that free movement of capital does not prevent the application of national provisions 'which distinguish between taxpayers who are not in the same situation with regard to their place of residence or with regard to the place where their capital is invested'. The TFEU also contains rules regarding indirect taxation and procedures for harmonization through secondary legislation. The fact that secondary tax legislation is enacted by the Council alone has attracted some criticism from national doctrine, as approval of tax laws by the legislature is a classical principle linked to consent on the levy of taxes through representation.

An analysis of ECJ case law shows that the word taxpayer appears in 346 judgments.[5] The frequency of the use of the word varies depending on the subject of the cases. There is no general concept of taxpayer in EU law, and most of the tax Directives do not refer to taxpayers. They make use of concepts such as 'company' or 'taxable person' instead. The ECJ tends to apply secondary law concepts, but 'taxpayer' is used in relation to most of the discrimination issues on non-harmonized matters and when analysing taxpayers' rights or procedural guarantees and principles.

3.1 Direct Taxation Harmonization: Directives Regarding Companies

Council Directives 2011/96/EU (parent–subsidiary), 2003/49/EC (interest and royalties) and 2009/133/EC (cross-border restructuring operations) establish specific tax benefits (exemptions or tax deferrals) in order to promote conditions that are analogous to those of a common market. Their aim is to guarantee tax neutrality for cross-border operations. Council Directive (EU) 2016/1164 (the anti-avoidance tax Directive, or ATAD) compels MSs to create a comprehensive framework of anti-abuse measures, as it was considered that tax avoidance distorts market competition. The personal scope of these four Directives is established on the basis of national legislation.

For example, Directive 2011/96/EU applies to every 'company of a Member State' that takes one of the forms listed in the Directive (taken from national law), that is considered to be resident in a MS according to its tax legislation and double tax conventions, and that is subject to one of the (national) taxes listed in the Directive.

[5] This includes only judgments (not orders or other documents) of the Court of Justice (not the General Court or the Civil Service Tribunal) from 1954 to 30/11/2017. However, in 83 (almost one quarter) of these judgments, the word 'taxpayer' is used not by the ECJ itself, but in national legislation which is quoted; or by the referring national court, in cases of prejudicial questions; or by the parties in the procedure.

Another example is the ATAD. This applies to 'all taxpayers that are subject to corporate tax in one or more Member States'. As 'taxpayer' and 'corporate tax' are not further defined, national concepts will apply. Here, EU legislation operates in a very similar way to double tax conventions: the OECD Model, which constitutes the standard among EU countries, also relies to a large extent on national legislation.[6] An exception is Article 7 ATAD, on controlled foreign company rules, which will apply to 'entities' and not just 'taxpayers'. This includes trusts and partnerships controlled by a taxpayer (Rigaut 2016, p. 501). EU law therefore has an impact on national decisions regarding whether entities without legal personality should be treated as tax transparent or not, which is a traditional tax issue.

3.2 *Indirect Taxation Harmonization: VAT*

Council Directive 2006/112/EC, on VAT, lays down all the fundamentals for this levy. The word 'taxpayer' cannot be found in the English version. The Directive uses the concept of 'taxable person' in Article 9, and 'persons liable for payment of VAT' in Title XI, chapter 1, section 1. The most general definition of a taxpayer is a person who is liable to tax. Articles 192a to 205 of the Directive therefore define the concept of taxpayer for VAT purposes. According to the general rules, a taxpayer is any taxable person carrying out a taxable supply of goods or services, any person making a taxable intra-Community acquisition of goods or any person recognized as liable by the MS of importation.

'Taxable person' is an EU concept that refers to 'any person who, independently, carries out in any place any economic activity, whatever the purpose or results of that activity'. The concept has been described as the subjective element of the tax event (Falcón y Tella 1998, p. 153), but it is also a personal status with relevance for the functioning of the VAT system. There are specific inclusions in the concept and exclusions from it, or authorizations directing the MS to make inclusions or exclusions. The objective of these, whether implicit or explicit, is to avoid tax distortions.

In order to achieve tax neutrality, the tax has to be shifted along the supply chain. Taxable persons therefore have to charge VAT as part of the payment received for the goods or services they provide; they also have a right to deduct the VAT that was charged to them. Even if this sounds paradoxical, in most cases VAT taxable persons are not taxed: they just help to levy the tax. This system has allowed the EU legislator to disregard the link between the taxpayer and the event on which the tax burden falls. This has led to a distinction in some national doctrinal definitions of taxpayer, between legal taxpayers (in VAT, taxable persons) and factual taxpayers (consumers who bear the tax burden).

---

[6] For example, the OECD Convention model applies to 'persons who are residents of one or both of the Contracting States' and 'the States take their stand entirely on the domestic law' (Art. 4 OECD Comm. 2014).

4 Taxpayers as Catalysts for Economic Integration

Individuals are defined as taxpayers—even if this term is not always used—by EU law because they undertake activities that are relevant for the common market. This means that the status of taxpayers in national law is modified (through the enactment of Directives or by ECJ case law) to the extent that, and in the fields in which, their activities are of interest to the common market. As stated above, this is mostly done to guarantee neutral tax treatment. The VAT mechanism, based on a duty to charge the tax and a right to claim a deduction, is one of the best examples.

Does EU law influence ability to pay, which is a core tax principle? Or do national tax principles and EU rules follow parallel lines, which never touch? The ability to pay principle belongs to the constitutional tradition of a majority of MSs.[7] Even though scholars have made several attempts to extract an ability to pay principle from EU Treaties and general principles (Englisch 2014), this principle has not been applied as such by the ECJ. However, European integration has partially modified the traditional juridical definition of taxpayer by altering the scope of the ability to pay principle. The ECJ analyses whether MSs apply this principle without distinction to internal situations and cross-border transactions (Vanistendael 2014, p. 122). This is linked to the ECJ's understanding of national taxpayers as catalysts for economic integration, which confers a new function on them within the EU context.

The consequence has been described as the emergence of a 'status of the EU-based non-resident' which shapes their tax liability (Ruiz Almendral 2008). The landmark *Schumacker* judgment[8] stated that workers who are resident and live in one MS but obtain the major part of their income in another should be treated as residents in the second state. Otherwise, they would not be able to apply their personal allowance or other tax benefits anywhere. The judgment has been criticized because it fails to take into account the welfare benefits received from the state of residence (Chalmers et al. 2006, p. 725), maybe because of the prevalence of the economic element in EU law (social policy is, essentially, a competence of the MS in the terms of Article 5 TFEU).

The critical importance of the *Schumacker* judgment is that it shatters the well-established principle that only residents should be taxed on their global income. Other traditional differences between the income taxation of residents and non-residents have since then been abolished by ECJ jurisprudence, provided that non-residents are residents in some EU state. The non-comparability of the two groups is a traditional assumption in international tax law, but the ECJ has rejected this and forces MSs to justify non-comparability on a case-by-case basis.

As for taxpayers' procedural rights and obligations, in the absence of specific EU rules, Member States can establish their own legal frameworks. When there is an

[7] Ability to pay has been recognized as a constitutionally relevant principle (explicitly or by judicial activism) in 14 of the 28 MSs, while in five more it is an important guiding principle (Englisch 2014). However, 'there is [no] consensus in any form among the Member States on the *implementation* of the principle of the ability to pay in national tax systems' (Vanistendael 2014, p. 121).

[8] Judgment of the Court of 14 February 1995, *Schumacker*, C-279/93, ECLI:EU:C:1995:31.

exercise of taxpayers' rights that derive from an EU source, the procedural rules have to comply with the principles of equivalence and effectiveness. It is interesting to mention that there is EU legislation regarding administrative cooperation which has an impact on taxpayers' status. We will focus on procedures for the exchange of information. This is a complex legal system, in which EU Treaties, secondary legislation, national rules and bilateral agreements between MSs are involved. The definitive adoption of the EU Charter of Fundamental Rights has a key impact, as the implementation of EU law by a MS entails the application of the Charter. In proceedings of this kind, a taxpayer has an obligation to cooperate with the tax authorities provided they comply with the applicable legal requirements. The fundamental right to be heard does not confer either the right to be informed of a request for assistance or the right to take part in the administrative proceedings. Taxpayers are entitled to challenge the legality of a decision, but this does not entail a right to access the whole of the request for information. Taxpayers' status here offers a tension between the need for rights and guarantees, on the one hand, and the exclusion of individuals from proceedings in order to ensure their efficacy, on the other. Some principles or rights—such as proportionality or the protection of private data—might be applicable at any time and the intervention of the taxpayer happens *ex post*.

5 Conclusions

There is no general concept of a taxpayer in EU law. Taxpayers are subjects of EU interest when a cross-border operation with tax implications takes place. From a national perspective, taxpayer status is linked to the ability to pay principle, political representation and belonging to a community. Conversely, EU definitions of taxpayers reflect the competences of the EU in the tax field (promotion of a common market and protection of competence). Hence, the core elements of the national concepts are only indirectly affected by EU law.

The principle of the legality of tax (expressed in the motto 'no taxation without representation') is eroded as a consequence of the transfer of sovereignty to the EU institutions, which results in a loss of law-making powers for national legislatures. Also, secondary tax legislation is enacted by the Council, which does not represent EU citizens directly.

The ability to pay principle is not substantially modified as such, but its scope has become broader as the ECJ does not presume there is non-comparability between residents and non-residents from another MS. The status of the EU non-resident taxpayer has been created, which is one of the most important impacts of the EU on the status of a taxpayer.

Tax Directives create rights and duties for taxpayers, and these are later made concrete by national legislation. To a large extent, the EU relies on national concepts of taxpayers in direct taxation Directives and is much more specific when regulating indirect taxation, which is coherent with the competences recognized in the Treaties and the thoroughness of EU secondary legislation in each case.

The EU's main objective is to ensure that tax regulations are economically neutral, so taxpayers' rights and obligations are formulated and interpreted from this point of view. On the other hand, the status of taxpayers regarding administrative cooperation mechanisms is affected by the need to prevent the individuals from knowing that a procedure affecting them is taking place. However, some rights are also recognized, and the EU Charter has an emerging role in this matter.

References

Chalmers, D., Davies, G., & Monti, G. (2006). *European Union law. Text and materials*. Cambridge: Cambridge University Press.

Englisch, J. (2014). Ability to pay in European tax law. In C. Brokelind (Ed.), *Principles of law: Function, status and impact in EU tax law* (pp. 439–464). Amsterdam: IBFD.

Falcón y Tella, R. (1998). *Introducción al Derecho financiero y tributario de las Comunidades Europeas. Servicio de Publicaciones de la Facultad de Derecho*. Madrid: Universidad Complutense/Civitas.

Rigaut, A. (2016). Anti-Tax Avoidance Directive (2016/1164): New EU policy horizons. *European Taxation, 56*(11), 497–505.

Ruiz Almendral, V. (2008). Entre la discriminación y la armonización: el régimen fiscal del no residente en España a la luz del derecho comunitario. *Revista de Contabilidad y Tributación, 307*(57), 3–68.

Santos, B. S. (2002). *Toward a new legal common sense: Law, globalization, and emancipation*. East Kilbride: LexisNexis Butterworths.

Vanistendael, F. (2014). Ability to Pay in European Community Law. *EC Tax Review, 23*, 121–134.

Teacher

Monica Cocconi

1 The Open Method of Coordination in Education

The process of European integration between national systems is increasingly clear in the field of education, in the absence of a precise conferral of competences. Under Art. 6 TFEU, the Union only acts by supporting and coordinating national policies: 'The Union shall have competence to carry out actions to support, coordinate or supplement the actions of the Member States. The areas of such action shall, at European level, be: … (e) education, vocational training, youth and sport'. The European initiatives in this area, which were first legitimized by the case law of the European Court of Justice, mainly rest on the open method of coordination. This method drives national education systems towards common goals, without undermining their choices on content and organization (Cocconi 2006).

The open method of coordination, designed by the Lisbon Council to extend European integration to non-economic sectors such as education, can be described as a form of soft law. Indeed, the purpose of this process is primarily to assist Member States in the progressive working out of their policies, and to promote autonomous implementation at the national level, within the limits set by the common guidelines.

However, convergence between national administrations is conceived as a side effect of this development. The aim of the results achieved through coordination is only to foster emulation between the Member States, rather than to introduce control at the EU level.

In other words, collaboration between the states aims to identify the practices that are worth adopting, by imitation, by other administrations, as well as to improve the performances of these administrations.

M. Cocconi (✉)
University of Parma – Department of Engineering and Architecture, Parma, Italy
e-mail: monica.cocconi@unipr.it

A. Bartolini et al. (eds.), *Dictionary of Statuses within EU Law*,
https://doi.org/10.1007/978-3-030-00554-2_72

Nevertheless, the method of open coordination might also lead to an improvement in national education systems; in particular, this method could have a positive influence on the subject of this analysis—the status, recruitment and training of teachers (Cortese 2016, p. 151).

2 Absence of the Requirement of Citizenship for Access to the Profession

One of the main goals of the European Union's action in the field of education is to promote the transnational mobility of teachers. This objective has almost been achieved because of the narrow interpretation by the European Court of Justice of the restrictions on the freedom of movement in relation to employment in public administration, under Art. 45(4), TFEU.[1]

In order to promote this mobility, the Court built the concept of public administration on the nature of the duties and responsibilities of civil servants, rather than on whether the system was subject to a public or a private body of law.

Consequently, under Art. 45(4) TFEU, public administrations are those involved in the 'direct or indirect participation in the exercise of powers conferred by public law and duties designed to safeguard the general interests of the State or of other public authorities'. The European Court has held that only these tasks imply the existence of that special relationship of allegiance to the state that forms the foundation of the bond of nationality and hence can set a limit on the exercise of the fundamental freedom of movement.

According to the Court, teaching is not characterized by the exercise of such powers and public responsibilities, and therefore Member States cannot impose a nationality criterion on teachers, under Art. 48(4) TFEU.

3 Fair and Easy Access to Quality Education in Europe

The focus on 'quality education', in order to make students' access to the labour market easier and more flexible, has also legitimized an active role for the EU, albeit through the European method of coordination and cooperation between the states, especially as concerns the recruitment and training of teachers.

In 2002, teachers' professional development was acknowledged by the Commission as a key element of the European education strategy; a Working Group, composed of representatives from the 31 countries participating in the 2010 Work Programme on Education and Training, was set up to identify ways to improve the

[1] See ECJ, 2 July 1996, C-473/93, Commission v Grand Duchy of Luxemburg; C-173/94, Commission v Kingdom of Belgium, C-290/94 Commission v Republic of Greece. Sulla nozione comunitaria di pubblica amministrazione definita dal giudice europeo, see Cassese (1996, p. 915).

training of teachers and educators.[2] In the same year, the Barcelona European Council included the improvement of education and training for teachers and educators among the objectives listed for the improvement of school education systems in the Member States.

Furthermore, in 2007 the Commission underlined the key role of quality teaching and learning in the achievement of the Lisbon objectives of building a European knowledge society.[3] It highlighted the fact that schools have become more autonomous and open learning contexts, and teachers are increasingly accountable for the content, organization and control of the learning process as well as for their personal professional development throughout their careers.

Some scientific studies have highlighted the existence of a positive relationship between the ongoing training of teachers and pupils' achievements.[4]

In national education systems, this connection is enhanced by the greater autonomy of schools, which also ensures more flexibility for teachers in performing their function. On the other hand, autonomy demands more accountability and transparency in the organization and management of education by schools (Eurydice 2008).

At the same time, in order to promote fairer access for European students to education services, which is a key objective of the Union, teachers must focus on diversity and inclusion and meet the specific needs of disadvantaged learners, such as gypsies (travellers) disabled people and migrants.[5] The fact that education plays a leading role in enhancing the Union's social cohesion was reaffirmed by the European Council in March 2006. The European Council also recognized that education and training are crucial to prevent and tackle poverty and social exclusion and discrimination, and to build a foundation on which active citizenship rests. Education and training should thus step up efforts to improve access to quality learning for all. With the Paris Declaration of 17 March 2015, European education ministers called for action at all levels to strengthen the role of education in promoting citizenship, as well as the common values of freedom, tolerance and non-discrimination, in order to strengthen competitiveness and, above all, social cohesion within the European Union.

In 2004, the Council and Commission Joint Report on progress towards the Lisbon Objectives in the fields of Education and Training called for the development of common European principles for the competences and qualifications needed by teachers and trainers.[6]

---

[2] See Communication from the Commission: *Thinking education: Investing in skills to improve socio-economic outcomes,* Strasbourg, 20 November 2012, COM (2012) 669 final, and also the Council Conclusions on *Investing in Skills for Better Socioeconomic Results*, and *Annual Growth Analysis for 2013, March 5, 2013.*

[3] See Communication from the Commission to the European Parliament and the Council, *Improving the quality of teacher education*, COM (2007) 392 final.

[4] See, for example, Darling-Hammond et al. (2005, pp. 16–17, 20).

[5] See Joint Council and Commission *Report on the Implementation of the Strategic Framework for European Co-operation in Education and Training (ET 2020), 2015.*

[6] In November 2006, the Council stated that 'the motivation, skills and competences of teachers, trainers, other teaching staff and guidance and welfare services, as well as the quality of school leadership, are key factors in achieving high quality learning outcomes'.

These principles have been developed on the basis of the experience of teachers and educators across Europe. At EU level, it was agreed that teaching possesses these common characteristics: (1) specific skills are required: all teachers must have at least one degree awarded from a higher education institution; (2) it demands long-life learning: support must be given to teachers in order for them to continue their professional development throughout their careers; (3) teachers are required to exercise mobility, which is a central component of initial and ongoing teacher education programmes; and (4) teaching is a career based on collaboration: teacher training institutions should work in partnership with schools, local actors and professional trainers. These phases have been fundamental in developing a strategy to improve the quality of teacher training in Europe.

4 Reviewing and Strengthening the Professional Profile of All Teacher Professions

The European institutions have invited the Member States to review the effectiveness as well as the academic and pedagogical quality of teacher training, and to introduce coherent and adequate resources for the selection, recruitment, inclusion and professional development of teachers. Member States should draw up a framework outlining the skills and the professional profile of all teachers, including initial and continuing vocational education and training (VET) trainers. For this purpose, most Member States have developed national qualification schemes for teachers, and have linked these to the European Framework (EQF). Directive 2005/36/EC on the recognition of professional qualifications also provides for a legal framework to encourage the professional mobility of teachers.

The European Union also provides some direct initiatives to support these goals. Community programmes, such as Comenius and Erasmus, under the Socrates programme, as well as the Leonardo da Vinci programme, fund projects to promote the development of teachers' skills. At the same time, the Lifelong Learning Programme (2007–2013) supports teachers' mobility and cooperation projects between institutions.[7]

The European Social Fund is also an essential tool for supporting the modernization of education and training systems, including the initial and continuous training of teachers in the Member States.

In addition, long-term global strategies will be needed to select the most suitable candidates for teaching, with different backgrounds and experiences, bearing in mind that the profession suffers from a strong gender prejudice and does not offer attractive career prospects. European institutions also hope for the creation of broader education communities, not limited to teachers themselves but including representatives of civil society and other stakeholders, in order to create a better

[7] Decision No 2006/1720/EC.

climate for creativity and reconciliation between professional and social needs, and to promote students' well-being.

5 Digital Learning

High-quality education also requires teachers to have innovative pedagogical skills and digital tools, as acknowledged in the Communication of the Commission of August 2015.[8] Several Member States have taken initiatives in this area to increase the digital skills of teachers and students, and one third of them have introduced national strategies to encourage the digitalization of education.

Teachers acquire ICT teaching skills through initial training rather than professional development; it is essential to be able to manage the potential of new technologies in teaching, in order to stimulate and engage students. It will be necessary to spread new ways of learning, characterized by customization, participation, the use of digital media, collaboration, bottom-up practices, and the creation of digital content by both the student and the teacher.

Integrating technologies into education is essential for customized and flexible learning. Finally, it is important to introduce large-scale pilot projects in real situations that can define ways, times and places for the effective use of ICT in teaching and in ex post assessment procedures.

6 Investing Public Resources for the Improvement of Teaching

At European level, the recommendation is to preserve, rather than reduce, public investment in school education, especially in the training of teachers; nonetheless, the current economic crisis has forced governments to employ resources carefully, in order to achieve the best possible results. Therefore, the efficient use of public income is needed to recruit and support teachers. However, the European authorities consider that the ongoing training of teachers is a less expensive tool for improving the outcome of exams than lowering the number of students per class or changing the school timetable.

Ensuring that teachers' education is of a high quality is also essential for the effective management of national resources and for obtaining a good quality-on-the-job ratio: about two thirds of the public resources destined for education is absorbed by teachers' salaries (OECD 2005).

[8] COM(2015)408 final.

7 European Law and Teachers' Fixed-Term Contracts

A European Court ruling on the necessity, in national law, of actual reasons being given to justify the repeated renewal of fixed-term contracts for teachers, to prevent any abuse, had a great impact in Italy.[9]

The European Framework Agreement on Fixed-Term Work[10] also applies to teachers, and covers annual leave in public schools. In order to prevent the overuse of fixed-term contracts, the Framework Agreement requires Member States to contemplate some restrictive measures. First of all, it is necessary to indicate the reasons that justify the renewal of a contract, its total maximum duration and the number of renewals. Moreover, in order to ensure the full effectiveness of the Framework Agreement, a fine must be levied if there is overuse; such a measure must be proportionate, effective and dissuasive.

When the EU Court was asked to assess the compatibility of the Italian rules on education with the European Framework Agreement, it acknowledged the existence of an objective basis for the use of fixed-term contracts for the temporary replacement of workers for social policy reasons (sick leave, parental leave, maternity leave and others). This applies particularly in the field of education, since school services need to be organized to ensure a permanent ratio between the number of teachers and the number of students, which depends on a set of factors that it is difficult to foresee and control. Adjustments are necessary because teaching fulfils a fundamental right that is protected under the Italian Constitution; the organization of a school service therefore entails a certain degree of flexibility, which justifies the use of fixed-term contracts.

The existence of such reasons, however, was not sufficient for the European Court to rule that the use of fixed-term contracts was consistent with the Framework Agreement, because fixed-term contracts must also be used to meet temporary rather than long-term needs.

The uncertainty of the date of appointment of teachers and the absence of a fixed deadline for the organization of competitive exams are factors that make recruitment uncertain and therefore do not ensure that the application of objective reasons is in line with the European Framework Agreement.

---

[9] CJEU, C-22/13, C-61/13, C-63/13, C-418/13, Raffaella Mascolo and others v Ministero dell'istruzione, dell'Università e della Ricerca.

[10] Framework agreement on fixed-term contracts concluded on 18 March 1999 between the general cross-industry organisations (ETUC, UNICE and CEEP) and the Commission, attached to Council Directive 1999/70/EC.

8 Conclusions

The status of a teacher is not directly regulated under EU law, as the Union does not have specific competences in the field of education but only coordinates and supports the actions of the Member States. However, despite the protection of the freedom of movement, states can restrict access to this profession to their own citizens. In addition, with the European Quality of Learning Objective, the Union has promoted higher standards for teachers' recruitment and training, including updating this to the new digital technologies and enhancing the professional profile of teachers. Finally, the European Court of Justice has ruled against abuse in the renewal of teachers' fixed-term contracts, because this breaches the European Framework Agreement.

References

Cassese, S. (1996). La nozione comunitaria di pubblica amministrazione. *Gior. dir. amm.*, p. 10 ff.

Cocconi, M. (2006). *Il diritto europeo dell'istruzione. Oltre l'integrazione dei mercati.* Milano: Giuffrè.

Cortese, F. (2016). Education between European law and national law. In L. Ferrara & D. Sorace (Eds.), *Cultural unity and pluralism.* Florence: Florence University Press.

Darling-Hammond, L., Holtzman, D. J., Gatlin, S. J., & Heilig, J. V. (2005). Does teacher preparation matter? Evidence on teacher certification. Teach for America, and teacher effectiveness. *Education Policy Analysis Archives, 13*(42), 1–51.

Eurydice. (2008). *Teachers responsibility and autonomy in Europe.* Brussels: European Commission.

OECD. (2005). Teachers matter: Attracting, developing and retaining effective teachers. http://www.oecd.org/education/school/34990905.pdf

Technology Transfer Professional

Valentina Colcelli

1 Introduction

The European Union, starting with the Lisbon Strategy, has assigned a crucial role to the circulation and use of ideas between public research organisations, including universities and research centres, and industries.

The European Union has qualified itself as a "knowledge-based society". As a "knowledge-based society", research (the production of knowledge), education (the sharing of knowledge) and innovation (which transforms research and education into development) are the core of the whole European integration process (Cippitani and Gatt 2009).

Thus, knowledge transfer from the research sector to other sectors is one of the goals of the European Union's policies. This link has been highlighted since 2006 in the White Paper on Growth, Competitiveness, and Employment: The European Union adopted a broad-based innovation strategy aimed at improving the framework conditions for research and innovation (Keeling 2006).

In 2007, the European Research Area (ERA) began to be realised by the Green Paper on ERA (European Commission, "The European Research Area: New Perspective", Green Paper 4 April 2007). During 2008, through self-assessment exercises, the EU Council reaffirmed "the importance of strengthening scientific and technological bases across Europe and developing its competitiveness in pursuit of sustainable development including protection of the environment, and satisfying the needs of its citizens, by achieving a European Research Area (ERA) in which researchers, scientific knowledge, and technology circulate freely" (conclusions to the 2020 Vision for the European Research Area). There was a renewed emphasis on innovation and the close linkage between research and exploitation which was proposed in Horizon 2020.

V. Colcelli (✉)
National Research Council, IFAC Institute, Sesto Fiorentino, Firenze, 50019, Italy
e-mail: valentina.colcelli@cnr.it

A. Bartolini et al. (eds.), *Dictionary of Statuses within EU Law*,
https://doi.org/10.1007/978-3-030-00554-2_73

In any case, we must underline how after years "from its official formalisation, the ERA still suffered from problems due to the fragmentation of activities which remained a prevailing characteristic of the European public research base" (Adunmo 2011). Nevertheless, the framework, as mentioned above, has a broad influence on how universities and centres of research or enterprises try to assign themselves a new function in the Internal Market to face globalisation (Bozeman and Boardman 2013).

The European Union policy on technology transfer from universities and/or research centres to enterprise must also be analysed in light of Article 101 of the Treaty on the Functioning of the European Union (TFEU), which prohibits anti-competitive agreements and practices. In this framework, the European Commission adopted Regulation (EU) No 316/2014 on 21 March 2014 for the assessment of technology transfer agreements (and guidelines), through which a licensor permits a licensee to exploit patents, know-how or software for the production of goods and services.

The above-mentioned Regulation should cover only technology transfer agreements "between a licensor and a licensee, even if the agreement contains conditions relating to more than one level of trade, for instance, requiring the licensee to set up a particular distribution system and specifying the obligations the licensee must or may impose on resellers of the products produced under the licence" (Regulation (EU) No 316/2014, Whereas n. 6). At the same time, the Regulation applies "where the licensor permits the licensee and one or more of its sub-contractors to exploit the licensed technology rights, possibly after further research and development by the licensee and its sub-contractors, for the purpose of producing goods or services" (Regulation (EU) No 316/2014, Whereas n. 7).

In any case, "agreements on the joint execution of research work or the joint development of the results of the research, up to but not including the stage of industrial application, generally do not fall within the scope of Article 101(1) of the Treaty" (Regulation (EU) No 1217/2010, Whereas n. 5). These agreements are covered by Commission Regulation (EU) No 1217/2010.

The field of application of Regulation (EU) No 316/2014 is the litmus test for understanding the ways in which technology transfer activity works. To speak correctly about the relationships among universities and research centres and enterprises, we must consider that Regulation n. 316/2014 should not apply to licenses in the context of research and development, that is, cooperation contracts or agreements on the joint execution of research work or the joint development of the results of the investigation, up to but not including the stage of industrial application (Regulation (EU) No 1217/2010 Whereas n. 6).

The contracts/agreements mentioned directly above are widespread in a quite broad meaning of technology transfers among universities and research centres and enterprises. This consideration permits a short introduction on what a technology transfer is and how it works, sometimes based on a technology transfer agreement between a licensor and a licensee. Thus, starting from here, we can approach the definition of the status of a Technology Transfer Professional (TTP), which is deeply conditioned by contemporary EU law.

2 Mechanisms Enabling Technology or Knowledge Transfers

On the economic analysis side, there are two mechanisms enabling technology or knowledge transfers: market-based technology transfers in which knowledge is licensed or waves overpayment, and non-market technology transfers in which knowledge spills over across space and time and can be taken as a free lunch (Minniti and Venturini 2017). The transferred technology shall be innovative for the recipient.

Thus, promoting technology transfer means the circulation of goods (trade), the circulation of productive capital (FDI), and the circulation of ideas (patent and technology licenses), but also people's mobility across jobs and places, i.e., cities, regions, or nations (labour mobility and migration) (Minniti and Venturini 2017).

So, when people move from one firm to another, from one country to another, they bring their prior experience and knowledge to the new firm. This produces a valuable market for talented workers and innovators. Song et al. (2003) documented that labour mobility is more likely to result in interim knowledge transfer when the hired workers possess technological expertise distant from that of the hiring firm. In particular, learning-by-hiring can be useful when the hired workers are used to explore technologically distant knowledge rather than to reinforce existing expertise (Minniti and Venturini 2017).

In this sense, it is relevant to underline how the European Union policy on technology transfer covers a quite broad range of instruments to try to reach its goal of building the ERA. Thus, the researchers or workers involved in project H2020 such as Rise, during its "secondments", also realise a transfer of technology from universities to firms.

Technological transfer is a process which can be formally accomplished through the more traditional tools provided by a legal system, such as contracts and IPR rules, but—as we stated—also informally ("Learning by Doing" and "Learning from Others") (Polanyi 1990, pp. 135–136).

Seen in this context, the main EU funding programmes and the actors involved in their management (i.e., European Commission General Directions, Specialised Agencies) highlight how each of them contributes to promoting and enhancing the EU policy for research, innovation and technological transfer. The EU programmes and initiatives support the technology transfer and provide detailed insight into the role of universities and research entities within EU projects and initiatives aimed at promoting technological transfers.

In any case, we can say that the patenting system can also accommodate both purposes (more private innovation, more public knowledge). Usually, governments are interested in promoting innovation by granting adequate returns to innovators and, meanwhile, the innovation spreads through the society and the economy, thus prompting further innovation (Minniti and Venturini 2017). In general, it is not easy to handle both interests. Technological transfers more appropriately work in the field of the circulation of ideas: Ideas, patents and licensed technologies allow the acquisition of technical information about new products or production processes.

Knowledge transfers that materialise through employing patent documents do not rely on any physical conduit. In contrast to patents, firms may try to protect their innovation by secrecy.

So, in light of the European Union policy on research, innovation and technological transfer, "technology transfer is deemed to have been achieved once a licensing agreement, a joint venture agreement, a manufacturing agreement, and a commercial agreement with technical assistance has been signed" (Glossary T | Ipr Helpdesk, n.d., retrieved from https://www.iprhelpdesk.eu/glossary/T and https://ec.europa.eu/jrc/communities/community/tto-circle-community).

So, in the academic field as well, agreements in the area of Research and Development (R&D), to be qualified as technology transfer agreements, must concern the licensing of technology rights through investing in start-ups, the creation of spin-offs having high technological content and innovative business projects, not only in their technical aspects, but also through direct interactions with entrepreneurs and the identification of the selection criteria for business projects in which to invest.

Licensing sometimes occurs in the context of agreements such as R&D agreements, and usually, they include "scenarios where one party merely finances the research and development activities of another party. (….)" (Regulation (EU) No 1217/2010 Whereas n. 9) or "the joint exploitation of results can be considered as the natural consequence of joint research and development" (Regulation (EU) No 1217/2010, Whereas n. 9).

In any case, such agreements must "improve economic efficiency and be pro-competitive as they can reduce duplication of research and development, strengthen the incentive for the initial research and development, spur incremental innovation, facilitate diffusion and generate product market competition" (Regulation (EU) No 1217/2010, Whereas n. 4).

3 European Knowledge Transfer Offices (KTOs)

European Knowledge Transfer Offices (KTOs), or more generally, the Technology Transfer Offices (TTO), manage the knowledge transfer process. Their main activities are the protection of the research results, technology and market assessment, and promotion and commercialisation. With respect to their operating models, they are usually part of the university as an own unit, directly reporting to the rectorate. However, it could be a separate unit of the university that is a dedicated company owned by the university or service unit shared with other R&D organisations, which means a partnership with private third party(ies) (Private-Public-Partnership) (Conti et al. 2011).

In the case of the EU, "most European Knowledge Transfer Offices are young, with more than half, established after 2000. Furthermore, more than half have fewer than five employees. These results suggest that most KTOs in Europe are still developing their experience and capabilities by managing the IP produced by their affiliated university or research institute" (European Knowledge Transfer Report 2013—[pdf Document], n.d., retrieved from https://vdocuments.site/documents/european-knowledge-transfer-report-2013.html, p. 10).

At the same time, in European universities or research centres, business preparation for researchers or professors have not preparation in this field. In fact, from the point of view of the institutions generating knowledge, the problem of skills consists essentially in ensuring an adequate standard of skills among the research staff at all levels, and mainly among researchers at the initial stage of their training (such as scholarship holders and PhD students) who will become professional researchers in the public or private sector. This framework should involve learning and technology transfer through education.

So, despite the framework drawn by Regulation (EU) No 1217/2010, which takes into consideration transfer channels not based on IP/patents, but according to common understanding and Regulation n. 316/2014, a Knowledge Transfer Office realises its goal if knowledge is licensed or waves overpayment.

KTOs role in transfers not based on IP/patents is a difficult one. In an institutional IP ownership regime, KTOs are the guardians of this IP. However, their role in other transfer channels is limited: R&D collaborations, contract research, and consultancy services are fully within the responsibility of faculty and staff, and KTOs can do little to support them, except for influencing the framework conditions (…..). About start-ups, KTOs have few tools and means to influence as well: first of all, fostering entrepreneurial spirit and generating an entrepreneurial culture are institutional, regional or even national tasks and heavily influenced by other systems outside higher education and public research. Incubators and other supportive infrastructure are of little use without a steady flow of academic entrepreneurs. Second, as parts of the university administration, KTOs are not really close to the business sector themselves (which many try to remedy by outsourcing their start-up support activities). Third, for one of the most pressing problems of start-ups and academic entrepreneurship, the provision of seed and venture capital, PROs usually lack instruments and resources (European Knowledge Transfer Report 2013—Slideshare, n.d., retrieved from https://www.slideshare.net/UNU-MERIT-PRESS-OFFICE/european-knowledge-transfer-re, p. 10).

4 Dealing with the Definition of Technology Transfer Professionals' Status

Technology transfer activity is carried out in a firm or a university/research centre by the TTO/ KTO, or the TTP could be a professional. In any case, the TTP is a worker participant in the construction of the Internal Market related to EU society, which has tried to define itself as knowledge-based.

In particular, on the academic side, the TTP acts as the manager, f.i., of the relationships with all the stakeholders of the entire technological transfer cycle and enhances the scientific work outcomes having an industrial interest by intervening in the whole process from the identification of a need which triggers certain scientific research, to the development of application projects, until the achievement of innovative outcomes which, properly protected, can be transferred to industrial applications. Therefore, the expert for technology transfers for university/research centres facilitates and carries out the intermediation, which is peculiar to technological transfer entities, between scientific interests, entrepreneurial ones and the institutional system of reference (Conti et al. 2011).

Amalya and Adi (2017, p. 36) remembered that “over the past 35 years, the commercialization of academic research has become an increasingly prominent aspect of university activity. The participation of universities in technology transfer (TT) endeavours, mainly through patenting and licensing of research results, serves as an important trigger for a re-evaluation of the nature of the profession of academic scientists”.

TTP status could be defined starting from the definition born in US law. As matter of fact, “[a]s the market for patents has grown faster in the United States and Japan than within the European Union (EU) over the last 30 years (OECD, 2010), it is not surprising that previous explorative studies of IP intermediaries focused on specific areas in the United States, such as Silicon Valley and the Boston Route and Tokyo in Japan” (Benassi et al. 2012).

So, the TTP is an intermediary between the technology suppliers and users in the specific area of the European Union, according to its mission to create a knowledge society, and the Technology Transfer Professional could be considered an individual status that is conditioned by contemporary EU law.

Because a TTP is an intermediary that is well known in the US market, and the latter is not a creation that is completely new for the European Union market, the communitarian vision of its market has contributed to defining and implementing this kind of work. As a matter of fact, starting from the consideration made in par. 1, it is possible to understand how the European Union’s legal system impacts on the qualifications of Technology Transfer Professionals and how the new functions assigned to European universities in the Internal Market to face globalisation have contributed to reinforcing and defining this economic status in the European Union. A TTP links three notions that are very relevant in the European Union’s structure: the worker/professional, the internal market and the knowledge-based society (Conti et al. 2011).

We must remember that the European Union’s policy on support for research activities and technology transfers—and especially on technology transfer agreements and similar concerted practices—cannot be relegated to business around patents. Nevertheless, in spite of the broad definition of technology transfer activities, which is not solely referred to business activities to transfer patents, in the EU legal system, it is also necessary to remember that the main dissemination channel of knowledge is through licensing. Regarding the European Technology Transfer Offices circle—launched in 2011—a technology transfer is deemed to have been achieved “once a licensing agreement, a joint venture agreement, a manufacturing agreement, and a commercial agreement with technical assistance has been signed”

(Glossary T | Ipr Helpdesk, n.d., retrieved from https://www.iprhelpdesk.eu/glossary/T and https://ec.europa.eu/jrc/communities/community/tto-circle-community). Therefore, the TTP is an intermediary between technology suppliers and users who deals with ready-to-use technologies or technologies which have already been patented. They facilitate and carry out the intermediation, which is peculiar to technological transfer entities, between scientific interests, entrepreneurial interests and the institutional system of reference. They are specialised workers, and they are faced with the management and matching of European universities and business cooperation (Carayol 2003), as well as the interactions between HEIs and businesses for mutual benefit (Davey et al. 2011).

Only organisations whose TTP can assist their clients right up to the signature of an agreement can be included in the definition of the status, to the exclusion of those who provide only contact or information services.

Thus, the TTP certification guaranteeing the international recognition of the competence of practitioners in the European Union Internal Market was born (see EuKTS or ASTP-Proton).[1]

References

Adunmo, K. A. (2011). The European Research Area (ERA): Science, knowledge, research & innovation. Towards Europe 2020. *Diritto e processo*, 9–38.

Amalya, L. O., & Adi, S. (2017). Shifts in the organization and profession of academic science: The impact of IPR and technology transfer. *Journal of Professions and Organization, 4*(1), 36–54.

Benassi, M., D'Angelo, A., & Guido Geenen, G. (2012). IP intermediaries in Europe: A web content analysis. *Industry and Innovation, Taylor & Francis Journals, 19*(4), 307–325.

Bozeman, B., & Boardman, C. (2013). Academic faculty in university research centers: Neither capitalism's slaves nor teaching fugitives. *The Journal of Higher Education, 84*(1), 88–120.

Carayol, N. (2003). Objectives, agreements and matching in science–industry collaborations: Reassembling the pieces of the puzzle. *Research Policy, 32*(6), 887–908.

Cippitani, R., & Gatt, S. (2009). Legal developments and problems of the Bologna Process within the European higher education area and European integration. *Higher Education in Europe*, 385–397.

Conti, G., Granieri, M., & Piccaluga, A. (2011). *La Gestione del Trasferimento Tecnologico. Strategie, Modelli e Strumenti*. Milano: Springer.

Davey, T., Baaken, T., Galán-Muros, V., & Meerman, A. (2011). *Study on the cooperation between higher education institutions and public and private organisations in Europe*. Brussels, Belgium: European Commission, DG Education and Culture.

[1]ASTP-Proton is a non-profit organisation committed to knowledge transfers between universities and industry, and the Association of European Science and Technology Transfer Professionals (ASTP) is the European professional association for knowledge transfer (KT) (https://www.astp-proton.eu); EuKTS is an international non-profit association which has been established to support the development of knowledge transfers (KT) by increasing the standards, recognition, education, training and mobility of knowledge and technology transfer professionals across Europe and beyond (http://www.eukts.eu).

European Commission. (2007). The European research area: New perspective (Green Paper 4 April 2007).

European Knowledge Transfer Report. (2013). [pdf Document]. Retrieved from https://vdocuments.site/documents/european-knowledge-transfer-report-2013.html

Glossary T | Ipr Helpdesk. (n.d.). Retrieved from https://www.iprhelpdesk.eu/glossary/T and https://ec.europa.eu/jrc/communities/community/tto-circle-community

Keeling, R. (2006). The Bologna Process and the Lisbon Research Agenda: The European Commission's expanding role in higher education discourse. *European Journal of Education*.

Minniti, A., & Venturini, F. (2017). The long-run growth effects of R&D policy. *Research Policy, 46*(1), 316–326.

Polanyi, M. (1990). *La conoscenza personale. Verso una filosofia post-critica*. Milano: Rusconi.

Song, J., Almeida, P., & Wu, G. (2003). Learning-by-hiring: When is mobility more likely to facilitate interfirm knowledge transfer? *Management Science, 49*, 351–365.

Third Country National

Ibtisam Sadegh

1 Third Country Nationals in European Union Law

1.1 Creation and Regulation

The 1992 Maastricht Treaty was the first to introduce citizenship of the EU, which was later extended by the Treaty of Amsterdam. The Treaty on the Functioning of the European Union (TFEU) established that every person holding the nationality of a member state shall be a citizen of the union. EU nationals as citizens of the member states are afforded rights, freedoms and legal protections by EU law, which are conferred on all citizens of the union.[1] As a primary and individual right, citizens of the union enjoy freedom of movement; the right to move and reside freely within the territory of the member states. This right is extended to the European Economic Area (EEA)[2] and, through a series of bilateral agreements, to Swiss citizens.[3] Freedom of movement is one of EU's 'four economic freedoms', together with free movement of goods, services, and labour and capital, which allow nationals of an EEA country to reside and work in another member state on the same conditions as its own citizens.

The formation of the EU and the granting of freedom of movement to nationals of the member states, has created the individual status of TCNs; individuals who are not nationals of the EEA and Switzerland and are hence, excluded from freedom of

[1] European Union citizenship is additional to, and does not replace, national citizenship.

[2] Iceland, Liechtenstein and Norway are the only EEA member states outside the EU.

[3] Switzerland is the only EFTA member state which is not simultaneously also a member of the EEA.

I. Sadegh (✉)
Department of Anthropology, Faculty of Social and Behavioural Sciences,
University of Amsterdam, Amsterdam, The Netherlands
e-mail: I.Sadegh@uva.nl

A. Bartolini et al. (eds.), *Dictionary of Statuses within EU Law*,
https://doi.org/10.1007/978-3-030-00554-2_74

movement. The individual status of TCN was initially constructed as the flipside of EU laws and agreements produced a dichotomy between individuals who are union citizens and those who are nationals of states which are 'outsiders' in relation to the EU, EEA and European Free Trade Association (EFTA) agreements. As a result of the continual process of defining and redefining the EU borders and concomitant negotiations with EEA and EFTA member states, the EU (re)configures and (re)defines the individual status of EU nationals and TCNs. The scope and meaning of the status of TCN is in fact dependent on this process.[4]

The EU has also passed numerous directives that expressly recognise and in the process, regulate this individual status;[5] particularly laws dealing with TCNs' entry to and movement within the EEA member states.[6]

1.2 *Residence and Freedom of Movement*

EU legislation regulates TCNs' residence and mobility within the EU; TCNs already residing within the EU are granted preferential treatment over TCNs who are entering the EU for the first time. For instance, Directive 2003/109EC provides that TCNs who are long-term EU residents, may apply for permission to reside in a second member state after they have acquired long-term residence status in the first member state. And, Directive 2009/50/EC, which concerns highly skilled workers, establishes that once they obtain a Blue Card[7] in the first member state of residence, they may be allowed, after 18 months, to move to a second member state. Nevertheless, a second Blue Card in the second member state must be applied for and they must meet the same conditions that were required in the first member state. Similarly, *inter alia*, Directive 2005/71/EC and Directive 2004/114/EC target TCN researchers and students respectively and Directive 2014/36/EU establishes the conditions of entry and stay of TCNs for the purpose of employment as seasonal workers.

All directives allow member states considerable discretion in setting the requirements that must be met by TCNs in order to move and reside in a second member state, albeit being allowed to reside in the previous member state. When TCNs stay in the EU for longer than three months and their status does not fall within any of the established EU laws, such as the abovementioned regulating their position by virtue of their activities, national immigration rules apply. Consequently, some

[4] For instance, the entry of Croatia as the 28th member state means that Croatians no longer have the status of TCNs as they did pre-2013.

[5] Example, *inter alia,* Directive 2003/109/EC concerns the status of TCNs who are long-term residents.

[6] The EU also has funds for the 'Integration of Third Country Nationals' which aim at promoting the European Agenda for TCNs legally residing in the EU.

[7] A Blue Card is a work permit granted to highly-educated skilled workers to stay and work in a member state.

member states allow free entry and certain exemptions to TCNs possessing valid work permits or residence statuses in the member states of previous residence, other member states offer a facilitated process, whilst others require full, new applications satisfying all the requirements despite the valid permit issued by the member state of previous residence. In all cases, TCNs must go through national immigration procedures. In a nutshell, their mobility rights and freedom of movement are restricted.

1.3 *Family Members of Union Citizens*

Directive 2004/38/EC establishes freedom of movement and residence within the territory of the member states to all union citizens. The European Parliament and Council, clearly with the intention of securing full freedom of movement for union citizens, have extended this right to TCNs who are family members of union citizens. The subtitle of the directive provides that its provisions have 'EEA relevance', hence, it applies to all citizens of the EEA states as well as their TCN family members. TCNs, generally excluded from the enjoyment of freedom of movement, enjoy freedom of movement inasmuch as they are 'family members' of EEA citizens as defined under Article 2 of the directive.[8]

In the important case of *Metock v. Minister of Justice Equality and Law Reform*, the European Court of Justice (ECJ), interpreting the extension of freedom of movement to family members of union citizens, decided that TCN family members could enjoy freedom of movement even if they had previously been in EU territory without a legal status.[9] The ECJ ruled that member states cannot impose additional conditions to the directive. In accordance with the treaty, movement may be restricted on the grounds of public policy, public security or public health. Moreover, Article 3(1) of the directive establishes that its provisions apply only to those family members that fall within the abovementioned definition, who either accompany union citizens or move in order to join them.

The directive establishes that whilst union citizens can practice freedom of movement by making use of either a passport or an identity card, their TCN family members must possess valid passports in order to leave their EU country of residence. Moreover, on entry into the territory of a member state, TCNs who are family members of union citizens are not exempt from observing the visa requirements established by Regulation (EC) No 539/2001, which lists which TCNs must possess

[8] Being, (a) the spouse; (b) the partner with whom the union citizen has contracted a registered partnership, on the basis of the legislation of a member state, if the legislation of the host member state treats registered partnerships as equivalent to marriage and in accordance with the conditions laid down in the relevant legislation of the host member state; (c) the direct descendants who are under the age of 21 or are dependents and those of the spouse or partner as defined in point (b); and, (d) the dependent direct relatives in the ascending line and those of the spouse or partner as defined in point (b).

[9] C-127/08.

a visa when crossing the union's external border. The difference between TCNs who are and who are not family members of union citizens is that the former must possess a valid visa to enter EU territory, but will subsequently be exempted from visa requirements if they possess a valid residence card showing that they are family members of union citizens.

In conclusion, the individual status of TCN does not transmit absolute freedom of movement; nor is the freedom granted self-sustainable. It is clear that TCNs are not the main interest of the directive; the main purpose of the directive is to promote, facilitate and implement full free movement of all union citizens, and hence indirectly, in the process, rights were given to family members of union citizens who fall under the definition imposed by the directive. TCNs' freedom of movement is strongly correlated with the movement of the related union citizens. As a result, the directive does not apply to movements of TCNs which are not connected with the movements of the union citizens' family members; any rights conferred to the status of TCNs are rights derived from the exercise of freedom of movement of union citizens.

2 Third Country Nationals in Malta

2.1 Entry, Residence and Citizenship

Since Malta is a union territory, TCNs' entry is regulated by visa requirements based on Regulation (EC) No 539/2001; however, the precise entry requirements differ from one TCN to another on the basis of his or her nationality and diplomatic relations between the country of nationality and Malta. As already established, the issue of residence and work permits, and mobility rights when TCNs move to Malta from another member state, is generally regulated by EU legislation. In cases where TCNs' activities are not covered by any of the established EU legislation, their position is regulated by national legislation; national laws merely fill in the gaps permitted and left by EU directives. In the Maltese context, in alignment with the foregoing analysis, there are various transformations which occur to an individual who acquires a lawful status; new rights and duties are made contingent to acquiring a status of a lawful residency. TCNs who successfully obtain Maltese citizenship also acquire lawful residency, however the principal vehicle of obtaining citizenship is through marriage; access to which is itself, as will be shown below, dependent upon proof of a lawful status in Malta.

There are three possible routes for TCNs to obtain Maltese citizenship, which are: (1) citizenship through naturalisation. This takes place when TCNs, who have long-term residency status in Malta, successfully apply for and obtain citizenship after legally residing for a minimum of five consecutive years in Malta prior to the date of application. However, this route relies heavily upon the discretion of the Minister and entails satisfaction of national requirements. (2) Citizenship through the Individual Investor Programme; applicants who satisfy the criteria must, *inter alia*, pay 650,000 Euros to obtain a Maltese passport.[10] (3) Citizenship by contracting with a Maltese citizen a recognised marriage acquiring civil effects; this is the main route availed of by TCNs which neither involves large monetary investments nor depends heavily on Ministerial discretion (Zammit 2012, pp. 28–29). Married TCNs must supply proof of continuous residency in Malta with the Maltese spouse for at least five consecutive years following the celebration of a civil marriage.

2.2 *Right to Marry*

The ECHR was the first legal instrument to give effect to certain rights established in the Universal Declaration of Human Rights (UDHR), by making such rights, inter alia the right to marry, binding in Europe. The right to marry prescribed under Article 12 of the ECHR is drafted differently to Article 16 of the UDHR; allowing for some restrictions by national laws and raising questions on the extent of the margin of appreciation enjoyed by member states in relation to this right.[11] However, from early days, the right to marry has been described as fundamental, and numerous legal opinions and judgements have clearly provided that only limited scope is afforded to national laws to restrict its exercise (Harris et al. 2014).

In the Maltese Constitution of 1964, the right to marry is not specified as a fundamental right and Malta only formally recognised and bound itself to protect the right to marry upon ratifying the ECHR in 1967. Moreover, as the convention did not form part of ordinary Maltese law, it was only through the enactment of the European Convention Act 1987[12] that the protection of the right to marry was clearly extended to individuals as part of Maltese law.[13]

The Marriage Act of 1975 regulates the formalities, restrictions, validity and annulment of civil marriages in Malta, as well as giving civil effects to canonical marriages and other religious marriages celebrated according to the rites or usages of any religion or denomination recognised for the purpose of the same act.[14] One of the essential formalities of the Marriage Act is that the celebration of the marriage must be preceded by the publication of banns of matrimony by the Marriage Registrar. For the Marriage Registrar to proceed with the publication of banns, the

[10] TCNs who apply for the Individual Investor Programme must also buy a property worth at least 350,000 Euros or rent a property for 16,000 Euros per year and make an investment in stocks or bonds for 150,000 Euros.

[11] Article 12 of the ECHR: Men and women of marriageable age have the right to marry and to found a family, according to the national laws governing the exercise of this right.

[12] Act XIV of 1987.

[13] In the case *Raymond Gilford v. Hon. Prime Minister et al.* decided by the Maltese, First Hall, Civil Court on 22 April, 1997, the Court held that for the first time, in 1987, the right to marry was included as a fundamental right under Maltese law.

[14] In practice, only Church marriages produce the same civil effects as civil marriages.

registrar requests the birth certificates of the parties to be married and a declaration on oath made and signed by each of them stating that to their best of knowledge and belief there is no legal impediment to the marriage or other lawful cause why this should not take place.

Perhaps, due to marriage being the principal route by which TCNs can acquire a status to reside long-term in Malta and/or due to pressures by EU bodies to protect the Schengen borders,[15] the Marriage Registrar, relatively close to Malta's accession into EU,[16] included an additional prerequisite for the publication of banns, which does not materialise from the Marriage Act. The registrar demands proof of a valid status in Malta from each of the prospective spouses. Whilst EU nationals enjoy freedom of movement in Malta as EU territory, TCNs must prove their valid status to the registrar. The Marriage Registrar may thus justify his refusal to publish the banns merely on the basis that a TCN's prospective spouse possesses an expired visa or residence permit and is therefore illegally in Malta, even if the other prospective spouse is a Maltese or an EU national. There are various cases of rejected asylum seekers whose request for publication of marriage banns was rejected on the basis of their lack of legal status in Malta.[17]

Maltese courts have supported the Marriage Registrar's request that the applicants, for the publication of marriage banns, must have a valid legal status in Malta.[18] In the case of Ogunyemi and Sandra, involving a Nigerian man and a German woman, the court explicitly decided that the requirement of a valid status does not breach the fundamental human right to marry of TCNs. The judge held that the registrar's request for proof of a valid visa because Ogunyemi is a third party national, 'does not mean that the very essence of the right is being impaired'.[19] The court decided that the right to marry of both parties was still substantively respected by Maltese laws and policy even if the parties could not exercise such a right in Malta due to the parties not fulfilling the established conditions. The court highlighted that the applicants could always access their right to marry elsewhere by entering a contract of marriage in Germany or a third country.

Hence, TCNs in Malta often face a catch-22 situation as regards marriage and legal status; a recognised marriage is a principal means for a TCN to obtain a regular residence status in Malta but an irregular presence also prevents access to a recognised marriage. Ultimately, when such a scenario of refusal to publish the banns by the registrar involves transnational marriages between EU nationals and TCNs,

[15] Malta, located in the South of Europe, is the desired destination of many asylum seekers who try to reach EU territory from Libya, by crossing by boat across the Mediterranean Sea.

[16] Malta joined the EU in 2004.

[17] See Ombudsman. (August 2009). *The Right of Immigrants to Marry* (Case no. 28). Office of the Ombudsman Malta.

[18] See *Desira and Eltarhuni v. Director of the Public Registry et al.* decided by the First Hall, Civil Court on 24 February 2012 and *Dr Shields and Dong Mei v. the Attorney General and Marriage Registrar et al.* decided by the First Hall, Civil Court on 15 April 2015.

[19] *Ogunyemi Kehinde Olusegum and Sandra Wetterich v. Director of the Public Registry and the Attorney General* decided by the First Hall, Civil Court on 4 May 2010.

there is arguably a breach of the right to marry of the TCN as well as of the partner, national of an EU member state.

3 Conclusion

The specificity of the individual status of TCNs in EU law must be understood against the background of European citizenship, as in many ways the status of TCN still stands as that of a 'non-status' (Dal Lago 2009) being defined in negative terms as the status of those who do not qualify as citizens of the union. The various European legislations subsequently regulating the status of TCNs remain somewhat overshadowed by this starting point. Thus, the emergence of the status of TCN on the European stage mainly took the form of an afterthought, insofar as the need was subsequently felt to regulate the status of non-union citizens. The resulting status remains one which in many ways deprives the holders of rights, rather than creating new forms of legal entitlement.

European law has however granted certain rights and duties to postulated categories of TCNs who are defined by virtue of: (a) their proximity to EU citizens, i.e. EU citizens' family members as defined by EU law and influenced by national legislation in regards to registered partnerships; (b) the duration of their legal residence within the EU; and/or (c) their participation in specific fields of activities which are in themselves regulated by EU law. Hence, EU law grants rights to TCNs either directly by virtue of legislation aiming to regulate TCN status within the territory of the union or indirectly, in that TCNs receive subordinate rights which are auxiliary and an indirect consequence to the rights granted to union citizens. In fact, there is a strong interplay between EU nationals' and TCNs' rights and freedoms; the clear intention behind granting freedom of movement to TCNs, who are family members of EU citizens, is to fully secure freedom of movement to union citizens. However, the definition of 'family members' is restrictive and excludes *inter alia* future family members; i.e. TCNs and EU nationals who wish to contract marriage or a registered partnership where the host member state treats registered partnerships as equivalent to marriage.

Focusing on the right to marry of TCNs in the member state of Malta brings to fore the strong link between marriage and legal status, particularly within the European context. The interrelationship between TCNs' rights to marry and to exercise freedom of movement as well as the constraints which condition their access to such rights, provides a deeper understanding of the juridical implications of EU law on the individual status of TCN as a 'non-status'. As the Maltese courts reiterate quoting EU laws, when a TCN entering Malta from outside the EU attempts to access certain rights, he or she is required to show a valid status through a visa or some form of special permit. Specifically, in Malta the requirement of proving a valid status by TCNs who request the publication of marriage banns in order to contract marriage, illustrates that TCNs are perceived as 'outsiders' who can only access their right to marry once their status in Malta is regularised. Paradoxically, whilst marriage continues to be the principal route of acquiring a valid Maltese residence status, a valid status is a crucial requirement necessary to contract marriage in Malta.

In the last decade, Malta, like many other European countries, started to impose more restrictions on migration. Whilst Directive 2004/38/EC extends freedom of movement to TCNs who are already family members of union citizens, fortified by the extensive interpretation by the ECJ in the Metock case, the same cannot be said of individuals forming mixed couples composed of a union citizen and a TCN, who are still in the process of contracting marriage. Until these individuals marry or enter into a registered partnership (where the host member state treats registered partnerships as equivalent to marriage), they do not fall under the directive's narrow understanding of 'family member'. In practice, EU citizens' fundamental right to marry is completely ignored when it comes to granting them access to their right to marry TCNs; which is ironical considering that the aim of EU law is to fully secure freedom of movement for EU citizens. This can only be understood in the current European political context, where national rules concerning migration, citizenship and legal status have become ever more restrictive, and the fundamental right to marry is given a secondary position, particularly in regard to TCNs due to its implications for their freedom of movement once they come to be acknowledged as family members of union citizens. Thus, TCN status can serve to allow the discriminatory exercise of national laws to exclude TCNs, and in the process, undermine other EU laws which seek to guarantee all EU citizens access to their rights.

References

Dal Lago, A. (2009). *Non-persons: The exclusion of migrants in a global society*. Vimodrone: IPOC.

Harris, D., O'Boyle, M., Bates, E., & Buckley, C. (2014). In Harris, O'Boyle, & Warbrick (Eds.), *Law of the European convention on human rights*. Oxford: Oxford University Press.

Zammit, D. (2012). Consultative assessment on the integration of third country nationals. *International Organization of Migration*, 28–29.

Transgender Person

Anna Camilla Visconti

1 Gender Identity and Transgenderism: An Introduction

In order to understand the concept of gender identity, it is important to distinguish between the notions of 'sex' and 'gender'. While 'sex' primarily refers to the biological differences between women and men, 'gender' also includes the social aspects of the differences between genders (Martina 2017, p. 19). The notion of 'gender identity' suggests that the sex assigned to an infant at birth does not correspond to the innate gender identity the child develops when he or she grows up; it refers to each person's deeply felt internal and individual experience of gender, which may or may not correspond with the sex assigned at birth, and includes the personal sense of the body and other expressions of gender (i.e. gender expression) such as dress, speech and mannerisms.

The term *transgenderism* is an umbrella term for transvestites, transsexuals and transgenderists, who move between the sexes and genders and do not necessarily insist on specific medical treatment; they may have cross-sexual hormone treatment, but do not undergo gender reassignment therapy (Lorenzetti 2013, pp. 19–20; Currah 2006, pp. 3–31; Toukers 2011, pp. 134–139).

The British sociologists Richard Ekins and Dave King (Ekins and King 2006) have differentiated between four types of transgenderism, the first one being the traditional transsexual who exclusively wants to be transformed from male to female (*MtF*) or vice versa (*FtM*) in terms of role behaviour, bodily outfit and legal recognition. The second type oscillates between variably long phases of living as a male or a female. A third type negates the gender dichotomy and wants to belong to neither category, neither male nor female, but to an alternative third sex and gender. Finally,

A. C. Visconti (✉)
University "G. d'Annunzio" Chieti-Pescara, Department of Legal and Social Sciences, Pescara, Italy
e-mail: annacamilla.visconti@unich.it

A. Bartolini et al. (eds.), *Dictionary of Statuses within EU Law*,
https://doi.org/10.1007/978-3-030-00554-2_75

there is a fourth type, one that wants to escape sex and gender categories altogether (*gender queer*).

It was only in 1980 that the diagnosis of *Transsexualism* was included in the Diagnostic and Statistical Manual of Mental Disorders of the American Psychiatric Association (DSM) and it was used only in the DSM-III (1980) and the DSM-III-R (1987). In the DSM-IV (1994), *Transsexualism* was replaced by the diagnosis *Gender Identity Disorder*, and in the fifth edition of the DSM (DSM-5), published in May 2013, this diagnosis was replaced by the less stigmatising diagnosis of *Gender Dysphoria* (Vitelli et al. 2013, pp. 221–243; Kettenis et al. 2013, pp. 901–914; Zito and Valerio 2012, pp. 153–169).

The diagnosis *Transsexualism* was dropped from the DSM because it was considered to be too closely linked to hormonal and surgical sex reassignment, and did not sufficiently reflect the needs of all those persons suffering from transgender problems, many of whom did not wish to undergo the full range of surgical treatments that transsexuals would usually want to receive (Pfäfflin 2015, pp. 19–23; Ruppin and Pfäfflin 2015; Vitale 2001, pp. 121–141).

2 EU and International Framework on Gender Identity

The European Commission and several Council of Europe bodies have supported policy-driven research on transgender persons (Antonino 2016, p. 305). More specifically, through its Recommendation CM/Rec (2010)5, which was made to member states to specify measures to combat discrimination on grounds of sexual orientation or gender identity, adopted on 31 March 2010, the Council of Europe's Committee of Ministers stressed the need to collect and analyse relevant data to monitor and redress any direct or indirect discrimination on the grounds of gender identity. The recommendation even recognises that specific action is required in order to ensure the full enjoyment of the human rights in transgender persons.

In 2010, Equinet, the European network of equality bodies, published a report on the work of equality bodies in promoting equality for, and combating discrimination against, trans people at EU Member State level.

The European Parliament Resolution of 4 February 2014 on the EU Roadmap against homophobia and discrimination on grounds of sexual orientation and gender identity [PT_TA(2014)0062] is certainly meaningful; however, it found issue with (1) Recommendation CM/Rec(2010)5, (2) the EU Charter of Fundamental Rights, (3) the guidelines to promote and protect the enjoyment of all human rights by lesbian, gay, bisexual, transgender and intersex (LGBTI) persons, which were adopted by the Council of the European Union in 24 June 2013, and (4) the results of the European Union lesbian, gay, bisexual and transgender survey carried out by the Agency for Fundamental Rights (FRA). Furthermore, the resolution called on the Commission, member states and relevant agencies to work jointly on a comprehensive multiannual policy to protect the fundamental rights of LGBTI people, in addition to an action plan featuring, among other things, general provisions in the field of non-discrimination and actions specific to transgender and intersex persons.

In 2007, as part of a large scale international effort to promote international standards on sexual orientation and gender identity, a group of distinguished experts in international human rights law published the *Yogyakarta Principles on the Application of Human Rights Law in Relation to Sexual Orientation and Gender Identity.*

The Commissioner for Human Rights has endorsed the *Yogyakarta Principles* and considers them as an important tool to identify the obligations of states to respect, protect and fulfill the human rights of all persons, regardless of their gender identity [*Human Rights and Gender Identity*, CommDH/IssuePaper(2009)2]. Accordingly, in the issue paper cited "*Human Rights and Gender Identity*", the Commissioner for Human Rights of the Council of Europe adopted a stance against legally recognising the gender identity of transgender persons without them undergoing irreversible sterilisation surgery.

This principle is significant, given that sex reassignment surgery is usually the prerequisite of legally recognising the patient's preferred gender. In a small number of European countries there is no requirement to undergo hormonal treatment or surgery of any kind in order to obtain official recognition of the preferred gender, such as in Spain (ley 3/2007) and the United Kingdom (Gender Recognition Act, 2004). Nevertheless, in most Council of Europe member states, the individual has to demonstrate that (s)he has followed a medically supervised process of gender reassignment; that (s)he has been rendered surgically irreversibly infertile (sterilisation), and/or that (s)he has undergone other medical procedures, such as hormonal treatment; such requirements clearly run counter to the respect for the physical integrity of the person. To require sterilisation or other surgery as a prerequisite to enjoy legal recognition of one's preferred gender ignores the fact that, while such operations are often desired by trans persons, this is not always the case (Venturelli 2008, p. 752).

In Resolution 1728 (2010), adopted in April 2010, on the topic of discrimination on the basis of sexual orientation and gender identity, the Parliamentary Assembly of the Council of Europe called on member states to address some important issues, such as, among others, (1) "*ensure that the fundamental rights of LGBT people … are respected, in line with international human rights standards*"; (2) "*adopt and implement anti-discrimination legislation which includes sexual orientation and gender identity among the prohibited grounds for discrimination, as well as sanctions for infringements*" and (3) "*ensure in legislation and in practice their right to official documents that reflect an individual's preferred gender identity, without any prior obligation to undergo sterilisation or other medical procedures such as sex reassignment surgery and hormonal therapy*".

In this respect, Resolution 2048 (2015) on discrimination against transgender people in Europe, adopted by the Parliamentary Assembly on 22 April 2015, is certainly highly relevant. The resolution calls on the member states, among other things, to abolish sterilisation and other compulsory medical treatment, as well as a mental health diagnosis, as a necessary legal requirement to recognise a person's gender identity in laws regulating the procedure for changing a name and registered gender.

Furthermore, it is worth noting *The Yogyakarta Principles Plus 10* (YP + 10) were recently adopted on 10 November 2017. They are additional principles and state obligations on the application of international human rights law in relation to sexual orientation, gender identity, gender expression and sex characteristics and aim to document and elaborate the developments made since the original 29 Yogyakarta Principles were adopted in 2006.

3 Jurisprudence on Gender Identity

The European Court of Justice (ECJ) and the European Court of Human Rights (ECtHR) have pronounced significant judgments related to gender identity (Trucco 2003, pp. 371–383).

In particular, the ECJ's jurisprudence has outlined the way to open the door for the inclusion of trans people under EU gender equality legislation. Nevertheless, since the landmark case of *P. v. S. and Cornwall Country Council* (ECJ, case C-13/94), the ECJ's judgments (among others, such as *K. B. v. National Health Service Pensions Agency*, 2004, case C-117/01 and *Sarah Margaret Richards v. Secretary of State for Work and Pensions*, 2006, case C-423/04) concern cases of *MtF* or *FtM* gender reassignment. Therefore, the ECJ has not considered the needs of all those persons suffering from transgender problems, some of whom do not wish to undergo the full surgical intervention treatments that transsexuals generally want to receive. There is no precise reason not to extend the protection from discrimination to cover cross dressers or transvestites, people who live permanently in the gender 'opposite' to that on their birth certificate without any medical intervention. Protection from discrimination on grounds of gender identity, should, in fact, encompass not only transsexuals, but include cross dressers and transvestites.

As regards the ECtHR's jurisprudence, the Court has led the way in the progressive recognition of gender identity issues. From an initial closure phase (see, *Rees v. the United Kingdom*, 17 October 1986 and *Cossey v. the United Kingdom*, 27 September 1990), the ECtHR has embraced a more extensive approach (see, *case of B. v. France*, 1992; *Christine Goodwin v. the United Kingdom*, 2002; *Van Kück v. Germany*, 2003; *Grant v. the United Kingdom*, 2006; *L. v. Lithuania*, 2007; *Schlumpf v. Switzerland*, 2009; *Y.Y. v. Turkey*, 2015). Since the case *B. v. France* and, particularly, the leading case of *Christine Goodwin v. the United Kingdom*, the Court has, in fact, recognised the applicability of the Article 8, "right to respect for private and family life", of the Convention to significant cases related to trans persons' human rights issues, finding the violation of the provision in view of an international trend in favour of increased social acceptance of transsexuals and of legal recognition of the new sexual identity of post-operative transsexuals.

With specific regard to transgender persons, the recent *case of A. P. Garçon and Nicot v. France* (judgment 6 April 2017) should be noted; this case concerned three transgender persons of French nationality who wished to change the entries concerning their sex and their forenames on their birth certificates, and who were not allowed to do so by the courts in the respondent state.

The Court recalled its settled case law related to applicability of Article 8 of the Convention to trans people (see *Van Kück v. Germany*, § 69, 12 June 2003; *Schlumpf v. Switzerland*, § 77, 8 January 2009; and *Y.Y. v. Turkey*, § 56, 10 March 2015). The Court ruled that the concept of private life:

> includes not only a person's physical and psychological integrity, but can sometimes also embrace aspects of an individual's physical and social identity. Elements such as gender identity or identification, names, sexual orientation and sexual life fall within the personal sphere protected by Article 8 of the Convention (see *A. P. Garçon and Nicot v. France*, § 92).

The Court argued that the right to respect for private life under Article 8 of the Convention fully applies to gender identity, as a component of personal identity, and that it includes the right to self-determination, of which the freedom to define one's sexual identity is one of the most basic essentials.

With the present judgment, the Court commented again on states' procedures for the gender identity recognition and affirmed that recognising of transgender persons' gender identity subject to sterilisation surgery or treatment amounts to fully exercising their right to respect for their private life under Article 8, conditional on their relinquishing full exercise of their right to respect for their physical integrity as protected by Articles 3 and 8 of the Convention. Particularly, the Court reiterates its finding in *Y.Y. v. Turkey* to the effect that due respect for the physical integrity of the applicant (a transgender person whose request to undergo gender reassignment surgery was refused on the grounds that he had not demonstrated that he was permanently unable to procreate) precluded any obligation for him to undergo treatment resulting in permanent infertility. (see *A. P. Garçon and Nicot v. France*, §§ 131 and 133)

As stated previously, not all persons affected by gender dysphoria wish to, or can, undergo surgical treatments. Since sterilisation concerns an essential human bodily function, it has implications for multiple aspects of an individual's integrity, including their physical and mental well-being and their emotional, spiritual and family life (Whittle 2002). Accordingly, the obligation to undergo sterilisation surgery or treatment in order to have one's gender identity recognised amounts to a violation of Article 8 of the Convention.

4 Conclusions

In conclusion and in view of the above, the legal situation for transgender people varies widely across Europe. The document entitled "Trans Rights Europe Map, 2016", published on 22 April 2016 by the non-governmental organisation Transgender Europe, highlights the existence of three categories of countries. In the first category, no provision at all is made for official recognition; this is in clear breach of established jurisprudence of the ECtHR, as mentioned above. In the second and smaller category of countries, there is no requirement to undergo hormonal and/or surgical treatment in order to obtain official recognition of the preferred gender. The third category of countries, comprising most Council of Europe member states, requires sterilisation in gender identity recognition.

However, some of the problems that transgender people encounter have been acknowledged and good practices are increasing. A recent example of good practice is the *Gender Identity, Gender Expression and Sex Characteristics Act*, adopted by the Maltese Parliament in April 2015, which constitutes a milestone in EU framework on gender identity. The law establishes the right to recognition of a person's gender identity on official documents without the legal prerequisite of surgical and/or hormonal treatments or a mental health diagnosis. With the same aim, on July 15th 2015, the Irish Government passed the *Gender Recognition Act*, which provides a process enabling trans people to achieve full legal recognition of their preferred gender; on 17 June 2016, Norway passed a law allowing the change of legal gender solely based on self-determination.

The recent legal developments, thus, highlight a positive trend emerging in Europe in recent years toward abolishing forced sterilisation driven by developments in the understanding of transgenderism. In this perspective, European and international institutional actors involved in the promotion and defence of human rights have played a central role in favour of abolishing the sterility criterion, which they regard as an infringement of fundamental rights, in order to a better protection of transgender persons' fundamental rights.

References

Antonino, A. (2016). Il controverso itinerario dell'identità di genere. *Nuova Giur. Civ., 2*, 305–317.

Currah, P. (2006). Gender pluralisms under the transgender umbrella. In P. Currah, R. M. Juang, & S. Price Minter (Eds.), *Transgender rights* (pp. 3–31). Minneapolis: University of Minnesota Press.

Ekins, R., & King, D. (2006). *The transgender phenomenon*. London, United Kingdom: Sage.

Kettenis, J., Drescher, H., Meyer-Bahlburg, H., Pfäfflin, F., & Womack, W. (2013). Memo outlining evidence for change for Gender Identity Disorder in the DSM-5. *Archives of Sexual Behavior, 42*, 901–914.

Lorenzetti, A. (2013). *Diritti in transito. La condizione giuridica delle persone transessuali*. Milano, Italy: Franco Angeli.

Martina, L. P. (2017). *La prospettiva di genere. Un processo di normativizzazione politica mondiale*. Roma, Italy: Aracne editore.

Pfäfflin, F. (2015). Transgenderism and transsexuality: Medical and psychological viewpoints. In J. M. Scherpe (Ed.), *The legal status of transsexual and transgender persons* (pp. 12–23). Cambridge, United Kingdom: Intersentia.

Ruppin, U., & Pfäfflin, F. (2015). Long-term follow-up of adults with Gender Identity Disorder. *Archives of Sexual Behavior*. https://doi.org/10.1007/s10508-014-0453-5.

Toukers, K. (2011). Transgendering: Challenging the normal. In S. Seideman, N. Fischer, & C. Meeks (Eds.), *Introducing the new sexualities studies* (pp. 134–139). New York: Routledge.

Trucco, L. (2003). Il Transessualismo nella giurisprudenza della Corte Europea dei Diritti dell'Uomo alla luce del diritto comparato. *Dir. pubbl. comp. eur., 1*, 371–383.

Venturelli, A. (2008). Volontarietà e terapeuticità del mutamento dell'identità sessuale. *Rass. Dir. Civ., 3*, 732–783.
Vitale, A. M. (2001). Implications of being dysphoric: A development review. *Gender and Psychoanalysis. An Interdisciplinary Journal, 6*, 121–141.
Vitelli, R., Fazzari, P., & Valerio, P. (2013). Le varianti di genere e la loro iscrizione nell'orizzonte del sapere medico-scientifico: la varianza di genere è un disturbo mentale? Ma cos'è poi un disturbo mentale? In F. Corbisiero (Ed.), *Comunità omossessuali. Le scienze sociali sulla popolazione LGBT* (pp. 221–243). Milano, Italy: Franco Angeli.
Whittle, S. (2002). *Respect and equality, transsexual and transgender rights*. London, United Kingdom: Cavendish.
Zito, E., & Valerio, P. (2012). Le identità sessuali tra discorso clinico e discorso sociale. In R. Vitelli & P. Valerio (Eds.), *Sesso e genere: uno sguardo tra storia e nuove prospettive* (pp. 153–169). Napoli, Italy: Liguori editore.

Transsexual Person

Anna Camilla Visconti

1 Gender Identity and Transsexualism

In order to understand the concept of gender identity, it is important to distinguish between the notions of sex and gender. While sex primarily refers to the biological differences between women and men, gender includes the social aspects of the differences between genders, in addition to the biological elements (Martina 2017, p. 19). The notion of gender identity offers the opportunity to understand that the sex assigned to an infant at birth might not correspond with the innate gender identity the child develops when he or she grows up. It refers to each person's deeply felt internal and individual experience of gender, which may or may not correspond with the sex assigned at birth, and includes the personal sense of the body and other expressions of gender (i.e. gender expression), such as dress, speech and mannerisms.

The term *Transsexualism* was coined by Magnus Hirschfeld in the early 1900s to distinguish transsexualism from transvestitism and intersexual status (Hirschfeld 1910). In 1949, the term was again used by David O. Cauldwell in *Psychopathia Transexualis* to define the clinical picture characterised by a person's refusal of their biological sex. Finally, the term was used by Harry Benjamin in *The Transsexual Phenomenon* in 1966 (Benjamin 1968, p. 57 ff.).

It was only in 1980 that the diagnosis of *Transsexualism* was included in the Diagnostic and Statistical Manual of Mental Disorders of the American Psychiatric Association (DSM) as a psychosexual disorder (Celesti 1968, p. 175 ff.; Gerini et al. 2009, p. 236); this was used in the DSM-III (1980) and the DSM-III-R (1987). In the DSM-IV (1994), the term was replaced by the diagnosis *Gender Identity Disorder*, and in the fifth edition of the DSM (DSM-5), published in May 2013, this

A. C. Visconti (✉)
University "G. d'Annunzio" Chieti-Pescara, Department of Legal and Social Sciences, Pescara, Italy
e-mail: annacamilla.visconti@unich.it

A. Bartolini et al. (eds.), *Dictionary of Statuses within EU Law*,
https://doi.org/10.1007/978-3-030-00554-2_76

diagnosis was itself replaced by the less stigmatising diagnosis *Gender Dysphoria* (Vitelli et al. 2013, pp. 221–243; Vitelli et al. 2006, p. 281 ff.; Zito and Valerio 2012, pp. 153–169; Ruppin and Pfäfflin 2015; Pezzini 1984, p. 461 ff.; Vitale 2001, pp. 121–141).

Transsexualism is an alteration of the sexual instinct where an individual feels they belong to a sex that does not correspond with their biological sex and so they wish to undergo surgical treatment (Lorè and Martini 1988; Stanzione 1992, p. 874 ff.; Vecchi 1994, p. 9 ff.). These are the characterising symptoms of this particular kind of gender dysphoria; the second symptom marks the difference between transsexual and transgender. Both terms describe a person with the external genitalia and secondary sexual characteristics of one sex, but whose personal identification and psychosocial configuration is that of the opposite sex. Nevertheless, while a transgender person does not necessarily insist on specific medical treatment, the term transsexual means a person—affected by gender dysphoria—who is undergoing, intending to undergo or has undergone a medical operation resulting in gender reassignment (Pfäfflin 2015). These persons are indicated as transsexuals and are either *MtF* (*Male to Female*) or *FtM* (*Female to Male*) (Lorenzetti 2013, p. 20).

2 EU and International Legal Framework on Gender Identity

The legal status of transsexual persons has been widely conditioned by EU and international law. Gender identity issues have been addressed by directives, resolutions and recommendations and the EU Charter of Fundamental Rights, as well as by the jurisprudence of the European Court of Justice and the European Court of Human Rights (Antonino 2016, p. 305).

In 1989, the Parliamentary Assembly of the Council of Europe adopted a Recommendation on the Condition of Transsexuals [Recommendation 1117 (1989)]; the European Parliament issued a Resolution on Discrimination Against Transsexuals which called on EU member states to take steps to protect transsexual persons and to pass legislation to further this end.

The directive 2006/54/EC of the European Parliament and of the Council of 5 July 2006 on the implementation of the principle of equal opportunities and equal treatment of men and women in matters of employment and occupation (recast) includes discrimination arising from the gender reassignment of a person. In effect, the introduction of the so-called *Gender Recast Directive* replaced a series of EU Directives introduced and implemented by member states over the previous three decades, and constituted the foundation of the framework for the equal treatment of men and women within the EU.

Significantly, Recital 3 of the Preamble of this directive introduced an explicit reference to discrimination on the basis of gender reassignment for the first time in EU law. Gender identity was, in fact, not explicitly included in EU law until the

Gender Recast Directive. One of the reasons for this was that gender identity was not included in the list of grounds of discrimination in EU Treaties. Instead, as described in subsection 2.1, the source for the inclusion was a 1996 decision by the ECJ whereby the Court interpreted the ground of sex to cover gender reassignment.

In 2007, as part of a large scale international effort to promote international standards on sexual orientation and gender identity, a group of distinguished experts in international human rights law published the *Yogyakarta Principles on the Application of Human Rights Law in Relation to Sexual Orientation and Gender Identity*. The Commissioner for Human Rights endorsed the Yogyakarta Principles and considered them to be an important tool when identifying the obligations of states to respect, protect and fulfil the human rights of all persons, regardless of their gender identity [*Human Rights and Gender Identity*, CommDH/IssuePaper(2009)2].

On 31 March 2010, the Committee of Ministers of the Council of Europe adopted Recommendation CM/Rec (2010)5, which introduced measures to combat discrimination on the grounds of sexual orientation or gender identity; stating that "*[m] ember states should take appropriate measures to guarantee the full legal recognition of a person's gender reassignment in all areas of life, in particular by making possible the change of name and gender in official documents in a quick, transparent and accessible way*".

The European Parliament Resolution of 4 February 2014 on the EU Roadmap against homophobia and discrimination on grounds of sexual orientation and gender identity [PT_TA(2014)0062] is certainly meaningful; however, it found issue with (1) Recommendation CM/Rec(2010)5, (2) the EU Charter of Fundamental Rights, (3) the guidelines to promote and protect the enjoyment of all human rights by lesbian, gay, bisexual, transgender and intersex (LGBTI) persons, which were adopted by the Council of the European Union in June 2013, and (4) the results of the European Union lesbian, gay, bisexual and transgender survey carried out by the Agency for Fundamental Rights (FRA). Furthermore, the resolution called on the Commission, member states and relevant agencies to work jointly on a comprehensive multiannual policy to protect the fundamental rights of LGBTI people, in addition to an action plan featuring, among other things, general provisions in the field of non-discrimination and actions specific to transgender and intersex persons.

In Resolution 1728 (2010), adopted in April 2010, on the topic of discrimination on the basis of sexual orientation and gender identity, the Parliamentary Assembly of the Council of Europe called on member states to address some important issues, such as, among others, (1) "*ensure that the fundamental rights of LGBT people … are respected, in line with international human rights standards*"; (2) "*adopt and implement anti-discrimination legislation which includes sexual orientation and gender identity among the prohibited grounds for discrimination, as well as sanctions for infringements*" and (3) "*ensure in legislation and in practice their right to official documents that reflect an individual's preferred gender identity, without any prior obligation to undergo sterilisation or other medical procedures such as sex reassignment surgery and hormonal therapy*".

In this respect, Resolution 2048 (2015) on discrimination against transgender people in Europe, adopted by the Parliamentary Assembly on 22 April 2015, is certainly highly relevant. The resolution calls on member states, among other things, to abolish sterilisation and other compulsory medical treatment, as well as a mental health diagnosis, as a necessary legal requirement to recognise a person's gender identity in laws regulating the procedure for changing a name and registered gender. Furthermore, it is worth noting *The Yogyakarta Principles Plus 10* (YP + 10) were recently adopted on 10 November 2017. They are additional principles and state obligations on the application of international human rights law in relation to sexual orientation, gender identity, gender expression and sex characteristics and aim to document and elaborate the developments made since the original 29 Yogyakarta Principles were adopted in 2006.

3 ECJ's Jurisprudence on Gender Identity

The jurisprudence of the ECJ has led the way in the inclusion of trans people under EU gender equality legislation; the case of *P. v. S. and Cornwall County Council* (ECJ, case C-13/94) is the landmark in this field. The Court established that the scope of Directive 76/207/EEC on the implementation of the principle of equal treatment for men and women as regards access to employment, vocational training and promotion, and working conditions cannot be confined to discrimination based on the fact that the individual is of one sex or the other, and may include discrimination arising from the gender reassignment of a person. In fact, the Court ruled that the directive extended to discrimination based on the sex of the person, thus including the case of dismissal of a transsexual person related to her/his gender reassignment.

Another important decision of the Court was the case of *K. B. v. National Health Service Pensions Agency* (ECJ, judgment 7 January 2004, case C-117/01), where the Court ruled that the United Kingdom's legislation was incompatible with Article 141 EC since it, in breach of the ECtHR, prevents a couple from fulfilling the marriage requirement which must be met for one of them to be able to benefit from part of the pay of the other. The ECJ recalled an important decision of the ECtHR (*Godwin v. United Kingdom*) where the Court held that the fact that it was impossible for a transsexual to marry a person of the sex to which he or she belonged prior to gender reassignment surgery was a breach of their right to marry under Article 12 of the ECtHR.

The ECJ's ruling was significant in *Sarah Margaret Richards v. Secretary of State for Work and Pensions* (ECJ, judgment 27 April 2006, case C-423/04); the reference for a preliminary ruling concerned the interpretation of Articles 4 and 7 of Council Directive 79/7/EEC of 19 December 1978 on the progressive implementation of the principle of equal treatment for men and women in matters of social security. The applicant, a post-operative transsexual woman (MtF), had argued that the refusal to pay her a retirement pension from the age of 60 was a breach of Article

8 of the ECtHR, as well as discrimination as per Article 4 of Directive 79/7/EEC. Moreover, in accordance with case law, the right not to be discriminated against on grounds of sex is one of the fundamental human rights, the observance of which the Court has a duty to ensure. The scope of Directive 79/7/EEC cannot thus be confined simply to discrimination based on the fact that a person is of a particular sex. In view of its purpose and the nature of the rights which it seeks to safeguard, discrimination arising from the gender reassignment of a person is within the scope of that directive (see Council Directive 76/207/EEC, *P. v. S. and Cornwall County* Council). The Court argued that "[a]*s it arises from her gender reassignment, the unequal treatment to which* [the applicant] *was subject must be regarded as discrimination which is precluded by Article 4(1) of Directive 79/7. The Court has already found that national legislation which precludes a transsexual, in the absence of recognition of his new gender, from fulfilling a requirement which must be met in order to be entitled to a right protected by Community law must be regarded as being, in principle, incompatible with the requirements of Community law*" (see K. B., §§ 30 to 34) (§§ 30, 31). In accordance with the ECJ's settled case-law, the right not to be discriminated against on grounds of sex is, in fact, one of the fundamental human rights the observance of which the Court has the duty to ensure and it cannot be confined simply to discrimination based on the fact that a person is of one or other sex. The Court, therefore, underlined that the scope of the Council Directive 79/7/EEC is also such as to apply to discrimination arising from the gender reassignment and that Article 4(1) is to be interpreted as precluding legislation which denies a person who has undergone male-to-female gender reassignment entitlement to a retirement pension "*on the ground that she has not reached the age of 65, when she would have been entitled to such a pension at the age of 60 had she been held to be a woman as a matter of national law*". The ECJ thus ruled that equal treatment for trans people has to be applied on the basis of the acquired gender and not the sex given at birth (Vecchi 2001, pp. 343–354; Whittle 2002).

4 ECtHR's Jurisprudence on Gender Identity

The ECtHR applied the European Convention on Human Rights in significant judgments related to transsexuals' human rights issues (Trucco 2003, pp. 371–383). The Court has led the way in the progressive recognition of gender identity issues. After initially rejecting transsexuals' grievances (see *Rees v. the United Kingdom*, 17 October 1986 and *Cossey v. the United Kingdom*, 27 September 1990), the ECtHR has embraced a more extensive approach (see *B. v. France*, 1992; *Christine Goodwin v. the United Kingdom*, 2002; *Van Kück v. Germany*, 2003; *Grant v. the United Kingdom*, 2006; *L. v. Lithuania*, 2007; *Schlumpf v. Switzerland*, 2009; *Y.Y. v. Turkey*, 2015). In the case of *B. v. France,* the Court found for the first time a violation of Article 8, "right to respect for private and family life", of the Convention in a case concerning the recognition of transsexuals. The Court reached the conclusion that the refusal to amend the civil status register in the claimant's regard had placed her "*in a daily situation which was not compatible with the respect due to her private life*".

The leading case in this field is *Christine Goodwin v. the United Kingdom* (judgment 11 July 2002); the applicant complained of the lack of legal recognition of her changed gender and in particular of her treatment in terms of employment, her social security and pension rights and of her inability to marry. The Court found a violation of Articles 8 and 12 ECtHR, owing to a continuing international trend toward increased social acceptance of transsexuals (see also *I. v. the United Kingdom*, judgment 11 July 2002).

With specific regard to transgender persons, the recent *case of A. P. Garçon and Nicot v. France* (judgment 6 April 2017) should be noted; this case concerned three transgender persons of French nationality who wished to change the entries concerning their sex and their forenames on their birth certificates, and who were not allowed to do so by the courts in the respondent state. The Court recalled its settled case law related to applicability of Article 8 of the Convention to trans people (see *Van Kück v. Germany*, § 69, 12 June 2003; *Schlumpf v. Switzerland*, § 77, 8 January 2009; and *Y.Y. v. Turkey*, § 56, 10 March 2015). The Court ruled that the concept of private life:

> includes not only a person's physical and psychological integrity, but can sometimes also embrace aspects of an individual's physical and social identity. Elements such as gender identity or identification, names, sexual orientation and sexual life fall within the personal sphere protected by Article 8 of the Convention (see *A. P. Garçon and Nicot v. France*, § 92).

The Court argued that the right to respect for private life under Article 8 of the Convention fully applies to Gender Identity as a component of personal identity, and that it includes the right to self-determination, of which the freedom to define one's sexual identity is one of the most basic essentials (Sciancalepore and Stanzione 2002).

5 Conclusions

In conclusion and in view of the above, EU and international law has expressed strong condemnation toward discrimination on the basis of sexual orientation and gender identity, and strongly regrets that the fundamental rights of lesbian, gay, bisexual, transgender and intersex (LGBTI) people are not yet always fully upheld in the EU.

The analysis of EU and international settings highlights a positive trend toward the promotion and defence of transgender persons' fundamental rights, starting with the fields of equality and non-discrimination on the grounds of gender identity and gender expression. In this perspective, European and international institutional actors, as well as the jurisprudence of the ECJ and the ECtHR, have played a central supporting role in the implementation of anti-discrimination legislation, which includes sexual orientation and gender identity among the prohibited grounds for discrimination. EU institutional actors are thus working to coordinate and monitor the implementation and the exchange of good practices among member states.

References

Antonino, A. (2016). Il controverso itinerario dell'identità di genere. *Nuova Giur. Civ., 2*, 305–317.

Benjamin, H. (1968). *Il fenomeno transessuale, trad. it.* Roma, Italy: Astrolabio.

Celesti, R. (1968). Il problema medico-legale della schizosessualità. *Medicina legale e delle assicurazioni*, 175 ff.

Gerini, G., Giaretton, F., Trombetta, C., & Romito, P. (2009). Violenza, discriminazione e salute mentale in un campione di pazienti transessuali. *Riv. Sessuol., 4(33)*, 236–245.

Hirschfeld, M. (1910). *Die Transvestiten – eine Untersuchung über den erotischen Verkleidungstrieb mit umfangreichem casuistischem und historischem Material [The transvestites – A study of the erotic desire to cross-dress, with extensive casuistic and historical examples].* Berlin, Germany: Medicinischer Verlag.

Lorè, C., & Martini, P. (1988). *Aspetti e problemi medico-legali del transessualismo.* Milano: Giuffrè.

Lorenzetti, A. (2013). *Diritti in transito. La condizione giuridica delle persone transessuali.* Milano, Italy: Franco Angeli.

Martina, L. P. (2017). *La prospettiva di genere. Un processo di normativizzazione politica mondiale.* Rome, Italy: Aracne editore.

Pezzini, B. (1984). Transessualismo, salute e identità sessuale. *Rass. dir. civ.*, 461 ff.

Pfäfflin, F. (2015). Transgenderism and transsexuality: Medical and psychological viewpoints. In J. M. Scherpe (Ed.), *The legal status of transsexual and transgender persons* (pp. 12–23). Cambridge, United Kingdom: Intersentia.

Ruppin, U., & Pfäfflin, F. (2015). Long-term follow-up of adults with Gender Identity Disorder. *Archives of Sexual Behavior*. https://doi.org/10.1007/s10508-014-0453-5.

Sciancalepore, G., & Stanzione, P. (2002). *Transessualismo e tutela della persona.* Milano, Italy: Ipsoa.

Stanzione, P. (1992). Transessualità. *Enc. del Dir.*, XLIV (pp. 874 ff). Milano, Italy: Treccani.

Trucco, L. (2003). Il Transessualismo nella giurisprudenza della Corte Europea dei Diritti dell'Uomo alla luce del diritto comparato. *Dir. pubbl. comp. eur., 1*, 371–383.

Vecchi, P. M. (1994). Transessualismo. *Enc. Giur. Treccani*, XXXI (pp. 9 ff). Roma, Italy: Treccani.

Vecchi, P. M. (2001). Transessualismo e discriminazioni. *Familia*, 343–354.

Vitale, A. M. (2001). Implications of being dysphoric: A development review. *Gender and Psychoanalysis. An Interdisciplinary Journal, 6*, 121–141.

Vitelli, R., Bottone, M., Sisci, N., & Valerio, P. (2006). L'identità transessuale tra storia e clinica. Quale intervento per quale domanda. In P. Rigliano (Ed.), *Gay e lesbiche in psicoterapia.* Milano, Italy: Raffaello Cortina editore.

Vitelli, R., Fazzari, P., & Valerio, P. (2013). Le varianti di genere e la loro iscrizione nell'orizzonte del sapere medico-scientifico: la varianza di genere è un disturbo mentale? Ma cos'è poi un disturbo mentale? In F. Corbisiero (Ed.), *Comunità omosessuali. Le scienze sociali sulla popolazione LGBT* (pp. 221–243). Milano, Italy: FrancoAngeli.

Whittle, S. (2002). *Respect and equality, transsexual and transgender rights.* London, United Kingdom: Cavendish.

Zito, E., & Valerio, P. (2012). Le identità sessuali tra discorso clinico e discorso sociale. In R. Vitelli & P. Valerio (Eds.), *Sesso e genere: uno sguardo tra storia e nuove prospettive* (pp. 153–169). Napoli, Italy: Liguori editore.

User

Patricia Valcárcel Fernández

1 'User' as a Multi-Purpose Legal Term

The term 'user' is not exactly an unambiguous one, either in the common setting or in the legal sphere. The term has its roots in the Latin word '*usuarius*', which designates an individual who uses something, who avails himself of a good, or who is the recipient of a service. In the broadest sense, the user is usually presented as that person who uses the goods or services provided by producers or suppliers, whether public or private.

We shall now leave the common, colloquial setting aside and focus on the meanings of the word with legal significance. Thus, in the legal sphere, we can establish that, in recent history, regarding what concerns the European setting, the word 'user' reflects the development that the consideration of different countries' populations has undergone juridically until being transformed into citizens. This is a process that is most clearly apparent as of the eighteenth century and emerges most conspicuously throughout the nineteenth and twentieth centuries. It was in the framework of this period when two circumstances come about.

Firstly, the birth of modern public law, in particular, of administrative law. 'Subjects' are transformed into citizens and into recipients of services; the provision of which begins to be considered crucial for society and, thus, gradually, the public authority begins to regulate, guarantee, control and even assume the provision thereof. Secondly, the industrial revolution, which favours the emergence of the productive and consumer society wherein citizens acquire great prominence as the 'users' of goods and services produced by undertakings, and the need for a regulation of the rights of citizens as 'users' of these products becomes increasingly evident. Over time, the position of these citizens—users of these consumer goods and services—is identified with the label of 'consumers and users'. The role of these

P. Valcárcel Fernández (✉)
Department of Public Law, University of Vigo, Vigo, Spain
e-mail: pvalcarcel@uvigo.es

A. Bartolini et al. (eds.), *Dictionary of Statuses within EU Law*,
https://doi.org/10.1007/978-3-030-00554-2_77

'users', as economic agents in the final link of the consumption chain, is consolidated. Their role as clients in the free market of consumer goods and services with which to satisfy their specific needs.

From the foregoing, it follows that there are specifically two main perspectives to which the term 'user' can be linked: (1) As the recipient of services that are especially relevant in different societies. The intervention of the public sector thereupon makes its presence felt in a more or less intense way (Barrio García 2003). (2) As an individual who uses goods, products and services for general consumption. For this second group, the binomial 'consumers and users' have gradually been coined.

In this entry special attention will be paid to the meaning of 'user', which is linked to the notion of 'recipient' of those services and characterised by the general interest that they represent for society. In this regard, as well as in the framework of the European Union (EU), it is essential to speak of the category of Services of General Interest (SGI).

2 'Users' as Recipients of Services of General Interest (SGI)

From the very beginning, the construction of what is today the EU was based on one overriding notion: that of consolidating the creation of a single market between its members. This initial objective is based on the defence of a set of fundamental principles, foremost among which is that of free competition and the freedoms associated with the same, such as the freedom of establishment and the freedom to provide services.

Nonetheless, the consolidation of an undistorted internal market, based on the rules of free competition, has not impeded the provision of a rule such as that appearing in Article 106.2 of the Treaty on the Functioning of the European Union (TFEU). This article indicates the existence of certain services that, by virtue of the general economic interest that they embody, may be subject to regimes that are more or less exorbitant with regard to what is characteristic of free competition in the market. In relation, the rules of free competition in an open market need not be applied in an absolute manner. Obviously, the crux of the matter lies in clarifying when the exception could apply to an activity and, for example, in legitimating the State to grant rights of exclusivity or certain economic aid to one or more undertakings in exchange for assuming the provision of these services.

Article 106.2 of the TFEU shows that the concurrence of operators in different markets cannot entail a risk of the provision or supply of the so-called essential services not being guaranteed for the users at all times. Users must have the provision of these services guaranteed on the basis of a series of basic principles: generality or universality, continuity, equality and non-discrimination, quality and adaptation to progress.

Recognition of the importance that certain services represent for society began to gradually gain momentum in documents from the European Commission (the Commission). Particularly noteworthy is the Commission Communication from

1996 on *Services of General Interest in Europe*. It emerged clearly with the inclusion into the Treaty of Amsterdam (1997) of Article 16 of the Treaty Establishing the European Community, which elevated the guardianship of economic services of general interest to the highest level of European Community (EC) legal sources, as a principal to be protected.

Since then, there has been a constant trickle of EU texts looking into the line described. Article 36 of the Charter of Fundamental Rights of the European Union, in the group of rights pertaining to solidarity, goes as far as enshrining 'access to services of general economic interest'.

The European commitment to SGI and the users thereof became evident in the Treaty of Lisbon, which is accompanied by a Protocol on SIGs (i.e., Protocol 26). The current Article 14 of the TFEU is also grounded on recognising the pivotal position occupied by SIGs among the EU's common values, insisting on the fact that they contribute decisively to attaining greater social and territorial cohesion (Fiedziuk 2011).

Regarding SGIs, the following notions can be highlighted. Firstly, SGIs play a key role as one of the values shared by all European societies. They form an essential element of the European model of society and are essential for enhancing the quality of life for all citizens and for overcoming social exclusion and isolation. They touch on the central question of the role that public authorities play in a market economy, which ensures, on the one hand, the smooth functioning of the market and compliance with the rules of the game by all actors and, on the other hand, safeguards the general interest (in particular, the satisfaction of citizens' essential needs and the preservation of public goods where the market fails).

Secondly, SGIs are characterised by their great variety. Clearly, activities such as telecommunications, energy, postal services transport, refuse collection or providing populations with a water supply have little in common; nonetheless, they all share common force lines, which make it possible to identify a series of essential aspects that are comparable in their legal regime (González-Orús 2005). This is clear, for example, in the formulation of common principles of access to these services for users. However, the extensive range of SGIs means that special attention must be paid to the categories thereof that can be distinguished, such as:

(1) Services of General Economic Interest (SGEI), which in turn allow a dual distinction. The first distinction is that SGEI provided in exchange for remuneration and subject to EU competition and internal market rules. These SGEIs have a European dimension and habitually correspond to many activities provided by large network industries. They are regulated by specific European rules and are subject to internal market and competition rules. In the 1980s, the EU started to gradually open up the different markets for large network industries (i.e., telecommunications, postal services, electricity, gas and transport) in which SGEIs can be provided. A comprehensive regulatory framework has been adopted for these services, specifying public service obligations at a European level and, in particular, the rights applying to the users thereof. The second distinction is that SGEIs, with respect to which exceptions to the provisions of the Treaty can be

authorised when the strict application of market rules would hamper the procurement of essential and specific objectives of general interest. This may result in the recognition of aid compatible with EC Law or exclusivity rights for whoever assumes the provision thereof.

(2) SGI of a non-economic nature and services with no effect on trade. These services are not subject to specific rules on the internal market, competition and state aid from the European Treaties. They are subject to the EC rules applicable to non-economic activities and activities with no effect on intra-EC trade, including the fundamental principle of non-discrimination. Police and justice are examples of these SGIs.

Thirdly, in view of the aforesaid classification, Member States have several options for ensuring the provision of what are considered SGIs to users. These range from opening up the market to competition over imposing public service obligations up to conferring exclusive or special rights to single operators, with or without provision of funding.

Fourthly, there may be certain SGIs that do not lend themselves to a plurality of providers. Under such circumstances, public authorities are empowered to provide them or attribute the provision thereof to third parties through temporary concession contracts awarded through public tenders, and the framework of which exclusive or special rights or certain aid that does not distort competition may be recognised.

By way of conclusion, market freedom is not at odds with recognising the existence of certain sectors, in which regulations that limit, define and elaborate on it, can be admitted. The general principle of prohibiting restrictions on the free movement of services currently stated by Article 56 of the TFEU has a fixed limit in Articles 14 and 106 of the TFEU, namely, in SGIs.

The solution imposed in the definition of the scheme of these services is aimed at the ever-difficult search to strike a balance between these SGIs and users: a genuinely complex balance that does not allow generic responses and is materialised by taking into account the specific particularities of each type of service in question. Thus, the core idea of the current European model of SGIs depends on different parameters. Those SGIs whose liberalisation process started on the initiative of community institutions in the 1990s in certain economic sectors, which are currently subject to EU-imposed regulation, would be SGEIs with harmonised European regulation.

Within the EU, it has been recognised that Member States may consider certain services as SGIs, even though they may have an economic content and have an impact on the market. The EU cannot oversee such a decision, except in cases of a 'manifest error' by the State in classification. SGIs without harmonised European legislation are subject to the primary regulation of the national authorities that define their legal status and the public intervention resources for guaranteeing the provision thereof. This does not mean, however, that certain provisions from European law are not applicable to them. All SIGs, economic or non-economic, are subject to certain provisions of the TFEU and to the secondary legislation, such as the principle of non-discrimination and free movement of people, as well as the procedural rules for public procurement.

It is not always easy to establish a clear boundary between SGIs. Non-economic SGIs would be those with respect to which the State fulfils its function in the social, cultural, educational and healthcare settings. They are services that are provided to the population and the users, and they are essentially funded by the State, owing to which the compensation that direct users may pay to offset their cost.

SGEIs without harmonised European regulation are subject to the TFEU rules on the internal market and competition, although these rules may be waived if justified, pursuant to the TFEU rules (i.e., Article 106.2) and jurisprudence from the Court of Justice of the EU (the 'Court'). These exceptions allowed by the TFEU would enable public authorities to recognise exclusive rights for companies providing such services to the extent considered necessary to accomplish the entrusted mission. The EC authorities' role is to control the proper need for these State measures and the proportionality thereof. The operation of these services frequently differs from one Member State to another.

3 Basic Principles of the Recognition of Rights to Users of SGI as Citizens

While SIGs are manifold and varied, the rights of users with regard to each of them must, to a good degree, be defined in a specific manner, addressing each type of service individually. Nonetheless, the general principals upon which the recognition of rights for users of services of this type are based can be identified. Thus, strictly from the perspective of the citizens who are potential 'users' of SGIs (*uti universi*), mention must be made of the following three principles.

The first principle is the access to the service. One acknowledged merit of SGIs lies in their validity as an instrument of integration, re-distribution and social cohesion. This value has been attained principally through the application of the principles of equality in access thereto recognised for users. One of the techniques established for ensuring this equality of access is that relating to 'universal service' (Sauter 2008). This is intended to ensure that identical services are provided to all users entitled to benefit from them, and in the most universal manner possible. This entails making these services available to all users, with no type of discrimination that may affect disadvantaged social groups or users who are geographically dispersed or distant from large cities. In any case, this equal access is not at odds with the diversity of SGIs, to which they will have to be adapted, or with the different needs and preferences that, with regard to the same, may arise in users depending on their economic, social, geographic or cultural situation.

The principle is the cost of SGEIs. There are a number of possible solutions for financing the costs of providing SGIs, either by resorting to a market price system that allows providers a return, taking the increased cost entailed by continuity and regularity into account, or by establishing a political price system, subsidising the cost difference through taxation. The type of SGI we are faced with will determine the manner in which its cost is assumed by users thereof. Thus, the cost of certain SGIs, particularly those of a non-economic nature, is met through public budgets.

In the case of SGIs of an economic nature, a number of different possibilities are available. Of note is the use of the aforesaid 'universal service' technique, which is a mechanism not only for guaranteeing the universal access to all users of the service, but also for regulating how to meet the cost of the provision thereof for the economic operators offering them, without increasing the cost for users. This technique guarantees the provision of certain services to all users requesting them, irrespective of their geographic location, with a specified quality and at a reasonable price.

The third and final principle to consider is the service quality and continuity. The rights of users of SGIs to the maintenance of provision is the inherent consequence of their status as essential services and, thus, of essential coverage. Access to these services at a reasonable cost implies enjoying the provision under certain conditions of regularity (i.e., continuity of service), of contemporaneity (i.e., adaptation to the users' needs and incorporation of technical advances) and at suitable levels of quality.

The concern for quality shows that the centre of gravity lies in the user and demonstrates that the aim is to ensure service improvement objectives, both generally and specifically for each service. The best solution for the changing and varied needs of users must be constantly sought. Moreover, service quality is guaranteed through evaluation and periodic control. The evaluation must be multi-dimensional.

References

Barrio García, G. A. (2003). Servicios públicos y ciudadanos: el usuario ante el nuevo servicio público (Public services and citizens: The user in front of the new public service). *Anuario da Facultade de Dereito da Universidade da Coruña*, (7), 125–154.

Fiedziuk, N. (2011). Services of general economic interest and the Treaty of Lisbon: Opening doors to a whole new approach or maintaining the status quo. *European Law Review, 36*(2), 226–242.

González-Orús, J. M. (2005). *Servicios de interés general y artículo 86 del Tratado CE una visión evolutiva (Services of general interest and Article 86 of the EC Treaty an evolutionary vision)*. Madrid, Spain: Universidad San Pablo-CEU.

Sauter, W. (2008). Services of general economic interest and universal service in EU law. *European Law Review, 33*(2), 167–192.

Voluntary

Carlos Vidal Prado

1 Introduction

A multitude of organisations are involved in the support of volunteering across the globe. Two major international organisations, the United Nations and the Council of Europe, have been especially active in supporting and promoting volunteering, particularly since the end of the 1990s.

The importance of volunteering has long been acknowledged by the EU. The celebration of the European Year of Volunteering in 2011, which triggered a series of documents, studies and resolutions by the Commission, Parliament and the European Economic and Social Council, was definitive for the momentum and promotion of volunteering. The European Year of Volunteering contributed to the evaluation of voluntary actions as important instruments for social, territorial and intergenerational cohesion.

An analysis of national surveys and reports on volunteering identified by key stakeholders in the Member States indicates that there are between 92 and 94 million adults involved in volunteering in the EU. This in turn implies that between 22% and 23% of Europeans aged over 15 years are engaged in voluntary work (GHK 2010, p. 7).

C. Vidal Prado (✉)
Faculty of Law, Universidad Nacional de Educación a Distancia (UNED), Madrid, Spain
e-mail: cvidal@der.uned.es

A. Bartolini et al. (eds.), *Dictionary of Statuses within EU Law*,
https://doi.org/10.1007/978-3-030-00554-2_78

2 Volunteering in EU Law and the European Voluntary Humanitarian Aid Corps

Humanitarian aid volunteering in the EU is regulated by Regulation (EU) 375/2014 of the European Parliament and of the Council of 3 April 2014, which established the European Voluntary Humanitarian Aid Corps ('the EU Aid Volunteers initiative') as a framework for joint contributions from European volunteers to support and complement humanitarian aid in third world countries; additionally, international humanitarian emergencies are also addressed.

The regulation defines what is meant by volunteer ("a person who chooses freely and without pecuniary motivation to engage in activities that benefit a community and society at large"), 'EU Aid Volunteer' ("a candidate volunteer who has been selected, trained in accordance with specific standards, procedures and reference criteria, assessed as eligible and registered as available for deployment to support and complement humanitarian aid in third countries"), and "humanitarian aid" ("activities and operations in third world countries intended to provide needs-based emergency assistance aimed at preserving life, preventing and alleviating human suffering, and maintaining human dignity in the face of man-made crises or natural disasters. It encompasses assistance, relief and protection operations in humanitarian crises or their immediate aftermath, supporting measures to ensure access to people in need and to facilitate the free flow of assistance, as well as actions aimed at reinforcing disaster preparedness and disaster risk reduction, and contributing towards strengthening resilience and capacity to cope with, and recover from, crises").

The objective of the initiative is twofold; on the one hand, to contribute to strengthening the Union's capacity to provide needs-based humanitarian aid aimed at preserving life, preventing and alleviating human suffering and maintaining human dignity. On the other hand, to strengthen the capacity and resilience of vulnerable or disaster-affected communities in third world countries, particularly by means of disaster preparedness, disaster risk reduction and by enhancing the link between relief, rehabilitation and development.

Most international literature on the subject tends to analyse the role of voluntary activity based on its contribution to social or economic life (Benlloch Sanz 2016). As stated previously, volunteering derives its essential value from its contribution to active citizenship, and its effects are often difficult to quantify: social commitment, a feeling of belonging, identifying with society, solidarity, a feeling of responsibility for society and the promotion of social cohesion are all difficult to measure. The economic value of voluntary activity should also be quantified, as proposed by the United Nations in its Handbook on Non-Profit Institutions in the System of National Accounts. This is also in line with the Union's emphasis on sustainable development, which strives for a global system in which environmental sustainability, solidarity and democracy are promoted alongside economic success.

Volunteers make an essential contribution in promoting social cohesion and environmental activities, as well as the reintegration of (long-term) unemployed persons into the job market, and this needs to be measured. This is highlighted in the Opinion of the European Economic and Social Committee on Voluntary activity: its role in European society and its impact[1] and in the European Parliament resolution of 22 April 2008 on the role of volunteering through its contributions to economic and social cohesion.[2]

In the aforementioned paragraphs, in the interests of preparing individuals for voluntary activity, the European Economic and Social Committee "feels that it would be useful to highlight the relationship between civil society and schools. In primary education, more attention must be paid to educational activities aimed at developing social awareness and involvement in solving social problems of general interest".

In this resolution, the European Parliament itself said that the further consolidation of the common European approach to volunteering would create more opportunities for mobility and employability for young people by allowing them to acquire useful skills; the relevance of the added value of knowledge and competences acquired through volunteering contribute to the volunteers' curricula vitae and their working life and so must be recognised as an experience of learning and non-formal and informal work. It could also be argued that the competences acquired by young people during their volunteer work should be included in the Youthpass (European Skills Passport), which links to Europass, which would ensure that volunteering is not seen as an alternative to formal training but an activity that complements it; including volunteering work in both the Youthpass and Europass would successfully increase the mobility of volunteers at both local and national levels.

In line with the previous paragraph, the European Economic and Social Committee maintains, in its opinion, that volunteering plays a special role in combating youth and long-term unemployment, as well as generally in relation to workers entering the labour force. Volunteers can accumulate important experience and knowledge in demand in the labour market and build up a network of contacts. Apart from activities in the social sphere and in health care, which are traditional areas for voluntary activity, volunteers can also acquire key competences and knowledge in areas like publicity, communications, self-expression, social skills, management and vocational training. They have the opportunity to try out various social roles, to learn to make the right decisions, to solve problems, to assimilate into different work cultures and to demonstrate their sense of justice and leadership qualities. Voluntary activity can form an important part of a person's CV and career.

Therefore, volunteering is an important non-formal and informal learning instrument that complements formal learning, education and training. It follows that it also serves to improve the opportunities available to people interested in the labour market, especially young people.[3]

---

[1] 2006/C 325/13, OJ C 325/46, 30.12.2006.

[2] (2007/2149(INI)) http://www.europarl.europa.eu/sides/getDoc.do?pubRef=-//EP//TEXT+TA+P6-TA-2008-0131+0+DOC+XML+V0//EN.

[3] Opinion of the EESC on Voluntary activity: its role in European society and its impact (2006/C 325/13), num. 4.6.2.

In coherence with this, the EESC calls on Member States to eliminate labour law shortcomings which prevent the use of volunteers in carrying out important work in the public interest, especially in the event of disasters. The EESC considers that all too often employees are still dependent on the goodwill of their employer, for instance to give them time off work.[4]

Several resolutions of the European Parliament have insisted on this line to facilitate voluntary mobility and cross-border EU activities[5]; additionally, there are also documents created by the European Commission which broadly follow the same lines and that speak of the positive impact of volunteering in employment (European Commission 2014; Natali and Pavolini 2014).

3 Internet-Mediated Volunteering

Volunteering can be promoted and developed through the use of online tools (European Volunteer Centre 2011). The internet offers a virtual space for volunteers and supports the growth of voluntary action through advertisements and easy, swift communication. Online volunteering redefines the concept of community and opens possibilities for cooperation between people who are physically distant. In this context, it allows people to exercise remote volunteering with their communities, but those communities not be defined, then, by the physical environments they inhabit but by their connections to groups that share common interests and a vision of the common good.

Despite the advantages offered by virtual volunteering, it cannot be ignored that it also presents risks and challenges (Cravens 2014, pp. 27, 34, 39, 41); the difficulty of creating electronic links between the volunteer and the target, the need for specialised technical training of both the volunteer and the recipient as a condition for the effectiveness of volunteer work and the demand for a personal wage structure higher than in other forms of volunteering are some examples.

4 Volunteering as Part of Corporate Social Responsibility

On the other hand, volunteer activity and employee volunteering are initiatives conceived by the European Commission as part of corporate social responsibility. The Commission considers employee volunteering to be an expression of corporate social responsibility.[6]

---

[4] Ibid., num. 4.6.7.

[5] European Parliament resolution of 12 June 2012 on recognising and promoting cross-border voluntary activities in the EU (2011/2293(INI)) and European Parliament resolution of 10 December 2013 on volunteering and voluntary activity in Europe (2013/2064(INI)).

[6] Communication of 20.09.2011 from the Commission on EU Policies and Volunteering: Recognising and Promoting Cross-border Voluntary Activities in the EU, COM/2011/0568 final, 2.2.6.

Some studies have made clear the need to establish community-building measures so that companies become involved in what the Commission terms "corporate volunteering" (GHK 2010, pp. 19, 68).

At the European level, the European Commission is making significant advances in the promotion of volunteering among its employees. In 2011, the Communication on EU Policies and Volunteering: Recognising and Promoting Cross-border Voluntary Activities in the EU stated that "in 2011 the Commission launched initiatives that seek to promote volunteering amongst its staff. These include intranet web resources for staff with information on volunteering opportunities, good practices and practical guidelines for staff wishing to engage in voluntary activities".

5 Volunteering in Relation to Routes of Formal and Informal Learning at EU Level

As previously stated, at the European level the declaration of 2011 as the European Year of Volunteering was a significant turning point; it not only enabled the realisation of numerous activities on the continent but, above all, it generated numerous documents that have been very important for the roadmap. After analysing some of the Commission's previous documents, we now focus on the relationship between the recognition of volunteering and the validation routes of formal and informal learning at EU level.

In particular, and in relation to the validation of non-formal learning, the "European Guidelines for Validating Non-Formal and Informal Learning" recognised the significance of adult learning in the third and voluntary sectors for the development of skills and competences. These sectors are administratively independent of both the public education system and the labour market, though both provide valuable learning contexts to formal education and the labour market. The validation of adult learning from the third and voluntary sectors raises the question of how to more closely align formal education and the labour market while, at the same time, safeguarding key attributes of independence and the concept of volunteering (European Commission 2015).

Some European countries have followed the recommendations of the European Guidelines and have progressed from theory to practice.

Experiences as a Volunteer Pass in Germany, VSkills in Scotland or ACTIVOL and Vol + in Spain[7] are clear examples of this. In the case of Vol + in Spain, the participation of the company consists in the intervention of experts in human resources to accompany the volunteers throughout the competences certification process.

In Europe, between 10% and 40% of the population are involved in volunteering and European institutions promote that the different administrations consider this

[7] http://www.plataformavoluntariado.org/formacion/course/index.php?categoryid=2.

work of the volunteers as a method of improving personal skills and a way of upholding the welfare state (GHK 2010, pp. 58, 65–66).

In short, in the framework of the European Union there have been great impulses and advances, especially in the last two decades, for Member States to recognise "non-formal" and "informal" training both at an official level and in the labour market.

Multiple political initiatives, recommendations and approvals from the Commission or Council of Europe have been adopted that centre around the recognition and validation of continuous learning and informal and non-formal learning. The effort of the third sector in general and the voluntary movement in particular, on the other hand, has managed to enter into the European political agenda by ensuring that volunteering is viewed as a way of acquiring learning and therefore of acquiring competences. Currently, volunteer organisations are represented in the debates to provide their own opinion on the recognition and validation of competences and skills.

One of the most important results of the European Year of Volunteering was the Policy Agenda for Volunteering in Europe (P.A.V.E.),[8] which offered "recommendations for a more efficient and effective European policy framework to support and promote volunteers, volunteering and volunteer-involving organisations and their partners". The recommendations included proposals for action echoing the aspects of volunteering policies that demonstrate European values, provide a vehicle for active citizenship and contribute to economic and social-capital growth.

Social entities have appreciated the work of volunteers in many ways. However, voluntary action should show other types of recognition associated with the learning that their task has given them. The Council Recommendation of 20 December 2012 on the validation of non-formal and informal learning[9] referred to this knowledge, which moves away from regulated training:

Non-formal education and training: Education and training which takes place outside the formal system either on a regular or intermittent basis.

- Non-formal learning, education and training which takes place outside the formal system either on a regular or intermittent basis. It is a learning derived from planned activities (in terms of didactic objectives and duration) in which there is some form of support for learning (such as, for example, a relationship between student and teacher).

The third sector has extensive experience offering different kinds of courses to improve volunteer capabilities: compulsory basic training courses for volunteers, specific courses for each of the groups with which they will be working, courses on new technologies and online training tools, etc.

- Informal learning: Learning resulting from daily life related to work, family or leisure. Informal learning is part of non-formal learning. It is often referred to as

[8] http://issuu.com/european_volunteer_centre/docs/pave_spanish_translation_by_fasvol-final.

[9] 2012/C 398/01, OJ C 398/1, 22.12.2012.

experience-based learning and can, to a certain degree, be understood as accidental learning. Informal learning can be unintended from the point of view of the learner. The experience, knowledge, skills and abilities that volunteers obtain as a result of their own voluntary action would be framed in this type of learning.

As the European Guidelines for validating non-formal and informal learning point out, volunteering experience generates wider knowledge, skills and competences that often remain invisible. From an individual perspective, the experience of volunteering represents an opportunity for validation that generates benefits in terms of jobs and studies.

References

Benlloch Sanz, P. (coord.). (2016). Comentarios a la Ley 45/2015, de 14 de octubre de Voluntariado. In A. Sempere Navarro & R. de Lorenzo García (Eds.), *Comentarios a las Leyes del Tercer Sector de Acción Social y del Voluntariado* (Vol. II). Madrid: Thomson Reuters-Aranzadi.

Cravens, J. (2014). Internet-mediated volunteering in the EU. Its history, prevalence, and approaches and how it relates to employability and social inclusion, European Commission. In *JRC Scientific and Policy Reports*. Bruxelles: Publications Office of the European Union.

European Commission. (2014). *Employee volunteering and employee volunteering in Humanitarian Aid in Europe*. Retrieved March 18, 2018, from http://ec.europa.eu/echo/files/euaidvolunteers/EUAV_Study_Employee_Volunteering_Europe_FINAL_en.pdf

European Commission; Cedefop. (2015). *European guidelines for validating non-formal and informal learning*. Retrieved March 21, 2018, from http://www.cedefop.europa.eu/en/publications-and-resources/publications/4054

European Volunteer Centre. (2011). *The future of volunteering: Concepts, trends, visions*. CEV Multi Stakeholder Symposium. https://issuu.com/european_volunteer centre/docs/tallinn_report_final

GHK, Educational, Audiovisual & Culture Executive Agency. (EAC-EA). Directorate General Education and Culture (DG EAC) (17.02.2010): *Volunteering in the European Union. Final Report.*

Natali, D., & Pavolini, E. (2014). *Comparing (Voluntary) Occupational Welfare in the EU: Evidence from an international research study*. Brussels: European Social Observatory.

Vulnerable Person

Paula Poretti

1 Introduction

The paper aims to explore the term 'vulnerable person' as defined in the available literature and other relevant sources, as well as international and EU instruments. Vulnerability is universal in that the threat of harm in the form of physical damage from injury or disease affects all human beings to varying degrees at different points in time. It is also particular and experienced uniquely by every person due to differences in the magnitude and potential of vulnerabilities at the individual level (Wiesbrock 2015, p. 74). The traditional approach towards the concept of vulnerability identifies certain groups in society who have specific characteristics. These groups of vulnerable persons are children, elderly people, the poor, the Roma, minorities, migrants, asylum seekers, the imprisoned or persons in detention, and disabled persons. Hence, a wider definition of the term 'vulnerability' would include all of the aforementioned categories. A narrower understanding of 'vulnerability' would confine it to just one category, emphasising its specific characteristics. Perhaps the most widespread and socially accepted notion of 'vulnerability' is that for persons with disabilities.

According to the more recent legal literature, vulnerability should not be interpreted narrowly, i.e. in a manner that only takes account of certain groups in society which are considered to be 'vulnerable'. Instead, vulnerability should be understood as a particularly dynamic concept that encompasses, but also transcends, the notions of minority groups (Ippolito and Iglesias Sánchez 2015, p. 1).

P. Poretti (✉)
Faculty of Law, J.J. Strossmayer University of Osijek, Osijek, Croatia
e-mail: pporetti@pravos.hr

A. Bartolini et al. (eds.), *Dictionary of Statuses within EU Law*,
https://doi.org/10.1007/978-3-030-00554-2_79

2 From a Traditional Approach Towards the Modern Understanding of the Vulnerability of Persons with Disabilities

The protection of vulnerable persons, understood as a fundamental human issue (Salm 2016, p. 7) is currently one of the topics that is being widely discussed at the international and EU levels. The starting point of the discussion on persons with disabilities as vulnerable persons is the understanding of persons with disabilities as holders of rights who are capable of making free and informed decisions within the limits of their capacity, and not passive recipients of care and attention (Bergeron 2015, p. 4). This is clearly a paradigm shift from the traditional understanding of a person with disabilities as a person in need of a charity-oriented, medically-based approach concerning his vulnerability. Namely, at the international level, for a long time, disability has been considered as a medical condition. The traditional approach towards the appropriate terminology reflects this. Most terms used in the MS, such as *behinderte Menschen* (Germany), *persona con disabilità/invalido* (Italy), *adultes handicapés* (France) or *osoba s invaliditetom* (Croatia), only focus on the specific characteristics of persons which place them in an inferior position to the 'normal' healthy population. Although it is difficult to find an adequate and appropriate term, the legal literature highlights a consensus on the necessity to avoid terms which are based on the incapacity, limitations or disturbances persons face due to their disabilities (Marinčić 2008, p. 200). A more affirmative terminology should be introduced which focuses on the interaction among psycho-physical impairments; a person with disabilities as a whole person; the individual barriers which the person faces, as well as the effects of the environment surrounding the person (Marinčić 2008, p. 203). This would be in line with the efforts to introduce a more 'situational approach' towards the vulnerability of persons with disabilities which respects the fact that the vulnerability of these persons is not always grounded in their disabilities (Schotch 2000, p. 215; Wiesbrock 2015, p. 93). However, the legal framework which regulates the protection of persons with disabilities at the national level in the different MS lacks a coherent approach towards the concept of the vulnerability of persons with disabilities. The variety of instruments applicable at the national level amounts to different levels of protection for persons with disabilities in the MS. This undermines legal certainty in national as well as cross-border situations concerning persons with disabilities. Hence, the need for a more harmonised approach at the international and EU level has been detected.

The first step in this direction was taken with the adoption of the UN Convention on the Rights of Persons with Disabilities (hereinafter: CRPD) in 2006. Prior to the adoption of the CRPD, only soft law instruments regulated the human rights of persons with disabilities at the international and EU levels.

The effect of the adoption of the CRPD is threefold. From 30th March 2007 to the present, 175 States have ratified/accessed the CRPD, and it is considered to be the most comprehensive human rights treaty of the twenty-first century.[1] At the EU level, the fact that the EU is a party to the CRPD has resulted in the acknowledgment that the relevant EU legal framework and policy should reflect the standards of protection introduced through its provisions. In addition, the MS should make efforts to adapt their existing or adopt new legislation which follows the model focused on persons with disabilities as holders of human rights and freedoms as provided by the CRPD. Many of the targeted instruments at the national level are EU instruments created by the EU legislature with the aim of promoting the Single Market and advancing consumer protection.

The CRPD introduced a new 'social model of disability' which implies respect for the human rights of persons with disabilities and the promotion of their inclusion and participation in society (Wiesbrock 2015, p. 72). In order to comply with its main principles, the state parties should ensure reasonable accommodation for persons with disabilities in accordance with Article 5(3) CRPD. Thereby, Article 2 defines reasonable accommodation. Regardless of the expected potential of the CRPD to drive the harmonisation of the rights of persons with disabilities as vulnerable persons at the EU level, the MS are not necessarily able to fulfill all of their obligations successfully. For example, in its concluding observations to the initial report of Croatia on the implementation of the CRPD from 2015, the Committee was concerned that there is a lack of understanding of the concept of reasonable accommodation and universal design in the fields of education, health, employment and construction in Croatia.

Besides the compliance of the MS with the obligations which arise from the ratification of the CRPD, the approach towards defining and understanding the concept of the vulnerability of persons with disabilities at the EU level is decisive in determining the level of adequate protection which will be granted within the national legal system. Hence, the concept of the vulnerability of persons with disabilities will be discussed in the next chapter.

3 Vulnerability of Persons with Disabilities Under EU Law

In the EU, the legal framework affecting persons with disabilities was developed under the influence of the market integration policy, first in the soft-law instruments, but more recently, with a broader integration of the human rights dimension in primary and secondary EU legislation. The initial step was taken with the introduction of the Communication on disability in 1996, but it was only after the entry into force of the Lisbon Treaty and the binding force of the EU Charter on Fundamental Rights (arg. *ex* Article 26) that a number of legal guarantees were ensured for persons with disabilities (Wiesbrock 2015, p. 82). The main problem present both at the EU level

[1]The number of States which had ratified/accessed the CRPD as of November, 28th 2017. Information available at https://www.un.org/development/desa/disabilities/convention-on-the-rights-of-persons-with-disabilities.html.

and in the MS legislation is the number of instruments which regulate the different rights of persons with disabilities, as well as the incoherent approach towards their regulation.[2]

However, a vast majority of the instruments which address the protection of persons with disabilities at the EU level are directly connected to the removal of obstacles for the proper functioning of the Single Market and the realisation of the four freedoms. The first among these instruments is Directive 2000/78/EC, which obligates the MS to eliminate discrimination against persons with disabilities in relation to employment and occupation. Other instruments in the field of free movement, competition, the protection of the environment and many others, which directly or indirectly address disabilities, also affect the legal position of vulnerable persons at the EU level. The jurisprudence of the Court of Justice of the European Union (hereinafter: CJEU) was the first to recognise the need to change the approach towards the vulnerability of persons with disabilities at the EU level. The initial definition of a disability as a 'limitation which, as a result of physical, mental or psychological impairments, hinders the participation of the person in professional life'[3] was replaced by a notion more in line with the CRPD of 'disability as the result of the interaction between the individual's impairment and the barriers created by society'.[4] However, it seems that this has not contributed to the equal recognition of the concept of the vulnerability of persons with disabilities at the EU level. For now, the concept of vulnerability is furthered exclusively through the EU policy on market integration and consumer protection. Namely, recent developments in the field of EU consumer protection legislation have been marked by a differentiation between the concepts of the 'average'[5] and the 'vulnerable'[6] consumer. The very distinction of the concepts of an 'average' and a 'vulnerable' consumer serves as means for a better understanding of a certain commercial practice, a level of standards of safety for products or standards for distance or off-premise contract as being adequate in the case of an 'average' consumer or in need of alteration in respect of 'vulnerable' persons. This ensures special protection for consumers due to their 'mental or physical infirmity, age or credulity',[7] the fact that they are 'particularly vulnerable to the

[2] For example, in Croatia, the legal position of persons with disabilities is regulated in a number of instruments, i.e. the CRPD (Official gazette MU, 6/07, 5/08), the Anti-discrimination Act (Official Gazette 85/08, 112/12), and the Disability Ombudsman Act (Official Gazette 107/07), while their employment possibilities are regulated by the Professional Rehabilitation and Employment of Persons with Disabilities Act (Official Gazette 157/13, 152/14).

[3] Case C-13/05 *Sonia Chacón Navas v Eurest Colectividades SA* [2006].

[4] Joined Cases C-335/11 and C-337/11 *HK Danmark* [2014]; Case C-363/12 *Z v A Government Department and theBoard of Management of a Community School* [2014].

[5] According to the CJEU's jurisprudence, the 'average' consumer is reasonably well informed, reasonably observant and circumspect.

[6] The CJEU's jurisprudence also recognised the concept of a 'vulnerable' consumer who is entitled to a higher level of protection. See also Wiesbrock (2015, pp. 83–85).

[7] Art 5(3), as well as recital 19, of the Unfair Commercial Practices Directive's preamble.

risks posed by the products under consideration',[8] or 'are particularly vulnerable, because of their mental, physical or psychological infirmity, age or credulity in a way which the trader could reasonably be expected to foresee'.[9]

However, two problems regarding the current concept of the 'vulnerability of persons with disabilities' as consumers as defined in EU law can be detected. The first, revealed in the legal literature, concerns 'vulnerability' stemming from 'mental infirmity' or 'credulity', which cannot be clearly defined or determined, due to which there is no clear notion of how the average member of a group of either 'mentally infirm' or 'credible' consumers could be assessed. In addition, the concepts of 'physical' and 'mental' infirmity are not in line with the CRPD, although the concept of disability, as contained in the Consumer Rights Directive, should be understood and interpreted according to the CRPD.[10] The second problem is acknowledged in court practice and concerns the fact that the national courts and enforcement authorities seem rather reluctant to apply the special rules of Article 5(3) Unfair Commercial Practice Directive (hereinafter: UCPD) to consumers needing more protection. Article 5(3) UCPD is not frequently used in the decisions of the relevant authorities and courts. The main explanation appears to be that the average consumer benchmark was designed and is clearly perceived as the normal consumer benchmark, the vulnerable consumer being an exception that should be interpreted strictly. Moreover, where practices are directed to a particular target group, the *modulated* average consumer benchmark applies, i.e. the benchmark of the average member of that target group (as set out in Article 5(2)(b) *in fine* UCPD). The national courts and enforcement authorities tend to apply the *modulated* average consumer benchmark, instead of the 'vulnerable consumer' benchmark of Article 5(3) UCPD. The fact that consumers do not form a homogenous group justifies a different assessment of the unfairness of a practice targeted at a particular group of consumers (Directorate-General for Justice and Consumers 2017, pp. 43–45). In addition, the findings from the research on the national practices in the MS confirm that the concept of 'vulnerability' is still vague and widely used in a broader context (i.e. not necessarily regarding unfair commercial practices) in respect of persons with mental or physical diseases, but also other vulnerable groups in society (Directorate-General for Justice and Consumers 2017, p. 44). In Croatia, for example, the concept of a 'vulnerable consumer' has been introduced through the transposition of the UCPD in the Croatian Consumer Protection Act (arg. *ex* Article 32/2). However, its insufficient use in court practice has resulted in no genuine effect on the protection of persons with disabilities as consumers (Poretti 2017, pp. 180–182).

[8] Recital 8 of the Product Safety Directive's preamble.

[9] Recital 34 of the Consumer Rights Directive's preamble.

[10] Joined Cases C-335/11 and C-337/11 *Jette Ring and HK Danmark* [2013], paras 37 to 39; See also Wiesbrock (2015, p. 87).

4 Conclusion

Although the vulnerability of persons with disabilities has been tackled under EU law, a specific legal framework providing protection for persons with disabilities is still missing. 'Vulnerability' as a separate concept is still not defined in EU law or by its case law. At the EU level, the protection of persons with disabilities is being developed through the distinction of the concepts of an 'average' and a 'vulnerable' participant in the market immanent in EU consumer law. Thereby, in assessing the effect of the efforts to provide protection for vulnerable consumers, it should not be disregarded that EU consumer protection policy and legislation have developed as a part of the measures aimed at promoting market integration. Hence, the limitations of the scope of protection provided to persons with disabilities under the concept of 'vulnerability' are largely influenced by several factors which all stem from the market integration policy. Being developed under EU consumer law, 'vulnerability' is construed as a broad concept, implying the protection of different potentially vulnerable groups of consumers such as children, the elderly, and the poor or indebted, with persons with disabilities being just one possible group among them. In this sense, it is possible to agree that it is not clear which groups of consumers can be categorised as 'vulnerable', as EU law fails to differentiate between various groups of 'vulnerable' consumers and the kinds of additional protection that they should be granted (Waddington 2013, p. 16).

At the same time, when assessing the 'vulnerability' of persons with disabilities, the courts of the MS are not obligated to take into account the specific situation of an individual. Instead, the national courts usually apply the typical categories of consumers, without considering the situational vulnerability of persons with disabilities, which is not caused by such persons' impairment, but by the social barriers which are imposed by human behaviour or an unadjusted environment. In addition, in situations in which the courts should provide additional protection due to the vulnerability of consumers, the requirements of the functioning of the internal market emerge as a limit on the scope of protection awarded to them. However, in order to question such practices of the national courts before the EU Courts, the CRPD and its requirement that the state parties take all appropriate measures to provide access to persons with disabilities to the support they may require in exercising their legal capacity (arg. *ex* Article 12/3) cannot be directly relied on in exercising EU law.[11]

In terms of other EU instruments which could be invoked or serve as a basis for enhancing the protection of persons with disabilities, the possibilities are limited. Although the European Consumer Agenda included the concept of vulnerable consumers, it failed to further its development or application. From the current activities of the EC in setting the new consumer programme for the next period, it is not

[11] Case C-363/12 *Z v A Government Department and the Board of Management of a Community School* [2014], para 90.

possible to foresee whether any developments should be expected.[12] Because the concept of the protection of persons with disabilities will most likely continue to be observed through the goals of the market integration policy as the European Disability Strategy has implied, the restrictions on its effectiveness should be accepted. Namely, the main problem is the fact that it is difficult to expect instruments related to consumer protection, which also serve the aim of market integration, to focus on the real needs and circumstances of persons with disabilities or the practices and attitudes they face in the same manner as the CRPD. In this sense, in order to ensure a high level of protection for persons with disabilities at the EU level based on the social model of disability, the introduction of a concept of social vulnerability in binding EU legislation should be advocated. Only such an approach would guarantee a shift in the practice of the national courts, as well as the possibility for the EU Courts to prevent legal, physical or social obstacles in the MS which prohibit persons with disabilities from acquiring the same level of protection and exercising their rights and obligations as 'fully equal' members of society.

References

Bergeron, J. (2015). *Draft report with recommendations to the Commission on the protection of vulnerable adults (2015/2085(INL))*. Bruxelles: Committee on Legal Affairs.

Directorate-General for Justice and Consumers. (2017). *Study for the fitness check of EU consumer and marketing law, Main report* (pp. 1–467). European Union: Directorate-General for Justice and Consumers.

Ippolito, F., & Iglesias Sánchez, S. (2015). Introduction. In F. Ippolito & S. Iglesias Sánchez (Eds.), *Protecting vulnerable groups: The European human rights framework* (pp. 1–20). London: Hart Publishing.

Marinčić, M. (2008). Jesu li osobe s invaliditetom "invalidi?" Pitanje konceptualne naravi, ali i potreba izjednačavanja mogućnosti. *Društvena istraživanja Zagreb, 17*(1–2), 199–221.

Poretti, P. (2017). *Study for the fitness check of EU consumer and marketing law, Final report Part 3-Country reporting-Croatia* (pp. 151–194). European Union: Directorate-General for Justice and Consumers.

Salm, C. (2016). *Protection of vulnerable adults study, European added value assessment*. Bruxelles: European Parliamentary Research Service.

Schotch, R. K. (2000). Models of disability and the Americans with Disabilities Act. *Berkeley Journal of Employment and Labour Law, 12*, 213–222.

Waddington, L. (2013). *Reflections on the protection of 'vulnerable' consumers under EU law* (Working Paper 2). Maastricht: Maastricht University.

Wiesbrock, A. (2015). Disability as a form of vulnerability under EU and CoE law: Embracing the 'social model'? In F. Ippolito & S. Iglesias Sánchez (Eds.), *Protecting vulnerable groups: The European human rights framework* (pp. 71–94). London: Hart Publishing.

[12]The DG Justice and Consumers of the European Commission commissioned two interlinked evaluations in 2017 which will provide an adequate basis for considerations regarding the new programme.

Waste Producer and Waste Holder

Valentina Colcelli

1 Introduction

The statuses of waste producer and waste holder fluctuate between the polluter-pays principle and the qualification of given products such as waste or "derived-by-products" for the production of renewable energy. In any case, both of the statuses have a function and a definition related to their purpose in the internal market that the EU seeks to build. In this sense, the starting point for the relevance of the statuses of waste producer and waste holder is that the European Union has become a leader in international environmental governance over the past two decades, replacing the United States (US) as the most prominent green *demandeur* in international politics (Versolmann 2016).

Directive 2009/28/EC, Directive 2011/92/EU and Directive 2012/27/EU are usually identified as the second generation of EU legislation on renewable energy and biomass plant localisation. These core directives relate to the Member States' obligations to remove the non-cost barriers, and in particular, the administrative barriers to the increased deployment of renewable energy systems (RES) (Article 13) (Szulecki et al. 2016).

Furthermore, the European Parliament adopted a resolution on the Council's position at its first reading with a view to the adoption of a directive of the European Parliament and of the Council amending Directive 98/70/EC relating to the quality of petrol and diesel fuels and amending Directive 2009/28/EC on the promotion of the use of energy from renewable sources (10710/2/2014—C8-0004/2015—2012/0288(COD)). Thus, the EU institutions, starting on 28 April 2015, began working on a new fuel quality and renewable energy directive. In the framework of the EU fight against climate change (European Commission 2000), the EU attempted

V. Colcelli (✉)
National Research Council, IFAC Institute, Sesto Fiorentino, Firenze, 50019, Italy
e-mail: valentina.colcelli@cnr.it

A. Bartolini et al. (eds.), *Dictionary of Statuses within EU Law*,
https://doi.org/10.1007/978-3-030-00554-2_80

to accelerate the existing policy approach toward biofuels with a view to reducing its dependency on foreign sources of energy, reducing greenhouse gas (GHG) emissions, and supporting farmers' incomes by providing new outlets for agricultural products. As a result, it adopted Directive EC 2009/30, which aimed to promote the use of biofuels or other renewable fuels for transport.

The EU biofuels legislation includes three important sustainability criteria. These sustainability criteria are set out in the Renewable Energy Directive adopted in 2009. For biofuels, the corresponding criteria are set out in the Fuel Quality Directive (Directive 2009/30/EC). The sustainability principles are the overarching goals that the individual producers should strive to achieve.

In this complex legal framework, what could potentially be "waste" has become a factor of production consumed in the green energy production process, and it is not only related to waste disposal. The waste producer and the waste holder are the main economic actors in the supply related to waste disposal and who are involved before a given substance can be qualified as "waste" in other production processes such as the renewable energy system.

2 Definitions of Waste Producer and Waste Holder in Directive 2009/28/EC

For the purposes of Directive 2008/98, a "waste producer" means anyone whose activities produce waste (original waste producer) or anyone who carries out pre-processing, mixing or other operations resulting in a change in the nature or composition of this waste.

Article 3 of that Directive provides in point 6 that a "waste holder" means the waste producer or the natural or legal person who is in possession of the waste.

> So far as concerns the financing of the cost of management and disposal of urban waste, inasmuch as a service provided on a collective basis to a body of 'holders' is involved, the Member States are obliged, under Article 15 of Directive 2008/98, to ensure that, in principle, all the users of that service, in their capacity as 'holders' within the meaning of Article 3 of that directive, collectively bear the overall cost of disposing of the waste (see, by analogy, judgment of 16 July 2009, Futura Immobiliare and Others, C-254/08, paragraph 46) (Case C-335/16, point 25).

Therefore, according to Case C-335/16, the concepts of waste holder and waste producer are linked to a financial obligation arising from their contribution to the production of that waste: "(24) Under Article 14 of Directive 2008/98, and in accordance with the polluter-pays principle, the costs of waste management are to be borne by the original waste producer or by the current or previous waste holders. The waste holders are subject to this financial obligation due to their contribution to the production of that waste (see, by analogy, judgments of 24 June 2008, Commune de Mesquer, C-188/07, paragraph 77, and of 16 July 2009, Futura Immobiliare and Others, C-254/08, par, 45)".

It is possible to avoid paying the tax only if the waste producer or the waste holder disposes of the waste independently, and accordingly, to be exempted from liability for the payment of a municipal tax for the disposal of waste if it is not precluded by national legislation under which no provision is made and that legislation meets the requirements of the principle of proportionality (Case C-551/13).

In any case, the waste producer must always be identifiable, and the "inevitable consequence of the administrative tracking procedure provided for in Article 18 of Regulation No 1013/2006 is that the consignee of the shipment will be made aware of the name of the waste producer and no derogation may be inferred from that regulation" (Case C-1/11, Interseroh Scrap and Metals Trading GmbH v Sonderabfall-Management-Gesellschaft Rheinland-Pfalz mbH (SAM)). Thus, the intermediate dealer is required to enter the name of the waste producer in Field 6 of the shipment document according to Article 18(4) of Regulation No 1013/2006, with potentially damaging consequences. "The person who arranges for the shipment and the consignee to keep the information covered by Article 18(1) of that regulation for at least three years from the date when the shipment starts. The necessary consequence of those provisions is that the consignee of the shipment receives all of the information contained in the shipment document, and will therefore be made aware inter alia of the name of the waste producer … as required by that regulation" (Case C-1/11, Interseroh Scrap and Metals Trading GmbH v Sonderabfall-Management-Gesellschaft Rheinland-Pfalz mbH (SAM)). This right prevails over any national law that requires information concerning the waste producer to be treated as confidential, since it is generally acknowledged that an undertaking's sources of supply are business secrets, which are not protected as a fundamental right. On the other side, the protection of human health and the environment against the harmful effects caused by the collection, transport, treatment, storage and tipping of waste are fundamental rights that must be protected.

However, the definitions that we can find in the Directives do not fully define the statuses mentioned above, because of the strong relationship between "waste management"[1] and the meaning of waste, and the lack of a clear definition of the latter.

3 Intent to "Discard" as the Criterion for Defining Who Is a Waste Producer or Waste Holder in Light of the EU Renewable Energy Strategy

According to the EU legal framework on waste and its function for the EU policy related to green energy production, the statuses of waste producer or holder are linked to what "waste" means and turn on the meaning of the word "discard" (Case

[1] According to point 9 of Directive 2008/98, "waste management" means the collection, transport, recovery and disposal of waste, including the supervision of such operations and the after-care of disposal sites, and including actions taken as a dealer or broker.

C-129/96 Inter-Environment Wallonie [1997] ECR I-7411, paragraph 26). Thus, the "intent" of the producer or the holder is the only criterion capable of clarifying "who is who" and "what is what".

Specified waste materials or raw materials resulting from an extraction or manufacturing process whose production was not the primary intention of that process may be regarded not as a residue, but as a by-product, which the undertaking does not seek to throw away according to Art. 3 of the Directive on Waste (Directive 2006/12/EC of The European Parliament and of the Council Of 5 April 2006). This is a moment in which the circulation of such materials in the internal market may suffer severe limitations, so it is very relevant to clarify the meaning of "waste" and how to manage it for the purpose of Directive 2008/98.

According to Art. 3 of the Directive on Waste, "waste" means any substance or object that the holder discards or intends to or is required to discard.

Therefore, the scope of the term "waste" turns on the meaning of the word "discard" (Case C-129/96 Inter-Environment Wallonie [1997] ECR I-7411, paragraph 26).

The Directive does not provide any decisive criteria for determining the intention of the holder to discard a given substance. The Court of Justice has been asked on several occasions for preliminary rulings on whether various materials are to be regarded as waste.

The question of whether or not a given substance is waste must be determined in light of all the circumstances (C-9/00, Palin Granit), regard being had to the aim of the Directive and the need to ensure that its effectiveness is not undermined (ARCO Chemie Nederland, paragraphs 73, 88 and 97). However, the concept of waste cannot be interpreted restrictively.

As a "derived by-product" in the internal market, a given substance shall cease to be waste, within the meaning of point (1) of Article 3, when it has undergone a recovery or operation in which the principal result is the waste serving a useful purpose by replacing other materials which would otherwise have been used to fulfil a particular function, or waste being prepared to achieve that function, in the plant or in the wider economy.

The Court of Justice has provided some indicators from which it may be possible to infer the holder's intent. Therefore, it appears that in addition to the criterion of whether a substance constitutes a production residue, a second relevant test for determining whether or not that substance is waste according to the above-mentioned Directive is the degree of likelihood that the substance will be reused, without any further processing prior to its reuse. The EU Court stated (Case C-147/15) that sometimes, one "must take into consideration the circumstances surrounding the backfilling operation in order to determine whether the operation would have gone ahead even in the absence of waste other than extractive waste. Thus, for instance, the fact that the operator of the quarry at issue in the main proceedings acquires such waste in exchange of payment to the waste producer or holder may indicate that the main objective of the operation in question is the recovery of such waste (see, to that effect, judgment of 13 February 2003 in Commission *v* Luxembourg, C-458/00, paragraph 44)".

If in addition to the mere possibility of reusing the material, there is also a financial advantage to the holder in so doing, the likelihood of reuse is high.

In such circumstances, the substance in question must no longer be regarded as waste that its holder seeks to "discard", but as a genuine product.

Because the waste's qualification as a "derived-by-product" stems from the holder's intention, its interpretation by the public powers affects such goods' free movement in the internal market.

First, in many of the Member States' legal systems, the burden of proof for the demonstration of the nature of the derived by-product moves to the holder, assuming judicial or administrative contestation (f.i. in the Italian legal system according to the criminal case Cass. Pen. Sez. III n.16200/2014). Because the qualification of waste as not being discarded, but as a biomass derived by-product is a derogation from the general rule established by law, the burden of proof regarding the existence of the conditions for the qualification (of biomass as a derived by-product) must be met by the one who requires the application of the exception.

Second, the limitation may be imposed properly by a government decision (Hansen et al. 2002).

If, according to Article 35 TFEU (Export Barriers), waste for recovery should be permitted to freely circulate within the EU market without restrictions, any possible limitation could be based on the respect for the fundamental requirements concerning waste management set out in Article 13 of the Waste Directive. Thus, waste management must be carried out without endangering human health and without harming the environment. As explained in Joined Cases C-418/97 and C-419/97 ARCO Chemie Nederland and Others [2000] ECR I-4475, paragraphs 36 to 40, the term "discard" must be interpreted in light of the aim of Directive 75/442 (the old Waste Directive reformed in 2006). This aim, according to its third recital, is the protection of human health and the environment against harmful effects caused by the collection, transport, treatment, storage and tipping of waste. Also, Art. 191 TFEU (old Article 174(2) EC) provides that Community policy on the environment must aim at a high level of protection and must be based, in particular, on the precautionary principle and the principle that preventive action should be taken (Edward 2013).

It must, therefore, be concluded that waste, whether recyclable or not, is to be regarded as "goods" whose movement, according to Article 30 of the Treaty, must, in principle, not be prevented (Case C-2/90 Commission of the European Communities v Kingdom of Belgium).

Even if the national measure could be justified by reasons relating to the protection of the environment (Case C-203/96 Chemische Afvalstoffen Dusseldorp BV and Others v Minister van Volkshuisvesting, Ruimtelijke Ordening en Milieubeheer), no action of a purely economic nature can justify barriers to the fundamental principle of the free movement of goods (Case C-120/95 Decker [1998] ECR I-0000, paragraph 39) (Engle 2008).

In this case, the EU should verify the compatibility of national or regional legislative decisions with the fundamental freedom of the circulation of goods in the internal market.

4 Definition of Biomass and Farmers as Waste Holders, Waste Producers or Suppliers of Biomass-Derived By-products

To explain in a more concrete manner why it is not easy to identify the meaning of waste, and thus, who is a waste producer or waste holder, we can use the example of a farmer, when she/he decides to supply a plant with her/his biomass for energy production.

According to European Union policy on the use of energy from renewable sources, biomass utilisation is an energy source that provides opportunities, related to f.i. (a) the exploitation of an endogenous resource, (b) that does not have an endemic dependence on price variations due to constraints in the global markets and to external geopolitical stability, and (c) can contribute appreciably to the creation of direct jobs in raw materials management and in the supply of energy products to consuming companies.

The greatest potential for renewable energy proceeding from agriculture stems from the use of the non-edible portions of crops.

The definition of biomass established by Art. 2 of Directive 2009/28/EC is not sufficient to qualify it as a juridical good, which, as such, can freely circulate in the EU market. Its qualification must be reconstructed through concentric passages, taking into consideration the EU legal framework on the use of biomass for energy production and waste treatment.

Biomass is the biodegradable portion of products, waste, and residues of a biological origin from agriculture (including vegetal and animal substances), forestry and related industries, including fisheries and aquaculture, as well as the biodegradable portion of industrial and municipal waste (Art. 2 of Directive 2009/28/EC).

The same legislative definition of biomass incorporates the concept of waste. However, waste is a concept that is even broader than the definition of 'biomass' present in Art. 2 mentioned above. Because the sources of waste are so diverse, it is convenient to consider the valorisation of biomass waste for different uses.

(1) Thus, starting from the EU framework on biomass legislation, which is likened to energy production, and according to Art. 2, paras.1 and 2, Directive 2008/98/EC on waste, biomass is not waste, but rather is a good moving freely in the internal market, if it is faecal matter and if it is not covered by paragraph 2(b) of Art. 2 Directive 2008/98/EC on waste. The reference to the letter b) of Art. 2 cited refers to the concept of "land (*in situ*) including unexcavated contaminated soil and buildings permanently connected with land".
(2) Straw and other natural non-hazardous agricultural or forestry material used in farming and forestry.
(3) Straw and other natural non-hazardous agricultural or forestry material utilised for the production of energy (if this is biomass that is not processed), but also if the production of energy is realised by starting with such biomass processed by methods which do not harm the environment or endanger human health.

(4) Animal by-products including processed products covered by Regulation (EC) No 1774/2002 (Animal by-products Regulation), except those which are destined for incineration, a landfill or use in a biogas or composting plant.
(5) Carcasses of animals that have died other than by being slaughtered, including animals killed to eradicate epizootic diseases, and that are disposed of according to Regulation (EC) No 1774/2002.[2]

Outside of the list above, biomass must be considered to be waste.

Waste is perhaps a concept that is even broader than the definition above because it applies to any biomass-derived by-product (Cheyne 2002).

As waste, biomass can still have a second life.

Because the term "biomass" has an unclear and univocal meaning, this has an impact on a farmer's qualification as a waste producer, waste holder or supplier of biomass-derived by-products.

5 Conclusion

For the purposes of Directive 2008/98, a "waste producer" means anyone whose activities produce waste (original waste producer) or anyone who carries out pre-processing, mixing or other operations resulting in a change in the nature or composition of this waste, and a "waste holder" means the waste producer or the natural or legal person who is in possession of the waste. In any case, according to the EU renewable energy policy, a given substance that could potentially be "waste" could become a factor of production consumed in the green energy production process, and thus, is not only related to waste disposal. However, the Directive does not provide any decisive criteria for determining the intention of the holder or producer to discard a given substance. The scope of the term "waste" turns on the meaning of the phrase "discard", and this has an impact on the qualification of the statuses mentioned above and on the rights and obligations related to them. The EU Court of Justice has identified some elements that are useful in understanding the producer/holder waste's intent.

References

Cheyne, I. (2002). The definition of waste in EC law. *Journal of Environmental Law, 14*(1), 61–73.
Edward, V. (2013). A review of the Court of Justice's case law in relation to waste and environmental impact assessment: 1992–2011. *Journal of Environmental Law, 25*(3), 515–530.

[2] It should be underlined that Regulation (EC) No 1774/2002 (Animal by-products Regulation) was repealed by Regulation (EC) No 1069/2009.

Engle, E. (2008–2009). Environmental protection as an obstacle to free movement of goods: Realist jurisprudence in Articles 28 and 30 of the E.C. Treaty. *Journal of Law & Commerce, 27*, 113.

European Commission. (2000). *European Climate Change Programme (ECCP)*. Final Report https://ec.europa.eu/clima/sites/clima/files/eccp/first/docs/final_report_en.pdf

Hansen, W., Christopher, M., & Verbuecheln, M. (2002). *EU waste policy and challenges for regional and local authorities*. Berlin: Ecologic - Centre for International and European Environmental Research.

Szulecki, K., Fischer, S., Gullberg, A. T., & Sartor, O. (2016). Shaping the 'energy union': Between national positions and governance innovation in EU energy and climate policy. *Climate Policy, 16*(5), 548–556.

Versolmann, I. (2016, September). Decision 994/2012 and beyond: Assessing the driving factors of integration in the field of external energy policy. Paper presented at the UACES 46th Annual Conference Queen Mary University of London. https://www.uaces.org/events/conferences/london/papers/abstract.php?paper_id=370#.WziMIS1aZ0s

Woman

Cristina Elías Méndez

1 Introduction: Traditional Definition

The traditional legal definition of woman is based on the principle of formal equality of all persons before the law, which obviously covers legal equality between women and men. This basic principle governs, on the one hand, the internal law of the Member States, considering the democratic principles required to any State belonging to the European Union (EU). It also obeys the coherence of the democratic principles that govern it (i.e., Article 2 TEU). Progressively, the provisions aimed at the achievement of material equality have been incorporated into the *community acquis* of the EU Common Constitutional Law (Häberle 1993), but this does not diminish the important political and legal commitment that the EU has been making in several areas, as well as transforming and shaping the legal status of women in the EU.

The original Article 119 of the Treaty of the European Economic Community, which established the 'principle that men and women should receive equal pay for equal work', obeyed economic reasons of ensuring competition between companies. It should be remembered that it was not until 1997 that the Treaty of Amsterdam finally incorporated the right of equality as a fundamental right, including equality of treatment between women and men among the objectives and missions of the then European Community (Mangas Martín 2008). Gradually, the general development and process of including fundamental rights in the EU has also involved awareness regarding the importance of material equality between women and men, finally becoming one of the main features of fundamental rights in the EU.

In the following sections, we will detail the range of rights that are designed to achieve the effectiveness of real equality, which make up the current status of

C. Elías Méndez (✉)
Universidad Nacional de Educación a Distancia (UNED), Faculty of Law, Department of Constitutional Law, Madrid, Spain
e-mail: celias@der.uned.es

A. Bartolini et al. (eds.), *Dictionary of Statuses within EU Law*,
https://doi.org/10.1007/978-3-030-00554-2_81

women in the EU. We will also point out those aspects of equality that EU law has disregarded.

2 EU Law on Women's Rights

In the analysis of the legal status of women in the EU, we will not study the reference norms and sentences in chronological order; instead, we will study them in hierarchical and typological manner: beginning with primary law, then descending to the secondary and finally devoting attention to jurisprudence. For reasons of space, we cannot be exhaustive in the description of secondary law or jurisprudence, so we will try to select the most relevant legal instruments and judgments that have been decisive in shaping the legal status of women in the EU.

2.1 Fundamental Principles of the Legal Status of Women in the EU

Non-discrimination and, specifically, gender equality are enshrined in the Treaty of the EU (TEU) as value (Article 2) and as an objective (Article 3(3)). It also enshrined in the Treaty on the Functioning of the EU (TFEU), which also formulates a principle of mainstreaming (Articles 8 and 10). Legislative procedures are regulated to adopt the principles and actions that combat discrimination based on sex, without prejudice to the measures adopted by the Member States (Article 19 TFEU). The Treaties also allow the EU to support and complement the Member States in the promotion of equality between men and women, with regard to labour market opportunities and treatment at work (Article 153). Article 157 TFEU requires the Member States and the EU to ensure the application of the principle of equal pay for equal work or work of equal value, and it enables Member States to take positive action in order to ensure full equality in the workplace.

It is also necessary to address the analysis of the provisions of the Charter of Fundamental Rights of the EU (the Charter), which is not a chronological point of departure but an essential arrival, after a long struggle for rights and freedoms in the European project. From a legal point of view, what is included in the Charter is especially relevant considering its legal binding force (i.e., 'the same legal value as the Treaties', according to the recognition granted by the Treaty of Lisbon, as provided in Article 6 TEU). From a material perspective, the rights and freedoms—regarded as most important in the context of the EU—have been chosen to be included in such a relevant document.

In Title III of the Charter, which is devoted to equality, we can find the consecration of formal equality (i.e., equality before the law; Article 20), and the forbiddance of discrimination on grounds of sex (Article 21). Article 23 specifically proclaims equality between women and men in all areas, highlighting the areas of employment, work and pay. In addition, it expressly adds a provision that allows (i.e., 'constitutionalizes', if we adopt the perspective of the quasi-constitutional character of the Charter) positive actions.

In Title IV of the Charter, under the heading 'solidarity', we find two relevant provisions. Thus, Article 33 departs from a classical principle of protection of the family, but also consecrates—in a more innovative way—the reconciliation of family and professional life as an objective, which is specified in the right of any person to protection from dismissal for a reason connected with maternity, the right to paid maternity leave and the right to parental leave following the birth or adoption of a child. Article 34 recognises the entitlement to social security benefits and social services (e.g., benefits and services that pertain to motherhood), in accordance with the rules laid down by EU law and national laws and practices.

Thus, the main pillars of equality between women and men in the EU are set up. Building on the principles of formal equality and the prohibition of gender discrimination, the importance of achieving equality in all areas is emphasised; thus, justifying a principle of mainstreaming, which is especially applied in the workplace. The legal basis for the introduction of positive actions is also provided. In the context of solidarity, which refers to the social dimension of the EU, it has been decided to consecrate the objective of reconciling family and professional life, which is specified into concrete measures in the fields of work and social aids.

It is also convenient to make reference to the European Pillar of Social Rights, the recent declaration of the EU on social principles and rights, whose legal force lies at the moment in its formal proclamation. Among its twenty formal principles, there are several of interest for effective equality between women and men. Thus, the second principle is specifically dedicated to equal treatment and opportunities between women and men in all areas, in addition to reiterating the classic principle of equal pay. The third principle refers to the principle of equal opportunities, regarding employment, social protection, education and access to goods and services available to the public, regardless of, among other things, gender. It also contains the commitment to promote equal opportunities for underrepresented groups to achieve real equality.

The ninth principle (work-life balance) is of great interest, because it specifies a series of measures for the achievement of material equality. We highlight this provision for the formulation of a principle of flexible working arrangements for parents and people with caring responsibilities and the formulation of a right of access to care services that are linked to the social character of the EU and the Member States. Likewise, the encouragement of a shared responsibility between men and women in the fulfilment of their caring responsibilities should be underlined. Also, principle 11, which proclaims the right of children to affordable early childhood education and good quality child care, can benefit gender equality policies and access of mothers and fathers to the labour market. Finally, principle 15 proclaims that women and men shall have equal opportunities to acquire pension rights.

The documents accompanying the European Pillar explain the problems detected and the data that justify the introduction of these measures (European Commission 2018):

> Measures to address gender inequalities include ensuring equal treatment in all areas, including employment and addressing gender gaps in pay, earnings, pensions as well as gender stereotypes. A more equal use of work-life balance arrangements between the sexes has also been shown to have a positive impact on women's employment. Policies in this area include access to adequate leave arrangements, flexible working arrangements and access to care services.

2.2 *Secondary Law*

As previously stated, making an exhaustive analysis of EU gender equality legislation is not possible, due to space restrictions. We try, therefore, to analyse secondary law regulation, following a double criterion of thematic and type of source. The first main area of interest for EU law has been, on the basis of the old Article 119 of the Treaty of Rome, the working conditions—although initially from a strictly liberal perspective, without including social rights (Balaguer Callejón 2005). The subjects of employment and entrepreneurship continue to be one of the major areas of European gender law, which has progressively been extended to other social aspects. Thus, we emphasise the strict labour-scope of the Directive 2006/54/EC, Directive 2010/41/EU and, among others, the Communication from the Commission (COM (2007) 424), tackling the pay gap between men and women.

In the social field, it is worth mentioning Council Directive 92/85/EEC, which sets out the basic rights of all women before and after pregnancy in the EU. Council Directive 2010/18/EU states that parental leave must be granted for at least four months as an individual right of both parents. Council Recommendation 92/241/EEC addresses childcare as a necessary element for work-life balance for men and women. Council Directive 79/7/EEC aims to ensure progressive implementation of the principle of equal treatment for men and women in matters of social security.

Beyond this field, Council Directive 2004/113/EC implements the principle of equal treatment between men and women outside the employment market, in the access to and supply of goods and services. Following, among others, the Council Resolution of 29 May 1990 on the protection of the dignity of women and men at work, the European Commission approved in 1992 a code of practice on sexual harassment (Official Journal L 49 of 24.02.1992) to clamp down on sexual harassment at work. It is also worth mentioning the Commission Decision 2000/407/EC, which relates to gender balance within the committees and expert groups established by it. We should also point out the Communication from the Commission (COM(2012) 615 final of 14.11.2012) with regard to gender balance in business leadership.

Another Communication from the Commission relating to 'A Woman's Charter' (COM(2010) 78 final, not published in the Official Journal) lists the principles of equality between women and men, justifying a gender-mainstreaming approach and explaining the strategies adopted by the Commission for gender equality: equal economic independence; equal pay for work of equal value; equality in decision making; dignity, integrity and ending gender-based violence; and promoting gender equality beyond the EU. These strategies form a framework for the coordination of action in all areas of EU activities, which remain valid from 2016 to 2019 (European Commission 2015). Finally, we can recall that a number of institutions specifically working in favour of gender equality have been set up, mainly the European Institute for Gender Equality (Regulation EC, No 1922/2006) and an Advisory Committee on Equal Opportunities for Women and Men (Commission Decision 2008/590/EC).

As we can see, the rights of non-discrimination in the labour sphere and, in some cases, in the social field, are consolidated and guaranteed through the binding force of directives. However, the only incipient progress in the fight against sexual harassment or gender balance in leadership positions within the public and private spheres are mainly reflected in mere soft-law instruments.

2.3 *Case Law*

The European Court of Justice, in line with its significant work in favour of fundamental rights, has also set important precedents against gender discrimination in its judgments. As in the case of EU secondary law, we do not intend to be exhaustive, but we do intend to undertake a selection of the most significant precedents (Consejo General del Poder Judicial 2018; Gómez Sánchez 2015; Mangas Martín 2008). The activity of the EU Court is obviously consistent with the principles and rights that are enshrined in EU law, which explains why a significant number of sentences are devoted to the main issues listed in the previous section.

First of all, we can, therefore, distinguish a jurisprudential line dedicated to the interpretation and application of the principle of equal pay. Thus, the *Defrenne* case (ECJ, 8 April 1976, C-43/75, *Defrenne v Sabena*) confirmed that this principle has a direct effect and must be guaranteed by the national courts. The EU Court also noted that there is discrimination in the differentiated pay for part-time staff, which is predominantly female (based on a doctrine which goes from the *Jenkins* case (ECJ, 31 March 1986, C-96/80) to the *Bötel* case (ECJ, 4 June 1992, C-360/90) and then to the recent *Espadas Recio* Sentence (ECJ, 9 November 2017, C-98/15). It is also worth mentioning the *Danfoss* case (ECJ, 17 October 1989, C-109/88)—a doctrine confirmed in *Enderby* (ECJ, 27 October 1993, C-127/92)—which establishes the reversal of the burden of proof when a company applies a system of pay that lacks transparency. The special attention given to indirect discrimination that involves the greater presence of women in part-time work and their different treatment is also addressed in the cases *Nimz* (ECJ, 7 February 1991, C-184/89), *Gester* (ECJ, 2 October 1997, C-1/95) and *Elbal Moreno* (ECJ, 22 November 2012, C-385/11).

The *Marshall* case (ECJ, 11 November 1997, C-409/95) was a very relevant sentence, correcting and improving the *Kalanke* doctrine (ECJ, 17 October 1995,

C-450/93). In *Marshall*, the Court established that positive discrimination actions are correspondent to the principle of non-discrimination. The *Badeck* judgment (ECJ, 28 March 2000, C-158/97) added that the regulations for the promotion of women in public functions are also correspondent to the principle of non-discrimination.

The protection against discrimination, due to pregnancy or maternity, has been specified in cases such as *Dekker* (ECJ, 8 November 1990, C-177/88), *Habermann-Beltermann* (ECJ, 5 May 1994, C-421/92), *Webb* (ECJ, 14 July 1994, C-32/93) or *Mahlburg* (ECJ, 3 February 2000, C-207/98), but also in *Brown* (ECJ, 30 June 1998, C-394/96), in which the dismissal of the worker occurred during pregnancy and was motivated by absences due to incapacity for work derived from it. The *Paquay* judgment (ECJ, 11 October 2007, C-460/06) establishes the prohibition of notifying a dismissal decision, because of pregnancy or the birth of a child during the protection period, as well as adopting preparatory measures for that decision before the said period expires. The *Thibault* case (ECJ, 30 April 1998, C-136/95) regarded discriminatory not to count the days of absence for maternity leave, for purposes of professional promotion.

The Court of Luxembourg ruled in its judgment, *Association Belge des Consommateurs Test-Achats et al.* (ECJ, 1 March 2011, C-236/09), a preliminary ruling on the validity of Article 5.2 (parental leave) of Directive 2004/113/EC, denying that a provision may allow Member States to maintain—without limitation—an exemption from the rule of unisex premiums and benefits. Judgment *Gueye and Salmerón Sánchez* (ECJ, 15 September 2011, C-483/09) settles preliminary questions referred from Spain, concerning protection measures for victims of gender violence.

The EU Court has made, through its jurisprudence, important work in favour of the guarantee and effectiveness of the rights that make up the legal status of women in the EU; in specific cases, applying European norms but, at the same time, having a positive impact on their development and consolidation (Freixes Sanjuán 2014).

3 Current Legal Status of Women in the EU

The starting point of women's legal position in the EU is equality before the law and, therefore, the formal equality of rights and obligations with respect to men. This legal status was strengthened as fundamental rights were gaining strength in an EU whose origin was limited to economic reasons. Early on, the prohibition of wage discrimination was included in the Treaty of Rome, a measure that was frozen in time as the sole reference to gender discrimination until the approval of the Treaty of Amsterdam. However, gradually, the development of this principle, on par with other rights and freedoms, and concern for the effective equality between men and women led to strengthening equality measures, which have experienced a significant development in social areas; thus, transforming the traditional juridical definition of women in the EU.

Currently, gender equality is a fundamental value and an objective of the EU, as well as a fundamental right; thus, the fight against gender discrimination must permeate all its policies and actions. Its enunciation is embodied and specified in the right of women in the EU to equality before the law, in the prohibition of gender discrimination and in the equality on all areas—especially in the fields of employment, work and pay. Measures of positive discrimination of the less-represented gender are allowed.

Overcoming a purely formal and liberal approach in the fight against discrimination has also led to the proclamation of the reconciliation of family and professional life as an objective, which is specified in the right of every person to be protected against any dismissal for a cause related to motherhood, as well as the right to paid maternity leave and parental leave due to the birth or adoption of a child. A right of access to social security benefits and social services, in the case of maternity, is also formulated. Thus, the social perspective of the EU is shown in these dimensions and placed at the service of achieving real equality.

An important number of directives have established a minimum of rights, aimed at the protection of maternity and against the discrimination to which it may give rise. It is a principle of non-discrimination that has also extended to social security and access to goods and services. Other fields in which progress has been made, although mostly with a mere persuasive nature, have been the combat against sexual harassment at work, the promotion of gender balance in public and business leadership and the reinforcement of the role of women in the development cooperation policy of the EU. The right of adequate leave for parents and persons with care responsibilities, the right of flexible working conditions and assistance services, the promotion of shared care responsibility between women and men, the right of children to affordable and good quality child care and equal opportunities to acquire pension rights are formulated as social principles in the European Pillar of Social Rights.

The conglomerate of rights that the *community acquis* has provided to women in the EU is, without a doubt, relevant, and has helped to strengthen their legal position. Deficiencies have been detected, however, regarding the effectiveness in the application of these rights. In the more developed fields (e.g., labour and social), despite the literal wording of the legally binding rule, in certain cases only the concrete claim of the particular before the European Court of Justice has achieved the respect and effectiveness of the right. In this area, the duration of parental leave for the care of minors and dependents and the promotion of co-responsibility should be further improved.

On the other hand, with regard to the newest and less developed areas on gender equality in the EU, the deficits can be explained because their instruments lack legally binding force, thus remaining at the mercy of the effective will of the Member States. This way, some fields (e.g., sexual harassment, parity in decision making or balanced participation in public and private spheres, gender violence or gendered language) have traditionally been neglected in Europe and only sectorial or promotional measures have been taken.

In any case, it is undeniable that the legal status of women in the EU enjoys a leading level of formal and material recognition in the global context. Moreover, it has been a driving force for the improvement of the legislation of the Member States, building an important set of rights on which to move forward.

References

Balaguer Callejón, M. L. (2005). La Constitución europea y la igualdad de género. *Revista de Derecho Constitucional Europeo, 3*, 273–290.

Consejo General del Poder Judicial. (2018). Igualdad de género. Jurisprudencia internacional. http://www.poderjudicial.es/cgpj/es/Temas/Igualdad-de-Genero/Legislacion-y-jurisprudencia/Jurisprudencia-internacional/

European Commission. (2015). *Strategic engagement for gender equality 2016–2019*. http://ec.europa.eu/anti-trafficking/sites/antitrafficking/files/strategic_engagement_for_gender_equality_en.pdf

European Commission. (2018). *Towards a European Pillar of Social Rights*. https://ec.europa.eu/commission/sites/beta-political/files/gender-equality-work-life-balance_en.pdf

Freixes Sanjuán, T. (2014). La igualdad de mujeres y hombres en el derecho de la Unión Europea: Especial referencia a la Jurisprudencia del Tribunal de Justicia de la Unión y del Tribunal Europeo de Derechos Humanos. In I. P. Gosálbez, L. R. Martín, & A. G. Costa (Eds.), *Integración europea y género* (pp. 15–65). Madrid: Tecnos.

Gómez Sánchez, Y. (2015). *Constitucionalismo multinivel. Derechos fundamentales*. Madrid: Sanz y Torres.

Häberle, P. (1993). Derecho constitucional común europeo. *Revista de Estudios Políticos, 79*, 7–46.

Mangas Martín, A. (2008). Cincuenta años de igualdad de trato entre mujeres y hombres en la Unión Europea: Balance. In F. Aldecoa (Ed.), *Los Tratados de Roma en su cincuenta aniversario* (pp. 283–324). Madrid: Marcial Pons.

Worker

Stefano Giubboni

1 Notions of the Worker in EU Law

EU law still lacks a general definition of a worker—or of an employee—and therefore it does not outline the related statutory protection except in a partial and sector-specific way. The reason behind is that, historically, within the EU legal framework, worker status, as well as the related notion, has been defined with a view to ensuring that workers (and their family members) enjoy the freedom of movement within the common (and later internal) market. A notion that was likely to be somewhat generalised has thus been gradually developed by the Court of Justice of the European Union (CJEU) with a view to identifying the subjects entitled to the freedom of movement, now enshrined in Article 45 of the Treaty on the Functioning of the European Union (TFEU) and in relevant secondary legislation (cf. Nogler 2009; Supiot 1992).

The worker status has therefore been defined, at least at an initial stage, with a view to creating the common labour market and to guaranteeing one of the four fundamental freedoms of movement within the Union. As early as in the mid-1970s, following the development of the first round of Community social policies, the statutory protection regime for workers has been gradually complemented with elements not directly aimed at the integration of the market, through the establishment of some minimum protection standards common to the national legal systems. However, that stage, too, featured the prevalence of instances for that type of harmonisation that Massimo D'Antona defined as 'functionalist', referring to its long-lasting orientation towards the creation of the common market and, in particular, the establishment of rules aimed at preventing distortions of competition engendered by social dumping (D'Antona 2000). This was reflected in a breakdown of the notion of employment in the framework of social harmonisation policies: Indeed, a

S. Giubboni (✉)
Department of Political Sciences, University of Perugia, Perugia, Italy
e-mail: Stefano.giubboni@unipg.it

A. Bartolini et al. (eds.), *Dictionary of Statuses within EU Law*,
https://doi.org/10.1007/978-3-030-00554-2_82

European notion of employment emerged, once again thanks to the case law of the CJEU, only from the directives that D'Antona defined as 'cohesive'—to differentiate them from the functionalist ones, the former being aimed at promoting the Union's autonomous social values (and not directly targeted at regulating the market).

Therefore, the special functional connotation in the notion of the worker initially elaborated in the framework of EU law still marks a clear difference from the historical development of labour law in the Member States (cf. Countouris 2007; Deakin 2004; Supiot 1994). The substantial difference is to be found in the rationale and function of the Community and EU definition of a worker and of employee status. On the one hand, the national labour law systems—either in basically general and unitary terms, or following a case-by-case and sector-specific approach—are centred on notions of a worker or an employee that meet the need to include a protection regime in the contractual relationship (cf. D'Antona 1989 and Supiot 1992). On the other hand, EU law develops such a notion mainly with a view to guaranteeing that workers enjoy the freedom of movement in the common market.

This is a distinguishing connotation and—in some ways—a genetic characteristic of EU labour law: Any notion intended to guarantee and promote workers' access to the common labour market lacks, as famously stated by Federico Mancini, that 'criticism of an unequal relationship' that embodies—in all the national legal systems—the very essence of a definition of employment aimed at including in employment contracts a statutory protection regime that is able to overcome the original power asymmetry between the parties (Mancini 1988, p. 33).

Moreover, EU law—which features a case-by-case approach to definitions—does not contain a single definition of a worker. Such notion varies based on the sector of application taken into account and, notably, on the type of source or area of law. In an attempt to rationalise and mainstream this variable pattern of references, scholars have suggested differentiating between two notions: a first one (the only to be a properly EU notion) that is relevant for the purposes of the free movement of workers; and a second one, which is to be developed based on the 'subsidiarity' approach, i.e. by the national law systems, since it is 'essential to the application of some protection regimes of Community labour law' as defined in the Member States' legal systems when transposing EU harmonisation directives (Lunardon and Tosi 2005, pp. 93–94).

On the one hand, the broad *stricto sensu* EU notion of employment—developed by the CJEU pursuant to Article 45 TFEU with the goal of standardising the conditions for the application of workers' freedom of movement within the internal market—also tends to wield its influence in areas other than the one it stems from, and in particular, within the two primary spheres of harmonisation that Massimo D'Antona defined as 'cohesive': the set of fundamental principles and rules on equal treatment and equal opportunities between men and women (and, at a later stage, the new non-discrimination principles), and the legislative framework on the protection of health and safety in the workplace. On the other hand, the notion of the migrant worker relevant for the application of the coordination of the national social security regimes—a notion that was initially not differentiated from the one stemming from Article 45 TFEU—soon began to become more and more autonomous, leading to the progressive (and by now complete) differentiation between the two notions (from, respectively, a labour law and a social security perspective) of the worker.

In light of such remarks, it is necessary to differentiate between three different notions of the worker that are relevant to EU law (cf. Giubboni 2007, 2017). The first notion (the only one to be of a *stricto sensu* EU nature) underlies the uniform application of the fundamental freedom of movement pursuant to Article 45 TFEU, although tending to extend its application outside its area of origin. The second notion, which is historically linked to the first one (albeit now substantially autonomous), is relevant for the purpose of coordinating the Member States' social security systems. The third notion, whose identification is the responsibility of the national legal systems (albeit in compliance with a set of limitations established by the supranational legislature), is intended to outline the scope of application of a significant part of the labour law directives, in particular, those featuring 'functionalist' harmonisation goals.

2 Worker Status and Freedom of Movement

According to consistent case law, which consolidated during the 1980s, in order to determine the scope of application of Article 45 TFEU, 'the essential feature of an employment relationship is that a person performs services of some economic value for and under the direction of another person in return for which he receives remuneration. The sphere in which they are provided and the nature of the legal relationship between employee and employer are immaterial as regards the application of Article 48 [later Article 39 of the Treaty establishing the European Community (TEC) and, finally, Article 45 TFEU]' (CJEU, 3 July 1986, case C-66/85, *Lawrie-Blum v Land Baden-Württemberg*).

The need to fix the notion at the EU level—without prejudice to the necessary ascertainment, by the national courts, of the actual existence of the requirements for the classification of a working relationship as employment—had already been outlined in the initial case law on this matter. As early as the famous *Unger* case, the CJEU had ruled that the term 'worker', as per former Articles 48–51 of the Treaty establishing the European Economic Community (TEEC), as well as the phrase 'wage-earner or assimilated worker' used in Regulation No 3[1958] to define the scope of application of the coordination of social security systems, 'has [...] a community meaning' (CJEU, 19 March 1964, case C-75/63, *Unger v Bedrijfsvereniging voor Detailhandel en Ambachten*): 'the establishment of as complete a freedom of movement for workers as possible' falls under the 'foundations of the Community', and the necessary consistency in the application of such principles would be jeopardised if national legislatures were responsible for determining the scope of the provisions on which such principles are based. If their meaning were to be inferred from internal legislation, 'it would therefore be possible for each Member State to modify the meaning of the concept of "migrant worker" and to eliminate at will the protection afforded by the treaty to certain categories of person'.

In its case law (cf., for instance, cases C-344/87, *Bettray v Staatssecretaris van Justitie*, of 31 May 1989, C-3/87, *The Queen v Ministry of Agriculture, Fisheries and Food, ex parte Agegate*, of 14 December 1989, C-337/97, *Meeusen*, of 8 June 1999, and C-138/02, *Collins*, of 23 March 2004), the CJEU constantly refers to the three objective criteria (relevant to the actual development of the relationship and regardless of the way it has been qualified by the parties) with a view to identifying the scope of application of Article 45 TFEU. These criteria are: (a) the 'effective and genuine' nature of the service (personally) performed; (b) the subjection to the authority (direction) of the recipient thereof (in which the employment relationship truly emerges *stricto sensu*); and (c) the fact that the service is paid for (and thus the payment, in any form whatsoever, of remuneration).

It should not be surprising that, in the framework of Article 45 TFEU, when defining the notion of a worker, the CJEU puts more emphasis not on the employment relationship itself (considered in a broad sense), but rather on the fact that the relationship consists in the provision of services against payment, and mainly on the effective and genuine economic nature of the services performed by the subject. It is primarily thanks to the extensive interpretation of such criteria (rather than on the basis of the broad notion of employment) that the CJEU has managed to easily encompass the patchwork of flexible, atypical, and non-standard work patterns that have been thriving since the end of the 1970s and have become the main form of access to employment in several EU countries over the last decades. Although uncertainties as to the classification of work patterns have been growing within the national legal systems, the CJEU could easily bring different types of work (part-time arrangements, on-demand work, casual work, temporary agency work, fixed-term or seasonal employment, apprenticeships, etc.) within the scope of application of Article 45 TFEU.

3 Worker Status and Coordination of Social Security Systems

The notion of worker that is relevant to the access to the system of coordination of the national social security regimes pursuant to Article 48 TFEU is centred on the status of socially insured persons and is no longer bound to the employment contract or employment relationship. The notion of a worker from a social security perspective—relevant for the purposes of the EU coordination rules (and, now, of Regulation (EC) No 883/2004)—has indeed been separated from the labour law-related notion. The gap between the two notions opened following the shift—which had been almost fully outlined in the abovementioned *Unger* judgement—from the concept of 'worker' to the one of 'socially insured person'.

The 'shift from the notion of worker to that of insured person' (Andreoni 1996, p. 533) determined a gradual differentiation of the two notions (the labour law-related one and the social security-related one) in two main directions, both of which are consistent with the functions of the rules aimed at coordinating the national social security systems. On the one hand, that differentiation led to a partial renationalisation of the social security-related notion of worker, which is shaped by EU law in a far more limited way than the notion enshrined in Article 45 TFEU. On the other hand, when stripping the social security-related notion of any reference to the employment contract or employment relationship, it pushed the latter towards the gradual generalisation of the subjective boundaries of the system of coordination of social security regimes (Article 2 of Regulation (EC) No 883/2004 extends the provisions on the coordination of social security 'to nationals of a Member State, stateless persons and refugees resident in the territory of a Member State who are or have been subject to the social security legislation of one or more Member States, as well as to the members of their families and to their survivors').

4 Worker Status and Social Harmonisation

As already stated, the notion of an employee, developed in the framework of the freedom of movement as per Article 45 TFEU, wields its influence in other fields, particularly in the primary spheres of harmonisation that Massimo D'Antona defined as 'cohesive'. The CJEU has long stated that the criteria developed with regard to Article 45 TFEU are also useful in defining the notion of a worker for the purposes of equal treatment, particularly between male and female workers. Indeed, Articles 45 and 157 TFEU feature the same rationale, which justifies the use of the same broad EU and functional definition of a worker (cf. CJEU, 13 January 2004, C-256/01, *Allonby*). Both provisions embody, in two areas of utmost relevance (citizenship and gender), a fundamental principle of EU law, or more accurately, an actual meta-principle of the supranational legal system, such as equal treatment and non-discrimination, now enshrined in Articles 20 and 21 of the EU Charter of Fundamental Rights.

Whereas antidiscrimination law tends to overcome the boundaries of employment with a view to 'outlining a relevant sphere of protection around the individual as such' (Chieco 2002, p. 58), the legislation on the protection of health and safety in the workplace considers the employee as the main subject in relation to the protection guaranteed by the supranational legal system. However, in this field as well (which sees the application of the broad EU notion of a worker, developed pursuant to Article 45 TFEU), there are strong calls for the extension of the protection beyond the boundaries of employment.

The remarks apply to the set of rules on working time, since Directive 93/104/EC (now Directive 2003/88/EC, Working Time Directive) refers in principle to the same definition criteria as Directive 89/391/EEC. Similarly, in the framework of Directive 92/85/EEC (Pregnant Workers Directive), the CJEU defined the concept of a female worker on the basis of the objective criteria that characterise the employment relationship, identifying its essential feature as the circumstance in which 'a person performs services for and under the direction of another person, in return for which he receives remuneration' (CJEU, 20 September 2007, case C-116/06, *Kiiski*).

Instead, the scenario consisting of the partial harmonisation measures adopted in fields other than those analysed so far provides significantly different indications. Outside the regulatory areas examined, the use of that 'subsidiary' notion of employment, determined by referral to the national labour laws, appears to prevail. The prototype of such a situation is represented by Directive 77/187/EEC (later replaced by Directive 2001/23/EC, Transfer of Undertakings Directive) on the approximation of the laws of the Member States relating to the safeguarding of employees' rights in the event of transfers of undertakings, businesses or parts of undertakings or businesses. In the absence of indications in the directive, the CJEU has clarified that its provisions 'may be relied upon only by persons who are, in one way or another, protected as employees under the law of the Member State concerned' (CJEU, 11 July 1985, case 105/84, *Foreningen af Arbejdsledere i Danmark v Danmols Inventar*). The notion thus has subsidiary value.

The reasons for an apparently unconditional referral to national law are to be found in the traditional interpretation according to which the Transfer of Undertakings Directive is aimed only at partial harmonisation. The same rationale—consisting of only partial and mainly procedural harmonisation—can also be observed in Directive 80/987/EEC (later Directive 200/74/EC and now Directive 2008/94/EC) on the approximation of the laws of the Member States relating to the protection of employees in the event of the insolvency of their employer. Although with some nuances, the same reasoning should be applied to Directive 75/129/EEC (replaced by Directive 98/59/EC) on the approximation of the laws of the Member States relating to collective redundancies.

Also, in the case of the directives on non-standard employment, the definition of an employee is of a subsidiary nature, i.e. it is entrusted to the national legislatures. Directive 97/81/EC 'applies to part-time workers who have an employment contract or employment relationship as defined by the law, collective agreement or practice in force in each Member State' (clause 2 of the framework agreement attached to the directive). Directive 1999/70/EC, in its clause 2, uses an analogous wording in order to define the scope of application of the rules on fixed-term employment contracts. Further, in Directive 2008/104/EC on temporary agency work, '"worker" means any person who, in the Member State concerned, is protected as a worker under national employment law' (Article 3).

5 Fragments of a Definition of Worker Status in EU Law

The analysis conducted so far on the different notions of employment that emerge from EU law suggests a complex picture, which is reflected in the definition of worker status in the EU legal framework. Taking a closer look, there is no status that can be defined univocally.

This confirms the correctness of what has recently been pointed out by careful observers on a more general level: The potential fragmentation of the status of the person in EU law essentially hinges upon the fact that such legal system shuns a unitary constitutional vision of the subject; it rather breaks down individuals' identities and roles, defining them based on the wide range of economic activities it regulates: 'EU law places the (many) Union's activities at the heart of the construction of the individual' (Azoulai et al. 2016, p. 6).

All of this explains why the worker is essentially considered, in the framework of the freedom of movement guaranteed by Article 45 TFEU, as a participant in the construction of the internal market. The protection granted to employees based on the patterns traditionally provided by national labour law systems has also been partially reshaped, as already recalled, by EU law, in particular through the harmonisation of social policies implemented between the second half of the 1970s and the end of the 1990s; however, this occurred in a very selective, sector-specific, inhomogeneous, and fragmented way. Therefore, it is impossible to identify—in the framework of EU law—an organic and unitary employee/worker status that is actually comparable, not only in terms of scope, with those defined in the national legal systems. And it is not by chance that the collective and redistributive dimensions (in terms of power and economic resources) are nearly absent (Article 153, paragraph 5 TFEU) from the fragments of statuses defined by EU law.

References

Andreoni, A. (1996). Sicurezza sociale. Sistemi nazionali e armonizzazione. In A. Baylos Grau et al. (Eds.), *Dizionario di diritto del lavoro comunitario* (pp. 527–557). Bologna: Moduzzi.

Azoulai, L., Barbou des Places, S., & Pataut, E. (2016). Being a person in the European Union. In L. Azoulai, S. Barbou des Places, & E. Pataut (Eds.), *Constructing the person in EU law. Rights, roles, identities* (pp. 3–11). Oxford: Hart.

Chieco, P. (2002). Lavoratore comparabile e modello sociale nella legislazione sulla flessibilità del contratto e dell'impresa. In P. Chieco (Ed.), *Eguaglianza e libertà nel diritto del lavoro. Scritti in memoria di Luciano Ventura* (pp. 47–87). Bari: Cacucci.

Countouris, N. (2007). *The changing law of the employment relationship. Comparative analyses in the European context*. Aldershot (Hampshire): Routledge.

D'Antona, M. (1989). La subordinazione e oltre. Una teoria giuridica per il lavoro che cambia. In M. Pedrazzoli (Ed.), *Lavoro subordinato e dintorni. Comparazioni e prospettive* (pp. 43–50). Bologna: Il Mulino.

D'Antona, M. (2000). Sistema giuridico comunitario. In B. Caruso & S. Sciarra (Eds.), *Opere. Scritti sul metodo e sulla evoluzione del diritto del lavoro–Scritti sul diritto del lavoro comparato e comunitario* (Vol. 1). Milan: Giuffrè.

Deakin, S. (2004). The comparative evolution of the employment relationship. In G. Davidov & B. Langille (Eds.), *Boundaries and frontiers of labour law* (pp. 89–108). Oxford: Hart.

Giubboni, S. (2007). Subordinazione e diritto del lavoro europeo. *Dir pubbl comp eur, 3*, 1433–1462.

Giubboni, S. (2017). *Diritto del lavoro europeo. Una introduzione critica*. Padua: CEDAM.

Lunardon, F., & Tosi, P. (2005). *Introduzione al diritto del lavoro. L'ordinamento europeo* (Vol. 2). Rome: Laterza.

Mancini, G. F. (1988). Principi fondamentali di diritto del lavoro nell'ordinamento delle Comunità europee. In *Il lavoro nel diritto comunitario e nell'ordinamento italiano. Proceedings of the conference held in Parma*. Padua: CEDAM.

Nogler, L. (2009). *The concept of 'subordination' in European and comparative law*. Trento: University of Trento.

Supiot, A. (1992). *Les notions de contrat de travail et de relation de travail en Europe. Rapport pour la Commission des Communautés Européennes*. Luxembourg: Office for Official Publications of the European Communities (Publications Office).

Supiot, A. (1994). *Critique du droit du travail*. Paris: PUF.

FSC
www.fsc.org
MIX
Papier | Fördert
gute Waldnutzung
FSC® C083411

Kolibri 360 GmbH
Ferdinand-Jühlke-Straße 7
99095 Erfurt, Deutschland
produktsicherheit@kolibri360.de